The Concise Encyclopedia of
ENGLISH AND AMERICAN
POETS AND POETRY

OTHER TITLES IN THIS SERIES

Archaeology
Modern World Literature

IN PREPARATION

Living Faiths
Music and Musicians
World History

Edited by
STEPHEN SPENDER and
DONALD HALL

The Concise Encyclopedia of

ENGLISH
AND AMERICAN
POETS
AND POETRY

Hutchinson of London

HUTCHINSON & CO (*Publishers*) LTD

178–202 Great Portland Street, London W1

London Melbourne Sydney Auckland
Johannesburg Cape Town

First published 1963
Second impression 1967
Second edition (revised in new format) 1970

This book has been set in Bembo, printed in Great Britain
on Antique Wove paper by Anchor Press, and
bound by Wm. Brendon, both of Tiptree, Essex

ISBN 0 09 098810 8

CONTENTS

Contributors   vii

Introduction   ix

Editors' note   x

GENERAL ARTICLES

American poetry   I

Anglo-Saxon poetry   8

Australian poetry   15

Canadian poetry   38

Classic and Romantic   51

Criticism and poetry   63

English poetry in Africa   97

'Everyman' and the miracle plays   99

Foreign influences on English poetry   101

Fugitive group   116

Hymns, songs and carols   133

Imagery   134

Imagism   139

Indian poetry in English   142

Metaphor   172

Middle English lyric   177

Music and poetry   185

Myth and poetry   187

New criticism   191

New directions in metrics   192

New Zealand poetry   197

Poetry and publishing—Britain   204

Poetry and publishing—United States   205

Popular poetry   209

Prosody, forms of verse, and some usages   215
Religion and poetry   252
Satire   263
Science and poetry   264
Society and the poet   283
South African poetry in English   285
Symbolism   298
Translation   311
For further reading   334
Notes on the contributors   368
Acknowledgments   375
Index of poets quoted   381
General index   383

CONTRIBUTORS

William A. Armstrong

Bernard Bergonzi

Marius Bewley

Carl Bode

Yves Bonnefoy

Buddhadeva Bose

Curtis B. Bradford

J. P. Brockbank

Christine Brooke-Rose

Vincent Buckley

Douglas Bush

Guy Butler

Glauco Cambon

Rivers Carew

Seymour Chatman

Nirad C. Chaudhuri

Stanley K. Coffman, Jr.

Nevill Coghill

J. M. Cohen

Patric Dickinson

Bonamy Dobrée

Maureen Duffy

David Ferry

Ian Fletcher

George Fraser

Northrop Frye

John Fuller

Thomas Jay Garbáty

Helen Gardner

W. H. Gardner

James Gindin

Geoffrey Grigson

Thom Gunn

Donald Hall

J. C. Hall

John Heath-Stubbs

Donald L. Hill

Geoffrey Hill

Arnold P. Hinchliffe

X. J. Kennedy

Hugh Kenner

George Kitchin

John Lehmann

Edward Lowbury

F. L. Lucas

George MacBeth

H. M. McLuhan

Louis MacNeice

Charles Madge

J. C. Maxwell

W. Moelwyn Merchant

Gerald Moore

Edwin Morgan

E. N. W. Mottram

Norman Nicholson

Walter J. Ong, S. J.

G. A. Over

Peter Pears

V. de S. Pinto

John Press

Kathleen Raine

John Crowe Ransom

Anne Ridler

W. W. Robson

Victoria Sackville-West

Louis Simpson

Sydney Goodsir Smith

Monroe K. Spears

Stephen Spender

Radcliffe Squires

Donald E. Stanford

C. K. Stead

W. Leonard Stevens

Anne Stevenson

R. S. Thomas

John Waller

Andrews Wanning

Vernon Watkins

Richard Wilbur

David Wright

INTRODUCTION

In this *Concise Encyclopedia* we have tried to collect information necessary to the student of poetry, and to represent the best contemporary
critical opinion. We believe that the present moment lends itself to an
attempt at ordering and revaluation, but we have not tried to impose a
critical uniformity on our contributors; the reader will discover
considerable diversity of approach and attitude. We have tried to make
a collection which represents the most intelligent of various approaches
and attitudes to poetry. We have not expected to collect judgments
which could be called final, and we realise that many of these opinions
will belong to our generation only. However, we face the prospect of
being outdated with some equanimity when we consider how interesting we would find a similar compendium from the eighteen-sixties.
But more important, we feel that the best articles here are of enduring
relevance.

We have sometimes deliberately dealt with aspects of a subject from
different points of view. For example, we have included a traditional
account of English prosody, and added as well an article about recent
prosodic discoveries made by linguists. In a similar way, on occasion,
we have tried to represent both English and American opinion; and in
some of our general articles we have deliberately called forth opposing
or complementary points of view.

In order to be *Concise*, we have found it necessary to put a brutal
limit on the number of words for each article. Our contributors sometimes felt that they were asked to condense the Holy Writ into a single
sentence. Also because of our limited space, we have omitted from our
list of poets many whom we would prefer to have included. We sent
our initial suggestions of contents to a good number of critics and
scholars, and we profited greatly from the suggestions they made.
Some of them more or less approved of our ideas to begin with, but
others expressed violent disagreement. We look forward to more controversy.

We have two sorts of articles here, the article with the name of a
poet and the article which pursues a general topic. In the articles on
poets we have tried to keep the biography to a necessary minimum,

and to emphasise the nature of the poet's artistic achievement, and to quote examples. The general articles are alphabetised by title among the articles about poets, but since not all the titles are predictable we have listed them separately on pages v–vi. The selection of general topics is somewhat arbitrary, as soon as one takes care of obvious necessities like the prosody of English verse. We have tried to choose topics which would allow contemporary critics to report on current literary theory and opinion; some of these articles are 'Imagery', 'Myth and Poetry', and 'Science and Poetry'. We have tried as well to find topics which call for broad historical treatment, like 'Foreign Influences on English Poetry' and 'Classic and Romantic'. Also we have wanted to note the tendency of English poetry, at this point, to develop in areas of the world outside England and the United States. We have articles about Commonwealth poetry, and articles about poetry written where English is a *lingua franca* spoken by the intellectual élite.

We have also included a short bibliography of suggestions for further reading, both works and criticism. For this, we are largely indebted to our contributors, many of whom have taken considerable trouble over compiling lists of titles relating to their articles in the *Encyclopedia*.

Stephen Spender
Donald Hall

EDITORS' NOTE

The printing of a poet's name in **bold type** in the text indicates that he is the subject of a separate article. There are similar cross-references at the end of many articles, especially in the case of individual poets who are discussed in one or more of the general articles. There are no such cross-references to 'Prosody, forms of verse, and some usages', since that article is too long, and mentions too many poets too briefly, for such a general reference to be of value. The reader who wishes to discover all significant references to a poet, or other topic, in addition to the principal ones, should consult the index.

With a few exceptions, quoted verse is printed exactly as it was written, even when spelling or syntax have become archaic to the point of obscurity. Words and passages that would be unintelligible to all but the specialist have been translated in footnotes. However, certain obsolete Old English letters have been transliterated for the benefit of readers unfamiliar with Old English; 'þ', for instance, has become 'th'.

Quotations are usually indented, but sometimes, for ease of reading, short quotations are printed in the main text in inverted commas as part of the sentence in which they occur. The end of a line of verse is then indicated by an oblique stroke:/.

A

Adams, Léonie [Fuller] (1899–), is an American poet and critic who shared the Bollingen Prize for 1955 with Louise **Bogan**. Her lyrics are executed with precision and taste, and her critics have never been able to decide whether she is more 'metaphysical' or more 'romantic'.   D.H.

Aiken, Conrad [Potter] (1889–), was born in Georgia. After attending Harvard, where T. S. **Eliot** was a fellow student and a member of the *Harvard Advocate*, he lived in England for many years before making his permanent home in Massachusetts. It was he who introduced Ezra **Pound** to the poems of T. S. Eliot, and with his astute critical articles he kept at the forefront of American poetical controversy in the second and third decades of this century. His criticism is collected in *A Reviewer's ABC* (1958).

More than any of his contemporaries, Aiken has specialised in the long poem, and perhaps he has lacked readers because of his addiction to an unfashionable genre. His verse is strongly musical, and gorgeous with imagery which has the quality of dream:

And in the hanging gardens there is
rain
From midnight until one, striking the
leaves
And bells of flowers, and stroking
boles of planes,
And drawing slow arpeggios over
pools.

His *Collected Poems* (1953) contains the best of his work in poetry. He has also written four novels, a collection of short stories, and an experimental autobiography.

Recognition has come slowly to Aiken in the United States, but he has received at various times the Pulitzer Prize and the National Book Award, and from 1950 to 1952 he was Consultant in Poetry at the Library of Congress. In 1954 he received the highest American award for poetry, the Bollingen Prize.   D.H.

Akenside, Mark (1721–70), English poet and physician, was born in Newcastle-upon-Tyne. His first volume of poetry was *The Pleasures of Imagination* (1744). He was frequently represented in Dodsley's 1758 collection by odes and 'inscriptions' abounding in classical allusions.   D.H.

Alabaster, William (1567–1640), an English Neo-Latin poet, was unknown for his English poems until these were discovered by Bertram Dobell in 1903. **Spenser** praised his unfinished epic poem to Queen Elizabeth in Latin hexameters.   D.H.

American Poetry. The American poem of native speech as well as local materials emerged only slowly from the New World. The British characteristics in colonial New England verse eased only gradually over two centuries into a poetry whose allegiances were less European:

Can we never be thought
To have learning or grace
Unless it be brought
From that damnable place?

These Revolution sentiments from Philip Freneau were to be theorised by **Emerson**: 'Why should we not have a poetry and philosophy of insight and not of tradition, and a religion by revelation to us, and not the history of theirs? . . . Why should we grope among the dry bones of the past, or put the living generation into masquerade out of its faded wardrobe? The sun shines today also.'

But theory outstripped the production of native poems which, as late as the nationalist Americanism of the nineteen-thirties, tended to be judged as documents of nationhood rather than as poems. **Poe** suffered in comparison with **Whitman** and the essential dialectic with Europe was repudiated. Private poetry-making developed in the seventeenth century out of the tensions of the cultured sensibility absorbed still in frontier and settlement physicalities, the defending and sustaining of life itself. It seems natural that the first poet should be a woman, and if Anne **Bradstreet**'s is necessarily minor poetry, arising from a largely public world of work and religion, where private pleasures were suspect, it remains a touching derivation from British models: her American voice is small but distinct, the native stresses already present in the tension between Puritan life in the wilderness and the intimate, embattled interior life.

Michael Wigglesworth's *Day of Doom* (1662), the ancestor of E. A. **Robinson**'s verse-novel of 1927, *Tristram* (in sales at least), enabled popular taste already to gloat over sadistic punishments for the non-elect, made easy-going by religious self-righteousness and the ballad metre. But *God's Controversy with New England*

shows the poet's elementary pride in 'dear New England! dearest land to me!' which precedes many American outbursts of this kind to come. The better poetry of Edward **Taylor** is more the private act but in spite of a certain nativeness of language, his theme—the dialogue of flesh and spirit—and his manner are those of the English seventeenth-century devotional poets.

Nor did emancipation of poetry automatically accompany the Revolution and the eighteenth-century enquiry: What is an American? Is a new poetry possible for the New World man or will it always be the Old World product transplanted? With this apprehension, in the huge expanding country, arose the endlessly complex problems of regionalism and the apparent choice an American should make between dead past and raw present. The search for an American poetry now took the primary form of opposition to the 'luxurious effeminacy' and 'pedantry' of European taste and its 'servile imitation' (Trumbull's *Essay on the Use and Advantages of the Fine Arts*, 1770). The native Shakespeare, whom **Melville** was still prophesying in 1850, would turn up soon; meanwhile nationalism battled with neo-classicism, which **Bryant** attacked, praising **Wordsworth** and urging that specifically American prosody (*Four Lectures on Poetry*, 1825) which William Carlos **Williams** is still trying to forward. Influential criticism between 1810 and 1835 prepared for Romantic transcendentalism by importing **Coleridge**'s Germanic notions, until American eighteenth-century moralism paralleled European Romanticism and W. E. Channing, friend of Coleridge, called for an American poetry 'which pierces beneath exterior life to the depths of the soul, and which lays open its mysterious working, borrowing from the whole outward creation fresh images and correspondences, with which to illuminate the secrets of the world within us'.

Then Emerson expressed the American quality latent in this not obviously native programme: 'America is a poem in our eyes'—poets should simply write it down and it would be both American and universal truth. Opposition to this simplification came in Poe's absolute aesthetic standards for the evaluation and composition of poetry, stressing formal unity and conscious reasoning, the structuring of desire through symmetry. Poetry is craftsmanship, intellectual, and culturally dependent on Europe. Yet nothing could be more American than Poe's inventions in *Ulalume* and the conception of *Eureka*. The New Englander, **Lowell**, attempted a common-sense bipartisan use of both objective beauty and regional inspiration, the American individual product under guidance from the humanitarian achievements and standards of the world. But in 1855 Whitman's *Leaves of Grass* opened up a form and feeling which was finally American beyond discussion. Here was poetry determinedly democratic, impersonally searching for the average American worker with whom to identify, and the American sense of things, and creating an idiom for the 'native-expression spirit', a poetry mirroring the People as it did not, Whitman claimed, in **Tennyson**, the tea-drinking aristocratic bard in the Old World's closed rooms. Whitman's bard was not a gentleman but 'an American, one of the roughs, a kosmos, / Disorderly fleshy and sensual . . . eating drinking and breeding'. In spite of the protests of genteel critics, Emerson found *Leaves of Grass* 'fortifying and encouraging'.

After 1900, Santayana represents those who preferred traditional form to Whitman's 'sunburnt' freedom. In 1915, however, Van Wyck Brooks in *America's Coming of Age* finds American poets, except Whitman, lacking 'Americanism'. At this very time T. S. **Eliot** and Ezra **Pound** escaped from the poetic desert of the United States—but to an English scene in which men of intelligence did not take up poetry in the endgame of Victorian romanticism. A revolution, parallel to the *Lyrical Ballads*, was overdue.

Looking back from this point, about 1912, the American poetic achievement is neither impressive nor consistently indigenous: the peaks tower above so much mediocrity. But there are at least three clear main lines of development which lead into the excellencies of the twentieth century: the meditative shrewd New England speech rhythms and interiorness of Emerson, Emily **Dickinson**, Robinson and **Frost**, which seems to descend from Mistress Bradstreet: the ratiocinative brilliance of Poe, Hart **Crane**, Wallace **Stevens** and Richard **Wilbur**, tracing back to the metaphysical brilliance of Taylor; and the pragmatic open forms and manifest cultural concern of Whitman, Pound, Williams, Robert Lowell's later verse and Allen Ginsberg, public voices which are the private voice of America rather as Thomas Wolfe designed his to be.

F. O. Matthiessen once defined American poets as those 'whose lives have been deeply shaped by American experience. They must have written in our language, since primitive Indian poetry belongs to an utterly different civilisation, and, like the foreign-language verse of our various immigrant groups, can reach us only diluted by translation'. It is not surprising that American poets have been obsessed with the desire to embody their personal incarnation of America in an inclusive epic—an impossibility achieved by a handful of masters. What Matthiessen called 'that chimera, the great Ameri-

3

can epic' caused poetic inflations from Bradstreet's Du Bartas imitations, through Barlow's *Columbiad*, to Robinson's verse novels. But the epic urge produced distinctive twentieth-century structures, unique in modern literature: Pound's *Cantos*, Eliot's *The Waste Land*, Hart Crane's *The Bridge*, Carl **Sandburg**'s *The People, Yes*, Williams' *Paterson*, Stevens' *Notes towards a Supreme Fiction*, and perhaps **MacLeish**'s *Conquistador* and Ginsberg's *Howl*. Here is a real American poetic achievement, expressing the American condition as the modern human condition, the extreme point beyond colonial verse, and apart from the mass of popular verse in cemeteries, almanacs, worksongs, jazz and 'pop' lyrics, and Revolution and Civil War songs, that affirmative popular voice of America practically unsuspected by Whitman and only thoroughly collected in this century by men like Sandburg and John and Alan Lomax.

The self-conscious professional American poet, like Freneau, for instance, sees himself frequently as a moulder, satiriser and myth-maker to the nation, concerned with timely public utterance on socially important matters. This is the laureate pose of Barlow, Emerson, Whitman, **Tate**'s *Ode to the Confederate Dead*, Sandburg and, especially, MacLeish. An Americanism appears too in Bryant's celebration of the continental geographical splendours and the land, and in **Longfellow**'s consolidation of popular myths— Evangeline, Paul Revere, Hiawatha, and the Hesperus. For Wallace Stevens, Whittier's *Snow-Bound* (1865) was a typical American poem: yet it is more an English-language description of New England life as 'Flemish pictures of old days' until line 212, when the American quality emerges in 'the red scourge of bondage' and:

We shared the fishing off Boar's Head,
And round the rocky Isles of Shoals
The hake-broil on the drift-wood
coals;
The chowder on the sand-beach made,
Dipped by the hungry, steaming hot,
With spoons of clam-shell from the
pot.

and in 'the square sail of the gundelow', the Indian and Civil War references, 'the boat-horn on Piscataqua, / The loon's weird laughter far away', and finally:

Before us passed the painted Creeks,
And daft McGregor on his raids
In Costa Rica's everglades.
And up Taygetos winding slow . . .

But the poem is not in an American idiom; the tone is not native as it is in, for instance, *Leaves of Grass*; it is, as Matthiessen observes, 'Our most thoroughly realised piece of early regionalism, and preserves with loving detail the essence of a self-contained way of life that the motor highway and the radio have now carried us beyond'. In the nineteenth century the native idiom appears mainly in popular and light verse, in Lowell's *Bigelow Papers*, for example. Robinson is one of the first to heal the division between literary and spoken verse languages. His *Man Against the Sky* versifies a *fin-de-siècle* sceptical naturalism in formal English, but in *Isaac and Archibald* and certain shorter poems, he achieves a dry laconic Yankee quality which is traceable in Emerson, Emily Dickinson and Frost. He found Whitman authentic but 'too pure for us—too powerfull pure, / Too lovingly triumphant, and too large'. He is for the future; meanwhile Robinson can manage:

Miniver mourned the ripe renown
That made so many a name so fragrant;

He mourned Romance, now on the
> town,
And Art, a vagrant . . .

The New England tone can be heard in
Emerson's *Hamatreya*—'To find the sitfast
acres where you left them'—and in *Days*:

> I, in my pleached garden, watched the
>> pomp,
> Forgot my morning wishes, hastily
> Took a few herbs and apples and the
>> Day
> Turned and departed silent. I, too
>> late,
> Under her solemn fillet saw the scorn.

In Emily Dickinson the tradition sounds
everywhere:

> I'm ceded, I've stopped being theirs;
> The name they dropped upon my face
> With water, in the country church,
> Is finished now,
> And they can out if with my dolls,
> My childhood, and the string of spools
> I've finished threading too.

Just as her 'neighbourhoods of pause'
looks forward to the methods of E. E.
Cummings, so do the Shaker hymns to
Gertrude **Stein**'s analytic repetitions; the
continuity is in the American linguistic
usage. No English poet wrote with the
daring of Emily Dickinson in the eighteen-
sixties:

> You've seen balloons set, haven't you?
> So stately they ascend
> It is as swans discarded you
> For duties diamond . . .

or Whitman about the same time:

> Steep'd amid honey'd morphine, my
>> windpipe throttled in fakes of
>>> death.

Frost's pace and tone is recognisably New
England, for example in the opening lines
of *The Wood-Pile, On Looking Up By
Chance at the Constellations*, and *Design*.
But his American ambitions are smaller
than those of Hart Crane whose *The
Bridge* is the first self-consciously major
poem to express the tensions and continui-
ties of the national culture, embodying
American history as mythical machinery,
and trying to make Brooklyn Bridge
the adequately flexible symbol of democratic greatness projecting into the high
future. Thirty years earlier, in their
Pennsylvania walks, while still students,
Pound, Williams, 'H.D.' (Hilda Doolittle)
and Marianne **Moore** were working out
a further American versification. **Imagism** may have failed because 'it lost
structural necessity', as Williams claimed,
becoming what Pound scorned as 'Amygism', the static province of Amy **Lowell**.
But imagist precision and concision pene-
trate the mature poems of Pound and
Williams. Marianne Moore went on to
create her idiosyncratically American
quantitative line and Pound explored the
potentiality of Whitman—'it was you
that broke the new wood'—and, with
Chinese ideogram forms, forged the
originality of the *Cantos*. Williams selected
local speech, pace and materials and fused
them in the intensely native collage of
Paterson. American poetry at last came
of age; craftsmanship and the freed line
had liberated the American voice. Gone
are the nightingales which even Columbus
noticed were not there, and gone the
poeticising rhetoric of the nineteenth
century.

To these major figures we may add the
native qualities of Sandburg, **Lindsay**
and Edgar Lee **Masters** speaking the
speech of the Middle West, E. E. Cummings in New York, and the Southern
irony and historic cultivation of John

Crowe **Ransom**. So that in 1950 Matthiessen rightly observed: 'we may not have had an American style in poetry as the French, for example, measure such things. We have lacked until very lately a formed critical tradition in anything like the European sense. But we have produced by now a body of poetry of absorbing quality. If this poetry reveals violent contrasts and unresolved conflicts, it corresponds thereby to American life.'

Even so, it is difficult still to isolate the typical American poem. Marianne Moore and Robert Penn **Warren** deny such a thing amid the variant styles, while Stevens believed there was 'an underlying difference of sensibility' but not of language. James Loughlin cites Williams' *Perpetuum Mobile: the City* as 'a very great modern American poem . . . entirely American and very un-English' in rhythm, diction and, above all, in its 'conception of what a poem is'. Certainly Williams emphatically promotes the native idiom in his search for 'the American Grain', holding that American English stems from Elizabethan England, modified by time and place 'to acquire a character differing greatly from that of present-day English', a difference in the pace of spoken language which determines elementary poetic form. 'Any art or work of art is always local and only national in its character by accident.' Therefore the poem in the American environment 'will have compact in it all those characteristics, psychological and otherwise, intonations, use of words, differing from British use, which makes our lives here of a separate character from the British equivalent'.

But to realise this essential 'we need a new prosody as much as we need a new social understanding—an expanded prosody, an enormously expanded understanding of the 'metrical core of speech" '.

Something of this difference clearly shapes Sandburg's *Threes* and Cummings' *Poem or Beauty Hurts Mr Vinal*, poems whose prosody are distinctly un-English. But Allen Tate takes a more critical attitude. Hart Crane, for him, is 'the archetype of the modern American poet whose fundamental mistake lay in thinking that an irrational surrender of the intellect to the will would be the basis of a new mentality'. The bridge of Crane's poem is America as 'a passage to new truths', an American myth of the heroic dream of a new Eden, but Crane was 'typical of the rootless spiritual life of our time', a man representing 'American life in this age. . . . His world had no centre, and the thrust into sensation is responsible for the fragmentary quality of his most ambitious work'. MacLeish's *Conquistador* (1932) fails in similar terms, as a typical modern and American poem, because its philosophy is 'personal and unarticulated. . . . The hero is concerned with his personal survival. He is modern and sentimental; not tragic and ironic'.

An American poet of the nineteen-thirties almost certainly would represent the confusion and violence in the West which led to 1939 and beyond. Yet, as Karl **Shapiro** wrote in *Essay on Rime* (1945): 'who / Except Hart Crane has tasted the pure manna / Of *Song of Myself*, the naked seed of rime?' National inspiration, local materials and speech, universal standards of craftsmanship, and the dialogue with Europe had produced good American poetry finally, but in a time of international dispute and indirection, with which America inevitably became involved and responsible. Pound's *Pisan Cantos* (1948) spring from the heart of this condition as Crane's *The Bridge* sprang from the nineteen-thirties, both men trying to affirm some personal warmth in a world of illiteracy and abused power which tempted a poet to reject humanity.

Ironically the human condition on the American continent in some measure prepared for this poetry. This was a land, as the expatriate English poet **Auden** remarks, where that intimacy of men localised in a homogeneous society within a humanised, mythologised and generally benevolent Nature was little known; a land still partly unsettled, where humanity shrinks before vast Nature, where 'the equality of men is not some dogma or politics or jurisprudence but a self-evident fact'. Mother Nature is replaced by a White Whale or Frost's 'great buck' (*The Most of It*) through which a man is confronted with a fiercely indifferent existential force. The American poet never really had the genial assurance of a Wordsworth, nor the acceptance of an urban community. American poetry shows the strain of a man talking to a small audience or none at all, a man whose justification is absolute individuality. 'The danger for the American poet', Auden believes, 'is not of writing like everybody else but of crankiness and a parody of his own manner.'

This partly accounts for twentieth-century poets' pride in those technical skills paramountly admired in industrial democracies, and always useful in America from frontier days onward; European amateurism in the arts is less favoured in the United States. The significant rebellion in Donald Allen's *The New American Poetry 1945–1960* opposes the substitution of acceptable techniques for speaking out in an empirical personal voice however raving and explosive, and represents the large section of American poetry revolting against what **Hopkins** called the 'Parnassian'. The typical poem of this newest generation is a highly charged personal declaration reaching for the transcendental at any cost in its rejection of convention in religion, politics and the academy. In the nineteen-fifties, thematic irresolution plus refinement of the poetic instrument tended to make the American poet no longer provincial, but a prey to conforming good taste insulating him from the overbearing vitality of his society.

Technically the best poets of the nineteen-sixties develop their forms from the practical example of Whitman, Williams, Pound, Louis Zukofsky and the essay 'Projective Verse' by Charles Olson, which formulates the poem as a field of experience and activity. Olson's own poetry extends some of Pound's devices into important new areas, and his influence is parallel to that of Lorca, Neruda, Mayakovsky and Tzara among younger poets who have released themselves from an exhausted tradition of academic form. The work of Allen Ginsberg has an international importance second to none in America, and his standard is backed equally by such distinguished poets of this Sixties Renaissance as John Ashbery, Kenneth Koch, Robert Creeley, Paul Blackburn, Michale Mc-Clure and Ted Berrigan. Their work contains a sense of the strains and commitments of poetry in an America radically at strife with itself, desperately trying to salvage its better civilisation in the face of the Vietnam war and the forces against Civil Rights. Inheriting their responsibility from the Thirties poets, the contemporaries speak for more than a provincial artistry: 'the sun shines today also'. And black poets are beginning to emerge with more than protest poetry in the narrower sense; the work of poets like M. B. Tolson and Leroi Jones is the spearhead of a poetic black power to come.

E.N.W.M.

Anglo-Saxon Poetry. The earliest vernacular verse, a remarkably distinctive and homogeneous body of work, was composed between the mid-seventh century and the Norman Conquest. The bulk of this poetry is preserved in four manuscript collections (known as the Exeter Book, the Vercelli Book, the Junius Manuscript, and the Beowulf Manuscript) written towards the end of the Old English period. Although the names of Cædmon (late seventh century) and Cynewulf (perhaps late eighth century) have come down to us, the works that can be confidently attributed to these two religious poets are few, and it is no disrespect to the uncertain Cynewulfian canon to say that the best Anglo-Saxon poems are anonymous.

In the structure of this verse, stress and alliteration provided the framework which after the Norman Conquest gave place to syllable-count and rhyme. Each line had four stresses and was divided into two half-lines by a caesura. The pattern of alliteration, whether consonantal or vocalic, coincided with stressed words, but did not include *all* stressed words; nor did it include an occasional bonus alliteration on an unstressed word. The first half-line had either one or two alliterating words, the second half-line had only one, e.g.:

Tha com of more   under misthleothum
Grendel gongan,   Godes yrre bær

(Now by the swirling bluffs from his
       wasteland
Grendel came stalking; he brought
       God's wrath)
      Beowulf, 710–11

Within each half-line the number of unstressed syllables was extremely flexible. Various rhythmic patterns were allowed, and the classification of these into five types by Eduard Sievers has been generally accepted, though there is still much argument about how far the reciter of the verse had to 'accommodate' unusually long or unusually short half-lines to a musical time factor—how far, in fact, the harp was an essential and regular accompaniment, or merely an introducer, occasional heightener, and end-marker. Harp or no harp, Anglo-Saxon verse has a strong, characteristically trochaic or dactylic beat, and this has proved sufficiently near the heart of the English language to be potentially re-assertable, long after **Chaucer** had ousted **Langland**, long after English verse had become predominantly iambic and syllabic. It breaks out time and again, in folk poems and ballads, in saws and nursery-rhymes, in the experiments of **Coleridge, Hood,** and **Hopkins,** and in its more deliberate revival by twentieth-century poets like T. S. **Eliot,** W. H. **Auden,** and Richard **Eberhart.**

Anglo-Saxon poetry is an oral poetry (though much of it was eventually written down in book form) and this is important. Judging it without reference to the methods of composition suited to oral delivery and aural comprehension is like judging plays without reference to the theatre. The use of stock formulas ('unlocked his word-hoard'), of kennings ('the whale's way'), and of periphrastic variation ('roads . . . shadowy thoroughfares . . . ancient foundations . . . dappled plains . . . fettered sea-bottoms'—these phrases describing, within a sentence of seven lines, the dry land that appeared when Moses divided the Red Sea, in the poem *Exodus*) implies a close relation between poet and audience, in which the Anglo-Saxon *scop* was expected both to speak within a bond of convention joining him to his hearers and to show his own powers of invention and variation.

Similarly, the habit of oblique and sudden allusion, often to persons or events in Germanic history familiar to his audience but obscure to us, shows the poet's easy and confident use of a shared inheritance in order to point some telling contrast or parallel. Whether it was secular poetry recited in the halls of noblemen and the courts of kings, or religious poetry recited behind monastery walls, it was something which had an acknowledged function in Anglo-Saxon society. The learned Alcuin might worry that the monks of Lindisfarne seemed to know as much about Ingeld the Heathobard as they did about Christ the Redeemer, yet this is itself a tribute to the pervasive significance of the *scop* and his lays. The minstrel-poet is represented again and again as a bringer of delight and happiness, a public focus for society's memories and hopes and fears, a central inhabitant of that bright warm Germanic hall islanded in the midst of darkness and lawlessness, enmity and the unknown.

The dominant genre is heroic poetry, and this is seen even in the large amount of poetry on religious subjects, where the influence of the ideals and conventions of the Heroic Age can usually be found, shaping character and action into forms acceptable to the Germanic experience. Most of the heroic verse, though composed in England, deals with Continental material—with stories of heroes, dynasties, and battles which the Anglo-Saxons brought with them to Britain and enjoyed recalling. These stories related mainly to events in Germany, Denmark, and Scandinavia during the turbulent years from the fourth to the sixth century. This was history, but it was history that frequently shaded off towards legend or incorporated elements of folklore. It reflected, however, a real society and a real view of society, and the force of the heroic poems can still be felt, with their code of fealty to prince or king, their tragic family clashes of incompatible loyalties, their stoic morality lightened by fierce brief joys.

Such is the background of the greatest Old English poem, *Beowulf*, an epic of some 3,000 lines dating probably from the early eighth century. But *Beowulf* is elegiac as well as heroic; like **Tennyson's** *Morte d'Arthur*, it seems to point to the end of a great fellowship. Although recent commentators have overstressed the Christian atmosphere of the poem, it remains true that the author was a Christian (who had perhaps also read Virgil) and that his admiration for the heroic worldly ideals was tempered by a deep sense of the transience of glory. It is no accident that he chose the Geats as the tribe his hero belonged to: a people who were to disappear from history in the wars with Sweden which are ominously foreshadowed at the end of the poem. We know nothing about the poet, but he was clearly a man of sensitivity and intelligence, and he is careful to present Beowulf not only as an exemplar of warrior virtues (shown in his fights with Grendel, Grendel's mother, and the dragon) but also as a kind, gentle, well-loved ruler whose last moments were a little consoled by his knowledge that he had ruled without treachery or perjury. The transformation of a traditional desperate heroism into a tentative, though still tragic, hope for human society is the *Beowulf* poet's contribution to heroic literature. His poem has a grave tenacious power, and is composed with considerable art:

Hafast thu gefered, thæt the feor ond
                   neah
ealne wide-ferhth weras ehtigath,
efne swa side swa sæ bebugeth
wind-geard, weallas. Wes thenden
                   thu lifige,
ætheling, eadig!

(What you have accomplished
Means men will praise you both far
                              and near
Whenever and wherever the sea beats
                              round
Earth's blustering cliffs. Warrior be
                              happy
While life is yours!)
                    Beowulf, 1221–5

It should be remembered, of course, that the solitary eminence of *Beowulf* may be deceptive. Tantalising epic fragments like *Finnsburh* and *Waldere* indicate that a great deal of this poetry has been lost. That there was a continuing tradition of heroic verse in England is suggested by the later application of it to native subjects in the tenth-century poems, *The Battle of Brunanburh* and *The Battle of Maldon*. *Brunanburh* celebrates a victory, *Maldon* a defeat; but it is in the latter poem that the fullest and most moving emphasis is laid on the heroic virtues of personal courage and doomed persistence.

In the religious poems, the aristocratic military code is transferred to the warriors of God, sometimes neatly, sometimes with incongruous effect. Prophets and apostles, saints and devils, Christ and Satan appear therefore in semi-familiar guise, with the Heroic Age never very far off either from Palestine or from Heaven, and this is in keeping with the poet-audience relationship in an England recently christianised. In the splendid *Dream of the Rood*, a strikingly dramatic meditative lyric in which the cross itself speaks and describes how Christ was crucified upon it, Christ is presented as a 'strong young hero', the leader of a *comitatus* of disciples. His actions are positive: he 'strips himself', 'mounts' the cross, 'embraces' the wood. A similar energy characterises the commanding figure of Satan in *Genesis B*: he appeals to his followers in Hell as his war-companions to whom he has once given princely treasures and who owe him service. In these two impressive poems, no doubt intensity is gained from the extreme situations—Christ on the cross, Satan in Hell—to which the poet has reacted imaginatively; but they also show the unexpected adaptability of the heroic ideal.

A different approach to the Anglo-Saxon audience is seen in the beast-fables, where religious instruction is given in a delightful allegorical form; *The Phoenix*, with its allegory of the Resurrection and its fine picture of the earthly paradise, and *The Whale*, which gives a naïve yet powerful symbolising of devilish deceptiveness, are the most notable examples.

The saints' lives (*Andreas, Elene, Guthlac, Juliana*) and the Biblical or Apocryphal narratives (*Genesis A, Exodus, Daniel, Judith*) are less valuable as poetry, though some vigorous description of action is found in *Andreas* and *Judith*. There are also one or two eloquent passages in *Christ* and *Christ and Satan*. The contrast between these mainly didactic works (some of them by Cynewulf, whose poetic reputation has been rather shakily built on attributions more than on the few poems he has actually signed) and the personal, deeply felt *Doomsday* (known alternatively as *Judgement Day II*—a late tenth-century poem) is particularly interesting because in the latter poem the Cynewulfian metrical grace has been broken up into various irregularities—like **Donne** after **Sidney**—which suit both the terrible subject and its penitential poet.

A distinctive feature of Anglo-Saxon poetry is the lyrical monologue, which in subject matter may overlap on either the heroic or the religious. *The Wanderer*, *The Seafarer*, *The Wife's Lament*, *The Husband's Message*, *Wulf and Eadwacer*, and *The Ruin* are a group of poems varying in value (and in certainty of text and interpretation) but all taking us into an area of human experience which has seldom been expressed with such pathos. Essentially it is the experience of loneliness: a masterless minstrel in exile, a sailor on the night sea, a woman parted from her husband, a husband from his wife, a woman from her lover, a man meditating alone on a deserted and ruined town. Images of desolation—snow and hail, screaming sea-birds, rain, crumbling walls —are everywhere presented as part of man's environment, just as separation and exile, and the physical danger of being unattached or friendless, having 'wolves for companions', always lie in wait in the precarious society of the Germanic migrations and settlements. Seafarer and wanderer may indeed bear eschatological overtones of the pilgrim soul banished from Eden and searching for Heaven; but they remain, in their basic strength, men of a historical time and place.

Hwær cwom mearg? Hwær cwom
  mago? Hwær cwom maththumgyfa?
Hwær cwom symbla gesetu? Hwær
              sindon seledreamas?
Eala beorht bune! Eala byrnwiga!
Eala theodnes thrym! Hu seo thrag
                 gewat,
genap under nihthelm, swa heo no
                 wære!

(Where has the horse gone? The rider?
          The treasure-giver?
The halls of feasting? Where are man's
              joys?
The dazzling goblets! The dazzling
            warriors!
The splendour of the prince! Ah, how
           that time
Has gone, has darkened under the
          shadow of night
As if it had never been!)
         The Wanderer, 92–6

For lighter entertainment, the minstrel could produce his *Riddles*, *Charms*, or *Maxims*. In these engaging poems, everyday life is reflected with realism and humour, sometimes with a grotesque fantasy. The *Maxims* (also known as *Gnomic Poems*) show a command of juxtaposition that is startlingly prophetic of cinematic cutting. In the *Riddles* the poet fixes by a cleverly misleading, yet often true and even lyrical description, some familiar object, conception, or living creature: a plough and a sword, a weather-cock and a battering-ram, a book and a bookworm, a badger and a cuckoo, gale and iceberg, horn and mead.

Moththe word fræt. Me thæt thuhte
wrætlicu wyrd, tha ic thæt wundor
               getrægn,
thæt se wyrm forswealg wera gied
               sumes,
theof in thystro, thrymfæstne cwide
ond thæs strangan stathol. Stælgiest
             ne wæs
wihte thy gleawra, the he tham
            wordum swealg.

(A meal of words made by a moth
Seemed to me when I heard the tale
Curious and phenomenal:
That such a mite like a thief in the
             night
Should swallow up the song of a poet,
The splendid discourse and its solid
            setting!
But the strange robber was none the
            wiser
For all those words and all that
            eating.)
        Riddle: Bookworm

But whether propounding a riddle, or re-telling a story of the Germanic heroes, or brooding on the first and last things of the Christian faith, the Anglo-Saxon poet remains, in a way that Wordsworth might have envied, 'a man speaking to men'. And whether lay or monastic, his audience kept a place for him. This is what gives Anglo-Saxon poetry its lasting qualities of dignity, moral force, and seriousness.   E.M.

Arnold, Matthew (1822–88), was the son of Thomas Arnold, the famous headmaster of Rugby. He was educated at Rugby, Winchester, and Balliol College, Oxford, where he won the Newdigate Prize for poetry. He held a fellowship at Oriel College, was for a time secretary to Lord Lansdowne, and in 1852 became inspector of schools, a position which he held until two years before his death. He married in 1852.

Arnold's first volume of poems, *The Strayed Reveller*, appeared in 1849, and was followed by *Empedocles on Etna* in 1852. Both of these he soon afterwards withdrew from circulation; but in 1853 he published a volume containing extracts from them. Later volumes appeared in 1855 and 1857; his frigid tragedy, *Merope*, was published in 1858. Most of his prose works appeared after 1860, the most important of these being the *Essays in Criticism* (1865 and 1888). He also published lectures *On Translating Homer* and *The Study of Celtic Literature*. His most important work of political and social criticism was *Culture and Anarchy* (1869). In later years he wrote on religion; the best known of these writings is *Literature and Dogma* (1873).

The young Arnold shocked or amused his contemporaries by his elegant dandyism, which developed into the famous 'urbanity' of his prose style. More important to the student of his poetry is the early and deep influence on him of the Romantic poets, especially **Byron**. Much of his poetry, as well as his letters to his close friend, A. H. **Clough**, reveals a conflict between his temperamental ro-

manticism and the strenuous moral earnestness he inherited from his father. If the 'Marguerite' of his 'Switzerland' and 'Faded Leaves' poems was an actual girl (which is not certain), this conflict was enacted in a love affair, and brought about its unhappy termination:

> Again I spring to make my choice;
> Again in tones of ire
> I hear a God's tremendous voice—
> 'Be counselled, and retire!'
>   *The Lake*

Whatever the biological facts, Arnold wrote comparatively little poetry after his early thirties. He entered instead upon a second and more immediately influential career as a literary and social critic, educational reformer, and religious thinker. He himself described his own poetic vein as a 'buried stream'.

The characteristic quality of much of Arnold's poetry is suggested by the opening of *A Summer Night*:

> In the deserted moon-blanch'd street
> How lonely rings the echo of my feet!
> Those windows, which I gaze at,
>   frown,
> Silent and white, unopening down,
> Repellent as the world:—but see!
> A break between the housetops shows
> The moon . . .

As so often in Arnold, poetic inspiration is symbolised by moonlight, which through 'a break between the housetops' brings a temporary relief from the 'repellent' world. Significantly, this is in a poem which deals, as Arnold the poet does not usually deal, directly with 'this strange disease of modern life'. The prose Arnold, with his insistence on 'seeing the object as it really is', may assail the Philistines with irony, banter, or persuasive exhortation; the poetic Arnold prefers to glide away from 'this uncongenial place' to a world 'far, far from here', where feeling is released by the song of nightingales, moonlight on moving water, and the contemplation of a serene, beautiful, yet poignant version of Greek legend.

Arnold's contribution to the classics of the schoolroom include *The Forsaken Merman* and *Sohrab and Rustum*, a self-consciously 'Homeric', though rather over-decorated, narrative poem. But grown-up readers seem to find *Dover Beach* more to their taste; feeling themselves, with the poet, 'on a darkling plain', 'where ignorant armies clash by night'. Next in popularity, perhaps, comes *The Scholar Gipsy*, with its attractive wistfulness and its memorable depiction of the beauty of the Oxfordshire countryside. Both of these poems show that 'self-commiseration' which Lionel Trilling finds characteristic of Arnold's best poetry. In Arnold this becomes a civilised sentiment, expressed with limpid melody. Yet Arnold himself was dissatisfied with his own work. He was aware that his finest inspiration came from the impulse which produced the song of Callicles in *Empedocles on Etna*; but he was obliged also to write the arid, dissonant, anguished meditations of Empedocles.

T. S. **Eliot** has described Arnold's poetry as 'academic', and it cannot be denied that Arnold's work has something of the prize-poem about it; at its best noble, sonorous, memorably phrased, it lacks the highest kind of technical originality. Moreover, Arnold is far from being always at his best, and his sad lapses of diction, rhythm, and 'ear' have often been noticed. But his positive virtues remain. He may be thought to belong to the same class of poets as **Marvell** or **Gray**, those who are not so much poets by vocation as highly civilised men who write poetry because it is an accepted mode of civilised expression. He was perhaps unlucky in that the tradition in which he wrote, unlike that of Marvell, or Gray in the *Elegy*, may not have allowed the complete realisation of his gifts.

Arnold's turning to prose is by no means a matter for unqualified regret; many readers today prefer his prose to his poetry. It is certainly clear that essays like *The Function of Criticism at the Present Time*, *The Study of Poetry*, and *Wordsworth* (to name no others) rank among the most lasting criticism written during the Victorian age.   W.W.R.

see also Criticism and Poetry *and* Foreign Influences on English Poetry

Auden, W[ystan] H[ugh] (1907–), was born at York, the son of a doctor. He was educated at Gresham's School, Holt, and Christ Church, Oxford. After leaving Oxford he travelled in Germany, and later worked as a schoolmaster and a writer for documentary films. *Letters from Iceland* (1937), written in collaboration with Louis **MacNeice**, is a short autobiography in verse up to 1936. Christopher Isherwood, who collaborated with Auden in three verse plays (*The Dog Beneath the Skin*, 1935, *The Ascent of F6*, 1936, and *On the Frontier*, 1938, and in a travel-book about China, *Journey to a War*, 1939) writes of Auden at school and at Oxford in his *Lions and Shadows* (1938). Auden visited Spain during the Civil War. In 1938 he went to the United States and later became an American citizen. He was Professor of Poetry at Oxford from 1956 to 1961. Auden has written libretti for operas by Stravinsky and Henze.

For many readers, Auden is the representative poet of the nineteen-thirties; and it seems likely that his place in literary history will be defined in some such terms. But Auden has by no means stopped writing since 1939, and it may well be that the division commonly drawn between his 'English' and 'American' phases may prove to be slightly artificial. None the less, there can be no doubt that his work underwent an important change from the nineteen-forties onwards, and J. W. Beach has shown in detail how Auden has revised his earlier work—sometimes even giving it a contrary sense—to bring it into line with his changed beliefs. Thus an interesting study could be written on the single word 'love' in Auden's poetry: to describe the fluctuations of its meaning would be to bring out the conversion of the poet's thought from an idiosyncratic Marxist-Freudian salvationism to an equally personal, if less evangelistic, form of Christianity. Just how significant are these restless disturbances of the ideological surface of Auden's poetry, is still an open question; but it is clear that a constant uneasy awareness of the 'climate of opinion' among sophisticated intellectual readers—the kind of readers who are most drawn to Auden's poetry—has played an important part in the composition of the poetry itself. For Auden's characteristic work has always shown an acute consciousness of 'the modern situation' as perceived by the intelligentsia of the time, and he himself has admitted that 'the preacher's loose, immodest tone' has been his chief temptation as a poet.

Yet much of Auden's early work, like the 'charade', *Paid on Both Sides*, had a markedly esoteric flavour; the poet was clearly drawing on private memories or obsessions to reinforce his imagery. This 'privateness' is indulged in the strange fantasy, *The Orators* (1932), sometimes to the point of irresponsibility. It was all the more noteworthy, therefore, that a poet

liable to such obscurity could also convey so vivid and lucid a sense of the general contemporary scene. Lines like these from *Birthday Poem* show Auden's gift for the memorable poetic reporting of the familiar present:

> August for the people and their
> favourite islands.
> Daily the steamers sidle up to meet
> The effusive welcome of the pier, and
> soon
> The luxuriant life of the steep stone
> valleys,
> The sallow oval faces of the city
> Begot in passion or good-natured
> habit,
> Are caught by waiting coaches, or
> laid bare
> Beside the undiscriminating sea.

But even in the most successful 'public' poetry of his early period Auden had a tendency to vacillate between a tone of facile knowledgeableness—the fashionable jargon of an eclectic culture—and an unabashed use of private reference, a self-consciously esoteric game. Some would judge that this tendency has remained in his later work, though expressing itself in somewhat different forms. Yet Auden's sternest critics must surely admit a certain power and vitality in a poet who became so influential that his highly personal mythology of imminent apocalypse, disease, death-wish, 'the Enemy', decaying industry, rusty machinery, the Railway, The Frontier...became common currency in the writing of the nineteen-thirties. This imaginary landscape is now so immediately recognisable and familiar that readers of Auden's generation may forget that it took a poet of his originality to create it.

Much has been written on the social background of the Left-wing poetry of the period; and no doubt it may be rightly related to the discontents, the mingled sense of guilt and frustration, among the upper, upper-middle, and professional classes in England after the First World War. But quite probably the distinctive character of this poetry, in so far as it was successful, takes its origin from the singular personal manner of Auden. Where Auden's enormous influence is concerned, then, criticism may have the same sort of problem as in dealing with his poetry: how to decide which of its distinctive qualities are merely representative of a common *malaise*, for which he was the spokesman, and which the reflection of a unique poetic personality.

The work of Auden's middle period, of which *For the Time Being* (1945) is perhaps representative, seemed to show a falling-off from the vivid, if sporadic, inspiration of his 'English' phase, and it was tempting at this time to find his most successful achievements in the field of light verse, a form of poetry in which Auden has always been interested (he edited the *Oxford Book of Light Verse*) and which in his hands, according to Kenneth Allott, expresses 'the normal Auden personality' suitably adapted to this mode. Certainly the lyrical gift shown in justly admired poems like 'Lay your sleeping head, my love . . .' was all the more welcome when it appeared here and there amidst much stodgy and mannered didacticism. *The Age of Anxiety* (1948), an ambitious 'eclogue' obviously aiming at a comprehensive poetic critique of modern maladies, perhaps marked the culmination (or nadir) of this didactic, generalising, moralising tendency. For although this poem contains some striking and penetrating observation and commentary, it is marred by curious immaturities and lapses of tone, and the general reaction to it was one of disappointment. Since *The Age of Anxiety* Auden has published nothing comparably ambitious in poetry. But a sifting of his later volumes reveals some impressively mature and serious poems (for example, the title poem in *The Shield of Achilles*) which show that his remarkable talent is by no means exhausted.

It is still too early to attempt even provisional summing-up of Auden's work. All that can be reasonably suggested is that the technical agility, and even virtuosity, which marked his poetry from the start has remained constant in his later development; while a certain sinister resonance, when the poet captured the mood of 'our time' without losing the unmistakable tones of his own personal voice, has departed from his writing. But he still remains the most widely influential and interesting poet of his generation.

W.W.R.

see also American Poetry *and* Foreign Influences on English Poetry

Australian Poetry. Australia's first recorded poet was Michael Massey Robinson, a gentleman convict who specialised in odes for royal birthdays, and who began publishing them in 1810. With him and Barron Field began that tradition of ambiguous response to the brute fact of Australia, which was to persist throughout the century. Their poetry is negligible, but it shows both a delight in the sheer freshness and isolation of the country and a revulsion from what some critics have called its 'utter contrariety'. These are the motifs which stir the sluggish stream of Australian poetry until the appearance of Adam Lindsay Gordon, Charles Harpur, and Henry Kendall around the middle of the century.

All three are interesting cases: Gordon for his oscillation between a verse of reckless action and one of easily evoked nostalgia; Kendall for the depth of his melancholy and the compulsive recurrence of his favourite images; and Harpur because, after all, his sense of the concrete and particular is not entirely muffled by the softening 'romantic' conventions which these poets made use of.

But no native tradition of any worth springs from any of them. The bush ballad, the vogue of which succeeded theirs, was such a tradition, but one whose relevance was limited to the social situation that called it forth. It was not until the turn of the century that any poet emerged for whom any substantial claims can still be made.

This was the era in which 'the big booming Australian voice', as one New Zealand critic has called it, began echoing everywhere. An elevated conception of rhetoric and a naïve conception of lyric took over, and ruled until the nineteen-thirties; indeed they are still surprisingly influential. Two of the reputations made in those decades can hardly remain permanent: those of William Baylebridge (1883–1942), a highly abstract affirmer of cosmic purposes, and Bernard O'Dowd (1866–1953), an almost equally abstract affirmer of social ones. O'Dowd is the better poet, but most critics agree that his early work is distorted by rant, and that only in his long poem *The Bush* (1912) does his vision of human destiny become transmuted into satisfying poetic terms. Hugh McCrae (1876–1958) was a more vital force. Most of his best work is in *Satyrs and Sunlight* (1928), a series of lyrical statements of the need for passion, in which there is a surprising play of wit. John Shaw Neilson (1872–1942) was an acknowledged naïf of fine but occasional penetration:

Listen! the young girl said. For all
Your hapless talk you fail to see

There is a light, a step, a call
This evening on the Orange Tree.
The Orange Tree

His collected poems appeared in 1934.

But the largest of all these poets was Christopher Brennan (1870–1932), most of whose interesting work was completed by 1900 and printed in *Poems* (1913). Between that date and 1960 there was no further collected edition, and Brennan's reputation has floated buoyantly on a stream of legend rather than on any critical analysis or debate. Now it seems clear that he is not the great international figure some Australians have thought him; but he is an important cultural fact. He claimed an affinity with Mallarmé; but he was also influenced by the Miltonic heaviness mediated to him, in its softer Keatsian version, by German Romanticism, and by the rhythms of the Celtic Twilight. His more ambitious metaphysical poems are clogged and opaque; and his lasting achievement is in a few lyrics and his sequence *The Wanderer*. In the latter sequence, with its Celtic gesturing, he steps clear from portentousness and embodies his own alienation in a myth of metaphysical wandering:

So I sit and muse in this wayside harbour
and wait
till I hear the gathering cry of the ancient
winds
and again
I must up and out and leave the embers of
the hearth
to crumble silently into white ash and
dust,
and see the road stretch bare and pale
before me:
again
my garment and my home shall be the
enveloping winds
and my heart be filled wholly with their
old pitiless cry.

When the 'Australian Renascence' came, under the influence of Norman Lindsay in the nineteen-twenties, it took a line directly opposite to European modernism, which was assailed for its 'decadence'. But out of this excitement emerged the two poets who were to bring into Australian poetry something of the modern precision and self-awareness: R. D. Fitzgerald and Kenneth Slessor.

Both are usually regarded as poets of the thirties, though Fitzgerald, a ceaseless experimenter, has kept on growing in stature until the present. Slessor, a poet endowed with a brilliant play of fancy, virtually stopped writing in 1938, after an increasingly tragic awareness of life had culminated in the fine and passionate elegy, *Five Bells*. His collected poems were contained in *One Hundred Poems* (1944), reprinted later with three additional short poems under the title *Poems* (1957). Fitzgerald, on the other hand, developed slowly, through a dogged application to the technical problems of presenting historical event and human incident. His best-known book is *Moonlight Acre* (1938), composed of two uneven sequences of lyrics and two more ambitious poems; but it is arguable that his best work is in *Between Two Tides* (1952), an epic of power and intrigue in Tonga of the eighteenth century, and *This Night's Orbit* (1953), a collection of shorter poems including the taut, experimental, memorable *Fifth Day*.

Not until after the war were the advances and experiments made by Slessor and Fitzgerald consolidated. Judith Wright and James McAuley both published their first books in 1946, Francis Webb and John Manifold in 1948. These post-war years may be regarded as the highpoint in Australian poetry. Judith Wright was immediately accepted and has been increasingly fêted ever since. The first substantial Australian poet to write under the influence of **Eliot**, she produced in *The Moving Image* (1946) a series of richly textured lyrics in which desperation at the loneliness of human beings is barely held in control. Her second book, *Woman to Man* (1949), is generally regarded as her finest achievement, containing as it does a set of lyrics concerning the conception and birth of her child:

This is no child with a child's face;
this has no name to name it by:
yet you and I have known it well.
This is our hunter and our chase,
the third who lay in our embrace.
Woman to Man

Her three later books have not made such an impact, although *The Two Fires* (1955) includes an important poem, *The Harp and the King*.

James McAuley, influenced as no other Australian poet has been by **Blake**, **Yeats**, and Rilke, introduced a very different note. In his first book, *Under Aldebaran* (1946), he used a variety of fixed forms to blend a quality of cerebration with a rigorously exalted statement of the ambiguity of the poet's rôle in life. Between that and his second book, *A Vision of Ceremony* (1956), he became a Catholic and became known as a 'classicist'. His later poetry is thinner in texture and more consciously graceful. Francis Webb, another Catholic, emerged as a wry experimenter with the dramatic monologue in his *A Drum for Ben Boyd* (1948). He has since published three further books, *Leichhardt in Theatre* (1952), *Birthday* (1954), and *Socrates* (1961). The themes which remain most persistent in his poetry are those of a self-exploration often violent and dangerous, and objectified in stories of physical exploration.

John Manifold, a Communist, has

published no book since *Selected Verse* (1948). His work as exemplified in that volume is characteristically taut, neat, and firmly stated.

Among the other poets now in their forties, the chief is Douglas Stewart, whose speciality is the gracefully cadenced creation of feelings trembling on the edge of consciousness; and among the younger poets, the most individual are probably Evan Jones, whose *Inside the Whale* appeared in 1960, and Gwen Harwood, who has as yet published no book.

But the most influential of all Australian poets is certainly A. D. Hope, a man who published his first book when he was well into middle age (*The Wandering Islands*, 1955). His more recent book, *Poems* (1960), included most of the best work in that volume. Hope's vision has been called both 'heroic' and 'contradictory', 'classical' and 'obsessive'. His tightly organised forms and smoothly moving rhythms

convey a view of man as balanced precariously between fulfilment and damnation. As he writes of Eve,

> The proud vicuña nuzzled her as she
> > slept
> > Lax on the grass—and Adam,
> > > watching too,
> > Saw how her dumb breasts at their
> > > ripening wept,
> > The great pod of her belly swelled
> > > and grew,
>
> And saw its water break, and saw, in
> > fear,
> > Its quaking muscles in the act of birth,
> > Between her legs a pigmy face appear—
> > And the first murderer lay upon the
> > > earth.
> > > *Imperial Adam*

In the short space of six years, he has had an enormous influence on Australian poetry, though it has not yet been fruitfully assimilated by younger poets.   v.b.

B

Barker, George (1913–   ), is considered a poet of the nineteen-forties rather than the nineteen-thirties, although he published his first volume at the age of twenty. But although his most typical work approaches the human condition at its symbolic roots in an ambitious visionary style influenced by **Blake** and the Surrealists, he has a fund of seriousness and genuine power of thought which places him nearer, say, to **Auden** than to Dylan **Thomas**. A poem like *Resolution of Dependence* is successful and moving because it keeps

under control that originality which elsewhere, as in the strange and much-maligned long poem. *Calamiterror*, produces the more characteristic Barkerian style, an imagery at once formal, simple, but colourful and often brilliantly horrific. His lyrics are much praised, and he has written other long poems of great interest, notably the Villonesque *The True Confession of George Barker* (omitted from the *Collected Poems*). Barker's poetry is often concerned with sex because this is to him, as a very individual Roman Catholic, a central element in the tragedy of human life. Most readers value him as a poet who is never evasive and who is technically most assured and inventive. Criticism of his poetry often centres on a certain unevenness of style and a careless use of symbols and images: this could be said of his most recent collection, *The View from a Blind I*. Nevertheless, Barker is one of the few considerable poets of the post-Auden era.   J.F.

Barnes, William (1801–86), born in the Blackmoor Vale of Dorset, is the unfairly neglected author of *Poems of Rural Life* in the Dorset dialect (1844, 1859 and 1863). Probably the apparent obscurity of his vocabulary, which affronts the eye but yields to the understanding, accounts for the obscurity of the poet.   D.H.

Barnfield, Richard (1574–1627), is the author of *The Affectionate Shepherd* (1594), a pastoral derived from Virgil, and other poems and satires. Two of his poems which were published in *The Passionate Pilgrim* were long believed to have been written by **Shakespeare.**

Beaumont, Francis (*c.* 1585–1616) and **Fletcher,** John (1579–1625), are figures inseparably linked together. After studying at Oxford and the Inner Temple, Beaumont became a dramatist, and his collaboration with Fletcher, the son of a clergyman, started about 1608 and continued until about 1613. Their early plays were probably written for boy actors but their later work was commissioned by the King's Men. After the retirement of **Shakespeare** and Beaumont, Fletcher became the principal dramatist of this adult company, though he frequently collaborated with Philip Massinger and other playwrights.

Comedies and Tragedies, the Folio published in 1647, attributes thirty-four plays and a masque to Beaumont and Fletcher, and the Folio of 1679 ascribes

fifty-two plays and the same masque to them. Research has shown, however, that they were the joint authors of only about twelve plays. Beaumont's constructive powers were superior to Fletcher's. Unlike Fletcher, he made frequent use of run-on lines in his blank verse and often introduced passages of rhyme and prose into his plays. These distinctive characteristics make it tolerably certain that *The Woman Hater, The Masque of the Inner Temple,* and *The Knight of the Burning Pestle* are entirely by Beaumont. The latter play is the finest of Elizabethan burlesques, offering a skilful parody of such fads as the bourgeois knight-errantry of Heywood's plays, the romantic marvels of popular ballads and romances, the rant of Senecan tragedy, and the naïve tastes of citizen audiences.

Neither of Fletcher's tragedies, *Bonduca* and *Valentinian,* is as well constructed as *The Maid's Tragedy,* which he wrote in collaboration with Beaumont. All three depend more on exciting events than characterisation and exploit extremities of romantic love, loyalty, tyranny, and pathos. The two dramatists collaborated best in the writing of tragi-comedy, which, according to Fletcher, deals with the danger but not the reality of death. *Philaster* and *A King and No King* well exemplify their skill in this type of drama. Set against romantic Mediterranean backgrounds, they work out a series of conflicts between love and honour which rise to their most dangerous climax at the close of the fourth act and are happily resolved in the fifth. Complications of plot are often achieved at the expense of consistency of characterisation, but the grace of the dialogue, the lyrical and pastoral interludes, the resourceful stage business, and the swift tempo of the action promote a temporary suspension of disbelief.

In several respects, Fletcher's comedies

anticipate the Restoration comedy of manners; his main theme is the warfare of the sexes, his hero is usually a clever rascal, and his heroine a witty upholder of feminine independence. Designed as a sequel to *The Taming of the Shrew*, *The Woman's Prize* shows how Petruchio is subdued by his second wife. In *The Wild Goose Chase*, which is probably Fletcher's best comedy, Mirabel is the 'wild goose' outwitted and won by ladies.　　 W.A.A.

Beddoes, Thomas Lovell (1803–49), was educated at Charterhouse and Oxford. While an undergraduate he published *The Improvisatore* (1821), an accomplished 'gothick' verse romance. After taking his degree, Beddoes proceeded to Göttingen to study medicine. Among the romantic poets who attempted to adapt Elizabethan tragedy to their own highly subjective idiom, Beddoes was the most successful. His first closet-drama, *The Bride's Tragedy* (1822), was enthusiastically received and the following year the poet met T. F. Kelsall, who immediately recognised his genius, and was to preserve many of the unpublished manuscripts towards which Beddoes himself showed such indifference. The years 1823 and 1824 were the most prolific and confident of the poet's career, witnessing the composition of many brilliant dramatic fragments. As H. W. Donner observes, their abandonment by Beddoes denoted rapid development rather than that faltering control of material underlying his many revisions of his major drama, *Death's Jest Book* (first draft, 1825–9). With its romantic irony, macabre and grotesque elements, *Death's Jest Book* was sourly received by Beddoes' friends, who advised against publication. The poet, recognising the play as his masterpiece, lost confidence, and his solitary habits and moods of depression were accentuated. Yet, though *Death's*

Jest Book contains striking scenes and single lines, its Elizabethan complexity of plot mutes its dramatic impact.

Apart from several rather unhappy visits to England, Beddoes' life was now spent in Germany and Switzerland, where he played a lively part in revolutionary politics. A group of fragmentary lyrics and prose pieces, *The Ivory Gate*, survives from these years. To the end the poet devoted himself to continuous, never completed, though often dazzlingly detailed revisions of *Death's Jest Book*.

The last of several suicide attempts was successful on 28 January, 1849. Beddoes' suicide, however, was not merely the result of psychosis; it was also doctrinal, for he was obsessed with the notion of death as spiritual maturity. This obsession charges his boldest and strangest images. Death is often depicted with a fierce terseness that recalls **Donne**:

> Millions have died that we might live
> this day

or his description of life as

> a single pilgrim
> Fighting unarmed against a thousand
> soldiers.

Beddoes never altogether realised his rich gifts, but dramatic fragments and isolated lyrics possess suggestive and incisive qualities that have won him choice admirers over the last sixty years.　　 I.F.

Belloc, Hilaire [Joseph Peter] (1870–1953), who was born in France but brought up in England, is best known in poetry for his nursey classics, like *The Bad Child's Book of Beasts* (1896) and *Cautionary Tales*. He also produced a small body of serious verse remarkable for its neat craftsmanship.

Benét, Stephen Vincent (1898–1943), was an American playwright, poet, novelist and short story writer who used American themes. In 1929 he was awarded the Pulitzer Prize for *John Brown's Body*, a long narrative of the Civil War which still enjoys considerable popularity in the United States. His poems are metrically various, and versatile in their use of different dictions.

Berryman, John (1914–), is an American poet, critic and short story writer, best known for *Homage to Mistress Bradstreet* (1956). and his *Dream Songs*. From an origin in the Audenesque thirties of American poetry, Berryman developed an involute, idiosyncratic style which has found its best expression in the eccentric, cryptic, moving sequence of *Dream Songs*. In 1965 he won the Pulitzer Prize. D.H.

Betjeman, John (1906–), has written several books of verse satirising, with bitterness yet nostalgia, English suburban life and love. Strong feelings treated wryly, detailed observation, and mastery of late-Victorian forms, which he turns ironically, characterise his best work. S.S. *see also* Popular Poetry

Binyon, Lawrence (1869–1942), was an English poet, dramatist and historian of Oriental art; his translation of Dante was praised by Ezra **Pound**. His *For the Fallen*, engraved on many English war memorials, was set to music by Elgar. D.H.

Bishop, Elizabeth (1911–), is an American poet, winner of a Pulitzer Prize, who lives in Brazil. Her poems often begin as quiet descriptions, somewhat in the manner of Marianne **Moore**, and end with a discovery of symbolic significance in the object or event described. D.H.

Bishop, John Peale (1892–1944), poet, essayist and novelist, was born in West Virginia. He was associated with Agrarian poets but was not primarily regional. His works include *Undertaker's Garland* (with Edmund Wilson; 1922), *Collected Essays* (1948) and *Collected Poems* (1948). D.H.

Blake, William (1757–1827), poet, painter and prophet, was born at 28 Broad Street, Golden Square, in Soho, London, on 28 November, 1757, the son of a prosperous hosier. When he was ten he was sent to Pars' drawing-school in the Strand, and four years later he was apprenticed to the engraver, Basire, there to learn the craft by which he afterwards lived. Blake's taste for Gothic art was formed at this time, while drawing the royal sepulchral monuments in Westminster Abbey for the Society of Antiquaries; and for comparative mythology through other of Basire's works, which included Stuart and Revett's *Antiquities of Athens* and Bryant's *Mythology*, for which latter he may have executed several engravings.

Poetical Sketches, printed in 1783 through the help of friends (notably Flaxman the sculptor), were written between 1768 and 1777. They show the influence of **Chatterton**, Percy's *Reliques*, **Ossian**, **Spenser**, and **Shakespeare**. In 1784 he married the illiterate daughter of a market-gardener, whom he taught to read, write, assist his engraving, and to see visions, a faculty that he himself possessed and which he believed to be latent in everyone. The marriage was childless but happy, Catharine Blake surviving her husband, who died in 1827 and was buried in Bunhill Fields. Blake and his wife lived at various times in Lambeth, South Molton Street, and Fountain Court off the Strand. The years 1800–04 were spent at Felpham on the

Sussex coast under the patronage of Hayley, friend of Romney and biographer of **Cowper**; but to this well-intentioned but galling protection Blake preferred hack work in London. From about 1820 to the end of his life he was enabled, by the help of a group of young disciples, Linnell, Palmer, Richmond, Calvert and others, to undertake his greatest works as an artist: his woodcut illustrations to Virgil, the twenty-two engravings to the Book of Job, and the illustrations to Dante.

Most of Blake's poetry was written before 1804, his latest work being *The Everlasting Gospel* (*c.* 1818). *The French Revolution* was printed in 1791 by Blake's friend and employer, the bookseller Johnson, but at the last minute not published on account of its Jacobin sentiments. A trial for sedition (in which he was acquitted) that brought to an end his stay at Felpham, suggests that Blake was never afraid of speaking his mind at whatever personal risk. Mary Wollstone-craft was among his friends, and he is said to have helped Payne to escape from England.

None of Blake's later writings was published in the ordinary way. He engraved his poems and aphorisms on marvellous pages decorated by designs, each copy coloured by hand, sometimes by Mrs Blake. These books, sold for a few pounds to a small number of friends and others, are now beyond price, as are his paintings, most of which were made to the order of his most constant friend and patron, Thomas Butts, a Swedenborgian. His writings include *There is no Natural Religion* (1788), *Songs of Innocence* (1789), *Tiriel* (1789), *The Book of Thel* (1789), *The Marriage of Heaven and Hell* (1793), *Songs of Experience* (1794), *Europe* (1794), *The First Book of Urizen* (1794), *The Book of Ahania* (1795), *The Book of Los* (1795),

The Song of Los (1795), *Vala* or *The Four Zoas* (manuscript, 1795–1804), *Milton* (1804–08) and *Jerusalem* (1804–?20). Most of these dates are approximate only. Besides these he wrote a burlesque, *An Island in the Moon* (?1809); *A Descriptive Catalogue* of his one exhibition, held at 28 Broad Street in 1809; and several manuscripts, the most important being the so-called Rossetti notebook, in which poems, fragments in prose and verse, and sketches for drawings were made over many years. Blake's *marginalia* are remarkable; among annotated works that have been preserved are Lavater's *Aphorisms*, two volumes of Swedenborg, Bacon's *Essays*, Berkeley's *Siris*, **Wordsworth**'s *Excursion*, Reynolds' *Discourses* and Carey's *Dante*.

Blake's lyrics were admired by **Coleridge**, Wordsworth and other notable contemporaries; they have the spontaneity of Shakespeare's songs, and a simplicity altogether deceptive, for they embody profound vision and complex philosophy. His so-called Prophetic Books are as forbiddingly obscure as the lyrics are apparently simple; yet in fact both are the work of the same mind, essentially imaginative and mythopoeic. Blake belongs to the romantic rise of imagination against rationalism, and his intellectual grasp of the issues involved equals, if it does not surpass, that of Coleridge. He attacked the scientific materialism of Bacon, Newton and Locke, in no way misled by Newton's professions of religion as to the real implications of his thought. The Prophecies all concern the spiritual condition of England, embodied in a multiform myth whose agents are the passions and faculties of the soul personified and revealed as the agents of history. Orc (passion) is manifested in rebellion against Urizen (reason), and Los (imaginative vision) labours for the regeneration of man through works of art. Tharmas, the physical man, plays a less important part. Each of these four 'Zoas' has a feminine 'emanation', the vehicle of the energy symbolised by the male. Blake realised that none of these faculties is the whole man; and in his attack on the rationalism of the Enlightenment created the monstrous figure of Urizen, the rational faculty that attempts to usurp the supreme government of man that belongs properly to the indwelling Logos, 'Jesus the Imagination' or the Divine Humanity present in and to man —a term borrowed from Swedenborg. Blake's Satan is the human selfhood or ego that opposes the influx of the divine spirit. Jerusalem is the soul of Albion, and Vala the Goddess Nature, *maya*, with whom he has fallen in love, to his undoing. (Scientific materialism is itself this infatuation; or, as he elsewhere says, 'Bacon's philosophy has ruined England'.) As a mythological expression of the mentality of his age Blake's myth is unerring in its penetration. His grasp of political events was clear, and his knowledge of history, philosophy and contemporary scientific thought extensive. His symbolism, once erroneously thought to be personal and subjective, proves on examination to be traditional, basically Neoplatonic, Biblical and alchemical.

His mythology is eclectic, for he believed that 'all religions are one', and that Christianity is the perfect expression of the one unanimous and universal tradition. He drew upon Greek, Norse, Celtic and even Indian themes, combining elements from several sources with an unerring insight into the metaphysical essence of symbols; as in his blending of Apuleius' Legend of Cupid and Psyche with the Biblical story of Solomon and the Fair Shulamite in his own myth of the love-story of the soul (Vala) and the divine

Eros (Luvah) told in Night IX of *Vala*, Christianised later in the story of Jerusalem and Jesus. The form of his long works is chaotic; he was always attempting, W. B. **Yeats** writes, to master the 'overflowing and bursting of the mind' with 'shining images' that amaze but bewilder. But the thought embodied is a consistent and comprehensive philosophy of the imagination. He resembles Coleridge in the ocean-like capacity of a mind that transcends formulation.

The notion at one time current that Blake was a self-taught eccentric has given place to an increasingly respectful recognition of the extent of his knowledge. What Nature was to Wordsworth, works of art were to Blake. 'He saw everything through art', Samuel Palmer recalled, 'finding sources of delight throughout the whole range of art'; while, as a critic, he was judicious and discriminating. He illustrated the works of many poets, including Young, Blair, **Gray**, Ovid, Shakespeare, **Chaucer**, Bunyan, and above all **Milton**, who was for Blake the ideal of the inspired poet, and whose influence is everywhere discernible in his writings. He was a Platonist and widely read in the Platonic tradition, from the Hermetica, Plotinus, Porphyry and Proclus to Berkeley. He read Plato, the Neoplatonists and the Orphic Hymns in the translations of Thomas Taylor, whom he probably knew well during his formative years. He also studied Swedenborg, Boehme, Cornelius Agrippa and the alchemists, especially Paracelsus, from whom he seems to have derived his doctrine of a 'marriage' of contraries. He read French, a little Latin and Greek, and learned Italian when over sixty in order to study Dante, who was as constantly in his thoughts in his last years as was Milton at an earlier period.

He despised Augustan poetic diction and was among the great innovators of verse. His lyrics have long been admired, but his use of long lines in the Prophetic Books is no less original and impressive. He called himself 'a true orator', and probably intended his verse to be declaimed. The trochaic pentameter is so frequent that it may be called his norm, but eight-stressed lines are frequent; the internal structure of his lines is variable, even to the use of 'sprung' rhythm, and is always organic. Ossian had upon Blake's verse a beneficial liberating influence; and **Chapman**'s *Homer* has also left its mark. Blank Verse he considered 'a monotonous cadence'. The strength, originality and organic quality of Blake's verse may be seen in this typical passage from Night II of *Vala:*

> What is the price of experience? Do
> men buy it for a song?
> Or wisdom for a dance in the street?
> No, it is bought with the price
> Of all that a man hath,—his wife, his
> house, his children.
> Wisdom is sold in the desolate market
> where none come to buy,
> And in the withered fields where the
> farmer ploughs for bread in vain.
> It is an easy thing to triumph in the
> summer's sun,
> And in the harvest to sing on the
> waggon loaded with corn.
> It is an easy thing to talk of patience to
> the afflicted,
> To speak the laws of prudence to the
> houseless wanderer,
> To listen to the hungry raven's cry in
> the winter season,
> When the red blood is filled with
> wine and with the marrow of lambs.
> It is an easy thing to laugh at wrathful
> elements,
> To hear the dog howl at the wintry
> door, the ox in the slaughter-house
> moan;
> To see a god on every wind and a
> blessing on every blast

> To hear sounds of love in the
> thunderstorm that destroys our
> enemy's house;
> To rejoice in the blight that covers his
> field, in the sickness that cuts off his
> children.
> While our olive and vine sing and
> laugh round our door, and our
> children bring fruits and flowers,
> Then the groan and the dolor are
> quite forgotten, and the slave
> grinding at the mill,
> And the captive in chains and the poor
> in the prison, and the soldier in the
> fields
> When the shattered bone hath laid
> him groaning among the happier
> dead.
> It is an easy thing to rejoice in the
> tents of prosperity:–
> Thus could I sing and thus rejoice:
> but it is not so with me.

A lifelong Christian, he was, with his friend Flaxman, an early member of the Swedenborgian Society. He was baptised, married and buried in the Church of England. In late life his friends were as shocked by his admiration of the Catholic Church and the Papacy as they were by the Jacobinism of his earlier years. But throughout his life he was consistent in his denunciation of scientific humanism and positivism, the cause of the Industrial Revolution that in his view ruined England. Poetry and prophecy were for Blake interchangeable terms, and he called 'false art' all naturalism, and whatever is not inspired by imaginative vision.   K.R.
see also Science and Poetry

Blunden, Edmund [Charles] (1896–), was born in Kent and educated at Cleave's Grammar School and Christ's Hospital. He served as a lieutenant with the Royal Sussex Regiment in France and Belgium, from 1916, returning to Oxford to take his degree when the war was over. From

1924 until 1927 he was Professor of English Literature at Tokyo University and from 1931 to 1943 was Fellow and Tutor at Merton College, Oxford. He was Professor of Poetry at Oxford from 1966 to 1968, and winner of the Queen's Gold Medal for Poetry in 1956.

He has published several volumes of prose and verse, and edited, among others, the work of **Clare, Collins, Hardy, Keats, Owen, Smart, Vaughan** and **Shelley.**

His early verse, inspired by the Kent countryside, owes much to Clare in verse forms, use of dialect words and imagery based on a close study of nature, and this period provides some of his best work. However, because he is always an observer not himself involved in the agricultural cycle, he lacks the vivid immediacy of Clare and is inclined to become merely descriptive.

His war poems do not have the bitter intensity of Owen's, but they are a faithful and sensitive record of that profound experience to which he returns repeatedly in his later work:

Be still, if these your voices are; this
                monolith
For you and your high sleep was made.
Some have had less.
No gratitude in deathlessness?
No comprehension of the tribute paid?
You would speak still? Who with?
           The Memorial

Since then he has been influenced successively by the poets he has studied. The verse has become weaker and there are an increasing number of compounds, combined with the duplication of adjectives, suggesting that the right word has eluded him. While his contemporary, **Graves,** has become part of the mainstream of modern poetry, Blunden has retreated into a linguistic backwater.

                      M.D.

Bogan, Louise (1897–), is an American poet, critic and lecturer born in Maine; she is poetry reviewer for *The New Yorker,* and she shared the Bollingen Prize with Léonie **Adams** in 1955. Her collected poems, which were published in 1955, reveal a talent for intense emotionality within precisely articulated forms. Her critical writings include *Achievement in American Poetry 1900–1950* (1951) and *Selected Criticism* (1955). A new collection of her poetry appeared in 1968 under the title of *The Blue Estuaries.*   D.H.

Bottrall, Ronald (1906–), is an English poet much praised by F. R. Leavis, in *New Bearings in English Poetry.* He has represented the British Council in Rome, Tokyo and elsewhere, and he was made a Fellow of the Royal Society of Literature in 1955.   D.H.

Bradstreet, Anne (?1612–72), was an English gentlewoman who arrived in New England in 1630. Her one volume of poems, *The Tenth Muse Lately Sprung Up in America . . .* (London, 1650), shows her to be largely derivative ('a right Du Bartas girle'). Her work indicates that a Puritan could combine piety and passion, and produce occasional lyrics remarkable in the context of pioneer New England. *see also* American Poetry   A.P.H.

Breton, Nicholas (?1545–?1626), wrote a considerable body of verse, of which the best was collected in *England's Helicon.* He had a lightness of touch in his short lyrics which is individual and which repays any reader's attention.   D.H.

Bridges, Robert (1844–1930), was born at Walmer in Kent. He was a doctor in early life, but was appointed Poet Laureate in 1903 and retained the position until his death. A tireless experimenter in metre, language and spelling-reform, he set out to found a new Classicism, based, according to Arthur Symons' review of one of his books of lyrics, on 'a thinking back as of one who really, in thought, lives in another age, to which his temper of mind is more akin'. Bridges thought back most often to the age of **Sidney** and **Campion**, though he resorted to the Greeks for the plots of some of his academic dramas, and took Lucretius as his model for the long reflective poem of his old age, *The Testament of Beauty*. He also learned something from the experiments of his friend, Gerard Manley **Hopkins**, whose poems he kept in his drawer for twenty-five years, in the belief that they were too radical to be published.

The best of Bridges is to be found in his shorter lyrics, which usually follow Elizabethan or romantic patterns. Though gently elegiac, they never reveal the cause of the poet's grief. Bridges' reticence was extreme. His sequence, *The Growth of Love*, contains interpolated sonnets which effectively disguise the story of the poet's love and loss. When writing *On a Dead Child*, a poem that recalls an incident in his medical training, Bridges refuses to show his feeling and ends on a coldly rhetorical note. *London Snow*, a purely visual exercise in modified Hopkins technique, is more moving, as are also some of the lyrics of his old age which recall childhood. Occasionally, as in *Low Barometer*, he has some of the haunted simplicity of Walter **de la Mare**:

The south-wind strengthens to a gale,
Across the moon the clouds fly fast,
The house is smitten as with a flail,
The chimney shudders to the blast . . .
And Reason kens he herits in
A haunted house. Tenants unknown
Assert their squalid lease of sin
With earlier title than his own.

Had the conservative reasoner and experimenter in Bridges been aware more often of these 'unknown tenants', his poetry might have been more compelling. As it is, a handful of the shorter lyrics and some descriptive passages from the curiously archaic *Testament of Beauty* are all that the modern reader will turn back to.

J.M.C.

Brontë, Emily (1818–48), the English novelist and poet, was one of the loneliest and strangest of English geniuses. She spent most of her life, apart from a visit to Brussels in 1842 during which she pined for home, at her father's lonely parsonage at Haworth on the Yorkshire moors. Her fame during much of the nineteenth century was overshadowed by that of her sister Charlotte, but most critics would now agree that her single novel, *Wuthering Heights*, has a depth, strength, and poetic intensity lacking, for all their vitality, in Charlotte's lively but much more conventional and sentimental novels.

In 1846, Emily published along with her sisters Charlotte and Anne a joint volume, *Poems of Currer, Ellis and Acton Bell*. Charlotte and Anne had no poetic gifts at all, and Emily, with a profoundly poetic spirit, had a good ear for rhythm and cadence but not much taste in language or feeling for construction. Most of her poems are more notable for isolated lines and stanzas, or for the fierce, proud, and lonely spirit that pervades them, than convincing as wholes. But for the reader who admires her great novel, or who has become interested in her extraordinary character, the poems express truthfully and movingly—if not beautifully or perfectly—her stoicism, her harsh but sincere religious attitudes, her passion for the Yorkshire moorlands, and a deep mystical yearning which seems impatient with the labour of shaping and polishing verse. There is a strange mixture of intimacy and distance in her writing, in verse, as well as in prose. She looks, in a sense, both back to **Blake** and forward to D. H. **Lawrence.**

An example of Emily's style, in which sincerity and intensity of thought and feeling never quite conquer the pedestrian metres of the hymnal or a fading romantic rhetoric, is this last stanza of *Last Lines*:

> Though earth and man were gone,
> And suns and universes ceased to be,
> And Thou were left alone,
> Every existence would exist in Thee.
>
> G. F.

Brooke, Rupert (1887–1915), was the son of a housemaster at Rugby School. In considering his poetry it is essential to separate Brooke from the myth which grew up after his death from blood-poisoning on the way to the Dardanelles in April, 1915. At that time he was virtually unknown. He had published one book, *Poems* (1911), which had been both attacked for its 'unpleasant' realism and praised for its tender and satiric strain. As Edward **Thomas** wrote: 'If readers live a little longer they may see Mr Rupert Brooke a poet. He will not be a little one.' Thomas had in mind such poems as *Menelaus and Helen*, *Lust*, or *Wagner* from which this is the last verse:

> The music swells. His gross legs quiver.
> His little lips are bright with slime.
> The music swells. The women shiver.
> And all the while, in perfect time
> His pendulous stomach hangs
>   a-shaking.

Brooke was a scholar of lively intellect; a Fellow of King's College, Cambridge; a Fabian Socialist; an active and practical man in literary affairs. To label him a 'war-poet' on the strength of five patriotic sonnets which caught the mood of the time is to misunderstand him. To regard him as typically 'Georgian' is also to misunderstand him, though this sobriquet was invented in concert with his friend, Edward Marsh. It was however 'E.M.''s taste that gave to subsequent anthologies of Georgian Poetry their particular flavour.

The myth of Brooke arose out of his own outstanding personal beauty allied to the fact that Marsh, as Winston Churchill's private secretary, was in a position to speak of him in the most influential political and social salons of the time. Brooke became a national symbol of noble sacrificial youth. This has done him considerable disservice as an artist. There is beyond doubt a communicable vitality in his poetry. When he died he had hardly begun to fulfil the promise of his first book; but in his latest poems there is abundant evidence of a genuine and original talent.   P.D.

Browne, William (1591–1643), is the author of the epitaph on the Countess of Pembroke ('Sidney's sister, Pembroke's mother') which has been attributed to Ben **Jonson.** His descriptions of nature are compelling, and won him the admiration of later, romantic poets.   D.H.

Browning, Elizabeth Barrett (1806–61), was born at Coxhoe Hall, Durham. By the early eighteen-forties her articles and poems had won the admiration of many readers, among them Robert **Browning,** whom she married in 1846. With her husband she lived and worked happily in Florence, an impassioned spokesman for Italian liberty and a favourite poet in England and America. Her eager humanitarianism, courage, and intellectual energy inform her famous protest against employing children in mines and factories, *The Cry of the Children* (1843), a poem which retains its power despite technical lapses and a characteristic prolixity. For modern readers *Casa Guidi Windows* (1851) and *Poems before Congress* (1860) are little more than records of her absorption in Italian life and politics. Her long romantic novel in verse, *Aurora Leigh*, a great success when first published in 1856, contains fine passages in keys unfamiliar to those who know only her love poems.

The forty-four *Sonnets from the Portuguese* (1850) explore and celebrate her enraptured love for her husband with an art unmatched in her other work. The first lines of Sonnet VII will illustrate their tone and sentiments:

The face of all the world is changed,
I think,
Since first I heard the footsteps of thy
soul
Move still, oh, still, beside me as they
stole
Betwixt me and the dreadful outer
brink
Of obvious death, where I, who
thought to sink,
Was caught up into love and taught
the whole
Of life in a new rhythm.

In the words of her biographer, Louise Boas, 'it is because the experience, though rare in such perfect form, is the universal ideal that her poems remain the perpetual voice of true lovers'.   D.L.H.

Browning, Robert (1812–89), was born in Camberwell, then a suburban village three miles south of the centre of London. His father was a clerk in the Bank of England, although he was also a learned man with a large collection of pictures and books. Educated primarily in his father's library, Browning also spent about six months at the newly organised University of London in 1828. Having decided that he wanted to be a poet and playwright, he was financially dependent upon his father until he married Elizabeth Barrett in 1846. His father or other relatives paid for the publication of his early poems. In 1846, Browning and Elizabeth Barrett eloped to Italy, living at Pisa and at Florence until she died in 1861. He then returned to London, becoming more successful and more idolised (the Browning Society was first established to praise and discuss his work in 1881) with every passing year. Browning died in Venice on 12 December, 1889, and was buried in the Poets' Corner in Westminster Abbey.

His first long poem, *Pauline* (1833), was a versified account of his own battle with religious scepticism and the rational influences of Voltaire. Strongly influenced by **Shelley**, he felt that poetry must record the central struggles within the poet's own mind and feelings. His second long poem, *Paracelsus* (1835), absorbs some of the confessional element in the dramatic portrayal of Paracelsus, the German Renaissance physician and scientist. The poem uses history to underline the conflict between knowledge and love. *Paracelsus* was praised by Walter Savage **Landor**, John Stuart Mill, **Wordsworth**, and others, but Browning's reputation disappeared with the publication of *Sordello* (1840), a long, highly obscure poem relating his theories on poetry, philosophy, love and Italian Renaissance history. He also attempted to write for the stage. Between 1837 and 1846 he wrote eight plays, three of which (*Strafford*, 1837; *A Blot in the 'Scutcheon*, 1843; and *Colombe's Birthday*, 1844), through his friendship with Macready, the famous actor-manager, were actually put on the stage. His plays were not successful, however, for their intricate verse and their emphasis on character did not satisfy the early Victorian demand for theatrical action and gore.

Browning also began to publish lyric poems, some as songs in the various plays (as in *Pippa Passes*, 1841), others independently in such volumes as *Dramatic Lyrics* (1842), *Dramatic Romances and Lyrics* (1845), and *Men and Women* (1855). Some of the lyrics reverberate with a hearty affirmation repellent to many twentieth-century readers:

> Kentish Sir Byng stood for his King,
> Bidding the crop-headed Parliament
> swing:
> And, pressing a troop unable to stoop
> And see the rogues flourish and honest
> folk droop,
> Marched them along, fifty-score strong,
> Great-hearted gentlemen, singing this
> song.
> *Cavalier Tunes*

In other short poems, Browning combines the lyric with a thematic narration. *The Last Ride Together*, for example, tells the story of a man's last drive with his love, though the story also demonstrates that life and any form of love are superior to all the arts as forces that give man pleasure and value. Yet the kind of lyrical form that conveys the narrative is both loose and jingling:

> I said—Then, Dearest, since 'tis so,
> Since now at length my fate I know,
> Since nothing all my love avails,
> Since all, my life seemed meant for,
> fails,
> Since this was written and needs
> must be—
>
> My whole heart rises up to bless
> Your name in pride and thankfulness!
> Take back the hope you gave—I claim
> Only a memory of the same,

> —And this beside, if you will not
> blame,
> Your leave for one more last ride
> with me.

The same volumes that contained these repetitious and sentimental poems also included many of Browning's most justly famous dramatic monologues. He developed the art of poetic treatment of human character in terse, compressed images. In *The Bishop Orders His Tomb at Saint Praxed's Church*, the dying bishop's instructions display all the rich sensuality, pride, and love for the artistic that characterise the Italian Renaissance:

> Peach-blossom marble all, the rare, the
> ripe
> As fresh-poured red wine of a mighty
> pulse . . .
> Some lump, ah God, of *lapis lazuli*,
> Big as a Jew's head cut off at the nape,
> Blue as a vein o'er the Madonna's
> breast . . .

Given historical or contemporary settings, the monologues often present casuistic arguments from characters most readers would regard as villains: the Duke in *My Last Duchess*, the narrator in *Mr Sludge*, 'The Medium', Don Juan in *Fifine at the Fair*. At other times, the monologues demonstrate a sensitive insight into failures, as in *Andrea del Sarto* in which the narrator reveals his inability to reach the kind of perfection he strives for in both his painting and his domestic life:

> There's what we painters call our
> harmony!
> A common greyness silvers
> everything—
> All in a twilight, you and I alike
> —You, at the point of your first pride
> in me
> (That's gone you know)—but I, at
> every point:

My youth, my hope, my art, being all
          toned down
To yonder sober pleasant Fiesole.
There's the bell clinking from the
          chapel-top;
That length of convent wall across the
          way
Holds the trees safer, huddled more
          inside;
The last monk leaves the garden; days
          decrease
And autumn grows, autumn in
          everything.

Because of the sympathy with which the protagonists are presented, readers have often assumed that something of Browning's opinions can be directly derived from the dramatic monologues. But even a famous statement like

Ah, but a man's reach should exceed
          his grasp,
Or what's a Heaven for?

in *Andrea del Sarto* is far more the painter's pathetic attempt at self-justification than Browning's philosophy. The poet, at his best, concealed himself behind the style and the terms of his characters.

In 1868 and 1869, Browning published his most extensive work, *The Ring and the Book*. Based on an account of a late seventeenth-century Italian murder trial that he had discovered on a bookstall in Florence, the long poem is a series of dramatic monologues interpreting the events from eleven different points of view (only one of which belongs entirely to Browning). Although the poet's sympathies are evident, for the murdered adultress and her lover seem almost like saints while the injured husband is both cruel murderer and melodramatic villain, each monologue is itself a thorough study of the character who delivers it. The verse is sometimes dull and repeti-

tious, although some of the fragments are terse and effective. Browning continued to write copiously, although in much of his later work, such as *Parleyings with Certain People of Importance* (1887), the compressed monologue has degenerated into the rambling essay. During his later years and for several decades after his death, critics and Browning Societies debated about what the poet's central message or philosophy was. From his looser, more essayistic poems, he seems to have advocated a belief that religious faith can conquer rational scepticism and favoured a kind of athletic spiritual vigour. Yet these simple faiths cannot explain the complex probings into human character apparent in his best dramatic monologues. Browning operated best under the severe restraints of a careful and faithful presentation of character, a guise of objectivity of a sort seldom understood and appreciated by the worshipping readers of his own day.   J.G.
see also Translation

Bryant, William Cullen (1794–1878), was born in Cummington, Massachusetts, and educated at Williams College. In 1817 the publication of his poem *Thanatopsis* laid the foundation of his sure, though not sensational, poetic fame. In 1825 he moved to New York, and in the following year became editor of the *Evening Post*, in which capacity he remained for more than fifty years—a partisan of Jacksonian Democracy, an influential voice in the affairs of the growing metropolis, and in his old age a picturesque and esteemed public figure.

Bryant's poetic output was small. The *Poems* of 1821 were followed, over his lifetime, by four other slim volumes of verse. He was primarily a poet of reflective lyrics, with only a few ideas and no wish to experiment. He expresses his thoughts sincerely, in carefully chosen language. In *Thanatopsis* and *To a Water-fowl* we find his favourite themes: the frailty and uncertainty of human life, and the permanence of nature. At times, as in this stanza from *To a Waterfowl*, the pathos and the sombre power of description raise the verse to a high level:

> All day thy wings have fanned
> At that far height, the cold, thin
> > atmosphere,
> Yet stoop not, weary, to the welcome
> > land,
> Though the dark night is near.

Some of Bryant's more facile poems, such as *Robin of Lincoln* and *The Death of the Flowers*, have found numerous readers. He is the author, also, of prose essays and lectures on topics ranging from politics to poetry, and of translations of the *Iliad* and the *Odyssey*.   L.S.

Burns, Robert (1759–96), was born at Alloway, near Ayr, the son of a gardener. His father took a small farm at Mount Oliphant but the land proved arid and stony although the whole family worked hard to make it a success. In accordance with Scots custom, Robert received a thorough education from the local school-master, a perceptive man who encouraged the boy to study further, and from an old housekeeper he learned many folk songs and legends.

The hard life continued until Burns was sixteen, when his father took a better farm and Robert was able to continue his education, studying surveying and eventually learning French. Burns' father died in miserable circumstances and he and his brother went into farming on their own but with so little success that Robert decided to emigrate. First, however, he published *Scots Poems chiefly in the Scottish*

Dialect, which was so well received that he went to Edinburgh instead and brought out another volume. With the proceeds from this he bought a farm, married, and then began to contribute regularly to James Johnson's *The Scots Musical Museum*.

In 1789 he was appointed exciseman and soon gave up his unlucky farming venture. He contributed to George Thomson's *A Select Collection of Original Scottish Airs* and there were two more enlarged editions of his poems. Just as it seemed that he had attained a life of reasonable comfort he contracted rheumatic fever and died after a year's severe illness.

Burns has for so long been regarded as the national poet of Scotland, to the neglect of such poets as **Dunbar**, Fergus-son and **Ramsay**, that it is difficult to assess his true place in English literature. As with all national heroes, legend has accumulated round him, obscuring what seems unsuitable: his inability to resist a pretty face, his strong anti-Calvinism and fierce revolutionary sympathies which nearly lost him his post as exciseman, but it is precisely those qualities which made him so considerable a poet.

His subjects are the local fairs, drinking parties, legends and gossip related at the fireside, and we hear them in the authentic voices of Burns and his neighbours.

> 'Twad be owre lang a tale to tell,
> > How monie stories past,
> An' how they crouded to the yill,[1]
> > When they were a' dismist:
> How drink gaed round, in cogs an'
> > > caups,
> > Amang the furms an' benches,
> An' cheese an' bread, frae women's
> > > laps,
> > Was dealt about in lunches,[2]
> > > An' dawds[3] that day.

[1]*yill*—ale [2]*lunches*—large pieces [3]*dawds*—lumps

and later:

How monie hearts this day converts
   O' Sinners and o' Lasses!
Their hearts o' stane gin night are gane,
   As saft as ony flesh is.
There's some are fou o' love divine,
   There's some are fou o' brandy,
An' monie jobs that day begin,
   May end in Houghmagandie[1]
     Some ither day.

He was an ardent, if usually humane, critic of the people and customs among which he lived. Sins of the flesh he forgave easily, as in *The Holy Fair*, but pride, spiritual and temporal, he satirised as unmercifully as **Pope**. It is a mistake to think of him as an untutored genius, standing outside the poetic tradition of his time. He was thoroughly grounded in grammar and syntax and knew most of the English and Scots writers who immediately preceded him, but his wit found best expression in his local speech; his attempts to write in the polished diction of the eighteenth century sound lame and pompous. The rhythms of Bible and sermon, however, appear frequently in his work, though usually with sardonic intention.

Lord, in thy day o' vengeance try him!
Lord, visit him that did employ him!
And pass not in thy mercy by them;
   Nor hear their prayer;
But for thy people's sake destroy them,
   And dinna spare!

But Lord; remember me and mine
Wi' mercies temporal and divine!
That I for grace and gear may shine,
   Excell'd by nane!
And a' the glory shall be thine!
   Amen! Amen!

[1] *Houghmagandie*—fornication

Burns' mastery of his verse-forms never failed, whether it was the complex *rime couée* of *Holy Willie's Prayer*, the rhyming couplet used with such skill in *Tam O'Shanter* or the simple quatrains of many of the songs. These are so well known that they have obscured the boisterous, satirical verse, which is so reminiscent of Villon in its exuberant enjoyment of life, but it was the craftsmanship of the early poems that made him able to write songs of such deceptive simplicity and freshness.

Some of them are revisions of traditional airs, others use only the chorus or title as a starting point. They supply the more intimate side of Burns' work, often connected with one or other of his love affairs, a forbidden meeting or its result, but they include drinking and patriotic songs of great vigour and the revolutionary *For A' That and A' That*. He enjoyed writing them so much that he refused any payment for them, preferring to live quietly among his neighbours rather than become 'the tenth worthy and the eighth wise man of the world'.   M.D.

Butler, Samuel (1612–80), was born of yeoman stock, and seems to have made a living from the age of fourteen as secretary to various well-heeled patrons, both Puritan and Royalist. His *Hudibras* (published in three parts in 1663, 1664 and 1678) spectacularly satirised the Puritans, delighted the King and Court, and made him a public personage. Yet tradition has it that he died in want, a further monument to Charles II's notorious ingratitude —and perhaps also to his own misanthropy, scepticism, and crusty honesty.

Hudibras drew upon a formidable wit and a capacious learning enlisted in the service of parody. In English poetry it embodied two geniune innovations: it re-discovered mock heroic, for the enlightenment of **Dryden**, **Pope**, and

Swift; and it converted the fluent or stately tetrameter couplets of **Marvell** and **Crashaw** to a loose, galloping metre pointed by colloquial diction and double and partial rhymes. The Errant Saints (replacing Knights Errant)

> Decide all controversies by
> Infallible artillery;
> And prove their doctrine orthodox,
> By apostolic blows and knocks; . . .
> Compound for sins they are inclin'd to,
> By damning those they have no mind to.

The two, of course, are complementary: the mockery of decidedly earthly Saints is paralleled by the stylistic swoop of pretension into bathos:

> And like a lobster boil'd the morn
> From black to red began to turn.

All Butler's liveliest work is in tetrameters: besides *Hudibras*, notably *The Elephant in the Moon*, a neglected poem which in its satire on the fantasies of scientists anticipates Swift in both matter and burlesque invention. Of his prose works the most noteworthy are the *Characters*, especially 'A Modern Politician', whose point has not yet been blunted.

A.W.

Bynner, [Harold] Witter (1881–1968), was an American author and editor. In 1916, under the pseudonym Emanuel Morgan, Bynner perpetrated the famous *Spectra* hoax with Arthur Davison Ficke. His works include *Selected Poems* (1936), *A Book of Lyrics* (1955) and *New Poems* (1960).

D.H.

Byron, [George Gordon Noel], Lord (1788–1824), was born in London, the son of Captain John ('mad Jack') Byron and Catherine Gordon of Gight. He was lame from birth, owing to a deformity in one leg (apparently a form of club-foot, or *talipes*). His father died while Byron was still very young, and the boy was brought up by his mother, a woman of violent and unstable temperament, in comparatively poor circumstances. He succeeded as sixth Baron Byron at the age of ten, inheriting the title from his grandfather, who had no surviving heir in the senior line. Byron was educated at Harrow and at Trinity College, Cambridge. *Hours of Idleness* (1807), a volume of comparatively slight undergraduate and earlier pieces, was violently attacked by some influential critics, partly because of Whig prejudice against Byron's aristocratic status. Byron avenged himself in *English Bards and Scotch Reviewers* (1809), an extremely telling satire in heroic couplets. Byron's tour in the Mediterranean from 1809 to 1811, which took him to Spain, Portugal, Greece and Turkey, gave rise to the first two cantos of *Childe Harold's Pilgrimage* (1812). These cantos began Byron's sensational popular success as a poet. They combined descriptive poetry in a manner not very remote from the eighteenth-century tradition with a fresh element, the presentation of the Byronic *persona*—the proud, lonely, melancholy wanderer through whose eyes these scenes are presented. On his return Byron took his seat in the House of Lords (where he made a memorable speech in defence of the Luddite machinewreckers) and became, handsome and carrying an aura of mystery, the idol of the fashionable drawing rooms.

Byron followed up the success of *Childe Harold* with such highly popular romantic narratives as *The Giaour* (1813), *The Bride of Abydos* (1813) and *The Corsair* (1814), in all of which the same typical Byronic hero is presented against a romantic Levantine background. *Hebrew Melodies* (1815) contains some memorable

33

lyrics, such as 'The Destruction of Senna-cherib' and of course:

> She walks in beauty, like the night
> Of cloudless climes and starry skies.

Byron's marriage to Miss Milbanke took place in 1815, but they were separated in the following year. Whether the separation came about because Lady Byron had discovered incestuous relations between her husband and his half-sister, Augusta Leigh, or for some other reason, is not certainly known, and probably never will be. At any rate, London society was scandalised, and Byron left England once more, this time for good. His travels took him to Switzerland and Italy, and he composed the third and fourth cantos of *Childe Harold* (1816, 1818). In imaginative power, they represent a considerable advance on the earlier part of the poem. But in *Don Juan*, the opening cantos of which were written between 1818 and 1820, Byron discovered a new and much more truly original vein. He rightly regarded this poem with far more seriousness than he did his popular romantic writings, and continued to work on it, in spite of the disapproval of his publisher, his friends, his mistress, Countess Teresa Guiccioli, and much of the public at large. For these looked upon the poem as a heinous and highly immoral work. *Don Juan* remained unfinished at Byron's death. While composing it he had continued to work his romantic vein both in narrative—notably *Mazeppa* (1819) —and in drama. Some of Byron's plays had some success on the stage in his day, but perhaps the most impressive, *Manfred* (1817) and *Cain* (1821), were not intended for the stage. They are dramatic philosophical adumbrations of the characteristic Byronic theme of titanic, cosmic defiance. *The Vision of Judgment* (1822), written,

like *Don Juan*, in the *ottava rima* stanza, is perhaps the finest of Byron's works, ranking with *Don Juan* as a great and original satire.

The outbreak of the Greek War of Independence opened the last brief chapter in Byron's career. He had always identified himself with the cause of the oppressed, whether at home or abroad. The Greek struggle for freedom captured his imagination, and in 1823 he set out to join the insurgents; in the following year he died, of fever, at Missolonghi. In his last lines, written when he completed his thirty-sixth year, he had said:

> If thou regret'st thy youth, *why live?*
> The land of honourable death
> Is here—up to the field, and give
> Away thy breath.

> Seek out—less often sought than found—
> A soldier's grave, for thee the best,
> Then look around, and choose thy
> ground,
> And take thy rest.

In the above account there has been space to mention only some of the chief events of Byron's brief life, and only some of his most striking works. He was a man of extraordinary dynamic energy, and wrote rapidly, not to say facilely, correcting and revising little. His personality gripped his generation with a mythic power, and for Europe at large he was the very symbol of the whole romantic movement. But here we meet a paradox. Byron was a champion of **Pope** and the Augustan values; he despised his great English romantic contemporaries, **Wordsworth, Coleridge,** and **Keats.** He thought far less highly of his own romantic pieces, which so captured the imagination of his contemporaries, than of *Don Juan*. Later criticism has at length come to agree with him here. *Don Juan* is great verse—but it is in a sense anti-poetic. The subjective, Byronic element is still there, but is tempered by irony, *panache*, and high spirits. *Don Juan* belongs essentially to the tradition of the novel, drawing especially on the eighteenth-century masters—Fielding, Smollett and Sterne.

The discrepancy between Byron's reputation abroad and the estimate of English critics has come to be notorious, though the gap is perhaps not so wide today as it was during the century following his death. English readers have inevitably been most sensitive to the faults of much of his poetry. It is sometimes technically weak, the diction undistinguished, the

thought second-rate. But these same English readers have also sometimes been less than sensitive to its passion and energy, and have brought irrelevant moral judgments to bear upon Byron's work. Criticism of Byron has been too much concerned with the biography and personality of the man—fascinating as these are in the problems and paradoxes they present—and not enough, at least until recently, with his work. Yet a high proportion of the latter still retains its vitality; and *Don Juan* at least, with its humour, humanity, and brilliant use of colloquial language, stands as a great work of literature. J.H-S. *see also* Satire

C

Cameron, Norman (1905–53), was a 'part-time' poet and translator who nevertheless achieved a distinguished if limited reputation. He published in Grigson's *New Verse*, and a collection, *The Winter House*, appeared in 1935, but his work is not obviously akin to that of other poets of the nineteen-thirties. Though his virtues of clarity and sense belong to the period, he has often the withdrawn and careful air of a poet who does not risk much. Some of the early poems are slight, with a classical touch; some later ones are looser, even comic. His best, however, such as *The Winter House* or *The Successor*, are strange and imaginative, and while in a sense no more personal than many of his neater ones, do strike one more forcibly for not being too obvious in their symbolism. As a whole his poetry is remarkable in its impact, for there are

fewer than sixty short pieces in the 1957 *Collected Poems*. He achieves his power and consistency by combining highly metaphorical forms with an honest plainness of style, the latter being a virtue which has made him known for his excellent translations of Rimbaud and Villon. There is a biographical introduction to his *Collected Poems* by Robert **Graves,** whose characterisation of his personality ('gentle, witty, clumsy, shrewd, overgenerous, and utterly reliable') has perhaps a useful bearing on his poetry. J.F.

Campbell, [Ignatius] Roy [Dunnachie] (1902–57), born in Durban, South Africa, was the first Colonial poet to achieve an international reputation. He won immediate recognition with *The Flying Terrapin* (1924), a long, flamboyant poem in which, as *The Times* reviewer noted, the influence of Rimbaud first became apparent in English verse. Unlike most of his contemporaries Campbell was a cosmopolitan and spent the best part of his life in Provence, Spain and Portugal; he was also expert at an astonishing variety of skills and at different times earned his living as a seaman, fisherman, horse-breaker, farmer, and bullfighter. Coming from a country still predominantly rural, Campbell could be described as a belated romantic in reaction against the Industrial Revolution and, like the great European romantics of the nineteenth century, the champion of individual man and foe of what Ortega y Gasset called 'the brutal empire of the masses . . . the common-place mind, which, knowing itself to be commonplace, has the assurance to proclaim the rights of the commonplace and impose them wherever it will'. Like those others—the list includes **Eliot, Pound,** Wyndham **Lewis** and **Yeats**—who questioned the assumptions of democracy in the period that saw the rise of Mussolini and Hitler, Campbell was often accused of being a Fascist, especially in view of his championship (as a Roman Catholic) of General Franco in the Spanish Civil War. His convictions led to his writing much satiric and polemic verse, such as *Flowering Rifle* (1936), but this is the least interesting part of his work. His best poems, which show the influence of Baudelaire and Rimbaud, are the lyrics and epigrams which appear in *Adamastor* (1930) and *Flowering Reeds* (1933). Such poems as *Tristan da Cunha, The Zulu Girl, Horses on the Camargue,* and *The Zebras* contain his individualistic outlook and beliefs with infinitely more economy and effect than his satires and polemics; particularly outstanding is *The Sling,* where he writes:

> I unread my books
> And learned, in spite of theories and
>   charts,
> Things have a nearer meaning to their
>   looks

Than to their dead analyses in parts
. . . Our light is in our heads; and we
                                    can seek
The clearest information in our hearts.

His best work is characterised by great forcefulness, energy, and a romantic imagery allied to an intensely personal vision. But in an age of experimental writing Campbell was satisfied to adhere to traditional forms of versification, with the curious result that his early poems now seem to date less than those of many of his more conscientiously modern contemporaries. In his later years he wrote little original verse of the quality to be found in *Adamastor*, but translated an enormous amount of poetry from a number of European literatures. His versions of the poems of Lorca and of St John of the Cross in particular are out-standing.   D.W.
see also South African Poetry in English *and* Translation

Campion, Thomas (1567–1620), was born in London, the son of a clerk in the Court of Chancery. He was at Peter-house College, Cambridge, from 1581 to 1584, and left without a degree. In 1586 he was admitted to Gray's Inn. It is thought that he served under the Earl of Essex during his expedition to France in 1591. In 1594 he contributed to a masque for the Christmas festivities at Gray's Inn, at which **Shakespeare's** *Comedy of Errors* had its first performance. He obtained a medical degree, probably at Caen in 1605, after which he practised as a physician in London.

Campion published five books of lute songs, both words and music, the first (1601) in collaboration with Philip Ros-seter; the other books belong to the later years of his life. He also published *Ob-servations in the Art of English Poesie* (1602), descriptions of four masques (one in 1607, two in 1613 and one in 1614), *Airs sung and played at Brougham Castle* (1612), *Songs of Mourning* (1613), *A New Way of making Four Parts in Counterpoint* (undated), and two books of Latin verse (1595 and 1619). In 1953, before these books were published, George **Peele** addressed Campion as one who 'richly cloth'st conceit with well-made words'. Other eulogies came from Francis Meres, from Samuel **Daniel** and from John **Davies** of Hereford who addressed a sonnet to Campion, praising his mastery of the 'various vaines of musick' and of medicine. Perhaps the crowning tribute was that of William Camden, who mentioned Campion with **Sidney, Spenser, Marlowe,** Shakespeare, **Drayton** and other 'most pregnant wits of these our times, whom succeeding ages may well admire'.

Nevertheless, Campion was soon forgotten and remained virtually unknown until the later years of the nineteenth century. In 1888 A. H. Bullen gave prominence to Campion's lyrics in an anthology and in the next year he published a collection of his writings. Many critics, among them George Saintsbury, discovered the excellence of these works. In 1895 Ernest Rhys described Campion as 'perhaps the one poet who comes nearest to fulfilling, in the genre and quality of his work, the lyric canon in English poetry'. The enthusiasm had not faded in 1932, when T. S. **Eliot** spoke of Campion as 'except for Shakespeare, the most accomplished master of rhymed lyric of his time', or by 1954, when C. S. Lewis wrote that 'with one exception, his poems can be divided only into the good and the better, or else into the more and less characteristic'. Campion the composer was re-established by Edmund Fellowes' edition of the song books (beginning in 1921).

'In these English ayres', wrote Campion, 'I have chiefly aymed to couple my words and notes lovingly together'. His poems are models of the song lyric, but they have an independent word music and a vitality of thought and feeling which raised them above most of the song and madrigal verse of the time. Their metrical designs and rhythms are fresh and varied:

> Kinde are her answeres,
> But her performance keeps no day;
> Breaks time, as dancers
> From their own Musicke when they
> stray.

> Love me or not, love her I must or dye;
> Leave me or not, follow her needs must I.

The distribution of contrast and echo in vowel sounds is finely balanced, and gives a formal perfection to the simplest lines:

> When to her lute Corrina sings,
> Her voice revives the leaden strings,
> And doth in highest noates appeare,
> As any challeng'd eccho cleere;
> But when she doth of mourning speake,
> Ev'n with her sighes the strings do
> breake.

In other poems (e.g. *The sypres curten of the night is spread*, and *When thou must home to shades of underground*) the emotion is stronger, but the language is cool and terse. Many lines have an epigrammatic quality:

> Though Bryers breed roses, none the
> Bryer affect.
> He that a truce embrace will finde
> To beauties faults must still be blinde.

Others' detachment suggests the present age:

> Vaile, love, mine eyes; O hide from me
> The plagues that charge the curious
> minde.

37

Balance, variety, irony and a faultless ear sometimes rescue these love poems from banality. In his religious poems such lapses do occur; nevertheless, one of his most memorable lyrics (*Never weatherbeaten sail*) is among the *Divine and Moral Songs*.

Campion called his English poems 'eare-pleasing rimes without Arte', and aspired for a time towards what he considered a more elevated style, the unrhymed, quantitative verse of Greece and Rome. His attempts to adopt these measures in English failed, but some of the verses with which he illustrated this thesis in the *Observations* (1602) are effective because they can also be scanned without distortion on an accentual basis. Though Campion's arguments are full of flaws (well answered in Daniel's *Defence of Rhyme*), they also reveal his passion for the correct balance of weight, stress, pitch and silence in each line of verse.   E.L.

see also Music and Poetry

Canadian Poetry. From the Colonial beginnings until 1920, Canadian poets accepted the fate of outer landscape as the formula for inner states of mind, if only because this pattern had been worked out by the romantics on the basis of Newton's *Opticks*. But Canadian landscapes, if used as equations for inner mental states, would yield some quite amazing results. Canadians could never bring themselves to accept the logic of their landscape as Roy **Campbell** did the landscape of South Africa. Had Canadians been daring enough to accept their landscape as the formula for mental states, they would have been projected into non-human orbits at once.

Corresponding to the Group of Seven in Canadian painting, we find E. J. Pratt and the Montreal poets who turned to Expressionism and observation of the outer processes of nature and urban commercial life. This meant a quite sharp break with picturesque poetry. Finally, corresponding to the new International Group in painting, are the Academic poets who consider that poetry is made from other poetry. Just as the painters became very much aware of other painters and publics, the poets have begun to notice varieties of poetry and reading publics. The result is a strong tendency towards what might be described as a dialogue in the arts. It even points towards the possibility of Canadian poets beginning to take the resources and traditions of language as their province.

The struggle to perceive some sort of autonomous centre of significance in Canadian expression is made difficult by the fact that a third of the small population is French-speaking. The English group, reading and speaking a principal literary language of the world, can scarcely discern the segment of its image or detect its own intonation in the mosaic of English. Conversely, the Canadian poet feels like an amateur radio-station operator who has to compete with a national network. The Canadian writer has never been encouraged to imagine that English, as a medium of experience and expression, was a personal responsibility and possession. But this situation is not even mainly due to the circumstances of marginal remoteness. Lack of confidence in the medium of English is also due to lack of community and conversation in an over-sized environment. Yet Robert **Frost** was able to use this very factor of lonely incoherence in North American speech in achieving many of his uniquely successful effects of laconicism amidst large silences.

Alienation from the medium of speech as such has been a special Canadian problem, because Canadians began to write poetry just when English poets had shifted the stress in poetry away from speech to the presentation of mental states by means of descriptions of landscape. Canada has a macroscopic landscape and a microscopic social life; and the coincidence of the new landscape poetry and the new Canadian settlement was not fortunate for the arts. Its shaping effect on Canadian poetry was noted by a reviewer as follows: 'For what emerges indubitably . . . is that Canada is a country where every prospect is so vile that the villainies of man are dwarfed by the assembled cruelties of rock, wind and snow.'

Writing in the second issue of *The Tyro* (1922) in an essay entitled 'The Three Provincialities', T. S. **Eliot** began by observing: 'It has been perceptible for several years that not one but three English literatures exist: that written by Irishmen, that written by Americans, and that composed by the English themselves.' By provinciality Eliot here indicates that uneasy state of groping towards identity and definition which was once referred to by a Canadian critic as 'the sense of our density'. When a remote section of population aspires to be in the mode, it involuntarily becomes provincial. When the same group simply assumes the right to innovate and to create without any regard to modishness, it becomes an authentic centre of culture. Canada has not yet approached this state, but the once provincial United States have done so.

The emergence of a North American, rather than a European, cultural centre offers new possibilities to Canadian poetry. It can now take the course which Eliot pointed to in the *Tyro* essay in 1922 as the way out of the three provincialities: 'It is a sign of the poverty and blindness of our criticism that in all three countries a mistaken attitude towards nationality has unconsciously arisen or has been consciously adopted. The point is this: literature is not primarily a matter of nationality, but of language; the traditions of the language, not the tradition of the nation or of the race, are what first concern the writer. . . . It is immaterial, from my point of view, whether English literature be written in London, in New York, in Dublin, in Indianapolis, or in Trieste.'

It remains to sample the principal modes and themes of Canadian poetry. In 1825 Oliver Goldsmith published *The Rising Village* in Halifax, Nova Scotia. It has been designated as 'Canada's first book-length poem in English'. Goldsmith, a connection of the Irish **Goldsmith**, was a son of a Loyalist who had left the American Colonies as a result of the American Revolution. Conscious of writing a kind of triumphant sequel to his grand-uncle's *Deserted Village*, he yet celebrates a different kind of desertion:

When, looking round, the lonely settler
                                    sees
His home amid a wilderness of trees:
How sinks his heart in those deep
                                solitudes,
Where not a voice upon his ear intrudes;
Where solemn silence all the waste
                            pervades . . .

This theme of stark isolation and human insignificance was to be repeated by Canadian poet and novelist alike for the next hundred years. What Pascal had shuddered at in the unsocial spaces of the heavens, the Canadian writer lived with at home.

In 1859, as Canada moved towards Confederation and unification by railway,

Charles Sangster, devotee of Thomas **Moore**, was writing of:

One voice, one people, one in heart
And soul, and feeling, and desire!
Re-light the smouldering martial fire
Sound the mute trumpet, strike the lyre.

But the industrialisation that made possible the national entity of Confederation in 1867 brought motives and patterns into daily life which were utterly at variance with the rural, colonial Canada that took so naturally to the poetry of the roman-tics. This matter is well discerned by Desmond Pacey in his *Creative Writing in Canada* (1951): 'The poetry of Lampman is the product of the impact upon a sensitive mind of the industrial revolution which occurred in Ontario in the late nineteenth century.' There is something almost quixotic about a Canadian re-buking industrialism in the nineteenth century. For whereas in England the industrial gesture was, in relation to the scene and resources, both brutal and des-tructive, Canadian industrialism was a puny gesture in a vast arena. Yet the poets and novelists rallied against it with pre-Raphaelite ardour. Writing of 'The Woodsman in the Foundry' Marjorie Pickthall registers protests and pathos:

Where the trolley's rumble
Jars the bones
He hears the waves that tumble
Green-linked weed along the golden
stones.

Where the crane goes clanging
Chains and bars,
He sees branches hanging
Little leaves against the laughing stars . . .

Canadian poets have never been disposed to wipe their hands across their mouth and laugh. The ability to yearn for pre-

industrial charm among the ice-floes and the blasted pines appears as an im-pressively rugged trait of the Canadian artist and writer. But it may have been no more than loyalty to British fashion.

By 1925 E. J. Pratt had established a delineation of natural force in *The Cachalot* and other poems which brought Canadian expression within the Expres-sionist phase. It is a companion poem as it were to Roy Campbell's *Flaming Terrapin*.

And when the cachalot out-wore
The squid's tenacious clasp, he tore
From frame and socket, shred by shred,
Each gristled, writhing tentacle,
And with serrated mandible
Sawed cleanly through the bulbous
head;

A. J. M. Smith and Klein, F. R. Scott and Earle Birney extended the same expressionist observation of process to the urban scene, having finally accepted, as it were, the displacement of the rural values and ways of Canadian life. The pattern of Scott's *Saturday Sundae* wryly asserts the inadequacy of the new con-sumer's paradise, deprived of the pioneer values:

The triple-decker, and the double-cone,
I side-swipe swiftly, suck the coke-straws
dry,
Ride toad-stool seat beside the slab of
morgue—
Sweet corner drug-store, sweet pie in
the sky.

The world of natural and urban pro-cesses alike traversed with tactile rather than visual stress—such was the new Canadian poetry and painting as it arose in the twen-ties to the fifties. In the fifties there ap-peared a new group that have been called the 'Academic' poets, partly because they have university posts but also because they consider that poetry is made out of other poetry. Some of them are much disposed, as a result of their close study of many writers, to enter into a kind of dialogue with other poets. And this tendency, so different from derivative adaptation, has led the Academic poets deeper into the world of language than Canadians have ventured before. Wilfred Watson, for example, matches his *An Admiration for Dylan Thomas* with *A Contempt for Dylan Thomas*:

poor Turleygod Thomas, his images
           askew
when men were making things of men,
           would hint
(being afraid no heaven can be true)
that thinghood is the heaven of the
           saint . . .

This would seem a most auspicious point at which to conclude a note on Canadian poetry. The emergence of a dialogue among the poets speaks of an entry into the world of the English language which is quite new. The long reign of the picturesque landscape may be over.

                            H.M.M.

Carew, Thomas (*c.* 1595–1640), son of a distinguished and well-connected law-yer, was by profession a courtier. His wit, indiscreetly turned against his patron, Lord Carleton, cost him his first job; but Charles I, says Wood, 'always es-teemed him one of the most celebrated wits in his court', and advanced him to the eminence of Sewer in Ordinary to the King.

Carew is usually associated with **Suckling** and **Lovelace** as a Cavalier Poet. But Suckling mocked him for an unbecoming care:

His Muse was hard bound, and th'
           issue of's brain

Was seldom brought forth but with
           trouble and pain;

and his poems are indeed more finished in form and diction, more elaborate in texture. The influence of the master craftsman **Jonson** is evident, as is also a somewhat muted strain of **Donne's** metaphysical conceits:

Aske me no more where Jove bestowes,
When June is past, the fading rose:
For in your beauties orient deepe,
These flowers as in their causes, sleepe.

The exquisite sound of the first couplet is capped by the philosophical image in 'causes', though its working out is less insistent than it might have been in Donne. Carew's discriminating aware-ness of his masters is shown by his tributes to Jonson, and particularly by the fervent *Elegy* which is incontestably the most penetrating contemporary appreciation of Donne's work.

Apart from the elegies and personal tributes, Carew's nearly constant theme is *carpe diem*; from such blunt assaults as *The Second Rapture*:

Give me a wench about thirteene,
Already voted to the Queene
Of lust and lovers . . .

through such *ad feminam* argumentation as *Perswasions to Love*, to such sly syllo-gisms as *Ingratefull Beautie Threatened*, few poets in English can have varied it more. The variations are emotionally raised above artful ingenuity by an implicit consciousness of the outrage to what is violated: innocence and honour, fidelity and matrimony. The key poem (usually omitted from anthologies as too scandalous) is the early *Rapture*, an antihymn that celebrates a religion of unfettered Love by appropriating with all deliberate blasphemy the traditional symbols:

Bathe me in juyce of kisses, whose
                                        perfume
Like a religious incense shall consume
And send up holy vapours, to those
                                        powres
That blesse our love . . .

In this exposure of opposite values, Carew is the obverse of **Crashaw**, who uses erotic imagery to solicit spiritual states. In this, and in the occasional sensuous richness of his verse texture and ornament, Carew comes close to a true Secular Baroque.   A.W.

Carroll, Lewis, was the pen-name of Charles Lutwidge Dodgson (1832–98). He was master of all types of comic verse, from the close parody by way of various types of fantasy to pure, inconsequential nonsense. Many of his best-known poems occur in *Alice's Adventures in Wonderland* (1865) and *Through the Looking-Glass* (1871). Some of these are parodies that have so long outlived the poems which prompted them that they seem to be Carroll's independent creations. This is true of *You are old, Father William*, the original of which is by Robert **Southey**, and of *'Tis the voice of the Lobster* which, like *How doth the little crocodile*, owes its inspiration to the *Children's Hymns* of Isaac **Watts**. As pure poetry, the nonsensical *Jabberwocky*, which has added several words to the English language and has been translated into several others, is the most accomplished, and the two ballads of *The Walrus and the Carpenter* and *The White Knight's Song* the most sustained. The White Knight's recital of the means by which he made his fortune slyly mocks at

everything from **Wordsworth**'s poetry to the first press advertisements:

His accents mild took up the tale:
  He said 'I go my ways,
And when I find a mountain-rill,
  I set it in a blaze;
And thence they make a stuff they call
  Rowland's Macassar Oil—
Yet twopence-halfpenny is all
  They give me for my toil.'

Carroll's masterpiece, *The Hunting of the Snark* (1876), is a nonsense ballad, romantically anti-romantic after the manner of Edward **Lear**, but not so transparent in its intention. The Snark is a less baleful Moby Dick, and the Bellman a more genial Ahab. Yet there are sinister undertones to the poem. All is not as light-hearted as it appears:

For the Snark was a Boojum you see

Though not so proficient a craftsman as Lear, Carroll had a far wider range. His poems exploit all the resources of colloquialism, mock-logic and contemporary allusion.   J.M.C.

Causley, Charles (1917–), a schoolmaster in Cornwall, was a seaman in the Royal Navy during the Second World War, and first came to notice through his war poems in *Farewell, Aggie Weston* (1951). He writes with extraordinary freshness, often in ballad form in the idiom of the ordinary man, from which the imagination can take vigorous wing. Also notable are *Survivor's Leave* (1953), *Union Street* (1957), and *Johnny Alleluia* (1961).   B.D.

Cavalier Poets. *See* Carew, Herrick, Lovelace *and* Suckling

Chapman, George (?1559–1634), was born near Hitchin, and is thought to have spent two years at Oxford and to have fought in the Netherlands before becoming known as a dramatist in the mid-fifteen-nineties. He later held a post in the household of the Prince of Wales until the Prince's premature death in 1612. Chapman published *The Shadow of Night* in 1594; it is a long, frequently obscure poem in praise of dark speculation and unconventional knowledge, sometimes thought to be the principal doctrine of a school of atheists that included **Marlowe, Ralegh**, Thomas Hariot the astronomer, and others as well as Chapman. The poem, whatever Chapman intended it to be, is crowded with turgid and recondite imagery. Chapman was genuinely devoted to science and learning. He once praised learning as that which 'turns blood to soul, and makes both one calm man'. In *Ovid's Banquet of Sense* (1595), Chapman's rich imagery, although still often clumsy and excessively intricate, is far more effective. He talks of 'the downward-burning flame of her rich hair' and describes the Thames:

And as by London's bosom she doth
fleet,
Casts herself proudly through the
bridge's twists,
Where, as she takes again her crystal
feet,
She curls her silver hair like amourists,
Smooths her bright cheeks, adorns her
brow with ships,
And, empress-like, along the coast she
trips.

Chapman finished Marlowe's *Hero and Leander* (1598). He approached this with some public awareness of his own cumbersome poetry, for he wrote, of Leander:

I in floods of ink
Must drown thy graces.

Nineteenth-century critics tended to feel that Chapman's complexities had spoiled Marlowe's poem. Contemporary critics, however, are more inclined to praise the richness and ingenuity of Chapman's verse. C. S. Lewis even feels that Chapman's verse is more appropriate for the later sections of the poem, for Hero's tormented grief for her departed lover, than Marlowe's would have been. Chapman also spent nearly thirty years translating Homer. His generally free translation made Homeric heroes resemble dashing Elizabethan courtiers. Unlike *Hero and Leander*, Chapman's *Homer* was praised much more widely in the nineteenth century than it has been in our own. Yet all of Chapman's verse, in both poems and plays, is marked by vigour, intelligence and intensity.   J.G.

see also Foreign Influences on English Poetry *and* Translation

Chatterton, Thomas (1752–70), was born in Bristol, where he lived until the last year of his life. By the age of ten he was writing precocious poems, among them verse satires. Before he was twelve he started writing medieval imitations, which he attributed to an imaginary fifteenth-century priest, Thomas Rowley. He wrote these partly under the influence of certain old manuscripts he had discovered, and partly under that of the eighteenth-century passion for the medieval evidenced by **Ossian** and Walpole's *The Castle of Otranto*. In 1770 he went to London, where he wrote a great deal but made little money. After four months there he killed himself with arsenic.

Chatterton's life is better known than his poetry. He satisfies the requirements of the romantic hero in that, firstly, he died young, secondly, society did not recognise him, and thirdly, in Macneile Dixon's words, 'his was a promise rather than a performance'. Nevertheless, when **Keats** finally rejected the style of **Milton**, with the famous remark that 'English must be kept up', it was to the English of Chatterton that he specifically referred. And as a footnote to Keats we can quote Bertrand H. Bronson: 'It is scarcely to the point that Rowley's language, strictly speaking, had no existence elsewhere than in his own mind and work. The same thing may be said, and truly, of **Spenser**'s language, and **Burns**' and **Hopkins**'—and even **Shakespeare**'s!'

What is difficult is to localise the specific evidence of talent, to separate the pastiche from the good writing. In a sense this is impossible, in that it is attempting to separate Chatterton from Rowley. As Bronson says, 'his emotional maturity, his finest aesthetic perceptions, his deepest inspiration, lay in Rowley'. And yet Chatterton was not Rowley, any more than **Pound** is Bertran de Born. The difference is that whereas Pound understands his relationship to Bertran de Born, pretending neither to us nor to himself that he *is* him, Chatterton does not attempt to understand his relation to Rowley. Thus it is Chatterton rather than Pound who is the hero of the senti-mentalists.

Though Chatterton seldom has a subject to bring alive, his writing is often vigorous in incidentals, as in the following stanza from *An Excelente Balade of Charitie*:

> Look in his glommed face, his
> sprighte there scanne;
> Howe woe-be-gone, howe withered,
> forwynd, deade!
> Haste to thie church-glebe-house, as
> shrewed manne!
> Haste to thie kiste,[1] thie onlie
> dortoure bedde,
> Cale, as the claie whiche will gre on
> thie hedde,

[1]*kiste*—coffin.

> Is Charitie and Love aminge highe
> elves;
> Knightis and Barons live for pleasure
> and themselves.

The last two lines would be clichés at any time, but there is considerable strength in the fourth and fifth lines.

Chatterton was immensely talented for his age, but the qualification 'for his age' cannot be omitted. What we can claim for him at his best is a rhetorical power that continually lapses into the nonsensical, a gift for description that treats medieval platitude as its chief ornament, and an energy that is founded in obsession.   T.G.

Chaucer, Geoffrey (*c.* 1340–1400), was born in London; his father, John, was a vintner who owned a house in Thames Street, a man of modest importance in the wine trade. He and his wife, Agnes, were so lucky as to secure a place as a page for young Geoffrey in the semi-royal household of Elizabeth, Countess of Ulster, later Duchess of Clarence. This was the beginning of his successful career as a courtier, and perhaps as a poet, for although there is no record of payments to him in respect of his poetry, the ability to entertain, or at least to read aloud, was among the things expected of an Esquire in a royal household, the rank he was presently to reach. There is in fact a manuscript at Corpus Christi College, Cambridge, showing Chaucer reading aloud to the Court of Richard II.

His name first appears in 1357, in the household accounts of his first employer. Two years later he was sent on active service to France, and was at once taken prisoner at 'Retters', near Rheims. Ransomed and returned to England in 1360, he was taken into the royal service, promoted to Valet in 1367 and to Esquire in 1368. His duties frequently sent him on missions and embassages to the Continent, in a minor capacity. Meanwhile, towards 1366, he had married a lady-in-waiting, Philippa de Roet. She was a sister of Catherine Swynford, the mistress and, ultimately, wife of John of Gaunt, the most powerful and cultivated man in the kingdom. He remained the poet's constant protector, and the last poem Chaucer ever wrote was addressed to his son, Henry IV; it was the poet's *Complaint to his Empty Purse*.

The two missions most important for his poetry were those on which he went to Italy in 1372 and 1378; these introduced him to the work of Dante, Boccaccio and Petrarch, a rich by-product of his official employment. From the official point of view there is no doubt he was an excellent public servant, honest and efficient: he was promoted in 1374 to be Comptroller of Customs and Subsidy of Wools, Skins and Tanned Hides in London; in 1385 he was made Justice of the Peace, and in 1386 Knight of the Shire, for Kent. In the following year, however, he lost all his offices, in the absence of his patron, Gaunt, who had gone off on a military expedition to Spain. Chaucer's wife died at about this time: these blows of fortune may have had good effect for us by freeing him for poetry. He began upon *The Canterbury Tales*. This unfinished masterpiece probably continued to occupy him to the end of his life.

The return of John of Gaunt in 1389 restored Chaucer to royal employment: he became Clerk of the King's Works (1389-91), in which capacity he must have met and worked with Henry Yevele, the greatest architect of the age. In 1394 he was once more in straits for money and was granted a pension; in 1398 King Richard allowed him an annual hogshead of wine, but he did not live long enough to draw it, for he died on 25 October,

1400, and was buried in Westminster Abbey, Yevele's masterpiece, not because he was a poet, but because he was a parishioner. There he has been joined by subsequent poets, in the Poets' Corner.

Chaucer lived at the centre of all the great doings of his day: he must have been in the thick of the Black Death, the Hundred Years' War, and perhaps of the Peasants' Revolt, to which he refers (*The Knightes Tale*) as 'the cherles rebellynge'. More importantly, he was in the thick of the cultural life of Christendom: he read fluently in Latin, French and, later, Italian; he was a distinguished astronomer and mathematician; he was up in the medicine and other sciences of his day; he loved reading and often tells us so, and what he read he remembered and quoted, or used in its Chaucerised forms. For he had an unusual capacity for assimilating and keeping alive his learning, which to him was 'auctoritee', to be held in reverence sometimes tinged with amusement. Against it he would weigh 'experience', gained not from books but from his busy life.

It is traditional and convenient to divide his life as a writer into three periods, though few of his poems can be exactly dated.

1. *The French Period* (1360-72). This may well have begun with his captivity in France; it includes what remains of his translation of the *Roman de la Rose*, a work that profoundly influenced his thought, feeling and technique, some other translations from French, and perhaps some of the now lost 'songs and lecherous lays' he confesses to in his 'Retracciouns' at the end of *The Canterbury Tales*. The gem of this period is *The Book of the Duchesse*, an elegy, couched in the form of an allegorical dream, to celebrate the death of his patroness, Blanche, Duchess

of Lancaster, who died in 1369. It is written with a high elegance of relaxed sentiment, in dream-like narrative form, adorned with every art of rhetoric that young and well-taught genius can bring to personal feeling; though elegiac, it has moments of high comedy and conversational exchange. As in so many of his poems, the poet himself is a central figure; he presents himself as a simpleton, his first trying-out of himself in this character, which reappears in other poems and reaches its full development in *The Canterbury Tales*. The poem is written in octosyllabic couplets that stumble here and there, but contribute a natural if jerky sweetness to the poem, long drawn-out though it be.

2. *The Italian Period* (1373–85). This includes *The Hous of Fame*, *The Parlement of Foules*, *Troilus and Criseyde* and the translation of Boethius; also the *Life of Seynt Cecyle* and *The love of Palamon and Arcite*, known to us respectively as *The Seconde Nonnes Tale* and *The Knightes Tale*; probably also certain other of the Canterbury Tales in their pre-pilgrimage form, for instance the story of Griselda, *The Clerkes Tale of Oxenford*.

The Hous of Fame and *The Parlement of Foules* are cast in the same dream-allegorical convention of French origin that marks *The Book of the Duchesse*, but are more ambitious in structure and content and make use of the work of Dante and of Boccaccio. The former poem is unfinished and concerns a journey to the House of Fame made by Chaucer, in the talons of a rather pedantic eagle, who sweeps him up above the clouds and lectures him on sound-waves and other matters. It is in octosyllabic couplets and for this reason thought to be earlier than *The Parlement of Foules*. The Parlement, which is in the stanza-form known as

'rhyme royal' of seven decasyllabic lines rhyming a b a b b c c, gives us more bird-language, for it includes a lively debate between eagles, a goose, a duck, a cuckoo and a dove, each talking after his kind, on the subject of mating; it is a poem for St Valentine's Day. In these two poems we see the first clear signs of Chaucer's genius in presenting character and idiosyncrasy through good talk. The duck, for instance, thus retorts upon the turtle-dove for its opinion that a lover should keep an eternal constancy to a dead mate:

'Wel bourded,'[1] quod the doke, 'by
        myn hat!
That men shulde loven alwey causeles.[2]
Who can a resoun fynde, or wit, in that?
. . . Ye, quek!' yit seyde the doke, ful
        wel and fayre,
'There been mo sterres,[3] God wot,
        than a payre!'[4]

The poem has a sensuousness, derived from Boccaccio, riper than the cool grace of *The Book of the Duchesse*; the description of Venus seems to anticipate Botticelli:

And on a bed of gold she lay to reste,
. . . Hyre gilte heres with a golden thred
Ibounden were, untressed as she lay,
And naked from the brest unto the hed
Men myghte hire sen[5]. . .

But the crowning work of this period is *Triolus and Criseyde*, translated and elaborated from Boccaccio's *Il Filostrato*, a poem which Chaucer saw as an example of Tragedy as Boethius (on whom he had been working) defined it—a transient happiness turned, by the hand of a malign Fortune, to misery and death. Chaucer's

[1] *bourded*—jested [2] *alwey causeles*—forever, for no reason [3] *sterres*—stars [4] *payre*—pair
[5] *sen*—see

poem throughout has the philosophic depth he found in Boethius that is lacking in Boccaccio. *Troilus and Criseyde*, as gravely as it is amusingly humane, is among the great narrative poems of the world; the interweavings of destiny and human character are traced with an understanding by which every reader feels himself enlightened; and when Chaucer has told his story of rapture and despair against the setting of the Trojan war, he steps aside to show it *sub specie aeternitatis*. Some hint of the quality of this poem may be given by quotation: first, to show a passage of high conversational comedy (with which it abounds), a stanza of advice from Pandarus as to how to write a love-letter:

'Towchyng thi lettre, thou art wys
                              ynough.
I woot thou nylt it dygneliche endite,
As make it with thise argumentes
                              tough;
Ne scryvenissh or craftily thow it
                              write;
Biblotte it with thi teris ek a lite;
And if thow write a goodly word al
                              softe,
Though it be good, reherce it nought
                              to ofte.'

(Touching your letter, you have sense enough; I know you won't make it pompous, as by being tough and argumentative. And don't write like a professional scrivener or show skill; blot it a little with your tears too. And if you happen on a good soft phrase, even if it is good, don't repeat it too often.)

Or to show ecstasy, this, from the account of the lovers' first night together:

Hire armes smale, hir streghte bak and
                              softe,
Hire sydes longe, flesshly, smothe and
                              white

He gan to stroke, and good thrift bad[1]
                              ful ofte
Hire snowisshe throte, hire brestes
                              rounde and lite;[2]
Thus in this hevene he gan hym to
                              delyte,
And therwithal a thousand tyme hire
                              kiste,
That what to don, for joie unnethe he
                              wiste.[3]

After the betrayal and death of Troilus, he is lifted above the planets to a sphere from which he can look back on the brittleness of the world and its affections, and laugh at the woe of those who grieve for him; then Chaucer turns to his royal young audience (King Richard was rising twenty) and speaks his conclusion, beginning thus:

O yonge, fresshe folks, he or she,
In which that love up groweth with
                              youre age,
Repeyreth hom fro worldly vanytee,
And of youre herte up casteth the visage
To thilke God that after his ymage
Yow made, and thynketh all nys but a
                              faire[4]
This world, that passeth soone as
                              floures faire.

And loveth hym, the which that right
                              for love
Upon a crois, ouer soules for to beye,[5]
First starf,[6] and roos,[7] and sit in hevene
                              above;
For he nyl falsen no wight,[8] dar I seye,
That wol his herte al holly[9] on him leye.
And syn he best to love is, and most
                              meke,
What nedeth feyned loves for to seke?[10]

3. *The English Period* (1386–1400). Between the Italian and English periods

---

[1] *good thrift bad*—begged a blessing on [2] *lite*—small [3] *what to don, for joie unnethe he wiste*—he hardly knew what to do for joy [4] *faire*—fair [5] *beye*—buy [6] *starf*—died [7] *roos*—rose [8] *nyl falsen no wight*—will be false to no one [9] *holly*—wholly [10] *seke*—seek

came a brief return to French dream-allegory in *The Legend of Good Women*. It was a command performance, ordered by the Queen, as a penance for what Chaucer (she thought) had implied about her sex in telling of Criseyde's falsity. The *Prologue* to this work is finely wrought and worth all the rest. The *Legends* that follow are his least successful narrative poems. The subject 'encumbered his wits' says **Lydgate**.

To convey the varieties of power displayed in his last great work, *The Canterbury Tales*, is impossible in a short space; a few salient features may, however, be noted. First, it is a triumph of imaginative organisation. The framing story of a pilgrimage to Canterbury permits a diversity of characters, united in a likely common purpose: Chaucer used this diversity to show a very full cross-section of English life, that includes a range of representative characters from Knight to Plowman, Parson to Pardoner, virgin Prioress to much-married bourgeoise, Merchant to Miller, from town and country, land and sea, university and shop, each pilgrim a type and yet also a highly idiosyncratic person; their diversity is England. But he also uses their diversity to make possible a diversity of tales: epical romance, *fabliau*, sermon, folk-tale, Saint's Life, beast-fable, 'tragedy' of the fall of Great Ones, tales from the classics, tales from the Orient, moral tales, histories, fairy-tales and even ghost-stories. Often the tales illuminate further the characters that tell them; but, considered from another point of view, they illuminate (for they represent) the main elements in the narrative-imagination of Christendom at that time; so, in their natural diversity *The Canterbury Tales* are an abstract and brief chronicle of England and Europe. In between tales there are lively comments and disputes among the pilgrims that keep alive the unexpected conflicts of character, the expected sequence of tales.

Certain themes recur and contribute to the sense of an organised, yet natural unity-in-debate, particularly the theme of the relationship between the sexes, in and out of matrimony. No English poet, or even writer, has anything like Chaucer's scope of insight in matters of sex; he shows as much understanding of a desire for chastity as for romantic passion, married love, or lusty fornication. He also understands misogyny. Above all he illuminates the problem of authority in marriage—who is to rule the roost. The Wife of Bath's solution is trenchant enough:

> And eek I praye Jhesu shorte hir lyves
> That wol nat be governed by hir wyves.

But the Franklin, no less true to his character, thinks:

> Love wol nat been constreyned by
>   maistrye.
> Whan maistrie comth, the God of Love
>   anon
> Beteth his wynges, and farewel, he is
>   gon!
> Love is a thyng as any spirit free.
> Wommen, of kynde,[1] desiren libertee,
> And nat to be constreyned as a thral;
> And so doon men, if I sooth seyen[2] shal.

A steady progress towards what may be called 'naturalism' may also be discerned in this work, based on what seems to be sharp, eye-witness observation of detail; for a quick example, a sanctimonious, hypocritical Friar, makes a predatory visit to a cottage, decides to sit down and make himself comfortable:

[1] *of kynde*—by nature
[2] *sooth seyen*—tell the truth

And fro the bench he droof away the
                                    cat.

The immediate stamp of authenticity
marks all that he has to tell us (in the flow
of his stories) about how life was lived
in the cities and villages, palaces and cot-
tages of the Middle Ages.

His greatest single accession of literary
power, in this work, not predictable from
his earlier poetry, is the ironical study of
several sorts of blackguardism; chief
exhibits are the Pardoner, the Summoner,
the Friar and the Miller; but there is also
a notable confidence-trickster alchemist
in *The Canoun Yemannes Tale*, and,
scattered through the tales, a number of
ingenious seducers. Chaucer blandly allows
them to expose themselves or each other
and makes no comment of his own.

Chaucer has a pervasive irony, seen at
its strongest and most subtle in certain of
The Canterbury Tales, notably those of the
Pardoner and the Merchant; if it were
possible to rank the Tales in order of
merit, these would be reasonable choices
to head the list, though *The Nonne
Preestes Tale* of Chantecleer and Pertelote
has a more universal appeal, and *The
Knight's Tale*, an aristocratic splendour of
conception.

Of his literary inventions, two are
outstanding: the brief portrait and the
autobiographical monologue. For the
latter may be instanced the Wife of
Bath's *Prologue* to her Tale, most sagacious
of his masterpieces in comedy, or the
Pardoner's *Prologue*, that confident self-
give-away. For the former, almost any
character taken at random from the
two-and-thirty pilgrims (if we include
Chaucer and the Host of the Tabard as
we should) as they appear in the General
Prologue will suffice; yet the finest and
most alluring of all his portraits is that of
Alison in *The Milleres Tale*:

. . . Fair was this yonge wyf, and
                                therwithal
As any wezele hir body gent[1] and smal
. . . Ful smale ypulled[2] were hire browes
                                    two
And tho were bent and blake as any
                                    sloo.[3]
She was ful moore blisful on to see
Than is the newe pere-jonette[4] tree
And softer than the wolle is of a wether.
. . . Ful brighter was the shynyng of
                                hir hewe
Than in the Tour the noble[5] yforged
                                newe
Hir mouth was sweete as bragot[6] or
                                the meeth,[6]
Or hoord of apples leyd in hey or heeth.
Wynsynge[7] she was, as is a joly colt,
Long as a mast, and upright as a bolt . . .

The original design (according to the
General *Prologue* itself) was that each pilgrim should tell two tales on the way to
Canterbury and two on the way back;
the Host of the Tabard was to be judge
and the winner to be rewarded with a
dinner at the expense of the others. But
there are only twenty-four Tales in all, of
which three are interrupted by other
pilgrims, and one (the Cook's) is unfinished. The Tales are written on so
large a scale (the work is over 17,000 lines
long) that to have accomplished the original design of some 120 Tales would have
been impossible. Even as a succession of
ten great fragments (as it has come down
to us in some eighty-four manuscripts)
it is a work of enormous energy and mag-
nitude, and the oft-quoted remark of
John **Dryden** remains its best summary:
'Here is God's plenty'.   N.C.
see also Foreign Influences on English
Poetry, Imagery *and* Science and Poetry

[1] *gent*—exquisite
[2] *smale ypulled*—plucked fine
[3] *sloo*—sloe   [4] *pere-jonette*—early pear
[5] *noble*—a silver coin
[6] *bragot, meeth*—drinks made with honey
[7] *wynsynge*—skittish

Cherbury, Lord. *See* Herbert, Edward.

Chesterton, G[ilbert] K[eith] (1874–1936), was a prolific English author of the gamut of literary forms. Of over a hundred published books, only some half-dozen were books of verse, yet his critics often contend that his poems represent him at his best.   D.H.

Churchill, Charles (1731–64), was born in Westminster, the son of a clergyman. He was educated at Westminster School and entered at St John's College, Cambridge, but never matriculated, probably because of the marriage he had contracted at the age of eighteen. (He later separated from his wife). He took Holy Orders, but became known for his extravagant and dissolute life, and as a great frequenter of the theatre. *The Rosciad* (1761), a satire on the actors of the day, saved Churchill from bankruptcy and made his reputation. *The Ghost* (1762–3) dealt with the so-called 'Cock Lane ghost'. The poem contains a hostile character-sketch of Dr **Johnson** as:

Pomposo, insolent and loud;
Vain idol of a scribbling crowd.

Churchill became a friend of John Wilkes and a member of the notorious 'Hell-Fire Club'. He resigned his Orders in the Church, and his later satires are political, written in the interests of Wilkes, with whom Churchill was also associated as part-editor of *The North Briton*. *The Prophecy of Famine* (1763) attacks Lord Bute and the Scots generally. Other victims of Churchill's satire were to include Hogarth and Smollett. *The Times* (1764) is an extremely outspoken attack on alleged homosexuality in high places. Churchill died in Boulogne, where he had gone to join Wilkes, whose radical opposition to the government had compelled him to flee to the Continent.

Churchill's poems are of considerable interest for the light they throw on the political and social scene of the day, but they lack the universality of great satire. Hailed in his day as 'The British Juvenal', he has since fallen to a large extent into neglect. We might perhaps regard Churchill as a forerunner of **Byron** rather than as a follower of **Dryden**. His last poem, *The Journey*, ends:

I on my journey all Alone proceed.

In this, and in some other passages, Churchill strikes a personal note, which points from the Augustan convention to something different.   J.H-S.

Clare, John (1793–1864), one of the few poets of romanticism who attainted a liberated purity of sensation and style, belongs in that regard to the company of **Blake, Landor** and **Wordsworth**, not the company of **Shelley** or of **Keats**, about whose cockneyism Clare remarked that 'when he speaks of woods, Dryads, Fauns and Satyrs are sure to follow'. Small, fair-haired, blue-eyed, a surviving twin, Clare was the son of a Northamptonshire farm labourer, self-educated, coming to poems by way of folk songs and **Thomson**'s *The Seasons*. He was stimulated by the strongest feelings of deprivation or exclusion. He watched the enclosure of common lands, an actual and symbolic exclusion from nature. He felt himself excluded from love, owing to the unattainability of his own ideal object, Mary Joyce:

Are the flowers the winter's choice?
Is love's bed always snow?
First Love

He was excluded from fame when London rapidly forgot the wonder of the peasant-poet and his first book of poems (1820). He was excluded from home, hope and identity, by consignment first to a private asylum in Epping Forest (1840–1), then to the public asylum at Northampton, as a manic-depressive (December 1841 until his death). His concern was a reconciliation of contraries; or at any rate to convince himself of the overriding power, if not of nature (to which, as to Mary Joyce, he was 'married'), or creative joy (the concept he derived from Wordsworth and **Coleridge**—see Clare's *Pastoral Poesy*), or love, then of the free mind. He reached in his second asylum, in or about 1844, an extraordinary resignation and self-realisation (*Love Lives Beyond the Tomb, Hesperus, I Am, To Mary: It is the Evening Hour*) and then a peak of exultancy, in his poem *A Vision*, of 2 August, 1844, which ends:

I loved but woman fell away,
   I hid me from her faded fame,
I snatch'd the sun's eternal ray
   And wrote till earth was but a name.

In every language upon earth,
   On every shore, o'er every sea,
I gave my name immortal birth
   And kept my spirit with the free.

                  G.G.

Classic and Romantic. In spite of complaints about their protean qualities, classic and romantic have remained usable and in many ways essential historical and critical terms. They frequently operate as a dyad, each implying the other as a correlative and polar opposite. Classic commonly refers to what is established, intellectually controlled, normative, clear, fixed, accessible, self-possessed, or, understood pejoratively, mechanistic. Romantic commonly refers to what is unexplored, imaginatively impelled, indefinable, diffuse, restless, remote, dynamic or self-creative. But if the terms are opposed, they are not simple negotiations of one another. Romantic is not simply non-classical, nor is classical simply non-romantic. Unskilful use of these dyadic terms often ignores the complexity of their relationship, which is a correlative of their history.

The term 'classic' is older than 'romantic'. The roots of its meaning against which 'romantic' developed its own significance are to be found in the Latin *classicus* (from *classis*, one of the social and political classes of Roman citizens), which Aulus Gellius uses to differentiate the 'high-class writer' (*classicus scriptor*) from the *proletarius* or low-class writer. The extension of this term to designate the ancient Latin and Greek languages as such was the result of an educational system based on the study of these languages when they had ceased to be vernaculars, that is, when they were learned only through formal schooling. Since this schooling singled out for attention chiefly the *classici* or high-class writers in the Latin and Greek literature, studying these languages and studying the *classici* became one and the same thing, and the languages themselves came to be styled 'classic' or 'classical'.

The 'romantic' picture is somewhat confused by the fact that this term, too, refers to Latin, since, with its cognates in other languages, it derives from a Latin adjective for 'Roman', *Romanicus*, from *Romanus*. The derivatives of *Romanicus* came to refer to vernacular Roman as against the older ancient Latin, and eventually to all the 'Romance' (Old French *romans, romanz*) languages, that is, to the medieval and eventually modern vernaculars developed from ancient Latin through Low Latin—Italian, Rumanian, Rhaeto-Romanic, Provençal, French, Catalan, Spanish and Portuguese. The long narratives of love and adventure in such languages popular through the Middle Ages came to be known as 'romances', and what went on in them was 'romantic'. From here the term romantic develops in various directions to mean romance-like, extravagant, absurd, unreal, or, in another series, highly imaginative, picturesque, or, in still another, having to do with the passionate love of man and woman with special reference to the tradition of courtly love, and so on.

By the late seventeenth century (France 1669, England 1674, Germany 1698), the term 'romantic poetry' or 'romantic literature' had come into use, as meaning romance-like poetry, referring to the works of Ariosto and Tasso and the medieval romances from which they derived. By the late eighteenth century the term romantic was active in ways in which 'classic' had never been and was being applied not only to poetry and criticism, but to manners, characters, and culture generally, and by the early nineteenth century its reference to literature was widely extended, particularly at first in Germany, the seed-bed of romanticism. **Shakespeare**, Cervantes and Calderon are styled romantic authors by Friedrich Bouterwek in 1801-05. With Friedrich Wilhelm Schlegel, his older brother August Wilhelm Schlegel, Madame de Staël, and others, romantic became a definitely programmatic term, associated with the progressive and Christian, and contrasted sharply with 'classic'.

From this point on, the term develops more and more the vagaries which led to Arthur O. Lovejoy's celebrated study 'On the Discrimination of Romanticisms' in *P.M.L.A.* (1924). In *Romanticism and the Modern Ego* (1943) Jacques Barzun has collected some of the interpretations given the term, such as a return to the Middle Ages, a love of the exotic, a revolt from reason, exaltation of the individual, exploitation of the unconscious, a reaction against the scientific mind, a revival of pantheism, of idealism, or of Catholicism, a rejection of artistic conventions, a liberation of emotion, a return to nature, or a glorification of force. Arthur **Symons**, in *The Romantic Movement in English Poetry* (1909), maintains that the great poets of every century but the eighteenth have been romantic. By the early twentieth century, beginnings of romanticism were discovered not only in Rousseau, but also in Kant (by Bertrand Russell and George Santayana), Francis Bacon (Irving Babbitt), the eleventh century (J. E. G. Montmorency), St Paul and/or Plato (H. J. C. Grierson), the *Odyssey* and, ultimately, the serpent in the Garden of Eden (Charles Whibley). The spread of the definitions here and the feasibility of this indefinite retroversion of romantic origins suggests that 'romanticism' was referring to a pervasive component of reality. And indeed the classic-romantic dyad was obviously reflecting in its own way oppositions caught in other pairs of terms recurrent in philosophical analyses: act-potency, form-matter, the one and the many, yang-yin (male-female). Apollo and Dionysus. In any complex state of affairs both elements in dyads such as these will be identifiable, often in a myriad of ways at once, and it is little wonder that romanticism could serve as a universal solvent of manifold phenomena. The efforts of Paul Elmer More and Irving Babbitt to make romanticism a somewhat villainous thing have antecedents, too, in the handling of these other pairs. The second of the members as here given tend regularly to be interpreted as evil, although on closer inspection this is not quite what they are.

The implication in Lovejoy's study that 'romanticism' and its cognates are hopeless designations meaning so many things that they mean nothing has yielded, as more recent reviews of the romantic-classic opposition have established, that these terms are certainly meaningful. However their profoundly elemental character when opposed to one another and the related fact that little, if any, literature or art can be qualified as classic to the exclusion of all romanticism or romantic to the exclusion of all classical elements demand that for effective use the terms be subject to careful contextual control. René Wellek, in two articles in *Comparative Literature* (1949), shows that the romantic movements of the late eighteenth and early nineteenth centuries in the various countries of Europe form 'a unity of theories, philosophies, and style' with a coherent group of ideas contrasting with earlier classic or neo-classic views, and that there was no misunderstanding about the term 'romantic' as referring to literature opposed to the neo-classic and drawing its inspiration from the Middle Ages and to some extent from the Renaissance. Wellek gives three criteria of romanticism: a view of poetry dominated by imagination, a view of the world dominated by an organic concept of nature, and a poetic style dominated by symbol and myth. Morse Peckham, in a *P.M.L.A.* article (1951), noting explicitly the importance of a fourth and related idea, the unconscious mind (attended to by **Wordsworth, Coleridge,** Carlyle, and a host of others), reduces the opposition of classic (or neo-classic) and romantic ultimately to that of mechanistic and organic cosmological views. Others have singled out as concrete manifestations of romanticism love of the remote, of what is free of the limita-

tions of 'that shadow-show called reality', confidence in intuition, delight in the marvellous or in mystery.

Although the term 'classic' is semantically older than 'romantic', the 'classic' became a burning issue only when romanticism emerged as an articulate ideal in the late eighteenth and early nineteenth centuries. Classic ideals and a general disposition to stress 'rules' had been maintained largely by the custom, virtually universal in Western Europe well through the eighteenth century and even later, of focusing all formal instruction in languages on Latin and some Greek, to the exclusion of the vernacular. The 'classical' ideals perpetuated largely through this educational system either directly or indirectly favoured certain characteristic persuasions. The literary genre was taken to be important in setting a writer's goal—a persuasion derived through Horace from the Greek doctrine of 'forms', Platonic and/or Aristotelian. Decorum or due measure was to be observed—another Horatian doctrine. Poetic invention (something like what romanticism was to style 'imagination') was to some degree to be chanelled through the places of invention the commonplaces or *loci communes*— a doctrine derivative from Cicero and Quintilian, highly operative in the Middle Ages, and reinforced by the Renaissance. Standard authors were to be imitated to some extent, although in such a way that their work was transfused with a new freshness—a doctrine which received maximum development when, after classical times, the only languages studied in school were ancient tongues foreign to all who used them and necessarily inviting close imitation in the process of being learned. The unities of time, place and action were to be observed in the drama—a typical late Renaissance and seventeenth-century persuasion deriving through Julius Caesar Scaliger from only partial antecedents in antiquity, but marking French 'classical' drama of the seventeenth century. The 'natural' was the 'universal' which gave appeal to literature.

Ancient Greek and Latin literature had more to it, even by its own account, than the bald statement of such views indicates, but 'romantic' elements in poetry and criticism, such as some of those in Homer or in Aristotle's *Poetics* or in Dionysius of Halicarnassus or in Longinus, got rather short shrift by comparison with these others which unmistakably dominated the classical world and were highlighted by the rhetorical tradition in the schools.

The Renaissance in England, as elsewhere, was marked by a renewed interest in classic Latin and Greek literature but remained close enough to the Middle Ages to continue medieval romance forms and their spirit, even in some of its most characteristic productions, such as *The Faerie Queene* of Edmund **Spenser**. The age generally noted as closest to the 'classic' ideals in England is the eighteenth century, referred to generally as neoclassic or Augustan. In this age, although 'following the ancients' (with some reserve) was a thing one talked about, 'classic' was not a term much in play. In *An Essay on Criticism*, a highly representative neoclassical document (although its doctrines of 'taste' and 'genius' show decidedly romantic elements), the youthful **Pope** makes an issue of 'following nature', of 'good' or 'common' sense, of 'discretion', 'just standards', the 'clear, unchanged, and universal', 'reason', and the 'rules of old discovered, not devised'—while allowing for 'nameless graces' which transcend these norms. But, although he identified the practice of the best ancient Greek and Latin writers with 'nature' herself, he does not make any issue of being

'classic' in temperament of performance.

Poets such as Wordsworth, Coleridge and **Byron**, although now known as English romantics, did not think of their own work as being of an explicitly romantic cut. The application of the term romantic to English literature of the late eighteenth and early nineteenth centuries begins slowly only at the mid-nineteenth century. In the English-speaking world, the greatest explicit attention was given the classic-romantic question in the early decades of the present century, when academic industry, fallen heir to the active late nineteenth-century contrast between romantic and classic, discovered without much trouble a pre-romantic age in the eighteenth century (and inevitably earlier and earlier), when romantic trends were as yet ill-defined but identifiable. From this discovery scholarship has moved to a greater and greater refinement of the issues.   w.j.o.

Cleveland, John (1613–58), was famous in his day for the fantastic ingenuity of his conceits, such as his query:

Why does my she-advowson fly
Incumbency?

He won renown for his Royalist satire, *The Rebel Scot*, and in his *Epitaph on the Earl of Strafford* he achieves a fine tragic intensity.   j.p.

Clough, Arthur Hugh (1819–61), an unduly neglected poet, though coming back into favour, was born in Liverpool; but in 1822 his father, a cotton-merchant, moved to South Carolina. Clough, however, after some schooling in Chester, went to Rugby, where he was subjected to the influence of Dr Arnold. As a scholar at Balliol (1837) he felt the full force of the Oxford Movement, but an innate scepticism, which grew in strength, made him relinquish the tutorship at Oriel to which he had been appointed. In 1849, after some travel, he became Principal of University Hall, a hostel of University College, London. In 1852 he went to Cambridge, Massachusetts, but after a year returned to London to become an examiner under the Education Office. His death was lamented by his friend Matthew **Arnold** in *Thyrsis*, which pays him tribute.

He is popularly known by his stoical poem *Say not the struggle naught availeth*, which, being too much quoted, is often foolishly derided. His main works are *The Bothie of Tober-na-Vuolich* (1848), *Amours de Voyage* (1849), these being in anapaestic hexameters, and *Dipsychus* (1850). The first two are really love-comedies, expressing a kind of hesitant timidity, the first describing a reading-party, the second, in epistolary form, an abortive love-affair in Rome. *Dipsychus*, in varying metres, often colloquial, is a kind of dialogue between the impulsive, intuitive, animal self and the social self, expressing with alert humour, and some wit, all the disunity of the Victorians torn between piety and agnosticism. It contains the fierce denial 'There is no God', and the frank avowal, 'How pleasant it is to have money'. The ambivalence of his attitude is well discussed in Bagehot's essay (*Literary Studies* II), but he scarcely mentions *Dipsychus*, a work extremely pertinent to our own time. Clough had considerable poetic, even lyrical gifts, as exhibited in *Ambarvalia* (1849) and *Mari Magno* (1861).   B.D.

Coleridge, Samuel Taylor (1772–1834), was born in Ottery St Mary in Devonshire, where his father was vicar, and was educated at Christ's Hospital, and Jesus College, Cambridge. From the latter he ran away for a time, and enlisted in the Dragoons; but he was discharged and returned to college. He formed a close friendship with Robert **Southey**, whose sister-in-law, Sarah Fricker, he married. With Southey he entered into what was to be the first of many abortive schemes. This was to emigrate to America, and found a utopian, communistic settlement, based on the principles of 'pantisocracy'. He also engaged for a period in Unitarian preaching. But Coleridge, like Southey and **Wordsworth**, was later to abandon his Radical ideas, both in politics and religion, becoming disillusioned with the French Revolution, and to embrace a conservative and Anglican position.

Coleridge had already begun to publish verse, some of it in collaboration with Southey. But the real turning point in his career came when, in 1797, he met Wordsworth at Nether Stowey in Somerset. The two poets planned together the *Lyrical Ballads* which appeared in the following year. This collection of poems, together with its Preface, is a landmark in the history of the Romantic movement in English poetry. Coleridge's principal contribution to the volume was *The Ancient Mariner*, which was written in 1797. This year has often been termed Coleridge's 'annus mirabilis', for it also saw the composition of *Kubla Khan* and of the first part of *Christabel*. These three poems represent the fullest expression of Coleridge's peculiar visionary imagination.

During the next two years, Coleridge visited Germany. This was very important for his intellectual development, for his own writings, lectures and conversation were to become the channel through which, to a very large extent, a knowledge of German Idealist philosophy was to reach England. From 1800 to 1804 he lived at Keswick, in Cumberland, to be near Wordsworth, with whom however he was later to quarrel. After a visit to Malta and Italy, he began his period of lecturing, on poetry and philosophy, in London, and in 1809 began editing his periodical, *The Friend*, which dealt with these subjects, as well as politics and religion. His most important prose work, the *Biographia Literaria*, containing some of his best criticism, appeared in 1817. Coleridge's last years were spent at Highgate, where he became well known for his continuous flow of brilliant but typically rambling talk.

Coleridge's mind was, without much doubt, *in potentia*, the most brilliant English mind of his generation. He was not only a great romantic poet and critic, but also, as we have said, the prime expounder of German philosophic thought for England. The influence of his religious and political ideas was to be far-reaching in the century after his death, in the spheres of Conservative political theory and liberal theology. But, though the corpus of his writings in prose and verse, together with the notes made by others of his lectures and conversation, is considerable, it presents a fatally flawed, incomplete and unsystematic impression. His work is full of half-realised hints and insights. Baffling as this is, it also makes him an intensely stimulating and fascinating study. Coleridge's inability to concentrate and to carry to full potentiality the expression of his genius was a cause of acute suffering to himself. The roots of it were in his temperament, aggravated by his long period of addiction to opium, which ruined his health and sapped his vitality. To this must be added, though they are contingent upon the other factors, the suffering caused by the breakdown of his marriage, his unhappy love for Sarah Hutchinson, Wordsworth's sister-in-law, as well as the quarrel with Wordsworth himself.

Of the three poems written in 1797 already referred to, only *The Ancient Mariner* is a completed whole. It is undoubtedly one of the greatest poems of the romantic period. It can be appreciated by children as a simple tale of adventure and marvels, yet at the same time its imagery can sustain a complex symbolic interpretation. G. Wilson Knight has termed it Coleridge's *Purgatorio*, and this is not inept. Fundamentally the theme of the poem seems to be one of despair and grace, sin and the promise of redemption brought about by the Mariner's acceptance of the blessedness of life in all its aspects:

Beyond the shadow of the ship,
I watched the water-snakes . . .

A spring of love gushed from my heart,
And I blessed them unaware!
Sure my kind saint took pity on me,
And I blessed them unaware.

That self-same moment I could pray . . .

Whether the two unfinished poems, *Kubla Khan* and *Christabel*, will also bear the weight of the symbolic exegesis which several recent critics have put upon them, is perhaps not quite so certain. These two poems, like so much of Coleridge's work, may be regarded as significant for what they suggest, and for the later historical developments in poetry to which they point, rather than—beautiful as these fragments are—what they actually achieve. *Christabel*, for instance, makes use of a metre based on stress and not on syllable-counting, and thus anticipates **Hopkins'** theory of 'sprung rhythm'. *Kubla Khan* was presented by Coleridge himself, as a 'psychological curiosity'. He was, in fact, a pioneer in the discovery and exploitation of the unconscious, and this poem looks forward to later Symbolism and Surrealism.

It would be a mistake, however, to regard Coleridge as only the poet of his 'annus mirabilis'. The sense that his imaginative genius was failing him dogged him for the rest of his life. The crisis is explored in *Dejection*, originally intended as an answer to Wordsworth's *Ode on Intimations of Immortality*, and not unworthy to stand beside it. Much of Coleridge's other work is diffuse, and over-rhetorical, evincing the inevitable sense of strain his personal despair entailed upon him. But to the attentive reader it will reveal with extraordinary poignancy the workings of its author's remarkable mind. It is also marked by great delicacy and accuracy of natural observation. Coleridge is particularly sensitive to images of light, flame, and clouds—in which phenomena, indeed, he had a scientific interest.　　　　　J.H-S.
see also Criticism and Poetry *and* Science and Poetry

Collins, William (1721–59), was born in Chichester, the son of a hatter, and was educated at Winchester and Magdalen College, Oxford. While still at Oxford he published *Persian Eclogues* (1742), and later came to London, where he hoped to earn a living by writing. His *Odes* (1747) attracted very little notice. Collins' struggles with poverty were brought to an end by his inheriting a small fortune. But, according to **Johnson**, it was the shock of this sudden change in circumstances which unhinged his mind. He suffered from violent melancholia, and died insane in his native Chichester. His longest poem, the *Ode on the Popular Superstitions of the Highlands* (written in 1749), appeared after his death.

Collins' poems are few in number, but show a very delicate sensibility. His models are the Greek lyric poets and **Milton's** early verse. He is frequently coupled with **Gray**, whom he influenced, as a forerunner of the Romantics. But the latter, including **Coleridge** and **Wordsworth**, vehemently acclaimed Collins' superiority over Gray. He had, however, a less certain ear. His *Ode to Evening*—

> If ought of oaten stop, or pastoral song
> May hope, chaste Eve, to please thy
> 　　　　　　　　　　pensive ear,
> 　Like thy own solemn springs,
> 　Thy springs and dying gales,

handles an unrhymed lyrical metre (in fact first used by Milton in his translation of Horace's *Ode to Pyrrha*) with great skill. There are many equally delicate touches in his other Odes.

Like that of Gray as well as that of many other poets of their generation, Collins' verse is apt to be crowded, even to excess, with abstract personifications. Nevertheless, by means of an apt and fresh image, he frequently shows the power of bringing this convention to new life. The following lines from the *Ode on the Passions* will serve to illustrate this:

> . . . *Cheerfulness,* a nymph of healthier
> 　　　　　　　　　　　　hues,
> Her bow across her shoulders flung
> Her buskins gem'd with morning dew,
> Blew an inspiring air, that dale and
> 　　　　　　　　　　thicket rung,
> The hunter's call to *Faun* and *Dryad*
> 　　　　　　　　　known . . .

A notable poem is the *Ode on the Poetical Character*; it implies a view of the Imagination as essentially divine in its creativeness, which goes far beyond eighteenth-century categories and anticipates those of **Blake** and Coleridge.

That Collins' career as a poet was cut

short by madness is certainly tragic. Though his achievement is slight, it hints at extraordinary potentialities.

J.H–S.

Corbet, Richard (1582–1635), was Bishop of Oxford and Norwich. He was renowned for his joviality, and was the subject of numerous anecdotes. A friend of Ben **Jonson,** he was known at the Mermaid Tavern for his ability to extemporise verse. On the page it is less of a performance, but confident and enjoyable. D.H.

Cotton, Charles (1630–86), who was born in Staffordshire, was famous during his lifetime for publishing the first English translation (1685) of Montaigne's *Essays* and for writing the second part of Walton's *The Compleat Angler*. His nature lyrics, especially *Retirement* and *Ode to Winter*, were admired by **Wordsworth, Coleridge** and Lamb. D.H.

Cowley, Abraham (1618–67), was the son of a London stationer, and was educated at Westminster and Trinity College, Cambridge. Joining the Court at Oxford in 1644 he subsequently served the Queen in France until the Restoration as 'cypher-secretary' and diplomatic emissary, which in 1655 led to his arrest in England as a spy. He was released two years later and was restored to his fellowship. He retired in 1664 and died three years later at Chertsey.

Cowley's obsequies at Westminster Abbey were the most splendid yet granted a man of letters, and for a generation afterwards he was idolised. **Denham** hailed him as the English Virgil and as **Spenser**'s and **Jonson**'s superior; together with **Shakespeare** and Spenser, he was one of **Milton**'s three favourite poets; **Dryden** wrote, in 1672, 'he is an authority

sacred to me'. Yet his vogue rapidly diminished, and in 1737 **Pope** could ask, 'Who now reads Cowley?'

Perhaps better than any contemporary, Cowley exemplified the literary fashions and intellectual interests of his period. His extraordinarily precocious *Poetical Blossoms*, published when he was fifteen, reflected his study of Spenser. *The Mistress* (1647) was influenced by Jonson and **Donne** in uneasy combination. His chief work, *The Miscellanies* (1656), included the unfinished epic, *Davideis*, the irregular Pindaric Odes, and the gay and sparkling *Anacreontics*. According to Dr **Johnson**, 'Such an assemblage of diversified excellence no other poet has hitherto afforded'.

In his effort to capture Pindar's 'rage' we see Cowley anticipating Dryden's magniloquent oratory; and the magniloquence remains, though modulated, in his later work, as witness a fragment from his fine *Hymn to Light*:

> Thou in the Moon's bright Chariot
> proud and gay,
> Dost thy bright wood of Stars survay;
> And all the year dost with thee bring
> Of thousand flowry Lights thine own
> Nocturnal Spring.

Cowley commands respect not as a metaphysical, but as a learned, serious artist who, anticipating the Augustans, speculated in poetry of effervescent wit, clarity, and brilliance upon Hobbesian ideas and discoveries of the new science. A classicist of Horatian temper, he also created models for over a century of English odes. W.L.S.
see also Foreign Influences on English Poetry

Cowper, William (1731–1800), was born at Great Berkhampstead, where his father was rector. After the death of his mother, when he was six, he was sent first to a local boarding-school and then to Westminster School in London. In 1749 he began to study law, but his career in that profession had little success and ended in 1763 with an attack of madness during which he suffered from the delusion that he was inevitably damned. After treatment in an asylum at St Alban's, he met the Unwins, a pious, evangelical family, with whom he went to live, first at Huntingdon and then at Olney. There he remained until nearly the end of his life, when his cousin, John Johnson, took him and Mrs Unwin to East Anglia. He died at East Dereham in Norfolk.

In spite of the melancholy of his disposition, Cowper is primarily a poet of pleasure—of the quiet, ordinary, everyday pleasures of the countryside. He did not begin to write with any purpose until he was forty-nine, when his first productions were six rather dull *Moral Satires*. Then, in a time of unusual lightness of spirit, he followed up the playful suggestion of a friend (Lady Austen) that he should write about the sofa. The result was *The Task*, a long, discursive poem in blank verse, the theme of which is summarised in its most-quoted line: 'God made the country, and man made the town'. *The Task* contains much comment on late eighteenth-century concerns, expressed in a rhetorical style which soon made Cowper a powerful voice in the humanitarian movement. Today, the poem's principal merit lies in its fresh and entirely unaffected attitude to nature. While other poets of the time tried to compete with the painter in constructing landscapes in verse, Cowper was content to record his impressions in a series of vivid and accurately detailed vignettes. Of the Rose of Sharon, for instance, he wrote:

Hypericum, all bloom, so thick a swarm
Of flow'rs, like flies clothing her slender
                                         rods,
That scarce a leaf appears.

He had, moreover, an engaging gift of humour, and is the author of much quiet, accomplished light verse. But among his many occasional pieces there is heard, here and there, an undertone that gives, even to the slightest lyric, both a poignancy and an unexpected subtlety of melody:

The poplars are fell'd, farewell to the
                                         shade
And the whispering sound of the cool
                                    colonnade,
The winds play no longer, and sing in the
                                        leaves,
Nor Ouse on his bosom their image
                                      receives.

At other times, he expressed his personal tragedy more directly, as in *The Castaway*, where he identifies his own fate with that of a drowning sailor:

Obscurest night involv'd the sky,
    Th' Atlantic billows roar'd,
When such a destin'd wretch as I,
    Wash'd headlong from on board,
Of friends, of hope, of all bereft,
His floating home for ever left.

Cowper's translation of Homer, made after the publication of *The Task*, is now little read, but a few of his *Olney Hymns*—such as 'Oh! for a closer walk with God' and 'God moves in a mysterious way'—written at the suggestion of John Newton, curate at Olney, have a strength of language and breadth of imagery which puts them among the best and most widely known of all English hymns.

Perhaps because his poetry lacks complexity Cowper has not received much attention from modern critics, but his life continues to intrigue biographers. In particular, they dispute about the effect on the poet of his religious beliefs. Hugh l'Anson Fausset and Lord David Cecil argue that Calvinism warped his talent and drove him to madness, while Norman Nicholson holds that his religious experiences 'lifted him like a love affair above day-to-day monotony', and points out that signs of madness had appeared long before Cowper came into contact with the Evangelical Revival. All these critics acknowledge the attraction of the poet's personality as revealed both in the verse and in his universally admired correspondence.   N.N.

Crabbe, George (1754–1832), was born at Aldeburgh, Suffolk, the son of an exciseman. He was trained as a physician and practised in his native town, but in 1780 came to London to seek his literary fortune. Here he attracted the attention and patronage of Edmund Burke, and also of Dr **Johnson**. His first published poem was *The Library* (1781), which was followed by *The Village* (1783). In this latter poem Crabbe discovered his highly original vein of poetic realism. It is a description of the contemporary village scene in deliberate reaction against any conventional pastoral idealisation.

I grant indeed that fields and flocks
                              have charms
For him that grazes or for him that
                              farms;
But, when amid such pleasing scenes I
                              trace
The poor laborious natives of the place,
And see the mid-day sun, with vivid ray,
On their bare heads and dewy temples
                              play;
While some, with feebler heads and
                              fainter hearts,
Deplore their fortune, yet sustain their
                              parts,

Then shall I dare these real ills to hide,
In tinsel trappings of poetic pride.

Before the appearance of *The Village*, Crabbe had been ordained. He returned as parson to Aldeburgh, and from 1781 to 1789 served as chaplain to the Duke of Rutland. In 1814 he was appointed Vicar of Trowbridge in Wiltshire. *The Parish Register* (1807) was a more extended piece of realistic documentation. The same volume included *Sir Eustace Grey*, a dramatic monologue of considerable power, dealing with the hallucinations of a mind unhinged by debauchery and remorse followed by a Methodist conversion. In his later volumes, *The Borough* (1810), *Tales* (1812) and *Tales of the Hall* (1819), Crabbe widened his scope as a narrative poet. He was a master of the short story in verse, at a time when the short story had not yet been fully developed as an independent art-form in prose. His later work takes its subject-matter mainly from the life of the provincial middle-classes and the squirearchy.

Crabbe's verse has seldom had full critical justice done to it, though his admirers have included **Byron**, Jane Austen, **Tennyson**, Edward **Fitzgerald** and, in our time, E. M. Forster. Superficial critics have been too ready to make fun of his occasional prosiness, his rather heavy-handed heroic couplets, his equally rather heavy-handed moral bias, and his tendency to melodrama. Against these should be set his powerful and vivid natural descriptions, his frequent psychological penetration, his irony and humour, and his strong sense of social criticism. Writers of textbook histories of English literature have found it convenient to pigeon-hole Crabbe as a 'pre-romantic'. But he is a realist, not a romantic. In his work the Augustan tradition shows a renewed vitality, pointing in a direction not taken by the romantic poets, but to be followed up rather by such novelists—likewise provincial in inspiration—as George Eliot and **Hardy**. J.H–S.

Crane, [Harold] Hart (1899–1932), was born in Ohio. After working a short time in his father's business, he moved to New York. In 1926 he published a collection of short poems, *White Buildings*, and in 1930 a long poem, *The Bridge*. In 1928 he went to Europe, but after six months was expelled from France for brawling. In 1932, after a year in Mexico, he committed suicide by throwing himself from the ship taking him back to New York.

In Crane we find the romantic attitude to language at its most valuable. Connotation takes over many of the traditional functions of denotation, but it does not do so recklessly. The effect is of a rich concentration rather than of the dissipation of meaning that we find in most other late romantic writers.

And yet this great wink of eternity,
Of rimless floods, unfettered leewardings,
Samite sheeted and processioned where
Her undinal vast belly moonward bends,
Laughing the wrapt inflections of our
                                              love;
Take this Sea, whose diapason knells
On scrolls of silver snowy sentences,
The sceptred terror of whose sessions
                                              rends
As her demeanors motion well or ill,
All but the pieties of lovers' hands.

This is the start of 'Voyages II', in *White Buildings*, which Yvor **Winters** has called 'one of the most powerful and one of the most nearly perfect poems of the past two hundred years'. 'Voyages' is a series of six love poems addressed to a young sailor, in which the sea is equivalent to love as a large unbounded force, and in which the relation between tenor and vehicle is so subtly balanced that it is difficult to say which, sea or love, is tenor, which vehicle. Thus the culmination of the romantic symbol is the product and accompaniment of the culmination of romantic utterance.

In *The Bridge* Crane attempted to write the American epic. At its best, as in the lines to Brooklyn Bridge or the conclusion to 'The River', it has the strength of his earlier poetry:

Damp tonnage and alluvial march of
                                              days—
Nights turbid, vascular with silted shale
And roots surrendered down of moraine
                                              clays:
The Mississippi drinks the farthest dale.

But, as Allen **Tate** says, 'the fifteen parts of *The Bridge* taken as one poem suffer from the lack of a coherent structure, whether symbolic or narrative: the coherence of the work consists in the personal quality of the writing—in mood, feeling, and tone . . . It is a collection of lyrics, the best of which are not surpassed by anything in American literature'. Most critics agree with Tate. R. P. Blackmur remarks that 'Crane had the sensibility typical of Baudelaire and so misunderstood himself that he attempted to write *The Bridge* as if he had the sensibility typical of **Whitman**'. There is in fact a considerable conflict between the local control of the best writing and the explicit philosophy of uncontrol set out by the work as a whole.

Few of the poems written between *The Bridge* and his death are considered of importance, apart from *The Broken Tower*. T.G.

see also American Poetry

Crane, Stephen (1871–1900), poet, journalist, fiction writer and pioneer of realism in American fiction, was born in New Jersey and spent most of his life in upstate New York. He is best known for *The Red Badge of Courage* (1895) and *The Open Boat* (1898), a short story. He anticipated by twenty years the free verse of American poets during the First World War.

Crashaw, Richard (?1612–49), a Londoner by birth, stands apart from the English Metaphysicals, showing little influence of **Donne** and considerable affinities with the Baroque poets of Italy. Beginning as a High Anglican, in reaction from a Puritan father, he left a Cambridge fellowship to follow Queen Henrietta Maria to Paris. Living in exile, he joined the Roman Catholic Church, was appointed to a Cardinal's household, quarrelled with his fellow servants, and ended his life in a very minor post.

Crashaw's poetry is uneven. At times as magnificent in style as any poet of the century, he fell easily into absurd bathos or empty rhetoric. A bachelor and celibate, he was most eloquent when addressing his ideal of saintly womanhood, Mary Magdalen or Santa Teresa. Yet there is no conception of female character in any of his poems, which are built from loosely associated successions of conceits, each stanza a separate unit. One of his finest sacred pieces, *The Weeper*, though intended as an address to the penitent Magdalen, should more properly be called *Tears*, since Crashaw was not concerned with her as a woman or with the nature of her conversion from sinner to saint, but solely with the flowing of her eyes, upon which he elaborates with a fervour that looks forward to romanticism:

Does the day-starre rise?
Still the starres do fall and fall.
Does day close his eyes?
Still the FOUNTAIN weeps for all.

Let night or day doe what they will,
Thou hast thy task; thou weepest still.

Alas that only a few stanzas before these same eyes have been compared to

Two walking baths; two weeping
motions;
Portable and compendious oceans.

In his translation of the first book of Marino's *La Strage degli Innocenti* (The Massacre of the Innocents) Crashaw rises at times to a grandeur that forestalls that of *Paradise Lost*, and easily surpasses his original, for many of his best lines have no pretext in Marino's thinner and more contrived verses. He is at his finest in the passage where Lucifer looks down in horror and anger at the Birth in the manger:

Hee saw how in that blest Day-bearing
Night,
The Heav'n rebuked shades made hast
away;
How bright a Dawne of Angels with
new Light
Amaz'd the midnight world, and made
a Day
Of which the Morning knew not:
Mad with spight
Hee markt how the poore Shepheards
ran to pay
Their simple tribute to the Babe, whose
Birth
Was the great Businesse both of
Heav'n and Earth.

Here, as in parts of *The Flaming Heart, A Hymn to . . . Sainte Teresa, The Hymn in the Glorious Assumption of Our Blessed Lady, The Weeper*, already mentioned, and the almost frivolous *Wishes to his (supposed) Mistresse*, Crashaw by dint of fervour transcends the limits of the conceited style to achieve greatness. Most of his other work, however, with the

exception of a poem or two in Latin and the accomplished *Music's Duel*, is undistinguished.   J.M.C.
see also Foreign Influences of English Poetry

Criticism and Poetry. The literary critic, said A. E. **Housman,** is 'the rarest of the great works of God'. It would certainly seem that there have been far fewer critics than great poets. Three only, in the almost unanimous opinion of those qualified to judge, supply what critical currency there is for the discussion of the Classics: Lessing, Goethe and Matthew **Arnold.** And where English poetry is concerned, modern taste has been almost entirely formed by T. S. **Eliot,** as it was by Arnold in the not too distant past. It is true that something commonly called 'criticism' is produced in every age by people who are by no means masters of that art; this ranges in quality from the humblest forms of book-sorting or literary gossip to the more pretentious examples of 'interpretation', 'appreciation', or 'balanced views' produced by the distinguished middlemen without whom the current of opinion would not circulate. But for all these the original ideas of the great critics, more or less interpreted, seasoned, or garbled, have provided the primary stimulation. There is good reason, therefore, for not trying to offer a guide to that dreary museum called 'the History of Criticism'. Some of the criticism written by the *epigoni* of the past performed a useful function in its day, a little of it can even now be read with profit and pleasure as a chapter in the history of ideas, or for its own sake (one thinks of a Rymer or a Dennis) as racy and vigorous literature. But it has little to offer as *criticism*. For living thought in criticism we must go to the masters.

All the great critics of poetry have been poets; but not necessarily, or even usually, great poets. **Shakespeare,** the supreme poetic intelligence of Europe, has left us no criticism; and many other great poets have given us only incidental observations and passing insights, which, though priceless in value (we may think of the magnificent criticism scattered in the letters of a **Keats** or a Gerard Manley **Hopkins**) do not by themselves suffice to form that structure of thought which is required before we should talk of great criticism. This is not to deny a powerful critical gift to these poets, or to other poets who have left us no critical observations at all. *Their* criticism was done in the actual process of composing their poetry. It was then that they made the judgments, and took the decisions, which it is left to the formal critic to infer and to describe explicitly. But only this formal criticism can intelligibly be discussed here.

Aristotle deserves his traditional fame as the Father of Criticism. (The view that what Aristophanes in *The Frogs* was offering, or thought he was offering, should be called 'criticism' needs only to be stated—for those who have read that play—to be refuted.) But the *Poetics* itself, and still more its influence in the Renaissance and the seventeenth century, belong to the history of ideas, not to living criticism. Aristotle's brief and telegraphic treatise, variously augmented, misunderstood, mangled, or modified, provided European criticism with verbal currency for three centuries. Read with the aid of scholarship, and without its Renaissance accretions, it can still provide stimulus and nourishment; after all, Aristotle's thinking in general may almost be called the paradigm of intelligence. But the proviso about scholarship is important; the *Poetics* is a special, and specially difficult, Aristotelian study. And a scholarly reading is bound to bring out that there is no agreement about the exact meaning of any of Aristotle's famous *dicta*.

A list of 'classical' critics will invariably also include Quintilian and Horace. Quintilian is historically important, particularly for exhibiting in a notable form that Roman confusion of poetry with rhetoric which has been such a baleful influence in the history of criticism. Horace's so-called *Art of Poetry* is a charming poem and a repertory of memorable tags. But neither of these, nor the anonymous author, conventionally called 'Longinus', who wrote on 'the Sublime', can be now said to have critical value, since they cannot now help us to get our minds clear about the poetry we read, or write; the attempt to 'apply' them to modern critical problems may be left to examination candidates.

Medieval and Renaissance criticism does not even have this conventional standing. This is as it should be, since much of it is deeply infected by Roman fallacies. It would seem, fortunately, that the good poets of those times (despite what some American scholars would have us believe) paid very little attention to the manuals of rhetoric which are what mostly figure in literary histories as the 'criticism' of the day. But these manuals must have had some influence, and this must have been largely bad. For they generate the error which can be briefly characterised as follows: it is assumed that you and I have much the same thoughts as Shakespeare, but unlike Shakespeare we lack the capacity to dress them up poetically; by studying So-and-So's manual we can learn how to do this, and so can become as good as Shakespeare. Nearly all that is valuable in these rhetorical treatises is merely the crystalisa-

tion of the practice of good poets; and good poets have usually learned from each other, without the aid of academic intermediaries. There are undoubtedly techniques, tricks, ways of doing things in poetry, which can be learned; but they are best learned, as the practice of good poets shows, from actual and not from theoretical models.

It may be objected that the Elizabethan critics deserve something better. But there was an immense discrepancy between the poetic theory and the poetic practice of that age. The Elizabethan critics seem to have been too preoccupied with the technical problems which are naturally to the fore in a period of poetic revival, to notice that a great literature was rising around them, of an orginality which transcends any talk about 'technique'. The most famous critical work of that age, **Sidney**'s *Defence of Poetry* (as it is commonly, if inaccurately, called), is a noble plea, couched in terms suitable for the gentle public which Sidney was addressing, on behalf of the high claims of poetry upon the civilised man, its essential role as a constituent of the good life. This plea is one that it is expedient and traditional for critics to make from time to time, though it might be argued that in making it they are acting as public moralists rather than strictly as critics. Sidney did this admirably for his time, but his time has now passed, and for his apologia to command attention as living criticism it would have had to have shown a depth and force of thought about poetry which was perhaps impossible for an Englishman at that stage of the development of English literature; or, if it had been possible, Sidney would have had to have been a Shakespeare. Much livelier criticism in this period is to be found in the record of Ben **Jonson**'s conversations with **Drummond** of Hawthornden; as with Robert **Graves'** Clark Lectures, even the table-talk of so excellent a poet must command respect. But Jonson's observations are too fragmentary, too dogmatic, and too post-prandial to constitute a body of coherent critical thought. Their great merit is one commonly found in the *obiter dicta* of good poets; an ability to distinguish, and a sharpness in bringing out the distinction, between what is alive and what is dead.

It would seem, then, that Dr **Johnson** was right to name as the founder of English criticism, not one of the earlier writers, but John **Dryden**. Dryden deserves the attention given to him in literary histories. He was the chief inaugurator of that age of English poetry which is known as 'the eighteenth century', but may be more accurately defined as the period between the publication of *Samson Agonistes* (1671) and that of *Lyrical Ballads* (1798). The poetic theory and practice of that time seem to us to have been involved in various grave errors, although its best poets were capable of transcending them. For full understanding of this period the study of Dryden is indispensable. In his poetry he was the first great 'Augustan' master; in his criticism he was a writer of admirable prose, of that flexible modern kind which he helped to introduce into English literature, and a man capable of independence, vigour, and distinction in his taste. Thus he was the author of the first really judicious and discriminating account of **Chaucer**, a passage which, with all its obvious historical limitations, remains a remarkable piece of criticism; he lent his splendid support to the institution of the cult of Shakespeare; and he was among the foremost of the wits who recognised the genius of **Milton**. Yet Dryden perhaps should not number among his many titles to fame the rare distinction of being one of

the great critics. He offers us, as a critic, much pleasure and some instruction, but he is not one of those who give us what may be called, in that metaphor which is more than a metaphor, *light*. He is often wise, sane and judicious; he is rarely illuminating. In part this is because, inevitably, much of his criticism has 'dated', in that he addressed himself to problems that do not now concern us, and spoke of them in a critical idiom that is no longer ours. But this to some degree may also be said of Johnson, who should surely be numbered among the few great critics. It is rather that there is a 'hand-to-mouth' quality about Dryden's thinking, an ultimate want of fundamental concern; criticism for him was too completely a department of manners; and depending as he did on the French critics of his time for what ideas about critical principle he had, his place in the history of criticism—apart from his vigorously independent particular judgments—is that of an intellectual middleman.

Samuel Johnson is the first critic of the past who can still be read for his direct value as a critic. Formed as his taste was in the 'Augustan' period, his bias and limitations are definite and obvious, but the increased study of his criticism makes us dwell upon them much less. He stands above all for common sense and humanity, standards not lightly to be dismissed when we are assessing the permanent value of his criticism of the 'Metaphysical' poets, or the validity of some of his strictures on Milton. But he also stands for the application of intelligence to literature; and this entails the recognition that 'poetry is poetry and not something else'; it is to be judged as art and not, or not primarily, as matter for edification. Johnson, unfortunately, is mainly remembered for those few judgements of his with which everyone disagrees. It is not to be denied that his remarks on *Lycidas* reveal his deficiencies as a critic. But his candour and forthrightness, his freedom from convention, which are apparent in those unlucky remarks are, in general, evidence of his greatness. The *Preface to Shakespeare* is a classic of criticism; if we could imagine an educated man who had not read Shakespeare and had no notion why Shakespeare is ranked so supremely high among poets, here would be the unimprovable statement to which to refer him. Its very temperateness and balance, which must have irritated an age of incipient bardolatry, only make its total testimony to the genius of Shakespeare the more impressive.

Johnson, though always concerned with critical principle, cannot be summarised; it might be said that in this combination of resistance to summary with concern for principle we have the mark of the great critic. All that can reasonably be done here, to suggest his quality, is to give an example of his characteristic way of relating poetry both to life in general and to the individual—in this case, Dryden—who writes it.

In a general survey of Dryden's labours, he appears to have a mind very comprehensive by nature, and much enriched with acquired knowledge. His compositions are the effects of a vigorous genius operating upon large materials.

The power that predominated in his intellectual operations was rather strong reason than quick sensibility. Upon all occasions that were presented, he studied rather than felt, and produced sentiments not such as nature enforces, but meditation supplies. With the simple and elemental passions, as they spring separate in the mind, he seems not much acquainted; and seldom describes them but as they are complicated by the various relations of society, and confused in the tumults and agitations of life.

What he says of love may contribute to the explanation of his character:

Love various minds does variously inspire;
It stirs in gentle bosoms gentle fire,
Like that of incense on the altar laid:
But raging flames tempestuous souls
                                        invade;
A fire which every windy passion blows,
With pride it mounts, or with revenge it
                                        glows.

Dryden's was not one of the *gentle bosoms*: Love as it subsists in itself, with no tendency but to the person loved, and wishing only for correspondent kindness; such Love as shuts out all other interest, the Love of the Golden Age, was too soft and subtle to put his faculties in motion. He hardly conceived it but in its turbulent effervescence with some other desires; when it was inflamed by rivalry, or obstructed by difficulties; when it invigorated ambition, or exasperated revenge.

He is therefore, with all his variety of excellence, not often pathetic; and had so little sensibility of the power of effusions purely natural, that he did not esteem them in others. Simplicity gave him no pleasure; and for the first part of his life he looked on Otway with contempt, though at last, indeed very late, he confessed that in his play *there was Nature, which it is the greatest beauty.*

We do not always know our own motives. I am not certain whether it was not rather the difficulty which he found in exhibiting the genuine operations of the heart, than a servile submission to an injudicious audience, that filled his plays with false magnificence. It was necessary to fix attention; and the mind can be captivated only by recollection, or by curiosity; by reviving natural sentiments, or impressing new appearances of things: sentences were readier at his call than images; he could more easily fill the ear with splendid novelty, than awaken those ideas that slumber in the heart.

'Nature', 'the genuine operations of the heart', 'natural sentiments', 'those ideas that slumber in the heart'—the association of these terms is significant. Johnson is here appealing to criteria which, whatever the variations in critical idiom, must surely be regarded as essential and permanent. At the same time it would be a mistake to suppose that in thus reiterating and renewing the 'classical' tradition (that great poetry gives us 'just representations of general nature') Johnson is limiting poetry to 'what oft was thought but ne'er so well expressed'. On the contrary, he elsewhere explicitly disagrees with this well-known *dictum* of **Pope**, on the ground that it limits the poet's originality of expression. His own principal criteria for a good poem, as they emerge in the *Life of Cowley*, are that it should be 'natural and new'; and so, while he severely disparages what he regards as the perverse straining for novelty in the 'Metaphysical' poets, he gives no sanction to platitude. Thus, after the famous (and surely unsurpassable) description of **Gray**'s *Elegy* as abounding with 'images which find a mirror in every mind, and with sentiments to which every bosom returns an echo', Johnson continues:

> The four stanzas beginning 'Yet even these bones' are to me original: I have never seen the notions in any other place; yet he that reads them here, persuades himself that he has always felt them. Had Gray written often thus, it had been vain to blame, and useless to praise him.

Johnson is commonly counted as an anti-romantic critic, but in passages like these he defies classification; the axiom to which he appeals here is surely no different from Keats' 'I think poetry should surprise by a fine excess and not by singularity: it should strike the reader as a wording of

his own highest thoughts, and appear almost a remembrance' (letter to Taylor, 1818).

This permanent element in Johnson's contribution to criticism appears also in his destruction, in the *Preface to Shakespeare*, of the dogma of 'the Unities', a passage which Stendhal borrowed without acknowledgment to exalt Shakespeare above Racine for the benefit of the young romantics. There is, then, nothing academic or conventional about Johnson's criticism. At the same time, Johnson strives to give a more than individual weight to his judgments. In his capacity as critic, as in his capacity as moralist, he seeks to appear as the spokesman of society; his poise is judicial, and the final court of appeal he recognises is 'the common reader'—by which he means the consensus of the educated public. This poised assurance, this judicial gravity, in Johnson is strictly inimitable. It is not only that we have no Johnson today; the situation to which a Johnson could address himself has changed. Attempts at the Johnsonian tone would nowadays be solemn mockery. Johnson is serious, but not solemn; he can take easily for granted the most important literary conventions, since they, like the moral and religious conventions, are invested for him with a sense of absoluteness. It is in this respect that his criticism may be said to belong to history. But in the downright vigour of his mind, the wisdom, breadth and general sanity of his critical thinking, Johnson still appeals to us across the ages.

If Dryden is rightly called the founder of English criticism in general (he was the first, according to Johnson, to 'determine upon principles the merits of composition'), the critic who most deserves to be called the founder of *modern* criticism is **Coleridge**. Johnson can show sensitivity

67

as well as his characteristic incisiveness; but his analysis even at its best has not the peculiar *inwardness* of Coleridge. And it is this inwardness, obviously related to Coleridge's preoccupation with psychology, which characterises his best criticism (**Shelley** aptly called him 'a subtle-souled psychologist'). Some exponents of Coleridge would prefer to stress his theoretical preoccupations. But, quite apart from the fact that as a philosopher and theorist Coleridge owes a heavy debt (and one which he deplorably grudged to acknowledge) to Schelling, the Schlegels, Schiller, and others, Coleridge's theories are hardly coherent enough, and engage too little with the actual practice and analysis of poetry, to be consolidated into a system; I. A. Richards' ostensible attempts, in *Coleridge on Imagination*, to systematise him turns out in fact either to ignore what Coleridge said, or to translate it into the vocabulary (which Coleridge would certainly have rejected) of a revived utilitarianism. Coleridge at his best shows an intensity of interest in poetry which could only have come from his own deep reflection on the experience of composing it, and from a sustained and loving familiarity with the best work of other English poets—neither of which priceless assets is fairly suggested by the common description of him as pre-eminently the 'philosophical' or 'theoretical' critic. At his best he provides a model for the analysis of poetry which is as remote from inappropriate utilitarianism as it is from that inspection of 'texture' carried on independently of meaning which (fairly or unfairly) is associated with the name of Edith **Sitwell**.

Only one example, perhaps welcome because it is not too familiar, can here be given of Coleridgean analysis; it is a discussion of the poetic and dramatic effects of the first scene of *Hamlet*:

Compare the easy language of common life, in which this drama commences, with the direful music and wild wayward rhythm and abrupt lyrics of the opening of *Macbeth*. The tone is quite familiar;—there is no poetic description of night, no elaborate information conveyed by one speaker to another of what both had immediately before their senses—(such as the first distich of Addison's *Cato*, which is a translation into poetry of 'Past four o'clock and a dark morning!');—and yet nothing bordering on the comic on the one hand, nor any striving of the intellect on the other. It is precisely the language of sensation among men who feared no charge of effeminacy for feeling what they had no want of resolution to bear. Yet the armour, the dead silence, the watchfulness that first interrupts it, the welcome relief of the guard, the cold, the broken expressions of compelled attention to bodily feelings still under control—all excellently accord with, and prepare for, the after gradual rise into tragedy;—but above all, into a tragedy, the interest of which is eminently *ad et apud intra,* as that of *Macbeth* is directly *ad extra*.

In all the best attested stories of ghosts and visions, as in that of Brutus, of Archbishop Cranmer, that of Benvenuto Cellini recorded by himself, and the vision of Galileo communicated by him to his favourite pupil, Torricelli, the ghost-seers were in a state of cold or chilling damp from without, and of anxiety inwardly. It has been with all of them as with Francisco on his guard,—alone, in the depth and silence of the night; ''twas bitter cold, and they were sick at heart, and *not a mouse* stirring'. The attention to minute sounds—naturally associated with the recollection of minute objects, and the more familiar and trifling, the more impressive from the unusualness of their producing any impression at all—gives a philosophic pertinency to this last image; but it has likewise its dramatic use and purpose. For its commonness in ordinary conversation tends to produce the sense of reality, and at once hides the poet, and yet approximates the reader or spectator to that state in which the highest poetry will appear, and in its component parts, though not in the whole composition, really is, the language of nature. If I should not speak it, I feel that I should be thinking it; —the voice only is the poet's—the words are my own. That Shakespeare meant to put an effect in the actor's power in the very first words—'Who's there?'—is evident from the impatience expressed by the startled Francisco in the words that follow—'Nay, answer me: stand and unfold yourself'. A brave man is never so peremptory, as when he fears that he is afraid. Observe the gradual transition from the silence and the still recent habit of listening in Francisco's—'I think I still hear them'—to the more cheerful call out, which a good actor would observe, in the—'Stand ho! Who is there?' Bernardo's inquiry after Horatio, and the repetition of his name and in his own presence, indicate a respect or an eagerness that implies him as one of the persons who are in the foreground; and the scepticism attributed to him:

Horatio says 'tis but our fantasy;
And will not let belief take hold of
     him—

prepares us for Hamlet's after eulogy on him as one whose blood and judgment were happily commingled. The actor should also be careful to distinguish the expectation and gladness of Bernardo's 'Welcome, Horatio!' from the mere courtesy of his 'Welcome, good Marcellus!'

Now observe the admirable indefiniteness of the first opening out of the occasion of all this anxiety. The preparation informative of the audience is just as much as was precisely necessary, and no more;—it begins with the uncertainty appertaining to a question:

HOR: What, has *this thing* appear'd
     again to-night?

Even the word 'again' has its *credibilising* effect. Then Horatio, the representative of the ignorance of the audience, not himself, but by Marcellus to Bernardo, anticipates the common solution—''tis but our fantasy!' upon which Marcellus rises into

This dreaded sight, twice seen of us—

which immediately afterwards becomes 'this apparition', and that, too, an intelligent spirit, that is, to be spoken to! Then comes the confirmation of Horatio's disbelief:

Tush! tush! 'twill not appear!—

and the silence, with which the scene opened, is again restored in the shivering feeling of Horatio sitting down, at such a time, and with the two eyewitnesses, to hear a story of a ghost, and that, too, of a ghost which had appeared twice before at the very same hour. In the deep feeling which Bernardo has of the solemn nature of what he is about to relate, he makes an effort to master his own imaginative terrors by an elevation of style—itself a continuation of the effort— and by turning off from the apparition, as from something which would force him too deeply into himself, to the outward objects, the realities of nature, which had accompanied it:

BER: Last night of all,
When yon same star, that's westward
     from the pole
Had made his course to illume that part
     of heaven
Where now it burns, Marcellus and
     myself,
The bell then beating one—

This passage seems to contradict the critical law that what is told, makes a faint impression compared with what is beholden; for it does indeed convey to the mind more than the eye can see;

whilst the interruption of the narrative at the very moment when we are most intensely listening for the sequel, and have our thoughts diverted from the dreaded sight in expectation of the desired, yet almost dreaded, tale—this gives all the suddenness and surprise of the original appearance;—

> MAR: Peace, break thee off; look, where it comes again.

Note the judgment displayed in having the two persons present, who, as having seen the Ghost before, are naturally eager in confirming their former opinions,— whilst the sceptic is silent, and after having been twice addressed by his friends, answers with two hasty syllables—'Most like',—and a confession of horror:

> It harrows me with fear and wonder.

> O heaven! words are wasted on those who feel, and to those who do not feel the exquisite judgment of Shakespeare in this scene, what can be said?

Coleridge, then, is to be honoured as the first great practitioner of 'close analysis'. The fact that this has become somewhat discredited by later critics' dull and unimaginative performances cannot detract from the sensitiveness and penetration shown here by the author of *The Ancient Mariner*.

But Coleridge's place in literary history, even when he is judged solely as a critic, needs further definition. In literary history he cannot be separated from **Wordsworth**; the two stand together, *Dioscuri*, who carried out the revolution in English poetry signalised by the publication of *Lyrical Ballads*. Wordsworth's great Preface, which must have owed so much to his close association with Coleridge, is perhaps the finest single piece of criticism produced by that movement. To some

extent its importance must be seen as that of a historical document, or as throwing light on Wordsworth's own poetry; but it also contains memorably phrased truths about diction, metre, and the nature of poetry which cannot be said to 'date', although there are other things in their context which inevitably and honourably have receded into the past.

Apart from these aspects of Coleridge in which he is the inseparable associate of Wordsworth, what does he contribute to living criticism? The answer must lie in notes, fragments, *marginalia* rather than in sustained pieces of classical work. The *Biographia Literaria* is no more a *book*, essentially, than the miscellany of lecture-notes which Coleridge did not prepare for publication. It is disordered, even chaotic. Coleridge was a genius, but his mind was undisciplined. He knew too much, and could formulate his thoughts too readily; and some of his formulations have not worn so well as the immortal 'willing suspension of disbelief for the moment, which constitutes poetic faith', or the other unforgettable phrases with which he has enriched the vocabulary of criticism. Yet, even if we have to judge that his greatness as a critic lies mainly in hints, suggestions, *stimuli*, rather than in set-pieces of critical practice, it should at once be added that his best insights are incomparable. He was the most intelligent Englishman ever to apply himself to the criticism of poetry.

There were other good critics in the age of Wordsworth and Coleridge, some traditionalists, others innovators, but there is none who can rank with them as masters. The best of all, after Coleridge, was probably William Hazlitt, and with him seems to have died the possibility of a distinguished critic's addressing his audience as equals. For Matthew Arnold, the greatest critic of the Victorian age, does not do this. He speaks as a teacher. Perhaps this has been the typical note of English criticism since his day, doubtless owing to the profound political, social, and economic changes of which it was Arnold's special glory to take such intelligent cognisance. Arnold was preoccupied with social, ethical and religious questions. His claims for criticism in his famous essay on its 'function at the present time' were on behalf of the critical spirit in general, not specially on behalf of *literary* criticism. And even where literary criticism is concerned, there is some justice in T. S. Eliot's calling Arnold a propagandist for criticism rather than a critic. It is true that Arnold rarely dealt with his contemporaries (in print, at any rate), and that he was often more concerned with the moral and spiritual value of poetry in general—with 'the idea of great poetry' —than with demonstrating in detail exactly what makes poetry great, or good. But to talk of Arnold as a 'propagandist' is not wholly just. As Eliot says, he shows, in an essay like *The Study of Poetry*, that wonderful assurance, delicacy, and economy, that incomparably felicitous use of quotation, which belong to the great critics. A whole view of poetry is set out, without any appearance of strain or oversimplification, in a few brief pages. Arnold's discriminating 'touch', his way of making clear an important point of principle by means of a skilfully chosen example, are illustrated in the passage which follows, taken from his *Last Words on Translating Homer*. Here Arnold, having rejected the suggestion that Tennysonian verse is the appropriate medium for translating Homer, goes on to explain the nature of 'perfect simplicity' in poetry.

> When a genius essentially subtle, or a genius which, from whatever cause, is in its essence not truly and broadly simple,

determines to be perfectly plain, determines not to admit a shade of subtlety or curiosity into its expression, it cannot ever then attain real simplicity; it can only attain a semblance of simplicity. (I speak of poetic genius as employing itself upon narrative or dramatic poetry—poetry in which the poet has to go out of himself to create. In lyrical poetry, in the direct expression of personal feeling, the most subtle genius may, under the momentary pressure of passion, express itself simply. Even here, however, the native tendency will generally be discernible.) French criticism, richer in its vocabulary than ours, has invented a useful word to distinguish this semblance (often very beautiful and valuable) from the real quality. The real quality it calls *simplicité*, the semblance *simplesse*. The one is natural simplicity, the other is artificial simplicity. What is called simplicity in the productions of a genius essentially not simple, is, in truth, *simplesse*. The two are distinguishable from one another the moment they appear in company. For instance, let us take the opening of the narrative in Wordsworth's *Michael*:

> Upon the forest-side in Grasmere Vale
> There dwelt a shepherd, Michael was
>   his name;
> An old man, stout of heart, and strong
>   of limb.
> His bodily frame had been from youth
>   to age
> Of an unusual strength; his mind was
>   keen,
> Intense, and frugal, apt for all affairs;
> And in his shepherd's calling he was
>   prompt
> And watchful more than ordinary
>   men.

Now let us take the opening of the narrative in Mr Tennyson's *Dora*:

> With Farmer Allan at the farm abode
> William and Dora. William was his
>   son,

71

And she his niece. He often looked at
them,
And often thought, 'I'll make them
man and wife.'

The simplicity of the first of these passages
is *simplicité*; that of the second, *simplesse*.
Let us take the end of the same two
poems: first, of *Michael*:

The cottage which was named the
Evening Star
Is gone, the ploughshare has been
through the ground
On which it stood; great changes have
been wrought
In all the neighbourhood; yet the oak
is left
That grew beside their door; and the
remains
Of the unfinished sheepfold may be
seen
Beside the boisterous brook of Green-
head Ghyll.

And now, of *Dora*:

So those four abode
Within one house together; and as
years
Went forward, Mary took another
mate:
But Dora lived unmarried till her
death.

A heedless critic may call both of these
passages simple if he will. Simple, in a
certain sense, they both are, but between
the simplicity of the two there is all the
difference that there is between the
simplicity of Homer and the simplicity of
Moschus.

Arnold's lifelong effort to make his
fellow-countrymen use their brains was
not wholly wasted. Though he sometimes says 'we poor despised followers of
culture', the note is cheerful. But Arnold
had no manifest successor. Walter Pater

and Leslie Stephen were both, in their
different ways, distinguished critics, but
they were not his equal; and the critical
battles over aestheticism, and the contrary
tendencies, in the eighteen-eighties and
-nineties produced heat rather than light.
Arnold had some admirable academic
disciples, among whom may be counted
the fine Shakespearean interpreter A. C.
Bradley; but in the work of Sir Walter
Raleigh may be seen a gravitation away
from Arnold and his 'high seriousness'
towards Lytton Strachey and the note of
Bloomsbury. Criticism early in this
century was not in a strong position; no
critic had appeared to command the
literary scene with the authority that
Arnold had in his heyday. Between
Arnold and Eliot the greatest literary
critic was not a critic of poetry, but
Henry James, the first great critic in
English of the art of fiction.

T. S. Eliot's *The Sacred Wood*, the most
influential critical work of our day, came
out in 1920. It was long before the importance of Eliot's criticism was recognised, but its influence and authority have
been immense. There had been no comparable critic since Dryden. Eliot introduced a severity and astringency into
criticism which were long resented, but
which eventually compelled respect when
backed by the prestige gained by his
work in poetry. His best criticism, as
he himself has recognised, was 'a by-
product of his poetry-workshop', an
extension of the critical thinking which
went into the formation of his verse.
He was at his best when concentrating on
those qualities in seventeenth-century
poets and Jacobean dramatists who
seemed to him to have qualities dormant
in the nineteenth century, which it was
desirable to re-introduce into English verse.
In his later criticism, after he had established his own poetic style, some in-

cisiveness departed from his critical thinking. He became more and more preoccupied with his rôle of public moralist, and with the larger cultural, ethical and spiritual considerations which had also absorbed the thought of Arnold—although Eliot's attitude to these problems, founded upon religious orthodoxy, was very different from Arnold's. Eliot's influence, until recently immense, may be now on the wane. But it is still close enough for a detached historical view of it to be impossible. It has operated very variously; for instance, the most lively critical ideas in I. A. Richards' *Principles of Literary Criticism* (1924) derive from Eliot, but are associated there with a theoretical pseudo-scientific apparatus which Eliot would have by no means approved; while the work of F. R. Leavis, who superseded Richards as the dominant figure among the Cambridge University critics, began by a more or less unqualified acceptance of the new perspective of English poetry enforced by the recognition of Eliot's importance as a new and original poet, but has later developed into a conception of criticism, literature, and their relationship to the good life, totally distinct from anything said or implied in the work of Eliot, and deeply influenced by a writer so antipathetic to Eliot as D. H. **Lawrence**. Yet it remains true that the work of neither of these critics, nor that of Richards' brilliant pupil, William **Empson** (from whom descends the ingenious verbal analysis characteristic of the whole school of American 'New Critics'), is intelligible without a proper understanding of the vital presence of Eliot's work in the background.

As with all great critics, the precepts and practice of Eliot cannot be summed up in a formula. All that can be said in general terms is that his procedure, in his best essays, resembles that of Arnold,

rather than that of Coleridge, in the tactical use he makes of adroit quotation and the skilful passage, at the right moments, from specific observation to general reflection; but it conveys an impression of a greater austerity, crispness, and precision than Arnold's work—on its less congenial passages, and un-Arnoldian sourness and primness—and reflects what the critic obviously feels to be a more desperate cultural situation than that which Arnold had to confront. Eliot is also more insistent than Arnold that poetry is poetry and not a substitute for religion or morals, and this insistence has lent an excessive tartness to his dealings with his great predecessor (for instance, in *The Use of Poetry and the Use of Criticism*). But whatever its lapses or shortcomings, Eliot's criticism at its best must surely be ranked among the best criticism in the English language. His peculiar gift as a critic is his power to exhibit relationships of the most general and far-reaching kind between intimate qualities of versification, style and texture in poetry and the *ethos*, 'philosophy', or attitude to life of the poet. He practised a discipline of relevance which makes most criticism of the past (and indeed of the present) seem wordy, inconclusive, and vague. A fine example of this disciplined critical prose, with its deeply thought-out strategy of transition from particular poetic effects to larger and more general considerations, is to be found in his essay on Ben Jonson.

If you examine the first hundred lines or more of *Volpone* the verse appears to be in the manner of Marlowe, more deliberate, more mature, but without Marlowe's inspiration. It looks like mere 'rhetoric', certainly not 'deeds and language such as men do use'! It appears to us, in fact, forced and flagitious bombast. That it is not 'rhetoric', or at least not vicious rhetoric, we do not know until we are able to review the whole play. For the consistent maintenance of this manner conveys in the end an effect not of verbosity, but of bold, even shocking and terrifying directness. We have difficulty in saying exactly what produces this simple and single effect. It is not in any ordinary way due to management of intrigue. Jonson employs immense dramatic constructive skill: it is not so much skill in plot, as skill in doing without a plot. He never manipulates as complicated a plot as that of *The Merchant of Venice*; he has in his best plays nothing like the intrigue of Restoration comedy. In *Bartholomew Fair* it is hardly a plot at all; the marvel of the play is the bewildering rapid chaotic action of the fair; it is the fair itself, not anything that happens to take place at the fair. In *Volpone*, or *The Alchemist*, or *The Silent Woman*, the plot is enough to keep the players in motion; it is rather an 'action' than a plot. The plot does not hold the play together; what holds the play together is a unity of inspiration that radiates into plot and personages alike.

We have attempted to make more precise the sense in which it was said that Jonson's work is 'of the surface'; carefully avoiding the word 'superficial'. For there is work contemporary with Jonson's which is superficial in a pejorative sense in which the word cannot be applied to Jonson—the work of Beaumont and Fletcher. If we look at the work of Jonson's great contemporaries, Shakespeare, and also Donne and Webster and Tourneur (and sometimes Middleton), have a depth, a third dimension, as Mr Gregory Smith rightly calls it, which Jonson's work has not. Their words have often a network of tentacular roots reaching down to the deepest terrors and desires. Jonson's most certainly have not; but in Beaumont and Fletcher we may think that at times we find it. Looking closer, we discover that the blossoms of Beaumont's and Fletcher's imagination

draw no sustenance from the soil, but are cut and slightly withered flowers stuck into sand.

> Wilt thou, hereafter, when they talk of
>   me,
> As thou shalt hear nothing but
>   infamy,
> Remember some of these things? . . .
> I pray thee, do; for thou shalt never
>   see me so again.

> Hair woven in many a curious warp,
> Able in endless error to enfold
> The wandering soul; . . .

Detached from its context, this looks like the verse of the greater poets; just as lines from Jonson, detached from their context, look like inflated or empty fustian. But the evocative quality of the verse of Beaumont and Fletcher depends upon a clever appeal to emotions and associations which they have not themselves grasped; it is hollow. It is superficial with a vacuum behind it; the superficies of Jonson is solid. It is what it is; it does not pretend to be another thing. But it is so very conscious and deliberate that we must look with eyes alert to the whole before we apprehend the significance of any part. We cannot call a man's work superficial when it is the creation of a world; a man cannot be accused of dealing superficially with the world which he himself has created; the superficies *is* the world. Jonson's characters conform to the logic of the emotions of their world. It is a world like Lobatchevsky's; the worlds created by artists like Jonson are like systems of non-Euclidean geometry. They are not fancy, because they have a logic of their own; and this logic illuminates the actual world, because it gives us a new point of view from which to inspect it.

This assembly of passages from the great critics, in the manner of Arnold's 'touchstones', may serve as a reminder of what the best criticism is like. In our day the nature, status and function of criticism have been called into question. There are some who would dismiss it altogether in favour of scholarship and literary history. Others believe in the paramount value of 'interpretation'. Others, again, prefer that art of *belles lettres* into which the criticism of 'Bloomsbury', even at its best, as in Virginia Woolf or E. M. Forster, was apt to turn. Most ordinary readers are perhaps indifferent. Yet it seems clear that if there were to be no more criticism of the kind which has won it so high a traditional esteem in our culture, the quality of human life, as well as of literature, might suffer.   w.w.r.

Cummings, E[dward] E[stlin] (1894–1962), was born in Cambridge, Massachusetts, studied at Harvard, and remained thereafter within the New England tradition of quirky individualism. For his criticism of militarism while serving in an ambulance corps in 1916, the French interned him in the camp he describes in *The Enormous Room* (1922), an autobiographical novel affirming individualist outsider against state and masses. After little immediate success as a poet in New York, he studied painting in Paris until 1924, by which time he had some literary reputation. He won the *Dial* poetry prize in 1925, returned to Paris in 1930 and to New York in 1933. *Eimi* (1933) is his violent prose reaction from a tourist experience of Soviet collective life. He exhibited paintings in New York and Paris. *i: six nonlectures* (1953) was the informal record of his Norton lectures at Harvard. *Poems 1923–1954* received a citation from the National Book Award committee in 1955.

In forty years Cummings' poetry changed little in material or style, largely because his range is conservative and traditional: the nature-lyricist's kingdom of spring, love, youth, the oppressive 'them', hated cities, dawn and sun. His celebrated typographical innovations, including lower case 'i' and passages like

```
s (oon  &   there's
a                m  oo
)n
```

and the grasshopper lyric in *no thanks*, control simply the sound and speed of reading through visual impact that disguises conventional rhythms. Cummings' poems are clear to a fault and have little to offer the adult imagination beyond their initial pleasure. They are certainly not meant to be read more than three at a sitting. His ear for the vernacular is good, expecially in satirically abusive poems which support his recurrent little man against the slick, urban, commercial, political and military. The bland good taste of his erotic poems can sometimes rise from the sentimentality of April-love to genuine physical tenderness:

> i like kissing this and that of you,
> i like, slowly stroking the, shocking fuzz
> of your electric fur, and what-is-it comes
> over parting flesh . . .

Cummings reiterates an anarchic multiplicity of i's against the habitual and undiscriminating, but tarnishes his work as a whole with a vulgar lack of self-criticism. A certain arrogance is the hallmark of his love, social abuse and humane pity: he fails to suggest the complexity of love and society, the context of his simple and immediate pleasures. His best defence is W. C. **Williams'** *Lower Case Cummings*; his best poetry is always about the freedom of 'wonderful one times one' versus the oppression of 'this busy monster, manunkind' and social progress—'a comfortable disease':

if beggars are rich (and a robin will sing
his robin a song) but misers are poor—
let's love until noone could quite be
(and young is
the year, dear) as living as

i'm and as you're
—let's touch the sky:
with a you and a me
and an every (who's any who's some)
one who's we
E.N.W.M.

see also American Poetry

D

Daniel, Samuel (?1562–1619), was born near Taunton, studied at Oxford, and became a tutor for various children of the nobility. After 1603 he was frequently at court and some of his dramas were apparently played before the royal family. Daniel wrote tragedies (*Cleopatra*, 1593, and *Philotas*, 1604), masques (*Twelve Goddesses*, 1604, and *Hymen's Triumph*, 1615), long, patriotic and historical epics (*History of the Civil War between Lancaster and York*, 1595–1609), and a prose history of England. But his most famous works are the fifty-five sonnets called *Sonnets to Delia* (1592). Daniel's calm, even, dignified sonnets became a model for later writers. One of the most famous, which demonstrates his careful balance and technical skill, begins:

Care-charmer Sleep, son of the sable
night,
Brother to death, in silent darkness born:
Relieve my languish and restore the light,
With dark forgetting of my care's return;

and ends:

Still let me sleep, embracing clouds in
vain,
And never wake to feel the day's disdain.

Daniel could, at his best, handle paradox with an ease that few of his contemporaries could match. He was, however, less effective in conveying strong emotion. In *The Complaint of Rosamond* (1592), he versified the story of Rosamond, the mistress of King Henry II, who was poisoned by a jealous rival. At a crucial point in the story Daniel's measured verse seems completely inappropriate:

Look how a tigress that hath lost her
whelp
Runs fiercely ranging through the woods
astray,
And seeing herself deprived of hope or
help,
Furiously assaults what's in her way,
To satisfy her wrath, not for a prey.

Most critics have praised Daniel as an accurate, responsible, and intelligent historian. But his history makes dull poetry, often drawn out with documentation and patriotically moral reflection. Daniel also defended the importance of the literary life in *Musophilus* (1599) and wrote a critical pamphlet, *The Defence of Ryme* (*c.* 1603). The latter was in reply to **Campion**'s concern with metrics as the essential element in poetry and his attack on conventional prosody. Daniel felt that poetry should deal with content, that poems should be 'wiser'; he also defended rhyme and English metre. Yet for all his intelligent industry and his concern with 'matter', his reputation rests primarily on the 'manner' of his *Sonnets to Delia*.

J.G.

Darley, George (1795–1846), Irish poet, critic and mathematician, was educated at Trinity College, Dublin. His fairy opera, *Sylvia*, contains fine lyrics, but his best work is to be found in *Nepenthe*. Other works include several tragedies. D.H.

D'Avenant, Sir William (1606–68), reputedly **Shakespeare**'s godson, produced the first English 'opera', *The Siege of Rhodes* (1656), revived Shakespeare's plays and himself composed two dozen dramatic works. In 1650 the publication of his heroic poem, *Gondibert*, and of his *Discourse upon Gondibert* led to a controversy with Hobbes about the nature of poetry. The variety of D'Avenant's gifts as a lyrical poet is apparent in his beautiful song:

The Lark now leaves his watry Nest
And climbing, shakes his dewy Wings;

in the rhythmical invention of

Wake all the dead! what hoa! what hoa!

and in the measured gravity of *The Philosopher and the Lover: to a Mistress Dying*. J.P.

Davidson, John (1857–1909), a Scotsman, wrote plays, novels and poems in various styles, but he is best known for his rugged ballads and songs. His materialistic ideas and proletarian sympathies were ahead of his time. D.H.

Davies, Sir John (1569–1626), was educated at Winchester College and Oxford,

entered the Middle Temple in 1588 and was called to the Bar in 1595. *Orchestra* was published in 1596, but *Epigrams*, additional to C.M.'s translation of *All Ovid's Epistles* (1598), was burned by order of the Archbishop of Canterbury. *Nosce Teipsum* (1599) was followed only by small minor poems, such as *Hymns of Astraea* (also 1599). Davies was an M.P. in England, and in Ireland, where he occupied several important posts, including that of Speaker of the Irish Parliament. He was appointed Lord Chief Justice in 1626, but died suddenly before he could assume office.

Orchestra, or, a Poem on Dancing, in rhyme royal, ostensibly a poem in which Antinous tries to persuade Penelope to dance, is really a philosophical nature-poem, 'as truly "nature poetry" for the Elizabethans as **Wordsworth** was for the Romantics . . . if there is no personal passion in the poem, there is delighted and passionate contemplation', in C. S. Lewis' words. It is concerned, not with the music of the spheres, but with their motion:

Behold the world, how it is whirlèd
round!
And for it is so whirled is namèd so;
In whose large volume many rules are
found
Of this new art, which it doth fairly
show.
For your quick eyes in wandering to
and fro,
From east to west, on no one thing
can glance,
But if you mark it well it seems to
to dance.

Everything dances—the sun, the moon, the stars, the sea. The poem expresses a conception of the harmonious nature of the universe (see E. M. W. Tillyard: *Five Poems*, 1945, for a brilliant analysis).

The quatrain was for the first time

fully mastered in *Nosce Teipsum*, which is concerned with 'Human Knowledge', and 'The Soul of Man and the Immortality Thereof'. The end of the first part illustrates its quality:

> I know my soul hath power to know all
> things,
> Yet is she blind and ignorant in all;
> I know I am one of nature's little kings,
> Yet to the least and vilest things am
> thrall.
> I know my life's a pain and but a span,
> I know my sense is mocked with
> every thing;
> And to conclude I know myself a man,
> Which is a proud and yet a wretched
> thing.

Whence develops the argument for the immortality of the soul.

Severe in diction and imagery, this purely didactic poem is in marked contrast with the fancifulness of *Orchestra*; 'drab' as opposed to 'golden', in Professor Lewis' phraseology. But it has a sureness which makes it relevant to our own day, and carries with it a strong emotive element.   B.D.

Davies, W[illiam] H[enry] (1871–1940), was a Welshman (born in Newport) who spent six years as a tramp in America. The fresh yet sharp simplicity of his poetry is complemented by the direct and rough prose of the *Autobiography of a Super Tramp* (1908).   D.H.

Day Lewis, Cecil (1904–), English Poet Laureate 1968, like many English poets, is the son of a clergyman. He was educated at Sherborne and Oxford, and earned a living in the nineteen-thirties as a schoolmaster, during the Second World War in the Ministry of Information, and more recently as a director of a publishing firm. He writes detective stories under the pseudonym Nicholas Blake. In the nineteen-thirties he was generally grouped by critics along with W. H. **Auden**, Stephen **Spender**, and Louis **MacNeice** as a militant anti-Fascist poet. He had, however, a special interest in the heroic narrative poem not shared by the other three poets. Much of his poetry in the nineteen-thirties was, however, weakened by a too conscious imitation of some of Auden's more boisterous mannerisms and by a rather stridently didactic tone.

Since the nineteen-forties, Day Lewis' poetry has become more traditional in its manner and more personal, domestic, or 'literary' (he is fond of topics from classical mythology) in its themes. A long poem, *An Italian Journey* (1954), is full of skilful pastiche of the styles of **Hardy, Browning**, and **Clough**. Day Lewis is a lively and scholarly verse translator, his most notable achievement here being his version of the *Aeneid* (1942), in long, loose, but supple lines. He was Professor of Poetry at Oxford from 1951 to 1956 and Clark Lecturer at Cambridge in 1947. He is a copious and various poet, a little too apt to echo other men's voices, a little given to diffuseness, and perhaps never seeming, for all the range of his intellectual curiosity, to have anything to say that is centrally and passionately his own.

Day Lewis has exercised so many manners so skilfully that it is impossible to find a quotation that seems typical. But the following stanza, the meditation of a liberal sadly accepting the necessity of revolution, represents, in its skilful modulation of sound and dignified bareness of diction, one of his manners of the nineteen-thirties at its best:

> Move then with new desires,
> For where we used to build and love

Is no man's land, and only ghosts can
live
Between two fires.

G.F.

Dekker, Thomas (?1576–1632), is known almost entirely as a playwright, author of *The Shoemaker's Holiday* (1600), and *Satiromastix* (1602) in which he repaid Ben **Jonson,** with whom he had earlier collaborated, for the ridicule of himself in the latter's *Poetaster*. Dekker appears through his works one of the most sympathetic and charming of the Elizabethan playwrights.

D.H.

De la Mare, Walter (1873–1956), published his first collection of poems in 1907 under the pseudonym of Walter Ramal, but he soon established a wide popular reputation in his own name as a leading poet of the Georgian period with volumes like *The Listeners* (1912), *Peacock Pie* (1913), *Motley* (1918) and *The Veil* (1921). He was also known for his novels and shorter prose fantasies, for his critical essays, and for his anthology of poems for children, *Come Hither* (1923). He was awarded the Order of Merit in 1953.

De la Mare's main preoccupations are with childhood and (an intimately related interest; he was influenced by **Poe**) with the resources of fantasy. Of children he felt that 'between their dream and their reality looms no impassable abyss' and it is this area which he is concerned to explore and illuminate in many of his poems. His marked technical skills are employed to create a dream world which, although F. R. Leavis and I. A. Richards have criticised it for being escapist, is yet rarely seen out of perspective of the 'real' pressures which generate it and give it consistency and significance. It is no Arcadia but rather a threatened horrific world which, if a retreat, is a harshly

modified one, and one which has important emotional relations to reality.

His energy, however, often outdistances his poetic integrity, and then fantasy becomes mere fancy. He is also prone to facile patriotics, to sentimentality, and to hollow rhetorical gestures. In his more overtly realistic work, such as *Dry August Burned*, and *The Fat Woman* and in lighter satirical pieces like *The Feckless Dinner Party* he displays an accurate and compassionate grasp of human relations and these serve to remind one that though an original writer, De la Mare is not as limited as his popular image might tend to suggest.

J.F.

Denham, Sir John (1615–69) was born in Dublin. He was a supporter of Charles I during the Civil War. His best known poem, *Cooper's Hill*, is of importance for fixing the classical form of the heroic couplet, and also as furnishing the model of the late seventeenth-century and eighteenth-century topographical poem. He also wrote a tragedy, *The Sophy*, and various verse, mainly occasional.

J.H-S.

Diaper, William (1685–1717), was educated at Balliol College, Oxford. Ordained deacon at Wells in 1709, he later became curate at Brent and subsequently at Crick. In 1712 he published three small volumes containing the best work of his brief career: *Nereides*, *Callipaedia*, and *Dryades*.

An Augustan, he wrote with grandiloquence and 'decorum' and moralised upon the common themes; yet he was an original. His *Nereides* wrought a sea-change unique in the pastoral tradition: its sea-nymphs and tritons inhabit an undersea setting elaborated from extensive knowledge of marine life. Diaper is chiefly interesting, however, for his many passages in avowedly congenial 'mean style' that reflect his acute country-man's perceptiveness. In these his language and imagery are fresh; his vision minute, objective, and exact:

> The azure Dye, which plums in Autumn
> boast,
> That handled fades, and at a Touch is
> lost.
> W.L.S.

Dickinson, Emily (1830–86), was born in Massachusetts. As a map of movement her life looks threadbare, since she hardly left her family house at Amherst. More than most women's her life was interiorised, held between a confident Calvinist father —'his heart was pure and terrible', she wrote—and local society, New England small-town puritanism in decline. 'Pardon my sanity in a world insane', she wrote to a friend, and she withdrew enough to maintain a balance. If her 1875 poems may be used biographically her existence looks more like defiance, tension and the self-dramatisation of the pressures in her passionate and unreconciling nature. She was, therefore, as much isolated and alone —'Queen Recluse' Samuel Bowles called her—as most modern American writers have been. Discoveries that she knew three or four men more or less intimately, and hints in Jay Leyda's *The Years and the Hours of Emily Dickinson* (1960) that she may have been promiscuous, have at least warmed the earlier enigma of the crushed female curate. Two years in Amherst Academy and one at Mount Holyoake Female Seminary were enough official education for her oddly tough intelligence and her natural gift with words.

She wrote about twenty-five great short poems all within the romantic range of nature, God, immortality and sublimated passion. Since she did not write for money, did not give in to parish-magazine literariness, and did not yield completely either to faith or to doubt, she freely articulated 'the despair that is the essence of the human condition', and her talent for personal vocabulary and intimations of intimacy rarely subdued into orthodoxy:

> Of course—I prayed—
> And did God care?
> He cared as much as on the air
> A bird—had stamped her foot—
> And cried 'Give me'—.

Continually she can establish her independent self, treasured in quiet defiance and linked to those verities she is sure of—nature and death: her major work, reaching its climax in 1862, appears at the end of nineteenth-century Romanticism and religious upheaval:

> Nature and God—I neither knew
> Yet both so well knew me
> They startled, like executors
> Of my identity
> Yet neither told—that I could learn—
> My secret as secure
> As Herschel's private interest
> Or Mercury's affair.

'The soul selects her own society' and when death comes, as in the lyric Allen **Tate** calls 'one of the perfect poems in English', the poet is prepared rather than kneeling:

> Because I could not stop for Death,
> He kindly stopped for me;

Her deeper self appears sometimes barbarically vital:

> Proud of my broken heart, since thou
> didst break it,
> Proud of the pain I did not feel till thee,
> Proud of my night, since thou with
> moons dost slake it,

Not to partake thy passion, my
                                humility.

After 1862 it is said she dressed in white;
her poems compare her anguish to
Calvary; she shunned publication even
more (few poems did appear in her lifetime, anonymously). She relished her
'lone orthography' (*After a hundred years*).

Although her measures scarcely resist
the English Hymnal and popular jingle,
she avoided contemporary genteel convention through her eccentric linguistic
taste: 'Great streets of silence led away /
To neighbourhoods of pause'; 'Let no
sunrise' yellow noise / Interrupt this
ground'; 'Like trains of cars on tracks of
plush / I hear the level bee'; 'Adored with
caution—as a brittle heaven'. She can also
control a devotional simplicity with the
directness of **Herbert** or **Vaughan**:

I died for Beauty—but was scarce
Adjusted in the Tomb
When One who died for Truth was
                                lain
In an adjoining Room.

Out of more complex balance of language
resources—Latin and Saxon—she re-creates
a hackneyed commonplace in a short poem
of great power:

Presentiment—is that long shadow on
                                the lawn—
Indication that suns go down—

The notice to the startled grass
That darkness is about to pass—

But Emily Dickinson's finest poems are
dramatic anecdotes of psychological experience: *I years had been from home* tells
of a return in apprehension to a house
once familiar and now haunted by an old
self:

I fumbled at my nerve—
I scanned the windows o'er—
The Silence—like an Ocean rolled—
And broke against my Ear.

No sooner is the hand 'fitted to the latch'
than the nerve breaks; the speaker 'like a
thief' escapes the psychological moment.
Emily Dickinson wrote in a letter, 'I
sing, as the boy does by the burying
ground—because I am afraid'.

'Her poetry is a magnificent personal
confession, blasphemous and, in its self-
revelation, its honesty, almost obscene. It
comes out of an intellectual life towards
which it feels no moral responsibility.
Cotton Mather would have burned her for
a witch' (Allen Tate). Her weaknesses are
those of a too neatly repeated range,
probably arising from that lack of discipline in writing for an audience of her
peers, and an almost total reluctance to
resist habits of metre, vocabulary and
tone.

Yet not until Johnson's superb editions
of the poems and letters (1955 and 1958)
did a complete and accurate text of this
major poet become available.   E.N.W.M.
see also American Poetry

Donne, John (1572–1631), is a figure to
whom it is impossible to be indifferent,
either as a man or a writer. The debates on
his personality and his poetry have been
marked by warmth, even extravagance, of
feeling on both sides. We know more
about him than about any other English
poet before **Milton**, and during the last
fifty years he has been the object of intense
critical study. But the issues are not
settled and probably never will be. His
earliest biographer was Izaak Walton,
whose *Life of Donne* first appeared as the
preface to the *LXXX Sermons* of 1640 and
was added to and revised up to its final
version in 1675. Donne's own letters, his

portraits (no less than five are extant) and his self-revelations in his prose works complicate the simple outline of his life as drawn by Walton, and some would substitute for Walton's 'second Augustine' an egoistic careerist whose main motives were worldly. Others, struck by such facts as his disastrously imprudent marriage, his constancy as a friend, loyalty as a son and generosity, have excused his cynicism as the product of a naturally melancholy temperament and explained his apparent sycophancy as the *façon de parler* of his time. So with his poetry. Ben **Jonson** called him 'the first poet in the world in some things' and some critics have ignored the qualification while others have stressed it. The first group exalt him for his power to exercise the mind while striking to the heart; the second point to the fragmentariness of his achievement and declare that although he wrote some fine poems he does not, as the greatest poets do, 'add up'.

Donne was born in 1572 in London. He came on his mother's side from a family notable equally for loyalty to the Roman Church and for literary activity. His grandfather was John Heywood, epigram-matist and interlude writer, who married Sir Thomas More's niece. His uncles, Ellis and Jasper Heywood, were Jesuits, Jasper being also the translator of Seneca's tragedies. His younger brother was imprisoned for sheltering a priest and died in prison. Donne was brought up strictly as a Catholic and sent to Oxford very young to avoid having to take the oath demanded. He probably then went abroad, before finishing his education as a law student at Lincoln's Inn. Along with other ambitious young men he sailed with Essex on the Cadiz expedition in 1596 and in the next year on the unlucky Islands Voyage. On his return he found good employment as secretary to the Lord Keeper, Sir Thomas Egerton. At the close of 1601 he wrecked what looked like being a promising career of public service by a runaway match with the niece of Egerton's wife, Ann More. From this time to his taking of orders in January 1615 he lived a melancholy life, perhaps dependent on the charity of his wife's relations, later devilling for Thomas Morton in controversies with Catholics and seeking, without success, for a 'place' and, with more success, for patronage. There can be no doubt of his hope to achieve a secular career and of his reluctance to take orders. He finally gave way in response to the direct pressure of King James. There can also be no doubt that, having yielded, he found a deep satisfaction in the exercise of his ministry and was conscientious in the performance of his duties, particularly in the preparation of his sermons. He was appointed Reader in Divinity to the Benchers of his old inn in 1616 and in 1622 he became Dean of St Paul's. He preached frequently at Court and was chosen by Charles I to preach the first sermon of the new reign; but his finest sermons are those he gave on the great feasts in his Cathedral, where he was buried under a striking monument by Nicholas Stone. This stands today in the south transept, having survived the fire in which old St Paul's was destroyed. He is shown standing, wrapped in his shroud, awaiting the resurrection of the body.

Donne was by profession first a 'place-seeker' and then a divine. In neither profession was poetry likely to help him. Apart from the two *Anniversaries* (1611 and 1612), in which he celebrated the virtues of the dead daughter of his patron, Sir Robert Drury, and some funeral poems and verse-letters written to please the great, particularly Lady Bedford, his poetry was written for its own sake and circulated among his friends. There is very little evidence to suggest that, apart from the Satires, some Elegies and *The Storm* and *The Calm*, it was at all widely known during his life. It was collected and printed two years after his death, in 1633.

Except for a handful of poems (including three fine Hymns and three of the Holy Sonnets) Donne's poetry was written before he took orders. To the period before his marriage belong the five Satires, a group of Love Elegies, a good many familiar Verse-Letters, including the famous realistic narrative poems *The Storm* and *The Calm*, and probably some of the lyrics which go under the name of *Songs and Sonnets*. In 1601 he wrote what appears to be intended to be only the first canto of a long satirical narrative, in which he was to trace the transmigrations of the soul of the apple that tempted Eve. Not many poems can be dated with certainty in the years following his marriage; but it seems likely that a good many of the *Songs and Sonnets* belong to this period. (Some of them assume the presence of a King on the throne and must be after 1603.) From 1607 to 1615 Donne was writing divine poems, verse-letters and the two *Anniversaries*, with other Funeral Elegies, and was also busy with prose works: *Pseudo-Martyr* (1610) in which he attempted to persuade Catholics to take the Oath of Allegiance and which won him the favour of King James, *Ignatius His Conclave* (published in 1611 in both Latin and English), a Lucianic satire against the Jesuits, and *Biathanatos*, a learned, casuistical discussion of the lawfulness of some suicides, which he never published. After his ordination Donne's genius found expression in his preaching. Apart from some sermons he published only his *Devotions* (1623), meditations inspired by a serious illness in that year. After his death his son printed three folio volumes of sermons and also scraped the barrel by printing not only the fragmentary *Essays in Divinity*, but also *Biathanatos* and his father's *Juvenilia*, Paradoxes and Problems written many years before by 'Jack Donne' which 'Dr Donne' would have wished to be forgotten.

The distinction between 'Jack Donne' and 'Dr Donne' is Donne's own. He made it in a letter of 1619 when sending a copy of *Biathanatos* to a friend: 'It is a Book written by *Jack Donne*, and not by *D. Donne*: Reserve it for me, if I live, and if I die, I only forbid it the Presse, and the Fire: publish it not, but burn it not'. Most writers on Donne who have picked up this distinction use it to mean the distinction between the satirist, elegist and love poet on the one hand and the religious poet and preacher on the other, 'Jack' being licentious and the 'Doctor' moral and serious. But Donne himself plainly meant something quite different: the distinction between a book by a private individual and a book written by a professional person who speaks with the authority and responsibility that his profession gives and demands. In this sense virtually all Donne's poetry, whether amorous or religious, licentious or idealistic, is the work of 'Jack Donne'. It is poetry that was not intended for publication. Donne was, in Ben Jonson's phrase, a poet 'on the by'. He was not a poet by vocation as **Milton** and **Wordsworth** were; nor was he a professional man of letters, like **Dryden**. He feels no sense of responsibility towards a public who are to be taught 'the best and sagest things', nor has he any sense of responsibility towards his own calling or reputation as a poet. He writes as the mood takes him and as a theme seizes his imagination. The poem is its own justification, and if it totally contradicts what he has said in another poem this is of no consequence. We should be much disturbed if manuscript poems by Wordsworth came to light which deplored the limited outlook of country folk and expressed a longing for the delights of urban life; but Donne who has written more finely than any other English poet of the delight and glory of mutual passionate love has also written finely of love as a fraud, declaring that a woman possessed is mere dead flesh, with only the medicinal value his age ascribed to mummy. He can declare

> Only our love hath no decay;
> This, no to-morrow hath, nor yesterday,
> Running it never runs from us away,
> But truly keeps his first, last, everlasting day.

And, on the other hand,

> Hope not for minde in women; at their best
> Sweetnesse and wit, they are but
> *Mummy*, possest.

It is possible to construct a 'philosophy of love' from Donne's love-poetry if we take as 'serious' those poems whose sentiments we approve, ignoring the remainder or dismissing them as the exercises of a cynical wit. The distinction is not a critical one. In what sense is *A Valediction: forbidding Mourning* more serious than *The Apparition*?

Some of Donne's poems would seem to have been written to exercise his wit, to see what could be made by craftsmanship and ingenuity of invention out of an old or unpromising theme. Many of these are paradoxes in the old sense, that is defences of indefensible positions. He can argue that total promiscuity is justifiable, that it is better to marry an ugly woman than a beautiful, or, with more weight, that age is lovelier than youth.

Others are imitations, also in the old sense, that is free translations into the social and poetical idiom of his own day of classic poems and classic themes. Thus the fourth Satire translates Horace's meeting with a bore into the poet's meeting with a spy at Court, the magnificent lyric *The Sun-Rising* is inspired by Ovid's address to Aurora, and *The Canonization* wonderfully adapts to its own ends Ovid's boast that he is willing to die for love:

> Call us what you will, wee are made
> such by love;
> Call her one, mee another flye,
> We' are Tapers too, and at our owne
> cost die,
> And wee in us finde th' Eagle and the Dove.
> The Phoenix riddle hath more
> wit
> By us, we two being one, are it.
> So to one neutrall thing both sexes fit,
> Wee dye and rise the same, and prove
> Mysterious by this love.

> Wee can dye by it, if not live by love . . .

The distinguishing mark of Donne's poems, whether we call them cynical or serious, and whether we can point to a source or tradition that he is remoulding or no, is that he can give the accent of personal feeling and personal sincerity to whatever mood he adopts, so that he always sounds as if he 'means what he says'. He is never languid. This accent of truth is as conspicuous in the outrageous poems as in those which have been called 'serious' or 'sincere', the poems on the joys of mutual love and on the grief of parting; it is heard in such an opening as

> Who ever loves, if he do not propose
> The right true end of love, he's one that goes

To sea for nothing but to make him
sick;

or in

I long to talk with some old lover's
ghost
Who dyed before the god of love was
born;

or in

If ever any beauty I did see,
Which I desir'd, and got, t'was but a
dreame of thee.

We expect such versatility from a playwright and applaud him for making an Iachimo and an Imogen speak with equal conviction; but in a lyrical poet we expect consistency of feeling. And whereas in a play the total design will guide us in assessing the worth of views expressed by the characters, we have no such guide if we attempt to discover Donne's personal views from his poetry alone. If we want to know Donne the man, we must go to his life, his letters, prose works and sermons. These provide the context for Donne the artist.

The 'accent of truth' in the Elegies, Songs and Sonnets and Divine Poems is the result of the combination of a powerfully dramatic imagination, which renders every mood with its present intensity and not as it is in memory, and a natural gift for melodic phrasing. Donne wrote some exquisite songs; in his Satires he attempted to come as near to a prose rhythm as a poet can; and in a few poems, such as *The Apparition* or *Women's Constancy*, he wrote brief dramatic monologues, very close to the poetry of the stage. But his greatest poems are those in which dramatic speech is lifted towards song or song breaks down into dramatic speech, in which the urgency of the dramatic moment and the vigour of dramatic speech is combined with the

ecstasy or poignancy of lyric, in such affirmations as

Love, all alike, no season knowes, nor
clyme,
Nor houres, dayes, moneths, which are
the rags of time;

or outcries such as

O more then Moone,
Draw not up seas to drowne me in thy
spheare,
Weep me not dead, in thine armes . . .

He is so remarkable an artist that he deceives us into thinking he uses no art at all and is writing out of the experience itself, baring to us his 'naked thinking heart'. The third element in Donne's poetry is his famous wit, his power to make surprising comparisons and, having surprised us, to make us confess the comparison is just. The majority of his love-poems are 'persuasions' of one kind or another, in which dazzling displays of false logic, and heaped-up arguments by analogy lead to a desired conclusion.

This blend of passion as vivid as in drama with lyric intensity and intellectual agility commended Donne to readers of the twentieth century as a poet who felt and thought at once. He was contrasted with the Romantics and the Victorians, who were reproached for feeling and then thinking about their feelings, or merely feeling. But the attempt to make Donne's poetry a standard by which other poetry can be judged is absurd. Donne is *sui generis*. None of his followers in the seventeenth century caught more than tricks from him, and those modern poets who were most profoundly impressed by him, **Yeats** and **Eliot**, did not catch his accent. At the same time we have to explain why the twentieth century found Donne so peculiarly 'modern' and why

poets so different from him in temper and outlook found an inspiration, if not a model, in his poetry. The fundamental reason why Donne seemed so 'modern' was that he wrote with an imagination unfettered by the doctrine that poetry should both instruct and please.   H.G.
see also Imagery *and* Satire

Doughty, C[harles] M[ontagu] (1843–1926), an English traveller and the author of *The Dawn in Britain* (1906), a six-volume epic on the national consciousness, which is a remarkable and largely unappreciated poem. He is best known for his prose *Travels in Arabia Deserta* (1888).   D.H.

Douglas, Gavin (?1475–1522), Bishop of Dunkeld, was the author of *The Palice of Honour, King Hart* (both allegories) and the first complete vernacular translation of Virgil's *Aeneid* (completed in 1513), containing original *Prologues* to each Book. *Prologues* VII, XII and XIII are descriptions of Winter, Spring and Summer, revolutionary in being pure 'Nature' poetry 200 years before **Thomson**'s *Seasons*. His *Eneados* is all transposed to the harsh actuality of medieval Scotland, the blue Mediterranean becomes the grey North Sea.

> Til Eolus cuntrie that wyndy regioune
> A brudy land of furyus stormy sowne . . .
> In gowsty caves the wyndis lowde
> > quhissilling.
> > *Eneados* I, ii

Ezra **Pound** commented that Douglas was 'better than Virgil because he had heard the sea'.   S.G.S.
see also Translation

Dowson, Ernest (1867–1900), received a sporadic, mostly French education, after which, in 1886, he went up to Oxford; a

carelessness about sleep and food was to bring out latent tuberculosis and inherited nervous instability. Going down without a degree, he helped his father for several years to manage a small London dock. In 1892 and 1894 he contributed to the anthologies of the Rhymers' Club. In 1891 he fell unhappily in love with twelve-year-old Adelaide Folkinowicz. His mother committed suicide in 1894. Thrown on his own resources, Dowson began translating French memoirs and *romans noirs*. His first, most accomplished book *Verses* appeared in 1896. His life became progressively disorganised, and he died at Catford, London, on 23 February, 1900.

On his poetry Graham Hough comments 'a vague relapse into unction and dreams of a white purity, between bouts of quite other emotion . . . it achieves a faint wavering music which, however tenuous, is his own'. *Cynara* exemplified these qualities:

> I cried for madder music and for
> > stronger wine,
> But when the feast is finished and the
> > lamps expire,
> Then falls thy shadow, Cynara! the
> > night is thine;
> And I am desolate and sick of an old
> > passion,
> > Yea, hungry for the lips of my desire:
> I have been faithful to thee, Cynara!
> > in my fashion.

Dowson brilliantly controls the alexandrine and movingly juxtaposes his paradise of childhood and the Romantic Fatal Woman: Cynara as Adelaide and the dangerous reconciler of the contradictions of experience, of knowledge and mystery. Dowson preferred his prose to his verse; and his short stories possess a narrow distinction. His biography resembles the common eighteen-nineties myth of the *poète maudit.* Those responsible for elaborating it were principally Arthur **Symons** and W. B. **Yeats**.   I.F.

Drayton, Michael (1563–1631), always dependent on noble or royal patronage, wrote many different kinds of poetry throughout his long career. He began with sonnets, publishing *Idea's Mirror*, which contains the famous and brilliant 'Since there's no help, come let us kiss and part', in 1594. He then wrote conventional complaints (*England's Heroical Epistles*, 1597) and verse chronicles (*Mortimeriados*, 1596), and collaborated on a number of plays, all but one of which have been lost. In his middle period, Drayton worked on *Polyolbion* (1612, 1622), a long historical and naturalistic description, in alexandrines, of the whole of England. The poem includes lists of all English birds, beasts, rivers, and historical figures. At this time, much of Drayton's verse, like **Donne**'s, explored the imagistic possibilities of his anatomical and naturalistic observations. In one poem, *The Heart*, Drayton shares his loved one's heart in a directly physical and intricate way. He also wrote an historical poem glorifying the battle of Agincourt and a fantasy, *Nimphidia* (1627), grouping legendary and historical figures in a graceful version of Queen Mab's land. His later verse is far more reminiscent of **Herrick** than of Donne. One passage, from the pastoral *Shepherd's Sirena* (1627), demonstrates his later simplicity and delicacy:

> The Verdant Meades are seene,
> When she doth view them,
> In fresh and gallant Greene,
> Straight to renewe them.
> And every little Grasse
> Broad it selfe spreadeth,
> Proud that this bonny Lasse
> Upon it treadeth.

Drayton was a dedicated poet, frequently versifying his allegiance to poetry and his respect for his contemporaries. He particularly valued **Marlowe**, Ben **Jonson** and **Drummond** of Hawthornden. His great skill at a variety of poetic forms, despite his lack of unique genius, makes him both a distinguished artist in his own right and an excellent illustration of changing literary taste.   J.G.

Drummond, William, Earl of Hawthornden (1585–1649), Scottish poet and royalist, was one of the first Scots writers to use the London literary dialect. He also translated French and Italian lyrics. The title, *Poems: Amorous, Funerall, Divine, Pastorall: in Sonnets, Songs, Sextains, Madrigals* (1616), sums up his favourite subject and forms.   D.H.

Dryden, John (1631–1700), poet, critic and dramatist, was born at Aldwinkle in Northamptonshire, into a family of landed gentry, both his grandfathers being baronets. He was educated at Westminster School under Dr Busby, and in 1650 went to Trinity College, Cambridge, as a scholar. He took his degree in 1654, but seems to have remained at Cambridge till 1657, when he went to London to take up a government appointment provided by his cousin, Sir Gilbert Pickering, Chamberlain to Cromwell. From his schooldays he had written poetry, but the first of his verses to attract attention were his *Heroique Stanzas* (quatrains) of 1659, in memory of Oliver Cromwell, and *Astraea Redux* (1660), which hailed the Restoration of Charles II. In 1663 he married Lady Elizabeth Howard, sister of his literary friend, Robert Howard. From then until the last few years of his life he supplemented his meagre income mainly by writing plays, though between 1670 and 1688 he had the benefit of an irregularly paid stipend of £300 a year as Poet Laureate and Historiographer Royal. In his later days his income seems to have been derived from his varied translations, notably of Virgil. As Monarch of Wills' Coffee House, he dominated the literary scene in the last years of his life.

'I do not know', Dryden is reported as having said towards the end of his life, 'if posterity will think me a great poet; they will not be able to deny that I was a good versifier'. For the passion of his life was 'to reform the numbers of our native tongue', and throughout his life, in poems, plays and prose, he strove to create an ordered and expressive language. The literary language common in his early days was becoming more and more feeble, muddled, slack, or grotesquely inflated. Dryden, to quote T. S. **Eliot**, 'for the first time established a *normal* English speech valid for both verse and prose, and imposing its laws which greater poetry than Dryden's might violate, but which no poetry since has overthrown'. And Matthew **Arnold** said 'Here at last we have the true English prose, a prose such as we would all gladly use if only we knew how'. He is the first great critic in our language, and Dr **Johnson** was justified in maintaining that nobody ever found his critical writings tedious. His contributions to heroic drama, which he was careful to distinguish from tragedy, gave it a quality it would otherwise have lacked. Here, however, and in the bibliography, he will be considered only as a poet.

We do not go to Dryden for profundity, for subtlety, for exaltation: he is the great poet of generalities, not by any means shallow, and of acute comment on human behaviour. He is not original in thought— all his poetry except *The Hind and the Panther* is occasional—but the energy of his intellect flows over a wide landscape. He could mould the language to his many purposes, and what raises him to the rank of poet is 'the energy divine' he imparts in all that he writes: 'the wheels take fire' as **Coleridge** put it, 'from the mere rapidity of their motion'. Moreover, as **Landor** made **Southey** say: 'He is always shrewd and penetrating, explicit and perspicuous, concise where conciseness is desirable, and copious where copiousness can give delight'. But these qualities he did not achieve until the writing of his first great poem, *Absalom and Achitophel* (1681), for though his earlier poems disengage themselves from outworn conventions and promise what is to come, they are uneven. Dryden had learned from play-writing how to mould declamatory verse, both in rhyme and in blank verse, a declamatory verse which is still the best since **Shakespeare**'s. He could be magniloquent:

> Discourag'd with his death, the Moorish
> pow'rs
> Fell back; and, falling back were press'd
> by ours.
> But, as when winds and rain together
> crowd,
> They swell till they have burst the
> bladder'd clowd,
> And first the Lightning, flashing deadly
> clear,
> Flyes, falls, consumes, 'ere scarce it does
> appear. . . .
> *The Conquest of Granada*, 1672

Or he could achieve the simplicity of:

> How shall I plead my cause, when you,
> my Judge
> Already have condemn'd me? Shall I
> bring
> The Love you bore me for my
> Advocate? . . .
> . . . Speak, my Lord,
> For I end here. Though I deserved this
> usage
> Was it like you to give it?
> *All for Love*, 1678

It was the flexible combination of the two methods that gave power and spirit to his first great long poem, *Absalom and Achitophel*, of which one can sense the vigour in even a short extract from the character of Achitophel (Shaftesbury):

> For close designs and crooked counsels fit;
> Sagacious, bold, and turbulent of wit;
> Restless, unfixt in principles and place;
> In power unpleas'd, impatient of disgrace.
> A fiery soul, which working out its way,
> Fretted the pigmy body to decay:
> And o'r inform'd the tenement of clay.

This broad, almost genial, Varronian satire was followed by the biting, Juvenalian *The Medall* (1682), and the brilliant *Mac Flecknoe*, the first mock-heroic poem in the language.

And in that year appeared the first of the two great ratiocinative religious poems, *Religio Laici*, defending the position of the average Anglican layman, who 'plods on to *Heaven*; and is ne'er at loss'. The exordium illustrates all his happy skill in relieving the couplet with triplet and alexandrine, his mastery of 'the varying verse, the full resounding line', every word chosen for its 'sound and significance':

> Dim, as the borrow'd beams of Moon and Stars
> To lonely, weary, wandring travellers
> Is Reason to the Soul: And as on high
> Those rowling fires discover but the sky
> Not light us here; So Reason's glimmering ray
> Was lent, not to assure our doubtfull way,
> But guide us upward to a better day.
> And as those nightly tapers disappear
> When day's bright lord ascends our hemisphere;
> So pale grows Reason at Religion's sight;
> So dyes, and so dissolves in supernatural light.

The much longer, and more argumentative *The Hind and the Panther* (1687), in which Dryden explains his conversion to Romanism, is the most self-revelatory of his poems. In it he can exclaim:

> O sharp convulsive pangs of agonizing pride!

The fable varies in intensity, being at times grandly rhetorical, at others colloquial, and it is shot with satire. Here too, as everywhere, Dryden reveals himself as master of the telling line, as in:

> Revenge, the bloudy minister of ill,
> With all the lean tormenters of the will.

This quality was already apparent in earlier work.

He displayed his varied mastery in all the other modes occasion offered; the songs in the plays, rollicking or sad; the complimentary epistles, as to Dr Charleton, Congreve, or the bucolic one to his cousin, John Driden; the elegies and epitaphs, of which the ones on Oldham and Purcell, very different from each other in form, are the best known. Though he excelled in the heroic couplet, he could use the dactyl as in the rattling:

> After the pangs of a desperate lover,
> *An Evening's Love*, 1671

or the anapaest in the haunting melody of the first Jacobite lament:

> A Quire of bright beauties in spring did appear,
> *The Lady's Song*, printed 1704

He could set a pattern of monosyllabic colloquial ease:

89

I think or hope, at least, the coast is clear,
That none but men of wit and sense are
here: . . .
Prologue to *Cleomenes*, 1692

or such highly coloured passages as:

Th' avenger took from earth th' avenging
sword,
And mounting light as air, his sable
steed he spurr'd:
The clouds dispell'd, the sky resum'd her
light,
And nature stood recover'd of her fright.
Theodore and Honoria, 1700

He never faltered in his progress: he was,
as Congreve remarked, 'an improving
poet to the last'. This is manifest in the
splendid 'Pindaric' Odes, which earned
him the sobriquet 'glorious John', including as they do the one on Anne Killigrew (1686), the *St Cecilia Ode* of 1687,
which with solemnity modulated by
harmonies imitative of musical instruments, might be considered a practice
piece for the great *Alexander's Feast* of
1697. Here he uses his strength as a giant
tossing about his weapons, sometimes
perilously near burlesque (the piece has
been called 'immortal ragtime') ending
with the Grand Chorus:

At last divine Cecilia came,
Inventress of the vocal frame;
The sweet enthusiast, from her sacred
store,
Enlarg'd the former narrow bounds,
And added length to solemn sounds,
With nature's mother-wit, and arts
unknown before.
Let old Timotheus yield the prize,
Or both divide the crown;
He rais'd a mortal to the skies;
She drew an angel down.

A conclusion to be contrasted with the
sad yet hopeful disillusion expressed in

the *Secular Masque* he wrote a few days
before his death to adorn Vanbrugh's *The
Pilgrim*:

'Tis well an Old Age is out,
And time to begin a New.

Not only did he set the standard for
the next century, and beyond, by his
discipline in the couplet; but without his
Odes there would not have been those
of **Gray** or of **Wordsworth**. His strength
rises to the heights of imagination, and
today only a dullard would deny him
the name of a great poet.   B.D.
see also Criticism and Poetry, Satire *and*
Translation

Dunbar, William (*c.* 1460–?1521), was a
Scottish poet, born half a century after
the death of **Chaucer**. The essence of his
poetry (as of the poetry of **Henryson**,
Gavin **Douglas** and other so-called
'Scottish Chaucerians') is that its debt to
Chaucer nowhere overrides its own vigour
and originality. Dunbar goes beyond
Chaucer in variety of metre and verse-
forms, and though he considered Chaucer
'anamalit' and 'aureate', his own 'aureate
diction' is much more highly wrought and
full of neologisms than anything in the
English poet. *The Goldyn Targe* and *The
Thrissill and the Rois* are ceremonial
poems of this kind. The former is an
allegory in which the poet's shield of
Reason is no defence against Beauty's
arrows. The latter celebrates the marriage
of James IV to Margaret Tudor (they are
the 'thistle' and the 'rose'), and makes
full use of such conventions as the May
morning dream and the animation of
heraldry. A poem like *Ane Ballat of Our
Lady* has an extreme verbal formality
which derives from the French *rhétori-
queurs*:

Hodiern, modern, sempitern,
   Angelicall regyne!
Our tern inferne for to dispern
   Helpe, rialest rosyne.

His other religious poems (not solitary or devotional as in later tradition, but public and liturgical) are perhaps more successful, especially those on the Nativity and on the Resurrection ('Done is a battell on the dragon blak').

Dunbar is valued chiefly as a comic and satirical poet, who, when it suits the occasion, can make use of the full range of the vernacular. Where these elements also emerge in the religious poems the resulting strain of the grotesque also underlines the medieval aspect of his work (see *The Dance of the Sevin Deidly Synnis*). His satire found full expression in the court of James IV, a king who, though learned, preferred to encourage flying Abbots rather than poets (see the *Fenyeit Freir of Tungland* and *Birth of Antichrist*). The famous *The Tretis of the Twa Mariit Weman and the Wedo* begins in skilful and conventional natural description and confounds the reader with the ensuing realistic and phallic detail of the women's conversation about the trials of marriage (the poem is incidentally one of the last examples of the use of the old alliterative form). It is in the tradition of the *chanson à mal mariée*, but through twisting of forms almost approaches an Augustan vision of the sexual reality that lurks in the polite society of ladies 'as thai talk at the tabill of many taill sindry'.

His personal poems, ranging from the petitionary complaint to the feast of basically good-humoured invective to be found in the *Flyting of Dunbar and Kennedie*, are the main sources of our knowledge of the poet's life. Apart from his B.A. and M.A. at St Andrew's in 1477 and 1479, his visit to France in 1491, and (probably on an embassy) to London in 1501, little is definitely known about him. He seems to have been of good birth, perhaps at one time a novice in holy orders, and as a poet dependent upon court patronage. His work is varied, accomplished and concise (*The Twa Mariit Weman* is, at 530 lines, his longest piece). In his often saturnine humour, his love of the town (in spite of his satire upon Edinburgh), his clerical satire, his sense of the transitory nature of life (see *Lament for the Makaris* with the celebrated and eloquent refrain 'Timor mortis conturbat me') and even in such comparatively minor things as his hatred of 'dark and drublie' winter, there is much that is essentially medieval about Dunbar. He cannot of course approach Chaucer in stature, but, as C. S. Lewis has remarked, he has 'a resonant singing voice . . . and a goblin energy which Chaucer has not'.   J.F.

Durrell, Lawrence (1912–), was born in India and was educated at St Edmund's School, Canterbury; he has held Foreign Office posts in the Middle East. To his travel-books and his novels he brings more than a little of the poetic qualities he reveals in his volumes of poetry. With vivid imagery drawn mainly from the Aegean, and a pervading historical sense, he leaves in the mind images of a curious, fleeting beauty, though his later poetry tends to probe deeper into the emotions and the ground for living, his verse, among other matters

Telling of the concerns of time,
The knife of feeling in the art of love.

His verse publications consist of *A Private Country* (1943), *Cities, Plains and People* (1946), *On Seeming to Presume* (1948), *The Tree of Idleness* (1955), his verse play *Sappho* (1950), and *Collected Poems* (1960).   B.D.

Dyer, Sir Edward (1534–1607), was an English poet, musician and diplomat, best known for his ruminative lyric, 'My Mind to me a Kingdom is'. He was a friend of **Sidney**, whose pastoral, 'Join, mates, in mirth with me', is addressed to him as well as to Sir Fulke **Greville**. He held official positions in court. Contemporary accounts mention him as the author of poems which have never been discovered.   D.H.

Dyer, John (1699–1758), is best known as the author of *Grongar Hill*, an attractive scenic poem published in 1726. Later he wrote two didactic poems—*The Fleece* (1757) which concerns sheep and the wool trade, and *The Ruins of Rome*—which are less pleasant.   D.H.

E

Eberhart, Richard (1904–   ), was born in Minnesota, and educated at Dartmouth, Cambridge, and Harvard Graduate School. He has been tutor to a Siamese prince, taught at American schools and colleges, and instructed naval gunnery in the Second World War, since when he has been with the Butcher Polish Company, poet in residence in universities, founder of the Poet's Theater, and, after working for the Library of Congress and the National Culture Center, elected to the National Institute of Arts and Letters. In his poetry the conservative moralist is concerned with original sin, mortality and a stern God. The war had the inevitability of Cain. He identifies with nature in a nineteenth-century manner, receiving hope from childhood wholeness or a mystic vision. His nostalgic language leaned to English tradition until a more direct local speech emerged in *Burr Oaks* (1947) and the echoes of **Blake** and **Tennyson's** *In Memoriam* diminish. *Undercliff* (1953)— his ninth book (including *Selected Poems*, 1951)—is the peak of his development. The language is not particularly local

and here he has found it difficult to shed a literary-philosophical jargon. Although his verse has never been slickly fashionable his doggedly traditional themes tend to monotony. But the anecdotal scene can provoke freshness—as in *Seals, Terns, Time* (1953):

> The seals at play off Western Isle
> In the loose flowing of the summer tide
> And burden of our strange estate—
>
> Resting on the oar and lolling on the sea,
> I saw their curious images,
> Hypnotic, sympathetic eyes
>
> As deep elapses of the soul.
> O ancient blood, O blurred kind forms
> That rise and peer from elemental
> water, . . .

His verse is compelled by tension which produced his characteristic roughness, but the basis is a humourless old-fashioned dualism of thought and flesh. His poetry is drawn towards the intellectual and abstract; to overcome this tendency he induces in himself a visionary blaze that will consume everything but its own momentary revelation. His later books include *Selected Poems 1939-65* (1966), for which he was awarded a Pulitzer Prize, *Thirty-One Sonnets* (1967) and *Shifts of Beings* (1968).   E.N.W.M.

Eliot, T[homas] S[tearns] (1888–1965), like Ezra **Pound**, with whom he shares credit for establishing the direction of one of English literature's richest periods, appears to have at first contemplated an academic career. His early poems, including *Portrait of a Lady* and the first two *Preludes*, were epiphenomena of a graduate student's work at Harvard University (1909–10). *The Love Song of J. Alfred Prufrock* and *Rhapsody on a Windy Night* were written during a student year in Paris and Munich. For three more years (1911–14) he pursued further graduate study at Harvard in metaphysics, logic, psychology, philosophy, Sanskrit and Pali. When he went abroad in the summer of 1914 it was not to expatriate himself but to learn from the German academicians who in those days kept the academic conscience of the West. He had been only a few weeks at Marburg when war drove him to England, where his historic meeting with Pound was a picturesque incident in a year devoted to reading the Posterior Analytics at Merton College, Oxford. As late as 1916 he was concerned with sending back to Harvard his doctoral thesis on Francis Herbert Bradley; in the same year he made his London début, not as poet or literary critic, but as a reviewer of philosophic books. When (in 1915) his marriage to Vivien Haigh-Wood terminated his university career, he turned to schoolmastering.

His sense of literary tradition was shaped by the classroom, where curricula arrange monuments' into 'an ideal order', that ideal order which, he wrote in *Tradition and the Individual Talent* (1919), 'is modi-fied by the introduction of the new (the really new) work of art among them'. His sense of the poet's scope of operation was shaped by the philosopher, Bradley, whose 'immediate experience' erases any meaningful separation between the phenomena judged and the mind that judges, between the expression and the experience expressed, between the past as it was and the past as I imagine it. The past is altered by the present because the present alters the mind which, conceiving the past, gives it its only accessible existence. And the past which thus takes possession of the poet confers upon him great responsibilities, since 'not only the best, but the most individual parts of his work may be those in which the dead poets, his ancestors, assert their immortality most vigorously'.

These meditations were perfected during a time when, in alliance with Pound, Eliot was appearing in *avant-garde* magazines, undergoing Establishment abuse, and tirelessly experimenting with the subversion of traditional forms. Yet his immediate derivation, as his juvenilia show, was from **Tennyson** and **Swinburne**, who conferred meditative dignity and neurotic energy respectively on a medium which exploited far more the sounds and associations of words than their denotations. His first step was to effect a learned fusion between their procedures and those of **Webster** and Laforgue:

But though I have wept and fasted, wept
          and prayed,
Though I have seen my head (grown
     slightly bald) brought in upon a platter,
I am no prophet—and here's no great
                    matter;
I have seen the moment of my greatness
                    flicker,
And I have seen the eternal Footman hold
          my coat, and snicker,
And in short, I was afraid.

His second was to suppress, so far as possible, the personal fulcrum on which Laforguian ironies turn. In place of the dandy whom the mockingly erudite diction would imply, we are to intuit a tragically disengaged *persona* whose mind is become the echo-chamber of the West. The *tour de force* of this method is *Gerontion* (1919):

> After such knowledge, what forgiveness?
> Think now
> History has many cunning passages,
> contrived corridors
> And issues, deceives with whispering
> ambitions,
> Guides us by vanities. . . .

His third was to elevate into a principle of cinematic deliberateness the discontinuity which his verse originally owed to the concatenation of short, highly finished passages often composed at different times. In *The Waste Land* (1922) these three methods came to simultaneous apotheosis, to produce the most influential single poem of the early twentieth century.

By the time *The Waste Land* appeared, Eliot was securely if somewhat anonymously installed as an English man of letters: author of a volume of *Poems* and a book of essays, *The Sacred Wood* (both 1920), editor of *The Criterion* (1922–39), reviewer for *The Times Literary Supplement*, London correspondent for *The Dial* (1921–2) and the *Nouvelle Revue Française* (1922–3). In 1925 he left his post at Lloyds Bank and joined Faber & Gwyer, later Faber & Faber, the publishers, of which firm he remained an active director till his death.

So neither *The Waste Land* nor *The Hollow Men* (1925) could be said to have emanated from the cellars of Bohemia. Their complex involvement with the Bloomsbury milieu and with the world of official letters exacted, however, a spiritual toll which work at editing and publishing compounded. Not until 1930 (*Ash-Wednesday*) nor again till 1935 (*Burnt Norton*) did Eliot again write major poems. By then he had become a spokesman for the Established Church (in which he was confirmed in 1927, the year he became a British subject), written a powerful religious drama, *Murder in the Cathedral* (1935), and consolidated his *oeuvre* with *Selected Essays* (1932) and *Poems, 1909–1935*. During the war years, three more poems joined *Burnt Norton* to constitute his principal achievement, *Four Quartets*. Thereafter his energies were applied to verse plays. In 1957, ten years after the death of his first wife, he married Valerie Fletcher. His services to literature were commemorated by the Nobel Prize (1948) and the Order of Merit (1948).

In the growth and consolidation of his influence since the time of *The Waste Land* and *The Sacred Wood*, Eliot's critical and creative work have lent one another authority. His principal essays have placed in circulation a view of poetry not so much counter-Romantic as counter-Georgian, emphasising the critical intelligence as a creative faculty, the primacy of the poem over the poet, and the impersonal authority, incorporating and refreshing the authority of tradition, which the achieved work seeks to manifest. His verse, correspondingly, brings to the turned phrase and the weighty line of the Jacobeans a wit which, like **Marvell's**, and Laforgue's, testifies to a poised and active intelligence cool amid the ambient magniloquence:

> He, the young man carbuncular, arrives . . .

Here 'carbuncular' has both Miltonic resonance and Laforguian wit.

Here, said she,
Is your card, the drowned Phoenician
                                    Sailor,
(Those are pearls that were his eyes.
                                    Look!)

Here the quotation from *The Tempest*, like Eliot's other echoes and allusions, not only contributes to a macaronic texture in which a time of encyclopedic malaise finds expression, but also recovers for the first time since **Pope** a way of deliberately invoking the gone voices with which our voices seek to harmonise.

. . . Which is not to be found in our
                                    obituaries
Or in memories draped by the beneficent
                                    spider
Or under seals broken by the lean
                                    solicitor
In our empty rooms

Here, though the word 'lean' twangs home like an arrow, it invites us not to admire the author's cleverness but to peer past the proffered image at the shadows of ancient terrors, which are somehow released from the very language.
   Always the brilliance is subdued, sinewy, certain:

Here are the years that walk between,
                                    bearing
Away the fiddles and the flutes, restoring
One who moves in the time between
                            sleep and waking, wearing
White light folded, sheathed about her,
                                    folded.
The new years walk, restoring
Through a bright cloud of tears, the
                            years, restoring
With a new verse the ancient rhyme. . . .

Throughout, the colouration of a decided temperament which sets its signature on every line co-exists with the odd withdrawal of any affirmative personality. This quality, Hugh Kenner notes, 'has allowed his work to be discussed as though it were the legacy of a deceased poet', and like such a legacy it 'invades the reader's mind and there undergoes an assimilation which soon persuades us that we have always possessed it'. 'I do not know for certain', writes William **Empson**, 'how much of my own mind he invented, let alone how much of it is a reaction against him or a consequence of misreading him'.
   The poems have won their authority in another way, by the reduplicated persistence of their themes. They have many situations but a recurring plot, first stated when Prufrock imagines himself bursting into a drawing-room like Lazarus, 'Come back to tell you all, I shall tell you all'. This plot makes use of a man who has crossed the frontier and come back: Sweeney the uninvited guest at a ragtime soirée; the Magi back in a kingdom where they are no longer at home, their own lives having in turn been permanently invaded by what they saw; Becket undergoing accepted doom to the horror of the women of Canterbury; the man in *Burnt Norton* who has been granted the vision in the garden and is left to meditate its possibilities amid 'the strained, time-ridden faces'. In the later plays it is the dead who return, or their ghosts: in *The Family Reunion* guilt for the dead wife walks, in *The Cocktail Party* the wife herself is restored, Alcestis-like; in *The Elder Statesman* the protagonist must confront 'spectres from my past', in *The Confidential Clerk* a woman who knows the secret of his birth. The plays advance on the poems in one major respect: in the poems such apparitions trouble surfaces, in the plays they are instruments of liberation. The very explicitness of Eliot's spare dramatic verse

seems consecrated to defining the essential and blessed privacy of whatever it leaves unstated; for privacy is the condition of freedom.

These are not only appropriate themes for a poet who guarded his privacy all his life, they also determine his centrality for an age much preoccupied with its own relation to the past. 'History may be servitude', he wrote in *Four Quartets*, 'history may be freedom'. From the time of his first meditations on tradition, Eliot was much concerned with the fact that while history may be, as Gerontion finds it, a nightmare, civilisation is memory. To transfigure history's 'cunning passages, contrived corridors and issues' and 'the rending pain of re-enactment / Of all that you have done and been' into 'both a new world / And the old made explicit, understood', was the programme of his fifty years' endeavour in prose and verse.

> See, now they vanish,
> The faces and places, with the self which,
>   as it could, loved them,
> To become renewed, transfigured, in
>   another pattern.

Hence his utility in a time which presses us on all sides to obviate strain by disowning the past, and to exchange new worlds for old by disowning ourselves. The theme owes its nervous, persistent force, perhaps, to its alliance with his own displacement, which he strove all his life to prevent from being a facile expatriation. For he was born in St Louis, Missouri, in Mark Twain's lifetime, by Mark Twain's river, the youngest of seven children who bore a distinguished New England name; and he spent all his working life in London, always himself yet always camouflaged, cultivating with ardour, rigour and dry passion a method which made him the

most traditional, in the twentieth century, of those English poets whose speech was nourished by that of the fens, of the downs, of cathedral towns, and of the much-storied City.   H.K.
see also American Poetry, Criticism and Poetry, Foreign Influences on English Poetry *and* Imagery

Emerson, Ralph Waldo (1803–82), is a typical representative of the Brahmin caste of New England. He became a minister in 1829 but broke with the church in 1832 to become a lecturer and essayist. He lived in Concord, New Hampshire, at the centre of the group known as Transcendentalists.

Though better known for his essays, he felt himself to be essentially a poet, and his poems contain more compact expressions of all his ideas. E. A. **Robinson** is reputed to have called Emerson the greatest American poet. Indirectly he prepared the way for **Whitman**, but his poems have an uneven quality.

This is largely the result of the theory of a transcendental poet as a mere amanuensis catching the 'fugitive sparkles' obtained in seeking an 'original relation to the universe'; S. T. Williams has defined this poet's task as setting down in finite words the tale of his collision with the infinite.

Emerson's principal models were seventeenth-century English poetry and the Persians, Saadi and Hafiz, and his poetry—intellectual, metaphysical and frequently gnomic—reveals a symbolic view of the universe in which unity exists because of the presence of an Over-Soul. Emerson is generally thought to be limited by his virtues—the good Yankee virtues of self-reliance and optimism—in solving the dilemmas he explores.

His poems, like *Each and All*, usually convey a sense of 'ecstasy':

Beauty through my senses stole;
I yielded myself to the perfect whole.

It must, however, be admitted that 'ecstasy' frequently falls into obscurity or arid argument. A.H.

see also American Poetry

Empson, William (1906–), is the oddest English poet who wrote between the two World Wars. Probably his first book of criticism, *Seven Types of Ambiguity*, made more impact to start with than *Poems* (the first of his two books of verse, published 1935), but by the nineteen-fifties, when he was no longer writing verse, he suddenly appeared as the main influence on many of the younger poets. No one, however, can be compared with him when it comes to writing what he himself calls his 'clotted kind of poetry'. He practised in the most concentrated form those ambiguities which he had discovered in or read into the old masters. His early poems are compact of double or multiple meanings, glancing allusions, teasing syntax, puns and twists of all kinds (like some other professors he is a crossword puzzle addict) but, like the Metaphysical poets of the seventeenth century, his conceits are balanced or carried by a strong and simple, sometimes colloquial, diction and also by the regularity of his verse-forms and the hypnotic pounding of his rhymes. He is an extremely cerebral poet (he admits that he has very little visual sense though his comparison of paddy fields to bees' wings would seem to contradict this) and more than any of his contemporaries he has drawn upon the sciences not only for imagery but for structural ideas. His 'metaphysical' form of wit frequently is occasioned by trivialities, such as a camping girl cleaning her teeth into a lake, yet surprisingly he

is generally a humane and quite often a moving poet.

Empson's poems number less than sixty, in striking contrast with his prolific contemporary **Auden**, from whom, though they are both intellectual jack-daws, he also differs in his disinclination to missionise. The later Empson, seasoned in the Far East, is both more personal and less muscle-bound than the brilliant young man at Cambridge. There has been an increased use of refrain and he has taken the villanelle in particular out of the museum and, unlike some of his imitators, made this archaic form work. Throughout his career he has shown an extraordinary flair for the suggestive and memorable single line, sometimes aphoristic—'Those stay most haunting that most soon deceive', sometimes cryptic—'Crash is a cloth but poisons are all greens', sometimes para-doxical—'The heart of standing is you cannot fly', sometimes deceptively simple —'It seemed the best thing to be up and go'. Empsom is notorious for the lengthy notes he has written to many of his poems but, as he explains, 'it is impertinent to suggest that the reader ought to possess already any odd bit of information one may have picked up in a field where one is oneself ignorant'. His poetry is the gnarled product of a mind that delights in the more curious aspects of the universe. And of his generation he is probably unique in that he has not a trace of self-pity. L.M.

English Poetry in Africa. The earliest poetry in English written on the African continent is found in the South (*see* the entry on **South African Poetry in English**). In West Africa the expansion of education in English produced a first generation of poets in the nineteen-thirties and nineteen-forties, the best known of whom are Michael Dei-Anang and

Raphael Armattoe of Ghana and Dennis Osadebay of Nigeria (*Africa Sings*, 1944). Examples of their work can be found in Langston Hughes' anthology *Poems from Black Africa* and in Dr Olumbe Bassir's *Anthology of West African Verse*. In general their work suffers from a certain stiffness of diction and a pervading earnestness of tone which speak of strong influence from the hymn and from nineteenth-century prosody. Another early poet, Adebayo Babalola of Nigeria, makes more use of vernacular (Yoruba) imagery and cumulative line-by-line effect in his poetry, though this too suffers from the failure to find an English diction matching the vigour of the originals ('She fell against a plate; the plate broke not'). Writers of this generation are often known as 'The Pioneer' or 'Pilot' poets, after the two newspapers, *The Ashanti Pioneer* and *The West African Pilot*, in which their work often appeared. The most successful of them was Gladys Casely Hayford (d. 1950) who wrote, not in standard English, but in the English-derived Krio language of her native Freetown. Owing to the prejudice then existing against the use of Krio as a literary language, few of her poems were published during her lifetime.

With the nineteen-fifties comes the emergence of a new generation of poets, many of them educated in the universities of West Africa. University magazines, such as *The Horn* of Ibadan University, founded and edited by J. P. Clark, played a great part in encouraging their development. Still more important was the literary journal *Black Orpheus*, founded by Ulli Beier in Nigeria in 1957. The B.B.C. African Service also played a part in encouraging these poets to write. The best-known poets of this time are Gabriel Okara, J. P. Clark, Wole Soyinka and the late Christopher Okigbo in Nigeria,

whilst in Ghana there appeared the work of Kwesi Brew, George Awoonor-Williams and G. Adali-Mortty. Lenrie Peters of the Gambia may also be considered in this group. In general these poets avoid those broad statements of attitude about 'Africa', 'the black man' and 'the white man' which had characterised their predecessors. Their writing is concerned with the acute rendering of personal experience in particular places and times (e.g. Clark's *Night Rain*, Soyinka's *Death in the Dawn* or Okara's *Victoria Beach*). Their tone is also less pietistic than that of their predecessors and their technique far more sophisticated and flexible. Such external influences as their early work reveals are more modern ones and are such as might be associated with literary education, ranging from Hopkins, Yeats and Eliot to Dylan Thomas and Lorca. But all the poets mentioned have succeeded in developing voices of their own very different from each other, as well as bringing new experiences and sensibilities into English writing.

The nineteen-sixties have seen the emergence of new poets in Eastern and Central Africa, together with a real explosion of poetic talent in Nigeria. The most important work to date from East Africa is Okot p'Bitek's *Song of Lawino* (1966), which shares with the work of Awoonor-Williams an ability to draw strength and meaning directly from the vernacular poetic tradition of their respective Iwo and Ewe languages. Meanwhile the established poets have added to their reputations with volumes such as Clark's *A Reed in the Tide* (1965), Peters's *Satellites* (1967), Soyinka's *Idanre* (1967) and Brew's *The Shadows of Laughter* (1968). Interesting new talents in Nigeria and Biafra are Aig Higo, Pol N. Ndu, Okogbule Wanode and Michael Echeruo (*Mortality*, 1968). The last three have been somewhat affected by the powerful influence of Okigbo. This internalising of literary influences is itself an indication of how rapidly poetic maturity in English has come to areas of Africa where the language was known to few people a generation ago.   G.M.

'Everyman' and the Miracle Plays. Medieval drama started in the churches (*c.* 900) when parishioners began to act out stories from the Easter and Christmas services. These representations soon brought such multitudes that the services had to be moved to the church steps. Popular support of these religious 'plays' transferred them to the inn yards, and the craft guilds, having religious ties, competed in presenting them on feast days. These Mystery (Latin *ministerium*) or Miracle plays became pageants on Corpus Christi Day (1318–1580) being performed in groups or 'cycles' as in York, Chester and Wakefield where all the crafts presented plays from the Bible. The biblical stories are presented with much earthy, raw humour. Christ's Roman Crucifiers discuss their work most realistically. Such literary aspects are seen best in the Wakefield master's *The Second Shepherd's Play*. Mak, the sheep stealer, is caught and tossed in a blanket:

> For this trespas,
> We will nawther ban ne flyte

Bot have done as tyte
And cast him in canvas

An angel's voice ends the secular theme.

The Moralities appeared in the fifteenth century using actors for abstract qualities, Death, Greed, Envy, etc., the purpose being to teach and edify. The first play of many was *The Pride of Life* coming *c.* 1400, but unquestionably the best was *Everyman* (*c.* 1500) originating from an earlier Dutch source. Everyman, a rioter summoned by Death for his last journey, asks his friends, Worldly Goods, Fellowship, etc., to accompany him. All refuse; only Good Deeds goes with him to the grave:

> All earthly things is but vanity:
> Beauty, Strength, and Discretion do
> man forsake
> Foolish friends, and kinsmen that fair
> spake
> All fleeth save Good Deeds, and that
> am I.

Its tight unity and high dramatic quality have kept *Everyman* theatrically alive for centuries. The Moralities were not acted by guilds, nor in cycles, and do not fall within the continuity of English drama, yet they produced in *Everyman* a high spot, still eminently actable, of the medieval stage.   T.J.G.

F

Fairfax, Edward (? –1635), was one of the foremost translators of Elizabethan England. His version of Tasso's *Gerusalemme Liberata*, which he retitled *Godfrey of Bulloigne, Or the Recovery of Jerusalem*, turned it into an ornate Elizabethan poem, satisfying in itself but unlike Tasso. Ben **Jonson** censured him for it.   D.H.

Fearing, Kenneth (1902–61), was a poet of the American nineteen-thirties. His Marxist sympathies were expressed in a long colloquial line which often parodies advertising. Sarcasm was his most obvious quality, but he sometimes showed a strong compassion for the victims of a predatory society.   D.H.

Finch, Anne. *See* Winchilsea, Countess of.

FitzGerald, Edward (1809–83), the poet-translator of the *Rubáiyát of Omar Khayyám*, was born Edward Purcell in Bredfield, Suffolk, his name later being changed to that of his mother's family. Soon after graduation from Trinity College, Cambridge, FitzGerald retired to Suffolk, there to spend most of his life in leisured privacy. His marriage in 1856 to Lucy, daughter of Quaker poet Bernard Barton, soon ended in separation. He died at Merton, Norfolk. Though a friend of **Tennyson,** Thackeray and Carlyle, FitzGerald himself shunned fame. All his books, except *Six Dramas of Calderón* (1853) were published anonymously.

FitzGerald informed his *Rubáiyát* with a unity not found in Persian manuscripts. In his final selection and arrangement of 101 quatrains from the thousand or more attributed to Omar, he stressed the poet-astronomer's themes of fatalism and sen-

suous delight. The result emerged, as he wrote, 'ingeniously tessellated into a sort of Epicurean Eclogue in a Persian Garden'. Its vision of a mechanistic universe seemed to echo Victorian pessimism, in a previously unfamiliar stanza-form:

> And that inverted Bowl they call the
> Sky,
> Whereunder crawling coop'd we live
> and die,
> Lift not your hands to *It* for help—
> for It
> As impotently moves as you or I.

The *Rubáiyát* achieved its immense fame slowly: though almost ignored, the first edition (1859) attracted **Swinburne** and **Rossetti.** The fourth version (1879) is today best known.

In 1855 while rendering into Miltonic verse the *Salámán and Absál* of Jámí, FitzGerald had generously interpreted his prerogatives: 'It is an amusement to me to take what liberties I like with these Persians . . . who really do want a little art to shape them'. A similar freedom marked his Byronic versions of Calderón, and his *Agamemnon* (1865) and Oedipus plays (1880–1), into which he inserted new speeches. His methods, however, have defenders. Lafcadio Hearn called FitzGerald 'probably the best translator who ever lived', who translated 'only the spirit, the ghost of things'.

The charge of Gamaliel Bradford that FitzGerald lacked will-power to sustain a major work of creation (*Bare Souls*, 1924), overlooks the extent of FitzGerald's contribution to his materials. A recent biographer, A. M. Terhune, has indicated both FitzGerald's devotion to his craft and the complexity of his personality.

X.J.K.

see also Foreign Influences on English Poetry

Flecker, [Herman] James Elroy (1884–1915), was an English poet and dramatist who was particularly interested in Greece and the Orient. His *Collected Poems* (1918) show his successful concern with form and colour, but he is probably best known for his posthumous play, *Hassan* (1922). D.H.

Fletcher, Giles (?1588–1623), is known as 'the younger', as his father, of the same name (?1549–1611), was also a poet. The younger brother of Phineas **Fletcher**, he was educated at Trinity College, Cambridge, and became rector of Alberton, Suffolk. His *Christ's Victory and Triumph in Heaven and on Earth* celebrates the Incarnation, Temptation, Passion and Resurrection of Our Lord and is written in an abbreviated variant of the Spenserian stanza. It is highly baroque in style, and influenced the work of **Milton** and **Crashaw.** J.H.S.

Fletcher, John. *See* Beaumont and Fletcher.

Fletcher, Phineas (1582–1650), was the elder brother of Giles **Fletcher**. Educated at Eton and King's College, Cambridge, he became rector of Hilgay, Norfolk. His poetic style, like his brother's, is a rather baroque version of the Spenserian manner. His poems include *Piscatory Eclogues* and *The Purple Island*. The latter, written on a plan somewhat similar to Bunyan's *Holy War*, curiously combines moral allegory with human anatomy. J.H.S.

Ford, John (1586–1640), was a Devon-born Jacobean playwright of melancholy and often sensational drama. He collaborated with Dekker and Massinger. His most popular plays are *'Tis Pitty Shees a Whore* (1633) and *The Broken Heart* (1633). D.H.

Foreign Influences on English Poetry. Influences are a two-way traffic. Every poet learns his craft from his predecessors, and in turn provides inspiration for some of those who come after him. Literatures too teach and learn from one another. One may, like Italian in the Renaissance, leap two centuries ahead of its neighbours. But after leading the fashion for so long, Italian was outstripped in the sixteenth century, fell into mannerism in the seventeenth, and in the nineteenth took new life as a result of influence from France, Britain and Germany. Meanwhile French poetry, which had established itself before Italian, fell into exhaustion in the fifteenth century, when the writing of *ballades* and *villanelles* became a mechanical craft and, after accepting the delayed impact of the Italian Renaissance, led the literary fashions of Europe once more until the eighteenth century, when it again fell into exhaustion, from which it was rescued by the external shock of foreign Romanticism. Such generalisations are dangerous. Yet there are rhythms in national achievement and in the predominance of nations, which are easy to perceive but hard to understand. It is, however, safe to say that almost all poets, in almost all ages, have been familiar with the poetry of other languages, and have imitated it. Frontiers have never been impassable in the poets' commonwealth. New subjects and treatments have constantly been adapted from models in other languages; and in this poetic exchange English poets have always taken a leading part, receiving and giving in equal measure.

Latin has been a permanent influence on all the literatures of Western Europe, at least until the end of the nineteenth century, when its lessons were, perhaps, exhausted. Between the Renaissance and the birth of scientific education it is unnecessary to ask whether a particular poet has been affected by the examples of Catullus, Horace, Virgil and Juvenal. He knew them before he knew the poets of his own language. A more apposite question is: by what qualities in these masters was he most affected? The answer can be discovered by observing which of their poems he chose to adapt or imitate. Horace stimulated the Elizabethans to the writing of lyrical verse. **Campion**'s 'The man of life upright' and **Herrick**'s 'Gather ye Rose-buds while ye may' probably derive their original inspiration from him. Yet Horace for the eighteenth century was a satirist and a teacher of moral lessons, while by the present age, though less familiar, he is most admired as a master of poetic compression. Virgil too has undergone great variations of esteem. The Elizabethans saw him as a pastoral poet and a story-teller; **Dryden**'s *Aeneid* is a great neo-Classic poem, ample and heroic in proportions, whereas Jackson Knight's prose version of our own day reveals concentrated style and a wealth of double-meanings that escaped the notice of the Elizabethans and the Augustans alike.

While Latin poetry was a constant influence on the poetic growth of Britain and other European countries, Greek epic and drama were far harder to understand and assimilate. Although many poets since the Renaissance have imitated and equalled the best of the *Greek Anthology*, there has been no modern equivalent to Pindar's odes, nor any sign that his example has deeply affected any writer except the nineteenth-century German, Friedrich Hölderlin. 'Homeric' has been a term of praise sometimes lavished on the 'artificial' epics of the sixteenth and seventeenth centuries. But generally they owe much more to Virgil than to Homer, whose world is too far distant from our own to give us lessons in anything except the *grand style* advocated by Matthew **Arnold**. In the same way the essence of the Greek

drama escapes us, since we cannot take it as half poetry and half ritual, as it was for its original audience. Many poets—**Keats**, **Browning** and Arnold for instance—have tried to dispense with the literary spectacles through which men have always looked on their Greek ancestors. Their success has been, at best, partial.

Late Middle Ages
Until the Elizabethan age, English was a provincial literature which took lessons from across the Channel but had little to offer in exchange. In the Middle Ages, Latin was the language of learned poetry throughout Europe, and of all poetry in those countries that had not yet evolved syntax, vocabulary and literary techniques sufficient to permit the expression of subtle thought with brevity and variety. French was at that time the vehicle of narrative poetry, song, fable and comic story, and Italian of reflective and philosophical poetry, also of some more formal narratives. French and Italian were the principal heirs of the Troubadours, who had, perhaps under Arab influence, revived the writing of the vernacular lyric in the twelfth century. This had stimulated writing, not only in Italy and Northern France, but also in Germany and the North-West corner of Spain. But German and Galician-Portuguese poetry did not persist. Medieval English poetry grew up under the influence of Latin, French and Italian.

It was our singular good fortune that, although outside the area touched by the Troubadour revival, English did not have to wait as long as German, Polish or Russian to evolve its own poetry. Like Spanish, it was quickly drawn into the Western European orbit. Until the end of the twelfth century there is little evidence of poetry written in English. Some references to scandalous songs and dances to be heard and seen in churchyards suggest the existence of popular songs that have not survived. The court of that ill-matched pair, Henry II and Eleanor of Aquitaine, was nevertheless a centre of poetry and scholarship. She was a patron of Troubadours and minstrels, and he of such outstanding scholars as the English-born John of Salisbury. Among the poets in the Angevin circle was Marie de France, a relative of the royal family, some of whose *Laïs*, or short narrative poems, though written in French, told stories of Arthur's knights, a subject almost certainly of British origin. About Thomas d'Angle-terre, author of the romance of *Tristan*, little is known beyond the fact that he was an Englishman of Norman origins.

The English poetic tradition was no doubt working underground during Angevin times, and not entirely under Anglo-Norman influence. For when, towards the beginning of the thirteenth century, poems began to appear in the vernacular, an alliterative style akin to that of the Anglo-Saxon poets was in full use. Layamon's *Brut*, an expanded translation of Wace's French work, which in its turn was based on Geoffrey of Monmouth's Latin history of the English kings, descends directly from the seventh-century epic of *Beowulf*, the Teutonic ancestry of which probably goes back to the lays of the Germanic tribesmen described by Tacitus. This must be accepted as the true English tradition, modified perhaps by Welsh and Irish techniques, which were also alliterative. Everything else, in consequence, must be ascribed to foreign influences. The history of foreign influence, therefore, is almost equivalent to a history of English poetry itself.

'The English medieval lyric', writes M. J. C. Hodgart in an essay contributed to the Penguin *Guide to English Literature, I*,

'is a poor relation of the splendid continental art-form, through which many of the finest writers of the Middle Ages said what they most deeply felt. . . . English lyrics written during the thirteenth and fourteenth centuries are for the most part but imitations of an established European tradition; only with the carol of the fifteenth century does a native tradition of any originality begin to appear'. The famous 'Sumer is icumen in' is a home-made *Reverdie*, a version of a stock Troubadour and Northern French poem which welcomes the return of spring, and was probably in origin a dance-song. The commonplaces of the Provençal tradition, however, take on a certain freshness when expressed in the somewhat hobble-de-hoy English of

When the nyhtegale singes the wedes
          waxen grene,
Lef and gras and blosme springes in
          averyl, y wene . . .
          MS. Harley 2253

and there are moments too in these apprentice lyrics when the broad humours of those first reprehensible churchyard songs blow all polite Frenchified manners to the winds.

A lively business of translation from the Latin as well as French went on in the thirteenth and fourteenth centuries. Almost literal renderings were made of familiar Latin hymns, chiefly by friars who wished to incorporate them in their popular preaching. More than one English version has survived of such favourites as *Veni creator spiritus*, *Ave maris stella* and *Vexilla regis prodeunt*. Most of these, however, adhere too closely to the Latin to have much virtue as English poems. One of the first English poets, indeed, to leave his name beneath his work, Friar William Herebert, a Franciscan of Hereford who died in 1333, only allowed himself reasonable licence when translating from the Anglo-Norman. Though the Franciscans played a considerable part in the development of the carol and its adaptation from secular to religious uses, the bulk of their religious poetry is dull and conventional. Very seldom does the monkish poet strike such a spark from a worn flint as Friar Thomas Hales from the medieval commonplace of the *Ubi sunt*, the stock lament for the great figures of the past:

> Hwer is Paris and Heleyne
> That weren so bryht and feyre on
> bleo?[1]
> Amadas and Ideyne,
> Tristram, Yseude and alle thee?
> Ecter with his sharpe meyne,[2]
> And Cesar, riche of worldes fee?[3]
> He beoth iglyden ut of the reyne,
> So the shef is of the cleo[4]

The poem challenges comparison with Villon or William **Dunbar**. Generally, however, the finest English poems are those which, like 'Adam lay ibounden', 'I sing of a mayden' and 'Maiden in the mor lay', lie closest to folk-song. Ballad and carol were Britain's highest achievement in lyrical poetry. Some themes from foreign folklore were treated in the ballads, but, on the whole, these owed little to influence from abroad. Until the coming of **Chaucer** English was at its best when freest from imported mannerisms.

Of the three great English poets of the fourteenth century, **Langland** and the anonymous author of *Sir Gawayne and the*

Grene Knight stand firmly in the old alliterative tradition. The third, Geoffrey Chaucer, adapted all that was best in the continental poetry of his day to thoroughly English uses. Langland took much material, including the allegorical convention, from the common stock of Christian poetry; the poet of *Sir Gawayne* retold a story which, though of British origin, belonged to the folklore of Western Europe. But both wrote poems which were, in essence, provincial and Teutonic. Chaucer was a European, best known in his own day as the translator of the first part of the *Roman de la Rose*. For his contemporaries, as Professor C. S. Lewis observes in *The Allegory of Love* (p. 162), he was 'the poet of dream and allegory, of love-romance and erotic debate, of high style and profitable doctrine'; a title in reality more suited to the author of the original *Roman*, Guillaume de Lorris. But for his successors, Chaucer was, again in Professor Lewis' words, 'the "firste finder" of the true way in our language, which before his time was "rude and boystous"'.

On the one hand Chaucer was the last heir of the Troubadour tradition. Though the plot of *Troilus and Criseyde* was based on Boccaccio's realistic and worldly story, it was, in Professor Lewis' words 'by Il Filostrato out of Roman de la Rose'; his contemporaries were not entirely wrong. It is a far more medieval poem than its Italian model. Chaucer copied Boccaccio more faithfully, however, in the narrative convention which he used for the *Canterbury Tales*. But he improved on it. For the group of riders who set out for Canterbury in the Prologue of his poem are far more sharply characterised than the group of shadowy gentlefolk who took it in turns to narrate the hundred tales of the *Decameron*. In this foreign framework, the origins of which go back to the *Arabian Nights*, Chaucer

---

[1] *bleo*—countenance
[2] *sharpe meyne*—powerful company
[3] *fee*—goods
[4] *He beoth iglyden ut of the reyne, So the shef is of the cleo*—They have all slipped out of the realm, As the corn-sheaf has vanished from the hillside.

assembled a collection of tales which, in their turn, owe their inspiration to a variety of continental sources. Here we have the *romance* (*The Knightes Tale*, which is based on the *Teseida* of Boccaccio) the *fabliau* or popular story (the *Milleres* and the *Reves Tales*); the animal (*The Nonnes Preestes Tale*), the popular sermon or moral story (*The Pardoneres Tale*) and several other current types, including a parody of the stock minstrel's narrative (*Sir Thopas*). Chaucer is the supreme example of a poet who turns all the poetic commonplaces of his day to new uses, in many cases so improving on his models as utterly to transcend them. The individual quality which enabled him to do this was that concreteness and realism which are generally to be found in a new literature, and which were lacking in most of Chaucer's immediate models. An equally fresh treatment of old themes, many of them the worn Latin stock-in-trade of the wandering scholars or Goliards, is to be seen in the Archpriest of Hita's *Libro de buen amor*, a work some fifty years earlier than the *Canterbury Tales*, which occupies a similar position in the history of Spanish poetry.

Chaucer's debt to his French and Italian models was as heavy on the technical side as in the matter of subject and treatment. The verse couplet of the *Canterbury Tales* is two syllables longer than the stock four-stress French couplet of the *Roman de la Rose*, which he had used in his translation and in some other pieces. The longer form is undoubtedly more suitable to the rhythms of English. Nevertheless it must be partially credited to foreign influence, as must also the seven-line Rhyme Royal, the metre of the early French *ballades*, which Chaucer used in *Troilus and Criseyde*, but which did not take as natural roots in English as the iambic pentameter couplet. Chaucer's vocabu-

lary, too, is far richer in Latin and French derivatives than that of any of his predecessors.

The poetry of the next century, both English and Scottish, drew its chief inspiration from Chaucer. No further foreign resources were for the moment needed, though there is some trace of goliardic influence in William Dunbar's headlong invectives, and in **Skelton**'s often semi-macaronic doggerel. France could at the moment show Britain nothing new, and the Latin tradition of the Poor Scholars was almost exhausted.

The Renaissance

The impact of the Classical revival and the Petrarchan love-convention was slow. Sir Thomas **Wyatt**, long reputed England's first Renaissance poet, copied certain Italian mannerisms, though not with entire success, and attempted a few sonnets. His travels abroad on embassies to France, Italy and Spain might have made him a suitable interpreter of the new poetry, which was spreading from Italy by way of Lyons to Paris and through Barcelona into Spain. But the distance that separated this Tudor courtier from his Italian model can be judged from a mere two lines of one of his translations, picked out by Professor Lewis:

> Thes new kyndes of plesurs wherein
> most men reioyse
> To me they do redowble still off stormye
> syghes the voyce.

Wyatt's metres are seldom easy to scan. But these thumping, English-sounding verses were only passed off as Italianate thanks to the skilful doctoring they received at the hands of Richard Tottel, when he prepared them for inclusion in his *Miscellany* of 1557. The Earl of **Surrey**, whose work was also printed by Tottel, did not carry the new style much further. In his translation of two books of the *Aeneid*, however, which is Chaucerian rather than Virgilian in spirit, he made use of blank verse. Although the medium had already been attempted by Chaucer in his *Tale of Melibeus*, Surrey has always received the credit for adapting the standard blank-verse line directly from the Italian.

It was not till twenty years after the publication of Tottel's *Miscellany* that the Italian style began to be freely imitated in England. Sir Philip **Sidney's** *Astrophel and Stella* was the first English sonnet-sequence, and his *Arcadia*, with its incidental poems set in a prose narrative, is almost its only Pastoral. The influences to which Sidney and his contemporary, Edmund **Spenser**, were subject are difficult to disentangle. The Italian style had by their time become firmly established in France. Spenser's two greatest lyrics, *Epithalamium* and *Prothalamium*, show no obvious debt to France. They derive from a shadowy Pindar, and from the more immediate example of various Italian and modern Latin odes. But Spenser adapted Petrarch and du Bellay at once in his early sonnets, and in his *Amoretti* is more relaxedly English, in the manner of Surrey. In the *Faerie Queene*, moreover, to quote Professor Lewis once more, he achieved 'the fusion of two kinds, the medieval allegory and the more recent romantic epic of the Italians'. Neither Petrarch, Ariosto nor Tasso entirely deflected English poetry from its course.

After 1580 English poetry could never again be accused of provincialism. The last relics of the old alliterative style are to be found in such poets as Robert **Southwell**, who were the last to resist the new trends, and in the popular poetry and nursery-rhyme of the next century.

But henceforth English poets followed the same conventions as those writing in the Romance languages. The language at the same time adopted an increasingly Latinised vocabulary and syntax. Spenser's studied antiquarianism in these respects had less influence than the more cosmopolitan practice of Sidney, **Ralegh** and other courtier poets. The de-Teutonisation of the language, begun by Chaucer, was now brought to a happy conclusion, and English poets began to exercise an influence abroad equal to that which they accepted from their foreign contemporaries. Sidney's reputation as a scholar, if not as a poet, was international, and the visits to Germany of English dramatic companies at the beginning of the next century marks the opening of a two-way traffic in influence which has continued ever since.

Elizabethan drama was in essence an English product. Senecan tragedy and the Latin closet-dramas of the Renaissance dictated the form of a few academic plays, like those of Samuel **Daniel** and Fulke **Greville**. Plots were freely taken from abroad, and the prevailing taste for horror and bloodshed may have found a respectable precedent in Seneca. But the episodic nature of the loosely constructed five-act play, its mingling of comedy and tragedy, of verse and prose, and most of its conventions must have been improvised by the managers and stock playwrights to suit their audience and the conditions of their theatre.

The age was remarkable for the excellence, if not always for the accuracy, of its translators. But their style was that of their own day: they made no concessions to that of their original author. **Chapman's** *Iliad*, like the *Faerie Queene*, strikes a compromise between the medieval and the modern; his *Odyssey* has something of the polish that was to come with the

Restoration. Apparently Chapman did not think it wrong to render Homer's hexameters first by the old 'fourteener' and then by iambic couplets. Elizabethan translations from the Greek and Latin convey nothing of the brevity and compression of the ancient tongues. English spirit always triumphs over foreign material.

By the beginning of the seventeenth century an English quality of sobriety and moderation was beginning to emerge, which has ever since rejected the more extreme continental fashions. From the Baroque conceit to the disordered imagery of the surrealists, these have been adopted in England, if at all, only in a modified form. The Metaphysical poets, with few exceptions, maintained their independence of the advanced styles of their day. The artificialities of Marino, and the contorted Latinity of Góngora found imitators and translators among such minor Caroline writers as Thomas Stanley and Sir Richard Fanshawe. But the poems they chose to render were, on the whole, the least characteristic, and appear far less bold than in the original Italian or Spanish. So mild did they sometimes become in the process of translation that one of Góngora's sonnets to a rose appears under Fanshawe's name in the *Oxford Book of English Verse* as an original composition.

Two poets of this group, however, learned rather more on their travels abroad than the rest. Andrew **Marvell**'s use of the conceit at the end of his poem *Upon Appleton House* is as curiously original as anything by an Italian Marinist. It is no simple matter to conjure up the mental image portrayed in the lines which announce the final coming of night:

> And now the salmon-fishers moist
> Their leathern boats begin to hoist;

> And, like Antipodes in shoes,
> Have shod their heads in their canoes.
> How tortoise-like, but not so slow,
> These rational amphibii go!
> Let's in; for the dark hemisphere
> Does now like one of them appear.

This poem of Marvell's bears some relation to the continental poem on solitude, the *Soledad* of the Spaniards. His better known *The Garden* has many parallels also among the garden-idylls written in France and Spain. Marvell's style was, in general, less exaggerated than that of his continental contemporaries. Not only was he a puritan, but he was also in the habit of writing his poems first in Latin, a language which still exerted a restraining influence. Richard **Crashaw** also wrote Latin poems, but was far more Italianate in manner. His version of the first book of Marino's *Sospetto d'Herode* is free, yet its rhetoric is often more elaborate than that of the original. *The Weeper*, a poem addressed to the Magdalen's tears, is an extreme example of the Baroque style in English. On account of an underground affinity between the Baroque and the Romantic styles, it is also the ancestor of **Shelley**'s *To a Skylark* and of poems by **Patmore** and Francis **Thompson**, all of which owe something to the Italian Baroque form and manner of:

> Not in the euening's eyes
> When they Red with weeping are
> For the Sun that dyes,
> Sitts sorrow with a face so fair,
> No where but here did euer meet
> Sweetnesse so sad, sadnesse so sweet.

Cowley's *Pindarique Odes* are another example of a Baroque style which in his case masquerades as Classical. Pindar no doubt supplied Cowley with hints, but only the mannerisms of his own century could inspire him to choose as one of his subjects 'an extravagant supposition of two Angels playing a Game at Chess'. Cowley was an eccentric scholar but the poets who were to guide English poetry back to Classicism took a conventional view of the Latin poets. Indeed they often saw them through well polished French spectacles.

Milton, on the other hand, possessed a deep understanding of Classical literature, and knew how to achieve its equivalent in English. It may have been Tasso's example that persuaded him not to imitate the lax form of the *Faerie Queene*, but to adopt a neo-Classic strictness. He may have been influenced also by Camões' *Lusiads*, which he probably read not in Portuguese but in Fanshawe's excellent translation. The form of the last two books of *Paradise Lost*, indeed, in which Michael relates to Adam the future history of Man, closely imitates the scene towards the conclusion of the *Lusiads* in which Gama receives similar instruction from a Muse or Siren concerning the destiny of Portugal. Milton learned much from Tasso and Camões. But even in *Samson Agonistes*, which approximates to the form of a Greek drama, his manner is that of an Englishman. Though he strives to give his language the weight and sometimes the syntax of Latin, it is Spenser, Shakespeare and the Bible that count for most in his poetic ancestry. *On the Morning of Christ's Nativity* shows him the complete master of the Baroque manner, which he used in that poem alone, and then abandoned for ever.

The Classical Revival

The Restoration and the eighteenth century, a period of neo-Classicism, based their literary theory and practice on their understanding of the Latin poets, which was affected by Boileau's example in the field of satire and by Milton's in that of reflective and didactic poetry. The period began under French influence. Some of the courtly lyrical poets wrote love-songs in the *précieux* manner, while the writers of heroic verse drama, abandoning the Elizabethan tradition, took their plots from Tasso and Corneille. They preferred the French rhymed couplet to blank verse. Nevertheless, the purge of unsuitable language, instituted by Boileau in the name of Malherbe, had no parallel in England. The excesses of the Metaphysicals had been less than those of the French Baroque poets and *Libertins*. Dryden himself, beginning in a *conceited* style, greatly simplified his language as he matured, but made no black-list of coarse and unpoetic expressions. Consequently English poetry remained more robust than French, and by the end of the century had fully returned to its own tradition. **Waller**'s couplet, Milton's blank-verse line, and a less complicated version of Cowley's ode were its stock measures.

The eighteenth century saw an extension of scholarly interest to the non-Classical world, which was reflected at second-hand by its poets. **Pope**'s Homer represented an extreme attempt to endow a barbaric world with Augustan manners. By a reversal of taste, the mid-eighteenth century began to take an interest in the primitive and strange. Thomas **Gray** was not only well acquainted with Classical, French and Italian poetry. He also published, with a far more superficial knowledge of his models, some *Imitations of Welsh and Norwegian Poetry*. Yet there is nothing recognisably Welsh except the names in such lines as:

Dauntless on his native sands
The Dragon son of Mona stands

and even so the Latin, not the Celtic, form is used. MacPherson's **Ossian**, though now acknowledged to be largely a forgery, was nevertheless based on some knowledge of Gaelic models and some respect for the Highland tradition. Some early translations from the Persian by Sir William Jones, a Calcutta High Court judge who was master of twenty-eight languages, though not very poetic were at least genuine. Jones, however, too easily assumed that the idiom of Hafiz could be rendered in conventional eighteenth-century English. Thus he stimulated a taste for pseudo-Orientalism of the sort practised by William **Collins** in his *Oriental Eclogues,* which, as he admitted, might just as well have been called Irish. The convention, however, travelled abroad, and in the end stimulated the writing of one masterpiece, Goethe's *West-Östliche Divan.* But the Augustans were too much concerned to prove that their age was the reincarnation of Imperial Rome to pay serious attention to other civilisations. Having discovered the Noble Savage, they took pains to dress him in a Roman toga and full-bottomed wig.

The Romantics

The romantic poets, by contrast, valued the Noble Savage for what they believed to be his native qualities of simplicity and deep feeling. They were not greatly interested, however, in reading or translating what he had written. Their own minds seemed to them stranger territories than the Persia of Hafiz or the heroic Wales of Thomas Gray. Passages from **Blake**'s *Prophetic Books* might pass for translations from the language of some other world. Blake, however, was the first major English poet who knew no language but his own. Robert **Burns**, too, can have had little French and even less

Latin. Indeed, when he wrote in conventional Southern English he handled it like a dead language. **Wordsworth** shows few signs of an acquaintance with foreign literature, and Keats not only read his Homer in Chapman's translation but drew his Classical mythology from a dictionary. The English tradition was now strong enough to nourish its own poets. Spenser, **Shakespeare** and Milton were Keats' teachers; the Augustans, Cowper, **Thomson**, and perhaps Henry **Vaughan**, were Wordsworth's.

Coleridge and **Shelley**, on the other hand, had a greater breadth of reading. Coleridge had a good knowledge of German, which was now becoming important as a vehicle for poetry as well as for philosophical thought, and translated parts of Schiller's *Wallenstein.* Shelley read at least six foreign languages, but did not imitate his foreign models at all closely. *Prometheus Unbound* is no more Greek than *Samson Agonistes*; and both his Calderón and Goethe translations have a Shelleyan resonance, in which Calderón's characteristic figures of speech and Goethe's colloquialisms are alike swallowed up.

The influence of the new German literature on English was on the whole deleterious. Schiller's example was responsible for a number of grandiloquent historical dramas, long ago forgotten, and the Victorian historical ballad owes something to Uhland and his generation. English examples had been far more influential in the formation of German. Milton had stimulated Klopstock's *Messias*; Goethe had learned romantic history from Walter **Scott** and the writing of chronicle-plays from Shakespeare, and such English ballad collectors as Percy had sent the Germans in search of their own folk-songs and ballads. Finally, **Byron** presented not only Germany but the whole of

Europe with a model of the poet as his own hero, 'a man proud, moody, cynical, with defiance on his brow, and misery in his heart, a scorner of his kind'. The effect of Byron lasted for almost half a century, finally to be replaced by that of Baudelaire, who, while adopting a similar pose of dandyism, also looked into his own heart, as Byron had not.

Just as Chaucer made use of the whole French tradition to give English poetry the shock which impelled it out of the backwaters of provincialism into the mainstream of Europe, so Pushkin adapted the full resources of English poetry to the needs of his own language. Shakespeare, Scott, Byron, and even such a minor figure as Barry Cornwall, had something to contribute to the new poetry of Russia.

The Nineteenth Century

The patterns of interweaving influence were far more complicated in the nineteenth century than in any previous age. Communication was freer, scholarship was more adventurous, and scholars were more eager to discover the intrinsic qualities of past civilisations rather than to see in them only such features as agreed with their own. Their success was uneven. William **Barnes**, the Dorset poet, read and translated from the Welsh, the Italian and the Persian, and experimented with metres from all three literatures, which he successfully adapted to the needs of the dialect in which he chose to write. Edward **FitzGerald**, on the other hand, though equally familiar with his originals, was content to cut Calderón's plays to half their length and to rob his lines of every conceit. His *Omar Khayyám*, too, clothes the Persian poet in a strangely English garb. His easy fatalism, which deeply affected the minor poets of the nineties, is foreign only in a few external

mannerisms of expression. Some of the quatrains, indeed, are little more than an assembly of semi-biblical clichés.

> Ah, make the most of what we yet may
> spend,
> Before we too into the dust descend:
>   Dust into Dust, and under Dust, to lie,
> Sans Wine, sans Song, sans Singer, and
> —sans End!

This verse is no more than the compound of a well-known English proverb and a phrase from the Funeral Service. There is more than a little similarity between FitzGerald's adaptation from the Persian and Gray's from the Welsh.

The three greatest Victorian poets, **Tennyson**, Browning and Arnold, were all anxious to make a new approach to Classical poetry. Tennyson achieved a certain Virgilian sweetness in such poems as *Ulysses* and *Tithonus*, and was also successful in his attempts to write quantitative verse in the Latin manner. Browning's versions of the Greek drama break with the eighteenth-century habit of seeing the Greeks through Roman eyes, but his rough-hewn verse fails to convey the ritual element in Aeschylus and Euripides. He is predominantly interested in character as they were not.

Both Tennyson and Arnold attempted to find an English equivalent for the Homeric line. Both made specimen translations. Tennyson's are good but do not suggest that his complete *Iliad*, had he attempted one, would have been better than the Earl of Derby's. Arnold came nearer to the desiderated *grand style*, both in his original poems, *Sohrab and Rustum* and *Balder Dead*, and in such passages as that translated from the sixth *Iliad* in which he speaks of the coming day:

>   when sacred Troy shall go to
> destruction,

Troy, and warlike Priam too, and the
people of Priam.

Had Arnold translated the *Iliad*, the full
impact of Homer might have struck
English poetry. For his fragments show a
mastery of the 'barbarous hexameter'
greater than that of any other poet. His
attempts to interpret Celtic literature, on
the other hand, were almost as unsuccessful as Gray's.

The Pre-Raphaelite movement attempted to naturalise several foreign influences
that had not yet had their full effect in
England. They failed, much as their
favourite FitzGerald failed, by their
inability to avoid cliché. Their poetic
language invariably suffers by its deliberate
remoteness from the spoken tongue.

D. G. **Rossetti**'s translation of Dante's
Vita Nuova and of a selection of lyrical
poems by Dante and his contemporaries
have a Romantic imprecision of vocabulary and a fade-away weakness in their
rhythms that gave the Italians the appearance of minor poets somewhat given to
melancholy, and cheated them once
more of their full impact on English
poetry. Chaucer had valued Dante as a
scholar but could make little of him as a
poet. Milton admired the *Divina Commedia*, but *Paradise Lost* would have been
no different had he never read it. Shelley's
Triumph of Life and Keats' revised *Hyperion* are fragments that show the great
lesson in compression and clear symbolism
that Dante had still to offer to English
poetry. Rossetti, however, presented those
qualities in the Italian master and his
contemporaries that had least importance
for the development of English poetry.
William **Morris**, too, was unfortunate in
his importations. As a theorist, he longed
to revive the Teutonic constituents in
English and to minimise the refinements
that had been derived from French. But

his *Beowulf* and his retelling in verse of
the saga of Sigurd the Volsung are
merely self-conscious exercises in the
writing of an artificial style. It was too
late for English poetry to learn anything
from these primitive sources. At best,
Morris encouraged the invention of
other pseudo-archaic styles, like that of
C. M. **Doughty**.

The nineties marked a temporary
weakening of the English poetic tradition.
Romantic poetry was exhausted: the
Classics seemed to have yielded their
last secrets, the Pre-Raphaelites had
prepared the ground for this defeatism,
and for the cult of Verlaine, the most
melancholy and the least vital of the
French symbolist poets. The poetry of
Ernest **Dowson**, Lionel **Johnson** and
other contributors to the *Yellow Book*
repeats this music-in-a-minor-key, which
for a while seemed more important
than that of Baudelaire or Mallarmé.
French was once more a fashionable
influence at the end of the century, and
refinement was for a while valued above
robustness.

The Twentieth Century

The immediate reaction from this decadence was to a new vogue for style,
whether in **Belloc** and **Chesterton**'s
light-hearted revival of the fourteenth-
century French *ballade*, or in the writing of
verse-dramas that could never be staged.
Later there came a brief Georgian revival
of the Wordsworthian interest in country
places and simple people.

W. B. **Yeats**, the most important
poet of the first quarter of the century,
knew little of foreign poetry. Even the
Irish legends of which he made use were
known to him only in English versions, or
in adaptations by his friends. His symbolism
was a personal amalgam from which
foreign literary influences were almost

entirely absent. Yeats was, however, with the possible exception of Blake, the first poet in Britain since pagan times whose thought was founded neither on Christianity nor on a revulsion from Christianity. The Theosophy which informs many of his later poems does not follow the exposition of Mme Blavatsky. Yeats drew on a number of writers, occultists of the seventeenth and nineteenth centuries, whose teachings had never affected English poetry before. Their influence, however, was limited to Yeats' own circle and they have no importance in the general history of poetry.

Ezra **Pound**, on the other hand, a poet of less achievement than Yeats, has been far more active in his search for foreign techniques with which to revive the dying English conventions. An American and an imperfect scholar, Pound raided Greek, Chinese, Anglo-Saxon, Italian and Provençal literature for poems that contrasted with the drab and sober writing of the Georgians. In translating them he used a somewhat Victorian poetic vocabulary derived from Browning and the Pre-Raphaelites. The influence of these explorations on his own poetry and on the more important writing of T. S. **Eliot** was considerable. Arthur **Waley**'s translations from the Chinese also revealed a wide new territory to his readers. While his form, a sparingly assonanced *vers libre*, has been inspiring to his fellow-translators, it cannot be said that he has brought any Chinese influence to bear on contemporary poetry.

The prevailing influences in the second quarter of this century have been those French symbolists whom the nineties failed to appreciate.

T. S. Eliot's early debt to Jules Laforgue hardly lasted beyond the epoch of *Prufrock*. *Vers libre* is a medium hard to acclimatise to English, and Eliot soon turned to a free blank-verse. Yet the tissue of quotations and cross-references, and the frequent breaks and changes of tone in *The Waste Land*, and the *Quartets*, owe something to the style of Laforgue's *Derniers Vers*, and to Mallarmé as well. For the progressions of both these poets was dictated, like Eliot's, by what I. A. Richards has called 'the music of ideas'.

Rilke's *Duineser Elegien* follow the same music, and it is the same French influence that worked through him on the poets of the thirties. Rilke's close texture and his device of using things or features of the landscape as 'objective correlatives' (or symbols) of a mood or state of mind was closely imitated by W. H. **Auden**. A comparison between Auden's 'To settle in the village of the heart', and its immediate model, Rilke's 'Ausgesetzt auf den Bergen des Herzens', reveals the basis of an essential element in Auden's style. Such a typical late poem as *In Praise of Limestone* exploits Rilke's method, but works it out in greater detail than Rilke himself ever attempted. He was undoubtedly the greatest influence from abroad on the English poetry of the thirties. Native influences, from Gerard Manley **Hopkins**, Wilfred **Owen**, Yeats and the study of Saxon and medieval poetry, contributed to the rediscovery of the old alliterative line and to various experiments in its revival. Indeed, the outstanding technical achievement of the last thirty years has been the discovery of satisfactory substitutes for the full rhyme, which is outworn, and of textures that are neither strictly regular nor absolutely free. In this foreign influences have been secondary to those from our own early tradition.

During the last forty years a great number of contemporary foreign poets have been read and translated. Yet none has been influential except Rilke. Apollinaire, Lorca, Pasternak, and a number of American poets—Wallace **Stevens**, Robert **Frost** and Robert **Lowell**, in particular—the poets of modern Greece, the German Expressionists and the French Surrealists have been accepted with interest and enthusiasm, yet direct imitation of them has rarely been attempted. The English tradition has once more become self-reliant. Its resistance to the influence of Surrealism has been remarkably strong. A movement which has bedevilled the poetry of France and of some Spanish-speaking countries, granting licence for every kind of looseness and obscurity, has found hardly any followers among English poets. A few pieces by David **Gascoyne** and George **Barker** show its influence, and Dylan **Thomas** practised the free association of images for which its theory provides. But all these three poets have preserved a formal sense deeply rooted in the English tradition. Surrealism can teach us nothing that Blake did not know, and can lead to no more compelling imagery than that of the Romantics.

The Channel has once more become a boundary which isolates, rather than a frontier across which ideas pass. A certain mutual influence exists between the more academic poets of Britain and the United States. But the best that is being written at the present time is almost completely English in ancestry. Philip **Larkin**, Thom **Gunn**, Ted **Hughes** and R. S. **Thomas** show no evidence of foreign reading. Peter **Redgrove** alone, among those at present coming forward, seems still to be affected by Rimbaud, a poet whose lesson has so far proved unassimilable.

The history of English poetry has been one of an early assimilation of ideas more fully worked out by foreign poets, followed by a period when more influence was exerted abroad than was received at home. Now an appropriate equilibrium has been achieved, and the exchange is small. All countries are, however, more aware of what is being written abroad than ever before, and an outstanding poet in any language would now probably influence the whole world of poetry within a few years. At present no such poet appears to exist.   J.M.C.

Frost, Robert [Lee] (1874–1963), was born in San Francisco, California, but the death of his father when he was eleven necessitated the removal of the family to Lawrence, Massachusetts, and Frost's poetry has been based largely on a sensitive awareness of a New England environment. After attending high school at Lawrence he matriculated at Dartmouth College but left after a few months. In 1893 he married Eleanor White and two years later entered Harvard University, leaving once again without receiving a degree. After eleven years of trying various jobs, during which he was unable to gain recognition for his poems, he decided to stake his future in a bold move. In 1912 he sailed with his wife and four children for England. He rented a farm near London and struck up friendships with a number of British poets, including Rupert **Brooke**, Wilfred Gibson and Edward **Thomas**. More importantly, in England Frost found a publisher for his first two books—*A Boy's Will* (1913) and *North of Boston* (1914). Both publications were received enthusiastically, and when he returned to America in 1915 Frost found himself an established poet.

While Frost never relaxed his suspicions about academic narrowness, which had twice driven him from colleges as an undergraduate, he frequently found a place in college communities as teacher or poet-in-residence. Eight books which followed *North of Boston* are contained in the comprehensive edition, *Complete*

Poems of Robert Frost, published in 1949. The Pulitzer Prize for poetry was awarded four times to him, in 1924, 1931, 1937 and 1943.

Though the increasing acknowledgment of Frost's greatness permitted John Crowe **Ransom** to refer to him at midcentury as a 'major' poet, Frost contributed surprisingly little to twentieth-century poetic technique. In a period of metrical experiment his clean iambic arrangements seem closer to **Chaucer** than to T. S. **Eliot**. His reputation rests not upon innovation but on the fidelity of his metaphors and his powers of observation and the essential probings of his themes.

The range of Frost's poetry runs from the short, self-contained lyric to longer, dramatically profiled works. In the lyrics, the relationship between poet and the natural objects within the poem are entirely self-sufficient; still they suggest an enlarged interpretation, as in the first quatrain from *The Pasture*:

> I'm going out to clean the pasture spring;
> I'll only stop to rake the leaves away
> (And wait to watch the water clear, I
> may):
> I sha'n't be gone long.—You come too.

While the third line readily belongs to the probabilities of the action it nevertheless encourages speculation, so that the poem may seem to cast its regard on other matters than cleaning springs. Such an extension results, however, not from a schematic symbolism but from an aura of normal association, or what Austin Warren has called Frost's 'natural symbolism'.

The longer poems, both narrative and dramatic, tend to establish themselves primarily through the monologue. Indeed, they show an attitude remarkably close to that of Robert **Browning**. That is to say, they move relentlessly towards a spiritual or psychological illumination of the past. And, like Browning's, Frost's characters are incapable of change. Thus, in the best known of Frost's narratives, *The Death of the Hired Man*, the old handyman, returning to die at the farm where he has worked only when he could find no more attractive work, is surrounded by the opposed attitudes of the young farmer and his wife. 'Home', Warren says, 'is the place where, when you have to go there, / They have to take you in.' His definition opposes Mary's: 'I should have called it / Something you somehow haven't to deserve'. Though the hired man's death shocks the two into an emotional sympathy it does not cause the attitude of either to change. If Frost's narratives lose dramatic elements in such static arrangements they nevertheless faithfully and poignantly delineate the elements themselves. As he says in *Hyla Brook*, 'We love the things we love for what they are'. This love extends to man and the manifestations of nature alike. Indeed, for this, more than for any other reason, though man and nature are often antagonists, in Frost's poetry they are ultimately inseparable.

Because Frost turned with joy and understanding to the natural objects of New England, he was often called a New England nature poet. The phrase does not precisely mislead, but neither does it lead to precision. In nature and New England Frost sought not the eccentric, the peculiar nor the local, but that which shares a common bond with all life everywhere. He cannot then, any more than Thomas **Hardy**, be called a regionalist. His own term for himself, 'environmentalist', perhaps does justice.

The environment itself is that of a total, encompassing nature, a cosmos. He envisages man first as reacting to an intimate, palpable nature, hard but filled with the surprises of beauty—the delight which leads to wisdom. In his intimate environment he looks 'into the crater of the ant' or longs to feel the 'hurt' of earth pressed against the whole of his body. Beyond this happy environment, however, lies the less communicative universe of remote stars and quantum physics. And here, as in *The Star-Splitter*, Frost shuttles back and forth between extreme positions, from the belief that the stars inspire lofty thought and the almost anti-intellectual feeling that they are irrelevant to human life. Or he may attempt to force a relationship between this outer nature and human life by claiming that within himself extend more frightening voids than the vast distances between stars.

This configuration of tentative attitudes dogs many of Frost's best poems and emerges as a controlling design of motives. In, for example, *Birches* Frost begins by saying that he likes to think the bent trees result from 'some boy's swinging them'. Then he admits that such is not the case, that in fact it is 'ice storms'. The first reason is wishful fantasy, the second is austere fact. Behind the fantasy-reason stands the desire for man to have an effect upon unsympathetic nature. Moreover, the fantastic reason alone supports the central metaphor of the poem.

> I'd like to go by climbing a birch tree
> And climb black branches up a snow
>   white trunk
> *Toward* heaven, till the tree could bear
>   no more
> But dipped its top and set me down again.
> That would be good both going and
>   coming back.
> One could do worse than be a swinger
>   of birch trees.

A similar pattern of fantasy and truth appears in *After Apple-Picking* where for a playful moment he says that

> I cannot rub the strangeness from my
>   sight
> I got from looking through a pane of
>   glass
> I skimmed this morning from the
>   drinking trough
> And held against the world of hoary
>   grass.

Yet the real reason for his vision of 'magnified apples' is the repeated task of the harvest. Again in *Mending Wall* where, though hunters and weather are the reasons for the wall's falling down, Frost is pleased to suggest 'elves' and beyond that 'something . . . that does not love a wall'. This 'something', like the ladder in *After Apple-Picking* or the tree itself in *Birches* appeals to a higher authority than either fantasy or fact. The appeal, scarcely clarified or made more than a gesture, nevertheless insists, throughout the opposition of nature-as-it-is and nature-as-man-would-have-it, upon the importance of human aspiration.

Because his poetry tolerated opposing points of view Frost was charged, especially by Yvor **Winters**, with an irresponsible, Emersonian relativism. That there is some truth in the charge of relativism must be confessed; that it is the whole truth is open to question. In *West-Running Brook* a young married couple discuss the phenomenon of a brook which runs counter to the normal direction and which in itself contains a current running counter to itself. The wife takes the view of the fantasist who at heart assumes that man and nature have common sympathies. The brook's counter-current, she says, is 'waving to us'. The husband takes two views: one, that the wave is unconcerned with human affairs; and second, that the 'contraries' of the brook epitomise the whole character of the universe. At the end of the poem, it is true, the separate views are approved: 'Today will be the day of what we both said.' But the ending also seems to move towards an attempt to fuse the fantasy of human wish with the cold fact of inhuman nature in such a way as to suggest that ultimate truth contains both views. If that is so, then Frost's relativism was preliminary to an intimation of a single principle that both composes and transcends blind nature and visionary man. R.S. *see also* American poetry

Fugitive Group. The Fugitive group of poets flourished from 1915 to 1928 in Nashville, Tennessee. Most of them were students or teachers at Vanderbilt University during some part of this period, though the group was not sponsored or recognised by the university. Numbering sixteen at the most, they met frequently to talk philosophy and to read and criticise each other's poetry. From April 1922 to December 1925 they published and largely wrote (the most important outside contributors were Hart **Crane** and Robert **Graves**) *The Fugitive*, a 'little magazine' of verse and occasional criticism.

The three leading members were John Crowe **Ransom**, Donald Davidson (1893–), and Allen **Tate**. Ransom, the oldest of the group and teacher at Vanderbilt of most of the others, was the first to come to full maturity as poet and critic; he tended inevitably to dominate the group, though not without stubborn opposition. Tate, a brilliant champion of the modern and experimental style, was the radical of the group and Ransom's frequent opponent in controversy—usually amicable, though some acrimony crept into their exchange (published 1923) over **Eliot**'s *The Waste Land*, which Tate defended against Ransom's strictures. (A dislike of the obvious or the sentimental and an inclination to irony were, however, as characteristic of Ransom as of Tate,

and to varying degrees of the whole group.) Davidson, a man of great personal warmth and loyalty, mediated between the other two both personally and intellectually, and was one of the chief forces holding the group together. These three, aided later on by Robert Penn **Warren**, the youngest member, did most of the editorial work, though manuscripts were selected and policies decided by equal vote of the whole group. The other members were diverse in background and interests. Principal hosts for the meetings were James Frank, wealthy merchant, and Sidney Hirsch, eccentric occultist and Orientalist. Two members who established literary reputations were Merrill Moore, psychiatrist and most indefatigable of sonneteers, and Laura **Riding** of Louisville, the only non-resident and only woman. Andrew Lytle and Cleanth Brooks arrived too late to be members but were decisively influenced by the group.

After nineteen issues the group felt that the magazine had done its essential work; the routine of putting it out was proving increasingly burdensome, especially to the leading members who were now well embarked on their literary careers. It was therefore terminated, though the group continued to write poetry and meet to read it. Their final publication was *Fugitives: An Anthology of Verse* (1928), a selection from the magazine with an approximately equal amount of new verse by the members.

The Fugitives were not regionalists: though the name 'Fugitive' was deliberately enigmatic and ironic, it was intended to suggest both the poet as wanderer and outcast from society and also a rejection of the genteel sentimentalities of Southern literature; as the Foreword to the first issue proclaimed, '*The Fugitive* flees from nothing faster than from the high-caste Brahmins of the Old South'. They did ot, however, engage in the kind of simple-minded and whole-hearted revolt against the past and against their society that was so characteristic of the period (and especially of little magazines). From the beginning, the leading members had found the New South slogans of Industrialism and Progress as distasteful as the falsities of the sentimentalised Old South. The Scopes trial (1925), in spite of its absurdities, brought to a focus the conflict between the scientific and religious attitudes which they felt to be the fundamental issue facing the South, and the misrepresentation and denigration of the South in accounts of the trial led them to a re-examination of Southern history. By 1927 the three leading Fugitives had committed themselves to a defence of the principles of the Old South, interpreted as a traditional and religious society. Joined later by Warren (alone of the Fugitives) and by a number of other scholars and writers, they began a campaign to preserve the values of the Agrarian South against the inroads of Industrialism that eventuated in the symposium *I'll Take My Stand* (1930). Though there is a definite relation between the two, the Agrarians were thus distinct in membership and purpose from the Fugitives.

Although it is doubtful whether *The Fugitive* can be said to have inaugurated anything like a Southern literary renaissance, it did give the lie to Mencken's description of the South as the 'Sahara of the Bozart'. And the major Fugitives—Ransom, Davidson, Tate, and Warren, together with the half-Fugitives Brooks and Lytle—have, as teachers and editors, as well as by the example of their own writing, had an enormous influence on younger Southern writers.   M.K.S.

Fuller, Roy (1912–), who is now a solicitor, served as a naval rating in the

Fleet Air Arm from 1941 to 1946. Though in the nineteen-thirties a left-wing propagandist, his first volume, *The Middle of a War* (1942), was concerned mainly with the war, as was his second, *A Lost Season* (1944). He wrote, to quote R. N. Currey, 'with a dry precision of events which he tried to see in political perspective', as of

> . . . the destruction of Europe by its
>   councils, its unending justification
> Of that which cannot be justified, what
>   is done.

In his next two volumes of poetry (he is also a novel-writer), *Epitaphs and Occasions* (1951) and *Counterparts* (1954), he widened his range and expanded his technique, hazarding even a roundel and a villanelle. He has come to full richness in *Brutus's Orchard* (1957), which contains poems of greater depth in varying metres, including experiments in the sonnet. *The Ides of March*, suggesting the title of the book, is a dignified and moving piece about any man who has 'caught the times like a disease', and has to choose where he stands, Brutus saying to himself 'I merely choose what history foretells.' Fuller has considerable powers of description, usually by deft suggestion:

> A clouded sky at dusk, the dirty red
> Of grazed skin: slightly furred, the trees
>   as though
> Drawn with a fine pen on a still-damp
>   wash.

Many of his poems are concerned with the problems of and the validity of the poet, as in *Poem to Pay for a Pen* (*Counterparts*), or, in his last book, the dialogue between the Poet and his Talent. There is now hesitation in his judgments, *Ambiguities* stating 'I only know / That pity is the best that I can show'.

He was elected Professor of Poetry at Oxford University in 1968.   B.D.

G

Gardner, Isabella (1895–), is an American poet, formerly an editor of *Poetry*, who is married to Allen **Tate**. Her *Birthdays from the Ocean* (1955) and *The Looking Glass* (1961) contain poems of great concentration and intensity. Her poems are often brief but they have the range and tone of lyrics rather than of epigrams.　　　　　　　　　　D.H.

Gascoigne, George (?1539–77), was the son of a wealthy and powerful family, studied at Cambridge and then attempted careers at court, in the law, and in the army. He was never successful, perhaps because of several imprisonments, but he was regarded by his contemporaries as a man of spirit and talent. His lyrics were first published in *A Hundred Sundry Flowers* (1573), although scholars are not certain that all the poems in the volume were his. Some use devices such as alliteration in an elementary and mechanical way:

> Then Craft the crier call'd a quest,
> Of whom was Falsehood foremost fere,
> A pack of pickthanks were the rest,

but others, such as *A Strange Passion of a Lover*, demonstrate a graceful lyrical style:

> The which to thee dear wench I write,
> That know'st my mirth but not my
> 　　　　　　　　　　　　　moan:
> I pray God grant thee deep delight,
> To live in joys when I am gone.

Gascoigne showed great versatility in his short literary career. He wrote a pastoral play, *The Supposes* (1575), which was modelled on Ariosto's work and influenced the sub-plot of **Shakespeare's**

The Taming of the Shrew. He also wrote a tragedy, *Jocasta* (1575), a satire, *Steel Glas* (1576), and an heroic romance, *Tale o Hemetes the Hermit* (1575). His critical work on English verse, *Certain Notes c Instruction* (1575), presents one of the firs explanations of how conceits operate and advocates poetic 'invention' to avoid the obvious or trite. Gascoigne reformec during his last year or two and wrote a temperance tract called *Delicate Diet fo dainty-mouthed Drunkards* (1576).　J.G.

Gascoyne, David (1916–), is an English poet influenced by surrealism. He wa precocious, publishing at first in the mid-thirties. He remains the English autho who has most absorbed the experiments o the modern movement in France.　D.H.

Gay, John (1685–1732), is the author of a long poem, *Trivia* (1716), and the popular *Beggar's Opera* (1728), which capture the spirit of eighteenth-century London. Bertolt Brecht adapted the latter when he wrote his *Die Dreigroschenoper*. Many of Gay's short poems, whether extracted from plays or independently written, show a sprightliness which has not grown dim.　　　　　　　　　D.H.

Gilbert, [Sir] W[illiam] S[chwenck] (1836–1911), was the collaborator of Sir Arthur Sullivan, with whom he wrote numerous musical plays. His librettos are characterised by skilful rhyming and resourceful verbal invention. He was also the author of comic poems, *The Bab Ballads*, and some fine parodies.　　　　　　　　　D.H.

Golding, Arthur (?1536–?1605), was an Elizabethan translator, whose best known work is his version of Ovid's *Metamorphoses* (1565–7). Written in 'fourteeners', it was used by **Shakespeare**, and in our

ay has been highly praised by Ezra
Pound. Its great virtue is the clarity
with which Ovid's mythological stories
are told, but it does not reflect the wit and
sophistication of the original.   J.H-S.
See also Translation

Goldsmith, Oliver (?1730–74), was born
in Ireland of English parents. After
desultory study in Dublin and Edinburgh
and wanderings on the continent, he
failed as a physician in London and
became a hack writer, entering Samuel
Johnson's circle. Fame rewarded him
not only as poet but as essayist (*The Citizen
of the World*, 1762), novelist (*The Vicar of
Wakefield*, 1766), and playwright (*She
Stoops to Conquer*, 1773).

That Goldsmith had to exist by his pen
may account for the slight quantity of his
poetry. He once remarked that 'to court
the draggle-tail Muses' was a luxury he
could ill afford. But *The Traveller* (1764)
and *The Deserted Village* (1770) enjoyed
great contemporary favour, and his
reputation as poet still rests mainly on these
two works. *Retaliation*, with its satiric
profiles of Garrick and other club
members, *Song* ('When lovely woman
stoops to folly'), and such comic verse as
the mock-elegy on Mrs Mary Blaize,
foreshadowing **Hood** in its puns, also
remain in anthologies. In *The Traveller*,
echoing Popean antithesis, Goldsmith
sets forth his idea of compensation: that
material and intellectual progress under a
Tory régime will counterbalance a declin-
ing poetry and a thinning populace. *The
Deserted Village*, with its familiar portraits
of preacher and schoolmaster, sadly depicts
the break-up of pastoral England after the
Enclosure Act:

Along the lawn, where scatter'd hamlets
                                                 rose,

Unwieldy wealth, and cumbrous pomp
                                                 repose;

Macaulay attacked the poem for anachro-
nism, for mingling English and Irish
village life in 'monstrous combinations'.
Among recent defenders is Robert **Graves**,
who calls it 'a true poem', signalling its
parallels to Irish minstrel songs (*The
Crowning Privilege*, 1955).

Against Boswell's portrait of 'poor
Nolly Goldsmith', the inspired bumbler,
may be set the considered respect of Dr
Johnson, whose Latin epitaph declared
that Goldsmith had adorned all he
touched; and who observed, on his
friend's dying so far in debt, 'Was ever
poet so trusted before?'   X.J.K.

Gower, John (1330–1408), came of a
Kentish family, and knew **Chaucer**, who
called him 'Moral Gower'. Though he
was highly regarded, little is known about
him. Gower married for the second time
in 1398, soon after going blind. He is
buried in St Saviour's Church, Southwark,
his effigy resting on his main works, the
Speculum Meditantis, *Vox Clamantis*, and
Confessio Amantis.

Gower wrote in three languages, the
Speculum (Mirour de l'Omme) of sins and
vices, in French; the *Vox*, an admonish-
ment to different social ranks, in Latin;
and the *Confessio* in English. His versatility
in language did not match his poetry,
which was of barely unrelieved didacticism, excepting the *Confessio* (1390) where
he realises that teaching must go with
pleasure. A lover confesses to Genius, a
priest to Venus, who lectures him on all
Seven Sins and violations of Courtly
Love. The *Confessio* is a frame story, its
strength lying in the tales, 'exempla'
which illustrate the teaching. Here Gower
tells a good story, having a diction

balanced, elegant, and touching on rhythmic beauty:

Under an hell[1] ther is a cave
Which of the sonne mai noght have,
So that no man mai knowe ariht
The point between the dai and nyht
There is no fyr, there is no sparke
Ther is no dore, which mai charke[2]
Whereof an yhe scholde unschette,[3]
So that inward ther is no lette.[4]

Gower wrote in octosyllabic rhymed couplets, in the *Confessio* as many as 34,000. A man of no genius who had technically perfected his art, Gower today is treated with respect, though he is little read.   T.J.G.

Graves, Robert [Ranke] (1895–), above all a poet, is also author of *Goodbye to All That*, one of the best modern autobiographies, and of numerous historical novels. He served in France with the Royal Welch Fusiliers during the First World War. In the early nineteen-thirties he settled in Deya, Majorca, and has lived there almost uninterruptedly (except during the period 1937–45) ever since.

As the reader of his autobiography will realise, Graves is a poet independent of the movements and influences of his time. He might be described as a one-man resistance movement against the formidable poetic-and-critical apparatus of **Eliot**, the mythological rhetoric of **Yeats**, the pretensions and opinionatedness of Ezra **Pound**. Graves is, in fact, probably a finer scholar than any of these, so that his refusal to ballast his poetic self with his didactic self is quietly impressive, and in fact it seems likely that his example will weigh more and more. By now, there

[1] *hell*—hill [2] *charke*—creak
[3] *yhe scholde unschette*—eye should open
[4] *lette*—obstacle

must seem to many readers a fusion in Robert Graves' poetry of personal experience which is poetic with individual expression which is unique, in a time when other poetry contains so many elements of intellectualisation. The attempt to make poetry a vehicle for modish self-conscious critical awareness is absent in Graves. At the same time, this personal integrity realised in poetry is the result of a lifetime's self-editing and paring away from his own work of whatever in his past the poet considers to misrepresent his 'poetic seriousness'. It could be argued that Graves has just as much a *persona* or mask as poets like Eliot, Pound or Yeats of whom he disapproves, but whereas with them the *persona* is artefact, with him it is the image of a wholly private and wholly poetic Robert Graves.

One of the most curious things about this poet is that there is no authentic Graves canon. Various volumes published as collected poems, either for his whole life, or of a few years previous to publication, simply bring up to date the Graves image. *Collected Poems* (1938) and *Collected Poems* (1961) are both highly selective. So there is the paradox that the modern English poet of the purest poetic integrity is also the one whose works are least integrated into a whole.

As the revealing Introduction to *Collected Poems* (1938)—when the poet adopted the views of Laura **Riding**—shows, looking back on his own output the poet sees many unsatisfactory excursions of a poetically impure kind, even into 'behaving like a Churchman', 'though I had ceased to be a Christian'. In fact, as the erratic but marvellous prose work *The White Goddess* shows, it has been a lifelong aim of Graves to discover a single outside theme which corresponds to a single inner poetic truth. This has been found in the revived ancient idea of the

Muse to whom the poet addressed his poetry, and whose reality he actually experiences in love. 'My thesis is that the language of poetic myth anciently current in the Mediterranean and Northern Europe was a magical language bound up with popular religious ceremonies in honour of the Moon-goddess, or Muse, some of them dating from the Old Stone Age, and that this remains the language of true poetry—"true" in the nostalgic modern sense of "the unimprovable original, not a synthetic substitute".' From this arise Graves' polemics against poets whom he regards as false, for example, Virgil, **Milton**, and all those of his contemporaries who do not share his views.

Graves' poetry at its best has a gnarled, odd, twisted texture like the trunks of the olive trees where he lives in Majorca, and a power of evocation which is truly magical. It is real moon-poetry but written by a man of learning, passion and tough common sense who is a contemporary. He has the superb ear and command of language which can raise a poetry based on close observation of nature and human psychology to diction which seems prophetic:

Be assured, the Dragon is not dead
But once more from the pools of peace
Shall rear his fabulous green head.

The flowers of innocence shall cease
And like a harp the wind shall roar
And the clouds shake an angry fleece.

s.s.

Gray, Thomas (1716–71), was born in London of middle-class parents, and educated at Eton and Peterhouse College, Cambridge. At Eton he became close friends with Richard West (whose early death was to inspire a moving sonnet) and with Horace Walpole. He accompanied the latter on a continenatal tour from 1739 to 1741, crossing the Alps to Italy. Emotional tensions led to their parting company, though they were subsequently reconciled. Gray returned to Cambridge, where he was appointed Professor of History and Modern Languages in 1768. His life was that of a shy, rather spinsterly don, the butt of undergraduate ragging; what he described as his 'leucocholy' or 'white melancholy' made him a prey to indolence and frustration. He has left us his charming and characteristic letters, and a small number of English and Latin poems. Their quality is such as to give Gray a unique and permanent place.

Of his English poems, *The Elegy Written in a Country Churchyard* (1750) possesses a universality of appeal beyond the rest. Essentially it belongs to a recognisable eighteenth-century *genre*—the meditation on mortality, to which Blair's *Grave*, **Young**'s *Night Thoughts* and Hervey's prose *Meditations among the Tombs* also belong. Nor is its feeling for idealised country landscape anything very out of the ordinary for mid-eighteenth-century taste. But Gray handles the quatrain with great rhythmical subtlety. Above all the whole poem is informed by deep and highly personal feeling. In 1742, when he began the *Elegy*, Gray was saddened by his quarrel with Walpole, the death of his mother and of West; and worried about his future and his material prospects. These private concerns nowhere explicitly enter the poem, but they serve to crystallise what would otherwise be a purely generalised emotion. It is this that gives to the poem its curious half-articulate Romanticism, as in the image of himself as the 'hoary-headed Swain' may recall him:

Hard by yon wood, now smiling as in
scorn,

Muttering his wayward fancies would
he rove;
Now drooping, woeful-wan, like one
forlorn,
Or craz'd with care, or cross'd in
hopeless love.

Of Gray's other poems, the most notable
are his odes. They are highly literary, and
owe their inspiration to **Milton**'s minor
poems and to Greek lyric poetry. It is true
that Gray's rather heavy poetic diction,
and his over-use of personified abstractions
(his two chief faults) are alien to the
true Greek spirit. But the poems have an
aesthetic quality and a music of their own.
Lord David Cecil aptly compares the
description of Venus in *The Progress of
Poesy* (1759) to 'some radiant, florid
ceiling painted by Tiepolo':

Slow melting strains their Queen's
approach declare:
Where'er she turns the Graces
homage pay;
With arms sublime that float upon the
air,
In gliding state she wins her easy way.
O'er her warm cheek, and rising bosom,
move,
The bloom of young Desire, and purple
light of love.

The Bard (1757) is a 'Gothick' poem,
reflecting Gray's studies in Welsh literature. The evocative use made of proper
names well illustrates the musical qualities
of his verse:

Mountains, ye mourn in vain
Modred, whose magic song
Made huge Plinlimmon bow his
cloud-topt head.

Of Gray's other odes, some are touched
by the same personal melancholy which
marks the *Elegy. On a Favourite Cat*

drowned in a Tub of Gold Fishes is in a
lighter vein; it is an enduring piece of
bric-à-brac, almost perfect of its kind.

J.H-S

Greene, Robert (?1560–92), was an
Elizabethan 'university wit' whose realistic
prose remains more vigorous than most
of his poetry. 'Weep not, my wanton' is
his best-known lyric, and *Friar Bacon and
Friar Bungay* his most remembered play.

Greville, Sir Fulke, Lord Brooke (1554–
1628), was educated at Jesus College,
Cambridge, and became a courtier and
favourite of Queen Elizabeth. He was a
friend of Sir Philip **Sidney**—whose life
he wrote—and of Bacon, and held
government office under both Elizabeth
and James I, who created him Lord
Brooke in 1621. Greville was murdered
by a discontented servant in 1628.

Sidney's influence is apparent in *Caelica*,
a sequence of 109 'sonnets' (though only
forty-one are true sonnets), on a variety of
themes, amatory, philosophical and religious. The early poems are written in a
manner fairly close to **Spenser** and
Sidney, but in Greville's mature work, in
Geoffrey Bullough's words, 'the tone is
deliberately kept low, the vocabulary
commonplace and the imagery never
more than necessary to make the point'.
This restrained, almost prosaic style is also
evident in Greville's two long didactic
poems, *A Treatie of Humane Learning*
and *A Treatie of Warres*. In these poems
Greville's pessimism, his Calvinistic cast of
mind, and his scepticism about human
activity, are very apparent. His other
principal works in verse are the tragedies,
Alaham and *Mustapha*, which Charles
Lamb described as 'political treatises, not
plays'. The following lines from *Mustapha*
present, in essence, Greville's attitude to
life:

Oh wearisome condition of Humanity!
Born under one Law, to another bound:
Vainly begot, and yet forbidden vanity,
Created sick, commanded to be sound.

C. S. Lewis has called these 'four lines of such precision and such sombre melody that nothing can ever be added to them', and has said that the rest of Greville's works 'are little more than an attempt to say the same thing'.   B.B.

Guest, Edgar [Albert] (1881–1959), was an English-born American newspaper poet who achieved very considerable popularity. His poems were widely syndicated in the United States and collected in *Heap o' Livin'* (1916), *Just Folks* (1917) and *Life's Highway* (1933).   D.H.
see also Popular Poetry

Gunn, Thom (1929–), is an English poet who lives in San Francisco, California. His poems are regular in form and ingenious in plot or conceit. He has consistently chosen existential themes concerning will and action. More recently he has experimented with syllabic metres.   D.H.

H

Hall, Donald (1928–), American co-editor of this *Encyclopedia*, has published three books of his poems. He has also written two prose books and had edited several anthologies. He was poetry editor of the *Paris Review* from 1952 to 1961.
                                D.H.

Hamilton, Sir George Rostrevor (1888–), is a traditional lyricist and satirist whose *Collected Poems and Epigrams* appeared in 1958. Uncollected are *John Lord, Satirist* (1934) and *Crazy Gaunt* (1946), and several volumes of criticism, of which *The Tell-Tale Article* is of especial interest.   J.F.

Hardy, Thomas (1840–1928), was born in Dorset, educated by his mother and the schoolmaster until he commanded Greek and Latin, and has started his omnivorous general reading; was apprenticed to an ecclesiastical architect and by 1862 settled in London with a position. But there he was caught up in the intellectual uproar of that decade, when orthodoxy contended with two enemies at once, the Darwinians of local origin, and the Higher Criticism from the Continent. He lost his faith, and soon he was feeling his way, compulsively, into the vocation of letters. He began with verse—which he had practised since childhood—but the poems had no takers; he therefore turned to fiction, where success came quickly. The period of fiction lasted thirty years. Then he returned to verse and had another busy thirty-year period, which finished only with his death.

The *Collected Poems* contains more than eight hundred entries, which is volume enough. But there are other short poems; and there is the huge Napoleonic 'Epic Drama' of *The Dynasts*. All this amounts to a great body of verse.

Yet there is not exactly a consensus of critics affirming its greatness as art. Hardy's plain country matter, and his intellectual ideas, have a Victorian stamp. The novels fell into the right time. But the verse begins exactly where it left off in the eighteen-sixties, and projects itself far into our own century, indifferent to the new poetries which were engaging readers and critics; **Yeats'** poetry, for example, or that of **Pound** and **Eliot**, so exacting of its readers as to need all the critics' help. No, it is the many unprofessional readers, including incipient poets, who think Hardy is indisputably a great poet.

One large body of Hardy's verse enacts his favourite theological speculations into pure images of action; for example, *The Subalterns*:

I

'Poor wanderer', said the leaden sky,
    'I fain would lighten thee,
But there are laws in force on high
    Which say it must not be.'

II

'I would not freeze thee, shorn one', cried
    The North, 'knew I but how
To warm my breath, so slack my stride,
    But I am ruled as thou.'

III

'Tomorrow I attack thee, wight',
    Said Sickness. 'Yet I swear
I bear thy little ark no spite
    But am bid enter there.'

IV

'Come hither, Son', I heard Death say;
    'I did not will a grave
Should end thy pilgrimage today,
    But I too am a slave.'

V

We smiled upon each other then,
    And life to me had less
Of that fell look it wore ere when
    They owned their passiveness.

Surely that is as good today, and will be as good tomorrow, as it was in 1902.

Another example, this time more middling or average. After his wife's death,

Hardy wrote many poems in her honour. Such pieces are decent, as the world knows, but as a rule they arouse no great expectations in the reader. In *A Procession of Dead Days* (1922) the bereaved husband reviews a series of seven crucial days which ushered him into fresh stages of the relationship. But it is the physical morning characters of the days, rather than the intimate personal detail, which distinguish the stages. This is ingenious, and very agreeable. Thus the third day:

Enters the day that brought the kiss:
He brought it in his foggy hand
To where the mumbling river is,
    And the white clematis. . . .
It lent new colour to the land,
And ai the boy within me manned.

And the final day, which requires two stanzas:

In semblance of a face averse
The phantom of the next one comes:
I did not know what better or worse
    Chancings might bless or curse
When his original glossed the thrums
Of ivy, bringing that which numbs.

Yes: trees were turning in their sleep
Upon their windy pillows of grey
When he stole in. Silent his creep
    On the grassed eastern steep. . . .
I shall not soon forget that day,
And what his third hour took away.

Emma Lavinia Hardy had died that frosty morning, 27 November, 1912.

There are hundreds of passages good as these, and a score of poems good as the one first cited, in Hardy's big collection. His devotees fish them up incessantly. They know what they like.   J.C.R.

Hawker, Robert Stephen (1803–75), Vicar of Morwenstow in Cornwall, was a High Churchman and a forceful and eccentric character. His poems mostly draw their inspiration from the life and traditions of his native Cornwall. The best known is the *Song of the Western Men* ('And shall Trelawny die?'), but his striking epic fragment, *The Quest of the Sangraal*, should also be noted.   J.H-S.

Hawthornden, Earl of. *See* Drummond, William.

Hecht, Antony (1923–   ), is an American poet of wit and elegance. He teaches English Literature at Smith College, Northampton, Mass., and frequently reviews for the *Hudson Review*. His first volume, *Summoning of Stones*, appeared in 1954. *The Hard Hours*, new poems, with a selection from the older book, appeared in 1967 and won the Pulitzer Prize.   D.H.

Henley, W[illiam] E[rnest] (1849–1903), English poet and imperialist, is best known for his *Invictus*. His stark free verse is often striking, but is frequently guilty of attitudinising. As editor of the *National Observer*, he published **Kipling**'s *Barrack-Room Ballads*.   D.H.

Henryson, Robert (?1430–?1506), was one of the earliest of the 'Scottish Chaucerians' or 'makars'. With William **Dunbar**, **James I** and Gavin **Douglas**, he is credited with having introduced the themes and styles of European court poetry into Scottish literature. Little is known of his life except that he was a schoolmaster in Dunfermline where he was possibly connected with the cloister school at the Benedictine Abbey. Dunbar mentions Henryson in the *Lament for the Makaris* which was published in 1508, so it seems reasonable to assume that he died in the early fifteen-hundreds.

Henryson's major poems include the *Testament of Cresseid*, *Orpheus and Eurydice*,

a pastoral ballad entitled *Robene and Makyne*, and a book of *Morall Fabillis of Esope* which is considered by H. Henry Wood, Henryson's most recent editor, to be 'the greatest and most original' of his works. The fables are adaptations of popular beast tales—many of them not Aesop's—each one prefaced with a prologue and rounded off with a rhetorical *moralitas*. Their manner is humorous and colloquial. Henryson possessed not only a remarkable eye for detail but a natural sympathy for the animal world, that was rare among medieval poets. In the *Taill of the Uplandis Mous and the Burgess Mous*, for instance, the menu of the elegant town mouse is like that of a rich man 'Except ane thing, thay drank the watter cleir / In steid of wine, bot yit thay maid gude cheir'. *The Wolf, The Fox and the Cager*, the *Taill of Paddock and the Mous*, and the *Preiching of the Swollow* are equally good examples of Henryson's skilful handling of animal characters.

The *Testament of Cresseid* is a sequel to **Chaucer**'s *Troilus*. Cast aside by Diomede, Cresseid curses Venus and Cupid for bringing misfortune upon her. In revenge the gods strike her with leprosy. She dies hideous and deformed, unrecognisable even to Troilus, who rides past the leper house and is reminded by her look of his lost Cresseid:

Than[1] upon him scho[2] kest[3] up baith hir
           Ene[4]
And with ane blenk[5] it come into his
           thocht
That he sumtime hir face befoir had sene.
Bot scho was in sic plye[6] he knew hir
           nocht,
Yit than hir luik into his mynd it brocht
The sweit visage and amorous blenking
Of fair Cresseid sumtyme his awin darling.

[1] *Than*—then [2] *scho*—she [3] *kest*—cast
[4] *Ene*—eyes [5] *blenk*—glance
[6] *sic plye*—such a plight

The *Testament of Cresseid* is a short poem
—only eighty-six Chaucerian stanzas—
but its tragic stature is unmistakable.
Henryson has less pity for his heroine
than Chaucer and his tone tends to be
moralistic. His description is always
accurate; often, as in this passage describing
Cresseid's disease, it is positively grim:

The[1] Cristall Ene minglit with blude I
mak,[2]
Thy voice sa cleir, unpleasand hoir and
hace,[3]
Thy lustie lyre[4] ouirspread with spottis[5]
blak
And lumpis haw appeirand[6] in thy
face . . .

But Henryson was also capable of
lightheartedness, even of frivolity. In
Robene and Makyne, Robene returns,
contrite, to his mistress after having
previously rejected her advances. Very
coyly he is snubbed:

The man that will nocht quhen he may
Sall haif nocht quhen he wald . . .

It is a refrain that reappears in a number
of anonymous Scottish ballads.

One of the most beautiful of his poems
is the lyrical *Annunciation*, in which a
complex and musical metre suggests that
it may have been intended to be sung as a
hymn to the Virgin.

Forcy as deith is likand lufe,
Throuch quhome all bittir sweit is;
No thing is hard, as writ can pruf,
Till him in lufe that letis;
Luf us fra barret betis;
Quhen fra the hevinly sete abufe

In message Gabriell couth muf
And with myld Mary metis
And said, 'God wele the gretis;
In the he will tak rest and rufe,
But hurt of syne of yit reprufe;
In Him sett thi decret is.' . . .

(Forceful as death is gracious love
Through which all bitter things are made
sweet;
Nothing is hard, as writ can prove,
To him who love admits;
Love doth from sorrow shield us;
When from the heavenly seat above
The messenger Gabriel came down
And met with gentle Mary
And said, 'God well doth greet thee;
In thee he will take rest and peace,
And yet reprieve the hurt of sin,
In Him thy purpose is ordained.')

Critics have given Henryson a prominent place in Scottish literature. H.
Henry Wood maintains that he was
'without equal the greatest of the Scots
Makars' although he admits that Dunbar
was a more accomplished technician.
Kurt Wittig, in *The Scottish Tradition in
Literature*, concludes that, 'In his assimilation of European subject matter, of
Chaucer's conception of poetic art, and
of Scottish characteristics, Robert Henryson is one of the greatest poets of the
whole Scottish literature, perhaps the
greatest of all, and certainly the one with
the most marked personality'.   A.S.

Herbert, Edward, Lord Cherbury (1583–
1648), wrote poems which showed the
influence of **Donne,** but his philosophy
foreshadowed eighteenth-century Deism.
Probably one would hear more of his
agreeable and intelligent poems if it were
not for the superior genius of his younger
brother, George **Herbert.**   D.H.

Herbert, George (1593–1633), came of a
noble family, a branch of that of the Earls

---

[1] *The*—thy   [2] *mak*—see
[3] *hoir and hace*—rough and hoarse
[4] *lyre*—flesh
[5] *spottis*—spots
[6] *lumpis haw appeirand*—livid lumps have
appeared

of Pembroke. His elder brother was the poet and philosopher, Lord **Herbert** of Cherbury. Herbert was educated at Westminster School and Trinity College, Cambridge, in which university he was public orator. He was ordained, and was appointed rector of Bemerton, Wiltshire, in 1630, where he spent the remainder of his life. It must be realised that this choice of the life of a simple country parish priest was most unusual, at this time, in a man of Herbert's social position and connections. He was a man of singular piety and sanctity, and might be termed an all-but-canonised Anglican saint. Herbert's verse, nearly all of it devotional in character, is comprised in *The Temple* (1633). His prose *Remains* (1652) include *A Priest to the Temple*, consisting of practical and spiritual instruction for the country parson.

As a religious poet, Herbert takes a foremost place among the followers of **Donne**. Indeed, there is a sense in which his poetry is more central to the English tradition; for his verse has never lacked readers, while that of Donne was almost forgotten between the seventeenth and the present century. It is true that 'quaint' is the epithet that has most frequently been applied to Herbert's work. But his acrostics, his poems shaped in the form of wings or bells, have many parallels in the poetry of the baroque age—especially in the Latin poetry of the Jesuit writers of the Continent. His imagery—much of it homely in character—is likewise in the seventeenth-century emblematic tradition. Above all, Herbert writes for an audience thoroughly grounded, like himself, in a knowledge of the Bible and the liturgy, and quick to recognise allusions to them.

Herbert was intensely loyal to the ideal of the Church of England as a *via media* between the extremes of Rome and Geneva. But his piety is highly personal and at the same time universal, never sectarian in character. In some poems there are signs of conflict between the vocation he had followed and the temptation of worldly ambition. Thus, in *The Collar*:

> I struck the board, and cry'd, No more;
>   I will abroad.
> What, shall I ever sigh and pine?
> My lines and life are free; free as the
>   road.
> Loose as the Winde, as large as store,
>   Shall I be still in suit?
>
> . . . .
>
> But as I rav'd and grew more fierce
>   and wilde
>   At every word,
> Methought I heard one calling *Childe*;
>   And I replied, *My Lord*.

It is this personal and sincere emotion, combined with Herbert's sure but unobtrusive mastery of lyrical technique and colloquial diction, which lifts his work above any mere quaintness of minor metaphysical conceit, or any merely conventional expression of piety. J.H-S.

Herrick, Robert (1591–1674), poet of the religious generation of **Quarles**, **King**, Wither and **Herbert**, exhibited a temperament and a mastery in little of a very different order. He was born in London, and after a fatherless childhood was trained as a goldsmith, which was his family calling, and may be thought to have had its effect upon the kinds of poem he wrote, mostly brief and curt as ornaments, intricate in pattern, rhythm, rhyme and shape, filed and finished with a scrupulous attention:

> I must confess, mine eye and heart
> Dotes less on Nature, than on Art
>   *Art above Nature*

Instead of completing his apprenticeship, Herrick went to the University of Cambridge, took his degree in 1617; and in 1627, in some respects a most unlikely cleric, was ordained, receiving in 1629 the remote crown living of Dean Prior, in South Devon, on the fringes of Dartmoor.

Herrick both hated and execrated the circumstances of his country life, though he admitted retrospectively (*Discontents in Devon*) that he never wrote better than where he 'loath'd so much'. He was able to contrive, at any rate, his fastidious goldsmith's poetry out of a diversity of elements, pastoral high jinks and sentiment and metropolitan sophistication; the attraction of the 'maid' or 'virgin' (two favourite words), of the young unmarried, about to be married, or just married girl, and his own apparent impotence or disinclination (he never married); a playfulness, which would have been more frequently arch and distasteful in a less healthy age of poetry, and a professional self-certainty derived from Ben **Jonson**, his master and friend, who had been his senior by nineteen years; an extreme hedonistic openness to momentary sensation, and a mingled deference to Anacreon (see *The Vision*, and *The Apparition of his Mistress, Calling him to Elizium*) and to Horatian grace, measure and properties.

No one must expect from Herrick's celebrated love poems more than a love of exterior grace—

> Fain would I kiss my Julia's dainty leg,
> Which is as white and hairless as an egg
> *Her Legs*

which is about as far and as deep as his nature goes. Herrick is frank about himself: he is 'sieve-like', holding neither hot nor cold (*Upon Himself*), 'wisely wanton' (*To All Young Men that Love*).

'Wantons we are: and though our words be such', he says in a two-lined poem about poets, 'Our lives do differ from our lines by much', and another poem he begins with this immediate confession:

> I could never love indeed;
> Never see mine own heart bleed:
> Never crucify my life;
> Or for widow, maid or wife.

His amorous situations in poems about Electra or Julia are dreams, or what might be, *if*. They are not what has been; and one is reminded at times of the earlier love protestations of Ronsard, already prematurely deaf, yellow, grey and old, brilliantly celebrating a tradition rather than an experience of love; and celebrating with more fervour of a genuine experience the forest of Gastines, the products of the Vendômois, and the meadows and caves of the Loir. Against his distaste for Devonshire (and against the unreality of some of his pastoral trifles and frills) Herrick set poems of such admirable truth as *A Thanksgiving to God, for His House and His Grange*; against his frivolities, such sober yet lightly moving poems as *The White Island* and *His Litany, to the Holy Spirit*. His unpleasing epigrams are not so much 'nasty' as the expression of an incomplete man's disgust at nature unquickened by art (see *Neglect*), or rough and raw fact contradicting grace. Death also distressed him and haunted him—'Pass all we must the fatal ferry'. But temperament and consciousness of his art prevented a defeat, and Herrick has never been better summarised than by himself in *A Psalm or Hymn to the Graces*:

> Honour be to the Graces!
> Who do with sweet embraces,
> Show they are well contented
> With what I have invented.

In 1647 he was ejected from Dean Prior, though he returned there after the Restoration, and died in his vicarage in 1674. In 1648, in London, he collected and published nearly all his verse in the one volume *Hesperides* (with *Noble Numbers*), after meticulous revisions and after arranging or composing the volume, poem against poem, with an extraordinary care for variation of shape, kind and movement.   G.G.

Hill, Geoffrey (1932–), is a lecturer in the Department of English Literature at Leeds University. His poems achieve a formal perfection unparalleled by his contemporaries. The exactness of his epithets and the precision of his rhythms make a poetry of hard surfaces which reveal profound sources. His *For the Unfallen* (1959) earned him the Gregory Award for 1960.   B.D.

Hillyer, Robert (1895–1961), was an American poet of considerable technical skill within conventional forms. His *First Principles of Verse* (1938) is a manual of this skill. A winner of the Pulitzer Prize for Poetry, Hillyer wrote consistently but without obvious development.   D.H.

Hodgson, Ralph (1871–1962), was an English poet who lived for many years in Ohio. His often anthologised *Bull, Eve, The Bells of Heaven, Time You Old Gypsy Man* have been called Franciscan in feeling and Pre-Raphaelite in tone and colour.   D.H.

Hood, Thomas (1799–1845), was born in London and was the editor of various periodicals, including the *London Magazine*, the *Gem* and the *New Monthly Magazine*, as well as being a poet. His more serious poems, *The Song of the Shirt* (1843) and *The Bridge of Sighs* (1844) overshadow

the more sprightly *Odes and Addresses to Great People* (1884).   D.H.

Hopkins, Gerard Manley (1844–89), was born at Stratford, Essex, and educated at Highgate School, where he won the Poetry Prize with *The Escorial* and wrote his Keatsian *A Vision of the Mermaids*. As an Exhibitioner at Balliol College, Oxford, he was influenced by the Oxford Movement and in 1866 became a Roman Catholic. The following year he took a First in Classics and Philosophy.

Besides being a skilled draughtsman and verse-writer in the Pre-Raphaelite manner, he kept diaries and journals in which he recorded his experiments with words and his sensitive observation of that 'individually-distinctive beauty' in nature which he called 'inscape'. In 1868 he felt the call of the priesthood and became a Jesuit, at the same time renouncing the writing of poetry 'as not belonging to my profession'. Seven years later his rector encouraged him to write *The Wreck of the Deutschland*, a long ode in which his new 'sprung rhythm' and most of the other features of his profoundly individual mature style were firmly established. Its many notation-marks and other 'oddities' precluded publication; but although Hopkins remained unpublished in his lifetime, and was appreciated only by two friends— Robert **Bridges** (who preserved his manuscripts) and R. W. Dixon—he continued to produce significant work: magnificent paeans of joy and faith like *The Starlight Night, Hurrahing in Harvest, God's Grandeur* and *That Nature is a Heraclitean Fire*, and such poignant laments for the passing of 'mortal beauty' as *The Leaden Echo and the Golden Echo, Spring and Fall*, and *Felix Randal*. He was stimulated by a long correspondence with the above-mentioned friends and with Coventry **Patmore,** and his letters on poetry and poetics show his remarkable critical acuity.

Between 1877 and 1884 he served as parish priest, missioner, and teacher of classics in various English and Scottish cities and Jesuit colleges, and in the latter year was appointed Professor of Greek at University College, Dublin, where he died of typhoid in 1889.

Bridges deferred the publication of Hopkins' collected poems until 1918, when the revival of **Donne,** the 'loosening of rhythm' and the emergence of a new classicism had created the taste for a 'modern' Victorian whose intellectual concentration, emotional intensity and densely textured style was destined to exert a major influence on English and American poetry. In Hopkins it was the complete absence of verbal flabbiness, or, as David Daiches expressed it, 'the clear signs of words having been bent to their master's will, with no dependence on the general "aura" of poetic feeling' that 'attracted the new poets to him after 1918; here was that unified sensibility, that fusion of thought and emotion, which **Eliot** had found in the metaphysicals'.

As Hopkins' poetic vision is based (like **Herbert**'s and **Vaughan**'s) on his perception of God in Nature and Man, so his original style derives from his quasi-mystical concept of 'instress' and 'inscape'. His aim was to fuse in words the unique individual nature of the thing contemplated and his own immediate and unique perception of it ('the instress of the inscape'): 'instress is not only the unifying force *in* the object; it connotes also that impulse from the inscape which acts on the senses and, through them, actualises the inscape in the mind of the "perceiver" ':

It is the forgèd feature finds me; it is
the rehearsal

Of own, of abrupt self there, so thrusts
on, so throngs the ear.
'Henry Purcell', *Poems,* No. 45

Sprung rhythm is a flexible stress-rhythm using feet varying from one isolated stressed syllable to 'paeonic feet' of four syllables (´ x x x) or, for special effects, feet containing even more unstressed syllables, or the extra-metrical 'outriders' (x x, or x x x). This modification of Old English accentual verse was combined with a boldly elliptical or 'manipulated' syntax, an abundance of new compound words, and a rich phonal pattern of alliteration, assonance, internal rhyme and vowel-gradations, the total complex of style being organic, not ornamental—strictly functional in bringing out the 'inscape'. For instance, the first four words of *The Wreck of the Deutschland* fix precisely that aspect of God with which Hopkins is immediately concerned:

Thou mastering me
God! Giver of breath and bread
World's strand, sway of the sea;
Lord of living and dead;

Thou has bound bones and veins in me,
fastened me flesh,
And after it almost unmade, what with
dread,
Thy doing: and dost thou touch me
afresh?
Over again I feel thy finger and find
thee.
Poems, No. 28

Hopkins claimed that the 'oddities' in his poetry disappeared and that everything 'came right' when his verse was read aloud. This is generally true: a good reading convinces one of his almost overpowering lyrical and dramatic directness. Initial obscurity is usually due to deep or subtle but never to muddled thought. One has to look twice to see that in 'I steady as a water in a well, to a poise, to a pane' the function of *steady* is both verbal *and* adjectival, and admittedly his syntactical transpositions and violent ellipses are sometimes clumsy; but for the unbiased, intelligent reader Hopkins' meaning (as the poet himself said) will eventually 'explode'. His masterly imagery is usually clear and precise; but he sometimes employs overtones and deliberate ambiguities with astonishing effect, as in:

The Windhover
To Christ our Lord

I caught this morning morning's minion,
kingdom of daylight's dauphin,
dapple-dawn-drawn
Falcon, in his riding
Of the rolling level underneath
him steady air, and striding
High there, how he rung upon the rein
of a wimpling wing
In his ecstasy! then off, off forth on
swing,
As a skate's heel sweeps smooth on a
bow-bend: the hurl and gliding
Rebuffed the big wind. My heart in
hiding
Stirred for a bird,—the achieve, the
mastery of the thing!
Brute beauty and valour and act, oh,
air, pride, plume, here
Buckle! AND the fire that breaks
from thee then, a billion
Times told lovelier, more dangerous,
O my chevalier!
No wonder of it: sheer plod makes
plough down sillion
Shine, and blue-bleak embers, ah my
dear,
Fall, gall themselves, and gash
gold-vermilion.
Poems, No. 36

In line 1 *caught* means both 'caught in the act' and 'caught the inscape of'. The adjectival accumulation before *air* (l.3) inscapes the qualities, attributes, of the buoyant wind, while in 'High there' we hear a shout, 'Hi there!' The expression 'to ring on the rein' is from the *manège*, so that 'rung upon the rein of a wimpling wing' (l.4) suggests both a ringing flutter and also the bird's pivoting on the tip of a delicately pleated and curved wing.

The dynamic nature-poetry of the octave overflows into the symbolism of the sestet, which is addressed not so directly to the falcon as to Christ, as the subtitle indicates and, by collateral implication, to the poet's own heart: the bird becomes the symbol of Christ the King. But the Christ-hero was also a humble labourer in the field and a martyr; his earthly mission was doomed to succeed by failure. And the poet-priest himself (so sensual in his enjoyment of natural beauty) has a heart 'in hiding' which must imitate Christ—*his* 'chevalier'. Thus the keyword, the imperative 'Buckle!' explodes like a firework into three complementary meanings: (1) 'bring under one discipline';

(2) 'engage the enemy'; (3) 'bend, collapse under stress'. Physical prowess ('mortal beauty') is fine; but spiritual prowess ('immortal beauty') is a million times lovelier—and more dangerous: it is the beauty of sacrifice.

Many of Hopkins' later poems record, in astringent, concentrated language, his own sacrifice—spiritual desolations arising partly from ill-health and partly from psychological frustrations due to the very intensity of his self-dedication to the religious life. He reproached himself for a certain lack of success, as both priest and writer:

> birds build—but not I build; no, but
> strain,
> Time's eunuch, and not breed one work
> that wakes.
> *Poems*, No. 74

In the following sonnet of 1885 a personal sense of guilt, complicated by a feeling of undeserved separation from God, is 'instressed' with great power: the experience is universalised. We see also how Hopkins has reverted to 'standard rhythm' and a more austere Miltonic style:

> I wake and feel the fell of dark, not
> day.
> What hours, O what black hoürs we
> have spent
> This night! what sights you, heart, saw;
> ways you went!

> And more must, in yet longer light's
> delay.
> With witness I speak this. But where
> I say
> Hours I mean years, mean life. And my
> lament
> Is cries countless, cries like dead letters
> sent
> To dearest him that lives alas! away.

> I am gall, I am heartburn. God's
> most deep decree
> Bitter would have me taste: my taste
> was me;
> Bones built in me, flesh filled, blood
> brimmed the curse.
> Selfyeast of spirit, a dull dough sours.
> I see
> The lost are like this, and their scourge
> to be
> As I am mine, their sweating selves;
> but worse.
> *Poems*, No. 67
> W.H.G.

Housman, A[lfred] E[dward] (1859–1936), a brilliant classical scholar, and for many years Professor of Latin at Cambridge, published two slim volumes of poetry, *A Shropshire Lad* (1896) and *Last Poems* (1922), and in 1934 had privately printed at University College, London, *Three Poems*, consisting of *The Parallelogram*, The *Amphisbaena* and *The Crocodile*. In 1936, his brother Laurence edited *More Poems*.

His public poems are all short, composed with remarkable economy of words, and skilled metrical simplicity. The subjects he dealt with are the common universal ones, love, death, the brevity of life, disillusion, with occasionally a deep appreciation of, not so much the details of nature, as of its general sense. The poem *Bredon Hill* is well known:

> In summertime on Bredon
> The bells they sound so clear;
> Round both the shires they ring them
> In steeples far and near,
> A happy noise to hear.

> Here of a Sunday morning
> My love and I would lie,
> And see the coloured counties,
> And hear the larks so high
> About us in the sky.

On Wenlock Edge is equally famous.

His harping upon early death, of young lovers or soldiers, makes him easy enough to parody, but the starkness of his verse makes what he has to say extraordinarily poignant. In the poem *Eight O'Clock*, the man condemned to be hanged hears the steeple 'Sprinkle the quarters on the morning town': and then, with all the force behind the sound of the words, and an enhancing alliteration, he goes on:

Strapped, noosed, nighing his hour,
He stood and counted them, and
cursed his luck;
And then the clock collected in the
tower
Its strength, and struck.

There is always more behind the poems than the obvious meaning. 'Poetry is not the thing said but a way of saying it' he laid down in his Leslie Stephen Lecture, *The Name and Nature of Poetry* (1933). The poem *When first my way to fair I took* expresses all mankind's baffled aspirations, and the harshness of actuality, ending:

To think that two and two are four
And neither five nor three
The heart of man has long been sore
And long 'tis like to be.

His philosophy is stoical; several of his poems advocate the escape by the open door, namely suicide, if the dignity and value of life are wanting. Life has its glamour, with its 'drunkenness' of love or battling,

But men at whiles are sober
And think by fits and starts,
And if they think they fasten
Their hands upon their hearts.

In some sense he might be regarded as a chastened and epigrammatic **Keats**.   B.D.

Howard, Henry. *See* Surrey, Earl of.

Hughes, Ted (1930–), was born in Yorkshire and attended Cambridge University. His first book, *The Hawk in the Rain* (1957), already revealed his originality in word-choice and phrasing. 'What excites my imagination', he has written, 'is the war between vitality and death'. In *Lupercal* (1960) the reader feels all the impact of a really original poet, the animal pieces being so phrased as to cover a large part of human emotions.   B.D.

Hunt, [James Henry] Leigh (1784–1859), poet, playwright, critic, and author of the ubiquitous *Jenny kissed me* and *Abou Ben Adhem*, is now chiefly remembered for his many friendships, particularly those with **Byron, Keats** and **Shelley**—and for having early recognised, and first published in his *Examiner*, apprentice work by Shelley and Keats.   W.L.S.

Hymns, Songs and Carols. The English song has its real beginnings in the music of the lutenist composers of the sixteenth century, in the tradition of which **Shakespeare**, Ben **Jonson**, and **Beaumont** and **Fletcher** shaped the lyrics interpolated into their plays. The Restoration playwrights (Congreve and **Dryden**) continued this Elizabethan practice, but, after the eighteenth-century ballad-operas (such as **Gay**'s *Beggar's Opera*), song largely disappeared from English drama, though there is wit in the lyrics of the **Gilbert** and Sullivan operettas, while the music-hall songs of the same time have a vitality and rough humour which, later on, appealed to W. H. **Auden**.

The Elizabethan composers also excelled in liturgical music, thus encouraging poets like **Donne** and George **Herbert** to write anthems for performance in church. About the same time, also, congregational singing was introduced in the form of versification of the psalms into the metres of popular ballads and carols. Isaac **Watts** was one of the first writers of hymns to break away from purely biblical paraphrase, and his work has the breadth of imagery and the imaginative scope of a true poet. Charles Wesley, though less of a poet, handled a wider variety of subjects and metres with skill and verse and, sometimes, with real verbal felicity, while among the many other hymn-writers thrown up by the Evangelical Revival were William **Cowper**, John Newton, Philip Doddridge and James Montgomery. The Oxford Movement in the Church of England brought forward a number of hymn-writers of the second rank, such as J. M. Neale and Frederick Faber, but as the century advanced the art of hymn-writing declined into sentimentalism and doctrinal vagueness. Until recent times, however, hymn-singing remained an important part of English life, and, for good or bad, the hymn has had much influence on popular taste in verse.   N.N.

I

Imagery. Since every use of language is radically mimetic we can scarcely even say what imagery is not; the modes of statement with which we offer to contrast it themselves dissolve, on inspection, into gestures fully as imagistic as any image, and 'images' on the other hand resolve themselves into names: things named, qualities named, actions named. They are not, certainly, pictures; they are constructions made with words; any visual experiences that attend a poem the reader supplies, doubtless prompted by the words, but never obliged.

Yet it seems helpful to single out as 'images' certain intensities of detail; and to note that whereas the vividness of Homer's loud-roaring sea ($\pi o\lambda\acute{v}\phi\lambda o\iota\sigma\beta o\varsigma$ $\theta\acute{a}\lambda\alpha\sigma\sigma\alpha$) or Virgil's beneficent moon (*astrorum decus et nemorum Latonia custos*) is inextricable from particular words, their sound and the sensation of pronouncing them, by contrast other sorts of vividness will pass without disastrous loss into a wholly new set of words; the Shield of Achilles preserves its meaning in English, or the account of missiles coming down like falling snow. What will separate in this way from the language in which it was conceived we call imagery, not necessarily because there is anything to look at, or even think we are looking at, but by analogy with the fact that it is vision, not hearing, that specialises in distinguishing thing from thing or object from ground.

What is true of a particular language is also true of a particular system of ideas. 'Cherubim' participate in the abstractness of a theological system, but **Shakespeare**'s 'young-eye'd Cherubim' are, by a single stroke of the imaging faculty, not conventions referred to but realities named.

We are in the presence of an image when we are convinced that the words name some actual thing, and once we call it *what the words actually name*, dropping the pretence that it is an elaborate way of meaning something else, we can examine imagery with some confidence.

He clasps the crag with crooked hands

There is nothing to be said about this, except that the words mean what they say and that it is precisely our belief in these words, and in the poem's other words ('he stands' . . . 'he watches' . . . 'like a thunderbolt he falls') that allows the poem to work at all; for the words on their own terms seem to cohere, seem to posit a savage human lordliness, until that last strange statement, when a specifically human clasping, standing and watching is bafflingly compounded by a reckless but directed downfall. But there is no need to be puzzled, for at the top of the poem is written, 'The Eagle'. The poem, in fact, is like a riddle, with the solution given first. We may note that the Anglo-Saxons had both their riddles and their kennings, and question whether the puzzle element is ever wholly absent from imagery, which thrives, therefore, partly on unlikeness. Certainly the Renaissance explications of a stock comparison:

An endless wind doth tear the sail
                                              apace
Of forcèd sighs and trusty fearfulness;
A rain of tears, a cloud of dark disdain
Hath done the wearied cords great
                                              hinderance

read like ingenious answers to such questions as, Why is My State like that of a Ship in Perilous Storm Tossed on the Sea? And **Donne**, in the most famous of all 'metaphysical' images, cannot be absolved of providing not a Dantean focus of contemplation, but three ingenious answers to the problem, Why are Two Lovers like a Pair of Compasses? He is merely ingenious; he shifts the ground twice, noting, firstly, that the centre does not turn, secondly, that if you close the compasses the spraddled legs grow upright,

and thirdly, that the moving foot, when you are drawing a circle, ends where it began (though not, he avoids pointing out, where the stationary foot is). It would be meretricious were it not for the dramatic situation; the lady is on the verge of tears, and he is talking rapidly to get her attention on to something else. He offers us no such stable and self-sustaining mystery as the three rings in the last canto of the *Paradiso*, but rather the witty counterfeit of such a mystery.

Imagery that stays, that survived in memory our experience of the poem, untrammelled, accreting meaning—

Turning and turning in the widening
                                              gyre
The falcon cannot hear the falconer . . .

—this is something to distinguish from Donne's compass, since its relevance is independent of explication. So is the relevance of **Shelley**'s skylark, from which, in memory, the poem (which is like an extended explication) tends to drop away, leaving behind the self-sufficient image of aspiring creativity. Such an image may become a piece of the poet's terminology; Shelley uses his skylark as terminology when, in a different poem, he causes Adonais to 'outsoar the shadow of our night', expecting us to supply the unstated bird and intuit the earth's huge shadow, cast aloft just after sunset, but not yet high enough to touch the realm to which the bird has soared. Then 'envy and calumny and hate and pain', not being high fliers, circle in the thickening dusk below, and that dusk, being the world's shadow is 'the world's slow stain', from whose 'contagion' the soul of Adonais is secure because, not being an ornithologist's skylark but a poet's, it has mounted into remote space where the sun is never eclipsed. To say that it is not an ornithologist's skylark is to say that Shelley is not really willing to accept the limitations of his images; having administered their charge of suggestion, they are withdrawn. They are not, for that matter, even explicitly named; countless readers have thrilled to the stanza in question without noticing its structure of imagery at all.

And Shakespeare of course, from whom Shelley drew so much encouragement, regularly extends the resources of what we can see on his stage, not only by descriptive set-pieces ('The barge she sat in . . .') and explicit evocations—

> Let Rome in Tiber melt, and the wide
> > arch
> Of the rang'd empire fall

but by currents of language which, stating no specific image, awaken the sensibility's obscure musculature with the feel and touch of unnamed things:

> > All our service
> At every point twice done, and then
> > done double,
> Were poor and single business to
> > contend
> Against those honours deep and broad
> > wherewith
> Your Majesty loads our house.

Here, as F. R. Leavis has noted, the resisting force implied by 'contend', the half-sensual specifications of 'deep and broad', evoke a resistless current flowing from the King, the fount of honour. No one hearing the play will think clearly of water, but everyone senses a more than abstract embodying of meaning. Every use of language, we began by saying, is radically mimetic; Shakespearean unstated imagery lies, in its nervous force, close to the hidden springs of mimetic power.

Such language, very telling from a stage, involves the hearer at levels below

rational decipherment, a fact not abrogated by later rational scrutiny. **Keats** learned the way of such strange palpabilities:

> To bend with apples the moss'd
> > cottage-trees . . .
> To swell the gourd, and plump the
> > hazel-shells
> With a sweet kernel;

and learned to withdraw them into reportage:

> And full-grown lambs now bleat from
> > hilly bourn;
> Hedge-crickets sing;

managing, so, a diminuendo as the power of Autumn withdraws, and the power of the poem correspondingly recedes from mimesis to statement.

It is an important general truth that a very large proportion of English poetry works with imagery whose tug is only half explicit, or half explicable:

> Dust as we are, the immortal spirit
> > grows
> Like harmony in music;

The first line extends its equable iambics between two strong monosyllables, 'Dust' and 'grows', with 'the immortal spirit' as pulsating counterpoint to 'dust'. 'Dust as we are': dust, posited; 'as we are', three dwindling words, concessive; after these, the firm movement mounts. So cunning is this rhetoric of emphasis that we apprehend neither 'dust' nor 'spirit' in a Donne's explicit and defining way, and are willing to accept, and savour as contributing to the pervasive gravity, the strange simile **Wordsworth** provides for the spirit's growth: 'like harmony in music'. Everything depends on keeping 'grows' from too explicit a vegetable denotation; though the spirit grows like a plant from the dust, its growth remains the growth of an impalpability, not like a plant but like harmony, something the intellect apprehends without isolating it, something inherent in relations as definite as Euclid's between experiences as elusive as sounds. This verse makes sense by keeping its interrelations below the threshold of explication, so that Wordsworth can seem to descend from the plane of vision to that of commentary ('There is a dark inscrutable workmanship that reconciles discordant elements, makes them cling together in one society') without rupture of essential continuity.

It is clearly impossible to isolate the imagery of such a passage from the finesse of rhythm and diction that interpenetrates it. When T. S. **Eliot** noted that a mere change of 'sung' to 'sang' would ruin a line of **Tennyson**'s, he was pointing to a still subtler tension between image and embodiment:

All day within the dreamy house,
  The doors upon their hinges creak'd;
The blue fly sung in the pane; the mouse
  Behind the mouldering wainscot
                shriek'd,
Or from the crevice peer'd about.

This appears to do more than enumerate significant details; but in its metronomic adjustment of syllable to beat, in its confined measure, in its little morbid accuracies it establishes not merely decay but the precariousness of trance. Of the eighty-four lines of *Mariana*, fifty-six step among details of this order with sleepwalking sureness; the other twenty-eight enact seven times over an unwearingly varied refrain, and the poem's way of preoccupation with things, not merely the things it is preoccupied with, becomes utterly neurasthenic, like technique feeding on itself.

This effect is worth isolating by contrast. **Chaucer**, for instance, is not simply the dedicated technician; he likes to seem cheerfully aware of the sort of occasion on which technical elaboration is expected of him—

The dayes honour, and the heavenes ye,
The nyghtes foo—all this clepe I the
                sonne—

and when he has the sun set,

And white thynges wexen dymme and
                donne,

it pleases him to note that they take on this eerie aspect 'for lak of lyght'. Two stanzas later, therefore, he can set his famous nightingale outside Criseyde's window without committing the poem to tapestried glamour:

A nyghtyngale, upon a cedir grene,
Under the chambre wal ther as she ley,
Ful loude song ayein the moone shene
Peraunter, in his briddes wise, a lay
Of love, that made hire herte fressh and
                gay.

Though the nightingale sings of love, it does so 'in his briddes wise', so that the effect on Criseyde is Criseyde's business, not the bird's, and we have for our part no doubt how far we are to think ourselves committed to a pretty fiction. Chaucer is clearly closer than Tennyson to the classical tradition which distinguishes clearly its narrative from its illustrative material; though his nightingale, unlike a Homeric simile, is part of the narrative, he is clear about where its relation with the heroine's state of mind begins and ends. But Tennyson's Mariana

And ever when the moon was low,
  And the shrill winds were up and
              away,

> In the white curtain, to and fro,
>   She saw the gusty shadow sway.

is scarcely distinct from what she perceives.

To say this is not simply to compare two poems, or two poets, but to mark points in a complex evolutionary story at the latter end of which we find the image growing self-sufficient. It is significant that **Milton**'s epic similes weave in and out of his narrative in a manner quite different from that of Homer's vignettes:

> Nathless he so endur'd, till on the beach
> Of that inflamed sea, he stood and call'd
> His legions, angel forms who lay
>   intrans't
> Thick as autumnall leaves that strow the
>   brooks
> In *Vallombrosa*, where th'*Etrurian* shades
> High overarch't imbowr . . .

Though the formal point of comparison is the density of their compaction, the force of 'autumnall', the dark exotic sound of 'Vallombrosa', the pictorial suggestion of overarch'd shades, all help to determine our sense of the fallen angels; and yet another comparison with scattered sedge, and another with the floating bodies of Egyptians in the Red Sea, are to intervene before we rejoin the Legions with whom we have never really lost touch, and whose aspect Milton has not really described at all.

It is already (1667) perilous even in a formal epic simile to separate imagery from referent. By 1920 it is, notoriously, impossible; T. S. Eliot's Gerontion is not only the speaker of a poem full of imagery, but himself an image, the inclusive consciousness whose specialised inclusiveness is the theme and substance of the poem. The **Imagism** of the decade before *Gerontion* was a campaign for technical hygiene, but not really a revolution affecting the relation of image to meaning.

That relation had been undergoing for some centuries an evolution which Imagism abetted and clarified but did not either define nor, certainly, initiate.

The specifically twentieth-century factor in this evolution has been not any school or movement, but the sudden irruption into English poetry of certain modes and strategies not native to the English sensibility but to the American. American usage, for one thing, is far less conscious of etymology than is English; so that **Johnson**'s 'when a radical idea branches into parallel ramifications . . .' seems a more learned, a less idiomatic achievement to a reader at Harvard than to one at Oxford. The images implied by derivation have thus an air of deliberateness when an American poet employs them, which prevents their seeping osmotically into adjacent effects. On the first page of **Pound**'s *Pisan Cantos* we find:

> What whiteness will you add to this
>   whiteness, what candor?

Here the felicity of 'candor' is not casual but analytically exact. On the same principle, an American poet will be almost satirically conscious of levels of diction; in Pound's *Propertius* and many poems of Marianne **Moore**, the salient reality is a tone, secured by aggressively precise polysyllables. Into a milieu so unambiguously linguistic, images irrupt with a special air of deliberation. Marianne Moore's famous 'imaginary gardens with real toads in them' owes half its éclat to the sudden homely diction in a context arch with half-pedantries:

> . . . nor till the poets among us can be
>   'literalists of
>   the imagination'—above
>   insolence and triviality and can present

for inspection, imaginary gardens with
real toads in them,
  shall we have
it. . . .

The American language, moreover, is less conscious than the English of a continuous tradition of usage and allusion, which can cause the most trivial words to rustle with echoes, 'hung', in William Carlos **Williams**' phrase, 'with pleasing wraiths of former masteries'. The process of allusion is thus more deliberate. It is hard to tell whether the author of *The Cenci* knows his debt to *Othello* or not, but *The Waste Land* has notes. On the other hand, American poets can keep a page surgically free of allusion; and when it is no longer part of the poetic ritual to incorporate things named into a literary tradition, the bare act of naming them becomes almost mystically portentous:

> an old barn
> is peaked there also, fatefully,
> against the sky. And there it is
> and we can't shift it or change
> it or parse it or alter it
> in any way.

This is not only Williams' way of deploying imagery, but unmistakably American in its numinous austerity.

In recent years transatlantic cross-fertilisation has been especially rapid, so than an English poet like Charles Tomlinson has been assisted by the example of Williams, Moore and Pound to make fecund derivations from Wordsworth.

> The quiet deepens. You will not
> persuade
> One leaf of the accomplished, steady,
> darkening
> Chestnut-tower to displace itself
> With more of violence than the air
> supplies

> When, gathering dusk, the pond brims
> evenly
> And we must be content with stillness.

This works by simply enacting the interplay between the alert sensibility and the real; its theme, in fact, is the reality of the real, and the unselfconscious fidelity with which, at best, that reality can be apprehended, enunciated. As always in successful poetry the things named are real on the page: here in Wordsworth's way they are also collected into a landscape, the plausibility of which asserts their extra-literary reality too. Perception remains a mysterious act of homage; so does naming; and if from Wordsworth's time on poets have seemed recurrently to celebrate a mystique of perception, it is because they have thought it relevant in a time of prolonged crisis to devote attention to the central mystery which renders language mimetic, imagery substantial, and poetry possible.   H.K.

Imagism began as a promotional venture and became a real, if limited, concept of poetry. It started in 1912 when Ezra **Pound** sought attention for the poems of Hilda Doolittle and decided that a well-publicised school might effect this. He introduced *Les Imagistes* in an appendix to his *Ripostes* (1912) and saw to it that a number of published references to 'Imagisme' appeared in 1913. These included poems signed 'H. D., Imagiste' and, as interest in the 'school' grew, two articles in *Poetry* (Chicago) that have become its first manifesto. Next he collected contemporary poems he liked and published them in *Des Imagistes* (1914). In this year, however, leadership passed to Amy **Lowell**, who arranged for the publication of three more anthologies, called *Some Imagist Poets*, appearing annually from 1915 until 1917. H. D., Richard Aldington, F. S. Flint and Amy Lowell contributed to all four volumes; John Gould Fletcher and D. H. **Lawrence** to the last three; besides Ezra Pound, other contributors to *Des Imagistes* were William Carlos **Williams**, Ford Madox Ford, Skipwith Cannell, Allen Upward, John Cournos, and James Joyce.

Three manifestos offer a partial statement of Imagist aims. Flint's 'Imagisme' and Pound's 'A Few Don'ts' (*Poetry*, March 1913) define certain objectives and allude to others. According to Flint, Imagism meant directness in presentation, economy in choice of words, and a rhythm based on the musical phrase, articles of belief not radically unconventional. Pound added a description of the Image as 'that which presents an intellectual and emotional complex in an instant of time', and added: 'It is the presentation of such a "complex" instantaneously which gives that sense of sudden liberation; that sense of freedom from time limits and space limits; that sense of sudden growth, which we experience in the greatest works of art.'

Except for the particularity of the concept of the Image, most of these principles are general enough to be summed up as an interest in good, i.e. precise and expressive, writing. Later manifestos were almost as general. The preface to the 1915 *Some Imagist Poets* developed Imagist principles at greater length, restating the importance of concentrated effects and of exactness, identifying Imagism with *vers libre* and with the presentation of an image (here defined as hard, clear particulars rather than vague generalities or the cosmic). This was cautious enough, except that the reference to free verse, together with the example of the anthology poems, tended to involve Imagism in the *vers libre* controversy.

Imagism is best understood by observing Imagist poems:

The apparition of these faces in the
            crowd
Petals on a wet, black bough.
            Ezra Pound

    Whirl up, sea—
    Whirl your pointed pines
    Splash your great pines
    On our rocks,
    Hurls your green over us,
    Cover us with your pools of fir.
            'H.D.'

    She has new leaves
    After her dead flowers,
    Like the little almond tree
    Which the frost hurt.
           Richard Aldington

Grass blades push up between the
            cobblestones
And catch the sun on their flat sides
Shooting it back, gold and emerald
Into the eyes of passers-by.
            Amy Lowell

These suggest what Imagism meant to its poets and to its public. Imagist poems, for example, tended to *be* an image (grass blades, sea waves, faces in a crowd) and therefore focus attention on the image more than the manifestos do. Sometimes the image was developed descriptively as details were added; sometimes metaphorically by juxtaposition with another image (sea waves—pine trees; faces—petals). The poems were Images of the objective world or of the subjective one of feeling and impression. In either case, the school's name had some relevance, and seemed partially to account for Imagist subject-matter and brevity.

The force of Imagist poems was centripetal. They dealt with small things, giving a microscopic view of objects and feelings, a perhaps excessively scrupulous search for the exact and accurate detail. They seemed to reflect an extreme exclusiveness which shut out traditional broad concerns of poetry in favour of a radically limited view. This limitation was presumably related to Pound's preference for the one Image rather than voluminous works, and to Amy Lowell's rejection of the cosmic in favour of solid particulars.

In the poems the rhythms seemed less a major concern than the manifestos indicated. Conventional metrics gave way to more flexible principles, the cadence or the musical phrase, but this was in part because Imagist poems were often too brief to permit establishment of a very definite rhythmic pattern. In any case, the particulars of the image took precedence, though the rhythms often strongly underlined the image (as in the 'H. D.' poem), showing the possibilities of the freer forms.

Though T. E. Hulme had relatively little contact with the Imagists, and his direct influence on the movement needs to be minimised, he is probably responsible for some of its characteristics. Pound half-seriously linked his new school to Hulme by introducing *Les Imagistes* as descendants of a school which Hulme originated in 1909. He appended several of Hulme's poems to *Ripostes*. Hulme's verse thus becomes the first identified as Imagist, and it is strikingly similar to what was to follow in the anthologies.

A touch of cold in the Autumn night—
I walked abroad,
And saw the ruddy moon lean over a
                                        hedge
Like a red-faced farmer.
I did not stop to speak, but nodded,
And round about were the wistful stars
With white faces like town children.

Hulme's amateur metaphysics provide a rationale for modern art that has a bearing on Imagism. He insisted that the modern artist must give up most of his traditional claims to religious vision and that the poet in particular must concentrate instead on expressing the much more limited area of impressions and feelings encountered in everyday experience. As these cannot be conveyed by abstract statement, the poet has to force words to his use; he can do so only by bringing language close to the concrete, the clear, solid image, which alone speaks to us unequivocally and directly.

Hulme's image was analogy, two concrete images yoked to produce a special effect which reduces, deflates, at the same time as it provides a sense of sudden discovery or insight. This concept of the image in terms of a psychological experience equivalent to sudden vision or intuition is like Pound's (and Mallarmé's), though Pound does not owe it to Hulme. Its line is to **Eliot**'s objective correlative, after a brief existence in Pound's Vorticism, and then to the New Criticism's formalist concept of the poem as a single organic reality. Similarly with the irony of the Hulme image; it is found in some of Pound's poems of the Imagist period:

Like a skein of loose silk blown against
                                        a wall
    She walks by the railing of a path in
                            Kensington Gardens,
        And she is dying piece-meal
            of a sort of emotional anaemia.

The irony of this is in the 'image' of the last two lines, as they suddenly change the shape of the first two; but this, like the concept of form inherent in the doctrine of the Image, runs from Hulme to Pound and then to Eliot where it becomes basic to modern poetry, rather than from Hulme to Imagism.

An additional quality associated with Imagism is lent by Imagist translations and imitations of Chinese and Japanese poetry. Like Hulme's influence this element is peripheral but important; and it is more useful in understanding Imagism than a discussion of nineteenth- and twentieth-century French verse, which the Imagists also read and reflected. Pound related the ideogram to the image and the vital, metaphoric character of the Chinese language to his own theories of the Image and the Vortex. He translated Chinese poems, and, with other Imagists, imitated the small, selectively detailed image presented by the Chinese and especially the Japanese *haiku*. This poetry has an aspect of the unspoken that is alien to Imagism, but like Imagism it seeks minor effects through the concrete object.

Imagism so defined influenced succeeding poets only as a phase. It can be seen in Eliot, in Wallace **Stevens**, and in Hart **Crane**; its interest in things persists more significantly in the poems of Marianne **Moore** and William Carlos Williams, neither of whom, however, could be limited by the Imagist label. It has seemed to a number of poets a phase necessary in their development as craftsmen. In the history of twentieth-century poetry in English, it is also a phase, a minor but illuminating aspect of transition. Its closest parallels are with Impressionism (and perhaps with Realism) in the nineteenth century, but also, though less obviously, with the symbolism and post-Impressionism of the twentieth. Imagism confined the poet to things, surfaces, even to effects of light and shadow or to using things to express the severely limited materials of the impression made by the outer world. It also concentrated on form and the formal resources of language, and prepared English and American poetry for a concept of form that was to produce more radical and ambitious innovations.   s.k.c.

see also American Poetry

Indian Poetry in English. It may seem surprising that Indians, who have always had a firm poetic tradition in their own languages, should ever have tried to write verse in English. That they did so, was an outcome of the anglomania which seized some upper-class Indians in the early years of British rule. Sons (and sometimes daughters) were sent to England even before they had reached teenage, and there they spent all their formative years. Thus it was that English became the poetic vehicle of a number of gifted Indians, such as Aurobindo Ghose, better known as Sri Aurobindo (1872–1950), his brother Manmohan Ghose (1869–1924), Toru Dutt (1856–77), and Sarojini Naidu (1879–1949). Considerably before their time Madhusudan Datta had published *The Captive Ladie* (1849); but this was followed by poems and plays in his native Bengali, and the merit of these latter was so palpable that his English poems were snuffed out and Madhusudan was soon recognised as the founder of modern Indian poetry. This example, and the later and spectacular success of the Bengali writings of Rabindranath Tagore (1861–1941), have not deterred some Indians in each succeeding generation from trying their hand at English. In the early years of the present century English verse broke out in the nationalist camp itself, and also in Sri Aurobindo's hermitage at Pondicherry. Some of these writers, such as Harindranath Chattopadhyaya (1898–   ), the patriot, and Dilip Kumar Roy (1897–   ), the yogi, ran English and an Indian language together; others remained loyal to English while writing about Hindu mysticism or India's political aspirations.

There are still a few Indians (both parents natives) who claim English to be their 'best' language. What circumstances led to this inconceivable loss of a mother-tongue, or whether they had abjured it voluntarily, cannot be ascertained; but this section has in the present day produced a new group who are assiduously courting the Muse of Albion. A representative figure is P. Lal (1930–), who runs a Poetry Workshop in Calcutta and serves as publisher and publicist for what is now termed 'Indo-Anglian' poetry. The 'Indo-Anglians' differ in one important respect from the nineteenth-century pioneers; the latter's ambition was to become *English* poets in every sense of the word (for example, Manmohan Ghose's poem *April*, where the flowers of an English spring are mentioned in their order of appearance with a rather pathetic precision), and the former insist they are Indians writing in English. To the question, 'Why in English?' they give various answers, one of them being that English in an Indian language—which it is not— another being that English entitles them to a larger audience. According to the second argument, Dante should have written in Latin, and Pushkin in French; what would have happened if they had done so, is, however, indicated by the fate of **Milton**'s Latin, and Madhusudan Datta's English verse. The fact is that the 'Indo-Anglians' do not have a real public in India, where literature is defined in terms of the different native languages, and their claim can be justified only by appreciation in England or the United States. Here it must be noted that poetry translated into English from the modern Indian languages does not constitute English poetry written by Indians; hence it is a mistake to include Tagore, or the later Indian poets who have appeared in English versions, in 'Indo-Anglian' anthologies, as some editors are prone to do. An exception should also be made of Dom Moraes (1939–), who has become virtually an Englishman.

The best of Indian-English verse belongs to the nineteenth century, when Indians came nearest to 'speaking, thinking and dreaming in English'. In authenticity of diction and feeling Sri Aurobindo far outshines the others, but Toru Dutt's charming pastiche still holds some interest. As for the present-day 'Indo-Anglians', they are earnest and not without talent, but it is difficult to see how they can develop as poets in a language which they have learnt from books and seldom hear spoken in the streets or even in their own homes, and whose two great sources lie beyond the seven seas. A poet must have the right to change and re-create language, and this no foreigner can ever acquire. As late as 1937, **Yeats** reminded Indian writers that 'no man can think or write with music and vigour except in his mother tongue'; to the great majority of Indians this admonition was unnecessary, but the intrepid few who left it unheeded do not yet realise that 'Indo-Anglian' poetry is a blind alley, lined with curio shops, leading nowhere.   B.BO.

J

James I of Scotland (1394–1437), reigned as King of Scotland from 1406 to 1437. He was the author of *The Kingis Quair* (*c.* 1423) in Chaucerian stanzas henceforth called 'rhyme royal' in James' honour. He was possibly the author of *The Ballad of Good Counsel*.   D.H.

Jarrell, Randall (1914–65), who was born and educated in Tennessee, taught in universities and reviewed books for the *Nation*; he flew for the United States in the Second World War. *Selected Poems* (1955) celebrates the victims of our 'dark time' as examples of history and original sin: the airman alone 'in knowledge / Slight, separate, estranged', and the bewildered mother of *2nd Airforce* link fates with characters in myth and *Märchen*. The ideal America of justice and happiness (*For an Emigrant*) is as illusory as personal innocence. Dürer's *The Knight, Death and the Devil* instances our condition: 'the poetry arises out of it, plays upon it with pained intelligence, and falls back. We admire, but we are unrelieved; we miss the great exhilarations of art' (Robert Fitzgerald).

The genesis of one of his best pieces, the title poem of *The Woman in the Washington Zoo* (1960), is examined in *The Sad Heart at the Supermarket* (1962), his second book of essays. The cultural and literary criticism both here and in *Poetry and the Age* (1953) is witty and erudite; his concern and insight were exemplary in contemporary criticism. Jarrell's novel, *Pictures from an Institution* (1954), satirises small college life in America with inside knowledge and humorous malice.   E.N.W.M.

Jeffers, [John] Robinson (1887–1962),

was the son of a theologian and professor of classics. From 1924 until his death he lived in a stone house and tower which he built with his own hands near Carmel in North California. The values for which he stood are summed up in the Preface to *The Double Axe* (1948) as 'what might be called Inhumanism . . . the rejection of human solipsism and recognition of the trans-human magnificence'. The interest and the limitation of Jeffers lies in his explicit condemnation of almost all humane liberal values. He was against the last war: 'all the dogs in the kennel / Killing one dog'; he is against man himself: 'I would rather be a worm in a wild apple than a son of man'; and he looks to a future with 'the people fewer and the hawks more numerous'. His symbols are the hawk and the rock: 'bright power, dark peace; / Fierce consciousness joined with final / Disinterestedness' and these symbols recur through all his poems. His technique (long poems with long lines), his chosen landscape (the enormous mountains and lonely shores of North California) and his reading (Greek tragedy) all seem to strengthen and support his narrowly pessimistic vision. The very weakness of the arguments used in defence of his beliefs throws into relief the intensity and dogged consistency with which they were held. And the basic attitudes, though unchanged from *Tamar* (1924) to *Hungerfield* (1954), were constantly tested against the political events of the times. The German, Japanese and Korean Wars, the concentration camps and the invention of the atomic bomb all seemed to fit in with the disillusioned view of human nature which Jeffers had expounded in his *Selected Poetry* (1938). In fact, Jeffers was like an eighteenth-century Methodist preacher or an Old Testament prophet whose warnings of impending doom were belatedly fulfilled. He is a difficult poet to quote but the conclusion of his poem *The Eye* (*The Double Axe*) perhaps sets out his basic tenets as movingly as any passage in his work:

> Here from this mountain shore, head-
> land beyond stormy headland
> plunging like dolphins through the
>   blue sea-smoke
> Into pale sea—look west at the hill of
>   water: it is half the planet: this
>   dome, this half-globe, this bulging
> Eyeball of water, arched over to Asia,
> Australia and white Antarctica: those
>   are the eyelids that never close: this is
>   the staring unsleeping
> Eye of the earth; and what it watches is
>   not our wars.
>   G.MAC.

Johnson, Lionel [Pigot] (1867–1902), an Irish poet, is best known for *By the Statue of King Charles at Charing Cross* and *Dark Angel*, a stern expression of his Catholic faith. In Ezra **Pound's** *Mauberly*, he is said to have died 'By falling from a high stool in a pub . . .'   D.H.

Johnson, Samuel (1709–84), ponderous though he has appeared to later ages, was a brilliant conversationalist and a remarkably diversified writer-essayist, literary journalist, critic, biographer of poets, minor playwright, major editor of **Shakespeare,** lexicographer, moralising fiction and travelogue writer, as well as poet both in English and in Latin. Born at Lichfield, the son of a bookseller, and schooled at Lichfield and Stourbridge, he was forced by poverty to leave Pembroke College, Oxford, shortly before his father's death in 1731, and the next year took up teaching in school. After marrying in 1735 a merchant's widow twice his age, he abandoned schoolteaching in 1737 and settled in London, where he devoted the rest of his life to writing, often in close collaboration with publishers. He was granted a pension by George III in 1762 and made an honorary Doctor of Law by Trinity College, Dublin, in 1765. He died in London and was buried in Westminster Abbey. His *Life* by James Boswell (1791) has long been the most famous biography in English.

Johnson's poetry is more representative than original. It is of a piece with his poetic theory, which derives its strength and weaknesses from the central academic tradition. Poetry was to delight and instruct the common reader, furnishing him, in words neither low nor technical, rhetorically adorned truths which were 'general' —by which Johnson meant somewhat abstract, somewhat widely applicable, and perhaps somewhat hard to encompass. Johnson took the doctrine of imagination pretty bluntly—he wanted to be able to put his finger on what the poet was imitating. Poetry was not to feign too much, but should be closely enmeshed with the business of life, both the poet's— 'the biographical part of literature is what I love most', he told Boswell—and the reader's, whose ways the poet should 'aim to mend'.

The influence of school and university, in both of which Latin and Greek were taught but English was not, is strong everywhere in Johnson. His first printed work was Latin verse, a translation (1731) of **Pope's** *Messiah*, and his earliest major literary project, soon abandoned, was a history of Latin poetry from Petrarch to Politian (1734). Like his prose essays in the *Rambler* and elsewhere, his poems when not frank paraphrases or imitations of the classics, as his *London: A Poem* (1738) was of Juvenal, were commonly concerned with standard themes from the places or commonplaces or 'topics' (*loci communes*) out of which, since antiquity, schoolboys and writers generally had consciously drawn 'matter' of invention. At the opening of his long poem *The Vanity of Human Wishes* he maps his strategy quite explicitly topic by topic:

> Let observation with extensive view,
> Survey mankind, from *China* to *Peru;*
> Remark each anxious toil, each eager
> strife,
> And watch the busy scenes of crouded
> life;
> Then say how hope and fear, desire and
> hate,
> O'erspread with snares the clouded
> maze of fate.

Dislike of poetry which departs from proper topical treatment shows in his well-known, if qualified aversion to the 'metaphysical' poets as writers who, he explains in his life of **Cowley**, did not 'imitate' anything and who failed to show true wit, 'which is at once natural and new', and which 'though not obvious, is, upon its first production, acknowledged to be just'. In his *Lives of the Poets* (1779–81) he passes critical judgment freely, but circumstantially, with close attention to his poetical texts.

Johnson's early poems, written when he was at Stourbridge and at Oxford, are chiefly lyrical, but he turns to drama and satire, in *Irene* (1737) and *London* (1738), and to criticism in his *Prologue* (1747) for David Garrick's production of Shakespeare's *The Merchant of Venice*. The *Vanity of Human Wishes: The Tenth Satire of Juvenal Imitated* (1749), in scope his greatest poem, fuses classical resignation and Christian faith, but with all the joy of the latter gone, for Johnson's sincere piety is 'sicklied o'er' with a drab rationalism and his own recurrent despondency.

In the last two decades of his life, Johnson's poetry gains in both mellowness had immediacy, the latter showing less

in his sincere lament *On the Death of Dr Robert Levet* than in the high-spirited raillery of *A Short Song of Congratulation*, in ballad form, published posthumously in 1786.

This balladry belongs to Johnson's more relaxed later years. In his major pieces he used the heroic couplet, which he believed Pope had brought near perfection once for all, but the pithy metaphors and precision-tooled epithets which give Johnson's best prose something of the gnomic resonance of Sir Thomas Browne's and make Boswell's records of his conversation so fascinating are not seen at their best in his verses. Despite his adeptness with *le mot juste*, he is shorter-winded than Pope and less varied in his repertory of tones.   w.j.o.
see also Criticism and Poetry *and* Translation

Jones, David (1895–   ), was educated at the Camberwell School of Art and became a painter and draughtsman. He served in the Welch Fusiliers during the First World War, and in *In Parenthesis* wrote of some of the things he 'saw, felt and was part of' between December 1915 and early June 1916. As the publishers said, 'it is the *chanson de geste* of the Cockney and Welsh and the Welsh Cockney in the Great War', which could be described as 'an early epic'. Written in a medium which is neither prose nor verse but certainly achieves poetry, it has echoes of the Bible, of Welsh literature, and the epic. Some of the language might be called pastiche but for the power, and the depth of sympathy. A passage of brilliant description of nature can be followed by the ponderings of a soldier, or the feelings of many, often couched in army slang.

The Anathemata (1952) is a religious poem of larger scope, contemporary yet concerned with prehistory or the founding of London; it is epic and Christian, written in a highly disciplined free verse, in varied idiom. With both poems the notes should be studied.   B.D.

Jonson, Ben (?1572–1637), was born either in 1572 or 1573, possibly a month after the death of his father who may have been a 'reverend preacher'. He was schooled at Westminster under William Camden but was recalled in about 1588 to follow his step-father's trade as brick-layer. He served with the army in Flanders (probably in 1591–2 or 1596) and was working for Henslowe as actor and play-wright by 1597. He was married, perhaps in 1594, to Anne Lewis, and lost a daughter at six months and a son (both commemora-ted in poems) at the age of seven. In 1579 he was imprisoned for his share in **Nashe**'s seditious satire, *The Isle of Dogs*, and again some years later for his part in *Eastward Hoe*, while in 1598 he killed a fellow actor in a duel and only escaped hanging by pleading benefit of clergy. His work as poet, playwright and contriver of masques (often with Inigo Jones) won him wide reputation and high patronage, and culminated in the issue of the Folio *Works* in 1616. After 1616 his work for the theatre witnesses to failing powers and coarsening public taste, but the later poems continue to show an amplitude of 'gifts reserved for age'. In 1630 a quarrel with Inigo Jones temporar-ily lost him court patronage. But in spite of illness and paralysis, harassing criticism and debt, Jonson kept his identity, and his friends, until his death and burial in Westminster Abbey.

The 1616 Folio, which set an important precedent in the history of published drama and won social status for the play-wright, included nine plays, seventeen masques and entertainments, and two collections of poems—*Epigrammes* and *The Forrest*. Apart from *Bartholomew Fair* (1614, but omitted from the first Folio) there is little in the six plays and seventeen masques and entertainments added in the 1640 Folio to strengthen Jonson's claims on our attention, but *Underwoods*, the final collection of poems, carries some of his best work.

Jonson's art at its characteristic best allies popular with courtly qualities, Roman with English and literary with colloquial; the London player and play-wright continue to be present in the occasional poetry, while the plays honour canons of taste and decorum that belong to a highly sophisticated vision of society. Jonson recovers the vigour and the vulgarity of Augustan Rome as well as its refinement and sureness of touch, and as in the best English and Latin 'Augustan' writing, human animality is constrained by those judgments and lucid feelings that depend upon a confident understanding of the social functions of literature. The masterly seduction scene of *Volpone*, for example, not only exhibits command of the multiple relationships between lust and avarice in mercantile Venice (or London), it recalls poetry and drama to the service of instinctive life. Before his celebrated song, *Come my Celia let us prove*, Volpone brags of the part he played once in a comedy 'For entertainment of the great Valois': while Jonson's own art, in Catullan song and Marlovian hyperbole, at once sets 'sensual baits' for the puritan Celia and vindicates the libidinous knave against the rapacious merchant. In *The Alchemist* Jonson's very different insights enable him to effect by rhetoric and plot the strange transformations that the quack science itself tries to bring about—it sublimes and exalts and makes men fit for fellowship (see I, i, 63–79).

Epigrammes is close to the plays in spirit rather than accomplishment. While scarcely 'bold, licentious, full of gall' (as Jonson thought common expectation required), they have often a truculence of address ('Lord, how is Gam'ster chang'd! his haire close cut!') that signals energy rather than urbanity, and the model for manner and substance is most often Martial. *Inviting a friend to supper* is notable for its easy, talking, couplets; there are some astringent anti-commendatory pieces (*To Fine Lady Would-bee, To my Muse*) and many anticipations of success more effacingly won in later poems.

In *The Forrest* and *Underwoods* Jonson speaks, with wider command of moods and forms, for 'Wakefull reason, our affections king'. Here and in the commendatory poems (including the great encomium to **Shakespeare**) classical influences are mediated into the English poetic idiom with a conviction unimaginable fifty years earlier. The conviction springs not only from practice in the theatre and from patient scholarly emulation of classical models (Jonson's translations have been mocked for their pedantry, and the verse of *Catiline* and *Sejanus* is superbly laboured) but also from the kind of confidence Jonson can express in his patrons and in the traditions of the country house (*To Penshurst, To Sir Robert Wroth*). But there are elements other than those to which Jonson is apt to draw attention in his more social poetry and his critical *dicta* (as set out in *Timber*); there is an Orphic and contemplative strain: 'high, and noble matter, such as flies From braines entranc'd, and fill'd with extasies'. There are things to interest

Herbert (*A Hymne to God the Father*) and **Carew** (*A Celebration of Charis* with its exquisite masquerade *Her Triumph*), with pre-echoes of other voices from **Marvell's** to **Pope's**.

Jonson is a highly self-conscious poet, and he is aptly represented by a piece in which his role as a poet redresses his frustrations as a playwright and affirms the qualities of his ageing muse:

> Come leave the loathed Stage,
> And the more loathsome Age,
> Where pride and impudence in faction
> > knit,
> Usurpe the Chaire of wit:
>
> Inditing and arraigning every day,
> > Something they call a Play.
> Let their fastidious vaine
> Commission of the braine,
> Runne on, and rage, sweat, censure, and
> > condemn:
> They were not made for thee, lesse
> > thou for them.
>
> . . . . . .
>
> Leave things so prostitute,
> And take th'Alcaike Lute;
> Or thine owne Horace, or Anacreons
> > Lyre;
> Warme thee by Pindars fire:
> And though thy Nerves be shrunke,
> > and blood be cold,
> Ere years have made thee old,
> Strike that disdainfull heat
> Throughout, to their defeat:
> As curious fooles, and envious of thy
> > straine,
> May blushing sweare, no Palsi's in thy
> > braine.
> > *Ode to Himselfe*
> > J.P.B.

K

Kavanagh, Patrick (1905–67), Irish poet, son of a small County Monaghan farmer. After a period in London, Kavanagh made his home in Dublin in 1939. By then he had published his first book of verse, *Ploughman and other Poems* (1936), and an autobiography, *The Green Fool* (1938). With the publication of his long poem *The Great Hunger* (1942) he entered the front rank of Irish poets writing in English. Many critics consider him the most outstanding since W. B. **Yeats.**

Kavanagh was pre-eminently a chronicler of rural life. Directly or indirectly, his years on the land inspired most of his best work. Ideas of social commitment, however, found no place in his view of poetry. He asserted that 'a poet merely states the position and does not care whether his words change anything or not', although this should not be taken to imply that Kavanagh's attitude towards poetry was materialistic. He saw the role of the poet as akin to that of the seer. Poetry was 'a mystical thing, and a dangerous thing'.

The Great Hunger, despite some weaknesses, is Kavanagh's most sustained and powerful poem. It presents the land as a destroyer of the spirit and the hunger of Maguire, the protagonist, is not for food but for a fuller life. Among the fields which he strives to make fruitful Maguire's spiritual identity withers slowly and agonisingly, as Kavanagh's might have done if he had remained on his Monaghan farm. The poem ends in utter despair and later Kavanagh became critical of it, because he felt it was too tragic to be wholly authentic as a representation of rural life.

He had no reservations about the authenticity of *Tarry Flynn* (1948). This auto-biographical novel develops the theme of the misfit farmer from a humorous angle and is his best prose work. In the portrait of Tarry a fine balance is struck between the embryonic poet and the ineffectual young farmer. To his own community he appears to be a slightly ridiculous figure, but Tarry knows he has come 'through fields that were part of no earthly estate'.

This increased detachment towards his subject-matter had already been made evident in the poems of *A Soul for Sale* (1947). Most of these look back to his life on the land. They offer a sense of actuality which is remarkable, and although they are rich with emotion recollected in tranquillity, the poet's personality remains wholly unobtrusive. Thereafter Kavanagh began to change his style and in the opinion of many the alteration was for the worse, with the personality becoming increasingly the dominating element.

In 1952 he edited *Kavanagh's Weekly*, a polemical periodical written mostly by himself, of which thirteen numbers were produced. Two years later he brought an action for libel, which he lost, against *The Leader*, a long-established weekly. The poems collected in *Come Dance with Kitty Stobling* (1960), after appearing sporadically throughout the 'fifties, confirmed a suspicion aroused by these events that Kavanagh was becoming more concerned with the role of poet than with poetry itself. He was cultivating an attitude of 'not caring', which had been extended to his craft and resulted in a parade of indifference to form, as if the poems could be adequately sustained by the vigour of the personality. Kavanagh's effort to remake the man probably reflected a need to renew his inspiration, but in most respects the process proved detrimental to the work.   R.C.

Keats, John (1795–1821), was born on 31 October, 1795, and after October 1819 was too ill to write any serious poetry; thus the output of this great poet is comprised in a life of twenty-four years. The first child of a livery stableman who had married his master's daughter, he had two brothers, George and Tom, and a sister, Fanny. His father died in 1804, and his mother, who had married again, in 1810. The Keats boys went to school at Enfield, where John entered into a close friendship with the master's son, John Cowden Clarke. In 1810 Keats' guardian, Richard Abbey, apprenticed him to a surgeon at Edmonton, from where he could walk over to see Clarke at Enfield. There one day, probably in 1812, Clarke read him **Spenser**'s *Epithalamion*; Keats borrowed *The Faerie Queene*, and from that time was devoted to poetry. Although it was not till 1817 that he wrote to John Hamilton Reynolds, 'I find I cannot exist without poetry—without eternal Poetry—half the day will not do—the whole of it', it was true from the day he read Spenser. In 1814, from when his earliest poems date, he broke off his connection with the surgeon, but served for some time as a dresser at Guy's and St Thomas' hospitals, and obtained his apothecary's certificate. Some time in the autumn of 1816 Clarke introduced him to Leigh **Hunt** and his circle, where he met Haydon, Hazlitt and **Shelley**. By then he was writing much poetry, and at the end of the year he finally abandoned medicine, having come into possession of some of his patrimony.

Poems was published early in 1817, and Keats began to write *Endymion*, which he did variously in the Isle of Wight, Margate, London, Oxford, and Dorking, where he finished it in November. In the summer the brothers had taken rooms at Hampstead, where Keats met C. W. Dilke and Charles Armitage Brown. During that year Tom Keats developed consumption, and in March 1818 Keats went to Teignmouth to nurse him in place of his brother George, who sailed to America with a young bride. He settled Tom in their Hampstead rooms, and soon after the publication of *Endymion* in May, went for a walking tour in Scotland, but returned overtired in August to nurse his brother, who died early in December. Before then he had fallen deeply in love with Fanny Brawne, which gave rise to more unhappiness.

Nevertheless the twelve months from about 21 September, 1818, to almost the same day in the next year, were the most amazingly productive ones. During that time he wrote the poems contained in the volume *Lamia, Isabella, The Eve of St Agnes and Other Poems*, published in 1820, the other poems consisting of the great odes, and the first *Hyperion*. During that time he wrote his plays, *La Belle Dame Sans Merci* and also the second *Hyperion* but after abandoning that he wrote little else except for the light *The Cap and Bells*. Towards the end of 1819 he fell ill, the nature of his illness revealing itself by a haemorrhage on 3 February, 1820. The Brawnes took him in, but in September, refusing an invitation from Shelley to go to Pisa, he went to Italy with the artist Joseph Severn. They settled in Rome, where Keats died on 23 February, 1821.

Keats achieved his high spiritual state through complete self-abandonment to the sensations of the fugitive moment; and his immense poetic richness not only through his sense of word-music, but also because, as he advised Shelley to do, he loaded every rift of his subject with ore. His almost unbelievably rapid development can be traced not in his poetry alone, but also in his fascinating letters, the reading of which is essential to an understanding of him both as a man and a poet. For him the poetical character has no self, as distinguished from the Wordsworthian 'egotistical sublime'. He takes his being from his surroundings, thus 'what shocks the virtuous philosopher delights the chameleon poet' (to Woodhouse, 27 October, 1818). He had said earlier (to George and Thomas Keats, 22 December, 1817) 'what struck me in a Man of Achievement, especially in Literature, and which **Shakespeare** possessed so enormously—I mean *Negative Capability*, that is, when a man is capable of being in uncertainties, mysteries, doubts, without any irritable reaching after faith and reason' such as haunted **Coleridge**.

In *Poems* (1817) we find the very early Keats growing into the second phase of development, that is, when the 'infant or thoughtless Chamber, in which we remain as long as we do not think', opens into the Chamber of Maiden-Thought where 'we become intoxicated with the light and atmosphere', from which open many doors leading to dark passages (to Reynolds, 3 May, 1818). In the first poem, '*I stood tip-toe upon a little hill*' —originally '*Endymion*'—we get a vision, a tactual sense of nature, of 'the fair paradise of Nature's light': we also read of 'What Psyche felt, and Love, when their full lips / First touch'd'. It is all 'luxury', the deliciousness of soft grass and leaves. We must pass over the bulk of the poems, even the famous *On first looking into Chapman's Homer*, the Epistles, the sonnets to Haydon, and 'To one who has been long in City pent', with its lovely final simile of 'an angel's tear / That falls through the clear ether silently', to stress 'Sleep and Poetry'. Sleep, drowsiness, the receptive state in which the intellect does not interfere with being was always a favourite state with Keats, to which a

score of quotations may bear witness. Most important, perhaps, in this enchantingly sensuous poem of natural beauty and erotic glimpses is the question asked and answered by:

And can I ever bid these joys farewell?
Yes, I must pass them for a nobler life,
Where I may find the agonies, the strife
Of human hearts . . .

We have often heard 'Strange thunders from the potency of song' but

A drainless shower
Of light is poesy; 'tis the supreme of
power;
'Tis might half-slumb'ring on his own
right arm.

Yet the whole theme, and his own programme for the future, are diffidently expressed.

Endymion is a poem which yet can puzzle. It can be read as an erotic poem spoiled by the 'mawkishness' to which he confessed in his all too apologetic Preface, or as a Neo-Platonic allegory of the poet in pursuit of essential beauty. It is both. **Swinburne** complained of its being a 'weedy wilderness'; and at the time Keats' mind was, he told Shelley later, 'like a pack of scattered cards'. It is, here and there both in idea and technique, a little distressing, but these passages are a thousand times compensated for by the magnificences, the imaginative leaps. We need quote only part of the Hymn to Pan:

Be still the unimaginable lodge
For solitary thinkings, such as dodge
Conception to the very bourne of
heaven,
Then leave the naked brain; be still the
leaven
That spreading in this dull and clodded
earth

Gives it a touch ethereal—a new birth:
Be still a symbol of immensity;
A firmament reflected in a sea;
An element filling the space between.

Oddly, given his education, the classical myths seemed to Keats the best vehicle in which to convey his own intuitions.

In his last volume, *Lamia, etc.*, Keats had come to full maturity, not only spiritually but technically. *Lamia*, the tale of a serpent-woman derived from his much thumbed Burton's *Anatomy of Melancholy*, is written in the heroic couplets he had so far imperfectly mastered; but now, from studying **Dryden**, there are no upsetting ineptitudes. It is a splendid if rather horrifying tale from which the most famous passage can be abstracted without damaging the poem, that which begins 'Do not all charms fly / At the mere touch of cold philosophy?' for 'Philospohy will clip an angel's wings'. *Isabella*, from Boccaccio, in *ottava rima*, though accused of morbidity, is almost faultless, while *The Eve of St Agnes*, in the stanza of Spenser, is a wonderful piece of sublimated eroticism, of love escaping from coldness, brutality and death. But what gives this volume its assured immortality is the great odes; *To a Nightingale*, *On a Grecian Urn*, *To Psyche*, *To Autumn*, *On Melancholy*. Here, in Matthew **Arnold**'s famous phrase, 'He is with Shakespeare'. There is no need to comment on them here; they make their immediate appeal to every reader of poetry (though their inner meaning and mystery demand contemplation). Their form, though to some extent suggested by Dryden, is based on the sonnet form, one which itself Keats was always trying to vary. These are the great heights of Keats' genius, but it would be foolish to ignore the lighter poems in four stress, seven-syllable metre that everybody enjoys,

such as '*Ever let the Fancy roam*', written to his sister Fanny; or the '*Lines on the Mermaid Tavern*' addressed to 'Souls of Poets dead and gone'.

But in this volume the publishers included *Hyperion, a Fragment*, a poem in Miltonic blank verse that Keats had abandoned during the summer of 1819 to try to recast it in the form known as *The Fall of Hyperion: A Dream*, which also he gave up in September, since as he wrote to Reynolds (22 September) 'Miltonic verse cannot be written but in an artful, or, rather, artist's humour'. To a man who had said that 'if poetry comes not as naturally as leaves to a tree, it had better not come at all' (to Taylor, 27 February, 1818) the attempt was obviously doomed to failure. Yet it has tremendous things in it. Here Keats came to the full realisation of what he had suggested in the lines quoted from 'Sleep and Poetry', for here he is told that no men can usurp the height of poetry

But those to whom the miseries of the
world
Are misery, and will not let them rest.

'Call the world if you please "The Vale of Soulmaking" ', he had written to George and Georgina Keats in April 1819. He was illustrating it here.

The second *Hyperion*, full of echoes from Dante, is in a sense Keats' greatest poem: it could not succeed. As Middleton Murry said, 'he was trying to utter in the abstract, what can be revealed through the concrete', and Keats was trying to reveal the identity of truth and beauty, which the goddess on the Grecian Urn had declared. In another way too, perhaps, he had attempted the impossible: solitary thinkings can go up to the bourne of heaven, but not beyond; and, as he wrote to Reynolds (25 March, 1818):

It is a flaw
In happiness to see beyond our bourne—
It forces us in summer skies to mourn:
It spoils the singing of the nightingale.

For the imagination becomes 'lost in a sort of Purgatory blind'.

A few days after abandoning the struggle, while walking through the harvesting fields towards Winchester, Keats composed the gloriously serene, and rich, *Ode to Autumn*, as though after the struggles of his muse, and the terrible strains of his emotional life, he had entered the Cave of Quietude described in *Endymion*, the sudden release that comes after stress. Here he returned to Shakespeare, his most influential reading, though still aware of the 'eloping vowels' of Spenser. It can in itself justify the opening line of *Endymion*, 'A thing of beauty is a joy for ever'. He may have ceased to be before his pen had wholly gleaned his teeming brain, but this poem alone would make his fame secure.   B.D.
see also Imagery

King, Henry (1592–1669), was the son of John King, Bishop of London, and was educated at Westminster and Christ Church, Oxford. In 1616, he was appointed Prebendary at St Paul's, and, in 1642, following various preferments, Bishop of Chichester. Ousted by the Parliamentarians, his property sequestered, he led a persecuted and migratory life until restored to his bishopric in 1660. About 1617 he married Anne Berkeley, who died (*c*. 1624) after bearing him six children. Among his close friends were **Jonson**, Walton and **Donne**. He was Donne's executor.

King, like most Royalist poets, was so only by avocation; yet his range is surprisingly broad. Besides the usual love-poems, he wrote epigrams, 'para-

doxes', verse in Latin and Greek, a metrical version of the Psalms, commendatory 'letters' to friends, 'official' poems commemorating events at court, and many elegies, obituary and otherwise.

He was deeply influenced by Donne, 'rich soul of wit' whose 'awful fire' and 'clear brain' he admiringly commends. His other model was Jonson (the exquisite anthology-piece, 'Tell me no more . . .' is pure Jonson); and in his love-lyrics, King is impressively successful in harmonising the two influences. Many of these are expressed in Jonson's limpid verse deepened and enriched by Donne's witty and succinct development of the conceit. Like Donne, he juxtaposes colloquial and learned words with fine surprise. A quite typical example of the resulting style, pervasive in his work, is this fragment from *The Legacy*:

With this last ragge of my mortalitie
Let all my faults and errours buried be.
And as my sear-cloth rots, so may kind fate
Those worst acts of my life incinerate.

His serious poems, among them *The Surrender*, *The Legacy*, and his masterpiece, *The Exequy* upon the death of his young wife, demonstrate how congenial was Donne's method to King's vision and talent. Despite the embroidery of carefully elaborated conceits and the metaphysical reasoning, King's tender, self-sacrificing love, deep personal grief, and sustaining Christian faith shine clear and precise in *The Exequy*. Its music is lovely, and it attains a simple poignancy unmatched by Donne. Six years later in *The Anniversary* King again contemplates his loss, seeing it now as common to everyone:

Yet only he
Is Nature's true-born child who summes
his years

(Like me) with no Arithmetick but tears.
                                          w.l.s.

Kipling, [Joseph] Rudyard (1865–1936), was born in Bombay but was sent to England for his education when five years old. He returned to India at the age of seventeen, and worked as a journalist, publishing stories and poems along with reporting. His reputation spread, and upon his return to England in 1889 he was regarded by some critics as the coming man of literature.

He wrote prose and poetry concurrently, and copiously in both forms. The verse consists of some 550 pieces, which is remarkable. Not less so is the range of themes: ships and machines cheek by jowl with the Bengali Babu, and war and politics with love and nature. The moods are as varied. The famous barrack-room version of the romance in the East:

By the old Moulmein Pagoda, lookin'
                         lazy at the sea,
There's a Burma girl a-settin', and I
                know she thinks o' me;
For the wind is in the palm-trees, and
             the temple bells they say:
'Come you back, you British soldier;
         come you back to Mandalay!'

is no doubt typical Kipling, but so is the airman's defiance to the sun after flying at 1,000 m.p.h.:

We fleet, but thou stayest
   A God unreleased;
And still thou delayest
   Low down in the East—

      .   .   .   .   .   .

Storm on at that portal
   We have thee in prison!
Apollo, immortal,
   Thou has not arisen!

The variety springs from the very nature of Kipling's poetry, which is not 'literary poetry' but poetry in its earlier natural form in which it was the most powerful means of communication between mind and mind. So his poems are off-hand, impetuous commentaries on whatever struck him, and he always called them verse. It follows from this that poetry was Kipling's informal and impromptu expression, standing against his prose, the formal artistic expression.

Its appeal, naturally, is linked with the interest in his subjects and sentiments, much of which has only historical significance. But Kipling could also use current topics to express timeless English feelings, and some of the deepest, and in this he had two manners, one for and from the Englishman at home and the other for the Englishman abroad, especially in the tropics. The following is an example of the subtle and nuanced at-home manner:

England is a cosy little country,
Excepting for the draughts along the
                                     floor
And that is why you're told,
When the passages are cold:
'Darling, you've forgot to shut the Door!'

      .   .   .   .   .   .

Shut—shut—shut the Door, my darling !
Always shut the Door behind you, but
You can go when you are old
Where there isn't any cold—
So there isn't any Door that need be shut!
   And—
The deep Verandah shows it—
The pale Magnolia knows it—
And the bold, white Trumpet-flower
                            blows it:-
There isn't any Door that need be shut!

The manner abroad is rough and stark, as illustrated in the piece on the monkey, among many others:

So I answered:—'Gentle *Bandar*, an
        inscrutable Decree
Makes thee a gleesome fleasome Thou,
        and me a wretched Me.
Go! Depart in peace, my brother, to
        thy home amid the pine;
Yet forget not once a mortal wished to
        change his lot with Thine.'

Still, despite the reversionism of his art and the traditionalism of his moods, Kipling in one respect belongs to the future. He is the first poet of modern technology. As such he brought together old passions and new inventions. The *Recessional*, with its refrain:

Lord God of Hosts, be with us yet,
Lest we forget—lest we forget!

is a fusion of religion with politics; in *McAndrew's Hymn* the fusion is with machinery:

Lord, Thou hast made this world below
        the shadow of a dream,
An', taught by time, I tak' it so—
        excepting always Steam.
From coupler-flange to spindle-guide I
        see Thy Hand, O God—

Predestination in the stride o' yon
        connectin'-rod.

In this contemporary poets have not taken the cue from Kipling, perhaps because modern technology is yet a growing thing and cannot yet create its own romance. But when it is digested poetry is likely to have its chance, and Kipling his followers.   N.C.C.

Kunitz, Stanley (1905–), was awarded the Pulitzer Prize in 1959 for his *Selected Poems 1928–1958*. Earlier volumes include *Intellectual Things* (1930) and *Passport to the War* (1944). He was editor of *Twentieth-Century Authors*. Robert **Lowell** praises Kunitz's 'savage, symbolic drive'.   D.H.

Kyd, Thomas (?1557–95), was one of the university wits of the Elizabethan age. He wrote *The Spanish Tragedy* (1594) which influenced **Shakespeare** and contributed a line to T. S. **Eliot**'s *The Waste Land*. He may have written an Ur-*Hamlet*. His plays were dramatically more sophisticated than those which preceded him.

        D.H.

L

Landor, Walter Savage (1775–1864), having inherited a fortune, spent most of his last fifty years on the Continent, particularly in Italy. He was deeply interested in history; he both studied and wrote of the Greeks, the Romans, and the Renaissance Italians, attempting to re-create the personal emotions and ideals of past heroes. The best known of his

many dialogues involving historical characters is the series called *Imaginary Conversations* (1824, 1853). He also wrote poems in Latin and published five volumes of verse in English. He developed a smooth and varied blank verse, as in *Regeneration* (1824):

We are what suns and winds and waters
        make us;
The mountains are our sponsors, and
        the rills

Fashion and win their nursling with
                                        their smiles.

His poetry frequently deals with natural
phenomena observed minutely. Yet his
Romanticism is graceful and restrained;
in *Absence* (1831), he describes the sun:

How often have we watched him
                                        laying down
    His brow, and dropped our own
Against each other's, and how faint
                                        and short
    And sliding the support!

Landor's verse is often lapidary, and much
of his best known poetry is in the form
of epigram and epitaph, a number of the
latter devoted to himself. One, called
Epitaph at Fiesole (1831), shows both the
sentiment and the contained ease evident
in many of his shorter poems:

Lo! where the four mimosas blend their
                                        shade,
    In calm repose at last is Landor laid;
For ere he slept he saw them planted here
By her his soul had ever held most dear,
And he had lived enough when he had
                                        dried her tear.

One of his most famous poems is *Dirce*,
which is also certainly one of the most
charming epitaphs ever versified:

Stand close around, ye Stygian set,
    With Dirce in one boat convey'd!
Or Charon, seeing, may forget
    That he is old and she a shade.

                                        J.G.

Langland, William (*c.* 1332–1400), is the
name given by a fifteenth-century manuscript tradition to the author of *Piers
Plowman*. The poem itself is a series of
dream-visions; the Dreamer's name is
Will. If what it says of him is autobio-

graphical (and this has been disputed,
though many scholars accept it as partly
so) he was born towards the year 1332
somewhere near Malvern in Herefordshire
and sent to school there. 'Too weak to
work with sickle or with scythe', he took
Minor Orders, migrated to London and
lived in Cornhill with his wife and
daughter, making a precarious living by
singing psalms for the souls of those who
supported him. He lived long enough to
remark in the poem on the loss of his
hair, his teeth and his sexual appetite.

Piers Plowman survives in three forms,
known as the A, B and C Texts. From
historical allusions in them it is clear
that A cannot have been completed
before 1362 and B not before 1377. The
C Text cannot be so precisely dated, but
is later. B is a revision and expansion of A
(three times as long) that enormously
enlarges its scope and visionary power: C
is a rearrangement of B with some additions and omissions. It is on the whole
accepted that all three are the work of
William Langland and this was confirmed
by Professor Kane's book.

The poem is a great catholic vision of
the world and its true spiritual course, in
the midst of the sins, errors and miseries
of the fourteenth century, presented in
the form of a search for the answer to
its prime question 'What shall we do to
be saved?'. In its fuller form (B and C) it
is divided into four great sections: (1) *The
Vision about Piers Plowman*, (2) *The Life
of Do-well*, (3) *The Life of Do-better*, and
(4) *The Life of Do-best*. The first describes
the world as 'a fair field full of folk'
busily engaged in making a living (honestly and not) but ignoring the 'Tower of
Truth' above them (Heaven) and the
'Murky Dale' beneath (Hell). Repentance
preaches them a sermon and they are
moved to undertake a pilgrimage to
seek St Truth:

A thousand of men tho throngen
                      togideris[1]
Wepynge & weylyng for here[2]
                      wykkide dedis[3]
Criede vpward to crist and to his clene
                      modir[4]
To haue grace to seke treuthe: god
                      leue that hy moten![5]

Ignorant of the way to Truth, they take for their leader a simple Christian farmer who claims to know it: he emerges from the crowd and his name is Piers (i.e. Peter) Plowman. He sets them to work, to stave off Hunger, and is rewarded by a Pardon sent from Truth. It baldly states that those who 'do well' shall go into eternal life, those who do ill into eternal fire. The second section investigates the meaning of 'doing well', and this leads on to discussions of doing better and doing best. The third section continues the investigation and shows us Faith, Hope and Charity in the persons of Abraham, Moses and the Good Samaritan, and tells the story of the Incarnation and Crucifixion, and of Christ's descent into Hell to redeem the souls of the righteous that had lain there since the sin of Adam. This, the most splendid passage in the poem, ends with the Easter triumph in Heaven and on earth for Christ's conquest over Death and Hell. Mercy and Truth have met together, Righteousness and Peace have kissed each other: Langland sees these 'Daughters of God' as 'wenches' or 'damsels':

Tyle the daye dawed[6] this[7] damaiseles
                      daunced,

That men rongen to the resurexioun,[8]
                      and right with that I waked,
And called Kitte my wyf and Kalote
                      my doughter
'Ariseth and reuerenceth[9] goddes
                      resurrexioun
And crepeth to the crosse on knees and
                      kisseth it for a Jewel!
For goddes blissed body it bar for owre
                      bote[10]
And it afereth the fende,[11] for such is the
                      myghte
May no grisly gost glyde there it
                      shadweth!'[12]

The fourth section makes clear that Christ, when on earth, lived the lives of Do-well, Do-better and Do-best, and tells of the coming of the Holy Ghost and the founding of the Church. But the Church is overturned by Anti-Christ and the Seven Sins: Conscience and the Dreamer are finally left alone in desolation to seek through the world for Piers Plowman. So ends the poem.

The figure of Piers is enigmatic, but may be bluntly described as Charity in its human dress, the supreme example of which was the Incarnate Christ. The figure weaves its way through the poem, first as a plain plowman, then as the Good Samaritan and Jesus: finally as St Peter, to whom Grace gives the materials from which Piers (Peter) is to build the Church, as a barn for garnering the harvest of souls:

'By god! Grace,' quod Piers, 'ye moten
                      gyue timbre[13]
And ordeyne that hous ar ye hennes
                      wende.'[14]

[1] *tho throngen togideris*—then thronged together
[2] *here*—their [3] *dedis*—deeds
[4] *modir*—mother
[5] *god leue that hy moten!*—God allow that they may!
[6] *dawed*—dawned [7] *this*—these
[8] *rongen to the resurexioun*—rang the bells for Easter
[9] *Ariseth and reuerenceth*—arise and reverence
[10] *bar for owre bote*—bore for our good
[11] *afereth the fende*—puts fear into the fiend
[12] *there it shadweth*—where it casts a shadow
[13] *moten gyue timbre*—must give timber
[14] *ar ye hennes wende*—ere you go hence

And Grace gaue hym the crosse, with
the croune of thornes,
That Cryst vpon Caluarye for mankynd
on pyned[1]
And of his baptesme and blode, that he
bledde on Rode[2]
He made a maner morter, and Mercy it
highte.[3]
And there-with Grace bigan to make a
good foundement[4]
And wattled it and walled it with his
peynes and his passioun,
And of al holy writ he made a rofe[5] after,
And called that hous Vnite, holicherche
on Englisshe.[6]

It is in charity of heart that Langland
sees our salvation: Do-well, Do-better and
Do-best are all ways of charity and
Piers is a figure for each and all of them,
as Christ was, and as St Peter was, and as
a simple plowman can be.

The poem has many moods that range
from Hogarthian realism to Christian
sublimity. To those who know it best it
is the greatest religious poem in our
language. If its moral can be contained
in a single line from it, it is this:

'Lerne to loue', quod Kynde, 'and leaue
alle othre'.

(Learn to love, said Nature, and leave all
else aside.)

It is not known whether Langland
wrote anything else. *Richard the Redeless*,
another alliterative poem of the period,
is no longer considered his, but part of
the alliterative revival centred in the
West of England (roughly, Chester to
Gloucester) between 1350 and 1400. The
alliterative verse-form used by Langland

is a loose development of the somewhat
strict Old English form: the line is divided
medially by a caesura and united by alliterations, which always fall on strong stresses;
but if the fifteenth-century manuscripts
by which the poem has come down to us
represent substantially what Langland
wrote, he was an irregular versifier, as
can be seen from the extracts quoted.
There survive seventeen A, sixteen B and
nineteen C Text manuscripts. There is a
considerable body of political, homilectic
and religious verse, some of it alliterative,
coming to us from the later middle
ages, but no other such poem is in a class
with *Piers Plowman*; the only other
masterpiece in the alliterative style is
Sir Gawayne and the Grene Knight, which,
though it has religious overtones, is
mainly a study in morals and courtesy
in a world of Arthurian romance and
magical adventure.   N.C.
see also Satire

Lanier, Sidney (1842–81), was an American poet, musician, critic and novelist.
He is best known for his musical theory of
prosody, which is contained in *The
Science of English Verse* (1880). A number of
pleasant poems, notably *The Song of the
Chattahoochee*, survive as examples of
multiflorousness considered as an end
in itself.   D.H.

Larkin, Philip (1922–   ), published his
first collection of poems, *The North Ship*,
in 1945, and though it contained many of
his virtues—the lyrical conciseness and the
technical skill, for example, it seemed too
slight to achieve recognition, although
the longest piece, No. 20 (*I see a girl
dragged by the wrists*), is characteristic of
the maturest of his later work. His two
novels, *Jill* (1946) and *A Girl in Winter*
(1947), both concerned with the individual's

[1] *on pyned*—suffered on
[2] *on rode*—on the rood
[3] *maner morter, and Mercy it highte*—a kind of
mortar, and it was called Mercy
[4] *foundement*—foundation   [5] *rofe*—roof
[6] *Vnite, holicherche on Englisshe*—Unity, Holy
Church in English

problem of adjustment to society, enabled him to develop his powers of sensibility and accuracy of language, and seem to have determined the development his poetry has since taken, both in style (the meaningful clarity of diction) and in theme (the poet's isolation). His latest collection, *The Less Deceived* (1955), was widely acclaimed for its sensitivity, its honesty, its perfect ease of meaning and cadence, and the rare ability to pursue an observation to serious conclusions without being obscure. In his most famous poems, Larkin treats the nostalgia of a girl's photograph album, a young wife's maiden name or the value of defunct churches quite without sentimentality. In others, he develops the impact of his short lyric ('Going', for instance, or, in *Listen*, Vol. 2, No. 3, 'Days'). In all these poems there is an extraordinary quiet power due to his refusal to strike any kind of pose: the colloquialism is never pushed too far; his reasonableness never descends to logic-chopping; and he is not afraid of a bold image. All the poetic virtues of the nineteen-fifties seem contained in his work.   J.F.

Lawrence, D[avid] H[erbert] (1885–1930), the son of John Arthur Lawrence, a miner, and Lydia Beardsall, who was socially and intellectually her husband's superior, and the husband of Frieda Lawrence (née von Richtofen), was perhaps the most controversial English novelist of his time. His supreme poetic gifts are perhaps revealed more fully in passages of poetic prose in *The White Peacock*, *The Rainbow*, *Women in Love* and short stories such as *The Fox* and *The Prussian Officer* than in his poems. He wrote a few remarkable poems, in nearly all of which he remains an imperfect artist, though his failures, or his blemished successes, are often more interesting

than the irreproachable achievements of his more correct contemporaries.

The poems he wrote as a young man are extremely interesting as autobiography, being concerned with his passionate involvement with his mother, an early love-affair in which he was desperately attempting to escape from his mother and assert his own manhood. They culminate in the cycle *Look we have come through*, which celebrates triumphantly his love for Frieda Lawrence. In all these poems there is the vivid observation, emotional intensity, and revealing honesty, bursting through restraints of form, which characterise *Love on the Farm*. The following lines show Lawrence at his best in his poetry as painter using words with freedom and power to convey broad sensuous impressions:

> The rabbit presses back her ears,
> Turns back her liquid, anguished eyes
> And crouches low; then with wild spring
> Spurts from the terror of *his* oncoming;
> To be choked back, the wire ring
> Her frantic effort throttling:
>   Piteous brown ball of quivering fears!

It is evident in these lines that Lawrence gave little thought to technique, being content to accept the 'ing' rhymes as they flow from his pen. Technically he was more at ease with *vers libre*, where as so often in English and American poetry, the rhythms of the Authorised Version of the *Old Testament* instilled in him their pattern and metrics which had become almost instinctive.

The often quoted letters of 28 October, 1913 and 19 November, 1913 to Edward Marsh, in which he gives his views on technique, are more effective in their attack on the conventional forms and diction of the Georgian poet than in putting forward any seriously considered views of what he himself was attempting in poetry (e.g. 'I think more of a bird with broad wings flying and lapsing through the air, than anything, when I think of metre'). The Imagists claimed Lawrence as one of their number and, although this meant nothing to him, perhaps they were right in thinking that his greatest strength lay in an imagery which seems alive as the pulsing of a vein.

In *Birds, Beasts and Flowers* (1923), Lawrence wrote a cycle of free verse poems, whose subject-matter is exactly indicated by this title. These delightful poems achieve in free verse the detachment, humour, and affectionate identification of himself with tortoise, snake, humming-bird or flower, which he shows in the best of his travel essays. It is as though, while retaining his brilliance and quickness, he had taken a holiday from the greater intensities of being D. H. Lawrence.

In the last two years of his life Lawrence wrote down rapidly in notebooks a great number of poems, some of which are little more than jottings recording moments of irritation (there are several directed against British censors and policemen, from whom, with the closing of the exhibition of his paintings, and the banning of *Lady Chatterley's Lover*, he suffered a good deal at the time). Many of these doggerel rhymes retain their freshness and sharpness. He also wrote sombre and prophetic sketches of the doom of civilisation, one of the most effective of which is *The Triumph of the Machine*.

He was aware in these years that he was dying, and in a few of these poems he looks as deeply into the darkness of the grave as any poet has done. *Bavarian Gentians*, in which the blueness of the flowers that someone had brought to his bedside suggests the deep journey into infinity of death, has an intensity, a deeply

felt understanding of the Greek myths of the underworld, which seem the beginning of a new development in his poetry. This was sustained further in the deeply moving *Ship of Death*, of which there are several versions. Lawrence called a late volume of his poems *Pansies*, the title being a skit on Pascal's *Pensées*. This mixture of seriousness and jocularity illustrates his attitude to most of his poems, which were the notes of a storyteller. Lawrence was often a great poet in his prose and sometimes a remarkable poet even in his poems.   S.S.

Lear, Edward (1812–88), was born in Highgate and died at San Remo; he was a retiring Victorian gentleman who lived chiefly abroad, painted and wrote travel sketches. As a draughtsman he was exact and at times fanciful, and his landscapes have charm. As a comic poet, he developed the limerick, an epigrammatic verse form which originated in the eighteenth century, and of which he found an example in the form of a nursery-rhyme, now lost (though referred to by Dickens in *Our Mutual Friend*), concerning an old man of Tobago. Lear composed his limericks to please the grand-children of his friend, the Earl of Derby, and published them many years later in his *Book of Nonsense* (1846). They follow the simple formula whereby the rhyme-word of the first line, generally a place-name, is repeated in the last, as in:

> There was a Young Lady of Lucca,
>   Whose lovers completely forsook her;
>   She ran up a tree
>   And said 'Fiddle-de-dee!'
>   Which embarrassed the people of Lucca.

Later limericks are often more comic and are more elaborate in form. Lear's *Nonsense Songs* of 1871, on the other hand, are melancholy, fantastic inventions at the same time romantic and self-depreciatory. Lear had a remarkable mastery of metre, and talent for coining new words. Nothing, however, conceals his unhappy, defeated attitude. The world of the *Nonsense Songs* is a place of refuge of a shy man, and even the limericks frequently present poor and persecuted oddities, pursued and despised by the universal enemy characterised only as 'They'. Lear had a special love of animals, both real and imaginary. The happiest of his creations are, perhaps, the pelicans of *The Pelican Chorus*; the most philosophical the 'Pobble' who became reconciled to the fact that he had no toes, and the most portentously romantic the 'Dong with a luminous Nose' who loved and lost his 'Jumbly girl' in the poem to which he lent his name. Lear gave it all the resonance of a romance by **Poe**, and all the mockery of his own peculiar nature. He wrote a grotesque self-portrait 'by way of Preface', which began:

How pleasant to know Mr Lear!
Who has written such volumes of stuff!

Later generations have found it indeed pleasant to know him. J.M.C.

Lewis, [Percy] Wyndham (1884–1957), was an English painter, essayist, novelist and poet. He was first known, before the First World War, as leader of the vorticist school of painting; Ezra **Pound** was associated with him at this time. Later he edited *Blast*, and wrote a book of poems, *One Way Song*, which was praised by T. S. **Eliot**. D.H.

Lindsay, Vachel (1879–1931), was born and reared in Springfield, Illinois. He went to college in Ohio and later studied art in Chicago and New York. He gained renown as a poet about 1912 and soon became a famous lecturer and reader. His later work did not succeed, however, and in 1931, impoverished and despondent, he committed suicide.

Lindsay's convictions and attitudes were those of the Middle West—agrarian, democratic, evangelistic. He writes of old friends in Springfield whose gospel came from Swedenborg and Henry George, and his family were Campbellites. Among his heroes were Jackson, Lincoln and **Whitman**, and in his lectures he tried to inculcate the vision of a nation glorified and perfected by the wise co-operation of priests, statesmen and artists.

Many of his poems take on the rhythms of country oratory and set forth legends and folklore. He wanted most to create symbols of deep national import, as in his poems on Lincoln, John Brown, Johnny Appleseed, Kansas, and buffaloes. His most striking works are *General William Booth Enters into Heaven* (1912) and *The Congo: A Study of the Negro Race* (1914). Their powerful syncopated rhythms were new in poetry, and their scenes suggest mural painting. Just as characteristic, however, is his elegy on John Altgeld, liberal governor of Illinois during Lindsay's youth, which concludes

Sleep softly, . . . eagle forgotten, . . .
       under the stone,
Time has its way with you there and
   the clay has its own.
Sleep on, O brave-hearted, O wise man,
     that kindled the flame—
To live in mankind is far more than to
      live in a name,
To live in mankind, far, far more . . .
    than to live in a name.
         D.L.H.

see also American Poetry

Lodge, Thomas (1558–1625), a disciple of **Lyly**, trained as a lawyer and physician.

His romance, *Rosalynde*, was the source of **Shakespeare's** *As You Like It*. His poetry includes *Scilla's Metamorphosis* (1589), *Phillis* (1593), a sonnet sequence and *A Fig for Momus* (1595), a verse satire.　D.H.

Longfellow, Henry Wadsworth (1807–82), was born in Portland, Maine, and attended Bowdoin College. After three years in Europe studying French, Italian, Spanish and German he returned to teach modern languages, first at Bowdoin and then, from 1836 to 1854, at Harvard. He then retired from teaching to devote himself to writing.

Some of his poems were popular favourites even before the appearance of *Evangeline* (1847). *The Song of Hiawatha* (1855) and *The Courtship of Miles Standish* (1858) both had an immense and immediate success. His interest in American subjects was balanced by a lifelong devotion to European literature, culminating in his translation of Dante (1867–70); often native and foreign themes find expression in the same work. His verse was translated into most European languages, and he in turn translated from most of them.

His reputation, so high in his own day, suffered a severe reverse, from which it has never recovered, about the turn of the century. Readers with a taste for modern poetry are likely to find merit in his less typical work, where his eye is fixed on particulars and his intent, or at any rate his tone, is not too didactic. An example is *In the Churchyard at Cambridge*, praised for its urbanity by I. A. Richards as early as 1929. The speaker in the poem speculates as to the character of the lady introduced in the first stanza:

In the village churchyard she lies,
Dust is in her beautiful eyes,
　No more she breathes, nor feels, nor
　　　　　　　　　　stirs,

At her feet and at her head
Lies a slave to attend the dead,
　But their dust is white as hers.

　　　　　　　　　　　D.L.H.
see also American Poetry *and* Popular Poetry

Lovelace, Richard (1618–58), was an ardent royalist, soldier, poet and musician. His poems tend to be over-elaborate, with the notable exception of *To Althea From Prison* and the poems addressed to Lucasta.

Lowell, Amy [Lawrence] (1874–1925), who was born in Brookline, Massachusetts, was a corpulent, cigar-smoking Brahmin. *The Complete Poetical Works* (1955) reveal her devotion to what she considered to be the Imagist movement (Ezra **Pound** said that she had turned it into Amygism). Her prose works include *Tendencies in Modern American Poetry* (1917) and *John Keats* (1925).　D.H.
see also American Poetry

Lowell, James Russell (1819–91), is the American author of *A Fable for Critics* and many other poems. He was a professor at Harvard, first editor of *The Atlantic Monthly*, and a conservative influence on the taste of his time. His poems are often well made and always unoriginal.　D.H.

Lowell, Robert [Traill Spence] (1917–   ), was born in Boston; into what has been called the New England aristocracy. The Lowells are intellectuals who counted already two poets, an astronomer, and a President of Harvard. The Winslows, on his mother's side, are of old colonial distinction. He was educated at St Mark's School, Harvard, and Kenyon. Yet his youth passed in a storm of difficulties with his parents. He was high-strung and headstrong; they had the social position of their families, but, not having the means to live in the style expected of them, were generally in straits, and bickering. It was a bad hurt for a boy who would have revered all his elders if they were not unworthy. In 1940 he entered the Roman Catholic Church, whose authority he could respect. In the Second World War he accepted a prison sentence as a conscientious objector.

His first major book, *Lord Weary's Castle* (1946), introduced a poet of very great lyric power, and unusual mobility over the range of the forty-two poems. Many are about Lowells or Winslows, over whom his judgment poises. Others are set in European history, and the shrines and devotions of his faith. His stage is large, and he knows the faces of evil.

In *The Mills of the Kavanaughs* (1951) the long title-poem is the reverie of a widow who re-enacts the decline and fall of an old New England house in Maine. The shorter poems are extended too, and more perfected. In *Falling Asleep over the Aenid* an old New Englander on a Sabbath morning instead of going to Church curls up over his book, and soon in a dream-fantasy is Aeneas in Italy, attending the funeral rites of Pallas, a native prince. Here is one fragment; Aeneas has kissed the lips and the face seems to speak:

> 'Who am I, and why?'
> It asks, a boy's face, though its arrow-eye
> Is working from its socket. 'Brother, try,
> O child of Aphrodite, try to die:
> To die is life.' His harlots hang his bed
> With feathers of his long-tailed birds.
> His head
> Is yawning like a person. The plumes
> blow;
> The beard and eyebrows ruffle. Face of
> snow,

> You are the flower the country girls
> have caught,
> A wild bee-pillaged honey-suckle
> brought
> To the returning bridegroom—the
> design
> Has not yet left it, and the petals shine;
> The earth, its mother, has, at last, no
> help;
> It is itself. The broken-winded yelp
> Of my Phoenician hounds, that fills the
> brush
> With snapping twigs and flying, cannot
> flush
> The ghost of Pallas.

In places the poet's English is crisp and decisive like Virgil's Latin; but Virgil would hardly have indulged the grief, the *lacrimae rerum*, to such length and sweetness. If Virgil is to be imitated, it must be on Lowell's terms.

Life Studies (1959) is very different. It expresses the last disenchantment of the boy who had entered into his inheritance too fondly. In a long prose section he releases the family skeletons from the closet as if to disown them once and for all. The tone is bantering and indifferent. But as poet he registers one technical advance by employing free verse. The poems are mostly joyless. Yet there is *Dunbarton* recalling a childhood time with his beloved Winslow grandfather:

> Grandfather and I
> raked leaves from our dead forebears,
> defied the dank weather
> with 'dragon' bonfires.
> Our helper, Mr Burroughs,
> had stood with Sherman at Shiloh—
> his thermos of shockless coffee
> was mild and grounds;
> his illegal home-made claret
> was as sugary as grape jelly
> in a tumbler capped with paraffin.

> I borrowed Grandfather's cane
> carved with the names and altitudes

of Norwegian mountains he had scaled—
more a weapon than a crutch.
I lanced it in the fauze ooze for newts.
In a tobacco tin after capture, the umber
                    yellow mature newts
lost their leopard spots,
lay grounded as numb
as scrolls of candied grapefruit peel.
I saw myself as a young newt,
neurasthenic, scarlet
and wild in the wild coffee-colored water.

In the mornings I cuddled like a paramour
in my Grandfather's bed,
while he scouted about the chattering
                    greenwood stove.

But it is a harsh book. And what is to
come next? Happily, Lowell is engaged
again, this time in 'imitations' of other
poets in other languages. His version of
Racine's *Phèdre* appeared in 1961; *Imitations*, of the same year, contains versions
of poems by Homer, Sappho, Villon,
Baudelaire, Mallarmé, Rilke, Pasternak,
and others.   J.C.R.
see also American Poetry

Lydgate, John (?1370–?1449), the 'monk
of Bury' was born in the Suffolk town
of that name, entered the monastery of
Bury St Edmunds at fifteen and was
ordained priest in 1397. Elected prior of
Hatfield Broadoak in 1423, he was
working in Paris three years later but
returned to his abbey in 1434 to remain
they until his death.

It has been said that Lydgate outlived
his genius; in writing well over 100,000
lines he equalled or surpassed the work of
any individual medieval writer. His last
works were the expansive translation of
the *Troy Book* (1412) from Guido della
Colonna (commissioned, with the *Life
of Our Lady* (1421–2), by Henry V) and
the *Siege of Thebes* (1420–2) following
the French *Roman de Thèbes*. The *Pilgrimage of Man* (1426–30) and the *Fall of Princes*
(1431–8) both total over 50,000 lines.

Lydgate wrote 'occasional' poems for
mummings and royal entries into London.
There are hymns, sermons, and moral
poems (*Stans puer ad mensam* and his
Testament). His humour is lost in his wide
learning, although *London Lickpenny* has a
lively account of coneys and coney catching. The influence of **Chaucer** is felt
shortly after 1400 in the *Flour of Curtesy*
and the *Complaint of the Black Knight*,
with Chaucer's *Book of the Duchesse* as a
source.

Of greater worth are the lyric descriptions which flash forth occasionally, as
those of Mary, in the *Life of Our Lady*:

> For this is the flour, that god hym self
>   beheld
> The white lylye of the chosyn vale
> The swete Roose, of the fayre felde
> Which of colour wexyth neuer pale
> The violet, our langour to a vale
> Purpyll hewede, thorough mercy and
>   pety
> To secoure alle, that in myschief be.
>   I, 106–12

and on religious passivity:

> O thoughtfull herte, plunged in distresse
> With slombre of slouthe, this long
>   wynters nyght
> Oute of the slepe, of mortall hevyness
> Awake anoon, and loke upon the lyght.
>   I. 1–4

To appreciate Lydgate one must find
such passages, but to do so one must eat
through the mountain of porridge which
surrounds Cockaigne.   T.J.G.

Lyly, John (?1554–1606), was one of the
Elizabethan university wits. He is mostly
remembered for his euphuistic prose style,
for which he unwittingly supplied the
adjective when he wrote *Euphues*. Some
of his poems survive in anthologies,
and are notable for their tactful elegance.
                                        D.H.

M

MacDiarmid, Hugh (1892–), is the pseudonym of Christopher Murray Grieve, a Scottish poet who was born in Langhold, Dumfriesshire, and educated at the University of Edinburgh. He is a turbulent, visionary man who has devoted his life and his art to the defence of humanistic values, and has consistently worked to expose the fake, commonplace, selfish and pretentious elements in modern society. His dedication to the causes of the under-dog has made him a Communist and an internationalist. He was a founder of the Scottish Nationalist Party and has for a long time been editor of its quarterly, *The Voice of Scotland.* He has been a major influence in the establishment of a new idiom in Scottish poetry. He was a founder of the Scottish section of P.E.N. and for some time editor of *Northern Numbers,* an annual anthology of Scots literature. The University of Edinburgh awarded him an honorary LL.D. in 1957. In spite of his vehement anglophobia (which he lists under 'recreation' in *Who's Who*) he lived for some time in London, where he made a reputation as a journalist and broadcaster. Since 1933, however, he has lived principally in Scotland and in the Shetland Islands.

MacDiarmid has published twelve volumes of poetry and several volumes of translations. His best verse is lyrical, written in a dialect that combines ancient and modern Scottish with English. Although they are often difficult to understand without a glossary, his lyrics are without doubt some of the most genuine of the twentieth century. There is nothing in Scottish literature, outside the work of **Dunbar, Henryson** and **Burns,** that equals the poems of his early books,

Sangschaw (1925) and *A Drunk Man Looks at a Thistle* (1926).

From the latter book comes the poem, *O Wha's the Bride?*

O wha's the bride that cairries the bunch
O' thistles blinterin' white?
Her cuckold bridegroom little dreids
What he sall ken this nicht.

For closer than gudeman can come
And closer to'r than hersel',
Wha didna need her maidenheid
Has wrocht his purpose fell.

O wha's been here afor me, lass,
And hoo did he get in?
—*A man that deed or was I born*
This evil thing has din.

And left, as it were on a corpse,
Your maidenheid to me?
—*Nae lass, gudeman, sin' Time began*
'S hed ony mair to gi'e.

But I can gi'e ye kindness, lad,
And a pair o' willin' hands,
And you sall ha'e my breists like stars.
My limbs like willow wands.

And on my lips ye'll heed nae mair,
And in my hair forget,
The seed o' a' the men that in
My virgin womb ha'e met . . .

In another vein, MacDiarmid is a trenchant satirist. He scoffs at the modern 'bourgeois' lethargy of Scotland.

They cannot lear, sae canno move
But stick for aye to their auld groove
—The only race in history who've

Bidden in the same category
Frae start tae present o' their story
   And deem their ignorance their glory.

In his more recent poetry he has largely abandoned his lyric forms and his Scots language. The poems of his spiritual autobiography, *Lucky Poet*, published in 1943, are frequently prosy and argumentative. MacDiarmid himself describes the change as a 'turn from the poetry of beauty to the poetry of wisdom', but there is some question as to whether his poetry has become a suitable vehicle for propaganda. And like other passionately committed writers, the frustrations of unfulfilled hopes have introduced bitterness into his recent work, the worth of which is sometimes swamped in repetitious invective.

Nevertheless MacDiarmid remains, with T. S. **Eliot** and Ezra **Pound**, one of the most original voices of the twentieth century. His compatriot, Edwin **Muir**, called his lyric verse 'pure inspiration'. Sir Compton Mackenzie writes that MacDiarmid is 'the most powerful intellectually and emotionally fertilising force Scotland has known since the death of Burns'. A.S.

McGinley, Phyllis (1905–), was born a Canadian and now resides in the United States, where she frequently contributes her light verse to *The New Yorker*. An admirer of hers is W. H. **Auden**, who wrote an introduction to her collected poems, *Times Three* (1960). D.H.

MacLeish, Archibald (1892–), was born in illinois. In 1939 the librarianship of Congress and a Yale honorary degree marked a climax of his poetic and political careers formed from his Yale education, service in the First World War, Law School and teaching at Harvard, and law practice in Boston. Among more strictly literary events, one should mention a first poetry volume in 1917, expatriate writing in France in the nineteen-twenties, visits to Mexico for *Conquistador* which received a Pulitzer Prize in 1932, and *Collected*

Poems 1917–1952 which collected Pulitzer, Bollingen and National Book awards. During the Second World War he became Assistant Secretary of State. Later he was chairman of Unesco and in 1949 became Boylston Professor at Harvard.

MacLeish's exact achievement as poet is in debate. His poetic voice is elegiac, when personal (*Epistle to be Left in the Earth*), in the mood of sensibility seeking nourishment in the past. In theme and manner his successive volumes follow the interwar times: **Imagism**, **Eliot**, social awareness, political commitment and 'democratic rhetoric'. 'His instrument is of the very best make', wrote Edmund Wilson in 1927; he is the master of *terza rima* and the radio and TV play. From *Ars Poetica* (1926) through *Frescoes for Mr Rockefeller's City* (1933) to *The Secret of Freedom* (1959) his work maintains a difficult position where poetry and politics meet. As unofficial laureate of America he has reflected both anxiety and patriotism, melancholy and self-belief (*American Letter*). His 'indomitable eloquence' (Stanley **Kunitz**) does lack dramatic tension (Cleanth Brooks): apprehensive meditation is his forte:

> As for the nights I warn you the nights
> are dangerous
> The wind changes at night and the
> dreams come
> It is very cold
> there are strange stars near Arcturus
> Voices are crying an unknown name in
> the sky.
> E.N.W.M.

see also American Poetry

MacNeice, Louis (1907–1963), was one of the most considerable of the English poets of the nineteen-thirties. He claimed that 'the poet is only an extension . . . of the ordinary man', and proved this by his willingness to tackle any theme or

subject in a startling and vivid manner. His technical range and stamina are outstanding. His early collections, *Blind Fireworks* (1929), *Poems* (1935) and *The Earth Compels* (1938), are notable for their celebration of the vitality and variety of life. As a liberal humanist with a facility for sensual and pictorial writing, he was obviously at pains to find solid structures for the poetry that comes easily to him: many of his more successful pieces are philosophical, and others, like *Autumn Journal* (1938), a classic verse diary of the Munich period, are outstanding because they can transcend in detail and emotion the journalistic streak that sometimes lurks in his writing. Later works, like *Ten Burnt Offerings* (1951), are ambitious and rhetorical, but lost the impact he could give to the shorter lyric, always his most natural form (see, for instance, the wartime pieces *Meeting Point* and *The Streets of Laredo*). Two recent collections of short poems are *Visitations* (1958) and *Solstices* (1961). In these volumes his sharp observation and fine ear for a phrase mellowed somewhat, but the characteristic strength and flow of the earlier work is evident. He wrote plays, translated Goethe's *Faust* and the *Agamemnon* of Aeschylus, and was the author of a number of radio plays and scripts for the BBC. He was a lecturer in classics before the war, when he also wrote criticism and travel books, notably *Letters from Iceland* (1937) in which he collaborated with **Auden**.   J.F.
see also Translation

Macpherson, James. *See* Ossian

Marlowe, Christopher (1564–93), was born and schooled in Canterbury. He studied at Corpus Christi College, Cambridge, from 1580 to 1587, spending part of his time in government service and possibly spying; lived in Shoreditch for six years, and was stabbed to death in a Deptford tavern by one Ingram Frizer in the presence of two known government spies, in a dispute now seen to have had possible political implications. By repute an atheist, he had been summoned before the Privy Council and accused in a note by an informer of holding seditious and blasphemous opinions. Lady Audrey Walsingham and **Ralegh** (with whom Marlowe may have associated in a group concerning itself with science and comparative religion) have been suggested as possible instigators of his removal.

L. C. Martin recognises that the chronology of his works is disputed and keeps an open mind, but it is generally held that the translation of parts of Ovid's *Amores* and the lyric 'Come live with me . . .' ('The passionate Sheepheard to his loue'), in *The Passionate Pilgrime* (1599) and *England's Helicon* (1600, 1614) are Cambridge work, contemporary with *Tamburlaine* and *Dido*. The translation of the first book of Lucan's *Pharsalia* (*Lucans First Booke*, 1600) is sometimes seen as an early specimen of non-dramatic blank verse with magnificent passages foreshadowing the plays, or so good as to be later work in, as C. S. Lewis says, 'a new manner inspired by a congenial model'. The accomplished nature of the two sestiads of *Hero and Leander* (for which **Chapman** provided four additional sestiads) suggests a late dating—about 1593.

F. S. Boas argues that in Ovid Marlowe found a genius akin to his own and that the translation provided a discipline and influence preferable to that of Seneca. The influence persisted and the mythological decoration, episodic digressions and sophistication of the original Musaeus poem in *Hero and Leander* are Ovidian.

Hero and Leander, much the best of the late sixteenth-century erotic epyllia, has been variously assessed as, his 'highest work', 'more perfect . . . than any of his plays', adding 'a new dimension'; 'spiritually poor', a poem written in 'holiday mood', its conceits whimsical and 'not attempting any serious poetic effect'. A distinctive twentieth-century recognition, suggested perhaps by the remarks of T. S. **Eliot** on *The Jew of Malta* in *The Sacred Wood* (1920) has been of the mock-heroic element in the poem's 'detached cynical wit' which looks 'forward to **Donne**, rather than back to **Spenser**', and Marlowe's lovers, 'both beautiful and absurd, sympathetic and yet also ridiculous' are discussed by M. C. Bradbrook, who points to the comic and 'exultant ruthlessness' in Marlowe's attitude to Hero, 'Venus nun', who

> Vow'd spotless chastity, but all in vain;
> Cupid beat down her prayers with his
> wings,
> Her vows above the empty air he flings.

Such calculated hyperbole is seen to be Marlowe's characteristic effect by H. Levin, who traces an antithesis running through his work 'between creative and destructive energies', resolved metaphysically in the lovers' strife as it is 'metamorphosed into its opposite, which is love':

> She trembling strove: this strife of hers
> (like that
> Which made the world) another world
> begat
> Of unknown joy.

The poem challenges the ancients and the gods; the human is pitted against the divine.

To Douglas Bush this is an ambush for Marlowe's own heresies and, attacking eulogistic critics following **Swinburne**, who have seen Greek purity in the poem, he proceeds to define its Italianate Ovidian nature. Images are drawn from 'art and

fancy, rather than nature' and human values suffer. C. S. Lewis agrees, but for him this distinguishes Marlowe, for the better, from the **Shakespeare** of *Venus and Adonis*, where human values intrude. Marlowe, dehumanising, can 'disinfect' the story; he suppresses pathos and gentleness and celebrates a shameless sensuality. The poem has integrity and purity, in that the lovers 'have no experience apart from their desires' and we, sharing their experience, see the world 'transfigured by the hard, brittle splendour of erotic vision'. The Marlowe and Chapman sestiads, dealing with Innocence and Experience is ascending and descending movements, governed by Venus and Saturn, are to be read together. Ideally complementary, Marlowe celebrates 'Joy grauen in sence', Chapman adds 'like snow in water wasts' and in their different modes Lewis suggests there is an epitome of the progress Lewis suggests there is an epitome of the progress of poetry at the turn of the century.   G.A.O.
see also Translation

Marquis, Don[ald Robert Perry] (1878–1937), American journalist and poet, was the creator of the lower-case cockroach, archy, and cat, mehitabel. Many of his best characters appeared in his 'Sun Dial' column of the *New York Sun*. His humorous works include *Hermione* (1916) and the *Old Soak* series (1921 and 1934). They overshadow the serious *Poems and Portraits*.
                                                        D.H.

Marston, John (1575–1634), was imprisoned with Ben **Jonson** and John Chapman for their collaboration on *Eastward Ho* in 1605. He wrote plays alone and in conjunction with others, was both satirised and befriended by Jonson, and published erotic poems and satires before entering the Church in 1607.   D.H.

Marvell, Andrew (1621–78), was a poet of the school of **Donne,** and a writer of wit and restrained irony rather than of enthusiasm. Yet at the same time, with **Crashaw,** he comes nearer than any other English poet to the Continental Baroque manner of Góngora and Marino. Like them he brings the commonplace and the rare into sudden juxtaposition, and is more concerned with the texture than the content of his poetry. After leaving Cambridge, Marvell spent four years abroad, part of the time, at least, as a tutor, and visited France, Italy and probably Spain. Indeed, to judge by references to Madrid, its Retiro Palace and Bull Ring, and the Gardens of Aranjuez, he may well have spent some time in that city. Since, moreover, he applied somewhat later for the post of assistant in the Secretaryship for Foreign Tongues, the office which dealt with Oliver Cromwell's European negotiations, it is almost certain that he read and spoke several languages. Although these years of travel, and indeed the next half-dozen years of Marvell's life, are largely undocumented, it is reasonable to assume that he read widely and not in English alone. He had certainly a good mastery of Latin for he wrote several of his poems in that language before composing the English versions.

In early sympathies and beliefs Marvell was a Royalist. For a brief spell he even joined the Church of Rome, but was rescued from this by his father. A period as tutor to the daughter of Lord Fairfax, the victor of Naseby, who had retired to his estates after a disagreement with Cromwell, may have modified his standpoint. It was during Marvell's stay in Fairfax's Yorkshire house, Nun Appleton, that he wrote the majority of his lyrical poems. The poem *Upon Appleton House* itself displays many of his habitual characteristics: his use of architectural,

horticultural and topographical detail, for instance, and his Baroque play with colours. Marvell's favourite colour is green, the green of that garden of which he speaks in a shorter poem, *The Garden,* that must also refer to his stay at Appleton House:

What wond'rous Life is this I lead!
Ripe Apples drop about my head;
The Luscious Clusters of the Vine
Upon my Mouth do crush their Wine;
The Nectaren and curious Peach,
Into my hands themselves do reach;
Stumbling on Melons, as I pass,
Insnar'd with Flow'rs, I fall on Grass.

Mean while the Mind from pleasure less,
Withdraws into its happiness:
The Mind, that Ocean where each kind
Does streight its own resemblance find;
Yet it creates, transcending these,
Far other Worlds, and other Seas;
Annihilating all that's made
To a green Thought in a green Shade.

The garden is for Marvell a symbol of the primal innocence of Eden, and also a refuge, alike for the mind afflicted by metaphysical anxieties and for the State or the statesman involved in Civil War. The political implication of the garden comes out clearly in a passage from *Upon Appleton House.* In a sustained conceit, Marvell first shows the garden drawn up in martial array:

See how the Flow'rs as at Parade
Under their Colours stand displaid:
Each Regiment in order grows,
That of the Tulip Pinke and Rose,

and then pleads for the restoration of that Edenic serenity when

The Gardiner had the Soldiers place,
And his more gentle Forts did trace.
The Nursery of all things green

Was then the only Magazeen,
The Winter Quarters were the Stoves,
Where he the tender Plants removes.

The idea of the Divine gardener had become a commonplace. Marvell's use of detail is, however, highly individual. His is not a purely formal garden, such as one would find in the poetry of Southern Europe. It looks forward rather to the English landscape garden of the next century, which imitates the hand of Nature. Marvell makes much of cultivation; the melon, vine, nectarine and peach are all plants hard to acclimatise; and he describes the hayfield too, though in terms of architectural formality for which there are parallels in Continental poetry. Sometimes, too, Marvell will work out an entirely cold conceit, as in the conclusion of *Upon Appleton House*. Suddenly the whole baroque artificiality of the scene has to be stressed, and this Marvell does by indicating in conceptist fashion that evening is falling and it is time to break off his poem:

But now the Salmon-Fishers moist
Their Leathern Boats begin to hoist;
And, like Antipodes in shoes,
Have shod their Heads in their Canoes,
How Tortoise like, but not so slow,
These rational Amphibii go?
Let's in: for the dark Hemisphere
Does now like one of them appear.

The picture of the fishermen lifting their coracles and placing them on their heads is hardly the most likely to suggest the fall of evening. Actually the mere fact that they have stopped fishing is enough to do so. Yet if one thinks of Marvell's ending as a deliberate and baroque attempt to stress the fictitious and pictorial nature of reality, this apparently wanton artificiality appears right and fitting.

Marvell's more famous address *To his*

Coy Mistress is hardly less exaggerative in its language. Here the relative slowness of the opening, with the poet's affirmation:

My vegetable Love should grow
Vaster than Empires and more slow

is contrasted with the speed of the concluding invitation to his mistress to enjoy love while there is still time—the old commonplace of Horace's 'Carpe diem':

Let us roll all our Strength, and all
Our Sweetness, up into one Ball:
And tear our Pleasures with rough strife,
Thorough the Iron gates of Life.
Thus, though we cannot make our Sun
Stand still, yet we will make him run.

The off-beat reference to Joshua's miracle in the battle is typical of Marvell's baroque use of classical and biblical legend. Sometimes, as with the Continental poets, his references are very obscure. The funeral custom that he describes and the events in the sky to which he compares it remain alike ill-defined in his *Elegy for the Death of Lord Hastings*:

The Gods themselves cannot their Joy
                                        conceal
But draw their Veils, and their pure
                                        Beams reveal:
Only they drooping Hymeneus note,
Who for sad Purple tears his Saffron
                                        coat,
And trails his Torches through the
                                        Starry Hall
Reversed, at his Darling's Funeral.

There remains an impression of great beauty, tenderness and grief, which acquires in its last two lines a kind of fortuitous magic that looks forward to the Romanticism of **Keats**.

At other times, and particularly in *An Horatian Ode upon Cromwell's Return from Ireland*, Marvell achieves a classic severity. In praising Cromwell, however, he once more resorts to his garden imagery, though this time he reverses the moral to show how much has been done by one who left its green refuge for the world of affairs:

> Much to the Man is due.
> Who, from his private Gardens, where
> He liv'd reserved and austere,
> As if his highest plot
> To plant the Bergamot,
> Could by industrious Valour climbe
> To ruine the great Work of Time,
> And cast the Kingdome old
> Into another Mold.

But Marvell also gives a fair and dignified picture of the King upon the scaffold:

> He nothing common did or mean
> Upon that memorable Scene;
> But with his keener Eye
> The Axes edge did try:
> Nor call'd the Gods with vulgar spight
> To vindicate his helpless Right,
> But bow'd his comely Head,
> Down as upon a Bed.

From the classical poetry of occasion to such a piece of Góngoristic conceit as that *On a Drop of Dew*, Marvell's range is considerable. What he lacks in passion he atones for by a rare intelligence.

From 1657 Marvell followed a political career. He became a colleague of **Milton** in the Latin Secretaryship, and is said to have protected him after the Restoration. He was Member of Parliament for Hull from 1659 to his death. His later satires, though they contain forceful passages, are on a lower level than his lyrical poetry. His *Miscellaneous Poems* were published in 1681, ostensibly by his widow, Mary Marvell. There is, however, no record of his ever having married.

Marvell's poetry, comparatively neglec-ted until about forty years ago, was strongly championed by T. S. **Eliot** and has influenced English poets ever since. Strong traces of discipleship can be found in the early work of Eliot himself and in America John Crowe **Ransom** and his followers have studied Marvell's intellectual and ironic example even more closely. J.M.C.

see also Foreign Influences on English Poetry

Masefield, John (1878–1967), created English Poet Laureate in 1930, was awarded the Order of Merit in 1935. His first volume, *Salt Water Ballads* (1902), includes the famous *Sea Fever*. He is also the author of numerous plays and novels.

D.H.

Masters, Edgar Lee (1868–1950), born in Kansas, was a chronicler of Mid-Western Americana in prosaic verse. He was best known for his *Spoon River Anthology* (1915). Other works include *New Spoon River* (1924), *Selected Poems* (1925), *Poems of the People* (1936), verse drama, biographies, and *Across Spoon River* (1936), an autobiography. D.H.

see also American Poetry

Melvil, Herman (1819–91), the author of *Moby Dick*, spent the last thirty-five years of his life writing poetry. His *Collected Poems* shows qualities which remind one of Emily **Dickinson,** and *Clarel* is a kind of nineteenth-century *Waste Land* written, unfortunately, in Hudibrastics. A.P.H.

Meredith, George (1828–1909), is a poet of faintly equivocal fame, though he is beginning to claim renewed attention. The early *Poems* (1851) are largely exercises, notable only for the first version of the fine *Love in the Valley* and for other lyrics foreshadowing the mature Meredith's strenuously optimistic attitude to Nature, which he sees as kindled into divinity by the self-consciousness that is at once Man's 'glory and danger'. *Modern Love* (1862), a narrative in fifty sixteen-line sonnets, presenting an artistically distanced version of his unhappy first marriage, is his masterpiece:

> In tragic life . . .
> No villain need be! Passions spin the
>   plot:
> We are betrayed by what is false
>   within.

The tone ranges from sardonic to tender, lyrical to colloquial and epigrammatic; the fault is an occasional melodramatic vulgarity. Meredith was to fall under **Browning**'s influence: the button-holing attitude; the wantonly elliptic syntax. Yet later poems such as *Phoebus with Admetus*, a vivid re-enactment of a myth, are full of sensitive detail. Meredith was also successful in the sonnet and in humorous-pathetic poems of common life. The more ambitious philosophic pieces tend to the crabbed and disjointed.   I.F.

Merwin, W[illiam] S[tanley] (1927–), is a prolific American poet with command of a variety of dictions. Considerable translation may have helped to extend his range. From an early elegance and concentration on myth, he moved to a poetry which is more personal and more connected with daily existence, and more recently to a poetry of fantastic imagery related to surrealism.   D.H.
see also Translation

Metaphor. In a purely formal sense, a metaphor is a figure of speech in which one thing is referred to by the name of another, in such a way, however, that

the hearer or reader will recognise that it is to the other thing, and not to the thing named, that the speaker or writer intends to refer:

> Awake! for morning in the bowl of
>   night
> Has flung the stone that puts the stars to
>   flight.

It is thus a means of emphasising the inherent resemblance of the two things, and, if successful, the effect obtained is more forceful and direct than that of a simile, the related and much commoner figure of speech in which one thing is said to be like another. If taken literally, the metaphor says that one thing *is* another and not just that it is *like* another. By convention, metaphors are not taken literally; conventional metaphors are often no more than concise similes. Yet at the back of any active metaphor there remains the assertion of actual identity between two quite different things or between different orders of things. The metaphor seems to be saying that though the things appear different, in some essential way they are the same. And this feeling of an inward identity in spite of an outward difference is one to which the mind is able to respond, and one in which, in fact, it takes a peculiar delight.

Why this should be so is a subtle question, and it may be suspected that the explanations for it that have been given by philosophers, psychologists, literary critics and by poets themselves are only partially adequate. A fresh attempt at explanation will be made later in this article, but first an account must be given of the phenomenon of metaphor as it is manifested in poetry and in language generally.

To be sure, one of the distinguishing marks of poetic language is that it contains more active metaphors than ordinary language, and one of the characteristic aims of poetry is to activate or reactivate metaphors. But, as Aristotle was the first among many others to point out, metaphor is a basic method by which all language extends its range of reference. There are metaphors in colloquial speech, in workaday prose, in philosophical discussion, even in scientific theory. In such contexts they are as often as not used primarily for convenience and without seeking to arouse a conscious awareness of metaphorical paradox for its own sake. Such metaphors may be thought of as non-poetic; but metaphors which provoke the awareness of metaphor, whether occurring in the formal context of poetry or in some other context, may be thought of as *poetic metaphors*.

Let us consider, for a start, poetic metaphors outside formal poetry. Sir Richard Burton, in *First Footsteps in East Africa*, describing the verbal dexterity of one of his Arab companions, recorded that: 'If a grain of rice adhere to our beards, he says smilingly, "The gazelle is in the garden"; to which we reply, "We will hunt her with the five"', adding in a footnote: 'That is to say, "we will remove it with the five fingers". These are euphuisms to avoid speaking broadly and openly of that venerable feature, the beard.' The need to avoid open mention of the beard is made the pretext for a use of metaphor that is vivid and amusing. It may, of course, be used more seriously, for example in honorific titles such as the name of Shah Jehan's Queen, Mumtaz Mahal, 'Pearl of the Palace'; or indeed solemnly, as in many religious expressions where the metaphor is used to induce a sense of awe before mysteries which cannot be described in ordinary words. These are instances where it is felt to be necessary or fitting to speak of something metaphorically rather than directly, because the thing spoken of is too illustrious, or mysterious, or too closely bound up with feelings of modesty or shame, to be given its common name. The poetic effect of such metaphors is incidental to their function of providing an alternative designation, a form of disguise. But whenever language tends in this way to be used allusively and periphrastically, it is on the way to assuming a poetic form. The standards by which the use of metaphor is to be judged are likely to differ according to whether it is used inside or outside a formally poetic framework. Inside poetry, there is no limit to the use of metaphor, but metaphor is judged primarily by its *poetic* effect; it is superfluous or excessive only when it fails in this effect. Outside poetry, there is a place for metaphor even in a chaste style, but (*cf.* Aristotle's *Rhetoric* III, iii, 3–4) carried to excess it can lead to obscurity, absurdity and frigidity. Inside poetry, the human propensity to metaphor is indulged; outside poetry, it is limited and controlled.

After a poem has been composed and handed down, there may be dispute about what is the significant level of reference: whether it is to be taken at its face value or metaphorically, and if metaphorically, what the metaphor refers to. Thus the Confucian *Shih Ching* included poems that were part of an oral tradition of popular poetry, in a style resembling that of compositions which have been recorded in our own time among certain tribal peoples of Asia. They refer explicitly to natural events, the changing seasons, the call of birds, the flowering of trees, and so on. According to Confucius and other orthodox Chinese commentators, however, they were to be interpreted as having a moral or political significance, and as guides to the conduct fitting to those in superior positions. This interpretation is implausible. Almost certainly in the first genesis the poems were allusive love songs. (See Marcel Granet, *Festivals and Songs of Ancient China*; and Arthur **Waley**, *The Book of Songs*.) In poetry which is oral and spontaneous, composed among people at a simple level of social and technical organisation, there is a continuous play of metaphor between the objects of the natural world and the relations of the human world, especially those of love and courtship. In the more sophisticated poetry of a literary tradition, the primitive charm of natural objects is still felt, but these may well have become literary symbols rather than a part of everyday life. It is part of the creative task of literary poets to revive the latent force of the natural metaphors of primitive life.

In the words of Aristotle: 'The simile also is a metaphor; for there is very little difference. When the poet says of Achilles, 'he rushed on like a lion'', it is a simile; if he says, "a lion he rushed on", it is a metaphor; for because both are courageous, he transfers the sense and calls Achilles a lion.' (*Rhetoric* III, iv, 1.) Besides preparing the way for treating similes as though they were metaphors, this quotation draws attention to the lion-warrior metaphor which has been stressed not only in Homer and ancient Greek poetry but also in Western, middle-Eastern and African poetic traditions. In the social world of fables, whether those of Aesop or the *Panchatantra*, the lion is the king of beasts. The British lion is a national emblem not because there are, or have ever been, lions at large in Britain, but because British people like to think of themselves as lions. In poetry and fable, lions are not only brave and strong but magnanimous. This kind of identification of people with animals is of course less

intense than in those societies where totemic beliefs are actively present. In such a society it may be asserted that members of the lion totemic group *are* lions. Such assertions puzzled early observers and were part of the evidence put forward by Levy-Bruhl for his theory that the mentality of primitive people was 'pre-logical'. (See E. E. Evans-Pritchard, *Nuer Religion*, Chapter V, 'The Problem of Symbols'.) Moreover, natural species are regarded as lineages, just as lineages are regarded as natural species: the metaphor is reciprocal. Yet beyond this functional convenience, there must be other, deeper reasons of an emotional—or rather of a poetic—order for the persistent tendency of human beings to equate themselves with animals, and to find analogies between the natural order and the human order. It may be, perhaps, that we see in animals the embodiment or projection of our own emotional (or 'animal') selves.

A great distance has been travelled between the naked Nuer and the courtly world of **Spenser**'s *Faerie Queene*, but here too metaphors from animals, and particularly the lion-warrior metaphor, are of notable importance. They can serve here as an example of metaphorical development at the literary level. Spenser's declared object was to 'fashion a gentleman or noble person in virtuous and gentle discipline'. He undoubtedly believed that the qualities he admired went with blood and breeding and were aristocratic products. Yet, when his knights and gentlemen apparently fail, he continually brings in noble savages and wild animals to the rescue:

Among wild beasts in desert places bred
It is most strange and wonderful to find
So mild humanity and perfect gentle
                                    mind.

n the First Book, he is extolling the Aristotelean virtue of magnanimity, greatness of soul, represented at the human level by the Red Cross Knight and at the animal level by the Lion. In the first canto, the 'gentle Knight' is compared to a lion, while the 'lovely Lady', Una, whom he accompanies, is compared to the 'milk white lamb' she leads with her. But the Knight deserts the Lady, whom he sees (by illusion) in bed with a young Squire. As she wanders in search of him, 'Out of the thickest wood a ramping Lion' rushes on her, but amazed at her beauty, instead of devouring her 'kissed her weary feet/And licked her lilly hands, with fawning tongue', and thereafter 'with her went along, as a strong guard / Of her chaste person . . .' Una, accepting her lion as a knight, continues to think of her knight as a lion:

'The lion, lord of every beast in field'
Quoth she, 'his princely puissance doth
                                        abate.
But he, my lion and my noble lord,
How does he find in cruel heart to hate?'

The metaphor is thus harped on and teased into new forms. In the course of the *Færie Queene*, fighting heroes are compared to two rams; a griffon and dragon; two boars; a bear and tiger; a lion and unicorn; a lion, a bull, a tempest and an eagle; a fire, a bear and a falcon; two billows; two brigantines; two mastiffs; two tigers, a vulture and heron; two bulls; winds; a storm; a dolphin and seal; an eagle and goshawk; a kite and falcon; a tiger and lioness; a millstream; a bull, mastiff, hound and curdog; a lion and a deer, and so on.

The metaphors that occur in poetry, whether primitive or literary, are not a random collection of comparisons. There are regularities and preponderances in the things compared. In other words, the world of metaphor has a definite structure, not unrelated to the real world, but revealing a vision of that world based on primitive or basic imaginary conceptions. To show this in detail would require a great deal more quotation than is possible here. It has of course been recognised since the time of Aristotle that objects and abstractions are metaphorically personified and endowed with human features. It is not so generally realised that the human body is metaphorically conceived as a house or a world and that Man, House, and World form a series of imaginative parallelisms. Allied to these are the metaphors by which changes of physical state (liquefaction, petrefaction, vaporisation, etc.) are equated with changes of psychological state. Varying traditions and cultures give varying emphases to the basic metaphors, but in so far as men are physically and psychologically alike and have the same natural environment, there is a common basis for all metaphor.

From this brief treatment of the phenomenon of metaphor, we can now proceed to the attempt at an explanation of its peculiar attraction for the human mind. Metaphors have been 'useful' in extending the range of language and thought, but this does not explain the feeling of pleasure and liberation they provide. Accepting the notion (as developed, for example, by Croce) the aesthetic experience is a direct or unanalysed awareness of what is qualitative, the power of metaphor seems to be that it gives us a vivid sense of the quality of a particular object. But it does so by equating that object with another object. This at first sight is paradoxical, since the feeling of quality is the feeling of a specific identity. A possible explanation might be as follows. Any feeling of quality in relation to an object involves the possibility of one thing 'standing for' another thing, of one thing 'evoking' another thing. At a basic level, the two things are imagined as the *same*: at the elaborated level, to have the same underlying quality. Quality is thus interpreted as a name for the feeling attending a perception of identity between different objects.

The images that are the material of the world of metaphor are interchangeable symbols. None of them is simply itself. Each image contains or evokes others. Any object which evokes a metaphor-bearing image conveys a feeling of quality. The concreteness of aesthetic experience is a *multiple concreteness*, and it is this, as well as its relation to emotions and cathexes, which gives it its special character. Aesthetic pleasure is not simply the pleasure of emotional or cathectic satisfaction, though philosophers and psychologists have not fully succeeded in pinning down what else is involved. Even Freud, fruitful as has been his line of interpretation, was more concerned with the clinical significance of imagery and fantasy than with the human propensity to enjoy metaphor for its own sake. The satisfactions of poetry and the arts are not the same as the satisfactions of physical or emotional needs and desires, nor is their attraction completely explained by interpreting them as substitutions. If they are substitutions, they provide an additional satisfaction even to the most physically and emotionally satisfied person, and it is this additional element which we seek to explain. It is not to be explained either in a Benthamite way by its usefulness in making possible the framing of hypotheses and the process of cognitive exploration; the poetic pleasures of science and the intellect are to be distinguished from the satisfactions of scientific and intellectual achievement.

The pleasure of metaphor is best seen as lying in the sense of interchangeability. We get this sense not only from the verbal device of metaphor in poetry, but from any object or image or activity or personage when we take a poetic view of it. As soon as we do so, its identity is both heightened and dissolved. We discern within it, perhaps in part unconsciously, its metaphorical structure.

Interchangeability of activities, interchangeability of symbols, the knowledge and the feeling that there is more than one thing; that there are many qualities, that the mind and the senses can move and choose freely, that there is still exploration to be done and discoveries to be made—somewhere within this range (here stated abstractly, but in its poetic form experienced concretely) lies the compelling power or metaphor. Here too lies the strange and urgent priority which is given to poetry not only by poets (who may well be thought to have a professional or vested interest at stake) but by non-poets. Life without poetry means, in effect, life without metaphor. It is possible that only man, with his verbal endowment, has evolved to the point of metaphorical thinking; and it is possible that his distinctive gift of metaphor-making is no less crucially human than those of walking, talking and tool-making.   C.M.

Metaphysical Poets. *See* Carew, Cowley, Crashaw, Donne, George Herbert, Marvell, Religion and Poetry *and* Vaughan.

Meynell, Alice [Christiana Gertrude] (1847–1922), English poet and essayist, was born in London. She edited *Merrie England* with her husband, Wilfrid Meynell. Her poems reflect both her Roman Catholicism and the influence of Francis **Thompson**, whom she and her husband befriended and sponsored.

D.H.

Middle English Lyric. The whole genre of the Middle English Lyric must be divided into two parts, of which the first is the secular, the second the religious, lyric. The origin of the secular lyric in England is obscure. Anglo-Saxon poetry did not contain these short subjective, at times highly emotional poems. The search has turned to the south, to the Trouvères of northern France and to the famous Troubadours of the Provence and Aquitaine. Evidence of Provençal lyric (the *Aube* and the *Pastourel*) is slight in England, however, and the French *chanson*, following the conventions of courtly love, the knight wooing a haughty and aloof lady, is a cold self-analysis of the joys inherent in suffering the lady's cruelties.

The English secular lyric, a meagre collection, shows the French influence in only a few items. The majority, following the anonymity of oral folk poetry, is of a robust, earthy, often physical nature. The 'lady' is not aloof; the 'maid' is close. She is called a specific name, 'Alisoun', or the 'Fair Maid of Ribblesdale'. The Middle English lyric has a lusty, swinging quality, scarcely ever found in its French counterpart:

When the nyhtegale singes the wodes
waxen grene
lef ant gras ant blosme springes in Aueryl
y wene

The Provençal lyric treats of an aristocratic world; the English lyric speaks of common life, and the figures of speech are those that a common man would understand: maidens were the fairest ever made 'of blod ant bon', 'A wyf nis non so worly wroht; / when heo ys blythe to bedde ybroht', an old man who feels himself unwanted is 'fulle-flet' (one who fills the floor) or 'wayteglede' (one who stares into the fire).

Thomas Ely, a twelfth-century chronicler, quotes the earliest example of lyric poetry: 'Merrily sang the monks of Ely', composed by King Canute, and churchyard singing and graveyard dances were so popular by the end of the twelfth century that priests complained of hearing these all night. By the thirteenth century lyric poems had reached their strength in England. Most are short and meant to be sung. The reader will immediately notice the strong emphasis on the seasons which was, of course, a common literary convention of the time, albeit a refreshing one.

Spring: Lenten ys come with loue to
toune
With blosmen ant with
briddes roune,[1]
that al this blisse bryngeth.

Summer: Sumer is i-cumen in;
Lhude sing, cuccu!
Groweth sed, and bloweth
med,
And springeth the wude nu.
Sing cuccu!

Autumn: Nou shrinketh rose ant lylie-
flour
that whilen ber that suete
sauour[2]
in somer, that suete tyde;[3]

Winter: Wynter wakeneth al my care,
nou this leues[4] waxeth bare.

Love, in the sense of possession and marriage (as compared to suffering and frustration in the *Chansons*) is a very common theme, though the unfortunate and rejected lover is not absent from English verse:

[1] *briddes roune*—birds' song
[2] *whilen ber that suete sauour*—at one time bore that sweet scent
[3] *tyde*—time   [4] *this leues*—these leaves

With longyng y am lad,
On molde y waxe mad,
   a maide marreth me.

(With longing I am afflicted,
On meadow I grow mad,
   a maiden injures me.)

Romance conventions (blood-red mouth, lily-white skin) and repetitive phrases may be called flaws in the lyric; however those minor faults are outweighed by the spirit and the joy of poems which, with the later fifteenth-century ballads, gave rise to the idea of a 'merry England'. The very great mass of Middle English lyric is of course religious with sources in the liturgy, the Bible and Patristic writings. The line between the physical passion of the secular lyrics and the mystical ecstasy of the religious ones is often finely drawn and in the prayers to Mary 'Mother mild, fairest of all' secular echoes are very strong. All subjects of the Virgin's life were raw material for the lyrics, and she is often addressed as the intermediary between God and Man.

Blessed be thou, leuedy,[1] full of
          heouene[2] blisse,
suete flur of parays,[3] moder of mildeness,
preyze Iesu thy sone that he me rede ant
          wysse[4]
so my wey forte gon[5] that he me neuer
          misse.

The poems in praise of Christ are equally numerous.

Suete Iesu, king of blysse
myn huerte loue, min huerte lisse[6]
thou art suete myd ywisse[7]
Wo is him that the shal misse!

[1] *leuedy*—lady   [2] *heouene*—heavenly
[3] *parays*—paradise
[4] *rede ant wysse*—advise and teach
[5] *forte gon*—in order to go
[6] *lisse*—joy
[7] *suete myd ywisse*—sweet certainly

Here too, in themes of Christ as the heavenly lover, secular themes are paralleled. One may wonder how far the two lyric types may have influenced each other.

The popular, cheerful carols, usually associated with Christmas, came late in the fifteenth century, in addition to political and satirical songs. By this time the lyric, both secular and religious, was losing its spontaneous flavour. The anonymity of oral transmission with all the strength of the folk spirit behind it gave way now to the exact rules, conceits, and rhyme schemes which we associate with Elizabethan poetry.

          T.J.G.

Middleton, Thomas (?1570–1627), was a popular Jacobean dramatist, whose first known poem is *The Wisdom of Solomon Paraphrased*. He collaborated in writing plays with **Dekker**, Rowley, Munday and others. His plays, which move from the satirical to the romantic, contain lyrics of merit.   D.H.

Millay, Edna St Vincent (1892–1950), American Pulitzer Prize-winning poet in 1923, was a novelist (pseud. Nancy Boyd), and dramatist. Her *Collected Lyrics* (1943) contains selections from eight books which gained her a reputation as 'spokesman of the flaming Twenties'.

Milton, John (1608–74), was born in Bread Street, London, when **Shakespeare** was still living in the city. His father, a prosperous scrivener or notary, was also a composer of repute. From St Paul's School Milton went up to Christ's College, Cambridge (B.A., 1629; M.A., 1632). He had been destined to take orders but he came to rebel against a prelatical church. He had also rebelled against the Cambridge curriculum and after receiving his degree he spent nearly six years in more liberal studies under his father's roof. In 1638–9 he had some fifteen months abroad, mostly in Italy, and the welcome he received from Italian writers confirmed his belief in his vocation (at home he was known to few, though he had written a number of great poems, from the *Nativity* to *Lycidas*).

In 1640 Milton settled in London and began to take in private pupils. His ambition to write the great modern heroic poem gave way to his sense of religious and civic duty, and most of the next twenty years were devoted to prose. He began with five tracts against episcopacy (1641–2), four on divorce (1643–5), and *Of Education* and *Areopagitica* (1644); the latter remains a classic possession. In 1642 Milton had married the young daughter of a royalist squire. The rapid failure of the marriage added personal anguish to his arguments for divorce on the ground of incompatibility; the pair were, however, reunited in 1645. Milton's first political pamphlet, *The Tenure of Kings and Magistrates* (1649), which appeared shortly after Charles I's execution, led to his becoming Secretary for Foreign Tongues to Cromwell's Council of State. His function was to handle diplomatic correspondence and, as a supporter of the Commonwealth, to reply to royalist attacks. His chief works of this kind were the two Latin *Defences* of the English people (1651, 1654); labour on the first hastened the onset of blindness, which became complete in 1651–2, when Milton was only forty-three and the great poem was not yet written—although thoughts of his defence of liberty helped, along with his 'better guide', to sustain him. His early pamphlets had been fired by the vision of a new and greater Reformation, but a last plea for a free commonwealth, published boldly, not to say recklessly, on the very eve of the

Restoration, was a cry of disillusionment and despair.

As the champion of the regicide government Milton might well have shared the fate of its leaders, and he was in fact taken into custody, but his life was spared. Halfway through *Paradise Lost* (vii, 23–8) he could declare, in accents that are uniquely his, that he sang

> with mortal voice, unchang'd
> To hoarce or mute, though fall'n, on
> evil dayes,
> On evil dayes though fall'n, and evil
> tongues;
> In darkness, and with dangers compast
> round,
> And solitude; yet not alone . . .

The death of Milton's second wife in 1658 occasioned his last sonnet, one of his finest. He married again in 1663. His late years, if harassed by blindness, gout, loss of property, and some friction with his daughters, were passed in a quiet routine of meditation, composition, walking in his garden, music, listening to readers, and talking with many visitors. *Paradise Lost* appeared in 1667, *Paradise Regained* and *Samson Agonistes* in 1671, three years before his death.

He first learned his art in the Latin verse that was a normal collegiate avocation; and he sometimes revealed parts of his nature more fully in Latin than in English, as in the sensuous springtime intoxication of the fifth *Elegy* or in grief for his dead friend, Charles Diodati, in the *Epitaphium Damonis* (1639–40). His first great English poem, *On the Morning of Christ's Nativity* (1629), written just after his twenty-first birthday, was a jubilant hymn on the meaning of the Incarnation, the harmonious order linking earth and heaven; the mature artist was already apparent in the subject, the structuring of themes, the musical and mythological imagery, and the volume of sound. The less ambitious but not less enchanting *L'Allegro* and *Il Penseroso* (?1631) show the young poet shifting from the Spenserian manner to the courtly urbanity of **Jonson**, but he excels his master in delicate grace and suggestive overtones.

On his twenty-fourth birthday (1632) Milton, now an obscure student at home, preparing himself for the unknown future, wrote the sonnet, *How soon hath Time*, an earnest dedication of his powers to service under his 'great task Masters eye'. There followed two slow-paced, weighty poems, *On Time* and *At a Solemn Music*, both in the irregular form of an Italian madrigal, both contrasting the sinful discords of earth with the pure harmony of heaven. That contrast—Milton's lifelong vision of perfection—was the theme of the elaborate masque, *Comus*, presented at Ludlow Castle in September, 1634. The best key to the masque is the personal passage in the tract, *An Apology for Smectymnuus* (1642), in which Milton recalled some of his early reading and the growth of his ideal of chastity and love: he had moved from Ovid to Dante and Petrarch, to chivalric romance, to 'the divine volumes of Plato', and over all was the Bible. Love of the Good is positive, Platonic, and Christian. The Lady's reply to Comus' libertine arguments rises from the rational to the religious and impassioned, and the last lyrical couplet is at once a moral statement and an incantation:

Or if Vertue feeble were,
Heav'n itself would stoop to her.

So far Milton's poems had been songs of innocence; his first song of experience was *Lycidas*. It was his contribution—signed 'J.M.'—to a volume of elegies (1638) on Edward King, a young Canta-

brigian lost in a shipwreck in the Irish Sea. Milton had not been close enough to King to feel acute personal grief, but such an event brought home the ancient problem, 'Why should the just man suffer?' —though his own involvement is barely touched and the questioning of God's providence remains impersonal. Working as usual within a tradition, Milton re-creates it. Pastoralism is functional, not decorative. The two young shepherds who drove afield are carefree youth, unaware of a canker at the heart of things; the later floral catalogue is a deceptive solace, a vain escape from reality. The passionate dialectic is finally resolved, not by argument, but by the vision of rebirth in heaven. And the quiet conclusion, returning after nature's violence to normal order, is an acceptance of God's ways to men and the human condition. Milton exploited to the full the irregularities of the *canzone*, changes of pace and tone, images of water, pagan and Christian symbols from Orpheus to Christ. In its complex orchestration of a central conflict *Lycidas* is one of the miracles of poetry.

The occasional sonnets of 1642–58 comprise journalistic gibes at the Presbyterians, genial Horatian invitations to dinner (reminders of Milton's capacity for friendship), and the more exalted utterances on his blindness and his dead wife and public men and events. In Milton's hands, as **Wordsworth** said, the sonnet became a trumpet—'Avenge O Lord thy slaughter'd Saints'. Technically, the heroic sonnets point towards the grand epic style in such modes of elevation as periphrasis and inversion; and, despite the rhyme scheme, run-on lines and internal pauses give the effect of a massive paragraph of blank verse.

When Milton came, about 1657, to active composition of his long-postponed epic, he chose what a biblical age accepted as the first of the three supreme events in world history. The subject, through centuries of imaginative and theological treatment, had acquired embellishments, and a modern poet, like a Greek dramatist, could build on established associations. *Paradise Lost* has the theological framework (including some heresies) that Milton set forth in his big Latin treatise *On Christian Doctrine* (completed about 1658–60), but there Satan and the war in heaven, for instance, were allowed only a few lines. Modern views of 'myth' would seem to have largely blunted the conventional nineteenth-century charge against outworn fundamentalism, and the poem can be read as a grand myth on the conflict between good and evil in the heart of man and in human history; though a reader loses much who cannot bring to Milton—as to Dante—imaginative sympathy with belief in a divine order and the divine absolutes of good, of justice, love, and mercy. In casting his material in the mould of a traditional heroic poem (while repudiating traditional heroism), Milton faced obstacles which had been less troublesome for Virgil and had not existed for Homer. Thus God and the Son, as speaking characters, may seem to represent rigour and compassion respectively; but these are two integral attributes of Deity, and in his concern with divine justice upon sin Milton was at one with the whole Christian tradition (including Lancelot Andrewes).

In some large and obvious ways the pattern of *Paradise Lost* follows that of the *Aeneid*—the plunge *in medias res*, the roll-call and council of leaders, the recapitulation of the past and prophecy of the future, the use of celestial powers; and there is a kind of affinity between the two epic pictures of a 'world destroy'd and world restor'd'. But, as always, Milton re-created everything he imitated. Invocations of the Muse became moving prayers for divine aid. And Milton went far beyond the ancients in knitting his story and scenes together through a network of parallels and contrasts, large and small, literal and symbolic—light and darkness, order and anarchy, love and hate, creation and destruction, and so on.

If traditional epic concreteness had its disadvantages (most of which Milton triumphantly surmounted), it also made possible the tremendous figure of Satan. His great qualities are those of the ancient epic hero, raised to a superhuman degree, but they are wholly corrupted by egocentric pride and passion. Milton was daring in giving his first two books, books of sustained energy and splendour, to his cosmic 'villain'; yet, for all readers capable of understanding Christian values, Satan, from his first speech onwards, reveals his corruption—in the same way as Richard III, Iago, Edmund, and Macbeth do. At times Satan reminds us of some of these, as in his sardonic gloating over the ruin he is about to bring on Adam and Eve:

> Hell shall unfold,
> To entertain you two, her widest Gates,
> And send forth all her Kings.

But the conscious ironist is himself enveloped in irony, since, though he achieves his end and though history is to be a record of evil, invincible good exists.

Adam and Eve are likewise enveloped in irony. The Garden, on which Milton lavishes all the beauties of the traditional earthly paradise, is one more vision of perfection; yet we see it only under the shadow of Satan's presence. What is perhaps the most famous simile in English poetry gains part of its poignant beauty from its tacit anticipation of the fate of Eve:

> Not that faire field
> Of Enna, where Proserpin gathering
> flours
> Her self a fairer Floure by gloomie Dis
> Was gatherd, which cost Ceres all that
> pain
> To seek her through the world.

The fall is handled with potent dramatic insight. The superhuman pair sink in thought, feeling, act, and mode of speech to the human level; and our age should be qualified to appreciate the irony of a craving for godlike knowledge and power that issues in loveless lust. But man and wife are reunited on a higher level. And all Milton's grand pictures of Satan and the luridness of hell, of idyllic Eden, of interstellar space, converge and coalesce in the narrative simplicity and emotional complexity of the last lines, an 'emblem' of the human situation:

> They looking back, all th' Eastern side
> beheld
> Of Paradise, so late thir happie seat,
> Wav'd over by that flaming Brand, the
> Gate
> With dreadful Faces throng'd, and fierie
> Armes:
> Som natural tears they drop'd, but wip'd
> them soon;
> The World was all before them, where to
> choose
> Thir place of rest, and Providence thir
> guide:
> They hand in hand with wandring steps
> and slow,
> Through Eden took thir solitarie way.

In keeping with his exalted theme and the maintaining of aesthetic distance, Milton's language is stylised, like that of Homer, Virgil and Tasso. But a frequent impressionistic complaint is exaggerated; only about a quarter of his words are latinate, and the supposedly classical syntax is often English, colloquial, and

elliptical. Milton's free placing of words and phrases allows a rich variety of emphasis and does not obscure the sense. These effects are further enriched by his masterful re-creation of blank verse. The basic unit is the ten-syllable line, in which stresses vary continually in number, position, and weight, so that individual lines ring infinite changes on a half-heard iambic norm and are also infinitely variable elements in the fluid pattern of the paragraph. Rhythm is a main agent of Milton's expressiveness and, more than most poets, he needs to be read aloud.

The short sequel to *Paradise Lost* was a wholly different kind of poem, in a style of almost biblical plainness. *Paradise Regained*, often dismissed as cold, has all the heat of Milton's passion for righteousness. The emphasis is on Christ the man, the perfect exemplar of faith and obedience, of the truly heroic knowledge of which the repentant Adam and Eve had a glimpse. There is dramatic tension in Satan's increasingly desperate efforts to confirm his fear that he is confronting his destined conqueror. In the swift dramatic climax Christ's divinity is manifested to both Satan and himself.

Samson Agonistes, the one great English tragedy on the Greek model, has for its protagonist a human sinner, ordinary in everything but physical strength and a Hebraic conscience. (The drama is essentially Christian, though no specifically Christian tenet appears.) Beginning in self-centred misery, 'Eyeless in Gaza at the Mill with slaves', Samson rises through a series of encounters with the chorus, his father, Dalila, and the Philistine giant, to renewed and selfless faith and humility. Sophoclean irony is everywhere at work, from the title to the outcome of each scene. The blind Milton, in Restoration London, must have felt keenly the parallel between himself and his hero, but his

ersonal emotions are sublimated. The
irregular lines and rhythms have a massive,
sinewy idiom and movement which are
one more experimental phase in his
classical art:

Nothing is here for tears, nothing to wail
Or knock the breast, no weakness, no
                                                    contempt,
Dispraise, or blame, nothing but well
                                                    and fair,
And what may quiet us in a death so
                                                    noble.

To some readers the drama is the most
completely moving of Milton's works,
the *Lycidas* of his old age. In it, as in the
two epics, the erstwhile revolutionist
still has faith in God and the individual
soul, if not in England and mankind. D.B.
See also Foreign Influences on English
Poetry *and* Imagery

Moore, Marianne [Craig] (1887–   ), was
born in St Louis, Missouri, and her first
book, *Poems*, appeared in 1921. She is
now regarded as among the most distinguished of American poets, and in
1952 she received the Bollingen Award,
the National Book Award, and the Pulitzer Prize for her *Collected Poems*. In 1955
she was elected a member of the American
Academy of Arts and Letters.

Marianne Moore's poetry exhibits both
feminine delicacy and intellectual and
verbal precision. She frequently writes
about animals, particularly of an exotic
kind, though she often uses these subjects
to point obliquely some human moral.
She has a magpie-like facility for incorporating in her poems quotations that interest
her from a wide variety of sources—
travel books, newspaper reports, scientific
journals—and this reflects her belief that
everything is potentially material for
poetry.

The forms of her poetry are extremely

original; she makes considerable use of a
metre based on a fixed pattern of syllables,
rather than the normal repetition of
stresses, and she is fond of unaccented
rhymes. The opening of *Smooth Gnarled
Crape Myrtle* shows Marianne Moore at
her most characteristic, and provides a
good example of her capacity for minute
observation:

A brass-green bird with grass-
green throat smooth as a nut springs
                                                    from
  twig to twig askew, copying the
Chinese flower piece,—businesslike atom
  in the stiff-leafed tree's blue-
  pink dregs-of-wine pyramids
  of mathematic
  circularity. . . .

Randall **Jarrell** has written of Marianne
Moore: 'She is *the* poet of the particular—
or, when she fails, of the peculiar; and is
also, in our time, *the* poet of general
moral statement'.   B.B.

See also American Poetry *and* Imagery

Moore, Thomas (1779–1852), was born
in Dublin and educated at Trinity College
there. A close friend of **Byron**, he acquired
international reputation with the publication of *Lalla Rookh* in 1817. He is
remembered now for his songs, especially,
'Believe me, if all those endearing young
charms'.   D.H.

Moore, Thomas Sturge (1870–1944), was
an English poet, art historian and wood
engraver, and was a friend and correspondent of W. B. **Yeats**. Their correspondence has been published in an
edition by Ursula Bridge. *Selected Poems*
(1934) have been called 'severely classical
in tone, academic in expression and finely
chiselled'.   D.H.

Morris, William (1834–96), London-born English socialist and founder of the Kelmscott Press, was associated with the Pre-Raphaelite brotherhood and was a designer and craftsman, as well as a writer. His epic and lyric poems reveal an interest in Greek, Scandinavian and medieval legend. His prose works include *News from Nowhere* (1891).

see also Foreign Influences on English Poetry   D.H.

Muir, Edwin (1887–1959), was born in Orkney, the son of a crofter. When he was fourteen the family moved to Glasgow. After doing a number of menial jobs Muir came to London in 1919 and married Willa Anderson. Together they travelled extensively in Europe between the wars, collaborating in many translations, notably of Kafka. Later Muir worked for the British Council in Prague and Rome and was Warden of Newbattle Abbey College, Dalkeith. He died in Cambridge and is buried at Swaffham Prior. His *Collected Poems 1921–1958* appeared in 1960.

Muir did not begin writing poetry seriously until he was thirty-five, and then only after a period of Jungian psychological analysis. Although he wrote poems for almost forty years, it was not until the last ten years of his life that he achieved real recognition. After his death T. S. **Eliot** praised his literary criticism and considered that his poetry 'ranked with the best poetry of our time'.

Muir's poetry is most profitably read in conjunction with his *Autobiography* (1954). This was originally published as *The Story and the Fable* (1940), a title that expresses the essence of his thought. For he sees the outward story of each man's life as inextricably bound up with his dreams and ancestral memories. Thus the ancient myths, particularly those of biblical and Greek origin, had a great

fascination for him; his poems are a progressively deeper exploration of these archetypes of the unconscious.

Muir's poems, while often dramatic, owe little to verbal novelty or brilliant imagery, and are largely traditional in form. His work is generally sombre, reflecting the bare landscape and subtle tones of his native Orkney. Indeed, he remained to the end loyal to the pastoral tradition of his childhood:

> My childhood all a myth
> Enacted on a distant isle.
> Time with his hourglass and his scythe
> Stood dreaming on the dial.

Many of his poems are (to quote the title of one of his books) 'variations on a time theme'—profound reflections on the perpetual dissolution of experience in the temporal flux:

> Time takes the foliage and the fruit
> And burns the archetypal leaf
> To shapes of terror and of grief
> Scattered along the winter way.

Towards the end of his life Muir, although never an orthodox believer, found some release from these spiritual conflicts in the Christian religion. His last poems have an authority and breadth of vision rare in the poetry of their time.

                                                    J.C.H.

Music and Poetry. The problem of the relationship of words and music is a perennially vexed one. 'Sphere-born harmonious sisters—Voice and Verse' says **Milton,** but they have seldom held an equal status. To formulate a definitive table of how to set verse (whatever its pattern) is impossible. What will please the poet is unlikely to please the musician. Once poetry is set to a song it has to forfeit its independence and become music. It has to obey musical rules.

Poetry comes off best, it is most audible and free, when it is unaccompanied or freely accompanied, and uncluttered by other instrumental or vocal disciplines. We are told by St. Augustine that (in the fourth century) St. Athanasius had insisted that the Psalms should be chanted as near to speech and with as little warbling as possible. St. Augustine confesses to being excessively beguiled by the music at the expense of the text, by the singing instead of the thing sung. The struggle between voice and verse is already far advanced, and as far as the Church was concerned, music (assisted and, in the way of sonorities, almost formed by the acoustic of the great medieval churches) was for centuries in charge. The unaccompanied plainsong chanters had become so unbridled in their 'excrescencies' that they had to be restrained by Papal decree in 1577, and secular tunes had invaded the maze of polyphony. The Reformers were of course on the side of the Text. The peculiar gift of man, as distinct from the birds, said Calvin in 1543, is to sing knowing what he is saying. This is the antithesis of the *jubilatio*, a spontaneous improvised wordless utterance of joy, taken for the use of the early Church from labourers and sailors. It is clear that the early fathers wanted a mixture of this natural popular expression with serious learning.

The congregational hymn was the reformer's answer to polyphony, and many beautiful texts were married to fine tunes (some from abroad). Although popular music gave much to the Church, the text, of its nature, could hardly do so. The carol was long the musical meeting place of church and people, and the most famous piece of Early English music, the rota, *Sumer is icumen in*, was a perfect example of the fusion of popular and learned music, as well as being a wonderful setting of words.

But the full flowering of poet and composer did not come until later. Then the flood was rich. The madrigals and lute songs poured from the Elizabethan presses for thirty years in great variety. In madrigals, the composers followed the mood of the text very closely and the music was performed, according to Thomas Morley's instructions, freely and fancifully. In the Ayres, the music kept nearer to the rhythm of the words and relied on a seemingly artless melodic line. There are exceedingly few melismas in the Elizabethan lute songs. Thomas **Campion**, the lutenists' chief spokesman, was a charming composer as well as an exquisite poet, and the variety of his metric schemes and their perfect aptness for music have never been equalled. He held forth violently against 'rhyme' and strove to substitute classical metres, but in fact the vast majority of his song-lyrics are rhymed, and there is one setting only of Sapphics and that is more curious than successful. Thomas Morley's single book of Ayres shows a rather more learned musical approach to sole songs than Campion or Rosseter or Jones who were all men of the theatre. The giant of the group was John Dowland, a great lutenist as well as composer. His natural mood was melancholy (*semper Dowland, semper dolens*), and his big, sombre songs are not surpassed in any song-literature. The dramatic accentuation of *Sorrow stay* is masterly. On the other hand, *In darkness let me dwell* contains word-settings which can only properly be explained on the ground that the sentiment of the song is so distracted that elongation of short syllables, and quick repetition of dense words fit the mood.

At this time (*c.* 1600) there came the

great monodic revolution in Italy, which rejected polyphony on the grounds of the 'laceration' of the text, and, invoking Plato and the method of singing in ancient Greece, endeavoured 'the imitation of the conceit of the words', accompanied by figured bass (where a single bass instrument plays an accompanying line, to which figures are attached denoting the harmonic framework for a keyboard instrument). This soon led to the rise of the virtuoso singer and to the development of opera, where the text became divided, for musical and vocal reasons, into sections which were primarily informative (recitatives) and others which were intended to be expressive and more worked out musically. In the former the words were generally well served, while in the latter they became less and less important.

The domestic songs of the seventeenth century, plentiful though they are in Playford's publications, and supplied though they may be with exquisite lyrics by **Herrick**, **Waller**, and others, seldom reach very great heights. Henry Lawes' setting of words may have pleased Milton but, with few exceptions, his vocal lines are simple to the point of banality, and, though they ought to be enlivened in performance with tasteful musical ornaments, they are rhythmically not to be compared with those of Rosseter or even Campion. This comes simply from too great a respect for the words and a lack of musical genius, which certainly cannot be said of Henry Purcell or of his older contemporary, John Blow. Both these men wrote operas of surpassing beauty, and numbers of lovely and touching songs, using with the utmost subtlety the Italian-born forms of recitative and aria. In *Dido and Aeneas*, in particular, Purcell succeeded time after time in giving vivid dramatic character to Nahum Tate's adequate text by musical touches of

genius. Settings of lines such as 'See! See! your royal guest appears'; 'Fear no danger to ensue'; and 'Pursue thy conquest, Love', cannot be bettered for varied dramatic emphasis.

Weak syllables must be permitted an accent if the character of the musical situation demands. In many of the songs of Purcell and Blow the conventions ordained florid vocal illustrations to words such as 'fly', 'glory', 'piercing', 'fury' and the like, and in a generation this led to the absurdities of the Italian operas which Handel wrote for London and which in turn provoked the inevitable and healthy riposte of *The Beggar's Opera*, a simplified musical show which was the ancestor of **Gilbert** and Sullivan. Handel himself could set English magically when he was fired to do so. Milton, **Pope**, **Dryden**, **Gay**, and Congreve drew from him exquisite and apt melody, and the limpid monosyllables of 'Where'er you walk' have a perfectly just accent. 'Come and trip it as you go' from *L'Allegro* shows what Handel owed to Purcell in setting English, and Arne showed at the same time what could be learned from Handel.

Tragically enough, when English lyrical poetry flowered again, there were no composers to set it. The successful songs of the nineteenth century have verses of ludicrous mediocrity. A very occasional lucky setting of **Shakespeare** is the only relief from a succession of Bunns, Bayleys, Bellamys and Fitzballs. 'O no! we never mention her' is a fair sample. Sir Hubert Parry was determined to clean all this up, but though his good taste and good intentions cannot be denied, the melodic invention shown in his many song settings is not very great: the Irish Stanford succeeded better with an Irish poet. There followed a period of thirty or forty years in which the two poets most in use by composers were A. E. **Housman** and

Walter **de la Mare**, the one for his intensity, the other for his varied and subtle colours. Among successful settings of the first are those by Somervell, Vaughan Williams, John Ireland, and, finest, George Butterworth; of the second, those by Herbert Howells and Armstrong Gibbs. The Elizabethans were set very happily by Peter Warlock. By this time, the poets had not to fear that their words would not be respected; on the contrary, with the banishment of anything like a melisma, the danger was that the composer would only succeed in lifting them reverently into tonality—reverently but dully. This was partly due to Wagnerian declamation and partly to the influence of the folk-song revival, which, while it revealed the musical treasures we had almost lost, emphasised, in putting these on paper, the syllabic melodic setting of the words, and did not usually try to suggest the singer's own vocal contributions, effects, turns or twists—in fact jubilations—which folk singers have always used.

It was a natural feeling for this vocal expansiveness, which all good song composers must have, which led to Benjamin Britten's success in liberating song from syllabic shackles. With him the poet's words are respected and transformed; if the text is treated roughly it is for a good musical reason: e.g. **Auden**'s 'As it is, plenty' where false accents are used to underline an atmosphere of mechanical and shallow gaiety.

As to the future of songs. Unless serial composers for the voice are prepared to use less violent methods both towards the text and towards the voice, singing of new art songs may be expected to die. As there is no obvious place for singing in electronic music, reliance on the old repertory will be intensified. Singers should hardly be blamed if they go to jazz for their *jubilatio*.   P.P.

Myth and Poetry. A myth, in its simplest meaning, is a story about a god, or some being comparable to a god. Hence myths usually grow up in close association with religions, but, because they are stories, they also belong to literature, especially to narrative, fictional and dramatic literature with internal characters. It makes no difference to its relation to literature whether a myth is believed to be true or false. Classical mythology became purely literary after the religions associated with it died, but from a literary point of view we may speak of Christian or Hindu mythology even when the attitude towards it is also one of religious acceptance.

Most of the stories we call myths are ancient and arose in the period of oral tradition along with folk tales. Primitive cultures generally have in their oral tradition a special group of canonical tales which are regarded as particularly serious or important, as having 'really happened', or as being of special significance in explaining certain features of the society, such as a ritual or the origin of a tribe or class; these are myths. In structure, however, there is little to distinguish a myth from a folk tale. Such Classical legends as the story of Cupid and Psyche in Apuleius' *The Golden Ass* have many analogues in folk tale, and so have the Hebrew legends of the Creation, the Fall, and the Flood. The difference is that myths, because of their central and canonical importance, tend to stick together and form mythologies, whereas folk tales simply disseminate and interchange motifs. It is not any structural feature in the stories of Phaethon or Endymion that makes them myths, for we could—and do—have folk tales of the same kind: it is their attachment to a growing body of stories told about a sun-god and a moon-goddess, and the further attachment of these deities to Apollo and Artemis in the Olympian hierarchy, that make them myths.

The true myth, then, is an episode in a mythology, and a developed mythology tends to become encyclopedic, that is, to provide a complete set of stories dealing with a society's religious observances, its origin and its earlier history. A mythology, we may say, undertakes to tell the definitive story of how a given culture or society came to be what it is. Besides this, it supplies a number of episodic tales illustrating the relations of gods with one another or with man, usually with a cautionary moral. It identifies or interrelates the various gods of local cults; it sanctions the law by giving it a divine origin; it provides a divine ancestry for its kings and heroes. At a certain stage of development a mythology produces a theogony, a connected narrative beginning with the origin of the gods and of the departments of nature they personify, such as heaven and earth, the creation and original state of mankind, the inauguration of law and culture, and so on down to the writer's own time. Some theogonies carry on the story to the end of time and the future annihilation of the world. The theogonic narrative structure, as well as all the subordinate functions of myth just listed, occur both in sacred books, such as the Christian Bible, which have a major literary influence, and in literature itself, as in Hesiod, and Ovid's *Metamorphoses*. In the theogony a mythology has expanded into a story with larger religious and philosophical outlines, where we are reading about the origin, situation and destiny of mankind as a whole.

As a society develops, its myths naturally become revised, selected, expurgated or reinterpreted to suit its changing religious needs. An immense amount of editorial labour lies between the myths of the Old Testament and the same myths in their modern form. The more archaic stories are often felt to be in bad theological taste; as Plutarch says, gods represented as doing unworthy things are no gods. In this way is developed a tradition of explaining or accounting for myths. Myths may be interpreted as allegories illustrating moral truths. Hence the device known in Greek culture as *hyponoia*, the attempt, say, to save the faces of both Homer and Aphrodite by explaining the story of Hephaestus' net in the *Odyssey* as an allegory of something profound and morally respectable. Or mythology as a whole may be interpreted allegorically, as primitive science, as esoteric philosophy, as distorted history, or (since the rise of Freudian psychology) as sexually directed dream. The interpretation of myth, chiefly as moral allegory, was one of the cultural heavy industries of Western Europe between Plutarch and the late Renaissance, and it played a very important role in literature, as Renaissance poets were accustomed to make great use of such allegorical handbooks as Natalis Comes' *Mythologia* or Sandys' translation of Ovid. Similar handbooks were used by **Blake, Shelley, Keats** and Goethe in the Romantic period, and they were still being written as late as Ruskin's *Queen of the Air*.

For poets, however, myth remains primarily a story: its meaning is implicit in the story itself, and the poet's impulse is to retell the story, or invent a new one with the same characters. Plato, for example, ridicules *hyponoia*, but he uses his own myths, usually with the familiar names of Zeus and Prometheus. Whether a poet is interested simply in the story or in giving a particular meaning to the story will depend, of course, on his temperament and circumstances. But there are at least three reasons why myth has a distinctive connection with poetry.

In the first place, a fully developed mythology, especially one that has produced a definitive theogony or sacred book, provides the outlines of a total verbal communication. There is nothing about the duties, destiny, meaning or context of human life, nothing at least which can be expressed in words, that is not explained or provided for in the accepted myth. This is the normal attitude of an orthodox Christian or Mohammedan to the Bible or the Koran, and it is the usual attitude of all religions to their sacred books. The poet can seldom claim such authority, but if he is a poet of great imaginative scope, inclined to think deeply on the largest possible issues of life, and attracted to the genres of greatest range, such as the epic, he is likely to make his major poem a re-creation of a myth. **Milton**'s *Paradise Lost* deals primarily with the biblical myths of the creation and the fall, but of course the whole structure of biblical mythology, from the beginning to the end of time, is re-created in it. In Dante it is the sacramental system of the Church rather than the narrative of the Bible that is primarily re-created, but the same encyclopedic reconstruction of a traditional mythology has taken place. And whenever a poet chooses a theme of particular significance in expressing his conception of life as a whole, it is likely to be a traditional mythical theme. Shelley's *Prometheus Unbound*, **Byron**'s *Cain*, Victor Hugo's *Fin de Satan*, are random examples. Classical mythology is particularly useful to Western poets whenever doctrinal reasons prevent them from using the Bible: thus if Ariosto wishes to provide a mythical ancestry for his patrons, he will turn to Virgil and the Trojan War.

In the second place, myths are about gods, and gods are usually associated with some (or, as with Christ, all) aspects of the physical world. The association is

usually one of identity, expressed by metaphor: thus we speak of Apollo, in pure metaphor, as a 'sun-god'. Hence myth enables a poet to make an unusually full use of metaphor, of natural imagery, of an imaginative identification of human emotion and nature. If **Shakespeare**'s *Venus and Adonis* has been about more realistically conceived characters, like *Romeo and Juliet*, there might have been certain advantages, but the young poet would not have had nearly so much fun playing with his imagery and working out such associations as the 'solemn sympathy' between the crimson flower and the death of Adonis. And even when the explicit connection with myth is dropped, the metaphorical concentration of myth is likely to remain. Thus the language of myth tends to become the language of poetry. Keats' *Ode to Psyche* is explicitly addressed to a goddess; the odes to autumn and the nightingale are not; but Autumn with her hair soft-lifted by the winnowing wind is no less a goddess, and the nightingale no less a light-winged Dryad of the trees, even if not directly associated with what **Cowper** calls Philomela's 'mechanick woe'.

Finally, myths are stories about characters who, almost by definition, can do what they like—which means in practice what the story-teller likes. Hence myths are abstract literary patterns, stories told without adjustment to demands for realism, plausibility, logical motivation, or the conditions of limited power. Later on, in literature, these demands are met, but they are met only by 'displacement', that is, by adaptation of the mythical pattern to a realistic setting. Thus the plots of *Tom Jones* and *Oliver Twist* are realistic adaptations of stories of the mysterious birth of a hero that can be traced through New Comedy and Euripides to such myths as those of Perseus and Moses. New plots are not invented; the old plots are adapted, not because they are old, but because there is a very limited number of effective ways in which a story may be told, and the mythology which does not provide examples of the entire number is rare indeed. An author's awareness of the traditional affinities of his plot matters little. We know from the critical gossip surrounding T. S. **Eliot**'s *The Confidential Clerk* that its author was aware of its resemblance to Euripides' *Ion*, and of the mythical patterns behind that play; we have no reason to suppose Oscar **Wilde** or W. S. **Gilbert** equally aware of similar resemblances in *The Importance of Being Earnest* or *The Gondoliers*. The resemblances are based on the structural principles of comedy, not on the author's erudition.

The conclusion from all this is that a fully developed literature, as a whole, is what a fully developed mythology is in earlier ages: a total structure of imaginative verbal communication. It fills up its space more completely: a myth may recall an entire mythology to one familiar with it, but most literary works, unlike the *Divina Commedia* or *Paradise Lost*, give little indication, except of a very indirect and oblique kind, of the whole range of literary experience. Again, literary criticism does not have a word, or a conception, for literature as a whole which would have the same relation to individual works of literature that 'mythology' has to individual myths. It it had, the true relation of myth to poetry would be self-evident.   N.F.

N

Nash, Ogden (1902–   ), is an American writer of light verse. His sophisticated, unconventional and often whimsical poetry, frequently published in *The New Yorker*, is most popular with the eastern American upper-middle class it satirises.

D.H.

Nashe, Thomas (1567–1601), was the son of a minister in Lowestoft, Suffolk, and attended St John's College, Cambridge. He then went to London, where he became one of the most skilful and controversial pamphleteers of his day. He wrote an invective against women, *The Anatomy of Absurdity* (1589), and a satiric homily on the seven deadly sins, *Piers Penilesse, his Supplication to the Divell* (1592). He was

deeply involved in the Martin Marprelate controversy as the principal defender of established institutions against the puritanical Martinist's assaults. He also engaged in frequent public controversy with the Harvey brothers (*Strange News*, 1592, and *Have With You to Saffron Walden*, 1596), accusing them of pedantry, narrow-mindedness, and hypocrisy. Nashe was a master of invective, making his adversaries seem pretentious and ludicrous. He also wrote one of the first novels, a grotesque and picaresque comic tale called *An Unfortunate Traveller* (1594). His verse is equally forceful and effective. He wrote a long comic poem, *Summer's Last Will and Testament*, in which the dying summer comments on the world it leaves. The poem is full of sharp social observations:

Those that now serpent-like creepe on
                  the ground,
And seeme to eate the dust, they
                  crowch so low;
If they be disappointed of their pray,
Most traiterously will trace their tailes
                  and sting.
Yea, such as, like the Lapwing, build
                  their nests
In a mans dung, come vp by drudgerie,
Will be the first that, like that foolish
                  bird,
Will follow him with yelling and false
                  cries.

He satirised pedants, sycophantic poets, and people who claimed to be more than they were:

After eche nation got these toyes in vse,
There grew vp certaine drunken
                  parasites,
Term'd Poets, which, for a meales
                  meat or two,
Would promise monarchs immortalitie:
They vomited in verse all that they knew,
Found causes and beginnings of the
                  world,

Yet Nashe was not simply a bitterly intelligent iconoclast. *Summer's Last Will and Testament* also contains the famous song, 'Adieu, farewell earth's bliss', one of the most effective of all Elizabethan songs, with its sharp and graceful tolling of the passing of human experience. Two separate stanzas follow:

Beauty is but a flowre,
Which wrinckles will deuoure,
Brightnesse falls from the ayre,
Queenes haue died yong and faire,
Dust hath closde Helens eye.
I am sick, I must dye:
    Lord, haue mercy on vs.

Wit with his wantonesse
Tasteth deaths bitternesse:
Hels executioner

Hath no eares for to heare
What vaine art can reply.
I am sick, I must dye:
    Lord haue mercy on vs.

                        J.G.

Nemerov, Howard (1920–), is an American poet, critic and novelist. His first poems were sophisticated and literary in the extreme, and best when they were satiric. His later poems have become increasingly simple in language and straightforward in tone, at the same time as they have treated subjects of increasing complexity and import.

New Criticism. The expression has acquired wide currency since 1941, when the Southern poet, John Crowe **Ransom,** first published his book *The New Criticism*, in which he defined the main traits of an attitude in literary appreciation which had been taking shape on both sides of the Atlantic during the previous two or three decades. But the same designation had already appeared in 1910, with the brisk essay the Renaissance scholar, Joel Spingarn, devoted to the cause of pure literature unhampered by non-aesthetic considerations. The concordance is significant because Spingarn openly stated his indebtedness to the ideas of Benedetto Croce, who had relentlessly attacked extra-literary misconceptions in the domain of criticism, and argued for an evaluation focused on the specifically aesthetic aspects of the work of art. Ransom was aware of Croce, and certainly shared with the Italian philosopher a deliberate concern for the intrinsic values of poetry as against those elements which have only an indirect relevance to it; at the same time, his sources were manifold, and they included T. S. **Eliot,** whose early collection of essays *The Sacred Wood* (1920) marked a turning point in literary approach. Along with Eliot, Ezra **Pound** was a shaping influence on the 'New Critics' for his belligerent emphasis on style and design, firmly outlined since 1910 in *The Spirit of Romance*. Thus through Pound and his British inspirer, T. E. Hulme, the 'new critical' school is linked with the Imagist movement which exerted a purifying pressure on the language of modern poetry.

Unfair objections to the New Critics as an esoteric clique organised for the benefit of obscure poetry stem from the fact that they evolved a technical terminology to deal with the non-discursive phenomena of poetical language, and since modern poetry in any Western language has been concentrating precisely on those phenomena, the connection between New Critics and new poets was inevitable, though by no means conspiratorial. Thinkers like Aristotle and (to a lesser extent) **Coleridge** provided additional tools, hence R. P. Blackmur (*The Expense of Greatness*, 1940; *Language as Gesture*, 1952), tried to combine both sources in his quest for a philosophical foundation to his stylistic analyses, while R. S. Crane, leader of the 'Chicago Aristotelians', clung to the Greek alone. Certain of the terms introduced or revived are now commonplace, for instance Ransom's 'structure and texture', Allen **Tate**'s 'tension', Cleanth Brooks' 'paradox', William **Empson**'s 'ambiguity', Kenneth Burke's 'symbolic action', and of course T. S. Eliot's 'objective correlative', not to mention the general interest in symbol, archetype and myth. Of these writers, Tate, Brooks and Ransom were involved in the Southern **Fugitive** movement of the twenties, and they share with Eliot a 'reactionary' fondness for the lost Christian unity of Western culture. Others have little to do with any such ideology, and Empson, whose *Seven Types of Ambiguity*

appeared in 1930 in the wake of I. A. Richards' *Principles of Literary Criticism* (1924), is British. Frank Raymond Leavis, the most influential representative of New Criticism in Britain, is less theoretically oriented than either of his fellow-countrymen; his *New Bearings in English Poetry* (1932), *Revaluation* (1936) and *The Great Tradition* (1948) constitute decisive contributions to that exacting cult of close reading which has perhaps in Allen Tate (*Reactionary Essays on Poetry and Ideas*, 1936; *Reason in Madness*, 1941; *The Forlorn Demon*, 1953; *The Man of Letters in the Modern World*, 1955) and in Cleanth Brooks (*Modern Poetry and the Tradition*, 1939; *The Well-Wrought Urn*, 1947) its finest American devotees.

Like Croceanism in Italy, New Criticism has recently come under fire in the English-speaking countries because it is academically entrenched, or because it has upset certain traditional valuations by stressing the poetry of wit, complexity and paradox against any form of *naïveté*, exuberance or vagueness; the fact remains that, prejudices aside, these critics have really taught us 'how to read', and with an authority that derives in many cases from their personal acquaintance with the creative process.   G.C.

New Directions in Metrics. What is metre? Impulses in the poet's brain? Or in the reader's brain? Marks on paper? A concretion? An intuition? An abstraction? A fiction? What do we do when we scan?

Some modern metrists think that intelligent answers can be found only through scientific inquiry into the fundamental parameters of rhythm and language. Rhythm is an auditory percept and hence a subject for psychologists. [The most recent study of rhythm is Paul Fraisse, *Les Structures Rythmiques: Étude Psycho-*

logique (Publications Universitaires, Louvain, 1956).] In its elemental state, it is a series of acoustic events of equal duration, pitch, and loudness occurring at equal intervals, graphically representable as a series of dots of equal size separated by equal spaces: ‧‧‧‧‧‧ However, the mind is anxious for regularity: it does not insist upon perfect equalities but welcomes, as rhythmic, sequences of events which are slightly variant. The simple rhythm of equal events at equal intervals is called 'cardiac' or 'primary'. We more commonly experience 'grouped' or 'secondary' rhythm—‧ O ‧ O ‧ O ‧ O —where the more prominent event has some recurrent sound difference or combination of sound differences.

What is there in the sound structure of English words which allows them to be disposed into secondary rhythmic patterns? There are a variety of views, and any answer will be controversial. But linguistic controversy is better than linguistic naïveté. By definition, rhythm can be achieved in language only through arrangements of vocal sounds. These sounds can be studied from two points of view, phonetic and phonemic. Phonetics describes and measures features like quality, length, pitch, loudness, timbre, etc., without reference to function. Phonemics considers only those sound distinctions with semantic implications: the sound /k/ is a phoneme in English because it signals that 'cat' is not the same as 'gnat', 'bat', 'rat', 'mat', etc. Similarly, the phoneme /′/ (read 'stress') tells us that 'disease' is not the same as 'dizzies' (even though the other phonemes—/d/, /i/, etc. —are identical).

Secondary rhythm has three components: (1) a time continuum, (2) a set of acoustic events, and (3) prominence 'on' selected recurrent events. Graphically:

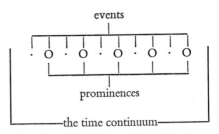

Since metre is a species of rhythm, our central theoretical question is: What elements of the language can function in metrical capacities?

1. Although language proceeds through time, time itself is not a distinctive feature in English, so the first element is given, but uninteresting. The space which a printed line of verse occupies is an obvious (though not an exact) analogue of the time it takes to recite.

2. The role of 'event' is played by the 'syllable'. Although serious problems have arisen in linguistically specifying syllable boundaries, there is little doubt that it is a linguistic unit. [There is no convenient summary of scholarship on the syllable. A good recent article is J. D. O'Connor and J. L. M. Trim, 'Vowel, Consonant, and Syllable—A Phonological Definition', *Word* IX (1953), 103–22.] And boundary determination seems unimportant to metrics: in **Wordsworth**'s

Ethereal minstrel! pilgrim of the sky

it is irrelevant whether minstrel is divided 'min-strel', 'mins-trel', or 'minst-rel'. All that matters is what is obvious, namely that there are two syllables. Poets have often altered syllable-count by various means: apocope ('th'army'), aphaeresis ('′tis'), vowel syncope ('med'cine'), consonant syncope ('de'l' for 'devil'), synaeresis ('many'a'=two syllables), synizesis ('being'=one syllable). Metrics needs to

193

describe these devices accurately and to decide upon their logical status. [Seymour Chatman, 'Comparing Metrical Styles', *Style in Language* (Technology Press and Wiley, New York, 1960), pp. 162–3.] Are they parts of the metre or of the performance?

3. The crucial problem in metrics is: What is prominence? Here we vitally need reliable linguistic insights. A plausible definition of ictus cannot be achieved without a genuine understanding of stress, accent, intonation and other linguistic features. Metrics as a phonetic problem is nothing new. Experimental phoneticians were attempting to discover the laws of metre in precise sound measurements in the nineteenth century. [Representative of early efforts are Ada Snell, *Pause: A Study of Its Nature . . .* (University of Michigan, Ann Arbor, 1918) and E. W. Scripture, *Grundzüge der englischen Verswissenschaft* (Elwert'sche Verlagsbuchhandlung, Marburg, 1929).] Despite the crudity of early instruments, it was soon possible to lay some idle prosodic ghosts, for example, the notions that syllable-duration is the only factor in prominence, that simple and exact temporal ratios (say 2:1) exist between 'long' and 'short' syllables, and that the mind possesses an elaborate timing device for scanning. By 1935, a phonetician [Wilbur Schramm, *Approaches to a Science of English Verse* (University of Iowa Studies, Series on Aims and Progress of Research, No. 46, Iowa City, 1935)] was able to record the duration, acoustic intensity, and frequency of a recitation by means of an electronic device that represented the recitation in diagrammatic form. Today we have devices like the 'sound spectograph' which will make even more accurate traces of acoustic phenomena.

But no matter how exactly and subtly

a machine traces, it cannot tell us what metre is, nor how we scan. Obviously, people were agreeing on scansions long before these machines were invented. Furthermore, although tracings usually confirm our intuitions as to the correct scansion, they have been known to show inconclusive or patently invalid distinctions. In one experiment, for example, in the word 'homeward', 'ward' was marked as longer and more intense than 'home' and at about the same frequency; but no metrist would approve of the scansion 'homeward'.

Why? Because the *phonemic* pattern is 'homeward'. Stress is a *potential*: regardless of the actual sound-features present in any individual articulation of a word, the syllable which is potentially prominent is the one that carries phonemic stress. The phonetics of stress are too complex to go into here; suffice it to say that all native speakers know where the stress falls on a multi-syllabic word if they know how to pronounce the word at all; we learn the stress-potentialities as part of our lexical repertoire. The normal phonemic command of their language is what enables people to scan, and it is in phonemics that we must seek to determine which features are utilised to signal prominence.

Not only is a clear knowledge of phonemic stress necessary to metrics, but also an understanding of how stress combines systematically with other features, like intonation (ups and downs in the voice, distinguishing, for example, 'He's here today' from 'He's here today?'), and juncture (ways of going from one sound to another—the features, for example, which allow us to distinguish 'Ice-cream' from 'I scream'). It is worthwhile to discuss the metrical implications of two analyses of English phonology. The first structural linguistic formulations of English metrics were based on the Trager-Smith phonology [George L. Trager and Henry Lee Smith, Jr., *An Outline of English Structure, Studies in Linguistics: Occasional Papers* 3 (Battenburg Press, Norman, Oklahoma, 1951). The first efforts to apply Trager-Smith phonology to metrical problems can be found in the symposium 'English Verse and What It Sounds Like', *Kenyon Review* XVIII (1956), 411–77.] Trager-Smith postulate four stress phonemes (primary /ˊ/, secondary /∧/, tertiary /ˋ/, and weak /˘/, from loudest to softest), four pitch levels (/4/, /3/, /2/, /1/, from highest to lowest), and four junctures (/♯/ falling and fading, /∥/ rising, /|/ level sustentional, and /+/ minimal, i.e. 'nitrate' versus 'night rate'). Trager-Smith metrists generally assume that ictus is *relatively* determined: the 'ictus falls on the syllable bearing the stronger of any two of the four stress phonemes' (i.e. the iambic foot is not 'weak-strong' but 'weaker-stronger'). Furthermore, 'When two instances of the same stress phoneme occur on syllables immediately following each other, the occurrence of the second in the sequence will be phonetically more "prominent" than the first' so that 'identical feet' (spondees and pyrrhics) are theoretically impossible. Taken to its logical limits, Trager-Smith metrics envisages 6,236 possible arrangements of stress, juncture and pitch features for the iambic foot (weak-weak plus /+/, weak-weak plus /|/, etc.) [Edmund L. Epstein and Terence Hawkes, *Linguistics and English Prosody, Studies in Linguistics: Occasional Papers* 7 (University of Buffalo, 1959), and Henry Lee Smith, Jr., 'Toward Redefining English Prosody', *Studies in Linguistics* XIV (1960), 68–76.]

But metre itself cannot be the totality of such variations; it is rather the common denominator in all performances and hence an abstraction from them. What is abstracted is precisely the relation 'weaker-stronger'.

Trager-Smith phonology is popular but not universally accepted. Some linguists have felt that there are not as many as four stress levels, and that stress itself is signalled not only by loudness but by pitch and length differences as well. The most provocative alternative analysis is that of Dwight Bolinger. [See particularly Dwight Bolinger, 'A Theory of Pitch Accent in English', *Word* XIV (1958), 109–49, and citations therein.] Bolinger, whose views are supported by interesting experimentation, distinguishes between (word-)*stress* and (phrase-)*accent* rather than between stress levels and pitch levels. Word-stress is the contrast signalled by potential syllable prominence (by whatever phonetic means) between words like 'insight' and 'incite'. Phrase-accent, primarily indicated by pitch change, is the larger prosodic relation between words, for example, differences like that between 'There's the *Spanish* teacher' (the teacher of Spanish) and 'There's the Spanish *teacher*' (the teacher who is Spanish). According to Bolinger, this is not a difference in stress, since 'Span-' and 'teach-' have word-stress in both sentences. Phrase-accent includes what is popularly called 'emphasis'—the prominence placed on certain syllables in a phrase: 'He's a nice boy' (normal emphasis), 'He's a *nice* boy' (emphasising his niceness), '*He's* a nice boy' (not someone else), etc. In this system, only multi-syllabic words are said to have word-stress; both monosyllables and multi-syllables may have accent.

The metrical implications of Bolinger's system can best be demonstrated by an example. Consider the first line of **Shakespeare**'s Sonnet XVIII. The 'events' are clear: there are ten syllables. As for 'prominence', one conceivable recitation might be marked as follows (using Trager-Smith symbols):

²Shàll Ì com³páre theè² | ²to a ˄ súmmer's³ dáy¹ ♯

The line would be iambic with trochaic substitution in the third foot, since every even syllable except the sixth is either stronger than or at least as strong as the odd syllable which it follows:

ˋ ˋ	ˋ ˊ	ˋ ˘	˘ ˄	˘ ˊ
˘ —	˘ —	— ˘	˘ —	˘ —

In a Bolinger scansion, only the bi-syllables 'compáre' and 'súmmer' contain word-stresses, while '-pare' and 'day' have phrase-accents. The same rendition might be marked:

Shall I compáre thee | to a súmmer's *day*

From the metrical point of view, only the second, fourth and fifth feet are *linguistically* determined, that is, determined for all possible speakers (the fourth and fifth because 'summer's' has stress on the first syllable and 'day' has accent, so that the adjacent syllables 'a' and '-er's' must, by the relativity principle, be examples of thesis). 'Shall I' and 'thee to' are linguistically indeterminate. Some speakers will give 'thee' slight (allophonic) prominence over 'to', some will give 'to' prominence, and some neither (hence pyrrhics *are* possible in Bolinger's system). 'Shall I' is even more interesting: its scansion clearly depends on semantic considerations. Pyrrhus entails neutrality of meaning. Motions toward accent on 'shall' suggest increasing degrees of amused hesitancy ('Shall I? Is it worth my effort? Can anything be gained from such a manoeuvre? Won't the comparison be laughably invidious, since you are so obviously superior?'). Insisting on iambus implies temerity, on the other hand ('My attempts to reflect your splendours must necessarily prove dismal, "so how should I presume"?').

It is noteworthy that both Trager-Smith and Bolinger metrics draw a clear distinction between the *metre* and the *recitation* or *performance*. [Fuller implications of this distinction are worked out in two striking contributions to *Style in Language*, by Rulon S. Wells (pp. 197–200) and Roman Jakobson (350–77). The importance of the distinction has also been noted by W. K. Wimsatt and Monroe Beardsley, 'The concept of Meter: An Exercise in Abstraction', *Publications of the Modern Language Association* LXXIV (1959), 585–98.] In both views, metre is a simple binary abstraction derived from the linguistic relations among adjacent syllables. But there are differences about what constitutes the basis for abstraction. Some would presume a single 'normal' performance. Others would 'recognise the inevitability of different recitations' and also the fact that these *may* or *may not* subsume the same metre. Some would define metrical complexity as the enormous number of possibilities whereby a foot may be actualised. Others take it to be the fact, and the semantic implications of, variant performances and scansions. The innuendoes and suggestions of different recitations are of great metrical and interpretational interest. [See Seymour Chatman, 'Linguistics, Poetics, and Interpretation: The Phonemic Dimension', *Quarterly Journal of Speech* XLII (1957), 248–56.] A metrical theory which is logically sound, linguistically well-informed, and semantically serviceable to literary criticism is a challenging prospect.

s.c.

see also Prosody, Forms of Verse, and Some Usages

New Zealand Poetry has been much possessed by questions of identity— questions which geography alone will not answer. The mature poetry of this island community is not the poetry of Englishmen removed twelve thousand miles but otherwise unchanged. Nor is it the product of some strange mutation of spirit induced by Pacific sun. Its practitioners have faced a peculiarly difficult task in attempting to explore, without naïve assertion, a quality of experience and hence of sensibility subtly different from that defined in the work of other English-speaking poets. To call this a 'task' is to suggest, of course, a self-consciousness which would exaggerate difference and lead to eccentricity. It is only by hindsight that the critic observes this delicate process of definition and differentiation.

During the past thirty years their poetry has made literature real to New Zealanders as it cannot be real to a colonial people: only those who are familiar with the artistic imagination at work on what they know, can turn with full appreciation to the literature of societies they have never experienced.

It is not surprising that New Zealand readers take little interest in their own nineteenth-century poets. These turned the eyes of strangers on the new, untamed landscape, alternately delighted and appalled by it. Sometimes they asserted a new, brave independence; more often a nostalgia for English gardens and cities; but they wrote always as Englishmen abroad, straining to catch the ears of their countrymen at home who remained pardonably indifferent. The two halves of the colonial Janus face may be represented at their weak best in one poem, *A Colonist in his Garden* by William Pember Reeves (1857–1932). On the one hand there is pride and confidence in the new land:

Here am I rooted. Firm and fast
We men take root who face the blast,
  When to the desert come,
We stand where none before have stood
And braving tempest, drought and flood,
  Fight nature for a home.

On the other there is a deep nostalgia which confirms that pride and confidence exist as gestures only:

Yet that my heart to England cleaves
This garden tells with blooms and leaves
  In old familiar throng,
And smells, sweet English every one,
And English turf to tread upon,
  And English blackbird's song.

The dialectic can hardly be said to have generated memorable speech.

For the lack of a colonial ballad tradition such as exists in Australia, few contemporary New Zealand poets feel anything but gratitude. Such a tradition, where it exists, is likely to persist in the popular mind, diverting attention from all poetry which insists on a complex and precise response to the particularities of local experience. In New Zealand the poets of the nineteen-twenties and thirties—the first of any substance to write as New Zealanders—stepped on to a stage peopled only by Colonial-Imperial wraiths, easily dismissed. The best of these new poets, and of those who have followed more recently, have turned the difficulties and dangers of their craft to a refining discipline, offering work which a surprisingly large number of their countrymen now read with pleasure.

The poems that R. A. K. Mason (1905–) published in the early twenties are the first in which we hear clearly the voice of a New Zealander concerned with himself and those about him, indifferent to national or regional postur-

ing, honestly and unselfconsciously tough
and direct:

> And so he brazened it out right to the
> > last
> > still wore the gallant mask still cried
> > > 'divine
> am I, lo for me is heaven overcast'
> though that inscrutable darkness gave
> > no sign
> indifferent or malignant: while he
> > was passed
> by even the worst of men at least
> > sour wine.

If art implies sophistication, Mason is
innocent of it. His strength resides, like
Wilfred **Owen**'s, in a belief that 'the
true poets must be truthful'. Like Owen
he is driven by angry pity for human
suffering: 'the poetry is in the pity'.
Mason has written little since 1939, but
his place among the founders of New
Zealand's mature poetry remains un-
disputed.

In the thirties four New Zealand poets—
A. R. D. Fairburn, Allen Curnow, Charles
Brasch and Dennis Glover—acquired
reputations which have grown with the
years. Fairburn (1904–57), the most
diverse, most uneven, most genial and
most obvious of them, had caught the
imagination of many New Zealanders
before his death. As conversationalist,
free-lance journalist, lecturer, broadcaster
and public speaker, he delighted by a
constant thwarting of expectation which
was also the basis of his wit as a poet:

> Her voice was a razor
> at the throat of quiet. She was slanging
> the foes of justice. The trouble was
> > there hadn't been a hanging.

Poetry and painting were accomplish-
ments of 'Our Sidney and our perfect
man'. It may be that the core of seriousness
in Fairburn was also a core of sentimental-

ity; if this is so then the poetry, which is
never separable from the man, must
bear that limitation.

Charles Brasch's poetry, unlike Fairburn's, contains nothing random, no
flashing wit. Brasch is essentially a poet
of the South Island, his imagination
shaped in the scrupulous assimilation of
that imposing landscape of lakes, fjords
and snow-capped mountain ranges. His
unremitting eye, turned upon the landscape, finds images of its own patience and
tenacity which in turn suggest a nation's
efforts to find and know itself. Fully
committed to his own country, yet
intensely aware of Europe, Brasch's
tranquil cadences are always lightly
tinged with regret:

> Remindingly beside the quays, the white
> Ships lie smoking; and from their
> > haunted bay
> The godwits vanish towards another
> > summer.
> Everywhere in light and calm the
> > murmuring
> Shadow of departure.

There is a singleness of tone, an elegiac
persistence, in Brasch's work, which is the
price of his unchallengeable exactness within a narrow compass of feeling.

Dennis Glover is a tough individualist,
his verse rugged and precise. His lone
characters—Harry, Arawata Bill, Mick
Stimson—are the masks through which
he speaks most impressively. They are
capable of a surprising range of feeling,
from a delicate lyricism to tough social
satire:

> Where all around us ancient ills
> Devour like blackberry the hills
> On every product of the time
> Let fall the poisoned rain of rhyme,
> > *sings Harry*;
> But praise St Francis feeding crumbs
> Into the empty mouths of guns.

Allen Curnow is perhaps the most considerable literary talent New Zealand has yet produced. As critic and anthologist he has been accused of a certain narrowness of judgment. But the introductions to his two anthologies remain the most brilliant and substantial critical statements so far made on the subject of New Zealand poetry; and his stature as a poet has never been seriously disputed. Curnow has insisted that only a poetry rooted in particular time and place can ever be more than local; that there is no short-cut to universality which by-passes what the poet knows and sees about him. With unfailing technical virtuosity, Curnow has gathered into his poetry the particularities of New Zealand landscape and society, its history, its inevitable consciousness of European antecedents, to form a mirror in which the New Zealander finds himself. One short poem must stand for a variety it cannot begin to represent. In *Tomb of an Ancestor* the local present is at odds with an historic past distant in space as well as time:

The oldest of us burst into tears and cried
Let me go home, but she stayed, watching
At her staircase window ship after ship
                                              ride
Like birds her grieving sunsets; there
                                    sat stitching

Grandchildren's things. She died by the
                              same sea.
High over it she led us in the
                        steepening heat
To the yellow grave: her clay
Chose that way home. Dismissed, our feet

Were seen to have stopped and turned
                        again down hill:
The street fell like an ink-blue river
In the heat to the bay, the basking
                        ships, this Isle
Of her oblivion, our broad day.
                        Heaped over

So lightly, she stretched like time behind
                                    us, or
Graven in cloud, our farthest ancestor.

Young poets appearing in the forties and fifties have been the first in New Zealand to feel they have antecedents who engendered a respect that made allegiance or rebellion possible. Their poems display a disinclination to repeat the particular successes of the previous generation, and hence a frequent turning to the urban—or suburban—scene, which they feel has remained largely unexploited in New Zealand poetry. Some repudiate any conscious interest in themselves as New Zealanders—a development which may seem healthy, but which leaves them open sometimes to peculiar distortions of perspective.

Among these recent poets, Kendrick Smithyman (1922–) is the most difficult, and may prove in time the most durable. He has the 'tough reasonableness' of the Metaphysical poet, and faces his countrymen with detached, unsentimental, ungrudging affection:

Harshly I would sing this death of a
                              changed heart,
    wayward I could sing for its born
                              people, being
    one knows no faith in them, being
                        perversely of them.

James K. Baxter (1926–) has been widely acclaimed in New Zealand. Lyric fluency and a habit of mind which finds its natural speech in metaphor are gifts dangerous as they are potent. Baxter's later publications show that he has these gifts fully under control.

Of this generation the historian, Keith Sinclair (1922–), and the journalist, Louis Johnson (1924–), are also interesting poets whose works in part reflect the professions they serve.   C.K.S.

O

Ossian is a transliteration of the name of Oisein, a legendary third-century Gaelic bard. To him, James Macpherson (1736–96) attributed *Fragments of Ancient Poetry Collected in the Highlands of Scotland and Translated from the Gaelic or Erse Language* (1760). Urged on by Scottish patriots eager to rediscover a national Homer, Macpherson produced the epics *Fingal* (1761) and *Temora* (1763). The works drew praise from **Gray**, the charge of fraud from Dr **Johnson**. Macpherson, who knew little Gaelic, appears to have woven his prose-poems in part from oral lore. But nostalgia for a primitive past, for warriors informed with what Macpherson called 'generous sentiments', gave the Ossianic poems timely appeal. Their impact proceeded upon the Continent, where Goethe was among their admirers. X.J.K.

Owen, Wilfred (1893–1918), the outstanding poet of the First World War, was educated at Birkenhead Institute and London University. At some time, as a tutor near Bordeaux in 1913–15, he showed some of his poems to Laurent Tailhade, who encouraged him. In 1915 he joined the army, went to France at the end of 1916, and was invalided home in June 1917. In hospital he met Siegfried **Sassoon**, who recognised his great gifts, and helped his poetic development. In August 1918 he returned to the Western front, was awarded the M.C., but was killed in action on 4 November. Sassoon collected his *Poems*, which were published late in 1920.

In a draft for a Preface, Owen had written:

> . . . this book is not concerned with
> Poetry.

> The subject of it is War, and the pity of
> War.
> The poetry is in the pity.

But there is nothing mawkish in his poetry; he identified himself with the men he wrote of, experienced with them. He submitted completely, as Middleton Murry said reviewing the book. There is a kind of serenity about even the most terrible poems, such as *The Show*: 'My soul looked down from a vague height with Death', though at the end Death shows him his own fresh-severed head. Shortly before his death he wrote to his mother that he came out again 'to help these boys . . . indirectly, by watching their sufferings that I may speak of them as well as a pleader can'. A notable example is his great sonnet *Anthem for Doomed Youth*. Even now, after all these years, his poems have an almost unbearable poignancy.

Such an effect could be achieved only by great poetic power, the sense of the musical value of words carefully chosen and rhythmed, such as he found in **Keats**, the poet to whom he was most devoted. Always pursuing metrical invention, his great triumph was in the dissonance which he used with such effect in *Strange Meeting*:

> . . . I mean the truth untold,
> The pity of war, the pity war distilled.
> Now men will go content with what
> we spoiled.
> Or, discontent, boil bloody, and be
> spilled.
> They will be swift with swiftness of the
> tigress,
> None will break ranks, though
> nations trek from progress.
> Courage was mine, and I had mystery;
> Wisdom was mine, and I had mastery;
> To miss the march of this retreating
> world
> Into vain citadels that are not walled.

He had the mastery, over his searing emotions and over the medium in which he resolved them. But his is not a despairing vision. As Edmund **Blunden** has said, 'A number of original and understanding essays or odes on human nature— for instance *Insensibility*, *Greater Love* or the more pictorial *Spring Offensive*— were written with singular devotion. Wisdom and art in them were united while the poet quite forgot his own case.'

The *Poems* (1931) edited, with a valuable notice, by Edmund Blunden, contains further interesting examples of his work, such as *Shadwell Stair*, which has interesting implications, but nothing which really adds to his stature. That his genius was of a high order is indisputable. Beyond his war poetry there is a vision of humanity, achieved through a daring poetic process, which places him above the circumstances in which he wrote, and renders him timeless.   B.D.

P

Parker, Dorothy [Rothschild] (1893–1967), was a critic, playwright, satirist born in New York. She was an editor of *Vanity Fair* in 1916–17. Her flippant but incisive wit attacks the cruel and the stupid. She wrote short stories as well as poems.   D.H.

Parnell, Thomas (1679–1718), was born in Dublin, educated at Trinity College, and became Archdeacon of Clogher. A member of **Swift**'s and **Pope**'s circle, his poems were collected after his death by the latter. Notable are the *Night-Piece on Death*, *Elegy to an Old Beauty*, *The Hermit* and translations of the *Pervigilium veneris* and Ausonius' *Cupido Cruciatus*.   J.H–S.

Patmore, Coventry [Kersey Dighton] (1823–96), studied as a painter before he became a poet. He was loosely associated with the Pre-Raphaelites, and published poems in *The Germ*. In 1849 he married, and in 1854 he published the first section of *The Angel in the House*, a long poem

in praise of married love. He became a convert to Roman Catholicism in 1864. In 1877 he published *To The Unknown Eros*, his best work. He was twice a widower, and was survived by his third wife. Among his friends he counted **Tennyson**, Ruskin and Gerard Manley **Hopkins**, with whom he carried on a correspondence which has been published.

In a collection of his poems published in 1886, Patmore wrote, 'I have never spoken when I had nothing to say, nor spared time or labour to make my words true. I have respected posterity; and should there be a posterity which cares for letters, I dare to hope that it will respect me.' His words are honest and the self-praise is accurate, but one looks with pity on the qualifying phrase. Patmore's poems, in their ruminative length and their calm diction, are largely ignored by a literate posterity. Yet here is what he asked for himself in the 'Proem' before *To The Unknown Eros*:

But chants as of a lonely thrush's throat
At latest Eve,
That does in each calm note

Both joy and grieve;
Notes few and strong and fine,
Gilt with sweet day's decline,
And sad with promise of a different sun

One may grant that he has described something of his condition, and that his poems exist to be read by those who appreciate his particular qualities: the coherence of his intellectual constructions, his accurate rhythms (frequently pseudo-Pindaric in metre), and his visions of an Eros both domestic and divine.

His most enduring prose is *English Metrical Law* (1878). T. S. Omond, in *English Metrists*, gives it 'a very high place among English studies of prosody'.

D.H.

Peele, George (?1556–96), went to Oxford and achieved a contemporary reputation as a lyrical poet before returning to his native London in 1581. Apparently attempting to gain preferment at court, Peele wrote courtly poetry, pageants, and plays, using conventional historical, legendary and pastoral themes. Critics generally acknowledge that *David and Bethsabe* (1594), a tragedy in blank verse, is his best play, but he also wrote *The Arraignment of Paris* (1584), a pastoral, *Edward the First* (1593), and *The Old Wives' Tale* (1595). He wrote a number of patriotic pageants, such as *Polyhymnia* (1590) and *The Honour of the Garter* (1593), consisting of even and dignified, but undistinguished, verse. His occasional verse, such as *A Farewell to Sir John Norris and Sir Francis Drake*, is simply pedestrian patriotism, unrelieved by wit or interesting imagery. His plays were apparently never popular, despite the fact that both **Greene** and **Nashe** praised him highly, and in his last years he was in constant poverty. His pageants also failed to earn favour or acknowledgment. He is best

known today for his early songs. These light lyrics, such as the following song from *The Hunting of Cupid* (1591), are sometimes skilful and graceful:

What thing is love? for, well I wot,
              love is a thing.
It is a prick, it is a sting,
It is a pretty, pretty thing;
It is a fire, it is a coal,
Whose flame creeps in at ev'ry hole;
And as my wit doth best devise,
Love's dwelling is in ladies' eyes;
From whence do glance love's piercing darts,
That make such holes into our hearts;
And all the world herein accord
Love is a great and mighty lord;
And when he list to mount so high,
With Venus he in heaven doth lie,
And evermore hath been a god
Since Mars and she played even and
                    odd.

J.G.

Pitter, Ruth (1897–   ), who was born at Ilford, Essex, is a poet of precise lyrics; in 1937 her *A Trophy of Arms* received the Hawthornden Prize for the best imaginative literature of the year. Her principal works are *First and Last Poems* (1927), *Spirit Watchers* (1940) and *The Bridge* (1945). *Ermine* (1953) has been described as 'mystic', with 'seventeenth-century affinity'. Recently published was *Poems 1926–66*. D.H.

Plomer, William (1903–   ), is a satirical poet with a sharp eye for character and social nuance. He is an accomplished lyricist, but his best work is in semi-dramatic or ballad form, a species of light verse at once graphic and bizarre. Many of his poems take some real or imaginary incident as a basis for extravaganza (e.g. *The heart of a King* where Dr Buckland inadvertently swallows the petrified heart of Louis XIV: here is a typically cool

and gracious absurdity). Other poems that make up his *Collected Poems* (1960) are ballads of London life (like *French Lisette* and *Mews Flat Mona*) and poems from Japan, Greece and South Africa (where he was born). He has also published fiction and biography.   J.F.
see also South African Poetry in English

Poe, Edgar Allan (1809–49), was the orphan child of two actors. He was taken into the household of John Allan, a Richmond, Virginia, merchant, and given a young gentleman's education in England (1815–20), in Richmond, and briefly at the University of Virginia (1826). Quarelling with his guardian, Poe ran away to Boston, where he enlisted in the army and published his first book, *Tamerlane and Other Poems* (1827). In 1830 he entered West Point Military Academy, hoping to redeem himself in his guardian's eyes, but the widowed Allan's remarriage ended Poe's hopes of an inheritance, and he left the Academy in 1831. Thereafter he subsisted by industrious magazine-work in Richmond, Philadelphia and New York, obliged by poverty to subordinate his poetry and fiction to the editorial and critical labours for which, until the success of *The Raven* in 1845, he was chiefly known. In 1836 he married his child-cousin, Virginia Clemm, and her death in 1847 destroyed his always precarious emotional balance. After two years of increasing distraction and dissipation, he was found dying, in October 1849, in a street in Baltimore.

Poe defined imaginative literature as 'that class of composition in which there lies beneath the transparent upper current of meaning, an under or *suggestive* one'. His short stories, accordingly, are allegories, though rarely of a perspicuous kind, and such celebrated tales as *Ligeia* and *The Fall of the House of Usher* are full but covert treatments of his fundamental and almost invariable theme: the struggle of the poetic soul to disengage itself from this fallen world, and to recover through visionary dream a conversancy with 'supernal Beauty'.

Poe's criticism treats this theme explicitly, assigning to art in general, and to poetry and music in particular, the function of momentarily estranging the soul from Earth, and launching it on 'a wild effort to reach the Beauty above'. Such being poetry's task, the poem must not, in Poe's view, appeal to the moral sense, or embody any ordinary human emotion; in so doing it would refer the reader to everyday earthly experience, and 'trammel the soul in its flight to an ideal Helusion'. Similarly, the poem must not be subservient to intellect, because factuality and logical clarity are inhibiting to vision. Finally, the poem must be short, because 'an elevating excitement' cannot long be induced or sustained.

Of Poe's fewer than sixty poems, not many are as 'realised' as the best of his fiction. Commonly, the subjects of the poems are those of the stories—the soul's loss of visionary happiness through earthly incarnation and the passing of childhood; the soul's nostalgia for an ideal beauty often personified as a lost beloved. The poems do not, however, concentrate upon the presentation of their subjects: while *The Haunted Palace* may possess some allegorical clarity and *The Raven* some narrative completeness, the verse generally has that deliberate 'indefinitiveness' which Poe praised in **Tennyson,** as well as that minimisation of the content which results from incantatory technique—from thudding metres and the hypnotic repetition of word, sound and phrase. Poe's typical poem is, in fact, a spell or charm in which the melodious attenuation of the subject matter is intended to induce an exhilarated feeling of unearthliness. The final stanza of *To One in Paradise* exhibits this strategy at its most compelling:

And all my days are trances,
  And all my nightly dreams
Are where thy grey eye glances,
  And where thy footstep gleams—
In what ethereal dances,
By what eternal streams.   R.W.

see also Symbolism

Poetry and Publishing—Britain. The complaint of poets that they have great difficulty in getting their work published in volume form is perennial. It is to a large extent justified; but the publishers have a formidable case for the defence. Except in times of war and its immediate aftermath, it has been extremely difficult, in this century at least, to persuade the British public to be interested in new verse that makes any serious demands upon its intelligence. Sales of one hundred copies or under for the first book of a poet who afterwards achieved some measure of fame have not been rare. The cold reluctance of booksellers, the discouragement of travellers and the consequent prospect of almost invariable financial loss have made some publishers unwilling to consider new poetry at all, while others have only undertaken their act of midwifery under firm guarantee or on commission. The more hopeful and enlightened publishers, who have not always been the most prosperous, have traditionally followed the policy of offering a contract by which the poet agrees to produce one, or perhaps two prose works of a more saleable kind in return for acceptance of his verse. These contracts in most cases do little good to the poet and none at all to the publisher (though

remarkable exceptions have been known). The prizes have, it seems, generally gone to those bolder houses which have been prepared to build up a poetry list without the illusory reinsurance of such package deals, but rather relying on the overall profitability of their other publications to absorb whatever losses poetry may involve them in. Even so, the establishment of a poetry list will require the most searching and expert scrutiny of all that is offered, because it is a lamentable fact of life that any given moment in every age there is an enormous mass of utterly feeble and spurious verse looking for some means of presenting itself to the public.

The experience of modern times is not, however, entirely without cheer, and in exceptional cases poets have been known, after years of struggle, to obtain a modest living from their volumes of poetry alone, and a modest reward for their loyal publishers. With the aid of the most recently developed channels of publicity, e.g. television, they have even soared into the best-seller class. The most likely ways in which a young poet will be able to find a hearing today are, first, by the sympathetic attention of literary editors who are ready to publish his work in their weeklies and monthlies well ahead of publication in book form; and, second, by appearing in an anthology of the work of a small group of like-minded young poets with a provocative introduction. Not all such anthologies have been without their meretricious side, but several have succeeded in their mediating task for the newcomer or near-beginner.

Modern British poets have sometimes had recourse to pamphlet publication through the agency of enthusiastic friends with private printing presses; but in general have shunned the Continental device of de-luxe illustrated editions intended to appeal to bibliophiles and art-lovers in the faint hope that they will include a few discriminating readers of poetry.   J.L.

Poetry and Publishing—United States.

In the United States modern American poetry may be dated from 1912, when Harriet Monroe founded *Poetry: A Magazine of Verse*. And the history of modern American poetry can be discussed without distortion in terms of its manner of publication. One of the reasons for the first wave of literary expatriates, before 1912, was presumably the utter vacuity of American editorship, still under the spell of the genteel tradition. But by the time Ezra **Pound** met T. S. **Eliot** in London, he was able to mail *The Love Song of J. Alfred Prufrock* to Chicago, and after some argument (Miss Monroe's taste ran to a blander product) see it in *Poetry*.

Other little magazines, like *The Little Review* and *Others*, thrived in the years of experiment. *The Dial* (1920–29) was the culmination and apex of them, but it was also a transitional periodical. In its deliberate catholicity (Pound and George Saintsbury in the same issue), in its size and handsome format, and in its air of quiet authority it resembled the forthcoming quarterlies. Magazines like the *Southern Review*, the revivified *Sewanee Review*, the *Kenyon Review* and the *Hudson Review* all included much criticism, and a poetry of wit and elegant skill. The contributors were for the most part professors, and many of the leading quarterlies have been associated with particular universities. *The Partisan Review* has been more generally intellectual than literary.

Book publication has mostly depended upon the charity of the New York publishers, but there has always been a certain amount of pamphlet publication, and some arts presses. In the nineteen-

thirties and forties James Laughlin's *New Directions*, with its annual anthologies and its distinguished regular list, furthered the cause of experimental poetry in a time of technical conservatism. Recently the number of small poetry publishers has increased; among them it is most necessary to notice *Jargon*, Jonathan Williams' press in North Carolina, which has first published the work of some of the best new poets.

Small literary magazines, as well as small publishers, revived in the late fifties—a phenomenon very much connected with a resurgence of experimentation. And some of the most recent quarterlies have banished criticism and substituted art, photography and literary or social journalism; *The Paris Review* and *Tri-Quarterly* are the most important of these. Recent innovations in techniques of reproducing print like cheap lithography, have led to a proliferation of small, sometimes idiosyncratic magazines. The orthodoxy represented by the University quarterlies is moribund.

But perhaps the most interesting recent phenomenon has been the emergence of university presses as major publishers of poetry. For a long time Yale's annual *Younger Poet* was the only book of poetry published by a university press. Then Indiana University Press started its distinguished series, to be followed by the University of Minnesota Press, the University of Chicago Press, Chapel Hill, and the Wesleyan University Press which alone prints four books a year. One may look ahead—with a pleasure not entirely unmixed—to a time when the university presses will print most of the poets and New York will no longer dominate the book publication of poetry.   D.H.

Pope, Alexander (1688–1744), was born in London. His father was a linen-draper, who had been a convert to the Church of Rome since young manhood. The penal laws passed against Roman Catholics at the accession of William and Mary seem to have been mainly instrumental in inducing Pope's father to retire from business and remove to Binfield in Windsor Forest, where the poet's boyhood was spent. Pope was educated privately by priests, and also read widely for himself. This application to study is said to have brought on the illness which, at the age of twelve, ruined Pope's health and left him deformed and stunted in body. He began to compose verses at a very early age; his *Pastorals*, written when he was sixteen (though polished later) were published by Dodsley in 1709. Highly conventional, they are nevertheless of considerable charm. There are true touches of natural observation, and the heroic couplet, which was to be Pope's medium in nearly all his work, is here given an almost lyrical quality:

> Where'er you walk, cool gales shall
> fan the glade,
> Trees where you sit shall crowd into a
> shade;
> Where'er you look, the blushing
> flowers shall rise,
> And all things flourish, where'er you
> turn your eyes.

The *Essay on Criticism* (1711) was a very different work. Here we have a young poet of high ambitions taking stock of his ideas as to the function of the critic and the nature of poetry. The *Essay* has sometimes been dismissed as derivative and conventional, but read against the background of the literary ideas of its time, and when allowance is made for Pope's inadequate critical vocabulary, it will be found to set forth a fundamentally consistent view, and to contain much that is of lasting value. Pope was now in London,

and a member of Addison's circle at Button's Coffee House. He also became involved in the beginnings of his numerous literary quarrels. The *Pastorals* had led to rivalry with Ambrose Phillips; an injudicious aside in the *Essay* had drawn a violent attack from the critic, Dennis. Against both Pope retaliated with deadly irony, and he pursued Dennis with merciless satire for many years. Biographers have too often represented Pope as a monster of vindictiveness. Modern research, however, has tended to rehabilitate his personal character. He was an extremely sensitive man, burdened with physical handicaps, and a member of a despised religious minority. The attacks made against him were often brutal in the extreme; he retaliated as he could, if he sometimes used devious and questionable means. Moreover, his intense devotion to the ideal of 'correctness' in poetry made him see bad writing in others as an offence in itself—a moral offence against the light of reason and clarity in human communications. He was always ready to encourage writers of real promise. And to the friends he loved he was capable of deep loyalty and tender affection.

It was inevitable that Pope, as a Roman Catholic and a Tory, should drift away from Addison and his Whig friends, and find a more congenial place in the Tory circle of **Swift** and Bolingbroke. But to his friendship with Addison must be largely attributed *The Rape of the Lock* (1712), for this rococo fantasy is thoroughly Addisonian in its spirit of light raillery. The incident which it treats with heroic mock-solemnity, the cutting off by Lord Petrie of a lock of Miss Arabella Fermor's hair, had threatened to cause a serious quarrel between their respective families, who were among Pope's Roman Catholic acquaintances. The poem was written for the purpose of composing this quarrel by making light of the whole business. The moral is in the speech of Clarissa in Canto V:

> But since, alas! frail beauty must decay,
> Curl'd or uncurl'd, since locks must
> turn to grey;
> Since painted, or not painted, all shall
> fade,
> And she who scorns a man must die a
> maid;
> What then remains but well our powers
> to use,
> And keep good-humour still whate'er
> we lose?

For those who abandon good-humour the baroque nightmare of the Cave of Spleen lies in wait.

Other poems of Pope's early period we must mention are *Windsor Forest* (1713) with its Claude-like landscape painting and its patriotic celebration of the Peace of Utrecht, and his two 'sentimental' pieces, the *Elegy on an Unfortunate Lady* and *Eloisa to Abelard* (both 1717). The last is a very interesting poem, in which, combining Ovidian rhetoric with an anticipation of the Neo-Gothic, Pope speaks nevertheless with real passion and insight into the human heart.

The first volume of Pope's translation of the *Iliad* had appeared in 1715. The task was completed in 1720, and followed by his *Odyssey* (1725–6) in which he had the assistance of other poets. Pope's *Homer* is a work of great rhetorical skill, immensely readable. It presented the image of Homer which his own age required, and if later ages have needed to make other translations, none has produced one that stands so securely in its own right as a work of English literature.

In 1719 Pope was able (with the proceeds of this translation) to buy the lease of his villa at Twickenham, where he resided for the rest of his life, spending his time on improvements to his house and grounds, in converse with his friends, in feuds and intrigues with his enemies, and above all in the writing and perpetual revision of his poetry. It is in this later period that Pope emerges as a great satirist, whose aim is essentially moral and humanistic. In the *Essay on Man*, the *Moral Essays* and the *Imitations of Horace* themselves, he assumes the Horatian *persona*—that of the detached, civilised observer of man and his foibles, basing his criticism of life on the classical doctrines of the mean and on good sense. Pope was able to do this because there was a real analogy between the stability of Rome under the *pax Augusta* and the condition of eighteenth-century England. The *Imitations of Horace*, therefore, are not merely imitative, though Horace is often followed very closely. In the Prologue to these Satires, *The Epistle to Arbuthnot* (1735), the material is wholly original, though the Horatian stance is still assumed. This is one of Pope's greatest poems, his apology for his own life and his vindication against his enemies. The famous satirical 'characters' of Bufo (Lord Halifax), Atticus (Addison) and Sporus (Lord Hervey) transcend any personal malice Pope may or may not have harboured, and fix for all time the portraits of an egotistic patron of bad writers, of a smooth, petty literary dictator, whose real talents were balanced by jealousy and moral cowardice, and finally of utter corruption and perversion at the very heart of society:

> . . . this bug with gilded wings,
> This painted child of dirt that stinks
> and stings;
> Whose buzz the witty and the fair
> annoys,
> Yet wit ne'er tastes, and beauty ne'er
> enjoys:

So well-bred spaniels civilly delight
In mumbling of the game they dare
                      not bite.
Eternal smiles his emptiness betray,
As shallow streams run dimpling all
                      the way.
Whether in florid impotence he speaks,
And, as the prompter breathes, the
                  puppet squeaks;
Or at the ear of Eve, familiar toad
Half froth, half venom, spits himself
                    abroad . . .

The *Essay on Man* (1732–4) treats of Man in relation to Nature as a whole. If we try to analyse it as a philosophical argument, it has obvious weaknesses, but if we read it as a quasi-lyrical vision of the Great Chain of Being, interpreted in terms of the Augustan concept of universal harmony and order in nature, it is an impressive, and above all, a memorable poem. In the *Moral Essays* (1731–5) Pope treats Man systematically in psychological, economic, and aesthetic contexts. Epistle III is notable for the famous satirical account of 'Timon's villa' —an example of the misuse of wealth and the perversion of taste.

In *The Dunciad* Pope employs the mock-heroic form he had so successfully achieved in *The Rape of the Lock* for a more ambitious and fundamentally more serious purpose. If Addison stands behind *The Rape of the Lock*, and Bolingbroke's philosophy behind *The Essay on Man*, it is the shadow of Swift (to whom it was dedicated) that falls across *The Dunciad*. It is an ironic prophecy of the return of Chaos, through the total corruption of literature by the commercial values of Grub Street, and the anti-humanistic pedantry of false scholarship. But the irony is no more light-hearted than is that of *Gulliver's Travels*. Pope does indeed feel that real values were threatened by the spread of bad writing and false

standards. It is recorded that Pope could not recite the famous closing passage without tears. What Pope envisages in that passage is a progressive derangement of the traditional hierarchy of the arts and sciences:

Thus at her felt approach and secret
                    might,
Art after *Art* goes out, and all is Night.
See skulking *Truth* to her old cavern
                    fled,
Mountains of Casuistry heap'd o'er her
                    head;
Philosophy, that lean'd no Heav'n before,
Shrinks to her second cause, and is no
                    more.
Physic of *Metaphysic* begs defence,
And *Metaphysic* calls for aid on *Sense*!
See *Mystery* to *Mathematics* fly!
In vain! they gaze, turn giddy, rave and
                    die.
Religion blushing veils her sacred fires,
And unawares *Morality* expires.

In the first version of *The Dunciad* (1728) it is Theobald who is crowned King of the dunces by the Goddess of Dullness. Pope's animus against Theobald arose out of the latter's criticism of Pope's edition of **Shakespeare**. But it should be realised that the quarrel between them (like Pope's and Swift's quarrel with Bentley) was fundamentally that between an imaginative and humanistic approach to literature and one that seemed merely mechanical and verbal. In *The New Dunciad* (1743) Colley Cibber was substituted for Theobald, and a fourth book was added, widening the scope of the satire to include the corruption of education, and the mania of collectors and *virtuosi*, as well as bad writers. Pope has been criticised for making this change, and for destroying the poem's unity of intention. But the appointment of Cibber as Laureate really had been an insult to poetry, and the extension of the subject-matter points rather than weakens the main theme. Though mock-heroic, the completed *Dunciad* really constitutes the true epic of the Age of Reason; and it realises terrifyingly—and we might say prophetically—how perilously human reason is balanced against the forces of Chaos.   J.H-S.

see also Satire *and* Translation

Popular Poetry. There is probably no more ambiguous term in the lexicon; the subjects it covers range, in one direction, from the medieval ballad to the American cowboy lament; in another, from the verses of Martin Tupper to those of Edgar **Guest**; and in a third, from the poetry of **Tennyson** to that of John **Betjeman**.

In its earliest sense, popular poetry is poetry *by* as well as *for* the people; and its words are usually sung. The origins of the English and Scottish ballads are obscure. No one knows who composed *Lord Edward* or *The Wife of Usher's Well*. But there are enough variant versions of many a ballad to argue that even if a single bard first had the inspiration, other bards and other groups soon reshaped it to suit a variety of individual tastes. The urge to share an emotion or incident in words and music is something deep within us. Through its promptings ballads have continued to be composed. It may be guessed that as early as the opening of the nineteenth century the spread of communication and the start of the popular press had put an end to the making of many ballads in the old way. Yet in the United States the isolation of the Appalachian mountaineers—the hill people of Tennessee, North Carolina, and Kentucky—kept the traditional ballad alive. Brought over from Great Britain, it was augmented and strengthened by local composition.

Our last balladist may have been the American cowboy. The mountain ballads were probably for the most part composed before the Civil War; the cowboy songs came after it. The cowboy had his heyday from about 1860 to 1880. Most of his ballads seem to date from that period. The pioneer in collecting them, John Lomax, believes that the main impulse for these ballads lay in the loneliness and monotony of the cowboy's life. He found that song made the day go faster, especially while driving cattle from Texas, along the Chisholm Trail, to Montana or Wyoming. The words and music for many of the ballads reflect his tedium and often its attendant pessimism; other ballads reflect his explosive celebrations at the end of the drive. Lomax's view of the origin of these ballads is much like that of the collectors of the medieval ballad. 'Whatever the most gifted man could produce must bear the criticism of the entire camp, and agree with the ideas of a group of men. In this sense, therefore, any song that came from such a group would be the joint product of a number of them.' It was probably through this process that such cowboy classics as *The Old Chisholm Trail*, *Home on the Range*, and *The Dying Cowboy* ('Oh, bury me not on the lone prairie') were developed.

For the origins of popular poetry in the second sense, poetry *for* but not *by* the people, we must go back to England and the early nineteenth century. It was then that the genuine popular press began, in the form of books and periodicals. With the expansion of the middle class, the gradual increase in leisure and the general spread of literacy, came the largest audience for poetry in the history of British publishing. The potential public swelled from thousands to millions. In the United States the situation was similar but developed more slowly; it was not till the mid-nineteenth century that mass publishing appeared.

We may ask what kinds of poetry appealed to this new audience. Though clear-cut categories are nearly always impossible, some distinctions can be made. There was, first of all, the kind of poetry that appealed to the largest class of all, and appealed to that class alone. Then there was the poetry that appealed to a still numerous class of readers with somewhat more taste and discrimination than the semi-literate mass. Lastly there was the poetry, composed by poets of enduring reputation, which had something to give to every level of reader from the most naïve to the most critical. These three categories and their poetry could be detected almost from the start, even though the individual readers and their favourite poets would die and be replaced by new ones. Here and there, as the decades passed, we might see one or two poets who exemplified a category better than all the others.

Guest is the classic example of the purely popular poet. He never strikes a chord which fails to vibrate in a hundred thousand bosoms. He is kindly, positive, optimistic, simple. He hymns the heart at the expense of the mind. He has a message for his mass of readers, a moral in every poem. Tupper, the most popular of his predecessors, has a somewhat more restricted range: the particular is more important to him. Where Guest's subjects are universal—home, mother, children, friends, with seldom a slip into the particular—Tupper often started his poem from a specific occasion such as Queen Victoria's birthday, the Great Exhibition of 1851, or the Battle of Waterloo. His popularity lay both in subject and treatment, yet it is worth noting that he chose his specific subjects so that they had the broadest appeal. In doing this, deliberately or not, he flattered the prejudices of many of his countrymen. For example, he wrote a poem called *The Anglo-Saxon Race*, which rang changes on 'The world is a world for the Saxon Race'. He wrote another with the revealing title, *Down with Foreign Priestcraft*, and another called *Energy*, which begins 'Indomitable merit of the Anglo-Saxon mind'. His poetry on domestic life was equally well adapted. His inspirational lyrics, along with his famous *Proverbial Philosophy*, had the same genial tone found in Guest. The two poets even chose the same titles once or twice. *All's for the Best*, sang Tupper in 1848; *All for the Best*, echoed Guest in the twentieth century.

Equally popular with Tupper, but superior to him in skill, were several English and American poets of the nineteenth century. Their subjects were similar to his but their treatment was more sophisticated. Mrs Felicia Hemans was the leading English poet in this category but she was surpassed by her American successor, Henry Wadsworth **Longfellow**. She had a womanly touch, with more than a trace of tears, which was well suited to the sentimentality of her Victorian audience. Her melancholy personal life, marred by the early death of her children and desertion by her husband, permeated her poems. Her titles include *Dirge of a Child*, *The Bride's Farewell*, *If Thou Hast Crush'd a Flower*. Longfellow's genius proved more robust, though his verses, too, were marked by sentiment. Despite the fact that his afflictions grew as great as Mrs Hemans' his masculine response was firmer and stronger. 'Life is real! Life is earnest', he exclaimed, 'And the grave is not its goal'.

With Tennyson we come to our last

and highest category. He represents the true poet, who has something to give everyone. For the great mass of his readers he has apparent simplicities of technique, and attitudes not unlike their own. For the group of readers just above that, he has subtleties and sophistications unrecognised by the crowd. And for the critics themselves he has the felicities of expression, if not the intricacies of thought, to which they respond with deep satisfaction. Tennyson fitted the temper of his time. In his splendid stanzas he cast the struggle and doubt of the Victorian mind and then its final optimism. Throughout his career he achieved a steady growth in literary reputation but it was not till the publication of *In Memoriam* that he won his widest public. In that long poem, however, he put all that his time was troubled by; and the result was the greatest popularity enjoyed by any of the high Victorians.

Tennyson's fame was grandly international ; so, less grandly, was Longfellow's. Mrs Hemans found her verses as well known, almost, in America as in her homeland; her *Casabianca* ('The boy stood on the burning deck') was read as a folk-classic in America. Tupper was much admired on both sides of the ocean. But when we reach the present we find no poet, either British or American, whose works are as widely enjoyed. There are no great popular poets living today, certainly none with international renown. And yet it would be unfair not to mention one special case, John Betjeman, whose reputation in England is unique. He remembers Victorian England lovingly; he values its high summers and its soot, its gardens and its railway stations. The notes he strikes are clear and plaintive. His poetry is often compassionate, sometimes morbid or pessimistic, and never proletarian. His work represents, in

sum, a minority report. It is the old against the new, in a country which still has a lingering love for the old. To a mass audience, he has little appeal, but England is a country literate enough to have a considerable group of sophisticated readers. They relish Betjeman. When he invokes destruction on the graceless town of Slough or laments the loss of London's Aldersgate Station these readers nod their heads in agreement; this is what they have often thought but never so well expressed.   C.B.

Pound, Ezra [Weston Loomis] (1885–   ), was born in Idaho, and spent the first twenty-three years of his life in America. Of the major poets of the twentieth century he is at once the most purely aesthetic and the most purely didactic, an odd combination which this on the whole anti-aesthetic and anti-didactic age has found hard to swallow. And he makes the mixture even more disconcerting with a weird sense of humour, sometimes schoolboyish ('My bikini is worth your raft', says the sea-nymph Leucothoe of the veil with which she saves Odysseus), sometimes uproarious in its gift for mimicry: 'Noigandres!' says a great Provençal scholar in Freiburg when asked what it means,

> NOIgandres!
> You know for seex mon's of my life
> Effery night when I go to bett, I say to
> > myself:
> Noigandres, eh, *noigandres*,
> Now what the DEFFIL can that mean!
> > *Canto* 20

And he often shows a comic self-awareness, not only of his own repetitions ('METATHEMENON / we are not yet out of *that* chapter'—*Canto* 77), but also of the very humour in his method of startling juxtapositions, as when, for instance, he is telling the story of Uang-iu-p'uh (a Salt Commissioner in Shensi who translated the Edict of K'ang Hsi into more colloquial Chinese for the people) but never seems to get round to it:

> And that Leucothoe rose as an incense
> > bush
> —Orchamus, Babylon—
> > resisting Apollo.
> Patience, I will come to the Commissioner
> > of the Salt
> > Works in due course . . .
> > > *Canto* 98

These three elements, aestheticism, didacticism and humour, are present throughout Pound's work, reinforcing each other as the poet and craftsman mastered the more and more recalcitrant material of his choice (which has been called many things, from simply 'flux' to an economic history of the world).

It is, however, also true, in a more superficial sense, to say that Pound moved steadily from the pure aestheticism of his early poems, which are often archaic and Pre-Raphaelite in diction and subject-matter, to the pure didacticism of the middle and later *Cantos*. These early poems were published between 1908 and 1921, when he lived in London and became the chief spokesman of the Imagist group. He also brought out *Cathay* in 1915 ('translations' from the Chinese) and *Quia pauper amavi* in 1918 (which included three draft *Cantos* and *Homage to Sextus Propertius*, a 'version' of Propertius still annoying to scholars though defended by poets). In 1920 he published his first truly modern poem, *Hugh Selwyn Mauberley*, a sad portrait of an imaginary pure aesthete in a modern world too philistine for him, and in a sense an ironic farewell to pure aestheticism:

> Non-esteem of self-styled 'his betters'
> Leading, as he well knew,
> To his final
> Exclusion from the world of letters.

Among many others, he met Ernest Fenollosa, an American authority on Japanese, and in 1920 edited his essay on *The Chinese Written Character* which, though in many ways wrong-headed, is important for Pound's poetic theory, especially his war on abstract vagueness. It was the friendship with Fenollosa that stimulated Pound's interest not only in the Japanese *haiku* (the influence of which can be seen especially in his otherwise Martialesque epigrams), but in the Chinese ideogram as a juxtaposition of particular images—a notion that was considerably to affect Pound's subsequent technique.

He then lived in Paris for four years, but finally settled in Italy, where he worked steadily at the *Cantos* (the first thirty were published in Paris in 1930), and wrote most of his critical and didactic prose: *How to Read* (1931), *ABC of Economics* (1933), *Make it New* (1934), *ABC of Reading* (1934), *Social Credit: An Impact* (1935), *Jefferson And/Or Mussolini* (1935). He was arrested in 1945 by the United States forces for his broadcasts on the Italian radio during the war, sent to Pisa and put in a barbed-wire cage. He was then sixty. There he wrote the magnificent *Pisan Cantos* which were later the occasion of the Bollingen Award (1949). In November 1945 he was flown to Washington to be tried for treason, was declared insane and remained in St Elizabeth's Hospital, Washington, for thirteen years, at first in unpleasant conditions but later with more privacy. He continued to work both at the *Cantos* (*Section: Rock Drill*, and *Thrones*) and further translations (a play by Sophocles and the Chinese *Book of Odes*).

He was released in 1958 and is now living in Italy.

Pound has been compared to **Browning**, at least for his use, in the early poems and as one of the fundamental principles throughout the *Cantos*, of the dramatic monologue by historical or legendary 'personae' with whom the poet temporarily identifies himself ('A poor clerk I, "Arnaut the less", they call me . . .'); and for his development of natural speech rhythms which were to change the whole tone of modern poetry ('Damn it all! all this our South stinks peace./You whoreson dog, Papiols, come!'). Even when he was not being idiomatic in the Browning vein, he did succeed in evolving a more natural, basically trochaic metre ('to break the pentameter, that was the first heave') which, together with a disciplined economy and judicious juxtapositions of the formal and the colloquial, were to become his strongest assets:

Come, my songs, let us speak of
                              perfection—
We shall get ourselves rather disliked.
                                    Lustra

Many critics, however, think that Pound really came into his own with *Hugh Selwyn Mauberley*:

        'His true Penelope
        Was Flaubert',
        And his tool
        The engraver's.

        Firmness,
        Not the full smile,
        His art, but an art
        In profile . . .

Indeed some critics maintain that *Mauberley* is Pound's only important poem. Pound in fact has been compared, not just with Browning, but with **Blake**,

in the sense that he is more generally admired for his shorter poems and some of the early *Cantos* (the anthology pieces), together with perhaps the most moving passages in the *Pisan Cantos*, while the *Cantos* as a whole, like Blake's Prophetic Books, are sighingly relegated to cranks and specialists. This view varies with the degree of familiarity, but on the whole most people 'can't take' the *Jefferson-Nuevo-Mundo Cantos* (31–41), the *Siena-Leopoldine Reforms* (5th Decad), the *Chinese Dynasties and Adams in Action* (52–71), *Rock Drill* (85–95) or *Thrones* (96–109), in which historical documents are translated or quoted (often with comic asides or in startling contexts), and including, later, much Chinese. Yet the *Cantos* are nothing if not consistent or, in Pound's own words, 'an epic poem which begins "In the Dark Forest", crosses the Purgatory of human error and ends in the light, "fra i maestri di color che sanno"'. *Rock Drill* indeed is flooded with light, not only that of his favourite 'light' philosophers, Ocellus, Erigena, Richard of St Victor and others, but visual, almost tangible light:

For me nothing. But that the child
    walk in peace in her basilica,
The light there almost solid.
                                Canto 93

Another comparison, as revealing, perhaps, as those to Browning and Blake, has been made between Pound and **Langland**. Both are extremely vital and rhythmic poets, both have written a vast and (apparently) plotless epic, both are fundamentally didactic and concerned, above all and at many levels of apprehension, with the purpose of wealth and the inevitably related corruptions of government, but through this with the basic needs of the human spirit; real wealth as a spiritual harvest of love, worked for celestially, ritualistically, agriculturally, politically and personally in every walk of life. Langland hammers at simony and bribery as the greatest evils, just as Pound hammers at usury, or money made from mere lending, without goods to back it, and not from productive work. Pound's phrase about the bank of Siena which was founded on 'the abundance of nature / with the whole folk behind it' (*Canto* 52) has a truly Langland ring, and Langland is ironical about Lombards and Jews for much the same reason as Pound is. Even more interesting is the parallelism in poetic method: both use an echoing orchestration; Pound's ideo-grammatic technique (the juxtaposition of disparate ideas, not merely in sentences but in whole cantos and whole groups of cantos) is the modern, metaphoric equivalent of Langland's constant shifting four-level allegory; his *periplus* or voyage of discovery among facts ('a sufficient phalanx of particulars') can be compared with Langland's unconventional use of the medieval dream-formula; and in both the concept of metamorphoses is vital.

Pound is not, however, a mere primi-tivist. It is true that his sources on economics, as on many subjects, are often old-fashioned. **Eliot** has said that his ideas as such are uninteresting, and he has been called a 'revolutionary simpleton' (by Wyndham **Lewis**), an 'uneducated revo-lutionary' (by **Yeats**), and 'a village explainer' (by Gertrude **Stein**). Yet few critics, so far, have examined these ideas in any expert detail. As Pound said in a broadcast after his release, 'every man has a right to have his ideas examined one at a time'.

It is true that he makes this difficult, even in his prose, by presenting them not discursively but ideogrammatically, and his view of history and the high achieve-ments of past civilisations is ideosyncratic and highly selective. The ratiocinative processes of eighteenth-, nineteenth- and twentieth-century civilisation are alien to him, and he works, in effect, by poetic intuition. This is what gives his poetry a disturbingly apocalyptic quality: just as in his early translations, he made 'howlers' but, uncannily and even through them, got at the spirit of the original, whereas his later translations (when he had learned more of the language in question) are less good in this way, so one often feels when reading even the most didactic passages in the *Cantos*, that he may in a very ultimate sense be right, as only a poet can be both right and wrong at the same time. Even on the question of economics, the present order may not last for ever, any more than feudalism did.

In the end, though, it is not even his ideas that matter but the 'ideas in action', that is to say, the poetry itself. The *Cantos* are difficult, but very rewarding, especially for those who are prepared to go a little way with the poet, follow him to his sources (which he usually gives) and see what he does with them. Above all, the *Cantos* represent a lifetime of reading, loving, suffering, and patient craftsman-ship. And as Pound himself says in *Thrones*: 'There is no substitute for a lifetime'.   C.B–R.

see also American Poetry, Foreign In-fluences on English Poetry, Imagism *and* Translation

Praed, Winthrop [Mackworth] (1802-39), an English poet of *vers de société*, was a Tory member of the House of Commons. His extraordinary facility with rhyme and stanza lent itself well to lighter subjects, but Praed was never able to write a serious or moving poem with comparable success.   D.H.

Pre-Raphaelites. *See* Patmore, Christina Rossetti *and* D. G. Rossetti.

Prior, Matthew (1664–1721), was born of a poor family in London, and was sent to Westminster and St John's College, Cambridge, by the Earl of Dorset who found him, as a boy, reading Horace in his uncle's tavern. Prior later became a successful diplomat, trusted by King William and Queen Anne, and helped to negotiate the Peace of Utrecht in 1713. He regarded his poetry as the scribblings of a gentlemanly amateur and published little until *Poems on Several Occasions* appeared in 1719. Although he did write some longer poems, he is best remembered for his light, unpretentious verses about man and society. In one poem, *An English Padlock*, he gracefully satirises foreign morality and claims that if an English husband fear his lady's fidelity, he need only watch the women on the Continent to be reassured. In another poem, *A Simile*, he compares young gallants to squirrels in cages:

Brought back, how fast so'er they go,
Always aspiring, always low.

The satire, the balanced line and the diminution of man's position, are frequent characteristics of Prior's poetry. He also relegated poetry itself to a secondary position in *A Better Answer* ('to Cloe Jealous'):

What I speak, my fair Cloe, and what
I write, shows
The difference there is betwixt nature
and art;
I court others in verse, but I love thee
in prose;
And they have my whimsies, but thou
hast my heart.

Yet, with all his deference and moderation, he recognised the limitations of an even, temperate life in a poem called *Epitaph*:

Without love, hatred, joy, or fear,
They lead—a kind of—as it were.

J.G.

Prosody, Forms of Verse, and Some Usages

I. PROSODY

Versification and numbers are the
greatest pleasures of poetry.
John Dryden

1. Introduction

The *New English Dictionary* defines prosody as 'the science of versification'; it is better to regard it, as Saintsbury did, as 'the study of the constitution of verses', or, better still, to look upon it with Lascelles Abercrombie as the way, or for that matter the ways, in which verse can be analysed. Evidently there can be no 'rules' of prosody which a poet must follow, though there are traditions which poets drop into because their effectiveness has been proved; there are measures which these traditions have stamped as natural modes of expression. Some poets rejoice in submitting themselves to a discipline, in wrestling with a challenge to craftsmanship; or they may try to add to the tradition, discover a new measure, as **Coleridge** attempted to do in *Christabel*, or invent a new prosody, as Robert **Bridges** and Gerard **Hopkins** did. Others pretend complete ignorance of this 'science', and would say with **Swinburne**, that master of versification: 'A dunce like myself measures verse . . . by ear and not by finger'. Necessarily, analyse the results as you will, it is the ear that dictates to the poet, just as it is by his ear that the reader will taste it.

Apart from whatever rhythmic impulse

215

may direct the poet, there are—within the scope of this article—two considerations that will influence his versification. The first was well stated by George **Gascoigne**, when in his *The Making of Verse* (1575), he advised the would-be poet:

> And in your verses remember to place every worde in his natural *Emphasis* or sound, that is to say, in such wise, and in such length or shortnesse, elevation or depression of sillables, as is commonly pronounced or used.

Beyond this, however, the poet will suit his words and their sequence to carry the *cadence*, or 'fall' of his phrase, a matter more vital than concurrence with any prosodic 'rule', perhaps cutting across the metre. More important to the poet, and therefore to the reader, is the sense conveyed by the run of the sentence, as in, say, **Drayton**'s

> Since there's no help, come, let us kiss
> and part,

or **Keats**'

> Be still the unimaginable lodge
> For solitary thinkings.
> *Endymion* I, 293–4

than by whatever prosodic system may be applied.

Nevertheless there are certain broad lines that make for clarification: certain terms are applicable which enable the discussion of poetry to be engaged in: we know what is meant when 'iambic verse' or 'dactylic measure' are spoken of, or 'accentual verse', and so on. In this article it is proposed to describe, first, the units of which verse—or prose for that matter—are composed, commonly called 'feet'; the divergent schools of thought concerning these; then the metres into

which these are woven, to be followed by illustrations of some of the forms employed, and finally some of the purposes to which they are put.

2. The Units of Verse

Verse is analysed, or, to use the common phrase, scanned, by counting. But what is it that is counted? The primitive method is to count the syllables, but syllabic scansion, while sometimes useful, does not carry the student of English poetry very far, though it is used by French prosodists for French poetry. It can sometimes act as a useful check; there can be no controversy about it, except, rarely, where *elision*, the slurring of a syllable, or a *redundant*, extra-syllable are indicated. At least it provides some terms which point to the nature of the verse being read—octosyllabic, decasyllabic, fourteener, and so on. And even those who favour one of the other main methods, are found sometimes to refer to 'dropped' or 'redundant' syllables.

English prosody has been bedevilled by the adoption of classical names and measures, on which the *quantitative system* is based, the 'foot' being composed of two lengths, long and short. Though early adopted, its limitations were soon appreciated, Samuel **Daniel** remarking in his *Defence of Ryme* (*c.* 1603):

> For as Greeke and Latine verse consists of number and quantitie of syllables, so doth the English verse of measure and accent.

This already indicated other systems of prosody. But whatever the objections to the quantitative method may be, classical nomenclature can be used with some validity; it at least allows one person to know what another is talking about, even should he adhere to the 'accentual' system. The most common units are as follows:

Dimeter, or duple metres:

Iamb	short – long $\smile$ –
Trochee	long – short – $\smile$
Spondee	long – long – –
Pyrrhic	short – short $\smile$ $\smile$

Trimeter, or triple metres:

Dactyl	long – short – short (like a finger – $\smile$ $\smile$
Anapaest	short – short – long $\smile$ $\smile$ –

Most metres can be analysed under these categories, especially the first and last two; but three-syllable, or trimetric feet, provide terms that are sometimes useful:

Amphibrach	short – long – short (two-short) $\smile$ – $\smile$
Tribrach	short – short – short (three-short) $\smile$ $\smile$ $\smile$
Molossus	– long – long – long – – –
Amphimacer	long – short – long (also known as 'cretic') – $\smile$ –
Bacchius, or Bacchic	short – long – long $\smile$ – –
Anti-bacchius	long – long – short – – $\smile$

There are some four-syllable feet which will be referred to later; but mostly these are usefully resolved into two two-syllable feet.

None of these, naturally, is an accurate time-measurement. A long syllable will vary in length according to the fullness of the vowel-sound, the number of consonants after the vowel, and the weight put on it according to the meaning. Anybody can see how the length of a 'long' syllable will vary by saying expressively:

When by the rout that made the
　　　　　　　　　　hideous roar,
His goary visage down the stream was
　　　　　　　　　　　　　sent,
　　　　　Milton: *Lycidas*, 61–2

The *caesura*, or 'gap', as Bridges preferred to call it, is a pause at some point in the line. At one time, according to classical rules it could be allowed, say, in the middle of the third foot of a five-foot line: but in English verse it can be placed anywhere to give variety, and to provide a pointer to the cadence. It can be short or long, shallow or deep if we adopt Edith **Sitwell**'s nomenclature. How it may give variation in rhythm may be illustrated by the light and deep caesuras in this passage from **Pope**'s *First Epistle of the First Book of Horace* (69–72):

To either India see the merchant fly,
Scared at the spectre of pale poverty!
See him, with pains of body, pangs of
　　　　　　　　　　soul,
Burn through the Tropic, freeze
　　　　　　　　　beneath the Pole.

There are light caesuras in lines 1 and 3, none in line 2, a deep one in line 4. The caesura may indicate the grammar, but grammar must not be allowed to dictate it. **Poe**, in his enlivening essay on prosody, *The Rationale of Verse*, argued that it should be regarded as a foot, consisting of a single long syllable, 'but the length of this syllable varies'. This would seem an unnecessary complication.

The objection made by opponents of the quantitative system is that those who employ it have to play so many tricks of 'substitution', 'licence', 'equivalence' and so on, as to make it seem too much like an elaborate game played for its own sake rather than for an appreciation of the verse, and, moreover, may so distort the versification to make it fit into

217

a rigid framework as to misplace the emphasis. Thus Saintsbury wrote in analysing **Tennyson**'s *The Dying Swan*:

> It brings out a scheme of *dimeters*, wholly iambic at the lowest rate of substitution, wholly anapaestic at the highest, mixed between. A few instances occur of the other usual and regular licences—trochaic and spondaic substitution, monosyllabic feet (*or* catalexis) and one or two of brachycatalexis, three feet instead of four.
>
> *Manual of Prosody*, 110

Catalexis, it should be explained here, means a 'cutting off'. A catalectic line is one where part of a foot has thus been cut off.

The other main school of prosody is the 'accentual' one, as upheld by Lascelles Abercrombie, though by no means fanatically. Here a foot depends upon accent—heavy or light—accent being made up partly of quantity, partly of pitch, but chiefly of stress, that is, the force of breath required. This would seem in many ways a preferable form of analysis, as it takes greater account of the rhythm, as will be developed later. It will be seen at once that this is a far more flexible way of determining feet. The general method does not differ very much, the difference being in deciding what is a foot.

Another school would wish to equate prosody with musical notation. This was carried to its extreme by S. **Lanier** in his *Science of English Verse* (Boston, 1880), but was put more acceptably by T. S. Omond in his extremely interesting and suggestive *A Study of Metre* (1907). Omond argued for isochronous periods to constitute a foot, whatever the proportions of longs and shorts. This might very well fit the theory of 'sprung rhythm', to be discussed later, developed before

that date by Hopkins, but not published till 1918. Musical discussion can on its side partake of prosodic terms, as when the second movement of Beethoven's Seventh Symphony is referred to as the dactyl-spondee movement. Now, having very briefly sketched out the main theories of the units of versification, it is time to move on to the next stage, the interweaving of the units into verse.

3. Metre

(*a*) GENERAL. Metre is the term used to describe the way the feet are organised, the object of this organisation being to establish a rhythm. It is the awareness of a continuous rhythm that enables the reader to distinguish poetry from prose. Prose, to be sure, has rhythms, but they follow no set pattern, unless we go to the not infrequent metrical effect often to be noticed at the end of sentences, analogous with the Latin *cursus*, as, for example, Sir Thomas Browne writing 'raise up the ghost of a rose', paralleled by Newton's 'lay all undiscovered before me', to give only two instances out of scores of possible ones. And, notoriously, copious writers such as Vanbrugh and Dickens often quite unconsciously drop into blank verse, 'that *prose mesurée*' as **Dryden** put it, 'into which the English tongue so naturally slides, that, in writing prose, it is hardly to be avoided' (Epistle Dedicatory of *The Rival Ladies*). Marked rhythms in prose are indeed to be fought shy of, except when a very emotive effect is desired, as in much of De Quincey.

The object of poetry, however, is precisely to arouse certain kinds of emotion, to induce a certain state of being, to break down the resistances the workaday mind offers to other than workaday notions, to enlarge the imagination into unaccustomed realms. Rhythm, in addition to imagery and so on, with which we are not here concerned, is a major agent in this. Exactly how rhythm works is a matter outside our present scope; suffice it to fall back on Coleridge's all-embracing phrase, 'the known effects of metre', since any reader innocent of experiencing these effects will not be addicted to poetry. It may be that it is an impelling sense of rhythm that drives a poet to utterance, just as with Rimbaud a poem first took shape in his mind through some folk tune running in his head. At all events, what must powerfully guide a poet in the form his verse takes is the rhythm which will best express his sense of being, his intuition, at the moment. Thus rhythm is designedly expressive.

And since the rhythm of most verse is of necessity *basically* composed of sequences of the same foot, metre is essential. If, however, this is unvaried, the effect becomes deadening, or is a jingle: it has got to be varied, though not so much as to destroy the basic pulse of the metre. Yet it is too often assumed that whatever variations a poet may contrive (or indulge in) the reader will always keep, somewhere beneath what he actually hears, a sense of the regular beat of the supposed metre. Whether this is so may well be questioned. Omond tells us:

'Mr Swinburne gives us as a heroic line the following:
   Illimitable, insuperable, infinite.
                   Elegy on Burton

That his ear was conscious of five periods when he wrote this line we need not doubt; but it is not easy for his readers to recognise them.'

He might have instanced from *Acactoria*, written mainly in heroics, such lines as:

   I would my love could kill thee; I am satiated.

or:

   Intolerable interludes and infinite ill.

Similarly, R. C. Trevelyan in his *Thamyris*, writes that when **Donne** wrote

   Blasted with sighs, and surrounded with teares

'his readers would be instinctively conscious of the number of the syllables, and so would not be disconcerted by the irregular distribution of the stresses'. In either case we might well ask: 'Why? What matters, surely, is the cadence'. But it is time to look at the metres themselves.

(*b*) DUPLE METRES. Probably the most important of these is the *iambic*, or *rising metre*, since it is the most commonly met with throughout the ages and in all poets. Its generic place in blank verse will be commented on later. For the moment a few obvious examples may be given:

   How vainly men themselves amaze,
   To win the Palm, the Oak, or Bays:
                   Marvell: *The Garden*

   Past ruin'd Ilion Helen lives,
   Alcestis rises from the shades
                   Landor: *Ianthe*

But a variation soon has to be made, so **Marvell** goes on:

   And their uncessant labours see
   Crown'd from some single herb or tree:

and **Landor**:

   Verse calls them forth; 'tis verse that gives
   Immortal youth to mortal maids.

A trochee is substituted for an iamb in the first foot of Marvell's fourth line and of

Landor's third, not only relieving the monotony, but adding force to the important word in each case. Variation can also be made from the start, as in **Wordsworth**'s *Lucy*:

> She dwelt among the untrodden ways
> Beside the springs of Dove,

'the' in the first line being an extra, or 'redundant' syllable. The poets of the seventeenth century would have elided the 'e' of 'the', and probably printed 'th'untrodden', though we today like to give the extra syllable its value. **Wordsworth** makes no trochaic substitution except at the beginning of the seventh line:

> Fair as a star, when only one
> Is shining in the sky,

bringing the emphasis on 'fair'.

The other duple metre is the *trochaic*, or *falling metre*, exemplified in Christopher **Smart**'s

> Now the winds are all composure,
> *St Philip and St James*

going oh, however:

> But the breath upon the bloom ∨

the syllable at the end of the fourth trochee being dropped (catalectic line).

One may instance a well-known piece of **Shelley**:

> Music, when soft voices die, ∨
> Vibrates in the memory ∨
> Odours, when sweet violets sicken,
> Live within the sense they quicken.

where, it will be noticed, the first two lines are similarly catalectic.

The *trochaic* is commonly supposed to be the milder, tenderer measure; it has 'a

dying fall'. Nevertheless a trochaic substitution at the beginning of an iambic poem often gives the vigour to what should in itself be vigorous. We can take **Jonson**'s

> Drink to me onely with thine eyes,
> And I will pledge with mine . . .

or **Lovelace**'s

> Bid me to live, and I will live
> Thy Protestant to be . . .

Yet this substitution would not appear to be necessary. One thinks of Francis **Thompson**'s:

> I fled Him, down the nights and down
> the days;
> I fled Him, down the arches of the
> years . . .

or of Allan **Ramsay**'s:

> My Peggy is a young thing,
> Just enter'd in her teens . . .

where nobody can say that the attack wants vigour. What, however, would seem to be of some importance is that for real force both the first and the last syllable of a line should be accented. We may take **Blake**'s:

> Tyger! Tyger! burning bright ∨
> In the forests of the night ∨

the effect being achieved by catalectic trochaics.

(*c*) TRIPLE METRES

(i) *Dactylic measure* ($- \cup \cup$) has never proved very successful in English verse, as was early recognised by the Elizabethan prosodists; the two 'short' syllables are an unfitting conclusion to most lines: usually a single or double catalexis has to take place, or a substitution. This we can see from **Browning**'s valiant efforts, as in *The Lost Leader*:

> Just for a handful of silver he left us, ∨
>   Just for a riband to stick in his
>   coat ∨∨
> Found the one gift of which fortune
>   bereft us, ∨
> Lost all the others she lets us devote ∨

Thus the dactyl, which would seem to indicate a good rattling measure with a strong attack, is usually found employed with other feet, as will be illustrated later. Nevertheless good dactylic verses have been written, the effect, however, being tender and meditative as might be expected with a falling rhythm, as in **Hood**'s *The Bridge of Sighs*, where alternate lines are dactylic:

> One more unfortunate,
> Weary of breath,
> Rashly importunate,
> Gone to her death.
> Take her up tenderly,
> Lift her with care;
> Fashion'd so slenderly,
> Young, and so fair.

Quantitatively the alternate lines are made up of two silent shorts, e.g. care ∨ ∨; accentually all the lines are two-stress. If we adopt the isochronous prosody, the matter is much plainer, such words as 'care' and 'fair' taking as long to say as 'tenderly' or slenderly'. But Hood can maintain the dactyl, and does so in several stanzas, as in:

> Touch her not scornfully,
> Think of her mournfully,
> Gently and humanly;
> Not of the stains of her,
> All that remains of her
> Now is pure womanly.

In this kind of triple-measure verse it is difficult to find instances that do not begin with an extra syllable: but English verse is full of such, syllables which make little or no difference to the sense. So in **Prior**'s:

> [As] Doctors give Physic by way of
>   prevention,
>   Matt alive and in health of his
>   Tomb-stone took care;

but the second line becomes

(ii) *Anapaestic measure* ($\smile\smile-$), which shares many characteristics of the dactylic variety. It also needs a little playing about with the odd syllable, perhaps at the beginning of the line, as in **Scott**'s:

> ∨ O, young Lochinvar is come out of
>   the west,
>   ∨ Through all the wide Border his
>   steed was the best;

where syllables are dropped, not added. Those examples might be placed in either category, with due substitutions and poetic licences. What matters is the swing of the metre. But where triple metre is concerned, whether the metre is brisk or the reverse depends upon the meaning, the tone. One may well call to mind, as a contrast to the two last instances, Dryden's Jacobite Lament, *The Lady's Song*, with its sad, haunting melody:

> A quire of bright beauties in spring did
>   appear,
> To chuse a May-lady to govern the
>   year;
> All the nymphs were in white, and the
>   shepherds in green,
> The garland was giv'n, and Phillis was
>   queen:
> But Phillis refus'd it, and sighing did
>   say,
> I'll not wear a garland while Pan is
>   away.

There the effect is this essentially accentual verse would seem to be gained by having a quantitatively very long syllable at the end of each line.

Quantitative prosody has its short-comings, but the ear can be misled if its owner is unaware of metrical possibilities, such as may be seen by the confusion between the anapaestic and the

(iii) *Bacchic measure* ($\smile$ — —). One can point to the tricky case of **Byron's**

> The Assyrian came down like a wolf
> on the fold,

which at first sight, or first reading, looks like the anapaestic measure, the good galloping measure, of Scott's *Young Lochinvar*. But Byron's poem is not in that sort of triple measure, being written in bacchics. Not to notice this is to lose the whole rich effect of the poem. Take the stanza:

> And there lay the steed with his nostril
> all wide,
> But through it there roll'd not the
> breath of his pride;
> And the foam of his gasping lay white
> on the turf,
> And cold as the spray on the rock-beating
> surf.

That, as catalectic anapaests, is mere jigging verse, inappropriate to the subject:

> $\smile$ And thére | lay the stéed | with his
>
> nós | tril all wíde,

but as bacchics it becomes:

> Ănd thēre lāy | thĕ stēed wĭth | hĭs
>
> nōstrĭl | āll wĭde, $\smile$

a really impressive rhythm, as W. P. Ker pointed out (*The Criterion*, October

1923), though Saintsbury had hinted at it. Quantitative prosody, that 'superstition' as Poe called it, may sometimes be extremely useful.

(iv) The *Hexameter*, which may be included under triple measure, is, as its name implies, a six-unit line; it is com-posed of dactyls and/or anapaests, with probably a shallow or deep caesura, as with:

> Two Patagonian apes with their arms
> extended akimbo.

'Barbarous hexameters', as Tennyson called them, are easily applicable to satirical feeling, as in the lines **Nashe** quotes in his *Reply to Gabriel Harvey*—who had wished to be remembered as the creator of the English form:

> But ah! what newes do you heare of
> that good Gabriel huffe snuffe,
> Knowne to the world for a foole, and
> clapt in the Fleet for a Rimer?

but at the same time it must be noted that, with anapaests in evidence,

> In the hexameter rises the fountain's
> silvery column,

but it always tends to be irregular, though in *The Courtship of Miles Standish* **Longfellow** could write consistent cata-lectic dactyls:

> Just in the grey of the dawn, as the
> mists uprose in the meadows,
> V.I.

and in the more famous opening of *Evangeline*:

> This is the forest primeval. The
> murmuring pines and the hemlocks,
> Bearded with moss, and in garments
> green, indistinct in the twilight,

where the comma after 'green' wipes out
the caesura between 'garments' and
'green', so that the rhythm is violently
changed. Dactyls also served **Southey** in
The Vision of Judgment, where he was
attempting hexameters as an 'innovation'
(see his Preface):

> Comfort I sought and support, and
> both were found in retiring
> Into that inner world, the soul's strong
> hold and her kingdom,
> Part I, last stanza

but this is apt to become monotonous.
Clough, in *The Bothie of Tober-na-
Vuolich*, and in *Amours de Voyage* used
the dactyl fairly regularly, but with considerable variation:

> We left in a hurry,
> Went from Milan to Como, three days
> before we expected.
> But I thought, if he came all the way to
> Milan, he really
> Ought not to be disappointed . . .
> IV, 65–8

But his 'uncle', in the amusing Prologue
to *Dipsychus*, hopes that this poem will
be in 'good plain verse, none of your
hurry-scurry anapaests, as you call them',
his objection being that you could never
be sure where the stress ought to come.
Clough, however, protests that 'a rude
taste for identical recurrences would
exact sing-song from *Paradise Lost*'.

(v) *Choriambics*, built on a four-syllable
foot, a trochee followed by an iamb
($- \cup \cup -$), is, in English, a rather clumsy
metre, though attempted with some
success by Swinburne in *Poems and Ballads
II*, the first foot being a trochee, the last
an iamb, the three middle ones being
choriambs:

> Love, what | ailed thee to leave | life that
> was made | lovely, we thought, | with
> love?

but the next we might think to begin
with a spondee:

> What sweet | visions of sleep | lured thee
> away | down from the light | above?

The form has not much importance in
English poetry. Nor has that of
(vi) *Galliambics*, about which prosodists
are a little reserved, mostly contenting
themselves with referring to the *Atys* of
Catullus. It has two impressive poems in
English, Tennyson's *Boadicea* and **Meredith**'s *Phaéton*, which opens:

> At the coming up of Phoebus the
> all-luminous charioteer,
> Double-visaged stand the mountains in
> imperial multitudes,

(vii) *Alcaics*, an old Greek metre modified by Horace, and which may be
regarded either as a quantitative or
accentual metre, has not been much
used, and not on the whole with much
success. Yet, resorting to Tennyson
again, the lines to **Milton** are well known:

> O mighty-mouth'd inventor of
> harmonies,
> O skill'd to sing of Time or Eternity,
> God-gifted organ-voice of England,
> Milton, a name to resound for
> ages . . .

(viii) There remain certain puzzles, indeterminate metres, such as **Swift**'s
Mary the Cook-Maid's letter to Dr Sheridan:

> Well; if ever I saw such another man
> since my mother bound my head,
> You a gentleman! marry come up, I
> wonder where you were bred?

> I am sure such words do not become a
>   Man of your cloth,
> I would not give such language to a dog,
>   faith and troth . . .

which might be doggerel were it not so clearly disciplined. **Dowson**'s *Non sum qualis eram* . . . one might call mixed; Saintsbury calls it a 'disputed scansion':

> Last night, ah, yesternight between her
>   lips and mine
> There fell thy shadow, Cynara! thy
>   breath was shed
> Upon my soul between the kisses and
>   the wine;
> And I was desolate and sick of an old
>   passion,
> Yea, I was desolate and bow'd my
>   head:
> I have been faithful to thee, Cynara!
>   in my fashion.

This he analysed as a 'sextet of Alexandrines with decasyllable (or brachycatalexis) in the fifth line, and with hypercatalexis, or double rhyme in the fourth and sixth'.

That is, one sees, an accurate analysis: but the question will naturally arise, 'How is this profitable?'. Is this not, rather, the dissection of a corpse than the lovelier apprehension of a living being? The point it might be pertinent to make is that one system of prosody is applicable to some kinds of verse, and another to other kinds. (See below on *Christabel*.) If quantitative analysis seems to desiccate the rhythm—and prosody should exist to enhance it—does any other system help better? It might be noted, parenthetically, that Saintsbury himself occasionally had to resort to syllabic analysis. The question is, how is verse actually read? It is not only a matter of cadence, but of emotional emphasis. Let us look at the last line of Dowson's stanza quoted

above. Does the reader say to himself 'I háve been faithful to thee . . .' or 'I have been fáithful to thee . . .'? Even the accentual system would seem to fail here. The line could be fairly adequately analysed under either system without the interpolation of the dactylic name 'Cynara'; but it would seem that the helpful system here is that of the isochronous period. The ear, again, would seem to be the only test.

4. Adventitious Aids

Alliteration, rhyme, dissonance and the refrain are also, or may be, an integral part of rhythm, and may help to determine the impact of verse.

(*a*) ALLITERATION, the repetition of a letter, usually a consonant, and normally at the beginning of several words in the same line, was to a large extent the basis of Anglo-Saxon and Middle English verse, as in **Langland**'s *Piers Plowman*, which opens:

> In a somer seson · whan soft was the
>   sonne,
> I shope me in shroudes · as I a sheep
>   were,
> In habit as an heremite · vnholy of
>   workes
>   (*Skeat's ed.*)

(where, incidentally, the early use of the caesura as a definite rule is exemplified). 'Apt alliteration's artful aid', as **Churchill** put it, has continued with varying degrees of popularity, partly as ornament, but mainly as emphasising the metre. It could be abused, as **Shakespeare**'s parody in *Love's Labour's Lost* rubs home:

> The preyful princess pierc'd and
>   prick'd a pretty pleasing pricket

It was tactfully used by Etherege in:

> It is not, Celia, in our power,
> To say how long our love will last . . .

But instances may be met with everywhere

(*b*) RHYME, when lines end with the same vowel-sound, followed by the same consonant, e.g. aid—fade, appeared early in Middle English verse, and would seem to be an important element in English prosody, enhancing the metrical sense, and bringing rhythmic phrases to a conclusion, even when the sentence structure overruns the line. It produces expectation, as well as adding to the musical effect, and can give just that sharpness to deliberately unrhythmic verse as to give it a bite it would otherwise lack. Daniel argues that it gives the poet wings, and, being the result of labour, must give added delight. For Dryden, one of its virtues was that 'it bounds and circumscribes the fancy', disciplining the poet's thought and language. It can, however, be somewhat speciously contrived to make bad poetry seem better than it is, and it does not add much to poetic value. Take a Donne 'Holy Sonnet', replacing the rhyming words with others of much the same meaning, and the sonnet does not suffer much: take rhyme out of much popular jingling verse and the poem as such disappears.

Double rhyming words are often employed, as in this passage from Christina **Rossetti**'s *The Bourne*:

> Underneath the growing grass
> Underneath the living flowers,
> Deeper than the sound of showers;
> There we shall not count the hours
> By the shadows as they pass.

Triple rhyme is also to be met with, though it tends to become comic, as deliberately so in Smart's:

> Thou valiant son of great Cadwallader,
> Hast thou a hare, or hast thou swallowed
>   her?

Byron used the double or triple rhyme for comic effect most happily in *Don Juan*. But that it can be used effectively is instanced by Hood's *The Bridge of Sighs* already quoted.

Internal rhyme, sometimes known as *leonine rhyme*, that is a word in the middle of a line rhyming with the end word, also occurs, as in Tennyson's *Leonine Elegiacs*:

> Low-flowing breezes are roaming the
>   broad valley dimm'd in the gloaming:
> Thoro' the black-stemmed pines only
>   the far river shines . . .

The effect can be fairly subtle, especially if the internal rhyme leaps from one line to the next; but if too marked it has the effect of dividing the line, making a quatrain or even sixaine (for an explanation of these terms see below) out of a couplet.

> When you're lying awake with a dismal
>   headache,
>   and repose is taboo'd by anxiety,
> I conceive you may use any language
>   you choose to
>   indulge in, without impropriety . . .

But these lines of W. S. **Gilbert** might just as well be written:

> When you're lying awake
> With a dismal headache,
> And repose is taboo'd by anxiety, etc.

T. S. **Eliot** imitates this with stimulating variations at the end of *Sweeney Agonistes*.

Eye-rhyme, when spelling corresponds but pronunciation does not, may sometimes provoke alertness, though it more often seems clumsiness, and does nothing towards the rhythmic effect. When over-used it is only an irritant.

(*c*) ASSONANCE, when words agree in vowel-sounds, but have different consonants, may sometimes be found in popular verse, as an imperfect form of rhyming. The variant, of some importance, used with triumphant consistency by Wilfred **Owen** in *Strange Meeting*, where the consonants agree but the vowels differ, is a form sometimes known as *dissonance*:

> It seemed that out of battle I escaped
> Down some profound long tunnel,
>   long since scooped
> Through granites which Titanic wars
>   had groined.
> Yet also there encumbered sleepers
>   groaned . . .

the ear being continually a little cheated of expectancy, this variation precludes any possible lulling effects of rhyme, and keeps the ear alert.

(*d*) The REFRAIN, burden, or chorus, usually at the end of a stanza, but sometimes in the middle as well, is the repetition of a line or phrase. It is often associated with the ballad, but does not occur there as often as is usually supposed. It is to be met with in the Victorian pseudo-ballad. It can be quite meaningless, a 'hey and a ho, and a hey nonny no' kind of chorus, or such a pastiche as **Morris'** 'Two red roses across the moon', rightly parodied by Calverley in 'Butter and eggs and a pound of cheese'. Yet it can be extraordinarily effective, either as reinforcing the emotion as in *The Lyke Wake Dirge* (to be quoted below) or in emphasising the rhythmical shape. **Yeats** used it increasingly, and in some twenty of his *Last Poems* employed it either to carry on the lilt of the verse, or to drive home the idea.

II. STRUCTURE

1. Line Measurement

Every reader of poetry would feel that the next step in rhythmic analysis is to see how far the length of a line is part of the rhythmic pattern, since we tend to pause at the end of a line as though the line itself constituted a unit, however complex. Or, indeed, however simple. T. S. Eliot's:

> Knock
> Knock
> Knock

at the end of *Sweeney Agonistes* is not the same as Hood's

> Work! Work! Work!

in *The Song of the Shirt*. And though perhaps the one-unit, or one-foot line is not strictly to our purpose—since the rhythmic effect is beyond the line—it may be of interest to notice **Herrick's** *Upon his Departure Hence*:

> Thus I
> Passe by,
> And die;
> As One
> Unknown
> And gon . . .

This is rare, though the two-unit, or four-syllable line, is fairly common, especially in early writers such as **Skelton**. But here is **Wyatt**, using iambs:

> With serving still
>   This have I wone,
> For my godwill
>   To be vndon.

Or with trochees:

> How shulde I
> Be so plesaunte
> In mye semblaunt
> As my fellows be?

That sort of metre is rare at the present day. Rather more common is the three-unit line, such as Thomas **Lodge**'s:

> My mistress when she goes
> To pull the pink and rose . . .

(*a*) But much more common, occurring so often in English verse as to make one consider it the natural English metre, is the four-accent, usually octosyllabic line, though there is a fairly frequent form of seven alternating with the eight, as in *The Dance*, by George Mason and John Earsden (1618):

> Robin is a lovely lad,
> No lass a smoother ever had.
> Tommy hath a look as bright
> As is the rosy morning light . . .

finally giving way to sevens only.

The seven-syllable line, with four accents, is fairly common. Ben Jonson employed it in most of the 'Charis' sections of *Underwoods*:

> Let it not your wonder move,
> Lesse your laughter that I love . . .

and **Cotton** was addicted to it. Donne used it, for example, in *Goe, and catche a falling starre*. That it is still a potent metre is made plain by Yeats' use of it, as in that section of *Under Ben Bulben* where he writes:

> Irish poets learn your trade,
> Sing whatever is well made . . .

varying a little with eights, and ending with a decasyllable:

> Still the indomitable Irishry:

where, nevertheless, the accentualists will claim, four stresses are maintained.

(*b*) The OCTOSYLLABLE goes back at least to **Chaucer**'s *The Hous of Fame*:

> Tho come another companye,
> That had ydoon the trayterye,
> That harme and greter wikkednesse
> Than eny hertë kouthë gesse . . .
>   III, 721–4

It served Wyatt, and, one might well say, the larger proportion of poets since then. Famous ones are Donne's *The Extasie*, and Bishop **King**'s *The Exequy*:

> But heark! My pulse like a soft drum
> Beats my approch, tells *Thee* I come;
> And slow howere my marches be,
> I shall at last sit down by *Thee*.

The great bulk of Marvell's poetry is in that metre, as is **Crashaw**'s *Hymn to Saint Teresa* and most of Swift's verse. It forms the basis of a good many quatrains, such as those of Tennyson's *In Memoriam*, and, varied with concluding sixes, of Smart's *Hymn to David* and Ralph **Hodgson**'s *Song of Honour*. Readers of poetry will find it at least as common as the ten-syllable line, for some reason regarded as normal for the English ear. But at this point it might be wise to suggest again that syllabic measurement is very rough and ready, though indicating decisive rhythm-lengths, and that all those mentioned can be analysed quantitatively, mainly trochaic-iamb, and, accentually, as four-stress lines.

In this connection it might be of interest to look at Coleridge's *Christabel*, composed in a four-stress (or accent) metre, which seems almost inevitably to give way to normal octosyllabics.

Coleridge said, erroneously, that the metre was 'founded on a new principle, namely counting the accents in each line, not the syllables. Though the latter may vary from seven to twelve, in each line the accents will be found to be only four'. Bridges (for a fuller account see his *Milton's Prosody*, Appendix F) hoped that by 'only' Coleridge meant 'not more than'. We may look at the poem:

> 'Tis the middle of night by the castle
> clock
> And the owls have awakened the
> crowing cock,
> Tu—whit!—Tu—whoo!
> And hark again! the crowing cock
> How drowsily it crew.

The difficulty there is in the fifth line. You can make four stresses only by reading 'drówsily', where the verse makes the stress, whereas the stress should make the verse. And this happens more than once, e.g.:

> She maketh answer tó the clock

But that paragraph already drops into octosyllabics:

> Sir Leoline, the Baron rich
> Hath a toothless mastiff bitch

and the end of the Conclusion to Part I, of twenty-one lines, is, except for a couplet in sevens, entirely in eights. The rest of the poem, regularly four-stressed, is almost entirely in normal iambic octosyllables, except for a few lines in anapaests:

> Bard Bracy! Bard Bracy! your horses
> are fleet,
> Ye must ride up the hall, your music so
> sweet . . .

But the four-accented octosyllable can easily become monotonous, and to avoid this the lines are sometimes varied with seven-syllable ones, as in Milton's *L'Allegro* and *Il Penseroso*:

> But com thou goddess fair and free,
> In heav'n ycleap'd Euphrosyne,
> And by men, heart-easing Mirth;   (7)
> Whom lovely Venus at a birth,
> With two sister graces more   (7)
> To ivy-crowned Bacchus bore.

Edward **Dyer**, indeed, opens his mainly octosyllabic *Grongar Hill* with a succession of almost unvaried sevens, occasionally interspersing a few as the poem goes on.

(*c*) NINE-SYLLABLE lines occur with some frequency. Blake used them largely in *The Immortal*:

> The Immortal stood frozen amidst
> The vast rock of eternity times
> And times, a night of vast durance,
> Impatient, stifled, stiffen'd, harden'd.

A four-accent line. Though sometimes used for whole poems, the nine-syllable line occurs more usually as a variant of the eight- or ten-syllable line.

(*d*) The DECASYLLABLE is not merely a line of ten syllables; it must, naturally, have a rhythm. Dr **Johnson**'s derisive:

> Put your knife and your fork across
> your plate

is not a line of verse, though Pope's:

> And ten low words oft creep in one
> dull line
> *An Essay on Criticism*, II, 346

surprisingly is, not only because of its setting, but because of two caesuras and metrically valid feet. It might be scanned:

And ten low words ‖ oft creep | in one
dull line,

iamb, spondee, iamb, iamb, spondee. Milton wrote *Paradise Lost* on a deca-syllabic system, but the accents and quantities are varied. Take II, 120–3. The first two lines are a Gascoigne-like jingle, preceded by others of the same kind; but the two last are probably some-thing as indicated:

Irreconcileable to our grand Foe,

Who now triumphs, and in th'excess of
joy . . .

yet they are all decasyllables.

The first important use of this metre in English was Chaucer's, in *The Canterbury Tales*, somewhat rigid iambics, with rhyme alleviating the peril of monotony. His method may be gathered from the Prologue:

A Clerk ther was of Oxenford also,
That unto logyk haddë long ygo.
As leenë was his hors as is a rake,
And he was nat right fat, I undertake.
285–8

He varies a little with an occasional nine or eleven, but is seldom so bold as in the first line of the Prologue:

Whan that Aprill with his shourës sootë

which might be analysed as two trochees, an anapaest and an antibrach.

(*e*) BLANK VERSE (the unrhymed deca-syllable) is even more important than the rhymed, since not only do many of our greatest poems exist in that metre, but it is also the medium for most of our greatest

drama. It is often referred to as the *iambic pentameter*, but its structure as such is subject to so much substitution that quantitative prosody can often be applied to it only with the utmost ingenuity.

How amazingly complex and varied Milton's blank verse is, readers of Saints-bury, Omond, or Bridges in his *Milton's Prosody* can amply appreciate. In spite of Poe's assertion that a metre must be thoroughly established before it can be departed from, we are conscious from the first line of *Paradise Lost*, irregular as it is, that we are subject to a compelling rhythm.

Of Man's | first | disobed | ience, and | the
fruit

'probably gives the line as it is naturally spoken by most people', to quote Aber-crombie. Then, when choosing almost anywhere we meet

Fall'n Cherube, | to be weak is | miserable
(157)

it is difficult to be conscious of an iambic basis. Yet the rhythm is there; it has been well established, though it might well be a decasyllabic line of three bars, or four accent units:

Fall'n Cherube   to be weak is   miserable.

But if monotony threatens, it is nor-mally avoided. Even Glover, accused of dulling the metre of his *Leonidas* by being too regularly iambic, varied con-siderably:

An aged temple with insculptur'd
forms

Of Jove's harmonious daughters, and a
train

229

Ŏf nīne brīght vīrgĭns . . .

VI, 234–6

which is, after all, in much the same muted measure as long tracts of *The Prelude*. **Thomson** in *Autumn* can ring splendid changes:

Who can recount what transmigrations
there
Are annual made? what nations come
and go?
Infinite wings! till all the plume-dark air
And rude resounding shore are one
wild cry.
1744 version, 866–9

There the last two lines, with their succession of longs, analyse them how you will, transform the metre.

A distinction must be emphatically made between dramatic blank verse and that offered for reading. Although in the latter it is by no means invariably a line with five accents, in developed dramatic blank verse it is, at its most effective, a three-stress line, as in **Marlowe's**:

And rĭde in tríumph through Persépolis.
Tamburlaine the Great

or Shakespeare's:

He smóte the sledded Pólacks on the íce
Hamlet

though it is often four when slowing-up is needed, or may even be six:

See see where Christ's blood steams in
the firmament!
Dr Faustus

Our first blank verse drama, *Gorboduc* (*c.* 1565), began bravely with Norton's (or **Sackville's**):

The silent night that brings the quiet
pause
From painful travails of the weary day

and kept it up equally bravely. But the object of dramatic blank verse is to provide a medium which the actor can speak easily, and which the audience can readily catch.

How far this varies from a norm can be appreciated by comparing the verse of a Shakespeare narrative poem (the sonnets are another matter) with almost any of his great speeches from at least his middle period. Take, at random,

O miserable lady! But for me
What case stand I in? I must be the
poisoner
Of good Polixenes; and my ground to
do't
Is the obedience to my master, one . . .
The Winter's Tale, I, 391–4

This, evidently, is to be spoken in the natural rhythms of speech, only generally controlled by the exigencies of metre.

Enjambement. It will have been noticed that with Chaucer the line and the sentence, or phrase, terminate together, a congruity named the *end-stopped* line, emphasising the line-end pause. This rigidity is overcome by continuing the sentence over the line, what is called *enjambement*. It is more than likely that the Elizabethan dramatists initiated this release. From Marlowe on they soon employed it, and it became common form. A good later example might be Wordsworth's:

This History, my Friend, hath chiefly
told
Of intellectual power, from stage to
stage
Advancing. . . .
The Prelude, 1805–6, XI, 44

It will be found in every kind of verse.

(*f*) The HENDECASYLLABLE (elevens) is not common in English verse, since, as Tennyson put it in his exercise in that form spiflicating the indolent reviewers:

So fantastical is the dainty metre.

It occurs incidentally in any decasyllabic verse which enjoys the 'poetic licence' of the unstressed extra syllable, or the *feminine ending*, but it is rare as a deliberate rhythm. We find it, as we might expect, in Swinburne:

In the month of the long decline of roses
I, beholding the summer dead before
me . . .
Poems and Ballads, I

(*g*) the ALEXANDRINE (twelve syllables) is far more important, and is often found, as in Drayton's *Polyolbion*, that neglected nature poem, and in Browning's *Fifine at the Fair*:

What price should you impose, for
instance, on repute,
Good fame, your own good fame and
family's to boot?
XI

but more usually it occurs as a variant of the heroic couplet (see below), especially to conclude a paragraph. It was extensively used so by Dryden, as in:

By haughty souls to humane honour
ty'd!
O sharp convulsive pangs of agonizing
pride!
The Hind and the Panther, III, 285–6

Pope used it more sparingly, feeling that too often

A needless *Alexandrine* ends the song,
That, like a wounded snake, drags its
slow length along.
Essay on Criticism, II, 356–7

(*h*) The FOURTEENER (theoretically seven iambic feet) occurs, according to Saintsbury, 'as almost the first equivalent of the old long Anglo-Saxon line in English'. He instances the *Moral Ode*, from which we may cull:

Ich am elder than ich was a winter and
eke on lore;

but the most famous example is **Chapman**'s *Iliad*:

Thus answer'd him: 'Polydamas, your
depth in augury
I like not, and know passing well thou
dost not satisfy
Thyself in this opinion; or if thou thinkst
it true,
Thy thoughts the Gods blind; to advise
and urge that as our due.

So it thumps on through twenty-four books, the rhymes only making it worse. But this measure soon split up in a two-line one, 8,6, which will shortly be discussed.

There is no logical limit to the length of any line, except what the ear will hold as rhythm. Browning in *Saul*, for example, resorting to what might be called fifteeners, varied with occasional fourteens or sixteens, the metre being mainly anapaestic, giving five accents, with the usual iambic or trochaic substitutions:

I know not too well how I found my
way home in the night.
There were witnesses, cohorts about me,
to left and to right,
XIX

A more perfect example may be found in Tennyson's *Locksley Hall: Sixty Years*

After. In a sense his Virgilian measure in *To Virgil* might be considered as in divided seventeeners, each set of two lines forming a single rhythmical unit:

> I salute thee, Mantovano,
>> I that loved thee since my day began,
> Wielder of the stateliest measure
>> ever moulded by the lips of man.

2. Some Metrical Devices

In nearly all verse the poet will resort to *fingering*, a delicate play with redundant or dropped syllables, the shifting of accent, and so on, which the attentive reader will instantly respond to as he reads. The later Yeats can be enjoyed for a beautiful use of this. But more definite attempts have been made to break away from too strait a prosodic cage, the first of which Bridges called:

(*a*) COUNTERPOINT. (See his *Milton's Prosody*, 'The Verse of Samson Agonistes' and Appendix F.) It really consists in inverting the stresses against the general run of the rhythm, inserting what seem to be dactylic lines among those of duple metre. Sometimes the stresses are to be understood, not heard. Each line needs careful analysis, and since this lengthy task is here impossible, the method may best be illustrated uncommented.

> This, this is he; softly a while,
> Let us not break in upon him;
> O change beyond report, thought, or
>> belief!
> See how he lies at random, carelessly
>> diffus'd,
> With languish't head unpropt,
> As one past hope, abandon'd
> And by himself given over;
> In slavish habit, ill-fitted weeds
> O're worn and soild;
> Or do my eyes misrepresent? Can this
>> be hee,

> That Heroic, that Renown'd
> Irresistible *Samson*? whom unarm'd
> No strength of man, or fiercest wild
>> beast could withstand.
>> *Samson Agonistes*, 115–27

(*b*) SPRUNG RHYTHM was invented by G. M. Hopkins, with support from Bridges, if, indeed, he did not think of it first. A fuller explanation than there is space for here may be found in 'The Author's Preface' to the posthumous edition of Hopkins' poems as published by Bridges. It might be argued that it is a kind of free verse (see below). It claims to be based on 'four sorts of feet: a monosyllable and the so-called accentual Trochee, Dactyl and the First Paeon. [The Paeon is a four-syllable foot—long, short, short, short.] Also lines can be "rove over", that is, for the scanning of each line immediately to take up that of the one before.' Further, there are '*hangers* or *outriders*, that is, one, two, or three slack syllables added to a foot and not counting in the nominal scanning'. It sounds too free to be verse, but in actual practice the rhythm is so marked as to constitute it such, and it follows Gascoigne's principle of bringing the emphasis where it is important. It is, in fact, a stress prosody. One example from *The Leaden Echo and the Golden Echo*:

> How to keép—is there ány any, is
>> there none such, nowhere known
>>> some, bow or brooch or braid
>> or brace, láce, latch or catch or key to
>>> keep
> Back beauty, keep it, beauty, beauty,
>> beauty . . . from vanishing away?
> Ó is there no frowning of these wrinkles,
>>> ranked wrinkles deep
> Dówn? . . .

It will be noted that the syllables to be stressed have often to be marked.

(c) FREE VERSE pretends to adhere to no 'rules', obey no 'law' except that of rhythm. All one need really say about it is that it is the erecting into a principle of what has for centuries been the practice of poets. It means the abandonment of all stanzaic form, yet each block of lines forms a definite rhythmic unit. Matthew **Arnold**'s *The Strayed Reveller* is an admirable example of controlled free verse—not such a contradiction in terms as the word 'free' might imply. Two unconnected 'stanzas' may be quoted:

> Who speaks? Ah! who comes forth
> To thy side, Goddess, from within?
> How shall I name him?
> This spare, dark–featured,
> Quick-eyed stranger?
> Ah! and I see too
> His sailor's bonnet,
> His short coat, travel-tarnish'd,
> With one arm bare!—
> Art thou not he, whom fame
> This long time rumours
> The favour'd guest of Circe, brought
>   by the waves?
> Art thou he, stranger?
> The wise Ulysses,
> Laertes' son?

and:

>   These things, Ulysses,
> The wise bards also
> Behold and sing.
> But oh, what labour!
> O prince, what pain!

The poems of D. H. Lawrence are mostly written in this controlled free verse.

When free verse throws off the control of the short rhythmic line, it tends to become heavily stressed prose. This may not make it any the less great utterance, but it does mean that it is deprived of the

aid of 'the known effects of metre'. The irregular lines are not 'verses' in any strict sense, but are carried along by a powerful metre of their own. Take Blake's *Vala, or the Four Zoas*, which has a vaguely iambic pulse:

> But Luvah and Vala standing in the
>   bloody sky
> On high remain'd alone, forsaken, in
>   fierce jealousy.
> They stood above the heavens, forsaken,
>   desolate, suspended in blood.
> Descend they could not, nor from Each
>   other avert their eyes.
> Eternity appear'd above them as One
>   man infolded
> In Luvah's robes of blood and bearing
>   all his afflictions;
> As the sun shines down on the misty
>   earth, such was their vision.
>   *Night I*

Or Whitman in *Leaves of Grass*, vaguely dactylic:

> Over the breast of the spring, the land,
>   amid cities,
> Amid lanes and through old woods,
>   where lately the violets peep'd from
>   the ground, spotting the gray debris,
> Amid the grass in the fields each side of
>   the lanes, passing the endless grass
> Passing the yellow-spear'd wheat every
>   grain from its shroud in the
>   dark-brown fields uprisen,
> Passing the apple-tree blows of white
>   and pink in the orchards,
> Carrying a corpse to where it shall rest
>   in the grave,
> Night and day journeys a coffin.
>   *Memories of President Lincoln*

There is the still freer verse of Ezra **Pound** in his *Cantos*.

3. Between Structure and Form

There are some groupings which while not one-line are rhythmic units which are not yet stanzas. Such are:

(*a*) the HEROIC COUPLET, strictly speaking rhymed iambic pentameters, 'riding rhyme'. The use is so common as to need no further illustration. In its earlier use each couplet was fairly strictly end-stopped, as with Chaucer, and with Marlowe in *Hero and Leander*. It was the stock form for Dryden and Pope, was adopted by Churchill in imitation. Browning used it with much enjambement in *Sordello*, and it was used again in its purer form in our own day by Roy **Campbell** in *The Flaming Terrapin*.

(*b*) POULTER'S MEASURE, which C. S. Lewis calls 'lumbering', is an Alexandrine followed by a fourteener; poulters, or poulterers, apparently giving an alternate fourteen to the dozen. Wyatt used it a good deal, as in *Spayne*, from Petrarch:

So febel is the threde that doth the
                                        burden stay
Of my pore lyff, in hevy plyght that
                                        falleth in dekay . . .

but it seems to have gone completely out of use.

(*c*) LONG, COMMON, AND SHORT MEASURE make up what look like four-line stanzas but would really seem to be pairs of well-known long lines split in two. They compose metres that can be used for tunes that everybody knows, and anyone wishing to see how these metres comply with popular requirements can read Isaac **Watts'** adaptations of the Psalms. As good an illustration as any is that of his versions of Psalm xxiii; 'The Lord is my shepherd; I shall not want'.

I. Long metre (8, 8).
      My Shepherd is the living Lord;
      Now shall my wants be well
                              supply'd;
      His providence and holy word
      Become my safety and my guide.

II. Common metre (8, 6). The
      fourteener split up.
      My shepherd will supply my need,
      Jehovah is his name,
      In pastures fresh he makes me feed,
      Beside the living stream.[1]

III. Short metre (6, 6, 8, 6).
      The Lord my Shepherd is,
      I shall be well supply'd;
      Since he is mine and I am his
      What can I want beside?

How strict this metre need be may admit of some doubt, for the most famous version of this Psalm is that of Sir H. W. Baker, in an 8,7 metre:

      The King of love my Shepherd is,
          Whose goodness faileth never;
      I nothing lack if I am His
      And He is mine for ever.
                          Hymns A & M, 197

Common measure, however, deserves its name. It is common to all sorts of poetry, notably the ballad. It is to be found almost anywhere in the canon, e.g. Wordsworth's *To the Cuckoo*, but here we might quote from Daniel:

      Come worthy Greeke, *Vlisses* come
      Possesse these shores with me;
      The windes and Seas are troublesome;
      And heere we may be free . . .
                          Ulysses and the Siren

and from Emily **Dickinson**:

      Because I could not stop for death,
      He kindly stopped for me;
      The carriage held but just ourselves
      And Immortality . . .
                          The Chariot

The name of **Housman** will occur to everybody.

[1] pronounced *strame* in the eighteenth century

III. SOME FORMS

It is obvious that systems of rhetoric or prosody are no arbitrarily invented tyrannies, but rather they are a collection of rules demanded by the very constitution of the spiritual being. And systems of prosody and rhetoric have never yet prevented originality from clearly emerging; the contrary—namely that they have assisted the birth of originality—would be infinitely more true.

Baudelaire: *The Mirror of Art,*
tr. Jonathan Mayne

Form itself is exciting, as any artist in any medium knows. Here we are concerned only to note how far prosody reinforces (rather than creates) form. Keeping this limitation in mind, some description, rather than analysis, is desirable.

1. General

The stanza, or staff, as it used to be called, is, apart from the whole poem— where the meaning-structure, rather than the rhythm is the appropriate focus—the next rhythmic unit. It can be of any conceivable shape, but there are some rhythmic groups which are part of the tradition which the 'spiritual being' has engendered. The first, obviously, is the two-line stanza, to be distinguished from the couplet, and it has been used to some effect, but it is not very common, perhaps because it is not very striking. The others are as follows:

(*a*) The TRIPLET, the three lines of which may be rhymed or not. Sidney Godolphin gives us, in not very strict iambic pentameters:

Vertue, and you, soe intermix that Wee
Believe you one with safer piety
than were the knowledge which is you,
which shee . . .
To the King and Queene

and Elizabeth Barrett **Browning**'s long octosyllabic *A Vision of Poets* is also rhymed:

He hears a silent gliding coil,
The snakes strain hard against the soil,
His foot slips in their slimy oil,

whereas Wallace **Stevens** often uses it unrhymed, and in rather freer verse:

Of medium nature, this farouche extreme
Is a drop of lightning in an inner world,
Suspended in temporary jauntiness.
The Bouquet

(*b*) The TERCET, a term sometimes incorrectly used for triplet, more strictly defines Dantesque *terzarima*, where the stanzas are connected by rhyme, thus: a b a b c b c d c . . . and so on. Dante ends each canto of the *Divina Commedia* with a quatrain, linking with the preceding tercet, thus: u v u v w v w. The tercets may be self-contained gramatically, but as often as not are linked by enjambement. Several instances occur on the canon, the earliest successful ones being perhaps those in Shelley's *The Triumph of Time*, or *Ode to the West Wind*:

Thou on whose stream, mid the steep
sky's commotion,
Loose clouds like earth's decaying
leaves are shed,
Shook from the tangled boughs of
Heaven and Ocean
Angels of rain and lightning: there are
spread
On the blue surface of thine aery surge,
Like the bright hair uplifted from the
head
Of some fierce Maenad, even from the
dim verge
Section II

but he ends each section with a couplet. Dixon's long poem *Mano* is in tercets, as

235

Prosody, forms of verse, and some usages

is Browning's not quite so long *Jochanan
Haddadosh* ('Jocoseries'), and William
Morris' *Defence of Guenevere*. Modern
examples are provided by William
Empson, and by Louis **MacNeice** in
his admirably sustained long poem *Autumn
Sequel*. Some have felt that the rhyme is
too insistent. Yeats, in *Cuchulain Com-
forted*, has dissonances rather than rhymes,
as has Archibald **MacLeish**. T. S. Eliot
goes further in Part II of *Little Gidding*,
experimenting with unrhymed *terza*
which, though not *rima*, have the same
rhythmic effect.

(*c*) The QUATRAIN, or stanza of four lines,
is perhaps the commonest in English
verse, quite apart from the poems in
common measure already noted. The
quatrain is usually self-contained, and is
more often than not decasyllabic. An
early instance is Sir John **Davies'** *Nosce
Teipsum*:

> For how may we to other's things attain,
> When none of us his own soul
> understands?
> For which the devil mocks our curious
> brain,
> When 'Know thyself' his oracle
> commands.

It is common in such long poems as it
is in shorter ones, and would seem to
be a convenient rhythmic unit, easily
handled by the poet, and readily taken
in by the reader. Other well-known
poems in quatrains are Dryden's *Annus
Mirabilis* and, of course, **Gray's** *Elegy
in a Country Churchyard*, in all of which
decasyllabics the rhyme-scheme a b a b
is maintained. Tennyson, in an octosyllabic
form borrowed from Lord **Herbert** of
Cherbury, adopted a b b a:

> When on my bed the moonlight falls,
> I know that in thy place of rest

By that broad water of the west,
There comes a glory on the walls.
In Memoriam, LXVII

FitzGerald, in *The Rubáiyát of Omar
Khayyám* adopted a further variant:
a a b a:

> And those who husbanded the Golden
> Grain,
> And those who flung it to the Winds
> like Rain,
> Alike to no such aureate Earth are
> turn'd
> As, buried once, men want dug up
> again.

Cotton's octosyllabic quatrains in *Winter*
rhyme a a b b:

> See where a liquid mountain rides,
> Made of innumerable tides,
> And tumbles headlong to the strand,
> As if the sea would come to land.

The same form is used by Shelley in *The
Masque of Anarchy*.

(*d*) After the quatrain the stanza is limit-
less, and limitlessly varied. There are
those of five lines, sometimes known as
the quintet; six, the sixaine; seven, the
septet; eight, the octave; and so on,
variously rhythmed and variously rhymed.
Take, as an example of variants, Robert
Greene's sixaine:

> Mars in a fury gainst love's greatest
> Queen
> Put on his helm and took him to his
> lance:
> On Erycynus' mount was Mavors seen,
> And there his ensigns did the god
> advance
> And by heaven's greatest gates he
> stoutly swore,
> Venus should die for she had
> wrong'd him sore.

and **Suckling**'s *A Ballad upon a Wedding*:

> Her feet beneath her petticoat
> Like little mice stole in and out,
>   As if they fear'd the light;
> But oh! she dances such a way,
> No sun upon an Easter day
>   Is half so fine a sight.

Shakespeare, again, has used it differently in *Venus and Adonis*.

(*e*) One form of the septet, rhyming a b a b b c c, is known as RHYME ROYAL, possibly because it was the measure of *The King's Quair*, by **James I** of Scotland. It was once extensively used, as by Chaucer in *The Prioress's Tale*; by Thomas Sackville in his Induction to a *A Mirror for Magistrates*, and by Shakespeare in *The Rape of Lucrece*:

> So she, deep-drenched in a sea of care,
> Holds disputation in each thing she
>   views,
> And to herself all sorrow doth compare:
> No object but her passion's strength
>   renews,
> And as one shifts, another straight ensues;
>   Sometime her grief is dumb and hath
>   no words;
>   Sometime 'tis mad and too much talk
>   affords.

It is the form used by Shelley in *Adonais*.

(*f*) The obvious form of the eight-line stanza is the OTTAVA RIMA, introduced from Italy, and used by Chaucer in *The Monk's Tale*. It consists of eight ten-syllable lines rhyming a b a b a b c c. It was used a good deal in the so-called romantic period, as by Keats in *Isabella, or The Pot of Basil*, and by Shelley in *The Witch of Atlas*.

(*g*) The SPENSERIAN STANZA consists of a decasyllabic octave with an alexandrine

added, the rhyme scheme being a b a b b c b c c:

> So passeth, in the passing of a day,
>   Of mortall life, the leafe, the bud, the
>   flowre,
>   Ne more doth flourish after first
>   decay,
>   That earst was thought to decke both
>   bed and bowre,
>   Of many a Ladie, and many a
>   Paramowre:
> Gather therefore the Rose, whilest yet
>   is prime,
> For soone comes age, that will her
>   pride deflowre:
> Gather the rose of love, whilest yet is
>   time,
> Whilest loving thou mayst be loved with
>   equall crime.
>   *The Bowre of Blisse*

It is unnecessary to go on. It will be seen that the number of lines in a stanza is little indication of its nature: the success will depend upon how far the rhythmic sense can be held together. There are two-line stanzas, and so on. **Vaughan** in *The World* carries off fifteen-line stanzas.

These forms can, of course, be infinitely varied, as by shortening the last line, usually giving the effect of finality, as Fanshawe does with his quatrains in his *Ode of 1630*:

> Now War is all the World about,
> And everywhere *Erynnis* reigns,
> Or else the Torch so late put out,
>   The stench remains.

So also, among hundreds of others, Keats' *La Belle Dame Sans Merci*.

The flexibility of the stanza could be illustrated by many, from, say, Skelton, of which one might choose *To Mistress Margaret Hussey*:

Merry Margaret,
   As midsummer flower,
Gentle as falcon
Or hawk of the tower:
With solace and gladness,
With mirth and no madness,
All good and no badness:
     So joyously,
     So maidenly,
     So womanly
     Her demeaning
     In every thing,
     Far, far passing
     That I can indite,
     Or suffice to write
Of merry Margaret
   As midsummer flower,
Gentle as falcon
Or hawk of the tower.

Where the rhythm is accentuated by the form, as it is in Vachel **Lindsay**'s *The Flower-fed Buffaloes.*

2. Some Special Forms

Sapphics is the only classical form which has produced much that lingers in the memory. The stanzas consist of three hendecasyllables and a decisive short one scanning $\smile\smile\smile\smile\bar{\smile}$. A well-known light example is Canning's *The Knife-Grinder*:

Weary Knife-grinder! little think the
               proud ones,
Who in their coaches roll along the
               turnpike-
Road, what hard work 'tis crying all day
  'Knives and Scissors to grind O!'

The serious sapphics attempted by the Elizabethans were dreary exercises, and if those written by **Cowper**, Swinburne, Bridges and **Hardy** scarcely rise above being, as Saintsbury says, *tours de force*, Watts' *Day of Judgement* triumphs:

When the fierce North wind with his
               airy forces,

Rears up the *Baltic* to a foaming fury;
And the red lightning, with a storm of
               hail comes
  Rushing amain down:

ending:

O may I sit there when He comes
               triumphant
Dooming the nations! then ascend to
               glory,
While our Hosannas all along the
               passage,
  Shout the Redeemer.

This corresponds more closely to the classical form which was weighty and melodious, as employed by Sappho herself or by Horace in, for example, the *Odes*, III, 18.

Forms derived from the Italian, or from French courtier poetry, some of which were considered in the last century as fit only for lighter verse, are often use by English writers for more serious purposes. We may begin with:

(*a*) the BALLADE, a poem of three octaves rhyming a b a b b c b c, and a quatrain, each ending with a refrain. The earliest example in our literature is Chaucer's 'Hyd, Absolon, thy gilte tresses clere', but this lacks the final quatrain. A complete, if slightly archaeized example is **Rossetti**'s translation from François Villon, *The Ballad of Dead Ladies*:

Tell me now in what hidden way is
  Lady Flora the lovely Roman?
Where's Hipparchia, and where is Thaïs,
  Neither of them the fairer woman?
Where is echo, beheld of no man,
Only heard on river and mere,—
  She whose beauty was more than
               human? . . .
But where are the snows of yester-year?

the final stanza running:

Nay, never ask this week, fair lord,
  Where they are gone, nor yet this
                       year,
Except with this for an overword, . . .
  But where are the snows of yester-year?

The quatrain usually ends with a more direct invocation to a prince or princess, as may be found in Swinburne's translations of Villon, or his own *Ballad of François Villon* (*Poems and Ballads* II), or in the admirable ballade Andrew Lang prefixed to his version of *Aucassin and Nicolette*. The ballade is, on the whole, an elegiac form.

(*b*) The RONDEAU consists of two stanzas, nine lines and six, with a refrain echoing the first line. A good example (here slightly modernised) is that by Sir Thomas Wyatt, that great introducer of metres and forms:

  What no, perdy, ye may be sure!
  Thinck not to make me to your lure,
    With words and cheere so contrareing,
    Sweet and sowre contre-weighing;
  Too much it were still to endure.
  Trouth is trayed where craft is in ure.
  But though ye have my hertes cure
    Trow ye I dote withoute ending?
      What no, perdy!

  Though with that pain I do procure
  For to forgett that ons was pure,
    With my hert shall still that thing,
    Unstable, unsure, and wavering,
  Be in my mynde without recure?
      What no, perdy!

A modification, the RONDEL, may be found in Swinburne's *Poems and Ballads* I and in his *A Century of Roundels*.

(*c*) The SESTINA was invented by Arnaut Daniel, and imitated by Dante and others. It consist of six sixaines, the concluding words of the first sixaine being repeated, in a perfect example in the same order, but at any rate the first line of each stanza taking up the end-word of the preceding one. It concludes with a triplet, employing three of the end-words in the middle of the lines, the other three at the end, again in the same order. It may be illustrated by quoting the first two stanzas and the final triplet of the sestina **Spenser** wrote in the August section of *The Shepheardes Calendar*, Cuddie's 'heavy lay':

Ye wasteful Woods! bear witness of
                 my woe,
Wherein my plaints did oftentimes
                 resound;
Ye careless birds are privy to my cries,
Which in your songs were wont to
              make a part:
Thou, pleasant Spring, hast lull'd me
              oft asleep,
Whose streams my trickling tears did
              oft augment.

Resort of people doth my griefs
              augment,
The walled towns do work my greater
                woe;
The forest wide is fitter to resound
The hollow echoes of my careful cries.
I hate the house, since thence my love
              did part,
Whose wailful want debars mine eyes of
              sleep.

          *

And you that feel no woe, when as the
              sound
Of these my nightly cries ye hear apart,
Let break your sounder sleep, and pity
              augment.

Swinburne, it goes without saying, has examples, even employing a double sestina in a speech in a play. Perhaps the best known in the language is **Kipling**'s *Sestina of the Tramp Royal*—'Speakin' in general, I 'ave tried 'em all,'. Ezra Pound includes 'Sestina; Altaforte' and 'Sestina for Ysolt' in *Exultations*, but these, though skilful, conclude with imperfect triplets. T. S. Eliot has a variant as Part II of *The Dry Salvages*, rhyming, not repeating, the words, except in the sixth stanza. There is, naturally, no final triplet.

(*d*) The SONNET, a term once rather loosely applied to short poems of an amatory nature, is now more strictly confined to mean a fourteen-line poem divided into two rhythmic units, an octave and a sixaine, the latter resolving the problem, or clarifying the emotion, expressed by the former. Originally from Italy, it was first introduced into English by Wyatt, imitating Petrarch, closely followed by **Surrey**. It is usually in decasyllables, but need not be, some of **Sidney**'s *Astrophel and Stella* sequence having a few sonnets in alexandrines, e.g. Nos. I, VI, LXXVI and LXXVII, while Shakespeare's No. 145 and those of Cotton, named 'Petrarchan Stanzas' are in octosyllables. Sonnets vary only in the rhyming system, but this is important. The octave, composed of two quatrains, may rhyme a b b a a b b a (Wyatt); or a b a b c d c d (Surrey and Shakespeare). Spenser in his *Amoretti* has a b a b a c a c, or a b a b b c b c. The characteristic sonnet sequences of this period—Daniel, Drayton, etc., follow this pattern. Milton, continuing Donne, has a b a b a c c a, as well as other arrangements.

More important are those of the sestet, since this is the final statement of the poem. Wyatt concludes e d d c e e. Surrey varies. His spring sonnet,

The soote season, that bud and bloom
forth brings

has only two rhymes throughout, the sestet being a b a b a a. Spenser also varies, perhaps linking the sestet with the octave, but, with Daniel, Drayton and the rest, giving a new rhyme to the last two lines, just as Shakespeare's sonnets end e f e f g g. Milton's sestets are more elaborate. He has, after a b b a a b b a, possibly c d c e e d, or c d c d c d. He rarely ends with a couplet. It is a mistake to talk about 'the Miltonic sonnet', as though Milton always wrote to one pattern.

On the whole the sonnet has followed one or other of these moulds. Keats, however, trying 'to discover a better Sonnet Stanza than we have', as he wrote to his brother George, enclosing the one beginning:

If by dull rhymes our English must be
chained

produced the triplet sequence a b c a b d c a b d e. In his sonnet *To Sleep* he again experimented. But the sonnet writers of the nineteenth century, such as Christina Rossetti, go back to one or other of the Elizabethan forms, but latterly Madeline Mason has published (1958) a sonnet sequence in a new form, *At the Ninth Hour*, of which the form is a b c a b c c d e d a e e a, but the distinction between the octave and the sestet is deliberately blurred.

The 'tailed sonnet', or *sonnetto caudato*, is one to which some lines have been added. It is not much used. The best instance in English is Milton's 'On the new forcers of Conscience', ending with the today pregnant line:

New Presbyter is but *Old Priest* writ Large.

The sixteen-line stanzas in which Meredith wrote *Modern Love* are often referred to as sonnets, but there is no justification for this.

(*e*) The TRIOLET is a short form of the rondeau, in the most common of which the first of eight lines is repeated in the fourth and seventh. But the repetitions are always syntactically different; they are not mere repetitions, but open up the meaning while at the same time preventing the rhythm from becoming wooden, e.g. Hardy's:

How great my grief, my joys how few,
　　Since first it was my fate to know thee!
—Have the slow years not brought to
　　　　　　　　　　view
How great my grief, my joys how few,
Nor memory shaped old times anew,
　　Nor loving-kindness helped to show
　　　　　　　　　　thee
How great my grief, my joys how few,
　　Since first it was my fate to know thee?

a successful example to be paired with Bridges':

When first we met we did not guess
　　That love could prove so hard a
　　　　　　　　　　master . . .

(*f*) The VILANELLE, lately come back into fashion, is more complicated. Like the triolet it depends on a repetition of lines. There are six stanzas (five triplets and a final quatrain), the first line of the first being repeated as the third of the second, fourth and sixth stanzas; the third line of the first being repeated as the last of the third, fifth and sixth stanzas. As in the triolet, the repetitions are syntactically varied, though as in the case of Dylan **Thomas'** exhortation to his father, the reader must help by shifting the accent:

Do not go gentle into that good night,
Old age should burn and rave at close of
　　　　　　　　　　day;
Rage, rage against the dying of the light.

Though wise men at their end know
　　　　　　　　　　dark is right,

Because their words have[1] forked no
　　　　　　　　　　lightning they
Do not go gentle into that good night.

Good men, the last wave by, crying how
　　　　　　　　　　bright
Their frail deeds might have danced in a
　　　　　　　　　　green bay,
Rage, rage against the dying of the light.

Wild men who caught and sang the sun
　　　　　　　　　　in flight,
And learn, too late, they grieved in on
　　　　　　　　　　its way,
Do not go gentle into that good night.

Grave men, near death, who see with
　　　　　　　　　　blinding sight
Blind eyes could blaze like meteors and
　　　　　　　　　　be gay,
Rage, rage against the dying of the light.

And you, my father, there on the sad
　　　　　　　　　　height,
Curse, bless, me now with your fierce
　　　　　　　　　　tears, I pray,
Do not go gentle into that good night.
Rage, rage against the dying of the light.

William Empson offers several examples, the famous one being *Missing Dates*, which begins: 'Slowly the poison the whole blood stream fills'.

(*g*) One especial form may be noted, the 'Burns metre'. This consists of six lines, 8, 8, 8, 4, 8, 4, rhyming a a a b a b, and appears to have come from Provence in the eleventh century. It occurs in English Miracle Plays, as in the York *Resurrection*:

Ah, blessed Lord, Adonai,
What may these marvels signify,
That here were showed so openly
　　Unto our sight
This day, when that the man gan die
　　That Jesus hight?

---

[1] text: 'has'

It has been much used by Scottish poets, such as Allan **Ramsay**, who offers an excellent example in his pastoral *Patie and Roger*. It is called after Burns because he made such extensive use of it as in *Holy Willie's Prayer, To a Haggis* and *To a Mountain Daisy*. The metre was aptly employed by Bridges in his poem *To Robert Burns (Later Poems)*.

(*h*) FREAKS. Certain forms have been used which would seem at first contact to be designed for the eye alone, stanzas shaped like wings or diamonds, etc. An exhaustive list may be found in Puttenham's 'Of Poets and Poesie' (see *Elizabethan Critical Essays*) but for our purpose here it will be enough to draw attention to **Herbert**'s *Easter Wings*, and the wing and diamond forms employed by Dylan Thomas in his series *Vision and Prayer*. Though these forms may seem purely designed for the eye, they have a rhythmic structure.

IV. SOME USAGES

Lyrical Poetry, to use Bagehot's excellent definition (*Essays on Hartley Coleridge*) 'is designed to express . . . some one mood, some single sentiment, some isolated longing in human nature.' Other kinds, the epic, narrative, contemplative, philosophic, engage life more as a whole, with its conflicting emotions. But the frontiers are necessarily vague. Is Gray's *Elegy* lyrical or contemplative? One might add another of Bagehot's dicta (*Essay on Wordsworth, Tennyson and Browning*): '[Lyrical] poetry should be memorable and emphatic, intense, and *soon over*'. The word 'lyrical' also implies something that can be sung, and we may begin with:

(*a*) The BALLAD, which early made its appearance in English poetry. It is a vague term. Its proper significance may be as Robert **Graves** argues, a social one local, with no known author. (There are those who claim that it was a communal product: but neither crowds nor committees make poetry.) It is probably oral, meant to go with a tune, need not be highly advanced technically, and it has no 'message'. Since the early eighteenth century, however, ballads have known authors, such as, to name only well-known ones, Mallet's *William and Margaret*, Coleridge's *The Ancient Mariner*, and Kipling's *Ballad of East and West*. It is much used today, by such as W. H. **Auden**, Charles **Causley**, Robin **Skelton**, and, a splendid example, Vernon **Watkins'** *Ballad of the Mari Lwyd*. It very often has a refrain, and is usually written in quatrains, often in approximation to common measure. It may tell a story, as does *Sir Patrick Spens*, or express an emotion, as does *The Lyke Wake Dirge*, which last may be partly quoted in illustration of its essential folk quality, the somewhat uncertain common measure, and the refrain. The tune, or at any rate *a* tune, is fairly well known:

This ae nighte, this ae nighte,
  —*Every nighte and alle*,
Fire and fleet and candle-lighte,
  And Christe receive thy Saule.

When thou from hence away art past,
  —*Every nighte and alle*,
To Whinny-muir thou com'st at last:
  And Christe receive thy Saule.

There are many variants of the metre, e.g. *The Twa Corbies*, which has a stanza of four octosyllabic lines. In fact there is no normal metre. Moreover the rhyme-systems vary. The five four-line stanzas of *Lord Randal*, in decasyllables, have the same end-word for each corresponding line throughout. *Edward, Edward* is in octaves, the second and fifth lines being refrains, the others rhyming rather imperfectly together, so that there are only three original lines in each stanza; e.g. Stanza vi:

'And what will ye leave to your bairns
      and your wife,
  Edward, Edward?
And what will ye leave to your bairns
      and your wife,
  When ye gang owre the sea, O?'—
'The warld's room: let them beg through
       life,
  Mither, mither;
The warld's room: let them beg through
       life;
  For them never mair will I see, O.'

(*b*) The ECLOGUE, the true meaning of the word being 'selection', but from Spenser onward falsely supposed to mean 'goat-herd's song', derives from the classics, notably the eclogues of Theocritus and Virgil. In form it is a dialogue, often about love, but apart from that embracing wide implications. Spenser's *The Shepheardes Calendar* is in that form. The eclogue had a great vogue at the beginning of the eighteenth century under the title of 'pastorals', such as those of Ambrose Philips and Pope, of Thomas Purney and William **Diaper**, mostly purposefully nostalgic of a golden age. **Gay** treated the form more realistically in *The Shepherds' Week*, while **Collins'** *Persian Eclogues* are somewhat different in idea, John **Davidson**'s *Fleet Street Eclogues* being markedly so. It might be considered that Southey's eclogues are a link between the pastiche and the modern.

(*c*) The ELEGY, by definition a song of lamentation or a funeral song, may take any number of forms, and provides some of the most famous poems in the language. It may be a distant, somewhat formal celebration of a person hardly known to the poet, such as Donne's *The Autumnal*, or not known at all such as Dryden's *Anne Killigrew* ode. They may be deeply personal, as King's *The Exequy*, or be tributes such as Dryden's *To the Memory of Mr Oldham*, or become through slight personal knowledge occasions for philosophical reflections, such as Milton's *Lycidas*, or Shelley's *Adonais*, or grow to be so through affection for the subject, as is Tennyson's *In Memoriam*, or Arnold's *Thyrsis*. Gray's *Elegy in a Country Churchyard* is really a contemplative poem.

(*d*) The EPITAPH is a very brief elegy, supposedly of a length that could be engraved on a tombstone. Notable ones are Ben Jonson's *On S.P.*, or his:

Farewell, thou child of my right hand,
      and joy;
  My sinne was too much hope of thee,
      lov'd boy,
Seven yeares tho' wert lent to me, and I
      thee pay,
  Exacted by thy fate, on the just day.
O, could I loose all father, now. For why
  Will man lament the state he should
      envie?
To have so soon scap'd worlds, and
      fleshes rage,
  And, if no other miserie, yet age?
Rest in soft peace, and, ask'd, say here
      doth lye
  BEN: JONSON his best piece of
      poetrie.
For whose sake, hence-forth, all his
      vowes be such,
  As what he loves may never like too
      much.

Perhaps the best known of all epitaphs is Marvell's *Enough, and leave the rest to Fame*.

(*e*) The EPIGRAM has come to mean a brief, witty poem, usually of a satirical nature. Often it is embedded in long poems, as in the famous couplet in **Butler**'s *Hudibras*, about those who

> Compound for Sins they are inclin'd to
> By damning those they have no mind to.
> I, I, 215–6

Such are to be found *passim* in Dryden or Pope. The epigram proper may be found admirably exemplified in the works of Donne, Jonson, Byron and so on. The turn of thought must be brief, and the best are in at most four lines. One of Byron's more savage ones runs:

> So Castlereagh has cut his throat!—the
> worst
> Of this is—that his own was not the
> first.

His 'The World is a bundle of hay' is too well known to need repeating. Epigrams continue to be written down to our own day, as by George Rostrevor **Hamilton**; there is the famous one by Roy Campbell *On Some South African Novelists*:

> You praise the firm restraint with which
> they write—
> I'm with you there, of course:
> They use the snaffle and the curb all
> right,
> But where's the bloody horse?

But the epigram need not be satirical, as witness Sir Henry Wotton's

> He first deceas'd: she for a little tried
> To live without him, liked it not, and
> died.
> *Upon the Death of Sir Albert Morton's Wife*

and Landor's perfect:

> Stand close around, ye Stygian set,
>   With Dirce in one boat convey'd!
> Or Charon, seeing, may forget
>   That he is old and she a shade.

(*f*) The EPISTLE, as its title implies, is basically a letter, possibly quite a familiar one, such as Jonson's *Inviting a Friend to Supper*, and is couched in ordinary language, as is Dryden's to Etherege, or Tennyson's in dedicating *Tiresias, and Other Poems* to FitzGerald:

> Old Fitz, who from your suburb grange
>   Where once I tarried for a while,
> Glance at the wheeling Orb of change,
>   And greet it with a kindly smile . . .

They may be more far-reaching, as is Pope's *Epistle to Dr Arbuthnot*, but even there the language can be colloquial:

> Shut, shut the door, good John! fatigu'd
> I said,
> Tye up the knocker, say I'm sick, I'm
> dead . . .

His *Epistles to Several Persons*, known as *Moral Essays*, are more solemn in manner. There, as in many other instances, e.g. Matthew Green's *The Spleen*, the words 'Epistle to . . .' merely serve as a dedication. Samuel Daniel in his *Certaine Epistles* is really writing philosophic poems, occasionally referring to the addressees, if only by throwing in a 'Madam' here and there, as in that masterly statement of stoicism, *To the Ladie Margaret . . .* which begins:

> He that of such a height hath built his
> minde,
> And rear'd the dwelling of his thoughts
> so strong,
> As neither feare nor hope can shake the
> frame
> Of his resolued powr's, not all the winde
> Of vanitie or malice pierce to wrong
> His setled peace, or to disturbe the same;
> What a faire seate hath he, from whence
> he may
> The boundlesse wastes and wildes of
> man suruay.

There are also imaginary letters, as Drayton's *England's Heroical Epistles*, or Pope's *Eloisa to Abelard*. The form is not extinct.

(g) NARRATIVE POETRY. A distinction must first be made between narrative poetry and the EPIC. The latter is an heroic poem, aimed at exhibiting through a narrative the nobler aspects of man and his relation with the Deity. Such are the *Iliad*, the *Odyssey*, and the *Aeneid*; *Beowulf*, and *La Chanson de Roland*; and, of course, *Paradise Lost* and *Paradise Regained*: many place *The Faerie Queene* in this category. Epics are rare, the latest with any claim to success being those of Southey. Apart from the few great ones, the most satisfactory have been the mock-heroic, such as Dryden's *Absalom and Achitophel*, and Pope's *The Dunciad*. Nor must the narrative poem be confused with the long meditative poem, such as Wordsworth's *The Excursion* and *The Prelude*, though these are strung together as narrative.

The object of a narrative poem, as its name implies, is to tell a story, perhaps swiftly, perhaps in a more leisurely way developing characters as it goes, and these objects must to some extent influence the prosodic form. Thus though most of Chaucer's *Canterbury Tales* is written in heroic couplets, his *Troilus and Criseyde* is written in rhyme royal stanzas, just as Daniel and Drayton resort to stanzas for their historical works. The poet of *Sir Gawayne and the Grene Knight* uses a kind of loose blank verse, but Kenneth Hare, in his modernised version, prefers stanzas.

If, however, the story itself, apart from meditation, is the goal, and where speed is desirable, the couplet, usually octosyllabic, seems to be the favoured medium, and was employed by Scott in *Marmion*

and other poems, by Tennyson in *Idylls of the King*, by Morris in *The Earthly Paradise*, by **Masefield** in *Reynard the Fox*, though he preferred stanzas in *Dauber* and *The Widow in the Bye Street*. Macaulay in *Lays of Ancient Rome* used stanzaic form in short iambic lines. Byron, where he thought speed was essential, used couplets, octosyllabic in *The Giaour* and *The Bride of Abydos*, decasyllabic in *The Corsair*, but where speed was of no account, as in *Don Juan*, he chose *ottava rima*, while for his more meditative *Childe Harold's Pilgrimage* he employed the Spenserian stanza, as did Keats for *The Eve of St Agnes*. Arnold's *Sohrab and Rustum* is in blank verse, but there the moral is more important than the tale. Browning achieved his dramatic effects in *The Ring and the Book* with blank verse, but where he required great speed, as in *How they brought the Good News from Ghent to Aix*, he rushed the story forward in good galloping anapaests in rhymed sixaines.

In short, there is no outstanding method. Subject matter, philosophic inference, seems to some extent to dictate to the poet what measure he will use. But even the philosophic meditative poem can have many forms; blank verse in Langland's *Piers Plowman*, the quatrain in Davies' *Nosce Teipsum*, blank verse again for Browning's *Pauline*, very individual accented blanks for Bridges' *The Testament of Beauty*—he used septets for *Eros and Psyche*—while Meredith used an interesting form of quatrain for *Earth and Man*.

(h) The SONG, possibly preceding the ballad, perhaps an offshoot from it, can take all sorts of forms, the single assumption being that this is verse fitting for a tune. It can be of the simplest, such as Carey's *Sally in our Alley*, in octaves of 8,7 with easy rhymes; or it can have the beautiful prosodic complexity of **Campion**'s:

> Rose-cheek't *Laura*, come
> Sing thou smoothly with thy beauty's
> Silent music, either other
>   Sweetly gracing.

Shakespeare's songs are immensely varied.

(*i*) The ODE is a development of the song, in classical times not always solemn, as can be seen from those of Horace; but in English poetry it implies something 'dignified or exalted' (*New English Dictionary*). It includes such things as Spenser's *Prothalamion* and *Epithalamion*, Wordsworth's *Immortality* ode, his *Ode to Duty*, and Tennyson's *Ode on the Death of the Duke of Wellington*. It is, in English poetry, on the whole, a hymn of praise, or at least of magnificence.

A distinction should be made between the ode as generally conceived, and the PINDARIC ODE. In the later seventeenth century the idea was prevalent that the 'Pindarique Ode' as a burst of passion, free and unrestrained. The theory certainly produced such magnificent odes as those of **Cowley**, notably the one on Hobbes, and Dryden's *Song for St Cecilia's Day*, and *Alexander's Feast*. Actually the Pindaric ode is a very strict form, consisting of strophe, anti-strophe, and epode, in unspecified numbers. Ben Jonson had sometimes adhered to this, calling the sections the 'Turne', the 'Counter-Turne' and the 'Stand', as in the one that contains as a 'turne' the famous:

> It is not growing like a tree
> In bulke, doth make man better bee:
> Or standing long an oake, three hundred
>   yeare,
> To fall a logge at last, dry, bold, and seare:
> A lillie of a day
> Is fairer farre, in May,

> Although it falle, and die that night;
> It was the plant, and flowre of light.
> In small proportions we just beauties see:
> And in short measures, life may perfect
>   bee.

In the midst of the seventeenth-century outbursts, Milton's nephew, Edward Phillips, pointed out in his *Theatrum Poetarum* (1675) what the form really was; and Congreve in his *Discourse on the Pindarique Ode* took the point up. Without detracting from Cowley and the others, he remarked that

> The character of these late Pindariques, is, a bundle of rambling thoughts, express'd in a like parcel of irregular stanzas, which also consist of such another complication of disproportion'd, uncertain, and perplex'd verses and rhimes.

His own examples are models of form rather than expressions of feeling.

Certainly the ode, whether called Pindaric or not, includes poems which are part of our consciousness, such as Keats' great odes, written in regular stanzaic form, to which we may add Hood's. They are not necessarily called odes. Swinburne's *Song for the Centenary of Walter Savage Landor* in fifty similarly shaped sixteen-line stanzas is certainly an ode; but the full-dress ode is not much in fashion at this date, since praise and exaltation are suspect. Yet it may be noted that Terence Tiller has recently published a 'Prothalamion' in a series of similar stanzas, suggesting that there is still life in the form.

V. CONCLUSION

What, it may be asked, is the object of prosodic studies? Firstly, as W. P. Ker suggested, much may be gained in the enjoyment of verse merely by noticing the metrical form, and he quotes Byron's:

> Could Love for ever
> Run like a river,
> And Time's endeavour
>   Be tried in vain—
> No other pleasure
> Like this could measure;
> And like a treasure
>   We'd hug the chain . . .

a form Swinburne adopted for his *Anima Anceps*. Such alertness will increase the reader's perception in, say, Housman's *Last Poems*.

But, as before hinted, the more stringent analysis of prosody, tacitly or subconsciously applied, may make the reader more sensitive to what the poet is striving to convey. Let us take three examples. Who, aware of prosodic possibilities would read Shelley's

> Away! the moor is dark beneath the moon

as marked, namely as a regular iambic pentameter? Surely it is to be read something as follows, a mixture of quantitative and accentual verse:

> Away! the moor is dark beneath
>   the moon,
> Rapid clouds have drank the last pale
>   beams of even.

Similarly, what are we to make of Tennyson's *Break, break, break*? One might suggest that it is read:

> Break break break
>   On thy cold gray stones, O Sea!
>   And I would that my tongue could
>   utter

> The thoughts that arise in me.

Basically an anapaestic measure.

Sometimes the poet can so adapt to his sense of the thing that no mistake can be made. Kipling's *Anchor Song* might illustrate this:

> Heh! Walk her round. Heave, ah, heave
>   her short again!
> Over, snatch her over, there, and hold
>   her on the pawl.
> Loose all sail, and brace your yards
>   aback and full –
> Ready jib to pay her off and heave
>   short all.

this complexity being faithfully followed through four stanzas, each gradually evolving into fairly regular anapaests.

Prosody, in short, induces the reader to pay attention, to listen to what he reads to himself, to catch the cadence, and so to get closer to what the poet is trying to convey. But the reading of poetry, just as much as the writing of it, is a subjective, rather than an objective experience. That is why it can be said of prosodists, more certainly than of any other group of men, 'two of a trade never agree'.   B.D.

see also New Directions in Metrics

Purcell, Edward. *See* FitzGerald, Edward.

Putnam, Phelps (1894–1948), was born in Boston. His published poems include *Trinc* (1927) and *The Five Seasons* (1930). He has been variously called a 'romantic of the hard-boiled school' and an 'acid realist'. His poems express modern philosophic problems in complex symbols. D.H.

Q

Quarles, Francis (1592–1644), was the
son of a minor official at Queen Elizabeth's court, and was educated at Christ's
College, Cambridge, and Lincoln's Inn.
Early in his career he paraphrased the
scriptures and translated many psalms
which he sent to John Winthrop in
Massachusetts to be incorporated in the
Bay Psalm Book (1640). Quarles did write
a poetic romance, *Argalus and Parthenia*
(1629), based on a tale from **Sidney's**
Arcadia, but most of his poetry was
religious. His most famous work is
Emblemes (1635), a series of devotional
poems, each prefixed by an appropriate
allegorical engraving. His devotional
verse is smooth and simple, as in *A Good-
Night*:

> Close now, thine eyes, and rest secure;
> Thy Soule is safe enough; thy Body
> sure;
> He that loves thee, he that keepes
> And guards thee, never slumbers, never
> sleepes.

The smiling Conscience in a sleeping
breast
Has only peace, has only rest:
The musicke and the mirth of Kings,
Are all but very Discords, when she sings:
Then close thine Eyes and rest secure:
No Sleepe so sweet as thine, no rest so
sure.

Emblemes, however, contains more variety
in both verse form and imagery. Quarles
uses the imagery of the compass to combine both sexual and religious devotion,
in a manner reminiscent of **Donne**, in
Canto VII, X:

> First franticks up and downe, from side
> to side,
> And restlesse beats his christall'd
> Iv'ry case
> With vaine impatience; jets from
> place to place,
> And seeks the bosome of his frozen
> Bride,
> At length he slacks his motion, and
> does rest
> His trembling point at his bright Poles
> beloved Brest.
> J.G.

R

Raine, Kathleen (1908–   ), was raised in
Northumberland and London and took
her degree at Cambridge in Natural
Sciences. In 1944 she became a Roman
Catholic. In what she regards as her truest
vein, she has sought to adumbrate aspects
of the eternal reality mirrored in the 'ever-
recurring forms of nature'. Her symbols,
when particularised, are drawn from a
northern landscape. Man she sees as a

child of nature, fashioned 'from substance
of star and ocean'. Yet he is more than
this:

> From a place I came
> That was never in time . . .
> . . . .
> Shall I know at last
> My lost delight?
> D.L.H.

Ralegh, Sir Walter (?1552–1618), was
born in Devonshire. After campaigning
in France and Ireland he became, in his

thirties, the Queen's favourite and one of the most influential men at the English court. In 1592, however, he spent a few months in the Tower for having seduced one of the Queen's maids of honour, whom, we are told, the Queen required him to marry. It was not until after his voyage to Guiana (1595) and his part in the expedition against Cadiz (1596) that he returned to favour. In 1603 James I gaoled him on the strength of confused accusations of treason. He remained in the Tower, writing his *History of the World*, till 1616, when he was released for a further voyage to Guiana, the failure of which led to his execution.

Few as his surviving poems are—his editor, Agnes Latham, attributes only forty-one to him—they serve as a kind of epitome of Elizabethan poetry. His earliest style bears resemblances to that of the *Mirror for Magistrates*: it is highly alliterative, full of compressed generalisation, and heavy with *sententiae* (e.g. 'Thus hope brings hap but to the worthy wight'). From this he moves towards the ornate metaphorical style made popular by **Spenser** and **Sidney**. But he also has a third style, harder to describe since it is inseparable from the poems themselves: it combines the directness of the early Elizabethan writing with the resonance of the later, and owes much besides to traditional ballads or sometimes—as in *Three thinges there bee*—to riddle poems.

From such poems as *The Passionate Mans Pilgrimage* and *The Lie*, it can be seen that the mark of this third style is a plainness of language which conveys deep emotion with care and exactness.

> And this is my eternall plea,
> To him that made Heauen, Earth and
> > Sea,
>
> Seeing my flesh must die so soone,
> And want a head to dine next noone,

Iust at the stroke when my vaines start
> and spred
Set on my soule an euerlasting head.
Then am I readie like a palmer fit,
To tread those blest paths which before
> I writ.

The framework of the ballad can serve to both intensify and control the feeling, as in these lines from *As you came from the holy land*:

> Know that loue is a careless chylld
> > And forgets promyse paste,
> He is blynd, he is deaff when he lyste
> > And in faythe neuer faste.

> His desyre is a dureless contente
> > And a trustless ioye
> He is wonn with a world of despayre
> > And is lost with a toye.

> Of women kynde suche indeed is the
> > loue
> Or the work Loue abused
> Vnder which many chyldysh desyres
> > And conceytes are excusde.

> Butt true Loue is a durable fyre
> > In the mynde euer burnynge;
> Neuer sycke, neuer ould, neuer dead,
> > From itt selfe neuer turnynge.

Walter Oakeshott says that Ralegh's poems 'were written for special occasions, the occasions most often being to please, or to pacify, the Queen'. This is scarcely an exaggeration. His longest poem, the manuscript of which was not discovered and printed until the nineteenth century, is entitled *The 11th and last booke of the Ocean to Scinthia*. It is a fragmentary draft, and it is possible that no preceding ten books ever existed and that the composition never progressed any further. Scinthia is the Queen, and it was almost certainly written in the Tower in 1592. It consists largely of an alternation between images of complete deprivation and images implying the richness of her favour: 'Shee is gonn, Shee is lost! Shee is fovnd, she is ever faire'. It is generally agreed that those of deprivation are the more impressive:

From frutfull trees I gather withred
                        leues
And glean the broken eares with misers
                       hands,
Who sumetyme did inioy the waighty
                       sheves
I seeke faire floures amidd the brinish
                       sand.

Ralegh's verse is distinguished from beginning to end by a grave melancholy, shown in the famous answer to **Marlowe**'s *Passionate Shepherd* and even in most of the love poems. C. S. Lewis speaks of the 'quietness, clarity, finality' of *Even such is time*, and the melancholy is indeed as far from self-pity as from the rage of **Swift**'s total rejections. It is a firm and clear-voiced acknowledgment of the uncertainty of life, the proximity of death, and the fact that Time 'makes hope a foole, and sorrow wise'.   T.G.

Ramsay, Allan (1686–1758), was a Scottish poet, wig-maker and bookseller. He had a pioneering interest in old Scottish and English songs, publishing several collections of these (e.g. the *Tea-Table Miscellany*, 1724–32). His own elegies and satires appeared in 1721, and his pastoral drama, *The Gentle Shepherd*, in 1725.   J.F.

Ransom, John Crowe (1888–), was born the son of a Protestant minister in Tennessee, obtained his B.A. at Vanderbilt University, and a bachelor's degree in *Literae Humaniores* at Oxford, where he was a Rhodes Scholar in 1913. Apart from two years in the field artillery in the First World War, he taught at Vanderbilt until 1937. More recently he has occupied the chair of poetry at Kenyon College, received the Bollingen Prize and the Russell Loines award, and been chosen Hon. Consultant of Letters at the Library of Congress.

Selected Poems (1945) omits his first volume, *Poems about God* (1919), and is drawn mainly from *Chills and Fever* (1924) and *Two Gentlemen in Bonds* (1927). Ransom helped to found and edit *The Fugitive* (1922–5), the organ of the highly influential Southern enclave which includes Allen **Tate** and Robert Penn **Warren**, and contributed to the Southern Agrarian manifesto-anthology *I'll Take My Stand* (1930) and to *Who Owns America?* He founded and edited the *Kenyon Review* (between 1939 and 1958). By 1945 he had become the acknowledged leader of the Kenyon New Critics; his critical work can be judged from *The World's Body* (1938), *The New Criticism* (1941), and *Poems and Essays* (1955).

Ransom's typical poem—*Painted Head, Antique Harvesters*—is the entertaining example of his critical concern for the poem as 'structure' and 'texture', as a 'tension' constructed of 'extension' and 'intension' which distinguishes poetic discourse from scientific utterance. He aims for the 'metaphysical' poem which refuses the separation of the physical abstract and the abstraction of ideas, and fuses thought into feeling through wit, in the manner **Eliot** taught his generation to admire in **Marvell** and **Donne**, and to imitate for poetic success. 'Science gratifies a rational or practical impulse', Ransom holds, 'and exhibits the minimum of perception. Art gratifies a perceptual impulse and exhibits the minimum of reason.' Perhaps this is why his metrics are far less ambitious than his cultivation of rhyme, music and diction, and, above all, a tone whose care and skill is his main contribution to modern poetry, when it is not mere pedantry. His technique constructs a diction and tone whose combination of literary-archaic and contemporary language is the texture for his thematic parallels between Southern agrarian aristocratism and urban, commercial democracy; the ambiguous conflicts between chivalric and senile values and the anti-values of the industrial wasteland.

If death and corruption are Ransom's frequent region of anecdote, the mixing of his poetic effects makes a redeeming awareness which prevents boredom. In *Philomela* the American poet in Oxford rehearses the European cult of the literary nightingale and finds himself dissonant: in Bagley Wood the bird's 'classics registered a little flat! / I rose, and venomously spat'. The concluding irony is a double disenchantment with the English poetic tradition and the poet's sense of his own unworthiness. A similar paradox of aloofness and involvement motivates his Southern poems:

> The little cousin is dead, by foul
> subtraction,
> A green bough from Virginia's aged tree,
> And none of the county kin like the
> transaction,
> Nor some of the world of outer dark,
> like me
> *Dead Boy*

Southern resistance to American change becomes the image of the world's change from agrarian class society to industrial democracy, and the adjustments in custom and value are the real root of Ransom's 'metaphysical' tension which he works out as textural ironies. His perpetually elegiac mode controls the harsh and coarse beneath the insistently intellectual lyric grace, in the manner of **Dryden** rather than Marvell:

> Their strokes and counters whistled in
> the wind
> I wish he had delivered half his blows
> But where she should have made off
> like a hind
> The bitch bit off his arms at the elbows.
> *Captain Carpenter*

But generally for Ransom body must weight the dualism of the human condition: 'To be a tragic ironist is to be aware sharply and grimly, but not too painfully, of the constant involvement of life with death':

> Practice your beauty, blue girls, before it
> fail;
> And I will cry with my loud lips and
> publish
> Beauty which all our power shall never
> establish,
> It is so frail.
> *Blue Girls*

Pain is to be controlled often through reductive metaphors—death is 'a brown study' or 'a gentleman in a dustcoat' or 'the forgetful kingdom'. Elegant balance protects Ransom from too naked an exposure to the irrational; his classical organisations fail to release that exhilaration of the truly metaphysical found in **Yeats**, for instance, or Hart **Crane**, or **Pound**. His poetry is brilliantly conscious —at best an order of high cultivation, at worst a finicking mosaic. The beautiful logic of the conceits in *Painted Head* is, with *Address to the Scholars of New England*, his finest achievement:

> Beauty is of body.
> The flesh contouring shallowly on a head
> Is a rock-garden needing body's love
> And best bodiness to colorify
>
> The big blue birds sitting and sea-shell
> flats
> And caves, and on the iron acropolis

To spread the hyacinthine hair and rear
The olive garden for the nightingales.
Painted Head

If Ransom's poetry 'represents the triumph of a richly plastic sensibility over an essentially small stock of "ideas" or "structures"' (Vivienne Koch), the achieved voice is unique: 'he has the personal seriousness that treats the world as it seems to him, not the solemnity that treats the really important things, the world as everybody knows it is' (Randall **Jarrell**). *see also* American Poetry, Fugitive Group, *and* New Criticism

Read, Sir Herbert (1893–1968), the son of a Yorkshire farmer, attended Crossley's School and the University of Leeds, and fought with distinction in France and Belgium. His many books include works of art criticism, literary criticism, aesthetics, political and educational philosophy, autobiography, a novel, and verse. As a critic he re-interpreted and defended romanticism through insights afforded by modern psychology and Marxist dialectics: ' "classic" and "romantic" . . . correspond . . . to the husk and the seed, the shell and the kernel. There is a principle of life, of creation, of liberation, and that is the romantic spirit; there is a principle of order, of control and of repression, and that is the classical spirit.' As a poet he was particularly concerned to keep form 'organic' rather than 'abstract' and to give their due to sentiments and emotions, images and rhythms that suggest themselves irrationally during composition. *The Gold Disc: An Elegy,* a set of reflections on his old age, concludes:

I too have heard the sounding rivers,
     the screech
Of amorous winds. But now the night
     is calm.
I listen to a music fraught with silence

To a solitude full of sound.
I have found the peace beyond violence
And gaze steadily into the gold disc that
     blurs all hard distinctions.
       D.L.H.

Redgrove, Peter (1932–), educated at Taunton and Cambridge, writes in the main of personal experiences enlarged by the imagination to be generally applicable. There is considerable power in what he writes; he sometimes deals with violence, but a deep humanity runs through works like *The Collector* (1959) and *The Nature of Cold Weather* (1961).   B.O.

Reed, Henry (1914–), is a writer of eloquent free verse influenced by **Eliot** (whom he brilliantly parodied in *Chard Whitlow*). His more serious poems are imaginative and dramatic, but it is as a gentle wit that Reed has become widely known. His sequence *Lessons of the War* is much anthologised as a melancholy and amusing complaint of the sensitive conscript. His slight but distinguished reputation as a poet is based on a single collection, *A Map of Verona* (1946). J.F.

Religion and Poetry Since the expression of man's deepest feelings is always in rhythmic form of some kind, we should expect to find a close connection between the religious and the poetic impulse: some would add the corollary that all poetry is in some sense religious. 'The difference between genuine poetry and the poetry of **Dryden, Pope** and all their school', wrote Matthew **Arnold**, 'is briefly this: their poetry is conceived and composed in their wits, genuine poetry is conceived and composed in the soul.' But Arnold's dogma does not take sufficient account of the fact that poetry is essentially a *making* (ποιεῖν, to make) with the material of words. Even if it be true that there is a moment of conception, of vision, which precedes the discovery of words in which to express it, the process of finding words must inevitably modify and shape the original thought. And words are common property, whose meanings are constantly changed in the rub of everyday usage. The perception of these truths led Michael Roberts to define poetry (in his Preface to *The Faber Book of Modern Verse*) as 'primarily . . . an exploration of the possibilities of language', which takes us a long way from the identity of religion and poetry.

If we look back to the primitive beginnings of any race, however, we see that poetry starts with some practical purpose in mind that can be called religious, whether of praise, propitiation, or incantation. Early sacred writings are in poetry, as the hymns contained in the 'Three Hundred Songs' of China (eleventh to sixth centuries B.C.), or the hymns to the Sun God of the Egyptian Eighteenth Dynasty (1580 B.C.). The sayings of the Delphic Oracle, we are told, were always conveyed by the priests in the form of verse—generally hexameters (and sometimes imperfect ones). The drama, too, begins as part of a liturgy: in the Greek Dionysiac mysteries which developed into the works of the great tragedians, and in elaborations of the Christian Mass at festivals, which developed into the miracle plays of the Middle Ages. But as the race grows and its activities become at once more varied and more specialised, poetry fulfils other functions and is more sharply separated from religion. A mystic who is also a poet will be likely to feel a clash between his need to identify himself with created beings for the purpose of his art, and his need to learn detachment from them if he is to follow the way of union with God, the *Via Negativa*. Thus, from

the present writer's *Golden Bird and Other Poems*:

> Saints move on the unbroken beam,
> But poets look with a refractory eye
> On decomposing light, and need to
> stray . . .

The poet's is the *Via Positiva*, the Way of Affirmation of Images (to use Charles Williams' term), and the union between the two ways implicit in Thomas **Traherne**'s work is hard indeed to attain.

When man begins to question the existence of his deity, his religious poetry is sometimes designed to persuade others (and often unconsciously himself) rather than to express a revelation: 'You ought to believe this', rather than 'That which we have seen with our eyes, which our hands have handled . . .' In other words, the didactic enters in, and 'we hate poetry that has a palpable design upon us', as **Keats** said. But leaving aside the subject of poetry which is bad because the poet has been lost in the propagandist, we must make a distinction between poetry which is the expression of personal religious feeling, and that which is designed for public worship: the latter will exclude 'personal' emotion and idiosyncrasy, as well as being typical of the race and age that produced it.

> Like as the hart desireth the water-
> brooks:
> so longeth my soul after thee, O God.
> *Psalm 42*

> Thee may I set at my right hand . . .
> For thee delightfully employ
> Whate'er thy bounteous grace hath
> given,
> And run my course with even joy,
> And closely walk with thee to heaven.
> Charles Wesley: *Forth in thy Name*

253

Both are expressions of desire for nearness to God, yet how different in tone and imagery!

To return to religious, as distinct from devotional, poetry, one may make a further distinction between the kind that is religious in a very general sense—concerned with some power or order felt to be greater than man himself—and the kind that expresses belief in some generally accepted doctrine. Dante's is the greatest of the latter kind, and his *Divina Commedia* embraces the whole of life, with its joys, sufferings and sins, relating it to the divine life and to man's existence after death. **Milton** is the English poet whose scope comes nearest to that of Dante, but when we think of English religious poetry, what probably first comes to mind is the directly lyrical expression of love and longing for God in the carols and laments of the Middle Ages, and then the poetry of the 'Metaphysicals', with perhaps the eighteenth-century hymns of **Watts**, **Cowper** and Wesley as a minor third.

In using Dr **Johnson**'s term 'metaphysical' (from his essay on **Cowley** in *Lives of the Poets*) to describe the poetry of **Donne** and others, we set aside the pejorative meaning which it had in his context, and have in mind chiefly their apprehension of the supernatural or abstract in sensuous terms. This is not exceptional in religious poetry, of course, since it is only by physical analogies that man can express his apprehension of the spiritual, and all mystical poetry has been accustomed to use the language of erotic love to describe the love between man and his maker. But the Metaphysicals were exceptional in the abstruseness of the thought which they brought within the sensual grasp, and the lightning mental swiftness with which their poetry moves between the supernatural and the natural.

If thy first glance so powerfull be,
A mirth but open'd and seal'd up again;
What wonders shall we feel, when we
                  shall see
    Thy full-ey'd love!
When thou shalt look us out of pain,
And one aspect of thine spend in delight
More then a thousand sunnes disburse in
                  light,
  In heav'n above.
    George Herbert: *The Glance*

Here the common action of looking is imagined as with extra-physical power: a mystical experience is translated into terms of sense, yet normal sense is transformed so that we do not feel the gulf between the supernatural and ourselves, as we inevitably do in such an anthropomorphic image as Isaac Watts' in *How bright those glorious spirits shine*:

And God the Lord from every eye
  Shall wipe off every tear.

To apply the term 'religious poet' to Milton and not to **Shakespeare** would make nonsense of it, and hence it is clear that we need a category which can include poetry that is (as was said above) concerned with some extra-human power or order, though not directly doctrinal. In this sense we can call *King Lear* a religious play, without needing to decide whether or not those critics are right who find a directly Christian reference there. And though we know that **Wordsworth** was a Christian believer, his best poetry is only religious in this general sense. **Shelley** in England, Leopardi in Italy, Rilke in Germany, are examples of poets whose work is religious in this sense: some of **Blake** could be claimed for either category.

With Shelley, we reach the point when poetry begins to be taken as a substitute for religion, a tendency which has persisted to the present day, and has been vigorously attacked by T. S. **Eliot**. In our age, however, it is as physician rather than as priest that the poet has been exalted—when he has been noticed at all. The supreme value in poetry has been seen in its performance of a kind of therapy for us, as I. A. Richards described it in his *Principles of Literary Criticism*, putting our nervous system to rights by unifying our impulses: perhaps after all this is not so far from the primitive purpose of incantation and propitiation, though the god is now not without but within.

Even apart from such theories, modern man is perhaps too sceptical of his own power to apprehend the Divine to attempt much poetry about the nature of God: he turns rather to the analysis of his own soul, and

> Elysium is as far as to
> The very nearest room

as Emily **Dickinson** wrote. Even Gerard Manley **Hopkins** achieves greatness in poems which express the agony of separation from God rather than in those which speak of union. 'O God of my perfect ignorance', in Delmore **Schwartz**'s apostrophe, is perhaps as near as most contemporary poets get to a statement about the nature of God. But our century has produced one religious poem which can stand with the great, and which in its lyrical passages does give us, however obliquely, an apprehension of the Divine: the *Four Quartets* of T. S. Eliot.   A.R.

Rexroth, Kenneth (1905–), is an excellent American translator of poems from Japanese, Chinese, Greek, Latin and Spanish. His early work was influenced by the Objectivist and Surrealist schools. Collections include *The Phoenix and the Tortoise* (1944) and *In Defense of Earth* (1956). *Collected Shorter Poems* appeared in

1967, and *Collected Longer Poems* in 1968.
    D.H.

Riding, Laura (1901–), published her *Collected Poems* in 1938, thus bringing together the contents of nine previous volumes published in close succession over a period of about ten years. She also wrote some essays on her contemporaries, the most impressive of them being *Anarchism is not Enough*; and she collaborated with Robert **Graves** in writing *A Survey of Modernist Poetry*, a book which—although today both the authors might disagree with it—remains one of the most interesting works on the subject.

Laura Riding's poetry is baffling and almost entirely neglected, although besides influencing Robert Graves, it also provided models for some of **Auden**'s poems in the nineteen-thirties. Perhaps it might be described as poetic philosophisings cut off in segments. When one considers a good deal of Nietzsche's writing, and today the poems of the French philosopher Jean Wahl, it will be seen that this account is not pejorative. On the cover of the *Collected Poems* what looks like an authoritative statement about Laura Riding's poetry consists mostly of negatives 'They are undiluted: no politics of psychology, no religion or philosophical sentiment, no scholastic irrelevancies, no mystical or musical wantonness. This does not mean that they lack any of the graces that it is proper to expect in poetry: they have memorable beauty of phrase, serene humour, and a rich intricacy of movement that redeems the notion of "pure poetry" from the curse put upon it by the aestheticians'.

They do indeed create a world of their own: intelligent, involved and abstract, they have a hypnotic atmospheric power which can involve the reader. Despite their impersonal tone the reader has the impression of intense personal seriousness, an anguish of being under the surface of sustained poetic argument. The pain of being a woman of genius is everywhere felt. s.s.

see also Fugitive Group

Robinson, Edwin Arlington (1869–1935), was born in Head Tide, and grew up in Gardiner, Maine (the Tilbury Town of his poems). The delicate youth immersed in classical poetry had to leave Harvard after two years, in 1893, when the family finances collapsed; but he had begun to develop as a poet there, and inherited more of the New England tradition as well as gaining contacts useful in later penury. He privately printed his first volume *The Torrent and the Night Before* at his own expense in 1896, just after his mother died suddenly of black diphtheria, attended and buried furtively by her three sons, since doctor and priest were frightened of the disease. Robinson's father, a storekeeper, was a spiritualist who experimented on his deathbed with table-rapping, flying books and furniture levitation, 'cutting my universe clean in half', the son claimed later, speaking of the 'living hell' of those months. One elder brother, Dean, took drugs and alcohol to relieve the strain of his country general practice, and the other, Herman, lost Robinson his share of the estate by investments and died of tuberculosis in Boston City Hospital in 1908. The poet himself was operated on for ear infections and mastoiditis believed to have been initiated by a schoolteacher's blow and resulting in deafness and a lifelong fear for his brain. Robinson's pessimism was not abstract: he regarded himself as an original unenergetic misfit: 'I was a tragedy in the beginning, and it is hardly provable that I shall ever be anything else. Just what manner of cave I may select for a time is of no importance.'

In middle life in New York his withdrawing temperament, failure to find publishers while working at odd jobs, and his poverty, reinforced his masochism. Nearly destitute in his forties, he drank and relied on friends who believed in his talent and had often to help him with money secretly. Public success came with *Captain Craig* (1902), a verse novel on themes of failure and resistance which are the stock material of his poetry. In 1903 he worked as a subway time-checker, but President Theodore Roosevelt was reading his work and provided him with a post at $2,000 a year and also persuaded Scribner's to reissue *The Children of Night* (1897). Robinson resigned his position when the Taft regime took office and in 1911 paid his first visit to the MacDowell Colony in New Hampshire, his future annual summer refuge until his death. *The Man Against the Sky* (1916) established him and he made enough money to live on, especially after the best-selling success of the verse novel *Tristram* (1927). He died of cancer in New York.

Robinson's genuine personal and *fin-de-siècle* gloom never reached tragic power: his reach is a dry irony and a finished lyricism without the grandeur of **Hardy**. His reading in classical and French poetry gave him the strength to resist the mediocre New York literary scene and to re-express the New England provincial inheritance. But infatuation with Arthurian medievalism and chivalric gothicry enervated his last twenty years of long narratives. His response to failure and small-town suffering goes into a series of very similarly dry and understated anecdotal accounts of half-feckless might-have-beens and local characters with a secret wayward triumph over circumstances. Robinson celebrates the provincial who believes he could have made his mark on the nation, had he got round to it. These characters are framed in a passive philosophy of regret and doom realised as a world of twilight lit by gleams, sunsets and the flash from armour and passion. Robinson 'began with autumn', said Edmund Wilson, 'and he has never had his rightful spring. He was old in spirit from the very first'. But he is accused by Yvor **Winters**—who otherwise praises him—of New England 'intellectual laziness': 'the type of mind which follows first guesses in matter of opinion and perception, with irritated contempt for opposing arguments, and which finds careful thinking beneath the dignity of a gentleman'.

The cycle of Arthurian verse novels has a certain Jamesian exposure of human relationships but Robinson's language is too laconically plain to do more than suggest life's little ironies, for example in the famous *Miniver Cheevy*:

Miniver cursed the commonplace
And eyed a khaki suit with loathing;
He missed the medieval grace
Of iron clothing.

His favourite and perfected sonnet form substituted for the mental framework he lacked: 'Robinson has no epos, myth, or code, no superhuman truth to tell him what the terminal points of human conduct are, in this age' (Allen **Tate**). His positive is nostalgia for the 'lost, imperial music' in the 'chaos of night' and vague hope for 'the coming glory of the Light' (*Credo*, 1894). His finest poem is not the Arnoldian and overpraised *The Man Against the Sky*, with its weak ambiguity of language and thought, but *Isaac and Archibald* (1899), a story of two old friends accepting life and death with wry autumnal charm. The poem rises to unusual power:

I could see
The forest and the sunset and the skyline,

No matter where it was that I was
          looking:
The flame beyond the boundary, the
          music,
The foam and the white ships, and two
          old men
Were things that would not leave me.
          E.N.W.M.

see also American Poetry

Rochester, John Wilmot, Earl of (1647–80), died at the age of thirty-three, but he crowded a great deal into this short life. The only son of Henry Wilmot, 1st Earl of Rochester, a cavalier general who helped Charles II to escape after the Battle of Worcester, he inherited the earldom on his father's death in 1658 and was educated at Burford Grammar School and Wadham College, Oxford. The king took a personal interest in him and gave him a generous grant which enabled him to travel for three years in France and Italy with his tutor, Sir Andrew Balfour. He appeared at court at Christmas 1664, and at once became a leading figure in the 'merry gang' of court wits, whose conversation delighted Charles II, but whose opinions and way of life shocked Puritans and old-fashioned Cavaliers alike. Shortly after his arrival at court he tried to abduct Elizabeth Malet, a beautiful heiress, and was imprisoned in the Tower. On his release, he served with distinction in the naval war against the Dutch, and married Elizabeth Malet in 1667.

In the years following his marriage he seems to have led a curious double life. On the one hand he was an affectionate husband and father and a popular landlord, and on the other one of the wildest rakes of the Restoration Court, 'Prince of all the devils of the town' and the hero of many escapades. He had a passion for the theatre and is said to have trained for the stage the great tragic actress, Elizabeth Barry, who became his mistress. Some of the scandalous stories told about him have been shown to be apocryphal and there is no reason to believe the old allegations that he persecuted either **Dryden** or Otway. In spite of his reckless life he was never a vulgar sensualist, and, as with **Byron**, whom he resembles in many ways, there was always a serious undercurrent in his character. At first he adopted the fashionable materialism of Hobbes but his mind was fundamentally religious, and, when his health declined in the late sixteen-seventies, he found it more and more difficult to get satisfaction from a life of pleasure. For a time he was in touch with the deist, Charles Blount, and in the winter of 1679–80 he took part in a series of frank conversations on religion with a Scottish clergyman, Gilbert Burnet, afterwards Bishop of Rochester. The commonly repeated statement that Burnet 'converted' him is false; what Burnet did was to put him into touch with a type of Christian humanism which he could understand and respect. In the spring of 1680 he collapsed while riding to his wife's estate in Somerset and was brought to his house at Woodstock in Oxfordshire. Here, as he lay on his death-bed, he had a religious experience which led to his conversion to Christianity and a solemn recantation of his past life.

Rochester was the one major poet among the Restoration wits. His reputation suffered from the blaze of notoriety that surrounded his life, and also from the fact that much pornographic trash was fathered on him after his death by dishonest editors. In the lyric he could play the fashionable game of the rococo pastoral with ease and charm, but in his best songs there is a union of intensity of feeling with perfection of form which recalls Catullus, **Burns** and Heine rather than Sedley and Dorset:

Absent from thee I languish still,
   Then ask me not, when I return,

The straying Fool twill plainly kill
   To wish all Day, all Night to Mourn.

His most impressive and memorable writing, however, is to be found in his satiric and realistic poems. Like **Swift** he is a great satirist because he has a drama in his soul. He has an artist's delight in the pageant of Restoration life which he paints with the power and gusto of a Hogarth in such poems as *A Letter from Artemisa, Timon* and *Tunbridge Wells*. Yet with another side of his mind he sees it as a 'universe of death', full of stupidity, affectation and cowardly betrayals. His *Maim'd Debauchee*, a dramatic monologue worthy of **Browning**, was rightly described by Charles Whibley as a 'masterpiece of heroic irony' and his poem *Upon Nothing*, possibly inspired by a passage in Hobbes' *Leviathan*, may be described as the last great metaphysical poem of the seventeenth century, rivalling the work of **Donne** in its fusion of subtle thought, imagination and irony.

A Satyr against Mankind, Rochester's most ambitious performance, is a unique expression in English poetry of the moral crisis of Western Europe at a time when the 'new philosophy' had shattered the old unified world-picture and man was seen as an isolated unit, miserable and insignificant in a hostile or indifferent universe. The passionate moral realism of the passage in which man is compared with the animals recalls and anticipates the spirit of the Fourth Voyage of Gulliver:

Be Judge your self, I'le bring it to the
                   test,
Which is the basest Creature, Man, or
                   Beast?
Birds feed on Birds, Beasts on each other
                   prey,
But Savage Man alone does Man betray.
Prest by necessity, they Kill for Food,
Man undoes Man to do himself no good.

With Teeth and Claws by Nature arm'd
they hunt,
Nature's allowances, to supply their
want.
But Man with smiles, embraces,
Friendships, praise
Unhumanely his Fellow's life betrays.

Rochester was rightly described by Voltaire as 'a man of genius and a great poet'. Like **Marlowe** before him and Byron and D. H. **Lawrence** after him, he is one of those dynamic spirits who disturb the complacency of their contemporaries by their intellectual daring and penetrating clarity of vision. v. de s.p.

Roethke, Theodore (1908–63) (pronoun-
ced ret'ke), was educated at the universities of Michigan and Harvard, and later taught at a number of institutions, becoming Professor of English at the University of Washington in Seattle.

The style of Roethke's first book, *Open House* (1941), and much of his second, *The Lost Son* (1948), is simple, vigorous and controlled, as can be seen from the following lines from 'The Return':

I circled on leather paws
In the darkening corridor,
Crouched closer to the floor,
Then bristled like a dog.
. . . A cold key let me in
That self-infected lair;
And I lay down with my life,
With the rags and rotting clothes,
With a stump of scraggy fang
Bared for a hunter's boot.

In his third book, *Praise to the End* (1951), he experimented with a kind of sophisticated nonsense verse:

Bring me a finger. The dirt's lonesome
for grass.
Are the rats dancing? The cats are.

Though sometimes such writing recalls the utterances of the Fool in *King Lear*, Roethke conceals his purposes where **Shakespeare** only half conceals his. There are, however, brilliant passages to be found in the book, as in the third section of 'I Cry, Love! Love!', which exemplifies with a sustained and delicate precision the 'anguish of concreteness' referred to earlier in the poem.

His poetry of the nineteen-fifties and sixties became more rational, but showed the strong and acknowledged influence of **Yeats.** He wrote in 1961:

What's madness but nobility of soul
At odds with circumstance?

lines which owe both style and substance to Yeats. John **Berryman** remarked, 'I think few critical readers will feel that his new self-reformation is as yet either at all complete or satisfying.' And while most readers applauded the work of Roethke's later period without reservation, some found the new literary influence constricting to his basic strength, which was the power to evoke the physical world.

t.g.

Rosenberg, Isaac (1890–1918), was born in Bristol, of Russian-Jewish immigrants. In 1897 the family moved to Stepney, in London's East End. According to Jon **Silkin** 'these two facts, his Jewishness and his poverty, form the base of an examination of his work'. Rosenberg originally intended to make painting his career, but by 1916 he was writing: 'I am convinced I am more deep and true as a poet than painter.' Between 1912 and 1916 he published, at his own expense, two pamphlets of poetry and a verse-play, *Moses*. All three have since been reprinted in *The Collected Works of Isaac Rosenberg*. He enlisted in 1915 ('against all my principles of justice . . .', 'Nothing can justify war.')

and was killed in France in April 1918.

Since his death Rosenberg has received some measure of acclaim, chiefly for his *Trench Poems* (1916–18) of which *Dead Man's Dump* is, perhaps, the finest and *Break of Day in the Trenches* the best known. Nevertheless, there is considerable critical disagreement about the merit of his poems. F. R. Leavis praises Rosenberg's 'astonishing technical skill' whereas Kenneth Allott considers that his poems are 'spoilt . . . by his appetite for the extravagant and his unpleasing poetic diction'.

Few readers would dispute that Rosenberg's immature work is often faulty. Even so, Allott's judgment is open to qualification, particularly with regard to the war poems, where bizarre images constitute a faithful rendering of the strained, unnatural conditions of trench-warfare. Writing from the ranks Rosenberg expressed dislike of **Brooke's** 'begloried sonnets'; and a powerful scepticism generates his best poetry:

Then we all sprang up and stript
To hunt the verminous brood.
Soon like a demon's pantomime
The place was raging.
See the silhouettes agape,
See the gibbering shadows
Mixed with the battled arms on the
       wall.
See gargantuan hooked fingers
Pluck in supreme flesh
To smutch supreme littleness.
See the merry limbs in hot Highland
       fling
Because some wizard vermin
Charmed from the quiet this revel
When our ears were half lulled
By the dark music
Blown from Sleep's trumpet.
     Louse Hunting

Here, imagery that at first might appear 'extravagant' is used to develop the macabre comedy. The skilful juxtaposing of elevated

and banal diction projects louse-hunting as a grotesque parody of heroic conflict. Rosenberg's is a considerable achievement:

So we crashed round the bend,
We heard his weak scream,
We heard his very last sound,
And our wheels grazed his dead face.
    Dead Man's Dump
       G.H.

Rossetti, Christina [Georgina] (1830–94), was the sister of Dante Gabriel **Rossetti**. Her Anglican piety deeply influenced her life and poetry. For some time she thought of embracing the religious life, and later rejected two suitors on religious grounds. Nevertheless, she remained closely associated with her brothers and their Pre-Raphaelite friends, and contributed to their magazine, *The Germ*. The title poem of *Goblin Market, and other Poems* (1862) scored the first big popular success for the new kind of poetry the Pre-Raphaelites were advocating. A fantastic narrative set in a fairy-tale world, it can be read as an allegory of Christian love and self-sacrifice, and it is typical of Christina Rossetti's work. So also is the title poem of *The Prince's Progress, and other Poems* (1866). This tale of a prince who, through irresponsible dallying by the way, never reaches his princess until too late, is poignantly symbolic of Christina's personal frustration:

Ten years ago, five years ago,
 One year ago,
Even then you had arrived in time,
 Though somewhat slow;
Then you had known her living face,
 Which now you cannot know.
The frozen fountain would have leaped,
 The buds gone on to blow,
The warm south wind would have
       breathed
 To melt the snow.

Other volumes appeared in 1872, 1881 and posthumously in 1896. They include romantic narratives, sonnets and lyrics, some of them devotional.

The key to much of Christina Rossetti's work may be seen in a deep-rooted conflict between her somewhat frozen piety and her richly sensuous nature. Nevertheless, her religious convictions give a central strength to much of her work, which is lacking in that of her brother. Her lyrics show a lightness of touch derived from ballad and folk-song, and a clarity of natural imagery. She is also not without an occasional quiet, very feminine humour.

J.H-S.

Rossetti, Dante Gabriel (1828–82), was early drawn towards both poetry and painting. In 1848, with Holman Hunt and J. E. Millais, he founded the Pre-Raphaelite Brotherhood, whose ideal was the patient fidelity to 'nature' of the Quattrocento painters. Though successful in both fields, Rossetti's own values were literary rather than artistic. Two of his most striking early poems, *The Blessed Damozel* and *My Sister's Sleep*, were contributed to the P.R.B. magazine *The Germ* (1850): the one a typical attempt in vaguely medieval terms to equate profane with spiritual love; the other, hauntingly evocative with its scrupulous Pre-Raphaelite minuteness. For some years Rossetti devoted himself to painting, though his *Early Italian Poets*, translations from the *Vita Nuova* and Dante's contemporaries, appeared in 1861. With their accuracy and versatility, these are, for some critics, Rossetti's major achievement. Two collections of original poems appeared in 1870 and 1881. Rossetti's later years were darkened by remorse—he blamed himself for his wife's suicide—by drug addiction and paranoia.

Haunted by Dante, Rossetti frequently attempted to follow his master in recon-ciling profane and spiritual love: a romantic version of Dante's synthesis of beauty and sanctity. Yet what was a reality in the morally coherent medieval world was self-deception in the uneasy speculative world of the nineteenth century:

Thy soul I know not from thy body,
                                        nor
Thee from myself, neither our love
                                    from God.

Rossetti really celebrates, as Nicolette Gray observes, love as God, not God as love. The sonnet-sequence *The House of Life* (1847–81) represents Rossetti's most ambitious attempt at Dantesque 'metaphysical' autobiography. Mrs Jane Morris, object of his devotion for many years, his wife and his mistress, Fanny Cornforth, appear here as incarnations of Beatrice and the Fatal Woman.

The defects in Rossetti's original work are narrowness of range, over-literariness, particularly in his ballads; over-dependence on easily won aural effects and mechanical alliterations. Yet his special note is unforgettable: sensuous brooding over mysterious, often ominous states of being, realised in such poems as *Willowwood*, *Paid on Both Sides*, *Sudden Light*, *Love's Nocturne*. Estranged from his age, Rossetti yet rejected 'art for art's sake', and his few poems on contemporary public themes—such as *Jenny*, for example, a study of a young prostitute—are vivid and intelligent. He left no formal criticism, but his scattered judgments are catholic and acute. In his best years, his personality was generous, fascinating and humorous (his limericks are early, admirable examples of their kind).

I.F.

see also Foreign Influences on English Poetry *and* Translation

Rowley, Thomas. *See* Chatterton, Thomas.

S

Sackville, Sir Thomas, Lord Buckhurst and Earl of Dorest (*c.* 1537–1608), was the only son of Sir Richard Sackville and Winifred Bruges. He was educated at Hart Hall, Oxford, and entered Parliament in 1557. He was appointed ambassador to France in 1570, and to the Netherlands in 1586, and from 1599 until his death he was Lord High Treasurer.

However, it is not so much for his official activities that we remember Thomas Sackville, as for his early achievements as a poet. It is much to be regretted that he ever deserted poetry for the conventional career of a wealthy young man of good family, related through the Boleyns to the Queen. In estimating his literary gift, it must be remembered that he was writing before **Spenser**, before **Marlowe** and before **Shakespeare**. In association with Thomas Norton, he wrote *Gorboduc*, or *Ferrex and Porrex*, an excessively dreary play which nevertheless has some claim to rank as the first tragedy in English blank verse; but in support of his better claim as a true poet we may quote a verse from the *Complaint of Henry Stafford, Duke of Buckingham*:

Midnight was come, and every vital
thing
With sweet sound sleep their weary
limbs did rest,
The beasts were still, the little birds that
sing
Now sweetly slept beside their mother's
breast,
The old and all well shrouded in their
nest;
The waters calm, the cruel seas did
cease,
The woods, the fields, and all things
held their peace.

v.s-w.

Sandburg, Carl (1878–1967), was born in Illinois of Swedish parents, and worked out his youth in labourers' jobs, the Spanish-American War, Lombard College, advertising, newspapers and Social Democratic politics. His first poems (1904) were immature and ignored, but he absorbed Chicago and the Middle West, created an image of 'The People' and took up **Imagism**: the result was *Chicago Poems* (1916) whose hearty industrial naturalism and social conscience, moody sentimentality and free-verse speech rhythms, and a strong American idiom, were reviled for emotional vulgarity and incompetent technique. But *Poetry* supported him and his reputation developed, even if his talent did not. This proletarian rhetorician became Harvard's Phi Betta Kappa poet in 1928, the year of his last major book of poems, *Good Morning America*. His energy thenceforward poured into a brilliant prose epic of Lincoln, his people's heroic centre, and into collecting song and folklore. *The People, Yes* (1936) combines original poetry with folk materials.

'Poetry', Sandburg claimed in 1928, 'is the achievement of the synthesis of hyacinths and biscuits': his own work is divided between the personal lyrical episode (*Fog*, *Bas Relief*) and the vigorous commentary on the industrial and agrarian scene, its workers and parasites (*Ossawatomie*, *Killers*). He assumed the part of the Whitmanian national bard but tended to narrow the variety of Americans into generalised attitudes about types and the masses in which documentary replaces insight. 'He is the lover of the plural' (**Aiken**), content too often to admit raw experience into poetry at its own level. His 'report on the people' is penetrated with loss of happiness (*Population Drifts*) and wasted opportunities. *Threes* (1920) contains some of his best writing—sardonic humour in local idiom and typical exacerbated radicalism: 'men with mustaches, sideburns, lilacs, told me the high golden words are: Mother, Home, and Heaven. . . . Years ticked off their say-so on the great clocks of doom and damnation'. His *Collected Poems* witness 'the vast unrealised possibilities of a native American radicalism that has never found its fullest expression' (Kazin).   E.N.W.M.

see also American Poetry

Sassoon, Siegfried (1886–1967), was educated at Marlborough and Cambridge. Before the First World War he had written *The Daffodil Murderer* and *The Old Huntsman* (published 1917). By then he had begun writing the passionately indignant war poems collected in *Counter-Attack* (1918) arising out of his war experiences as an infantry officer. He was awarded the M.C. By means of a taut, telling prosody, sometimes based on colloquialisms, reinforced by rhyme, he was deeply pitiful or scathingly sarcastic. Yet the grim horror of the war did not altogether kill his early romanticism, which mingled with his new realism in the slim pamphlet *Augustan Books of Poetry*, No. 18 (1926), where occurs the famous 'Everyone suddenly burst out singing'.

His *Collected Poems* (1947) were followed by *Sequences* (1956), combining three privately printed volumes. These express a resigned acceptance in which the sense of loveliness is not overwhelmed by disillusion. There are pieces here as striking and as memorably moving, as full of suggestion beyond the words as in his earlier work. Among such is his portrait of **Hardy** at Max Gate, in which 'Old Mr Hardy, upright in his chair' is suddenly replaced by 'the seer whose words the world had known'. Sometimes the old bitterness wells up:

Most minds decide to-day
That mercy does not pay.

His autobiographies, *Memoirs of a Fox-Hunting Man* (1927), *Memoirs of an Infantry Officer* (1930), *Sherston's Progress* (1936), and *Siegfried's Journey* (1945), should be read as a gloss on his poetry.   B.D.

Satire, a literary form of Latin origin, while setting out to ridicule and scorn particular abuses, generally aims, at least in principle, at the reform of public morals. Satire is present in **Langland**'s *Piers Plowman*, and in other medieval poems, though mixed with narrative and didacticism. Such a line as

Spera in deo is spoken of priests who
                                        have no
    spending of silver
                                Passus XI, 487

looks forward to the greater satire of the Augustans, and some passages of John **Skelton** have true satirical point. For the most part, however, Skelton is lighter-hearted than his models,

The famous poets satiricall
As Persius and Juvenall,
Horace and noble Martiall . . .
                            Against Garnesche

The Jacobean satirists, Joseph Hall, John **Marston** and John **Donne**, though closer students of these Latin masters, also lack single-mindedness. Donne in his *Satyre IIII* overwhelms a miserable courtier with such copious and fantastic abuse that the man is forgotten in the exuberance of the poet's invention:

    Towards me did runne
A thing more strange, than on Niles
                        slime, the Sunne
E'r bred; or all which into Noahs Arke
                                came;
A thing, which would have pos'd
                        Adam to name;

*

Stranger than strangers; One, who for a
                                    Dane,
In the Danes Massacre had sure been
                                    slaine,
If he had liv'd then; And without help
                                    dies,
When next the Prentises 'gainst Strangers
                                    rise.
One whom the watch at noone lets
                                    scarce goe by,
One, to whom, the examining justice
                                    sure would cry,
Sir, by your priesthood tell me what
                                    you are . . .

It is not until **Dryden**, who had studied
French models from de Régnier to
Boileau, and adapted their pointed style,
that English satire was capable of barbed
brevity. The poet Shadwell lives for ever
in Dryden's lines from *MacFlecknoe*.
Though all his writings may be forgotten,
he is immortalised in the character conferred upon him by Dullness:

Shadwell alone of all my Sons is he
Who stands confirm'd in full stupidity.
The rest to some faint meaning make
                                    pretence,
But Shadwell never deviates into sense.

John Oldham and the Earl of **Rochester**
stand beside Dryden at the beginning of
the Augustan age as able satirists in the
French manner. Alexander **Pope** continues
the tradition with greater wit and lighter
fantasy. His attack on Lord Hervey in the
Epistle to Doctor Arbuthnot is a sword-
thrust:

Satire or sense, alas! can Sporus feel?
Who breaks a butterfly upon a wheel?

Compared with this Dryden's passage on
Shadwell is like a bludgeoning.

Charles **Churchill** and Samuel **Johnson**
extend the history of satire, which culminates in **Byron**'s discursive novel in verse,

Don Juan. Here once more satire has become mixed with other ingredients, narrative, sentimental and personal. Detached
stanzas, however, such as that which
follows the speculation as to what would
have happened if Laura had been Petrarch's
wife, preserve the high tradition of moral
satire:

All tragedies are finish'd by a death,
    All comedies are ended by a marriage;
The future states of both are left to faith,
    For authors fear description might
                                    disparage
The worlds to come of both, or fall
                                    beneath,
    And then both worlds would punish
                                    their miscarriage;
So leaving each their priest and prayer-
                                    book ready,
They say no more of Death or of the
                                    Lady.

Since Byron there has been no verse-satire
on a high level.   J.M.C.

Schwartz, Delmore (1913–66), Brooklyn-
born poet, critic and teacher, has published
mixed collections of verse and prose in
which the two forms have complemented
each other. His more recent verse was
collected with the earlier poems in *Summer
Knowledge, Poems 1938–1958* which won
him the Bollingen Prize in 1960   D.H.

Science and Poetry. It is of some note
that, in the west, almost the first appearance
of a natural scientific world view was in
poetic form. Empedocles (*c.* 490–430 B.C.)
wrote a long poem, *Nature*, of which some
four hundred lines survive. He was a
philosopher, statesman and religious teacher, as well as a poet and scientist. His
contemporaries thought of him as a god,
and it has recently been suggested (by
E. R. Dodds in *The Greeks and the Irrational*)
that he was one of a group of Greek

exponents of the ancient and world-wide cult of shamanism, the role of shaman including those of poet, scientist, oracle, healer and magician.

Lucretius' great work *On the Nature of Things* is the outstanding example in literature of a sustained imaginative poem with a scientific subject matter. In it he pays tribute to Empedocles, but by his own time (c. 99–55 B.C.), the rationalist and largely materialist philosophy of Democritus and Epicurus had helped to separate science from its magical origins. Yet the atomic theory, which this philosophy expounded, was a kind of poetic hunch, without experimental evidence. Such metaphorical models have been indispensable to the development of the natural sciences. It is arguable that poets have contributed to the formation of sensibilities and imageries favourable to scientific work, especially in the early, inventive phase of a science, when only by inspired guesswork can a conceptual start be made.

Children and laymen have always been fascinated by the conjuring tricks of science, and we cannot rule out the possibility that scientists themselves are partly motivated by the satisfaction to be got from science as a form of play. At least we can be sure that those poets who have had an amateur interest in science have been largely lured by its magical potentialities, invisible influences, transmutations of substances, and explorations of the very large and the very small. To take a few scattered examples, **Chaucer's** *Treatise on the Astrolabe* (1391) demonstrates in prose the poet's interest in the motions of the celestial bodies, an interest which in scores of passages in his narrative poems is made poetic and dramatic. On the other side of the world, the Chinese poet, Po Chü-i (we learn from Arthur **Waley**) was in the ninth century A.D. carrying out unsuccessful experiments in alchemy which he described

with delicately realistic irony at his own expense. Nearer our own time, **Coleridge's** notebooks are full of what Kathleen Coburn has called 'imaginative chemistry'. He and **Shelley** read scientific books and made friends with scientists. One may conjecture that it was the aesthetic magic of natural phenomena, above all of transformations of physical state, that principally attracted them in the sciences.

Historians of science have pointed out how the founders of modern astronomy, Copernicus and Tycho Brahe, were (to quote Butterfield) 'driven by a mystical semi-religious fervour—a passion to uncover the magic of mere numbers and to demonstrate the music of the spheres' (*The Origins of Modern Science*, p. 63), while Newton himself was 'prepared to believe that gravity, which was otherwise so apparently unaccountable, represented the constant activity of a living being that pervaded the whole of space' (*ibid.*, p. 126). Such conceptions go back to Plato and Pythagoras, and before that perhaps to the shaman, the poet-magician of prehistory who was able to send his soul on voyages into the sky. The poetic imagination was one factor helping to make possible the discoveries of modern science. Scientific discoveries in turn have had multiple and sometimes contradictory effects on the sensibility of recent epochs. They could produce a sense of wonder, of apparition. They shook old images to pieces and opened up fresh fields of fantasy. On the other hand they were quantitative, mechanistic and rationalistic, with hostile implications for faith and vision. 'The seventeenth century, indeed, did not merely bring a new factor into history, in the way we often assume—one that must just be added, so to speak, to the other permanent factors. The new factor immediately began to elbow the other ones away, pushing them from their central position. Indeed, it began immediately to seek control of the rest . . .' (Butterfield, *op. cit.*, p. 190).

The literature of protest against science as deadly to the imagination is, whether justified or not, in itself an imaginative achievement. Poets and poetic prose writers like **Blake** and **Ruskin** were prepared not only to deny the validity of science— outside its own limited field—but also to propound their own 'true' versions of science, which are often beautiful and strangely enlightening. Goethe, it is well known, disputed the Newtonian theory of light and, with superb self-confidence, was ready to take on the scientist at his own game. But he marks an intersection between the poetic approach to science and the scientific approach to poetry. From his time to our own, the former becomes less practicable, the latter more insistent. The mid-nineteenth century saw a high point of tension and paradox in the relations between the two modes of perception. Science was in process of being routinised, poetry of being banalised. Poetic temperaments tried to break through the hardening crust. The most original scientists retained the essential poetry of the creative impulse. But with science had come large-scale industry, and new forms of power and machinery, new forms of politics, new forms of education. The complex situation cannot be surveyed in terms of 'science' and 'poetry' alone.

The history of the scientific approach to poetry is part of the history of aesthetics in general. Philosophic aesthetics were long dominated by the ideas of Plato and Aristotle about poetry and the other arts. It is in the seventeenth century and especially in the Age of the Enlightenment (1650–1750) that new formulations and searching questions on the subject of artistic creativity begin to be found. This development,

though largely philosophic, was linked to some extent with speculation, and some new knowledge, in psychology and physiology. Discussion about 'genius' and 'taste' can be traced to Gracián in Spain, La Bruyère in France, Shaftesbury in England, and Baumgarten in Germany— the latter being the first to use the word 'Aesthetic' as the name of a special science. The history of aesthetics takes up a large part of the important work by the Neapolitan philosopher, Benedetto Croce, first published in 1901 under the title *Aesthetic as Science of Expression and General Linguistic*. This may be regarded as the culmination of philosophic aesthetics, for although Croce speaks of aesthetics as a science, he is using this term in the pre-Baconian sense of 'branch of knowledge' rather than as meaning 'field of experimental inquiry'. In this he was following the eighteenth century Neapolitan philosopher, Vico, who had called his own work *Scienza Nuova*, the New Science. This Vico did in conscious challenge to Bacon's concept of science, his aim being to establish the existence in its own right of 'Poetic Wisdom', or, as Croce puts it, 'the autonomy of the poetic world'.

Croce himself is scornful of attempts to link aesthetics with human physiology, by those for example who 'have tried to deduce the pleasure of art from the echo of that of the sexual organs' (*op. cit.*, p. 83). Similarly he writes that 'Darwin's book on the expression of the emotions in man and animals does not belong to Aesthetic' (p. 95), and he has a chapter on 'Errors arising from the confusion between Physics and Aesthetic'. In fact, Croce, like Bergson, represents part of the reaction in philosophy against the viewpoint of positivism, according to which all human and social activity should be studied by the methods and in the spirit of the natural sciences. The 'science of Aesthetic' was then to some extent an attempt to break away from the sterile controversy between idealism and materialism by emphasising the direct, intuitive mode of knowledge.

But there have been parallel developments which, rightly or wrongly, have made claims to possessing a more genuinely scientific, a more 'positive', less 'metaphysical' approach to the understanding of poetry. Obviously there are many possible methods of analysing the content of the poem itself, in a more or less quantitative way, and this has become normal practice in certain types of literary criticism and analysis, though always open to the charge that by dissection of the poem you destroy its life. Alternatively, one may observe, record and analyse people's responses to poetic and artistic stimuli. 'Experimental aesthetics' may take the form of laboratory research on the effect of different stimuli, including sounds, words and images. Psycho-analytical writers have found in the imagery of poetry and myth a fruitful field for the exploration of the unconscious mind.

The explicitly sociological approach to poetry and the arts begins with Comte (1798–1857), for whom, as for Vico, these represented a survival from an earlier phase of cultural development. Poetic sensibility and expression, on this view, are more natural to primitive than to civilised mankind. One may compare the recent statement by a leading social anthropologist that 'the poetic sense of primitive peoples has not been sufficiently allowed for' (E. Evans Pritchard, *Nuer Religion*, p. 142). One may also compare the ironical comment of Peacock in *The Four Ages of Poetry* (1820) that 'A poet in our times is a semi-barbarian in a civilised community'. For Comte, however, even when society was run, as he expected, on completely 'scientific' lines, poetic myth and symbol would still be needed to make it palatable.

Moreover, intuitive, emotive responses in social and personal relationships were essential to his 'positive polity' and could be nourished through the arts.

Comte therefore had more 'use' for poetry than Bentham, to whom it was simply 'misrepresentation' (as it had also been for Plato in the Tenth Book of the *Republic*). Writers and intellectuals have been alternately attracted and repelled by positivism, and on the whole have reacted against it. Bergson coined the term 'scientism' to describe the pretentions of those who sought the prestige of natural science for inquiries in fields where they did not apply, such as aesthetics. Controversy continues as to the sense in which the social sciences can be said to be scientific.

There have however been some notable initiatives towards bridging what many have felt to be the widening gap between the scientific and poetic modes of sensibility. At Cambridge in the nineteen-twenties, I. A. Richards lectured in the School of English on a possible psychological basis for literary criticism and performed with his students the famous experiment described in his book, *Practical Criticism* (1929). Some Cambridge poets began to bring scientific terms into their poetry, in a manner recalling that of **Donne**. For a short time it seemed that a new synthesis might be possible, but though some exciting hybrids appeared in that highly cultivated soil, they did not propagate themselves elsewhere.

Moreover, other influences and initiatives were at work. Marx and Freud, each claiming the authority of 'science', loomed ever larger, sometimes in opposition, but, as interpreted by the surrealist movement, in a conjunction which provided a militant poetic attitude to all human life and activity. Claiming to base themselves on dialectical materialism and therefore on the search for reality in the objective world, for a few years (1930–32) the surrealists placed their movement 'at the service of the Revolution'. Simultaneously they were looking to the unconscious, newly explored by Freud, as the direct source of poetry and painting, which should be as 'automatic' as possible. Splendid as was the idea of so radical a reorientation of human effort, the talented surrealist group soon petered out, leaving a trail of mystifications and *objets trouvés*.

In the past ten years there have been a variety of movements that challenged convention, disowned society, rejected the past and sought new kinds of stimuli. There have also been new applications of scientific methodology to the interpretation of poetry and other arts, and new attempts, within poetry and the arts, to assimilate modern technologies. Thus we have the use of content analysis by D. C. McClelland and his associates to assess changes in the level of achievement-orientation in different societies at different periods through the imagery in their literature, the decoration on their ceramics, and so on. In the other direction, we have the composition of poems and graphics with the aid of electronic computers. Science, it would appear, has now become so dominant that poets and other artists are consciously or unconsciously led to simulate the activities and attitudes of the scientist. C.M.

Scott, Sir Walter (1771–1832), poet and novelist, was born in Edinburgh, the son of a lawyer, and was educated at the High School and University there. He studied law and eventually became a Clerk to the Court and Sheriff of Selkirk. His literary work, which was immense, occupied his leisure time. His first inspiration was the ballad, three imitations of which he appended to his *Minstrelsy of the Scottish Border* (1802–3). His first long rhyming romance, *The Lay of the Last Minstrel* (1805), is a more ambitious imitation of the Middle English lay, the metre for which he found in **Coleridge**'s *Christabel*. His other popular romances, *Marmion* (1808), and *The Lady of the Lake* (1810) have their highlights—the epic battle scenes in *Marmion* and the hunting scene in *The Lady of the Lake*—but the modern ear tires of the thudding octosyllables and the tawdry diction offends. The introductions to *Marmion*, however, especially the noble first in which the ardent patriot expresses his country's spirit in face of Napoleon's march through Europe, are excellent. Yet, if this were all, one might demur to the inclusion of Scott among the great Romantic poets, but in addition to the finer passages in the romances and the Introductions are the lyrics interspersed in the novels which succeeded the poetry. The best of these—Meg Merrilies' spells for birth and death in *Guy Mannering*, Cleveland's song from *The Pirate* ('Farewell! farewell! the voice you hear') and above all *Proud Maisie* from *The Heart of Midlothian*—justify John Buchan's claim that they 'have the desiderium of great poetry'.

Scott said '**Byron** bet me'. That was when *Childe Harold* announced a new poet who had none of Scott's inhibitions and who could exploit the exotic as Scott had exploited the age of chivalry. He wisely set about transferring to fiction the spirit of his romances on the more solid basis of history as seen through the romantic temperament. G.K.

Service, Robert [William] (1876–1958), was an English-born Canadian writer of ballads, and a novelist of frontier life. His *Collected Poems* (1944) include the celebrated *Shooting of Dan McGrew*. His autobiography, *Ploughman of the Moon*, appeared in 1945. D.H.

Shakespeare, William (1564–1616), was born in Stratford-upon-Avon, the son of a prosperous glover. Probably—the records for the period are lost—he attended the town Grammar School, and received there the traditional education of the day. His Latin may have seemed 'small' to Ben **Jonson**, and there is no good evidence that he had any Greek at all, but there is no reason to doubt that, as a seventeenth-century report has it, he 'understood Latin pretty well'. Whether as the same source asserts, he 'was a schoolmaster in the country', is more doubtful, but it is possible. The years after he left Stratford, where the last record is the baptismal entry for twin children on 2 February, 1585, are undocumented, and we next hear of him through the hostile description of him by Robert **Greene** late in 1592 as 'an upstart crow beautified with our feathers . . . an absolute *Johannes fac totum*'.

During his dramatic career, we hear little of him, and still less that directly illuminates his literary life, but this is not surprising, still less does it warrant doubts about his authorship of the plays. It was not yet the custom to write the lives of English men of letters unless, like **Sidney, Donne** or **Herbert**, they also had other claims to fame, and we have as much information about Shakespeare as we could expect to have about a popular dramatist of his day.

His life after 1592 can conveniently be sketched in terms of a few landmarks. After a confused period during much of which the London theatres were closed because of plague, he appears in a document of 15 March, 1595, as a leading member of the Lord Chamberlain's Men, and he continued to be associated with this company (renamed the King's Men in 1603) for the rest of his career. His increasing prosperity is attested by the grant of arms to his father (1596) and his own purchase of New Place, Stratford, in 1597.

In 1598 his name appeared for the first time on title-pages of plays, and in 1599 he was a part owner of the new Globe Theatre. After his father's death in 1601, he continued to buy property in Stratford, and seems to have paid longer visits to his native town until he eventually settled there in 1611. After the production of *The Tempest* in that year, there are only two plays, *Henry VIII* and *The Two Noble Kinsmen*, probably both collaborations with **Fletcher**, before his death in 1616. One theatrical event of 1608 that may have had some importance for his work is the opening of the Blackfriars Theatre, which offered more scope for spectacular effects and drew, perhaps, a more sophisticated audience. The King's Men, however, continued to play the same repertoire both there and at the Globe.

Apart from Shakespeare's very earliest years in the theatre, and apart from a few uncertainties later, the relative and even the absolute dating of his works is not in serious dispute. Greene's reference to him in 1592 as 'an absolute *Johannes fac totum*' implies versatility and, one would think, a fair body of work to his credit. Hence the more conservative view that would date only the Henry VI plays before 1592 is open to question. Some would now attribute up to ten plays to this early date, including both Histories, Comedies (*The Comedy of Errors, The Two Gentlemen of Verona* and *The Taming of the Shrew*) and Tragedies (*Titus Andronicus* and, possibly, *Romeo and Juliet*). The two narrative poems, *Venus and Adonis* (1593), and *The Rape of Lucrece* (1594) belong to the plague years; the *Sonnets*, collected in 1609, are of uncertain, and probably varying, date. 1594–1600 are the years of the later Histories and the central Comedies, and, among the Tragedies, *Julius Caesar* and *Hamlet* (probably 1600). After *Twelfth Night* (?1601), there is a period in which, apart from the so-called 'Dark' Comedies, *Troilus and Cressida*, *Measure for Measure* and *All's Well That Ends Well*, his work is exculsively in the field of tragedy, until a group of less sombre plays is ushered in by the probably collaborative *Pericles* (1607–8), and concluded by *The Tempest* (1611). *Henry VIII* and *The Two Noble Kinsmen* follow about 1613.

Shakespeare's earlier works are sometimes viewed too much as foreshadowings of his more mature writings. They are that, but they are also remarkable in their own right. Of the narrative poems, *Venus and Adonis* is an accomplished exercise in Ovidian vein, and the less unified *Rape of Lucrece* looks forward, in the treatment of Tarquin, to the exploration of the human soul in the later tragedies, especially *Macbeth*. But the non-dramatic work is of relatively minor importance, in spite of the abiding interest of the *Sonnets* and of the single excursion into something like metaphysical poetry, *The Phoenix and the Turtle*. It is in drama that Shakespeare appears from the first as an artist of remarkable assurance. The English history play, as a serious genre, begins and, virtually, ends with him. Even the recalcitrant material of the reign of Henry VI is given dramatic shape, at least in the last two plays (the first is of less certain authorship), and the commanding figure of the future Richard III is already powerfully presented in the great soliloquy of *Henry VI, Part iii*, with its rhythms of struggle and thwarting:

And I—like one lost in a thorny wood
That rents the thorns and is rent with
the thorns,
Seeking a way and straying from the way;
Not knowing how to find the open air,
But toiling desperately to find it out—
Torment myself to catch the English
crown.
III,ii, 174–9

Richard III itself, though the conception of the villain-hero's career had already been given dramatic outline in Sir Thomas More's *Life*, is something new in English drama: intricately woven melodrama, yet in a genuinely historical setting, which reaches at least the borders of tragedy in Richard's monologue before the battle:

I shall despair, There is no creature
loves me;
And if I die no soul will pity me:
And wherefore should they, since that I
myself
Find in myself no pity to myself?
V, iii, 200–203

In tragedy itself, Shakespeare was not so active in his early years. What is interesting is the enormous difference between his first two tragedies. *Titus Andronicus*, perhaps his earliest and certainly his least abidingly popular play, may be little more than an extreme representative of the tragedy of blood popularised by **Kyd**, but it shows constructive skill and vivacity beyond the powers of the lesser dramatists of the age. *Romeo and Juliet*, though it has its inequalities and uncertainties of tone, is another matter. Injudicious attempts have been made to bring it under philosophical theories of tragedy that may possibly apply to Shakespeare's later plays, but it remains unique: a play that makes it impossible for anyone ever again to write a tragedy of young love without provoking unfavourable comparisons—so much is it *the* poetic rendering of its subject. Romeo's last speech is perhaps the best example of the poetry that belongs to the young Shakespeare alone:

O, here
Will I set up my everlasting rest,
And shake the yoke of inauspicious stars
From this world-wearied flesh. Eyes,
look your last.

Arms, take your last embrace. And, lips,
                                        O you
The doors of breath, seal with a righteous
                                        kiss
A dateless bargain to engrossing death!
                                V, iii, 109–15

Comedy (with history) forms the greatest part of Shakespeare's early writing, and here it is not so easy to isolate the completely new as it is with the histories and *Romeo and Juliet*. He had an accomplished, if limited, predecessor in the field of sophisticated comedy in the person of John **Lyly**, and the early Shakespeare may, by comparison, seem sometimes more crudely farcical—as in *The Comedy of Errors* and *The Taming of the Shrew*—or even inept in his romanticism, as in *The Two Gentlemen of Verona*. But even *The Comedy of Errors*, perhaps the earliest of the comedies, is a remarkable piece of virtuosity in its construction, and by the time we reach *A Midsummer Night's Dream*, Shakespeare is capable of a wonderful harmony of contrasting elements—each group of characters living in a world of its own, yet held together by the magic of Puck and the unabashed self-possession of Bottom. One of Puck's last speeches shows the lyric strain in Shakespeare's early work:

Now the hungry lion roars,
And the wolf behowls the moon;
Whilst the heavy ploughman snores,
All with weary task fordone.
Now the wasted brands do glow,
Whilst the screech-owl, screeching
                                loud,
Puts the wretch that lies in woe
In remembrance of a shroud,
                                V, i, 360–67

It is in comedy that the middle period of Shakespeare's work follows on with least interruption from the first—*Love's Labour's Lost* and *A Midsummer Night's Dream*

bridging the gap between the earliest plays and *The Merchant of Venice*, with its successors up to *Twelfth Night*. Tragicomedy, which had been skirted (not very happily) in *The Two Gentlemen of Verona* and, in a sense, in the framework of *The Comedy of Errors*, is handled with assured craftsmanship in *The Merchant of Venice*, where the contrasting 'worlds' of Venice and Belmont give new richness to the inherited stories, and where Shylock—however romanticising criticism may have exaggerated the sympathy to be accorded to him—gives us, as part of the total structure, a new version of the villain-as-hero motif that had been at the centre of *Richard III*. The element of potential tragedy is perhaps not quite so well integrated in *Much Ado about Nothing*, brilliantly contrived though the intrigue is; and for the last two plays in this group, Shakespeare turns to a more unmixed comedy, though with a flavour of satire and, in *Twelfth Night*, a melancholy behind the gaiety.

Shakespeare's greatest comic creation, Falstaff, is placed in a context of history. Beginning with the simplest and most purely tragic of the whole sequence, *Richard II*, the second group of histories goes on to the most complex and wide-ranging achievement of Shakespeare's earlier career, the two parts of *Henry IV*. Falstaff, like Shylock, need not be sentimentalised, but he is the supreme example of the absurdity of trying to bring Shakespeare's greatest creations under some simple heading such as 'braggart soldier'. The rejection of Falstaff may be necessary, but for it also to be as potent as it is, what is rejected must be something vital and exciting. Certainly, in spite of all attempts to glorify him as a text-book hero-king, and in spite of the patriotic interest, genuine as far as it goes, Henry V as king makes only a relatively superficial appeal in the absence of Falstaff. It is understandable that, outside comedy, Shakespeare should now want to turn to a subject of less limited significance, as he does in the first of his mature tragedies, *Julius Caesar*. Here we have, in Brutus, the first example of the type of internal struggle which meets us soon after in the figure of Hamlet, as well as elements to be more fully developed in the portraiture of Macbeth.

Hamlet, the first of what are traditionally regarded as the four principal tragedies, comes within the same period as the so-called 'Problem Plays'—*Troilus and Cressida*, *Measure for Measure* and *All's Well that Ends Well*—and is sometimes included among them. It has certainly proved a problem for generations of interpreters, and is perhaps the most sheerly interesting play ever written: in **Johnson**'s words, 'The particular excellence which distinguishes it from the rest' of Shakespeare's plays is 'variety'. The second of the central tragedies, *Othello*, is, by characteristic contrast, the most concentrated and the most unrelievedly moving: nowhere in world drama is there such a good example of Aristotle's idea of a momentous error—simply getting things wrong—as a generating principle in tragedy. And in Othello's 'music', one side of Shakespeare's verse reaches its highest form:

> If it were now to die,
> 'Twere now to be most happy; for I fear
> My soul hath her content so absolute
> That not another comfort like to this
> Succeeds in unknown fate.
> II, i, 187–91

In *King Lear* and *Macbeth* (as later in *Antony and Cleopatra* and *Coriolanus*), successive plays alternate between a rich and complex structure and one with a greater singleness and depth of interest. *King Lear* is the play which most tempts us

to think of Shakespeare as giving a picture of the whole universe through a particular series of events, and it marks the highest point of the power of dramatic utterance through simplicity.

> Pray, do not mock me:
> I am a very foolish fond old man,
> Fourscore and upward, not an hour more
>   nor less;
> And, to deal plainly,
> I fear I am not in my perfect mind.
> . . . .
> Do not laugh at me;
> For, as I am a man, I think this lady
> To be my child Cordelia.
> IV, vii, 59–63; 68–70

In *Macbeth*, the stress is on the single soul in the grip of evil, with the impulse to good conquered but never wholly obliterated, and emerging in the imagery:

> And pity, like a naked new-born babe,
> Striding the blast, or heaven's cherubims hors'd
> Upon the sightless couriers of the air,
> Shall blow the horrid deed in every eye,
> That tears shall drown the wind.
> I, vii, 21–5

Antony and Cleopatra and *Coriolanus*, in spite of the richness of the one and the shapeliness and intense psychological interest of the other, perhaps mark some relaxation from their forerunners; and it is not surprising to find Shakespeare, constantly the experimenter, taking to a new type of play, to which the name 'romance' has been given. Like some earlier plays, these can be called tragi-comedies, in that death and disaster are threatened, but escaped by the major characters; but more peculiar to those plays are themes of separation, reunion and regeneration. The freedom of expressive rhythm in these last plays can be illustrated by such a passage as this from *The Winter's Tale*:

When you do dance, I wish you
A wave o' th' sea, that you might ever
      do
Nothing but that; move still, still so,
And own no other function. Each your
      doing,
So singular in each particular,
Crowns what you are doing in the
      present deeds,
That all your acts are queens.
     IV, iv, 140–6

The more formal and stately aspect appears in the abjuration by Prospero in which—though it is wholly a part of the play—readers have inevitably seen Shakespeare's farewell to the stage:

But this rough magic
I here abjure, and, when I have required
Some heavenly music—which even
      now I do—
To work mine end upon their senses that
This airy charm is for, I'll break my staff,
Bury it certain fathoms in the earth,
And deeper than did ever plummet sound
I'll drown my book.
    The Tempest, V, i, 50–57
       J.C.M.

See also Imagery

Shapiro, Karl [Jay] (1913–), American poet and critic, was Consultant in Poetry at the Library of Congress (1946–7) and editor of *Poetry* (1950–5) and of *Prairie Schooner* (1956–63). He became Professor of writing at the University of Nebraska in 1956. *Beyond Criticism* (1953) establishes his opposition to mythical, historical views of poetry. He was awarded the Pulitzer Prize for *V Letter* (1945). *The Bourgeois Poet,* 1964, was a departure from his early stanza-patterns, a collection of prose poems. *Selected Poems* (1968) collected the best of his work.   D.H.

Shelley, Percy Bysshe (1792–1822), was the son of Timothy, in due course Sir Timothy Shelley, Bt., and was heir to the baronetcy. To give a brief account of his restless and complex life is impossible. The barest outline is attempted here, and reference must be made to N. I. White's *Shelley,* and A. M. D. Hughes' *The Nascent Mind of Shelley.*

After school at Syon House, Isleworth, and at Eton, Shelley went to Oxford—where he chiefly dabbled in amateur science—but in March 1811 was expelled from his college for refusing to admit authorship of *The Necessity for Atheism.* Soon after, going to London companioned by Thomas Jefferson Hogg, he met sixteen-year-old Harriet Westbrook and, urged by compassion rather than passion, made a runaway marriage with her at Edinburgh in August. Leading a financially harassed life, they stayed in York, in Westmorland, Ireland, Wales and London, where Shelley made acquaintance with his hero, William Godwin. The Shelleys' daughter, Ianthe, was born in June 1813, and their son, Charles, in November 1814 (d. 1826). But by that time, in July, Shelley had eloped with Mary, the daughter of Godwin and Mary Wollstonecraft. Harriet committed suicide at the end of 1816, and shortly afterwards Shelley married Mary. Their first child, a girl, who lived only a few days, had been born early in 1815; their second, William, early in 1816 (d. 1819); Clara was born September 1817 (d. 1818); Percy Florence, who succeeded to the baronetcy, was born in 1819.

The Shelleys travelled continuously; after journeys abroad, they spent a little time in England, at first harried by debt, but later happily at Marlow. Early in 1818 they left England to live in Italy, where they stayed variously in Rome, Pisa, Leghorn and other places, Shelley's life being passed in writing, cultivating friendships, struggling with financial difficulties, and in boating. He was drowned early in July 1822 when his small yacht encountered foul weather.

His first publication was *Original Poetry, by Victor and Cazire* (1810), Cazire being his sister Elizabeth. Two Gothick novels followed, *Zastrozzi* (1810) and *St Irvyne* (1811). He issued some small poetical ventures, but his first distinctive work was *Queen Mab*, privately printed in 1813. He moved rapidly from Godwinian perfectibility and the contradictory determinism exhibited in this poem to the characteristic *Alastor* (1816). Here can be seen the influence of **Southey**'s *Thalaba* and **Landor**'s *Gebir*, and there begins to be seen his progress in philosophy through Hume and Berkeley to Plato. *Laon and Cythna* 'or, The Revolution of the Golden City', printed in 1817, was suppressed, and issued (revised) in 1818 as *The Revolt of Islam*, in twelve cantos of Spenserian stanzas. *Rosalind and Helen* appeared in 1819, as did *The Cenci*, Shelley's miscalculated bid for popular fame. Its subject was distasteful to theatre management; moreover, though written in the then fashionable pseudo-Shakespearean manner, the drama lacks change of movement or tension. Shelley's genius was far better suited to the 'lyrical drama' form of *Prometheus Unbound* (1820), which, in common with his previous volumes was printed 'with other poems'. *Oedipus Tyrannus*, 'or, Swellfoot the Tyrant' was issued alone in 1820. *Epipsychidion*, addressed to Emilia Viviani, appeared in 1821, as did *Adonais*, his tribute to **Keats**, which includes four remarkable autobiographical stanzas (xxxi–xxxiv). The last work printed in his lifetime was *Hellas* (1822), and he was at work on the gloomy, possibly pessimistic *Triumph of Life*, written in *terza rima*, at the time of his death. Mrs Shelley collected from his papers the *Posthumous Poems* which she published in 1824.

Shelley prefaced *Epipsychidion* with the lines:

My song, I fear that thou wilt find but
                                             few
Who fitly shall conceive thy reasoning,
Of such hard matter dost thou entertain;
Whence, if by misadventure, chance
                              should bring
Thee to base company (as chance may
                                        do),
Quite unaware of what thou dost
                               contain,
I prithee, comfort thy sweet self again,
My last delight! tell them that they are
                                        dull,
And bid them own that thou art
                                beautiful.

Nothing could more aptly express the difficulty of entering into the Shelley universe. Compared with him most of us, his readers, are 'base company'; and while from our earliest poetry-reading days we are entranced by the magical beauty of his song, what it contains is not easy to grasp. Thus the way to Shelley is through his lyrics, which seize upon us even though we do not really understand what he is hoping to convey. The lyric in *Posthumous Poems* that every schoolboy knows:

One word is too often profaned
    For me to profane it . . .

of which the second stanza runs:

I can give not what men call love,
    But wilt thou accept not
The worship the heart lifts above
    And the Heavens reject not,—
The desire of the moth for the star,
    Of the night for the morrow,
The devotion to something afar
    From the sphere of our sorrow?

in some sense provides a key to *Epipsychidion*, a great visionary poem some passages of which scandalised members of

that great sect
Whose doctrine is, that each one should
          select
Out of the crowd a mistress or a
          friend
Of all the rest, though fair and wise,
          commend
To cold oblivion . . .

But the further key must be sought in Plato's *Symposium* (which Shelley, with certain omissions, translated), in Dante, and in (another translation of his), Calderón's *El Magico Prodigioso.*

Shelley is at once a didactic poet and an exemplar of the pure poet. 'Didactic poetry', he said, 'is my abhorrence'; yet he ardently wished to reform mankind, to free it from custom, tyranny, and superstition. After the early *Queen Mab*, visionary enough, but with voluminous notes inspired largely by Godwin's *Political Justice* (he began to re-cast the poem as *The Daemon of the Universe*), his method was entirely that of 'pure poetry', which 'acts in another and diviner manner. It awakens and enlarges the mind itself by rendering it the receptacle of a thousand unapprehended combinations of thought. Poetry lifts the veil from the hidden beauty of the world...' (*A Defence of Poetry*, 1821). It is only in his obviously satirical works, such as the bitter *Masque of Anarchy* (1832), or the ludicrous *Swellfoot the Tyrant* that he speaks directly.

It is not readily evident what Shelley implies by his symbolism—what he meant by Daemon, cave, dome, veil, ship and so on (admirably treated in Neville Rogers' *Shelley at Work*). Even Heaven and Eternity do not carry the same meaning as they do in ordinary converse. Yet that need not matter for the first impact that his poetry makes. It does not disturb the reader when he comes to the fifty-second stanza of *Adonais*:

The One remains, the many change and
          pass;
Heaven's light forever shines, Earth's
          shadows fly;
Life, like a dome of many-coloured glass,
Stains the white radiance of Eternity.

although it includes the over-riding idea of the One and the Many. But then:

Until Death tramples it to fragments.—
          Die
If thou would'st be with that which
          thou does seek!

To die, as Keats did, is to be made 'a portion of that loveliness / Which once he made more lovely'.

A sense of this is given as early as *Alastor*, his first great poem, the pattern of all his greater works, allegorical, peopled with visionary figures, daemons and genii, illustrating abstract ideas, as in *Prometheus Unbound*, or *Hellas* (didactics disguised), though *Alastor* might be classed with the more autobiographical poems, such as *Epipsychidion* and *Julian and Maddalo*, in the last of which he portrays himself in a demented state. His philosophy of determined, stoical resistance to the conditions of living as imposed by a cruel deity and savage politics is expressed in the final speech of Demogorgon in *Prometheus Unbound*, where 'Gentleness, Virtue, Wisdom and Endurance' are what enable us

To suffer woes which Hope thinks
          infinite;
To forgive wrongs darker than death or
          night;
   To defy power which seems
          omnipotent;
To love, and bear; to hope till Hope
          creates
From its own wreck the thing it
          contemplates;
  Neither to change, nor falter nor
          repent;

This, like thy glory, Titan, is to be
Good, great and joyous, beautiful and
free;
This is alone Life, Joy, Empire, and
Victory.

It is a tremendous manifesto, but there is
no easy optimism in it.

Bagehot said that the best description of
Shelley's lyric is his own poem *To A
Skylark*, and this is largely true, though it
omits the deeply dejected ones such as
When the lamp is shattered, or O *world! O
life! O time!* Some of the best-remembered
lyrics occur in the longer poems, as 'Life of
Life! thy lips enkindle' (*Prometheus*), and
'The World's great age begins anew'
(*Hellas*). Many seem thrown off impulsive-
ly, such as the splendid *Ode to the West
Wind*; others embody a deep experience,
as *Hymn to Intellectual Beauty*; others again,
varying in depth, are occasional—to
Harriet, to Mary, to Jane, and so forth.
Most have Shelley's typical half-abstract
imagery, *Ozymandias* being a notable
exception. But nearly everywhere we
glimpse, through the veil of existence,
beautiful or painful, the loveliness that
accompanies a transcendental vision. B.D.
see also Foreign Influences on English
Poetry, Imagery, *and* Science and Poetry

Shirley, James (1596–1666), prolific auth-
or of fresh lyrics and often tired plays, was
a Londoner, and died as a result of the
Great Fire. His plays include *The Cardinall*,
The Gamester and *The Maid's Revenge*.
Narcissus (published as *Eccho* in 1618) is a
long, graceful narrative poem.   D.H.

Sidney, Sir Philip (1554–86), was born at
Penshurst in Kent; his father was Sir
Henry Sidney, three times Lord-Deputy of
Ireland, and his mother was formerly Lady
Mary Dudley, daughter of the Duke of
Northumberland, and sister of the Earl of
Leicester. He was educated at Shrewsbury
School and at Christ Church, Oxford, but
left without taking a degree. Between
1572 and 1575 he travelled widely on the
Continent; he witnessed the St Bartholo-
mew's Eve massacre in Paris, and was
painted by Veronese at Padua. In 1576 a
possible marriage was suggested between
Sidney and Penelope Devereux, daughter
of the Earl of Essex, probably the 'Stella' of
Sidney's sonnet sequence *Astrophel and
Stella*, but she married Lord Rich in 1581,
and in 1583 Sidney himself married
Frances Walsingham. Sidney became a
Member of Parliament in 1581, and about
this time was requesting Queen Elizabeth
for office. He appears to have felt himself
poorly treated by the Queen, and was
certainly short of money. In 1583 he was
knighted, and was appointed Governor of
Flushing in 1585. Sidney was fatally wounded in a skirmish at Zutphen in the
Netherlands in October 1586. His death
was regarded as a national tragedy;
Professor C. S. Lewis has described him as
'that rare thing, the aristocrat in whom the
aristocratic ideal is really embodied'.

As a poet, Sidney was associated with a
group including Edmund **Spenser**, Gabriel
Harvey, and Sir Edward **Dyer**, who aimed
to improve the standard of English poetry,
and to profit by the example of the best
poets of France and Italy. His major poetic
work was *Asrophel and Stella*, but Sidney is
also noteworthy as the author of *Arcadia*, a
long prose romance, and an extremely
important critical essay, the *Defence of
Poesy*.

Evidence of Sidney's apprenticeship as a
poet can be seen in his metrical versions of
the Psalms; these are of small poetic value,
but reveal the tireless interest in technical
experiment that characterised Sidney and
Spenser and other young poets of the time.
Thus, apart from two versions in *terza
rima*, each of the forty-three psalms is

rendered in a different stanza form. As an extreme example, the version of Psalm XV has only one rhyme throughout. The interest in experiment is equally apparent in the many poems that Sidney introduced into his *Arcadia* (written about 1580, though none of Sidney's works can be dated with any certainty; nor were any published during his lifetime). English poetry in the earlier sixteenth century had been marked by a lack of metrical range and variety, and it was the desire of Sidney and his friends to overcome this state of affairs that led to their concern with technical experiment. One attempted solution was to introduce into English the metres of classical poetry; Sidney has a number of examples, though the attempt was not successful. However, some of the other devices that Sidney used in the *Arcadia* poems were to prove more fruitful, such as his use of Italian rhyme-schemes. These poems show a great variety of forms: couplets, six-line stanzas, rhyme royal, sonnets, canzone, sestinas, *terza rima*. For the most part the *Arcadia* poems, which employ highly conventional pastoral material, must be regarded as poetic exercises. Nevertheless, a few of them do possess genuine poetic merit, such as the double sestina, 'Strephon and Klaius', where the lamentations of the shepherds become successively graver and more heavily repeated for ten stanzas until the climax when the cause of their grief is revealed. Another accomplished poem from *Arcadia* is the sonnet 'My true love hath my heart':

My true love hath my heart and I have
        his,
By just exchange one for the other
        given:
I hold his dear, and mine he cannot miss,
There never was a better bargain driven.
His heart in me keeps me and him in
        one;

My heart in him his thought and senses
        guides:
He loves my heart, for once it was his
        own;
I cherish his because in me it bides.
His heart his wound received from my
        sight;
My heart was wounded with his
        wounded heart;
For as from me on him his hurt did
        light,
So still methought in me his hurt did
        smart.
Both, equal hurt, in this change sought
        our bliss,
My true love hath my heart and I have
        his.

This poem, with its monosyllabic simplicity of diction and tightly logical structure, returning with a circular motion to its starting point, shows some of the fruit of Sidney's experimental labours.

Their final flowering, however, is only apparent in the mature achievement of *Astrophel and Stella*, which was the first Elizabethan sonnet sequence. 'Astrophel' and 'Stella' are usually identified with Sidney and Penelope Devereux, and it can be assumed that the sequence was written soon after Penelope's marriage to Lord Rich; this is suggested by a number of puns on the word 'rich'. Nevertheless, the work is not simply an autobiographical record, though romantically inclined critics have tried to see it as such. Astrophel and Stella are symbolic figures who transcend their origins in actual persons, and the work is not a story, but a sustained meditation, substantially about love, but also touching on public events, literary criticism, court gossip, and so on. Much of the material of the sequence, the imagery and verbal devices, is conventional matter from the Petrarchan tradition, but Sidney infuses life into it as he employs it for his personal ends. Physical events—the beloved's sign of favour or disfavour, a kiss, her absence, the hero's participation in a tournament—are mentioned at intervals and provide themes for meditation. The earlier poems deal with the conflict between reason and desire, while the later ones are more passionate, but the conflict constantly recurs.

Astrophel and Stella is characterised throughout by a blend of wit and sensibility, of intellectual brilliance and temperamental ardour. An apparent stress on personal feeling will be accompanied by a high degree of rhetorical organisation; this is evident in Sonnet V, where the central insoluble conflict is given intense dramatic expression:

It is most true that eyes are form'd to
serve
The inward light, and that the heavenly
part
Ought to be King, from whose rules
who do swerve,
Rebels to nature, strive for their own
smart.
It is most true, what we call Cupid's
dart
An image is, which for ourselves we
carve,
And, fools, adore in temple of our
heart,
Till that good god make church and
churchman starve.
True, that true beauty virtue is indeed,
Whereof this beauty can be but a shade,
Which elements with mortal mixture
breed.
True that on earth we are but pilgrims
made,
And should in soul up to our country
move:
True, and yet true that I must Stella
love.

The interest and value of *Astrophel and Stella* lies in the innumerable ways in which Sidney is able to vary his theme and

278

present the central situation. Its unique combination of convention and acute moral and psychological realism gives it a permanent validity. In Charles Lamb's words, Sidney's sonnets are 'not rich in words only . . . they are full, material, and circumstantiated'.   B.B.

Silkin, Jon (1930–), was educated at Wycliffe College and Dulwich; he was Gregory Fellow of Poetry, Leeds University, 1958–60. He is a visionary, compassionate poet, often, as he has said, using animals as a symbol for man's pain. His works include *The Peaceable Kingdom* (1954), *The Two Freedoms* (1958), and *The Re-ordering of the Stones* (1961).   B.D.

Simpson, Louis (1923–), was born in Jamaica, and received U.S. citizenship when he fought in the U.S. glider infantry during the war. He is the best American poet of the Second World War, and, perhaps because of his origins, has written most perceptively about America. He won the Pulitzer Prize in 1964 and, in 1966, published *Selected Poems*.   D.H.

Sitwell, Dame Edith (1887–1964), the daughter of Sir George Sitwell, Bt., and Lady Ida Sitwell, and the sister of Sir Osbert and Sacheverell **Sitwell,** both famous poets and prose writers. She and her two brothers were a formidable triumvirate who shocked the literary establishment in the early nineteen-twenties with their readings of their own poetry, their support of modern art and with their attacks on Georgian poets and current reviewers.

From the first, Edith Sitwell's poems showed her intense preoccupation with new rhythms and imagery, and the effects produced by building up patterns of consonants and vowels. Dame Edith was extremely preoccupied by the use of technical devices, as the Introduction to her *Collected Poems* (1957) shows. In this interesting Introduction Dame Edith asserts that the poems in *Façade* 'are abstract poems—that is, they are patterns in sound. They are, too, in many cases, virtuoso exercises in technique of an extreme difficulty, in the same sense as that in which certain studies by Liszt are studies in transcendental technique in music.'

But if these early poems belong very definitely to the period of cubism in painting and music under the influence of jazz (William Walton's music for *Façade*, and the ballet done after it, are a completely successful example of harmony among the arts), they also produce an atmosphere and feeling which are extremely personal. It is a strange world in which imagery, already strange but certainly justified as simile, is as it were pushed over the edge of the real into artifice. A characteristic example of this procedure is the lines from *Madame Mouse Trots*:

> Hoarse as a dog's bark
> The heavy leaves are furled.

Occasionally the peoms are revealing of the child-like, sensitive, perhaps intensely lonely poet, easily moved to intense pity by suffering, but also very capable of being moved (for example in *Gold Coast Customs*) to satiric indignation. Some poems, of which *Colonel Fantock* is outstanding, seem autobiographical and have an unexpected directness and simplicity.

During the Second World War Dame Edith rose to what many readers consider the height of her achievement. She wrote a series of poems which seem to point the anguish of the Air Raids from 1940 onwards to the agony of the Crucifixion. In *Still Falls the Rain* the artificiality and the rather brittle quality of some of the earlier poems has been replaced by a prophetic nobility of utterance:

> Still falls the Rain—
> Dark as the world of man, black as our
> loss—
> Blind as the nineteen hundred and forty
> nails
> Upon the Cross.

The tension of that time made suitable the great exaltation of this generalised utterance of reconciliation of man's inhumanity to man within the highest suffering. The only alternative to it which might have produced as impressive a result would have been concentration on the 'minute particulars' of suffering.

In her later poems the lines have tended to get longer, the emotions more generalised, the imagery crystalline, the tone more prophetic. There is a lack of detailed observation and a certain monotony. Nevertheless, in the *Elegy for Dylan Thomas* there is some close appraisal of the dead poet's achievement, and his personality is truly evoked. She was created D.B.E. in 1954.   s.s.

Sitwell, Sacheverell (1897–), is the younger brother of Edith and Osbert Sitwell. He was educated at Eton and attended Balliol College, Oxford, briefly before settling in London as a writer. His fifteen volumes of poems include long narratives on mythical or heroic subjects, dramatic monologues, and highly coloured, fanciful lyrics descriptive of scenes familiar and exotic. Their form is usually a flexible unrhymed line of varying length built up into elaborate periods. The lines below are taken from *Pastoral*, an evocation of life in pre-Hellenic Crete:

> They netted the dark water, and it
> sparked with fire,
> It shone, it gleamed, it glittered, it had
> scales of silver,

It was a shining dagger, hurled and
                                    quivering
That flashed in the meshes . . .

                                    D.L.H.

Skelton, John (*c.* 1460–1529), probably came from Cumberland or Yorkshire, though his origins are uncertain. He had achieved a scholar's reputation before 1490, when he was already laureate of Oxford; by 1493 he was laureate also of Cambridge and probably of Louvain. In 1490 Caxton praised his knowledge of Latin authors and his skill as a translator. By 1494 he was attached to the court of Henry VII and by 1498 had taken holy orders. By 1499 he was serving as tutor to Prince Henry, when Erasmus honoured him as 'the one light and ornament of British letters'. Appointed Rector of Diss in 1502, he retired about 1504 to Norfolk, where he developed his distinctive talents as a poet in the vernacular. He was appointed King's Orator in 1512 and returned to court. In his vast morality play *Magnificence* (1516) and in several lampoons written in 1521–2 he attacked Wolsey's character, policies, and influence so recklessly that he was probably forced for a time to make use of his right of sanctuary as a resident in Westminster. A reconciliation seems to have followed shortly afterwards, and several of his later poems are dedicated to Wolsey.

Though many of Skelton's works have not survived, it is clear enough that he was no humanist. At the very moment of the Renaissance and the Reformation he spoke, often in medieval terms, from a medieval standpoint—but with almost inexhaustible energy, wit, and independence. His first significant poems are the love lyrics written about 1490; there are also some fine religious poems of about 1498, the year when he became a priest. About 1498–9 he wrote *The Bouge of Court*, a satirical

dream allegory in rhyme royal which evokes vividly the fear-ridden existence of the courtier dependent on favour. Within the next five or six years he developed his unique verse-form, the Skeltonic: a short, jolting, vigorous line usually employing three stresses but varying from two to five or more, usually rhymed in couplets but often sustaining the rhyme for three or four lines or more. Latin is used freely with English, sometimes in hexameters broken at the caesura, sometimes in rhyming jingles. A lively example comes from perhaps the earliest surviving poem unquestionably in Skeltonics, *A Devout Trental for Old John Clarke* (1506–8):

> *Jam jacet hic* stark dead,
> Never a tooth in his head.
> Adieu, Jayberd, adieu,
> In faith, deacon thou crew!
> *Fratres, orate*
> For this knavate,
> By the holy rood,
> Did never man good:
> I pray you all,
> And pray shall,
> At this trental
> On knees to fall
> To the football;
> With, 'Fill the black bowl
> For Jayberd's soul.'
>   *Bibite multum:*
> *Ecce sepultum*
> *Sub pede stultum,*
> *Asinum, et mulum!*
> The devil kiss his *culum!*
> With, 'Hey, ho, rumbelow!'
> *Rumpopulorum,*
> *Per omnia secula seculorum!*

Philip Sparrow (before 1509), in which a young girl mourns the death of her pet sparrow and curses Gib the cat that killed him, owes its undoubted success to the perfect appropriateness of the metre to speaker and subject.

It was so pretty a fool,
It would sit on a stool,
And learned after my school
For to keep his cut,[1]
With 'Philip, keep your cut!'
  It had a velvet cap,
And would sit upon my lap
And seek after small worms
And sometimes white bread crumbs;
And many times and oft
Between my brestes soft
It would lie and rest;
It was propre and prest.[2]

The metre seems peculiarly effective also in expressing something of the desperate squalor and turmoil of the tavern episodes which make up *The Tunning of Elinor Rumming* (probably 1522). Skeltonics succeed again brilliantly in the two bitter attacks on Wolsey, *Colin Clout* (1522) and *Why Come Ye Not to Court?* (1522), where Skelton suggests the angry voice of the English people everywhere denouncing ignorance and corruption in church and state.

  And if you stand in doubt
  Who brought this rhyme about,
  My name is Colin Clout.
  I purpose to shake out
  All my cunning bag
  Like a clerkly hag;
  For though my rhyme be ragged,
  Tattered and jagged,
  Rudely rain-beaten,
  Rusty and moth-eaten,
  If ye take well therewith
  It hath in it some pith.

          *

  Thus, I Colin Clout,
  As I go about,
  And wand'ring as I walk,
  I hear the people talk.

Speak, Parrot (1512), in rhyme royal, is another attack on Wolsey, obscure but

often powerful, in which Parrot may, as H. L. R. Edwards has suggested, stand for the poetic faculty. Skelton wrote *The Garland of Laurel* (1523) chiefly to honour himself as a poet; the best parts of the poem are perhaps the interpolated compliments to several ladies.

Within the last thirty years poets and scholars have forced a revaluation of Skelton that is still in progress. What once seemed merely unplanned, endless or intolerable to the ear now charms and even instructs poets, including **Graves** and **Auden**, by its vernacular vigour, humour, and wisdom, its extreme unpretentiousness, its personal tone, its evident sincerity. The claim is made that Skelton's 'rhythmic spontaneity and flexibility is in fact a high technical achievement', and not only in the Skeltonics (John Holloway)—or even that he shows 'an exquisite mastery in the subtle modulations of rhythm and metre' (Peter Green). C. S. Lewis, however, finds Skelton's metre often chaotic, doubts that his 'artlessness' was deliberate, and concludes that 'the result is good only when he is either playful or violently abusive, when the shaping power which we ordinarily demand of a poet is admittedly on holiday or may be supposed to be suspended by rage . . .' Though scepticism may persist as to Skelton's metrical achievement, the earlier legend of the buffoon who applied his wits, as Puttenham said, 'to scurrilities and other ridiculous matters' is no longer credible. It must be conceded that behind the mocking, abusive, helter-skelter manner, Skelton was a deeply responsible man. The evidence lies not only in his defence of justice and religious truth, as he saw them, against a most dangerous adversary; it lies also in the close knowledge and compassion observable in his portraits of men and women of his time.   D.L.H.

---

[1] *cut* – distance, reserve
[2] *propre and prest* – handsome and alert.

see also Satire

Skelton, Robin (1925–), was educated at Pocklington School, and after serving in India during the war, at Leeds University. In *Patmos and Other Poems* (1955) and *Third Day Lucky* (1958) he displayed considerable mastery of form; in *Begging the Dialect* (1960) he showed himself able to break away from accepted diction. B.D.

Smart, Christopher (1722–71), was born in Kent but attended Durham Grammar School and Pembroke Hall, Cambridge, of which he was elected Fellow in 1745. He left Cambridge about 1749 to become the partner of a London bookseller and to make a name in Grub Street. He succeeded, but only by incessant and exhausting labours. From 1756 to 1763, though confined for madness, he wrote or planned his poems, including *A Song to David* (1763), his paraphrase of the Psalms, and his *Hymns for Children* (1765). Impoverished during his later years, he was aided by friends, but died a debtor in the King's Bench Prison.

In his own time his claim to a permanent place among the poets was thought to rest on his 'Miltonic' poems on 'attributes of the Supreme Being', often praised and several times reprinted in the eighteenth century. His miscellaneous magazine verse and prose were regarded then, as they are now, as of minor interest. *A Song to David* was neglected as the work of a disordered mind and omitted from the collection of his work published by his nephew in 1791. His *Psalms* and *Hymns* were not reprinted; his excellent verse translation of Horace (1767) was a commercial failure. In the nineteenth century the myth gained currency that Smart in a burst of insane exaltation had written one great poem and then relapsed into dullness. Not until 1949 was enough of his mature work re-published to demonstrate that *A Song to David* is no isolated miracle. At least the *Psalms*

and the *Hymns* form a not unworthy setting for it. In 1939 appeared an annotated edition of fragments, newly discovered, of a long religious poem by Smart, composed during his madness but never before published; in 1954 the manuscript was re-edited so as to clarify the structure of the poem and re-published as *Jubilate Agno*. This poem is not only a rich source of biographical information; it is remarkable also for its antiphonal design, its curious learning, and its Old Testament splendour.

Robert Brittain, one of Smart's recent editors, asserts that 'In scope, in intensity, in the precision and grace of their versification, his collection of religious poems is worthy to be set beside the work of our finest devotional lyricists'. His theme is not sin or self-doubt, but the praise of God, in which all living things unite in gratitude for life. His peculiar idiom reflects his interest in Hebrew poetry, Horace, and contemporary music. In its design, *A Song to David* is a complex, even an intricate poem, the work of a vigorous intellect in perfect order. Though its effect is cumulative, some sense of its powerful directness may be got from a quotation:

> Strong is the lion—like a coal
> His eyeball—like a bastion's mole
>   His chest against the foes:
> Strong the gier-eagle on his sail,
> Strong against tide, th' enormous whale
>   Emerges, as he goes.
> But stronger still, in earth and air,
> And in the sea, the man of pray'r;
>   And far beneath the tide;
> And in the seat to faith assign'd,
> Where ask is have, where seek is find,
>   Where knock is open wide.
>
> D.L.H.

Snodgrass, William Dewitt (1926–), was born in Wilkinsburg, Pennsylvania. He attended Geneva College and the State

University of Iowa. In 1958 he was the Hudson Review Fellow in Poetry. He now lives in Detroit, Michigan, where he teaches at Wayne State University.

Snodgrass's first book, *Heart's Needle*, won the $1,000 award in poetry of the Ingram Merrill foundation in 1959, and the Pulitzer Prize in 1960. His verse is mainly autobiographical and subjective, but the personal tone is offset by a skilful control of technique and frequent touches of humour.

After Experience was published in 1968.

A.S.

Society and the Poet. Poetry is a special part of language, and like all language, it is a shared system of symbols. By means of such symbols, it is possible for the individual to enlarge his experience and to have access to the generalised experience of the symbol-sharing group. In this sense, poetry depends for its production on society as well as on the individual. On the other hand, the poetic experience is one which we commonly perceive as private to our own subjectivity. With every such experience we enlarge our individuality, our privacy, at the expense of the public and the social. Whatever its origins, to some extent poetry has come to be a compensatory freedom to make amends for the constraints exerted on us by physical and social reality.

It is in this sense that poetry has quite correctly been called unrealistic and anti-social, while, conversely, poetry which aims at being realistically and socially acceptable runs the risk of becoming unpoetic. On the other hand, poetry and the other arts do not consist of pure, wish-fulfilling, *id*-releasing fantasy. The fantasy elements in them have been elaborated and worked over, according to the canons of a particular form or style, so as to make them into a system of symbols through which the poet or artist, as individual, can establish rapport with a group of other individuals for whom he aims to provide stimulus, pleasure, enlightenment, heightened perceptions, quickened emotions— all the ingredients that add up to a response at the aesthetic level.

The individuals with whom the poet is communicating make up a society of their own, small or large, with its own standards and conventions, whether they aim at strictness or freedom. These same individuals, and also the poet, are in addition members of societies in the ordinary sense, with all the ordinary obligations and facilities. They may, and usually do, feel that this ordinary sociality needs to be recognised in the constructed world of the poem. As a rule they also feel, more or less articulately, that the sort of recognition they give to the social reality should be given on their own terms and not on those of other people claiming to represent social obligation. They claim in fact the rights of a special social group, with language, aims and membership conventions of its own, existing, like any other voluntary group, within the at least partly involuntary framework of organised societies. All that is needed to join the special group concerned is the wish to do so, and access to the appropriate system of symbols.

The preceding paragraphs indicate the logic of the poet's position in a general way. It remains to look at some problems which have become pressing over the past few hundred years and which are especially acute at the present time. Revolutionary changes in society have modified the poet's role and made him more self-conscious. The greater the change, the greater the perplexities in which he finds himself. The positions taken up by poets towards social forces vary widely. At the extremes the poet (*a*) has nothing to do with society, and (*b*) places himself unreservedly at the service of social forces. But these positions break down in practice.

From the European poet's point of view, the French Revolution was a kind of secular apocalypse, in which a vision was glimpsed of a reconstructed society and a reconstructed humanity. From that time forward there were among poets those who aligned themselves not with society in its conventional existing shape but with social forces which they believed were going to transform it. It was next to impossible for any poet in England, France, Germany, Italy or elsewhere in Europe to escape feeling the pull of this romantic radicalsim, whatever solution, compromise or reaction was the outcome for him personally; whether he ended up on the left or on the right, or in a deliberately non-political position, whether his ideal society was in the past or in the future. Whatever his political sympathies, his temperamental tendencies were individualist and the part of his programme that he felt most strongly about was the liberation of the individual from social restraint. Of course, as one kind of 'tyranny' was overthrown, other kinds began to appear, especially the tyranny of 'bourgeois morality'. The anti-aesthetic implications of this morality were soon apparent to the poet, who often enough during the nineteenth century waged war against it, not only in his writing but in his life, and especially his private life. Conventional political sentiments, even liberal or socialist ones, were not in the same key as the spirit of poetic rebellion. 'Cunning and morality', wrote **Blake**, 'are not poetry but philosophy; the poet is independent and wicked; the philosopher is dependent and good. Poetry is to excuse vice and show its reason and necessary purgation'.

At a sublime level, the poetic rebellion is expressed in Milton's sympathy for the Fallen Angels, in Blake's antinomian prophecies, in Baudelaire's *Les Fleurs du Mal* and Rimbaud's *Une Saison en Enfer*. At the level of surface behaviour, it has often been expressed, especially since the French Revolution, by a certain wildness of demeanour, by eccentricities of hair, beard and dress, by a 'bohemian' way of life and so on. Traits which originated from personal idiosyncrasy have tended to become stylised as the insignia of anti-philistine, anti-bourgeois intransigence. Poets and artists may in this way be among those who start fashions, and these may ultimately spread to much wider groups and indeed may themselves end up as the conventional norm.

From the French Revolution to the Russian Revolution, poetic and political rebellion, though distinct, often overlapped. Each had its deviant minorities and each opposed itself to the existing values and institutions of society. The evolution of the class of 'intellectuals' took place during this period, a class of growing numbers and importance, including many other besides the poetic and political elements. The Russian Revolution, more thorough-going than the French, had the appearance of offering to poetic and intellectual rebels the possibility of a society which they could whole-heartedly support, abandoning their historical role of social opposition. However, Soviet society turned out to be more constraining than most of them had hoped; some reacted away from it, others went through psychological crises, and yet others did their best to conform.

Since the Second World War, the development in many countries of welfare socialism, the liquidation of colonialism, and the beginning of a slight 'thaw' in the Soviet system, have caused intellectuals, including poets, to reassess their position yet again. A posture of total revolt against society has seemed unreasonable, since the whole gigantic structure appeared to have built into it what might be called 'a sincere desire for amendment'. At the same time, it has been hard for most intellectuals, and especially poets, to feel intense enthusiasm for any of the variants of industrial society that exist, or even for any that seem likely to emerge in the short or middle term. Perhaps the attitude of poets to society nowadays is best characterised as one, not of identification, and not of rejection, but of watchful reserve. It is however more likely than it has ever been that the poet will, in a self-conscious sense, have 'an attitude to society'.

Such an attitude is an intellectual construction, and therefore not the most poetic part of the poet. Nor is it the same as the direct realisation of their fellow human beings achieved by, for example, **Chaucer** or Villon. For the poetic imagination *can* be turned on to people living their irreducibly complex lives and can convey a sense of their essential quality. This is a power that some poets share with some painters, novelists, dramatists, actors, and others whose art has a realistic tendency. It is not, in fact, very common to poets. It is at the same time one of the most precious gifts of the arts, since it can give back life where machinery, industry, rationality, organisation and drabness are tending to take it away. It is important therefore to distinguish the poetic imagination trained on a social canvas from what C. Wright Mills has called 'the sociological imagination'. In the social sciences it is possible, and desirable, to be imaginative, but the first need is to be systematic and rational. In poetry the first need is to be poetic and this need overrides every other.

A poet may gain something from sociology, from psychology, from politics, from philosophy, and so on. They are all part of the world he lives in. But they will not, in themselves, make his poetry more poetic. His excitement at finding them, at living in them, even at reacting against them, may be translated into the energy of his poetic output, if he is lucky, but he cannot count on their having this happy effect, and for many the consciousness of society and its unresolved problems weighs heavily, to the point of reducing them to silence.   C.M.

South African Poetry in English. The Republic of South Africa is a multi-lingual country with two official languages: Afrikaans (home language of one-and-a-half million Whites and half a million Coloureds), and English (one million). Africans (ten million) are divided into two main language groups, the Nguni (Zulu, Xhosa, etc.) and Suto (Tswana, Pedi, Southern, etc.). No one has pre-eminence, and although English is likely to become the *lingua franca*, it will be long before it will be the natural medium of expression for all groups. All African languages and growing literatures, for a variety of reasons, have a sectional flavour, are symbols of cultural and political rivalry. Most English and Afrikaans writers use their mother tongues, but, as in other parts of the continent, many Africans prefer English to their own language. This important phenomenon is treated under the entry on **English Poetry in Africa**. This article is confined to the poetry of the English section in South Africa and Rhodesia.

Thomas Pringle (1789–1834), a settler of 1820, writes on topics which will pre-occupy poets for a century: the indigenous peoples (*The Bechuana Boy*, *The Kaffir*); wild life (*The Lion Hunt*, *The Giraffe*) and the landscape treated as a symbol of freedom or the benevolent Nature of **Wordsworth** (Pringle, 1828: 'Man is distant, but God is near'; Gibbon, 1903: 'God is greater in the open, Little man is

285

less.'). Pringle demonstrates two major problems: firstly, how to use a language from one hemisphere to master experience in another. For instance, vocabulary; one is forced to borrow bizarre-sounding names, which may attract attention without evoking any picture of emotion. What will his European readers make of *quagga*? Pringle resorts to footnotes. A century has to pass before familiarity makes possible such images as **Campbell's** 'livid mambas of deceit'.

Secondly, how to transpose a European response to an apparently similar African stimulus. Thus he attempts a twilight poem (*Evening Rambles*) on the untamed frontier, but, with typical honesty, acknowledges his difficulties:

Now along the meadow damp
The enamoured firefly lights his lamp,
Link-boy he of woodland green
To light fair Avon's Elfin queen;
Here, I ween, more wont to shine
To light the thievish porcupine
Plundering my melon bed

None of his many imitators was prepared to face these problems. Not until the turn of the century do we find poets, such as Gouldsbury (Rhodesia) and Gibbon, practising a technique, which owed much to **Kipling**, capable of capturing both the primordial landscape and the encroaching industrial revolution. Here is Kipling (*Bridge Guard, Karroo*):

We hear the Hottentot herders
    As the sheep click past to the fold—
And the click of the restless girders
    As the steel contracts in the cold—

Voices of jackals calling
    And, loud in the hush between,
A morsel of dry earth falling
    From the flanks of the scarred ravine.

And the solemn firmament marches,
    And the hosts of heaven rise
Framed through the iron arches,
    Banded and barred by the ties.

More interesting is Kingsley Fairbridge (1885–1924) whose long and intimate knowledge of the bush, and of African custom and speech, keep his verse clear of a certain tiresome, extraneous picturesqueness. He is not taking snapshots of local colour. In F. C. Slater (1876–1954) the refreshing influence of native rhetoric and imagery is apparent:

Beautiful was Wetu as a blue shadow
That rests on the grey rocks
About a sunbaked hilltop:
His coat was black and shiny
As an isipingo berry;
Her horns were as sharp as the horns of
                        the new moon
That tosses aloft the evening star . . .
The black cloud that brought us white
                                rain
Has vanished—the sky is empty:
Our kraal is desolate:
Our calabashes are dry:
And we weep.

                    Lament for a Dead Cow

The Rhodesian poet, A. S. Cripps (1896–1952), failed to achieve this freshness. Arcadian pastoral trappings sit uncomfortably on tribesmen. He is at his best when outraged or prophetic.

The turning point in South African poetry comes in the nineteen-twenties, with the first poems of Roy Campbell and William **Plomer**. Both poets saw and accepted the primitive violence of Africa, which, centuries before, Camões had personified in Adamastor (*Lusiads*, Canto V). Both react against the sentiments and conventions which had obscured this fact:

Far be the bookish muses . . .
My task demands a virgin muse to string

A lyre of savage thunder as I sing
Campbell: *The Flaming Terrapin*

That was the Africa we knew
Where, wandering alone,
We saw, heraldic in the heat
A scorpion on a stone
Plomer: *The Scorpion*

They debunked the false values of white society, and the poetic clichés these gave rise to (Campbell: *Veld Eclogue*; Plomer: *The Pioneers*). Satire made its spirited début. They tackled the problems of technique differently, both with professional awareness and skill. Campbell, when faced with an awkward African creature, makes a virtue of necessity, exploiting its bizarre quality, for example, in *Dreaming Spires*, or by linking it with something long in poetic orbit, e.g. 'Those gaunt muezzins of the mountain tops / The grey baboons'. Plomer cultivates the neutral style:

Naked or gaudy, all agog the crowd
Buzzes and glistens in the sun; the sight
Dazzles the retina; we remark the smell,
The drums beginning, and the vibrant
light.

Now the edge of the jungle rustles. In a
hush
The crowd parts. Nothing happens.
Then
The dancers totter adroitly out on stilts,
Weirdly advancing, twice as high as
men.
The Devil Dancers

The pioneering, romantic phase ends with their vigour and intelligence, their contempt of the amateurish, their awareness of Europe and the great tradition of its verse. The veld is no longer a haunt for untrammelled souls, but fenced, overstocked, eroded—a symbol of a spiritual waste land. Above all, the African is no longer a picturesque stranger. Campbell sees

The curbed ferocity of beaten tribes,
The sullen dignity of their defeat.

Most White South Africans, however, continued to enjoy their colonial afternoon. The absence of an alert and interested audience or market started the exodus of talent: Campbell, Plomer, Van der Post, followed by F. T. Prince, Charles Madge, R. N. Currey and others, all of whom have written well, if briefly, out of their African experience. In most one can detect certain preoccupations natural to people born into a composite, unhappy society: an acute awareness of cultural incompatibilities, a fondness for travellers or explorers among strange lands and peoples, seeking a synthesis, and finding no more, perhaps, than themselves (Plomer: *A Traveller's Tale*; R. N. Currey: *Man's Roots*; Madge: *Poem by Stages*). The preoccupation persists in the next generation (Lerner: *The Desert Travellers*; Delius: *The Explorers* and *The Pilgrims*; David Wright: *A Voyage to Africa*; Guy Butler: *Livingstone Crosses Africa*).

Most of the post-war generation served in Europe and the Mediterranean, and all experience the tug of Europe. Few have surrendered to it. They are less impatient with their own country, and, for the first time, have started examining their own, not only others', behaviour with a critical eye.

These million English are a vague
communion
Indifferent to leadership or goal,
Their most accomplished children leave
the Union,
Search other countries for their cause or
soul.
Delius: *The Last Division*

287

I have not found myself on Europe's
maps,
A world of things, deep things I know
endure,
But not the context for my one perhaps.
Butler: *Home Thoughts*

This might be significant: a previous generation chose to be exiled from Africa rather than Europe: this has chosen differently. Commitment guarantees nothing, of course, and the poetry of a society in a state of acute and continuous crisis tends to be cluttered with journalistic circumstance and accident; but at least it makes preoccupation with mere technique impossible.

To ascribe the present weaknesses of South African Poetry—its lack of lyricism, its too insistent conscience, its metrical conventionality—to the cabinning, cribbing and confining effects of a society bound in by saucy doubts and fears is to beg the question; for good poetry is never merely a symptom, it is an agent. A change in society would change Africa's poetry. A major poet would change both.

Nevertheless the genuine struggle with words continues; and the work of N. H. Brettell (Rhodesia), Ruth Miller, Margaret Allonby, Roy Macnab, and, most notably, Sydney Clouts, shows the impulse to look in one's heart, and write.

During the middle sixties several new voices appeared—C. A. Fair, Elias Pater, Perseus Adams, Charl J. F. Cilliers, and Douglas Livingstone—to mention a few (see **Bibliography**). Interest in poetry has grown, stimulated by little magazines such as the quarterly *New Coin* (1966), *Ophir* (1967) and *Chirimo* (Rhodesia) (1968). *Contrast*, *Classic* (devoted mainly to writing by Africans) and *New Nation* are hospitable to verse. It is safe to say that the body of good South African poetry has grown appreciably, during the past decade.

Some of the best new poetry is intensely interior; and some poets so intense that any utterance which does not come *de profundis* is rejected as unpoetic. Equally frequent are poems which record moments of sensual contact with the usually alienated outer world. The charges of metrical conventionality, lack of lyricism, and a too insistent conscience no longer hold. There is plenty of experiment, and a growth in confidence and in competence.   G.B.

Southey, Robert (1774-1843), friend of **Wordsworth**, brother-in-law of **Coleridge,** and Poet Laureate for his last thirty years, was famous as the author of epics such as *Joan of Arc* (1796) and *Madoc* (1805) and of humane iconoclastic verses such as *The Battle of Blenheim* (1798). Although he shared Coleridge's theories about nature and Pantisocracy, his poetic use of nature was highly abstract. As he wrote in *The Holy Tree* (1798),

I love to view these things with curious
eyes,
And moralize:

Except for the occasional verse his position demanded, Southey later turned to biography (*Life of Nelson*, 1813; *Sir Thomas More*, 1829), history, and children's stories. Contemporary critics find him more interesting as illustrative of changing social and political doctrines than as poet.   J.G.

Southwell, Robert (1561-95), an English Jesuit, was hanged for treason. His most celebrated lyric is *The Burning Babe* which was much admired by Ben **Jonson**. A religious and mystical poet, his work often exhibits the influence of the popular Euphuistic style.   D.H.

Spender, Stephen (1909-   ), is an English poet who has acted as co-editor of this

Encyclopedia. He attended Oxford University, and as a poet has been associated with other Oxford poets of the nineteen-thirties: W. H. **Auden**, C. **Day Lewis**, and Louis **MacNeice**. Though these poets all showed some interest in Marxism and psycho-analysis, their similarities were in reality slight and their differences have increased with the years. Spender's poems have always been highly lyrical and personal; he has been concerned to express his emotions, whether his subject matter was subjective or objective.

His earlier books of verse were collected (and some of the poems revised) in his *Collected Poems 1928–1953* (1954). He has published an autobiography, *World Within World* (1951), considerable literary criticism including *The Destructive Element* (1935) and *The Making of a Poem* (1955), and fiction, of which the most recent example is *Engaged in Writing* (1958). He assisted Cyril Connolly in editing *Horizon*, and he co-edited *Encounter* from its foundation in 1953 till 1965.   D.H.
see also Translation

Spenser, Edmund (?1552–99), was born in London, of middle-class parents, and attended Merchant Taylors' School. In 1569 the schoolboy had translations from Du Bellay, in unrhymed verse, in the first English 'emblem book', *The Theatre for Worldlings*. In the same year he went up to Pembroke College, Cambridge (M.A., 1576), where the ambitious don, Gabriel Harvey, became his friend and mentor. In 1578–9 Spenser was secretary to John Young, Bishop of Rochester (ex-Master of Pembroke). In 1579–80, in London in the service of the great Earl of Leicester, he became acquainted with court life and with Sir Philip **Sidney** (the Earl's nephew) and the minor poet, Sir Edward **Dyer**. In 1579 Spenser dedicated to Sidney his first

book, the pastoral *Shepheardes Calendar*, which is commonly regarded as marking the inauguration of the golden age of Elizabethan poetry: he also married Machabyas Chyld, apparently his pastoral 'Rosalind'. For some unknown reason Spenser quitted Leicester's service in 1580 and went to Ireland as secretary to Lord Grey, the Lord Deputy. Except for three visits to England he remained in Ireland for the rest of his life, until 1593 as a busy official. For an Elizabethan, Ireland meant something like exile, but Spenser evidently came to enjoy his life there and to assimilate Irish lore. From 1588–9 he owned the estate of Kilcolman near Cork. In 1589, together with Sir Walter **Ralegh**, who had been his neighbour in Ireland, Spenser returned to England for the publication (and dedication to Elizabeth) of the first three books of *The Faerie Queene* (1590). The voyage, the world of the court, and much else were described in the pastoral, *Colin Clouts Come Home Againe* (dated 1591; published 1595). Spenser's first wife had died by 1591 and on 11 June, 1954, he married Elizabeth Boyle, a relative of Richard Boyle, later Earl of Cork; his bride was celebrated in the sonnets, *Amoretti*, and in the *Epithalamion* (published together in 1595). Books IV–VI of *The Faerie Queene* appeared in 1596. In 1598 Tyrone's rebellion and the 'spoiling' of Kilcolman and other estates brought the distressed poet, with despatches, to London. He died in January, 1599, within a few weeks of his arrival. He was buried in Westminster Abbey.

Of all the major English poets Spenser is nowadays probably the least appreciated and least read, but readers who neglect him miss a great deal. His historical claims upon us, while not his chief claims, are immense. His work embodies, far more completely than that of any other writer of his age, the modes and ideas of Renaissance poetry, classical and medieval. Continental and modern, religious and secular. He wrote in, and in some cases naturalised in England, the principal genres: pastoral, satire, elegy, reflective hymn or ode, wedding ode, sonnet and heroic poem. More than anyone since **Chaucer**, Spenser made English an integral and important part of European poetry (and admiring contemporaries could rejoice that England no longer lagged behind Italy and France). Yet his roots were thoroughly English. His first book was typical: in domesticating exotic pastoral conventions he used the title and pattern of an old farmers' almanac, took Chaucer as his tutelary genius, revived old and dialectal words, and, observing 'decorum', wrote ecclesiastical satires in a rough popular measure and style. And if Spenser was the confluence of preceding traditions, in thought and feeling as well as in technique, he was also the fountainhead of most later English poetry, from **Drayton** and others through **Milton** and on through **Shelley**, **Keats** and **Tennyson**.

But Spenser's immediate, intrinsic claims, which chiefly concern the reader of poetry, are also immense and unique. Some minor poems have varied attractions—the *April* eclogue in praise of Elizabeth, the charming fantasy, *Muiopotmos*, the general and topical satire, *Mother Hubberds Tale* (which the authorities suppressed), the Platonic-Christian *Four Hymns*, and above all the *Epithalamion* and the less personal and more dream-like *Prothalamion*. The *Epithalamion*, a microcosm of Spenser's sensibility and art, is surely the most beautiful love poem in the language. A processional pageant, in the form of an Italian *canzone*, it blends Irish actuality with classic myth, and ardent passion with a religious reverence that reaches its climax in a daring and triumphant echo of Psalm xxiv:

Open the temple gates unto my love,
Open them wide that she may enter in . . .

From the bride to the 'trouts and pikes' of the river Mulla, everything is transfigured by the poet-lover's ecstatic vision; for the wedding of Edmund Spenser, widower, and Elizabeth Boyle, spinster, is part of the creative process of a divine order. Yet there are sinister hints of the perils that encompass frail humanity.

The Faerie Queene was to have twelve books, each with its own protagonist and story illustrative of one of the 'Aristotelian' private virtues (and possibly twelve more on the public virtues!). The six completed ones dealt with Holiness, Temperance, Chastity, Friendship, Justice, and Courtesy —a spectrum very much of the Renaissance. Indeed the poem was avowedly a conduct book. Spenser was at one with his age in his didactic view of the heroic poets from Homer to Tasso; they all held up examples to be emulated or abhorred. In spite of modern prejudice, didactic seriousness—as in Dante—is by no means incompatible with great art, and Spenser's imagination and craftsmanship created a vision of life that embraces everything from religious and Platonic idealism to brutal realism.

The first book elaborates the story of St George and the dragon in the pattern of a morality play. The Knight of Holiness exemplifies Spenser's re-creation of romance motifs: 'the unpromising hero' becomes an untried Christian. He falls into sin and is rescued by Prince Arthur (divine grace), but, overcome by guilt, he yields to Despair and is saved from suicide by Una (true faith); after religious discipline he is able to accomplish his quest and kill the dragon (Satan). Bald summary, however, tells nothing of the pictorially or dramatically vivid and poignant scenes, the symbolic details, the suggestive phrases, the expressive rhythms. If the dragon is a fairy-tale dragon, its conqueror merges with Christ through a veiled allusion (I, xii, 13) in the manner of T. S. **Eliot**'s *The Waste Land*.

After the first book there is not much allegory in the strict sense of narrative with a sustained double meaning. For the most part Spenser, like a novelist, puts characters in situations that evoke moral reactions. Unlike a novelist but like other Christian humanists, he saw the natural reason as an ally of faith. So Guyon, the Knight of Temperance, fortified by Platonic and Aristotelian ethics, resists the offers of Mammon (II, vii) and the allurements of the Bower of Bliss, though his senses can be 'softly tickeled': the siren-song (II, xii, 32) is an oblique reflection of the poet's own craving for rest:

O thou faire sonne of gentle Faery,
That art in mighty armes mosts
                              magnifide
Above all knights, that ever battell
                              tride,
O turne thy rudder hither-ward a
                              while:
Here may thy storme-bet vessell safely
                              ride;
This is the Port of rest from troublous
                              toyle,
The worlds sweet In, from paine and
                       wearisome turmoyle.

In this whole canto Spenser's method of agglomeration produces an effect that economy could hardly achieve; the air of the Bower becomes heavy with corruption. Here all natural, wholesome things are perverted by artifice and evil; ivy is made of gold and 'Low his lascivious armes adown did creepe' (II, xii, 61). In the book of Chastity, among examples of courtly love and lust shines the radiant Britomart, the protagonist, whose goal is not a nunnery but marriage. She is a real woman, a cousin of **Shakespeare**'s heroines; she figures in eerie scenes (III, xi–xii) but, in

combat with her destined husband, she is red-faced and sweating (IV, vi, 19).

Romantic criticism has treated *The Faerie Queene* as a romantic tapestry, its author as an escapist dreamer and music-maker; and modern readers, assuming that Spenser is a nursery poet, have brushed past him on their way to **Donne**. Informed modern criticism has repudiated both attitudes; it sees both the 'sage and serious poet' Milton saw and a sophisticated and subtle artist. Though the poem has its flat or merely fairy-tale passages, it is not only more comprehensive but more difficult than the poetry of Donne. Interpretative difficulties in Donne exist chiefly in particulars and can be removed by editorial notes, but those in Spenser are of another and more complex kind. The main reason is not the elaboration or intricacy of narrative but the predominantly mythic quality of Spenser's imagination (a quality displayed on a small scale in the wedding odes). One rough proof is his creation of a world, a world that lives—if only on sufferance— even in the minds of people who have not read him. Everyone has some sense of that timeless, boundless fairyland of plains and dark forests and castles, of knights riding and fighting, golden-haired ladies captive or fleeing, heroes and villains, lovers and lechers, magicians and giants and monsters, a richly imaginary garden with very real and ugly toads in it; and this ever-shifting phantasmagoria is mirrored in the flowing stream of Spenserian stanzas. It is a world of flux and evil, in which only beauty and goodness and divine grace are fixed lights. In the most earthy or unearthly incidents, from the grim-grotesque *fabliau* of Malbecco (III, ix–x) to Sir Calidore's vision of the Graces (VI, x), a mythic aura invests substantial reality; the 'hundred naked maidens lilly white', who are 'dauncing in delight', are 'thumping' the ground. Sometimes we have a full-fledged philoso-

phic myth, as in the Garden of Adonis (III, vi) or the *Cantos of Mutability*. In the wholesome air of the Garden, so different from that of the Bower of Bliss, the idea of perpetual change is presented in terms first of abstract myth, then of the love of Venus (matter) and Adonis (form); and, though Time is the enemy of love and stability, change is accepted as a process of endless renewal. But in the fragment *Mutability*—a brief cross-section of Spenser's art, both grand and homely—the Christian poet, while clinging to orthodox faith in evolution under Providence, cries out against his own overwhelming vision of cruel and meaningless flux and prays for the peace of heaven. It was his last utterance.   D.B.
see also Criticism and Poetry, Foreign Influences on English Poetry, *and* Metaphor

Stein, Gertrude (1874–1946), was an American expatriate who lived at the centre of the Parisian art world from 1902 to 1946. Anderson and Hemingway were influenced by her simple and repetitive style. Her poems—and her prose, which was often difficult to distinguish from her poems—began to return to fashion in America in the late nineteen-fifties, when a number of young poets paid public homage to her.   D.H.
see also American Poetry

Stephens, James (1882–1950), Irish-born author of the prose fantasy, *The Crock of Gold*, was described by James Joyce as the only man capable of finishing *Finnegan's Wake* if he died before completing it. He was a poet of folklore and the supernatural.   D.H.

Stevens, Wallace (1879–1955), was born in Reading, Pennsylvania, and died in Hartford, Connecticut, in the same year that he was awarded the Pulitzer Prize in

Poetry for his *Collected Poems*. Stevens developed late as a poet, his first, most famous volume, *Harmonium*, not appearing until 1923, when he was already forty-four years of age. Educated at Harvard, he later studied law in New York, where he was admitted to the Bar in 1904. He joined the legal staff of the Hartford Accident and Indemnity Company in 1916, becoming vice-president in 1934—a position which he held until his death. The contrast between Stevens' roles in life has been remarked to the point of tedium, but Stevens himself, wandering between two worlds, seems to have reconciled them, or at least to have balanced them, without difficulty. However intensely he may have lived on the vice-presidential side of life, his dedication to poetry was complete. After *Harmonium*, thirteen years elapsed before the appearance of his second volume, *Ideas of Order* (1936). Then followed *The Man with the Blue Guitar* (1937); *Parts of a World* (1942); *Transport to Summer* (1947); *The Auroras of Autumn* (1950); a book of essays, *The Necessary Angel* (1951); and finally *The Collected Poems* in 1955. A large volume of poems, plays, and prose called *Opus Posthumous* was published in 1957.

There are few poets of the twentieth century who have written in English whose work on first acquaintance seems to present greater difficulties. But a resolute reading of *The Collected Poems* will illuminate the obscurities much sooner than an uninitiated reader could hope to achieve with **Yeats** or **Eliot**. Despite the exotic rhetoric, the wantonly fantastic images, the apparent freedom from the restraints of logic, one soon discovers that the central meaning of Stevens' poems is deeply traditional, and that his metaphors and symbols are consistently controlled by it.

His central meaning and single subject is the pre-eminence of the creative imagination, which includes the nature of poetry and of the symbol. When Stevens' obsessive concern with this subject matter is understood, much of the difficulty of his work disappears. We always know what to look for, or at any rate what we shall find. For example, he is describing the central act of perception, of imagination, in a poem from *Parts of a World* called *The Glass of Water*:

> Here in the center stands the glass. Light
> Is the lion that comes down to drink.
> >   There
> And in that state, the glass is a pool.
> Ruddy are his eyes and ruddy are his
> >   claws
> When light comes down to wet his
> >   frothy jaws
> And in the water winding weeds move
> >   round.

These symbols enact a whole complicated aesthetic. We are not told what it is; we fall through it as through an imaginative trap-door placed with diabolic cleverness. The symbols force us into an imaginative act, and by introspection into our own mind's working we find that Stevens has compelled his meaning on us. That meaning resembles **Emerson**'s aesthetic in *Nature*. Man knows nature (in which language and art are included) as a mediating symbol between him and a higher reality. The symbol becomes a transparency through which the mind moves out towards growth and intuitive knowledge. Matter and mind are tranquilly reconciled with each other in the medium of symbolic language. But while Stevens is concerned with the epistemological aspects of symbolism in a way that is characteristic of the twentieth century, his belief in the imagination is essentially romantic, and not really different from the faith of **Wordsworth** and **Coleridge**.

In *The Idea of Order at Key West*, Stevens relates how, walking at evening beside the sea, he heard a woman singing above the sound of the waves. Her song interpreted, and so made anew, the world in which she moved:

> It was her voice that made
> The sky acutest at its vanishing.
> She measured to the hour its solitude.
> She was the single artificer of the world
> In which she sang. And when she sang,
> >   the sea,
> Whatever self it had, became the self
> That was her song, for she was the
> >   maker. Then we,
> As we beheld her striding there alone,
> Knew that there never was a world for
> >   her
> Except the one she sang and, singing,
> >   made.

This is of course Coleridgean. The situation and meaning are also similar to Wordsworth's *The Solitary Reaper*, although Stevens follows the implications further and more explicitly than Wordsworth does in that particular poem. The imagination is a creative and plastic power that shapes and orders the universe of experience from moment to moment, and it is only in terms of the imagination that the poet lives. It is the only entry into life; indeed, it *is* life.

For Stevens the imagination must transcend the world of material reality, but the relation between them must not be severed. The imagination may transfigure the world of things, but it also takes its direction, perhaps its very life, from that lower world. They interact reciprocally, and that is why Stevens' poems are often filled with lists of itemised particulars as in a characteristic poem from *Parts of a World*, *The Man on the Dump*:

> The dump is full
> Of images. Days pass like papers from a
> >   press.

The bouquets come here in the paper.
So the sun
And so the moon, both come, and the
janitor's poems
Of every day, the wrapper on the can of
pears,
The cat in the paper bag, the corset, the
box
From Esthonia: the tiger chest, for tea.

In the quotidian world of his dulled responses, sitting on the dump of familiar and conventional images and beliefs inherited from his society, the man without imagination resembles one of Eliot's Hollow Men. But a visitation of imaginative vision, symbolised as so often in Stevens by the moon, can redeem even the dump:

That's the moment when the moon
creeps up
To the bubbling of bassoons. That's the
time
One looks at the elephant-colorings of
tires.
Everything is shed; and the moon comes
up as the moon
(All its images are in the dump) and you
see
As a man (not like an image of a man),
You see the moon rise in the empty sky.

Imaginative transfiguration extends here even to the old automobile tyres. But if the imagination begins with 'the janitor's poems', it always moves through them to something beyond. One recalls how Wordsworth in *Tintern Abbey* moved through the stages of intensified sensuous perception towards a deeper and more sublime insight into reality—a reality which was ultimately grounded in 'the mind of man'. Similarly, the man on the dump— the man surrounded by dead images and systems—through his imagination first animates the cold corpse of the world, and then transcends it. In this moment of transcendence the reality the poet encounters is the reality of his own mind, his essential self, which he now truly recognises for the first time:

One sits and beats an old tin can, lard
pail.
One beats and beats for that which one
believes.
That's what one wants to get near.
Could it after all
Be merely oneself, as superior as the ear
To a crow's voice?

The implications of this ultimate discovery of the self through imagination are revealed more clearly in the closing lines of *Final Soliloquy of the Interior Paramour*:

We say God and the imagination are
one . . .
How high that highest candle lights the
dark.

Out of this same light, out of the central
mind,
We make a dwelling in the evening air,
In which being there together is enough.

Ultimately, the self which is discovered through the imagination is not unrelated to the cosmic 'I' of **Whitman**'s *Song of Myself*, and it carries suggestions, especially in the last work, which take on a colouring distinctly mystical, as in the beautiful late poem, *Prologues to What is Possible*. Stevens' faith that God and the imagination are one is not essentially different from Blake's faith that 'God becomes as we are, that we may be as he is', and 'that the Poetic Genius is the true Man, and that the body or outward form of Man is derived from the Poetic Genius'. The meaning of Stevens' poems is not, after all, very different from Blake's in *The Divine Image*.

Perhaps the single work that defines his position most fully is the sequence of thirty poems, *Notes toward a Supreme Fiction*, published in *Transport to Summer*. The supreme fiction is of course the supreme truth—the imagination's insight to which the poem is servant and vehicle:

The poem refreshes life so that we share,
For a moment, the first idea . . . It
                                satisfies
Belief in an immaculate beginning
And sends us, winged by an unconscious
                                will,
To an immaculate end.

Stevens' tireless concentration on this theme can become monotonous when reading his poems in quantity. At his best, it has produced several poems among the finest in American literature, notably the early poem, *Sunday Morning*. But too often in the later and middle volumes it is content to remain an idea embellished with strange and costly rhetoric. Nevertheless, with the exception of Eliot, and possibly of **Pound** and **Frost**, Stevens is the most important American poet of the first half of this century. There are no other serious competitors. During the forties, the earlier image of Stevens as a dandy in verse gave place to the image of the philosophical poet, and critical articles proliferated during the fifties in American quarterlies and reviews. But while Stevens' major stature in American literature is beyond dispute, a deeper perspective of time is needed in his case for an exacting evaluation. His poems have a heady quality to which contemporary criticism is not yet quite inured.

M.B.

see also American Poetry

Suckling, Sir John (1609–42), was the son of James I's Secretary of State and comptroller of the King's household. After Cambridge, Gray's Inn, the Grand Tour, and knighthood, he became a professional soldier under Gustavus Adolphus of Sweden in the Thirty Years' War. He was later court poet and attendant to Charles I before becoming one of the first cavaliers to fight against the rebels in the English Civil War. Suckling wrote several plays, such as *Aglaura* (1638), but is most famous for his graceful, witty songs and love lyrics. The well-known song that begins 'Why so pale and wan fond Lover?' ends:

Quit, quit for shame, this will not move,
    this cannot take her;
If of her self she will not love,
    nothing can make her:
    the divel take her.

Although Suckling's easy, competent verse is seldom profound, he often displays sharp observation of paradoxical human qualities, as in *Loving and Beloved*:

For Kings and Lovers are alike in this
That their chief art in reigne dissembling
                                is. . . .
So we false fire with art sometime
                                discover,
And the true fire with the same art do
                                cover.

Often, his poems begin with a sharp dramatic opening:

Out upon it, I have lov'd
Three whole days together.

Beneath all the sharpness and courtly sophistication, Suckling retains a spirited earthiness. One of his best poems is *A Ballade Upon a Wedding*, praising the charm and gaiety of a country wedding, and he ends another poem in which he has asked for the ghost of a significant and spiritual love with the flat statement 'Give me the woman here'.

J.G.

Surrey, Henry Howard, Earl of (?1517–47), is said to have made good translations from Italian and Spanish poems when still a boy. He apparently had a stormy career at court, alternately placed in charge of important military expeditions and imprisoned for treason or intrigue. His poems, though circulated widely in manuscript, were not published until *Tottel's Miscellany* appeared in 1557. Surrey knew Italian well; he used his studies to regularise the metrics of English verse and develop smooth and elegant lyrics. His poetry has an appealing neatness, as in the concluding couplet of the sonnet, *Description of Spring*:

> And thus I see among these pleasant
> things
> Each care decays, and yet my sorrow
> springs!

Most contemporary critics do not find Surrey's poetry as forceful or as unique as that of Thomas **Wyatt**, his predecessor. He did, however, incorporate a measured balance into the line of the English sonnet, as in the conclusion of his famous poem on the death of his friend Clere:

> Ah! Clere! if love had booted, care, or
> cost,
> Heaven had not won, nor earth so timely
> lost.

Not all of his verse is elegant and precisely measured, for he did write an invective against the city of London when he was once arrested for breaking windows. But the invective is less characteristic than the grace of the concluding stanza of *A Praise of his Love*:

> Sith Nature thus gave her the praise,
> To be the chiefest work she wrought;
> In faith, methinks! some better ways
> On your behalf might well be sought,
> Than to compare, as ye have done,
> To match the candle with the sun.

J.G.

see also Foreign Influences on English Poetry

Swift, Jonathan (1667–1745), was born in Dublin. He was the greatest journalist and pamphleteer of his age, and one of the greatest satirists of any age. Among his best-known prose works are *A Tale of a Tub* (1704), *The Drapier's Letters* (1724), and *Gulliver's Travels* (1726). His famous irony is seen at its most brilliant in *An Argument against Abolishing Christianity* (1711), and the scathing *Modest Proposal* (1729). Swift's political writings were at first on behalf of the Whigs, but in 1710 he went over to the Tories, supporting their foreign policy in *The Conduct of the Allies*. He had taken holy orders in 1694, and in 1699 was given a prebend at St Patrick's, Dublin, and the living of Laracor. The illness (probably Ménière's disease) from which he suffered all his life became more pronounced in 1738, and for a time before his death he was insane. He was buried in St Patrick's with his own epitaph '. . . ubi saeva indignatio ulterius cor lacerare nequit' inscribed on his tomb.

The enigma of Swift's personality, and especially of his relations with 'Stella' (Esther Johnson) and 'Vanessa' (Esther Vanhomrigh), has attracted biographers, and his savage misanthropy has been much discussed. But Swift was found a gay companion by his close friends; and he won the love of **Gay, Pope,** and Arbuthnot. He detested 'that animal called man', but was able to love individual men and women. He was beloved by the Irish poor, whose cause he had defended against their exploiters. Though he derided conventional pietism he was a most conscientious dean and pastor.

Swift began his career as a poet in 1692, with 'pindaric odes' one of which, according to Dr **Johnson**, called forth **Dryden's** remark 'Cousin Swift, you will never be a poet'. After these ambitious but unsuccessful efforts Swift confined himself to light verse. Among his best pieces are the autobiographical *Cadenus and Vanessa*, the burlesque *Petition of Mrs Frances Harris*, *Verses on his own Death*, *On Poetry*, *a Rhapsody*, and, illustrating Swift's scatological preoccupations, *A Beautiful Young Nymph Going to Bed* and *Strephon and Chloe*.

Leslie Stephen said that whether or not Swift should be called a poet is 'a matter of terminology'. Certainly Swift never adopts the traditional great-poet manner; most of his verse is familiar and occasional; and even when it most obviously comes from the ironic author of 'Gulliver' we are less often reminded of his celebrated 'savage indignation' than of his favourite motto, Vive la bagatelle'. But he also had a didactic purpose, which he describes in the *Verses on his own Death*; here he indicates his own characteristic manner:

> His vein, ironically grave,
> Expos'd the fool, and lash'd the knave

and, while allowing that 'the Dean had too much satire in his vein', defends his satire:

> . . . Malice never was his aim;
> He lash'd the vice, but spar'd the name.
> No individual could resent,
> Where thousands equally were meant;
> His satire points at no defect.
> But what all mortals may correct;
> For he abhorr'd that senseless tribe
> Who call it humour when they gibe:
> He spar'd a hump, or crooked nose,
> Whose owners set not up for beaux.

The poem must be read as a whole for the appreciation of its typical Swiftian blend of gaiety, forcefulness, and astringency.

Very few authors have been equally great in prose and verse, and Swift is no exception. None of his poems has the richness and variety of satiric method shown, for instance, in the best parts of *A Tale of a Tub*. The lack of evocativeness in his phrasing, the limited movement of the octosyallabics in which he usually writes, the monotonous repetitiveness of his themes of decorum and common-sense, are serious limitations in Swift's poetry; while the dry manner in which he handles the gross subject-matter of poems like the *Beautiful Nymph* can even be found repellent. But within his self-imposed limits Swift can often score by his pungent reminder of uncomfortable truths. w.w.r.

Swinburne, Algernon Charles (1837–1909), poet, dramatist and critic, whose father was an admiral, and whose mother was the daughter of the Earl of Ashburnham, was born in London. But most of his early years were spent by the sea, either in Northumberland, where his grandfather had an estate, or in the Isle of Wight, where his father lived. His passion for the sea inspired many of his poems. He was educated at Eton and at Oxford, where he obtained many distinctions, especially in the classics. Brought up in a High Anglican, Oxford Movement atmosphere, he rebelled against this, became atheistical, and all his life detested kings and priests. He left Oxford in 1860 without obtaining a degree, travelled a little in Italy, where he met **Landor,** and a few years later was established in London, where he entered into Pre-Raphaelite circles. In 1880 he went to live in Putney with Theodore Watts-Dunton, as a haven, it would seem, from a wild life he was in danger of being engulfed in. His career is not marked by any other events.

On leaving Oxford he published two plays, *The Queen Mother* and *Rosamond*, which passed unnoticed. His plays, though they contain splendid poetry, will not be treated here. The magnificent *Atalanta in*

Calydon (1865) is, to be sure, a play, on the Greek model, but it is as a poem that it is chiefly regarded. It was at once popular, being full of Swinburne's vehemence, and the overwhelming onrush of his extremely skilful verse in a great variety of metres, the great choruses alone offering examples that are unforgettable, since they remain in the ear. There are such variations as:

Before the beginning of years
   There came to the making of man
Time, with a gift of tears;
   Grief, with a glass that ran.

Or:

Who hath given man speech? or who
                hath set therein
A thorn for peril and a snare for sin?

Or again:

O that I now, I too were
By deep wells and water-floods . . .

the dialogue also exemplifying many daring verse forms.

This work caused some scandal on account of its atheistical sentiments, as did, on account also of its erotic flavour, the at once hailed *Poems and Ballads* of 1866, including the famous lines in the *Hymn to Proserpine*:

Thou has conquered, O pale Galilean;
   the world has grown grey from thy
                breath;
We have drunken of things Lethean, and
       fed on the fulness of death.

Though this volume remains popular, with such poems as *Les Noyades* and *The Leper*, *Rococo* and *Dolores* are no longer the favourites that they were. It would seem that *Songs Before Sunrise* (1871), with its atmosphere of republican libertarianism,

is more in the taste of today, though some would stake out a claim for the *Tristram of Lyonesse* volume of 1882. But everywhere, in the two later *Poems and Ballads* (1878 and 1889) there are characteristic magnificences, as there are in the plays, especially *Erectheus* (1876).

Swinburne will always have a place in the canon by virtue of his overflowing energy, which, controlled by consummate craftsmanship, forces the reader to share the emotion of the poem. He had a passion for words, for rhythms, for the pungency of forms, but it is an all-too-common mistake to suppose that he allowed words to carry him away. They are always carefully chosen to convey the ethos of any particular piece, for Swinburne was an artist as well as a craftsman. He was not an original thinker, deriving many of his ideas from Mazzini, Baudelaire, and others; but he made such ideas his own with the passion that produces poetry. Some of his poems, such as *Hertha* in *Songs Before Sunrise*, are considerable intellectual feats.

He had, moreover, a deep feeling for certain aspects of nature, especially the sea, the actuality of which grew into a symbol, invested with a kind of mysticism. But if poems such as *A Forsaken Garden* (*Poems and Ballads II*) represent the best-known Swinburne, the actual ballads, the commemorative verses, and his pieces dealing with the universal emotions, including the love of children, all have an unmistakable Swinburnian tang. Yet perhaps one of the most memorable is the *Dies Irae*, composed when he was at Oxford, but printed for the first time in the *Posthumous Poems*, published in 1917. He may have been guilty of poetic excesses, but he was also capable of parodying these.   B.D.
see also Translation

Symbolism. In the widest meaning of the word, all poetry has always been symbolist, since the indirect expression of a feeling, a fact, or an idea, by means of real objects which have analogous resemblance to them, seems to be part of the very nature of language. Nevertheless, this type of knowledge was regarded with suspicion and neglected in the Western world, after Descartes and in the Age of Enlightenment, as a result of the influence of rationalist philosophies which were being developed at that time. Subsequently it was necessary for certain poets to rediscover the specific powers of analogy and symbol. And today it has become customary to reserve the term 'symbolist poetry' for the most important moment of this revival.

From what epoch exactly is it possible to date the beginnings of symbolist poetry? It must be emphasised that it had already been prepared by those who, notably in the eighteenth century, had retained the sense of a transcendent reality and of the participation of all existing things within a profound unity. These were the occultists, the alchemists, the Cabalists, and mystics such as Swedenborg (1688–1772) or Saint-Martin (1743–83), inheritors of the thought deriving from antiquity of Hermes Trismegistus and of the doctrine of Universal Correspondences which is exposed in the *Corpus Hermeticum*. But this form of speculation only became enduringly associated with poetic creativity in the first half of the nineteenth century, at the time when Romanticism had succeeded in imposing a new form of subjectivism on poetry. For a long time a decadent classicism, perhaps in France more than elsewhere, had put poets under the obligation of imitating only the most general aspects of nature; this could only result in making poetry an empty corpse, and in diverting the really effective forces of creativity from the poem. The Romantic movement reintroduced the connection between consciousness and existence, and presented the

problem of inventing suitable forms to realise this connection. Novalis (1772–1801), **Shelley** and **Blake** maintained the values of visionary experiences and the magical qualities of poetic intuition against the pretensions of science. **Coleridge**, in his *Biographia Literaria* (XIII), defines the imagination as 'a repetition in the finite mind of the eternal act of creation in the infinite I AM', and this is followed soon after by **Emerson**, representing the preoccupations of American transcendentalism, writing in his essay *The Poet* (1844) that nature is 'a temple whose walls are covered with emblems' and that 'the distinctions which we make in events . . . disappear when nature is used as a symbol'. Finally, **Poe** provided the bodily form for this intuitive theory in his poems, *The Raven* and *Ulalume*, which require mention because they have exerted a profound influence on the destinies of symbolism in Europe.

It was in fact under the star of Poe that symbolist poetry, properly called, developed. It would have appeared without him, no doubt, in an intellectual milieu excited by theosophy and illuminism, to which Balzac (with *Seraphita*, 1835, and *Louis Lambert*, 1839) had used his immense prestige to introduce Swedenborg, and where Eliphas Lévi was about to publish in 1856 the *Dogme et rituel de haute magie*. Shelley and Coleridge might, it is true, have been preferable as the initiators of the practice of symbolism in poetry. Nevertheless it would be wrong to think that Poe was nothing but an accident in the genesis of symbolism, for he gave to French poets that of which they were most in need, a new myth of the function of the poet. What caused the Romantic movement to be checked was that it had become enclosed within a communing which of itself provided no solution for the unhappy condition of man, which it was only capable of describing. And poets who together with Théophile Gautier (1811–72; *Émaux et Camées*, 1852), and later with the Parnassiens, tried to base their existence upon the cult of an unshakeable concept of the beautiful, in doing so cut themselves off from the true reality of life. Poe delineated an issue. For by his tragic destiny he appeared as the *poète maudit*, heir to the spirit of Romantic agony, accuser of false values. Moreover in teaching that the function of poetry was 'to reach the Beauty above', and above all in suggesting that this beauty appertains to the life, the divine nature, the mysterious essence of that which exists, he provided this struggle with a goal, and this agony with an explanation. If the poet is rejected, betrayed, destroyed by society, this is because he is the supreme 'savant', as Rimbaud will later assert, called upon by his feeling for analogy to the formidable task, denied to other men, of deciphering the absolute. This task of transforming reality, and the idea that it condemns the poet to solitude and suffering, are the essential traits of symbolist poetry in France.

They are to be found in the *Bénédiction* (1857) of Baudelaire as well as the *Tombeau d'Edgar Poe* (1877) of Mallarmé, and in a more familiar style in the *Poètes Maudits* (1884) of Verlaine, in which the misfortunes of several contemporary poets are described. And it was under the star of the same heroism that Mallarmé set out to justify the most singular and contestable aspect of Edgar Allan Poe, his concern with techniques which permit him to make, and even fabricate, poems. Language having the specific function of evoking transcendent reality, undoubtedly the poet is obliged to watch over the machinery of techniques which facilitate the evocation. Yet there is, as between Mallarmé and Poe, a misconception which covers over two tendencies in symbolist poetry which are

in fact basically different: for Poe is interested above all else—as Paul Valéry was later—in the psychology of the creation of the poem, whilst Mallarmé, giving 'a purer significance to the words of the tribe', sought to investigate the means for the metaphysical approach to the sacred.

However this may be, what in English is called symbolism (in France the use of this term is in general limited to a little group of poets who in 1886 explicitly adopted the name) is defined by the double concern with a metaphysical 'beyondness', an ideal, an 'azure'—and with a language which for the first time in history is conscious of its specific difference, accepting the necessity of inventing new ways of using words and of thus becoming separated, at least provisionally, from that which other men understand by it. The symbolist poet inaugurates, or, rather, confirms the divorce of the poet from society in modern technological civilisation.

Charles Baudelaire (1821–67) was the first to formulate in the sonnet entitled *Correspondances*, published in the first edition of *Les Fleurs du Mal* in 1857, the theory of universal analogy and of the universe as a 'forest of symbols':

La Nature est un temple où de vivants piliers
Laissent sortir parfois de confuses paroles;
L'homme y passe à travers des forêts de symboles
Qui l'observant avec des regards familiers.

Comme de longs échos qui de loin se confondent
Dans une ténébreuse et profonde unité
Vastes comme la nuit et comme la clarté,
Les parfums, les couleurs et les sons se répondent.

In *Les Phares*, as in several other poems, he has put this intuition into effect. But it would be dangerous to label him a symbolist for this reason, even in the widest application of the term, because if he has the sense of the spiritual world, of heaven, he has also that of the earth, and of the reality of the individual, of concrete existence of which he affirms the irreplaceable worth. The most penetrating aspect of his art is in his direct interest, without any kind of meditation, and not symbolic, in such or such a thing. His sense of sin would lead him to condemn in advance the 'angelism' of Stéphane Mallarmé (1842–98) who was most purely the poet of symbolism. From his first poems (*Les Fenêtres*, 1866) we see him rejecting all idea of narration or discourse. He demands of words that they should become separate from perceptible reality as music does, and at the same time he utilises the strictly musical resources of language. The word, for Mallarmé, is that which permits the evocation of the idea. His poetry is not symbolic in the sense in which a myth can expose some truth which is hidden in the depths of reality, but in that the word appears to him as the direct sign of the archetype of something. He leads us back into the intelligible garden which is evoked in the *Prose pour des Esseintes* (1885). But where is this garden? Does it have a real existence somewhere and is it the function of poetry only to evoke it, or must it go as far as trying to create it by the very act of its own existence? That Mallarmé himself dreamed of this is proved by his project for a *Livre absolu*, which would have provided the Orphic explanation of the earth, idea disembarrassed of matter and chance in the bosom of which it becomes lost—and also indeed of his last poem, *Un coup de dès jamais n'abolira le hazard* (1897), in which he confesses the failure of the undertaking.

The most radical symbolist idea was certainly this dream of re-creating spiritual reality, of which Coleridge, for instance, had only imagined the knowledge or the evocation by means of the symbol. By comparison with the great project of Mallarmé, other contemporary works remain secondary or partly foreign to the idea even of symbolism. Mallarmé's contemporary and friend, Paul Verlaine (1844–96), had an impressionistic sensibility marvellously attuned to evocative music, provided that what was evoked had as object only the human, even the 'too human'. He is much closer to the allusions to real objects which characterise the painting of a Monet or a Whistler than to the symbolist art of a Redon. Arthur Rimbaud (1854–91), ten years the junior of Verlaine and Mallarmé, in many other respects one of the great poets of the century, only made negative use of symbolism, requiring of analogy that it should establish arbitrary and harsh relations between existing realities (*Les Voyelles*, 1871) which can tear the veil away from appearances and thus reveal to us, not an ideal world at which his thought does not stop, but the profound 'fire' of reality. Jules Laforgue (1860–87) evokes the ideal only with the aim of treating reality ironically. And from 1885 to 1900 the poets who expressly take the name of symbolists—Jean Moréas, who in 1886 published the manifesto of the movement, Gustave Kahn, Maurice Maeterlinck, etc. —have above all else the quality of establishing that atmosphere of reverie which is affected and fabricated, against which, later on, Valéry and Claudel were to react.

Truth to tell, after 1890, symbolism, more and more closely associated with the spirit of 'decadence', became, from Ibsen to d'Annunzio, a European reality. And it was indeed in the Anglo-Saxon countries, once again, that its most recent forms of expression are to be found. It was not until 1899 that Arthur **Symons** published his *Symbolist Movement in Literature*, in which the chapter devoted to Jules Laforgue was to become one of the source influences of the work of T. S. **Eliot**. But already **Yeats**, to whom the book was dedicated, had established his position as the greatest symbolist poet of a generation destined to diverge from the position taken up by Mallarmé. The setback to French symbolism had been due essentially to the 'angelism' already mentioned, that contempt for earthly things which results in man separating himself from life and also from other men. In this manner the symbol itself becomes degraded, since true analogy only exists in a confrontation with life and action. Thence the mind comes to hesitate, without really being able to choose, between the bloodless reality dreamed by a Gustave Moreau, and the precious or perverse 'realism' of Des Esseintes (the famous hero of Huysmans) or the drawings of Beardsley. These are the two aspects of the secret 'Byzantium' in which the decadent poet tries to maintain his nostalgia

for escape. Yeats also affirmed an eternal Byzantium, but in the moment of doing so it became animated with his love for carnal realities. This means that the transition from the sensuous to the supersensuous is a drama which he lived, which becomes even the content of the work in his poetry; instead of evoking simply, or of trying to make exist, the 'Beauty above', his poetry expresses the direction which seeks to attain to this; Yeats achieves the transition between a symbolist poetry of essence, and a modern poetry of existence experienced in the very act of writing.

Y.B. *trans* S.S.

Symons, Arthur (1865–1945), was an English poet and critic, one of the most talented poets of the eighteen-nineties, and certainly an enormous influence on subsequent poetry. **Eliot** has acknowledged that it was Symons' *The Symbolist Movement in Literature* (1899) which introduced him to the poems of Jules Laforgue.

D.H.

see also Translation

T

Tate, Allen (1899–). American poet, critic and novelist; a member of the American Academy of Arts and Letters, a past incumbent of the Chair of Poetry in the Library of Congress, a former editor of *The Sewanee Review* and, from 1966, Regents' Professor of English in the University of Minnesota.

A Southerner, and an Agrarian, Tate was born in Kentucky and educated at

Vanderbilt University, Tennessee, where, together with John Crowe **Ransom** and Robert Penn **Warren**, he belonged to the celebrated **Fugitive Group**. Several critics, including Leonard Casper, have suggested that this group was fugitive, primarily, from a sterile provincialism, a debased 'legend', from the 'soft silken reminiscent life of the Old South'. Even so, Tate's dominant preoccupations have largely centred upon the Civil War and its consequences. In an early prose work, *Stonewall Jackson* (1928), he ascribes to the antebellum South that 'historical sense of obligation' without which 'society becomes a chaos of self-interest'. Powerful variants of this theme are presented in the novel *The Fathers* (1938; new edition 1960), in a number of essays and in *Ode to the Confederate Dead*. Tate has suggested that this poem's structure is 'the objective frame for the tension between the two themes, "active faith" which has decayed, and the "fragmentary cosmos" which surrounds us'.

As a craftsman, Tate may be said to utter the 'formal pledge' of art in the presence of 'aimless power'; the poems are parables of this persistent opposition. R. P. Blackmur, adapting Dr **Johnson**'s criticism of the Metaphysicals, has said that 'in Tate's poetry we have images of violence yoked together by form', and Cleanth Brooks has called Tate 'witty in the seventeenth-century sense'. Yvor **Winters** concedes less; he finds in this poetry, at times, 'merely a crudely stereotyped assertion of violent emotion'. Despite the prevalence of dry pun and paradox, Tate sometimes excites a *frisson* reminiscent of **Poe**:

There are wolves in the next room
           waiting
With heads bent low, thrust out,
           breathing
At nothing in the dark: between them
           and me
A white door patched with light from
           the hall
Where it seems never (so still is the
           house)
A man has walked from the front door
           to the stair.
         The Wolves
         G.H.

see also American Poetry *and* Isabella Gardner.

Taylor, Edward (*c.* 1642–1729), the son of a yeoman farmer, William Taylor of Sketchley, Leicestershire, England, emigrated to the Massachusetts Bay Colony in 1668. Unable to subscribe to the Act of Uniformity of 1662, he found at Harvard College, from which he graduated in 1671, an atmosphere congenial to his nonconformist Calvinistic religious principles. He served as Congregational minister in the frontier town of Westfield, Massachusetts, until his retirement in 1725.

Taylor left in manuscript over eight hundred quarto pages of poetry of which the most important works are *Preparatory Meditations* and *Gods Determinations*. The *Meditations*, dated from 1682 to 1725, and written at roughly two-monthly intervals as spiritual exercises in preparation for the administering of the Lord's Supper, are Calvinistic in doctrine, and in style they are often reminiscent of George **Herbert**'s poetry and, to a lesser extent, the poetry of **Donne**, **Crashaw** and **Vaughan**. Taylor's juxtaposition of colloquial and erudite diction, homely and cosmic similies and metaphors, and frequent echoes of Herbert's *The Temple* mark him as the last of the Metaphysical school of poets. The *Meditations* express an intense spiritual experience motivated by the conviction that as one of God's predestined elect he was the special recipient of divine grace. The topics most frequently chosen by Taylor are the sweetness of God's grace, the degradation of natural man by original sin, the humility and weakness of man before the glory of an absolutely powerful, sovereign God, the delights of heaven, the horrors of hell, the mystery of the incarnation, atonement and redemption, and the hope of salvation. He is most convincing on the subject of natural man and the hope for grace:

I'm but a Flesh and Blood bag: Oh! do
         thou

Sill, Plate, Ridge, Rib, and Rafter me
with Grace.
Meditation No. 30, First Series

The experience of divine grace is often expressed by the figure of a liquid running from the source, the Godhead, to the thirsty recipient:

Oh! Grace, Grace, Grace! this Wealthy
Grace doth lay
Her Golden Channells from thy
Fathers throne,
Into our Earthen Pitchers to Convay
Heavens Aqua Vitae to us for our own.
Meditation No. 32, First Series

Gods Determinations is a long allegorical poem, written in a variety of stanzaic forms, which attempts to justify God's ways to men within the framework of Calvinistic Puritan doctrine. Debates between personified Justice and Mercy and a Satan who comes roaring on the scene, may indicate the poet's familiarity with medieval drama. The poem describes the creation, the fall of Man, and the salvation of the elect after victory over the temptations of Satan. Some of the most moving poetry occurs in 'The Preface':

Who made the Sea's its Selvedge, and it
locks
Like a Quilt Ball within a Silver Box?
Who Spread its Canopy? or Curtains
Spun?
Who in this Bowling Alley bowld the
Sun?

D.E.S.

see also American Poetry

Tennyson, Alfred, Lord (1809–92), was born at Somersby, Lincolnshire. His father, who was rector of the parish, had been disinherited, and was an embittered man who became a chronic drunkard. From his father's side the poet was to inherit a melancholy, moody streak, and from his mother's his sometimes over-delicate refinement. Some of Tennyson's juvenile work appeared in *Poems by Three Brothers* (1827), together with that of his brothers, Frederick and Charles, both of whom were to become poets of considerable distinction. Alfred was educated by his father at home, and then went up to Trinity College, Cambridge. Here he became a member of the circle of young intellectuals known as the 'Apostles', of which Arthur Hallam, Tennyson's particular friend, was a leading light. *Poems, chiefly lyrical* (1830) was fiercely attacked by some of the leading critics of the day, but nevertheless contained some of Tennyson's best and most characteristic work, such as *Mariana*, with its reminiscences of the Lincolnshire landscape, and its evocation of a mood of melancholy and decay:

Upon the middle of the night,
Waking she heard the night-fowl crow.
The cock sung out an hour ere light:
From the dark fen the oxen's low
Came to her: without hope of change,
In sleep she seem'd to walk forlorn,
Till cold winds woke the gray-eyed
morn
About the lonely moted grange.

Hallam's death in 1833 was a profound emotional shock to Tennyson. *In Memoriam*, begun shortly after this, but not completed till 1850 (in which year Tennyson also married) records Tennyson's grief, and his struggle to attain to faith in immortality, in the light of the growing challenge to religion from contemporary science. The core of the poem is an imperfectly apprehended quasi-mystical intuition:

Aeonian music measuring out
The steps of Time—the scales of
Chance—

The blows of Death. At length my
 trance
Was cancell'd, stricken through with
 doubt.

In Memoriam, though it had been preceded by a further volume of *Poems* (1833), a two-volume collection in 1842, and *The Princess* (1847), made Tennyson's reputation, which was further consolidated by *Enoch Arden* (1864). He succeeded **Wordsworth** as Poet Laureate in 1850 and became increasingly accepted as the official poet of the Victorian age. Though much of his work in this capacity is conventional and second-rate in its thought, he never quite shed the more unconventional side of his nature, and his rare lyrical gift never deserted him. Thus among the numerous volumes which continued to appear regularly down to the time of his death, we may specially single out *Maud* (1855), which Tennyson himself always valued highly, but which was received with very mixed feelings by some of his admirers. It is an unequal poem, marred by a certain hysterical lack of control. But it represents a serious attempt to treat in poetic terms the horrors of contemporary industrialism, while its manner of telling a story through a series of lyrical monologues in free and varied metres anticipates some of the poetic techniques of the twentieth century.

The Idylls of the King, a series of poems which began with *Morte d'Arthur* in 1842, and was completed with *Balin and Balan* in 1885, represent, as a whole, Tennyson's most ambitious work. They illustrate very well both his strength and his weakness as a poet. Dealing with the Arthurian legend, and based mainly on Malory, it has often been complained that the medieval material is made far too genteel, while the morality is conventional, and the overall allegorical plan somewhat trite. Neverthe-

less, *The Idylls* contain passages of great beauty, and sometimes of a haunting wildness—for example, Guenevere's last sight of Arthur:

And even then he turn'd, and more and
 more
The moving vapour rolling round the
 King,
Who seem'd the phantom of a Giant in
 it,
Enwound him fold on fold, and made
 him gray
And grayer, till himself became as mist
Before her, moving ghost-like to his
 doom.

As to Tennyson's poetry as a whole, it is very difficult to deal adequately with it, or with full justice, in a brief article. His reputation has undergone curious vicissitudes since his poems first began to appear in print. His early volumes were fiercely attacked. They followed up the Romantic tradition of **Shelley** and **Keats**, and in the opening decades of the reign of Victoria, eighteenth-century criticism was still fighting a rearguard action. By 1850 the tide had turned, and at the time of his death Tennyson was generally accepted not only as a great poet but as a prophet and moral teacher. The twentieth century saw an inevitable reaction against this, as against almost everything Victorian. But more recently, Tennyson has been increasingly (and rightly) rehabilitated. This renewed appreciation, the way to which may be said first to have been pointed out by Sir Harold Nicolson, has tended to concentrate on the melancholy, sensuous, lyrical, romantic Tennyson, which was never quite submerged in the figure of the conventional bard. This is the Tennyson of *The Lotos-eaters, Oenone, Tithonus*, of the lyrics in *The Princess* and of the earlier-composed idylls; but also of such later poems as *Frater Ave atque Vale, Prefatory*

Poem to my Brother's Sonnets, Merlin and the Gleam, and *Crossing the Bar.* But this approach may involve its own dangers of over-simplification. The division between Art and Reality, prominent in much of Tennyson's work, was something entailed on the Victorian poets by the contemporary situation, and they can scarcely be blamed if they failed adequately to resolve the division. In two early poems, *The Lady of Shallot* and *The Palace of Art,* Tennyson shows himself aware of the dilemma. In the first of these, the Lady is destroyed when she turns from her magic mirror to the world of real men and women; but in the second, the Soul, withdrawing from Reality into the world of Art, discovers she has created for herself a nightmare of inner corruption. Tennyson must be given credit for an earnest attempt to come to grips with the problems, and with the scientific and other thought of his age. But unfortunately he often thought on a second-rate level. His real strength was emotional and intuitive.   J.H-S.

see also Imagery *and* Popular Poetry

Thomas, Dylan [Marlais] (1914–53), was born in Swansea, of Welsh parents, on 27 October, 1914. In 1936 he married Caitlin Macnamara, by whom he had two sons and a daughter. He died in New York on 9 November, 1953.

From the first, he set himself the task of remaking language in terms of his own vision. His first book, *Eighteen Poems* (1934), revealed an idiom, new to English poetry, whose concentrated force was easily adapted to the correspondence he sought between sexual imagery and themes of vast metaphysical range. The stubborn originality of his verse derived from a singleness of vision, at once Freudian and biblical, which remained fresh throughout his life, as though his eyes still remembered the Garden of Eden:

The force that through the green fuse
                    drives the flower
Drives my green age; that blasts the
                    roots of trees
Is my destroyer.   (v)

I sit and watch the worm beneath my
                    nail
Wearing the quick away.   (viii)

Light breaks where no sun shines;
Where no sea runs, the waters of the
                    heart
Push in their tides . . .
A candle in the thighs
Warms youth and seed and burns the
                    seeds of age.
                    (xiv)

In *Twenty-Five Poems* (1936) the sexual imagery was continued, the idiom finding lyrical expression in a more varied stanza form. Besides these poems, Dylan Thomas wrote stories whose imagery, sometimes marked by surrealism, influenced his verse. Twelve stories, together with sixteen new poems, formed his third book, *The Map of Love* (1939): these poems announce a new attitude to writing. The book ends with the poem for his twenty-fourth birthday:

Twenty-four years remind the tears of
                    my eyes.
(Bury the dead for fear that they walk to
                    the grave in labour.)
In the groin of the natural doorway I
                    crouched like a tailor
Sewing a shroud for a journey
By the light of the meat-eating sun.
Dressed to die, the sensual strut begun,
With my red veins full of money,
In the final direction of the elementary
                    town
I advance for as long as forever is.

In his subsequent fiction he wrote about real people. The autobiographical Swansea and Carmarthen stories of *Portrait of the*

Artist as a Young Dog (1940) and the first four chapters of a semi-autobiographical novel, *Adventures in the Skin Trade*, published posthumously in 1955, use the direct style of abundant comic invention which now gave life to his prose.

A much greater development was to follow, for during the war years Dylan Thomas wrote most of the poems for *Deaths and Entrances* (1946); *Fern Hill* and *Poem In October*, composed in stanzas of vivid colour and a compelling assonantal music, acclaimed life through the eyes of his boyhood, and in the dust of bombed London such poems as *A Refusal to Mourn the Death, by Fire, of a Child in London*, and *Ceremony After a Fire Raid*, reaffirmed the same faith through the eyes of a religious witness.

During and after the war he made films, and broadcast frequently. His one published film-script, *The Doctor and the Devils*, was written in 1947. His prose found its true mastery in the late broadcast scripts collected in *Quite Early One Morning*, and his rich voice made him a superb reader of these, and of poetry—particularly his own.

His last work, *Under Milk Wood*, a play for voices, was completed for radio a month before his death, but was still undergoing revision for stage and book form. In the six poems of *In Country Sleep* his lyricism reached its highest perfection. These and the *Prologue* to *Collected Poems* (1952) were all he finished in the last seven years. He left an unfinished *Elegy*. *In Country Sleep*, *In the White Giant's Thigh* and *Over Sir John's Hill* belong to a projected work to be called *In Country Heaven*, which was to have further parts, the theme of which he also planned to use as the basis of a libretto for an opera to be composed by Stravinsky. He was on the point of leaving New York for Hollywood for this collaboration when he died. v.w.

Thomas, [Philip] Edward (1878–1917), was born in London and was the eldest son of a clerk at the Board of Trade. He was educated at Battersea Grammar School, St Paul's School and Lincoln College, Oxford. In 1899 he married Helen, daughter of James Ashcroft Nobel, writer and critic; there were three children of the marriage, one son and two daughters. Thomas earned a precarious living by writing and reviewing. He enjoyed the society of most of the writers of his day, but the real background of his work was the fields and woods of southern England. He was killed in action near Arras in 1917.

Many contemporary writers began in verse and turned to prose. With Thomas the reverse happened. A lover of the countryside, he would wander, brooding among its ways, recording his impressions in sensitive prose. In most of the books not written too hastily to order there is a quiet but profound knowledge and love of the country, tinged with a half-racial, half-personal melancholy. He had also evinced a deep attachment to books early in his life.

The mere need to write for a living was not the only cause of Thomas' growing dissatisfaction: the poet within him insisted on recognition. Thomas' meeting with Robert **Frost** in 1913 was the turning point. Thomas already knew and admired Frost's poems. Frost in his turn appreciated the other's sensitive prose, and with his interest in colloquial speech, recognised the potential poetry of Thomas' writing. He showed him passages which could be read as verse and urged him to devote himself to writing actual poetry. Gradually Thomas began to do so, and in the last two years of his life expressed in verse all his love of nature in a way that was quizzical, sensitive and individual. It was a new facet of English poetry, this delicate movement of a poem, which expressed the sensitivity of a mind that was mostly so un-Georgian in its expression. Take, for instance, the first stanza of the poem *Adlestrop*:

Yes. I remember Adlestrop
The name, because one afternoon
Of heat the express-train drew up there
Unwontedly. It was late June.

This conversational yet terse style was to have great influence on later poetry. It is casual, completely un-romantic, yet flexible and capable of great development. It was a perfect medium for the quiet, wry, half-playful, half-melancholy musing which was so much a habit of Edward Thomas. 'When a poet writes', Thomas had said in *The Country*, 'he is often only putting into words what some old country-man has puzzled out among the corn in a long life-time.' He was himself a country-man at heart and much of his poetry was the fruit of some such 'puzzling out'. 'As for myself', he wrote in *Old Man*,

Where first I met the bitter scent is lost.
I, too, often shrivel the grey shreds,
Sniff them and think and sniff again and
try
Once more to think what it is I am
remembering.

But this conversational style, is as suggested above, capable of the sudden terseness of common speech. It is admirable for giving a sudden twist to the thought, for ending a poem in a way that leaves the palate tingling, as the cheek does from a sudden sting in the wind. *But These Things Also* ends:

and starling flocks
By chattering on and on
Keep their spirits up in the mist,
And Spring's here, Winter's not gone.

When Thomas met Frost, he expressed enthusiasm for the poetry of Ezra **Pound**.

Pound was one of the leaders of the Imagist movement, which aimed to counteract the blurred and sentimental tendencies of contemporary poetry. If Thomas was not actively or consciously involved in the movement, some of his phrases and images could hardly have failed to please its promoters.

I like the dust on the nettles, never lost
Except to prove the sweetness of a
shower.

That is how he closes *Tall Nettles*. And in *March the Third*, writing of the church bells and the birds' voices he says:

but the birds' songs have
The holiness gone from the bells.

Edward Thomas' poetry shows the union of a love of old things with a surprisingly modern sensibility. His most moving poem, *The Unknown Bird*, expresses not only the yearning of his own heart, but a too noisy world's consciousness of a lost or unattainable heaven. It begins:

Three lovely notes he whistled, too soft
to be heard
If others sang; but others never sang
In the great beech-wood all that May
and June.
No one saw him: I alone could hear him
Though many listened. Was it but four
years
Ago? or five? He never came again . . .

R.S.T.

Thomas, R[onald] S[tuart] (1913–), who graduated in Classics in theUniversity of Wales in 1935, has been a Welsh country parson since 1942. His six volumes of poetry all convey an initial impression of formal lucidity and direct statement; they are in fact increasingly penetrating expressions of ironic conflict, the partly bitter irreconciliation between the parson-artist and the people to whom he ministers, symbolised in the brutal yokel, Iago Prytherch. But the growth in stature and complexity in this figure, and the increasing compassion with which Thomas regards him in his later verse, is characteristic of the increasing significance of this distinguished poet.   W.M.M.

Thompson, Francis (1859–1907), English poet, was discovered by Wilfred Meynell, editor of *Merrie England*. Thompson's *Hound of Heaven* was published in it in 1891. His mystical, religious poetry shows the influence of **Patmore** and the seventeenth-century metaphysicals.   D.H.

Thomson, James (1700–48), was born at Ednam, Roxburghshire, Scotland, where his father was the parish minister. After studying at Edinburgh University he came to London in 1725. Here he composed *Winter*, the first part of *The Seasons* (1726–30). *Winter* was published on **Pope's** recommendation, and was an immediate success. *The Seasons* is a descriptive poem in Miltonic blank-verse, in four parts corresponding to the four seasons, to which was added a *Hymn*. The work as a whole is marked by richness of colouring and accuracy of observation, though it is burdened by a heavily rhetorical Miltonic diction. Of its four parts, *Winter* is the best, reflecting as it does the stormy wildness of the Scottish scenery of Thomson's boyhood:

Pleas'd, have I, in my cheerful Mode of
            Life,
When, nurs'd by careless *Solitude,* I
            liv'd,
And sung of Nature with unceasing Joy,
Pleas'd, have I wander'd thro' your rough
            Domains,
Trod the pure, virgin, Snows, myself as
            pure,

Heard the Winds roar, and the long
            Torrent burst;
Or seen the deep, fermenting, Tempest
            brew'd,
In the red, evening, sky.—Thus pleas'd
            the Time,
Till, thro' the opening Chambers of the
            South,
Look'd out the joyous Spring, look'd
            out, and smil'd.

The Seasons made Thomson's reputation, and through the influence of friends, he received a Government sinecure.

Thomson's best known other work is *The Castle of Indolence* (1748), an allegory in the style of **Spenser** of considerable charm. *Liberty* (1738) is more ambitious, but less readable. He also wrote several now-forgotten tragedies, including *Sophonisba* (1730). He is also often credited with the authorship of *Rule, Britannia!* which appeared in the masque *Alfred* (1740) written jointly with David Mallet.   J.H-S.

Thomson, James ('B.V.') (1834–82), a Scottish poet, is best known for *The City of Dreadful Night*, which was published serially in 1874. He was an admirer of Leopardi, **Shelley** and the German mystic, Hardenberg.   D.H.

Thoreau, Henry David (1817–62), American naturalist and essayist, born in Concord, of French, Scottish, Quaker and Puritan stock is known primarily for his narrative, *Walden*. His *Poems of Nature* (1895) incline toward scholarly doggerel, imitative of **Emerson's** gnomic style.

          D.H.

Tourneur, Cyril (?1575–1626), first attracted attention with his political parable in rhyme royal, *The Transformed Metamorphosis* (1607). He is best known as a playwright, for *The Revenger's Tragedy* and

The Atheist's Tragedy. Certain passages of his verse have attracted particular attention for their gloomy beauty.   D.H.

Townshend, Aurelian (*c.* 1583–*c.* 1647), was a London poet and the writer of two masques, performed at court in 1632. He was a friend of Thomas **Carew**, who dedicated a poem to him. Townshend described himself 'a poor and pocky poet ... glad to sell a hundred verse at sixpence a piece'.   D.H.

Traherne, Thomas (1637–74), was more famous for his prose *Centuries of Meditations* than for his poetry, and remained unknown as a poet until a notebook into which he had copied some of his poems turned up on a second-hand bookstall in 1895. Another manuscript, containing some of these poems and others in versions emended by Traherne's brother, Philip, was subsequently discovered in the British Museum Library, and the two selections were published in 1903 and 1910 respectively.

Traherne was a Herefordshire parson, educated at Oxford, who spent the last two years of his life as chaplain to Sir Orlando Bridgeman. He was a learned Platonist and a specialist in church history. But most of his poetry, as of his prose *Meditations*, reverts to a single experience: an immediate and deeply emotional apprehension in childhood of unity between himself and the world. This unified condition was the touchstone to which he brought everything that subsequently befell him. For him all origins were pure, all subsequent developments liable to corruption, from which they could only be rescued by 'Thought'—a term which Traherne used in the sense of religious meditation. His deepest love was of solitude:

> Remov'd from Town,
> From People, Churches, Feasts and
>   Holidays,
> The Sword of State, the Mayor's
>   Gown,
>   And all the Neighb'ring Boys;
>   As if no Kings
>   On Earth there were, or living Things.
> The silent Skies salute mine Eys, the Seas
> My soul surround; no rest I found, or Eas.
>
>   My roving Mind
> Search'd evry Corner of the spacious
>   Earth
>   From Sky to Sky, if it could find
>   (But found not) any Mirth;
>   Not all the Coasts,
>   Nor all the great and glorious Hosts,
> In Hev'n or Earth, did any Mirth afford;
> I pin'd for hunger at a plenteous Board.

Traherne was trying in vain to recapture the immediate vision of the countryside that he had known in childhood. He knew it was to be had, and that only his adult state of distraction stood in its way. To combat this adult state he purposely chose the straightforward childish words that he associated with the original experience. Here in his brother's revised version of the poem, which has not survived in its original form, the last line is a metaphysical antithesis. Traherne, however, seldom used this kind of language. The poem, *Shadows in the Water*, of which we have his own version, recalls another childish experience with a visual naïveté which guarantees its authenticity, yet with a subtlety of reasoning partly childish and partly based, perhaps, on a speculative passage of Plotinus:

> Beneath the Water Peeple drown'd.
> Yet with another Hev'n crown'd,
> In spacious Regions seem'd to go
> Freely moving to and fro:
>   In bright and open Space
>   I saw their very face;

Eys, Hands and Feet they had like mine:
Another Sun did with them shine.

'Twas strange that Peeple there should
walk,
And yet I could not hear them talk:
That throu a little watry Chink,
Which one dry Ox or Horse might
drink,
  We other Worlds could see,
  Yet not admitted be;
And other Confines there behold
Of Light and Darkness, Heat and Cold.

The picture of this looking-glass country implies that earth is a reflection of heaven, whose inhabitants can see the child through a chink in their world and watch over him. When the adult Traherne recalled by the aid of meditation the directness of his old apprehension, he knew that the roofs of heaven slope at the same angle as those of Hereford did when his uncle was Mayor and he a small boy, and heard the bells of Paradise ring with the old magic of West-country chimes. Like **Blake**, he realised that this mingling of childish and intellectual vision is man's natural inheritance. Traherne is consequently an enduring poet even when at times his language is flat, his metres clumsy and his imagery undistinguished; and he is never the better for his brother's improvements. He is seldom, however, on a level with his neighbour, Henry **Vaughan**, or with his own finest passages of ecstatic prose in the *Centuries*. With Vaughan he stands somewhat outside the Metaphysical school, but unlike him, he is idealogically close to the Cambridge Platonists and the community of Little Gidding. Traherne was strongly Anglican in viewpoint.   J.M.C.

Translation. Homer and Virgil founded the European epic tradition and the history of English translation is best studied in relation to them. The Renaissance came to represent these poets as 'Nature': not the best in their kind merely, but archetypes of all ambitious writing. One eighteenth-century critic, the Abbé Batteux, carried the equation to its extreme. The word arrangement of Greek and Latin being the order of nature implied that modern tongues should never deviate from that order except where constrained by requirements of sense, clearness and euphony. Thus a translation should accord in all parts, even length, with its original. Translation, though, is a dynamic encounter between two tongues and since ours is an uninflected language, dense with consonants and poor in rhyme—though too easy rhyme brings its own hardship—attempts to pursue closely the syntax, cadences and sound of other languages must be largely quixotic.

Dryden had previously insisted on a mean between metaphrase and paraphrase, and a contemporary of Dryden's, Lord Roscommon, blandly and reassuringly defined a more relevant principle, fidelity of tone:

Your author always will the best advise,
Fall when he falls, and when he rises, rise.

The eighteenth century defined a further principle: tact in choice of an original. It was insolent for a minor poet to meddle with giant originals; better to do Nonnus well, than Homer badly. **Pope**—greatest poet of his age—with proper reverence and freedom, translated Homer and 'imitated' Horace, for in Horace he recognised an affinity of temperament and a satiric vision close to Augustan concerns.

The eighteenth century witnessed also the rise of literary history: a recognition both of the pastness of the past and its continued presence. This conflicted with the static view of Homer and Virgil as archetypes and underlies already Pope's early, suavely optimistic *Essay on Criticism*:

> Know well each ancient's proper
> character:
> His fable, subject, scope in every page;
> Religion, country, genius of the age . . .
> Thence form your judgment, thence
> your maxims bring,
> And trace the Muses upward to their
> spring

and was to find full expression in the *Preface* to his *Iliad*.

Such relativism gave force and poignancy to two established modes 'Allusion'—the notion of adapting elements in a classical work—and the notion of writing a poem as Homer or Virgil might have written it had they been citizens of Augustan England—'Imitation'. Where the Elizabethan translator, with a limited sense of the past, had been comparatively free, the eighteenth century's freedom was haunted by the tragic paradox of a lost heroic age: Pope's epic plans were only fulfilled in translation. Translation thus becomes more complex; in Collingwood's phrase, a meeting the past half-way. Yet the divergences between, say, **Johnson**'s *Vanity of Human Wishes* and Juvenal in treatment of old age, Fate and Providence, conspire to throw the model into sharper relief. This remains more true of the twentieth century: **Pound**'s *Homage to Sextus Propertius* stands in just such a relation to his originals. *Fidus interpres* is a vulgar error. To preserve an original requires complete involvement in the life and idiom of one's own age. 'You must not', Samuel **Butler** remarks, 'skin him, stuff him and set him up in a case'.

For translation is also a dynamic encounter between two persons: the original poet and his translator. Triumphant translation has normally resulted where the translator has not been dominated by his original—as **Browning** was by

Aeschylus—for his role is not passive, but active. Ears too dazed by the surge and thunder of the *Odyssey* are not necessarily the best adapted to re-create the spirit of Homer in English. Of first importance are insight—the poet's 'way of looking'—and skill in one's own tongue. The best translators are good original poets, though there are examples of fine, parasitic talents like Edward **Fairfax** or **Fitzgerald**. Yet both treat their original with healthy boldness. Exact rendering is best accomplished in prose. 'A translation is at best a dislocation, a translation from verse to prose is a double dislocation', but 'further dislocations are necessary if an effect of deformity is to be avoided' (Butler).

Translation of past masterpieces is a responsible re-seeing of that past. The great moment in literature conquers a literary experience so completely that it cannot be afterwards expressed. By such a definitive gesture, though, each masterpiece encapsulates a vivid centre, peculiarly of its own culture, and transmits that through time. Just this non-verbal life the translator wishes to preserve. The analogy is perhaps with the author, revising his own work after a lapse of time, who finds his way back to the original experience behind the work. This defines the limits of interpretation. The experience itself is given; if he changes that he is not revising, but writing a new poem. 'Expression is once again open. One may well see an original in slightly different terms; may well come to feel that, in really accurate delineation, the stresses require to be arranged a little differently. So with translation. Translation as 'revision', almost as correction, pulling back the timeless object into the world of time, which is also the world of change' (D. S. Carne-Ross). Although the timeless object must be constantly brought back into the world of change, once given life there its life *as a translation* is necessarily limited. It must soon begin to distort its original and so leave its audience dissatisfied. All translation is provisional: prolegomenon to the never-to-be-written final interpretation.

Consciously or unconsciously, past translators have worked in this spirit. Homer has appeared as a different poet to different generations: **Cowper**'s 'tea-cup' temporarily displaced Pope's baroque Homer. Both were temporarily displaced by the eminently plain, rapid, direct and noble figment of **Arnold** (though that Homer never ran). T. S. **Eliot** waspishly remarked of Gilbert Murray's neo-Swinburnian Euripides: It 'has erected between Euripides and ourselves a barrier more impenetrable than the original Greek'. The translator of Eliot's generation was 'H.D.'. We can now recognise her work as inadequate for dramatic, though admirable still for lyric purposes: the quick images pointing to an original brilliantly and informally seen, as though for the first time. The so-called 'timeless' translation will inevitably resolve itself into 'colourless' as in the recent English New Testament with its refining of the forcible 'den of thieves' into the drearily neutral 'cave of robbers'.

Of major translations, Gavin **Douglas'** *Eneados* is historically the first. Its trenchancy is far from the emollience of Virgil. **Golding**'s *Metamorphoses*, **Marlowe**'s spirited *Amores*, **Chapman**'s Homer, Fairfax's limpid and supple Tasso, Harington's crude but lively Ariosto, between them possess all the exuberance and magniloquence of the best Elizabethan work, as May's Lucan, Sandys' Ovid, Stanley's Góngora and Anacreon, and Fanshawe's *Pastor Fido* retain the positive qualities of the diminished age that follows.

Chapman's Elizabethan robustness is crossed with Jacobean pessimism—compare his account of the war against Heaven with Pope's. Yet the authority of exuberance runs there and controls his charming sillinesses, though the purist may disdainfully point at Chapman's turning the biblical majesty of 'And Zeus troubled the deeps' into:

> Then all the tops he bottoms in the deeps
> And all the bottoms in the tops he steeps.

Similarly, Dryden's Virgil retains the coarse strength and theatrical dignity of its age—its leisured detail allowing one to remain uninvolved. With Lucretius, an original chosen with greater tact, Dryden's 'sullen sensuality' transforms the grave cosmic celebration of plenitude into something resembling a belly-laugh. This period's confidence carried colloquialism to the lengths of Samuel Butler. The grave baroque afflatus of later Wren, Hawksmoor and Handel finds its counterpart in Pope's *Iliad*. Two lines from the 'Milesian Intrusion' of Book XIV determine the poet's alertness to the almost Restoration Comedy insolence of his original. Zeus' falling asleep after being tricked by Hera into making love appears as:

> At length, with love and sleep's soft
> power oppressed,
> The panting thunderer nods, and sinks
> to rest.

The presence of Belinda's poet is clear, though the mock-heroic element works the other way: the Gods are now shown as vulnerable by aggrandisation. The comic-baroque functions as conscious parody: an overstressing of masked elements in the original. The nineteenth century, that golden age of diplomacy, offers us Lord Derby's unruffled Foreign Office Despatch on the Trojan War.

At certain times some authors become more amenable to translation than at others: talent and *Zeitgeist* coincide. The nineteenth century was better adapted to translate Virgil than Homer, despite the revival of Greek studies in its later years. Of Homer, we have extremes: the pomaded prose of Lang, Leaf and Myers and the exasperatedly brilliant 'Billingsgate' of Butler; **Rossetti**'s *Early Italian Poets*, **Swinburne**'s Villon and **Symons**' Verlaine remain the best Victorian examples of the art. What **Tennyson** would have made of Virgil—his English Idylls are virtually Augustan 'imitations' of Theocritus—and how **Clough** would have treated Horace, it is fascinating to conjecture.

In this century, translation has extended far beyond the classics and the Italian Renaissance. Our 'Imaginary Museum' attitude and the 'Paperback Revolution' are perhaps responsible. Homer's challenge has been answered by Lattimore. This version preserves the monotonously hypnotic ritual of epic, preserving also dispensable stock-epithets. Hector may be once or twice referred to as 'tamer of Horses'; consistent reference becomes ludicrous. The selections from the two epics, commissioned recently by the British Broadcasting Corporation, were by poets rather than linguists. This experiment restored an oral element, focusing the limitations and virtues of our period in translation. The novel remains still the dominant art-form and the more successful versions tended to the colloquial, rapid and psychological. Christopher Logue's fight between Achilles and the River-God Scamander was most commanding. Here grotesque and colloquial mingled, evoking the weird, animistic violence of the original. Logue owed something to Pound's oddly neglected achievement, for beside *Homage*, Pound has given us in *Cathay*—based on another's prose—perhaps the finest example of twentieth-century translation.

Greek drama has been best rendered by Americans: Dudley Fitts, Robert Fitzgerald and William Arrowsmith. Fitts' *Lysistrata* glimpsed in terms of persisting tension between Northern and Southern states of the Union—has been successfully staged. Fitts' and Fitzgerald's Oedipus trilogy has been criticised as 'over-literary'. Pound's *Women of Trachis* is painfully eccentric. Of English translations, **Mac-Neice**'s *Agamemnon* and Rex Warner's Euripides pioneered with the full resources of 'modern' verse. Neil Curry's *Bacchae* is another fine acting version. Penguin Classics verse translators, intimate with the optative rather than poetry, have been disastrous. Vellacott's Euripides is a model of the art of sinking when your author rises. Euripides would seem to have provided the metrical model for *The Lays of Ancient Rome*, the thudding Macaulay being as near a working equivalent to Greek metres as the translator could find in English.

For the first time since the seventeenth century, Spanish has become a popular field (oddly, Góngora's *Polifemo* was translated in the eighteen-sixties). E. N. Wilson's superb Góngora *Solitudes* makes the absence of further work regrettable. Roy **Campbell**'s and J. F. Nims' versions of St John of the Cross, Aubrey Bell's Luis de Leon, **Merwin**'s *Cid*, Lloyd's and Campbell's versions of Lorca demand mention—though everything Campbell translated turns univocally into Campbell's double-rhymes and bucking rhythms, even when these patently rupture the mood of his original. Ruth Speirs, Stephen **Spender** and J. B. Leishmann have finely interpreted Rilke, and Michael Hamburger's Hölderlin and Hoffmansthal are close and elegant. Edwin Morgan's Montale is also remarkable for combining fidelity to the Italian with a following of the sheerly physical curve of the original. Richard

Wilbur has given us Molière and a memorable Propertius elegy. Morgan has been successful with Scève, Tasso's madrigals and modern Russian verse. Chinese has been admirably served by **Waley**, Jenyns and Hugh Gordon Porteous; Arabic by Professor Arberry. John Heath-Stubbs has sensitively rendered Leopardi and **Gray**'s Latin epistle to Richard West. George Fraser's Cavalcanti and Tibullus are accurate and stylish.

Critical works on the subject are rare. Tytler's essay *Principles of Translation* (1791) first stressed the criteria of 'freedom' and 'ease' and contains good close criticism. Dryden's essays and the eloquent Preface to Pope's *Iliad* are classic. E. S. Bates' *Modern Translation* (1936) is a concise manual of theory. J. S. Phillimore's *Some Remarks on Translation and Translators* and J. P. Postgate's *Translators and Translation* are both useful, and there is a stimulating essay by Pound on the great English practitioners. Proudfoot's *Dryden's Aeneid and its Seventeenth-century Predecessors* should inaugurate a new critical approach.

I.F.

V

Van Doren, Mark [Albert] (1894–   ), is an American critic, novelist and Pulitzer prize-winning poet. He was Professor at Columbia University from 1924 to 1959, and Literary Editor of *The Nation* from 1924 to 1928.   D.H.

Vaughan, Henry (1622–95), a Welshman, spent two years or more at Oxford and afterwards went to London to read law, and for the last twenty years of his life practised as a doctor in his native county, Brecon, from which he derived his appellation of the 'Silurist' (the Silures were the ancient inhabitants of Brecon). He was a Royalist and strongly anti-Puritan. Like his twin brother, Thomas, Vaughan was greatly interested in chemistry and the Hermetic sciences. But he remained a devout Christian, deeply affected by nature, of which his vision was mystical. Thus he has affinities with **Wordsworth**, on whose *Immortality* ode he exerted some influence.

Vaughan's early poetry is conventional. His brooding on a charnel-house fails to arouse a shiver, his addresses to Amoret lack passion. In his one love-poem that has distinction, his address to his mistress 'on a Starry Evening', he shows himself less interested in her than in the divine order of the Universe, which alike controls the motions of the stars and the loves, lives and deaths of men. In his first two collections, *Poems* (1646) and *Olor Iscanus*, the best pieces are translations from the Latin. His religious conversion occurred some time before the publication of his sacred poems, *Silex Scintillans* (1650), which he reissued with the addition of a second part five years later. In the preface he delivered a strong attack against the Metaphysicals, objecting in particular to their importation of 'Foreign vanities; so that the most lascivious compositions of France and Italy are here naturalised and made English'. At the same time he declared himself a follower of 'the blessed man, Mr

George **Herbert'**, and begged leave to communicate his 'poor Talent to the Church'. Unlike Herbert, however, Vaughan is not a poet of the Church but of a personal vision expressed in terms that are not always Christian, but sometimes gnostic or neo-Platonic. Nevertheless his poetry also abounds in echoes from his declared master.

Vaughan's conversion reawoke in him certain memories of childhood. Moments of enlightenment in his maturity reminded him that as a child he had lived in a state of perpetual proximity to the source of light. Hence in many of his poems he speaks of a desire to travel not forwards but back:

O how I long to travel back
And tread again that ancient track!
That I might once more reach that
                                   plaine,
Where first I left that glorious traine,
From which th'Inlightened spirit sees
The shady City of Palme trees.

But at the height of his vision Vaughan glimpsed another direction that was neither backwards nor forwards; he saw Eternity in the figure of a ring, as he had already done before his conversion in his poem to Amoret on a starry evening. The theme recurs in the opening lines of *The World*:

I saw Eternity the other night
Like a great *Ring* of pure and endless
                                    light,
    All calm, as it was bright,
And round beneath it, Times in hours,
                                days, years
    Driv'n by the spheres
Like a vast shadow mov'd . . .

From this vision Vaughan found himself separated by a veil, which had been rent for Nature but which still blinded man. This he describes in addressing God in the last lines of his Hermetic *Cock-crowing*:

Only this Veyle which thou hast broke,
And must be broken yet in me,
This veyle, I say, is all the cloke
And cloud which shadows thee from
                                    me.
This veyle thy full-ey'd love denies,
And only gleams and fractions spies.

Gleams and fractions inform most of the poems of *Silex Scintillans*, which often drop from sublimity into pedestrianism as illumination is followed by a fresh falling of the 'veyle'. Vaughan's finest verses are sparks struck from the flint, as he himself indicated by the choice of his title. In contrast to the Metaphysicals he speaks directly without wit and word-play, and is not shy of echoing a phrase from Herbert or from the New Testament. Whereas the poetry of the school of **Donne** was predominantly intellectual, Vaughan's relies always on emotion. Metrically also, it is far less ingenious than much of the work of his contemporaries. Vaughan is close to **Traherne** in his interests, but a more accomplished poet. He has also affinities with a German contemporary, Paul Fleming, who was like him in blending Christian and neo-Platonic or Hermetic ideas.   J.M.C.

Viereck, Peter (1916–), is an American poet and historian who won the Pulitzer Prize for his first book of poems, *Terror and Decorum* (1948). An inveterate experimenter within the range of forms, Viereck has demonstrated more variety than depth in his subsequent poems.   D.H.

W

Waley, Arthur [David] (1889–1968), the outstanding translator of Chinese poetry, perfected a loose 'sprung rhythm' to which he adapted poems by a variety of poets over many centuries. Following the example of Ezra **Pound**, though with a scholar's knowledge of his originals, he published in 1918 his first selection of *170 Chinese Poems*, which he prefaced with an able defence of his method of translation. A further collection of short pieces in 1920 was followed by *The Temple* (1923) which contains poems of greater scope, which display subtle changes of mood and rhythm.

Essentially a poet of the nineteen-twenties, Waley appreciates the irony and understatement of his originals, yet is capable of capturing the sustained lyricism of the first-century poet, Chang Hêng, as successfully as the impressionism of Li Po and Po Chü-i. His biographical studies of the two latter poets contain many translated fragments that are comparable with the best in his selection from his earlier books, *Chinese Poems* (1946). His *The No Plays of Japan* (1921) contains some fine poetry, and he also published a number of prose translations from the Chinese and Japanese, including *The Way and its Power*, a subtle interpretation of the Tao Tê Ching. J.M.C.

see also Translation

Waller, Edmund (1606–87), was the richest poet known to English literature. To considerable inherited estates he added a wealthy heiress. He had to abduct her, as she was a ward, but through influence escaped punishment from the Star Chamber.

Waller became the youngest ever Member of the House of Commons by representing the Borough of Amersham at the age of fifteen. And he became 'Father of the House' before his death at eighty-one. He nearly diverted the course of history in 1643, when his 'Waller Plot' aimed to secure the City of London for Charles I during the Civil War. He was betrayed by a servant, but saved his life by informing on his accomplices and laying out £30,000 in bribes. Escaping with a fine of £10,000, he was exiled to France. Cromwell pardoned him in 1651. Charles II received him in 1660 and but for opposition would have made him Provost of Eton.

Intimate with kings and noblemen, statesmen and great ladies, Waller was essentially a court poet and a wit. His graceful dedicatory poems, on births and deaths, places and occasions, made him popular. His *Panegyric to My Lord Protector* was followed by an ode *Upon His Majesty's Happy Return*, as the times made it convenient. Not taken aback by Charles II's sardonic remark respecting the inferiority of the latter to the former, Waller replied: 'Sir, we poets never succeed so well in writing truth as fiction'. 'Waller', as **Pope** said, 'was smooth.' To which **Johnson** added: 'he was rather smooth than strong . . . The general character of his poetry is elegance and gaiety'. **Dryden** praised him for the excellence and dignity of his rhyme.

Today Waller is known mainly for his love of 'Sacharissa' (Lady Dorothy Sidney, eldest daughter of Robert, Earl of Leicester), whom he courted in vain, and for such timeless lyrics as *On a Girdle* and that beginning:

Go, lovely Rose!
Tell her that wastes her time and me
That now she knows,

When I resemble her to thee,
How sweet and fair she seems to be.

Nor should one forget his last poem, written in his final year, which ends:

The soul's dark cottage, battered and
decayed,
Lets in new light through chinks that
time has made;
Stronger by weakness, wiser men
become,
As they draw near to their eternal home.
Leaving the old, both worlds at once
they view,
That stand upon the threshold of the
new.

With this brave farewell, the 'smooth' and 'correct' poet withdrew from a life he had lived magnificently.

For the courtier, the politician, the rich man, it was very edifying; for the poet it came too late.   J.W.

Warren, Robert Penn (1905–), who was born in Kentucky, began as a poet in the **Fugitive Group** of Southern writers, and wrote under the influence of the Metaphysical poets. Later, after considerable success as a novelist, he took to writing a verse looser in construction and more directly concerned with emotion. His long narrative poem, *Brother to Dragons* (1953), was adapted and produced as a play. He has won both the Pulitzer Prize and the National Book Award, and in 1966 published his *Selected Poems*.   D.H.
see also American Poetry

Warton, Joseph (1722–1800), was an Oxford-educated headmaster and an astute critic of the 'correct' school of poetry in *Essays* on **Pope** (1756, 1782). He was the brother of Thomas **Warton.**   D.H.

Warton, Thomas (1728–90), was Poet Laureate of England in 1785. He was a professor of poetry and history at Oxford and a friend of Dr **Johnson.** In his *Poems*

(1777) he revived sonnet form, and he also wrote a three-volume *English Poetry* (1774–81) and *Observations on the Faerie Queene of Spenser* (1754). He anticipated Romantic poetry.   D.H.

Watkins, Vernon (1906–67), was a Welsh poet who drew on Welsh material and legend. His books of poems include: *Ballad of the Mari Lwyd* (1941), *The Lady with the Unicorn* (1948), *Selected Poems* (America: 1948), *The Death Bell* (1954), *Cypress and Acacia* (1959), and *Affinities* (1962).   D.H.

Watts, Isaac (1674–1748), a clergyman and the author of *Divine Songs for Children* (1715), which contains lines on the busy bee parodied by Lewis **Carroll**, and the metred *Psalms of David* (1719). His popular hymns include 'O God, our help in ages past'.   D.H.

Webster, John (*c.* 1580–*c.* 1638), was born free of the Merchant Taylors' Company, perhaps about 1580; but less is known of his life than of those of Sophocles or Euripides two thousand years before. In 1602–5 he collaborated with other dramatists, particularly with **Dekker** in *Sir Thomas Wyatt*, *Westward Ho!*, and *Northward Ho!*; but this was prentice-work. His outstanding decade, about 1610–20, produced *The White Devil* (*c.* 1611–12, published 1612); *The Duchess of Malfi* (*c.* 1612–14, published 1623); thirty-two new pieces in the sixth edition of 'Overbury's' *Characters* (1615); and *The Devil's Law-Case* (*c.* 1619, published 1623). Then he reverted to collaboration, in the lost *Late Murther of the Son upon the Mother* (1624; with Dekker, **Ford**, and Rowley); in *A Cure for a Cuckold* (*c.* 1625; with Rowley and, perhaps, Heywood); in *Appius and Virginia* (*c.* 1626–7; probably with Heywood); and perhaps in two other plays.

The rest of his work is unimportant—
a dull and derivative elegy on Prince
Henry (1612); a Lord Mayor's Pageant
(1624); and some prosaic commendatory
verses. By 1634 or 1638, he was probably
dead. Fitzjeffrey's *Notes from Black-Fryers*
(1617) assails 'crabbed Websterio' as a
costive, unintelligible, arrogantly hyper-
critical writer. Yet Webster's allusions to
fellow-dramatists, and theirs to him,
especially his friend Heywood's, suggest
that he was not always so 'crabbed'.

Webster lives by his *White Devil*, his
Duchess, and parts of his *Devil's Law-Case*.
Few read the rest. Quite reasonably, since
life is short. But this partial reading has
produced a falsely partial picture of him as
a sort of demon-sexton, supping man-
dragora and pillowed on skulls, amid
yews, ravens, and screech-owls. His other
works do not, however, suggest a Jacobean
Beddoes, **Poe**, or Baudelaire. The black
of Italianate tragedy suited his Muse; but,
as with **Byron**, it is rash to take modes
and moods for the whole man.

Even as tragic dramatist, Webster has
been most diversely judged. For Charles
Kingsley and William Watson, he was
morbidly demoralising—a public poisoner;
for Shaw, a 'Tussaud-laureate'; for
William Archer, 'Bedlam broke loose'.
Yet he moved Lamb to raptures; **Swinburne** and Stoll praised his stern moral
tone; Swinburne, indeed, did not fear to
name him with Aeschylus, Dante, and
Shakespeare. The truth, as so often, seems
to lie half-way.

Webster's strength is not in his plots—
these tend to gasp and wheeze by the fifth
act. Rather, the reader recalls the vibrating
intensity of single scenes—the breathless
trials in *The White Devil*, *Devil's Law-Case*,
Appius and Virginia; Brachiano's wooing of
Vittoria, and his quarrel with her in the
House of Convertites; the Duchess'
wooing of Antonio, or her discovery by
her insanely jealous brother. In his minor
dramas Webster is no more a thinker than
Scribe; even in his three chief plays his
philosophy seems mainly an embittered
despair. His only values are courage, compassion, and a clear-headedness that prefers
even cynicism to cant. Accordingly his
most living figures are dauntless women or
sardonic Machiavels.

Above all, perhaps, Webster's fame rests
on his style—its imaginative concreteness,
its concentrated vehemence, its subtle
rhythms. Hence, though a plagiarist more
unblushing even than **Goldsmith**, Sterne,
or Chénier, he seems often more original
than his originals. Few poets have had
more power to force the dullest sense to
feel, or hear, or see.

> Had I bin damn'd in hell,
> And should have heard of this, it would
> > have put me
> Into a cold sweat.

> I would have their bodies
> Burn't in a coale-pit, with the ventage
> > stop'd,
> That their curs'd smoake might not
> > ascend to Heaven.

> Millions are now in graves, which at
> > last day
> Like Mandrakes shall rise shreeking.

Of a blackamoor:

> Shee simpers like the suddes
> A Collier hath bene washt in.

As metrist, Webster strains the traditional mould of blank verse audaciously near
the breaking-point. Yet it does not break,
as with **D'Avenant** or **Suckling** it was
soon to do.

> On paine of death, let no man name
> > death to me,
> It is a word infinitely terrible.

We thinke cag'd birds sing, when
                    indeed they crie.

Today Webster is hard to act. Few actors can modulate his unearthly, elusive music; and we are less uncritically romantic than the Jacobeans. Except in brief scenes, Webster cannot rival Shakespeare as dramatist; and yet, as poet, there are moments when he can challenge Shakespeare himself.   F.L.L.

Wheelwright, John (1897–1940), was a Bostonian poet active in left-wing politics, and edited the magazine, *Poems for a Dime*. His eccentric poems were sometimes overshadowed in his lifetime by his eccentric manners, and the true originality of his sprightly verses is only beginning to be assessed.   D.H.

Whitman, Walt (1819–92), was born on Long Island ('fish-shape Paumanock') and his childhood was nourished there and in the old port of Brooklyn. After brief schooling he was apprenticed at the age of fourteen to a printer, the beginning of his career in the printing, editing and writing of newspapers which was only broken by a few intermittent years of school-teaching: 'one of my best experiences and deepest lessons in human nature'. His poetry at this stage was conventional and as sentimental as his temperance novel. Discharged from the editorship of the Brooklyn *Eagle*, for political reasons, in 1848, he travelled to New Orleans, a journey which opened up his provinciality to the experience of the Mississippi heartlands, Chicago and the Great Lakes. Back in New York, he wrote angry poems about liberty, frequented a circle of artists, and wrote and lectured on art theory. He absorbed opera, Egyptian antiquities, and the mass of international arts and crafts in the 1853 World's Fair, and bought real

estate, supported his family, and could have become fairly wealthy through his business sense. But in 1855 he rapidly assumed a prophetic role—the American poet of *Leaves of Grass*, his first volume of poems. Although the author's name was nearly concealed in the copyright line, the frontispiece showed the new bard, bearded, in shirt-sleeves, and showing his dark undershirt. The myth of Walt proclaimed

an American, one of the roughs, a
                              kosmos,
Disorderly fleshy and sensual . . .
          eating, drinking and breeding.

Leaves became his bardic scripture, augmented in a series of editions till his death, his one book in which the writer moved in tension between the man Whitman and the persona Walt, until he finally claims 'who touches this touches a man'. The new poems were attacked—'I expected hell, and I got it'—for their informal structures and their frank physicality. **Emerson** found in them merits which were 'fortifying and encouraging', but the *Boston Post* rejected these New England romantic verses as 'these foul and rank leaves of the poison-plants of egoism, irreverence, and lust'.

At thirty-five Whitman embodied the legend he required but his journalism had to continue. His working-man's dress became less symbolic when the 1857 depression left him poor. The third edition of *Leaves* contained the new *Out of the Cradle, Endlessly Rocking*, a more personal poem than *Song of Myself*, the earlier masterpiece: a Long Island boy watches love and death enacted in the lives of two mocking birds and becomes the poet, 'singer solitary'—'Never more the cries of unsatisfied love be absent from me'. *Bardic Symbols* records more of this personal crisis within the public image: 'I too but signify at the utmost a little wash'd up drift'. Yet beyond despair and a sense of failure, his typical resilience reasserts that 'before all my arrogant poems the real Me stands yet untouch'd, untold, altogether unreach'd'. Humility gives him strength to await the flow of his tidal vitality.

The portrait for the 1860 *Leaves* is Byronically confident and vulnerable, and *Protoleaf (Starting from Paumanock)* exposes the dividing aims of the poet at forty: to sing himself—'free, fresh, savage, / Fluent, luxuriant, self-content'; to 'write the evangel-poems of comrades and love'; to make 'a song of These States'; and to project an ecstatic vision of the New World recovery of Adam's innocence and power as part of 'A world primal again' with new politics, religions, inventions and arts. Parallel to these strained effusions, the *Calamus* poems express love in intimate personal terms. When Civil War broke out, Whitman had already warned America not to rely on union through legal papers and agreements. He did write his bad recruiting poem, but his transforming experience developed through his identification with the wounded in camp hospitals from 1862 onwards: 'There is something in personal love, caresses, and the magnetic flood of sympathy and friendship that does, in its way, more good than all the medicine in the world' (*Hospital Visits*). The war strengthened his poetry but germs and weariness sapped his health.

The war-poems in *Drum Taps* (1865) drew little attention and a *Leaves*-shocked Secretary of the Interior sacked Whitman from his minor government post. But in 1865 Whitman produced his great Lincoln elegy, *When Lilacs Last in the Door-Yard Bloom'd*, and in 1866 received his first strong defence in Ashton's *The Good Gray Poet*. Distinguished English appreciation and an edition of his poems came while he lived in unheated rooms in Washington. After 1868, his descent from 'the high plateau of my life and capacity' left only the essays in *Democratic Vistas* (1871) and some poems in *Passage to India* (added to *Leaves* in 1870). A passionate friendship with a young streetcar conductor was interrupted by a paralysing stroke (1873) from which he did not fully recover: 'My heart is blank and lonesome utterly'. On a hospitable farm his health improved for him to write *Specimen Days* (1882) and make a round of lectures and visits. With financial help he was able to live his last days in decent attendance and receive the final edition of *Leaves* on his deathbed..

The preface to *Leaves of Grass* announced the image of the frontier poet and an American poetry: 'here are the roughs and beards and space and ruggedness and nonchalance that the soul loves'. The 'sunburnt 'poet embodies the geography and spirit of his country and scorns the 'unmistakably genteel' Europeanised intellectual. He is 'self-reliant', despises the aristocratic tradition from **Shakespeare** to **Tennyson**, and in place of 'old theories and forms' offers symbolically fresh style and typography. His bardic utterance is a demand on the expanding nation, addressing no particular class and accepting the universe in Emersonian sympathy—'the attitude of great poets is to cheer up slaves and horrify despots'. Whitman's programme emerges in three statements: 'whatever satisfies the soul is truth'— 'One's self I sing, a simple separate person, / Yet utter the word Democratic, the word En-Masse' (1867)—'The moth and the fish-eggs are in their place; / The suns I see, and the suns I cannot see, are in their place'. *Song of Myself* continually documents the exact individual life in action—'I am the man, I suffered, I was there'—and, equally, the language ranges from the high philosophical to the intimate colloquial. 'In modern times what controlling, organising, selecting poet has created a world with as much in it as Whitman's, a world that so plainly *is* the world? Of all modern poets he has, quantitatively speaking, "the most comprehensive soul"—and, qualitatively speaking, a most comprehensive and comprehending one, with charities and concessions and qualifications that are rare at any time' (Randall **Jarrell**).

His language enacts his vision of the 'procreant urge of the world'—his imagery relates to the life and death processes and he wrote some of the best erotic poetry in English. *Leaves of Grass*, he said, 'is avowedly the song of Sex and Amativeness, and even Animality' (1888). Beyond the famous 'barbaric yawp' lies the mystical nature experience of *Song of Myself*, section 24—'Something I cannot see puts upward libidinous prongs; / Seas of bright juice suffuse heaven . . .'—and the dignified articulation of imagery and ryhthmic pacing of the Lincoln elegy, whose liturgical forms and almost brusque simplicities extend the tradition of *Lycidas*.

Whitman always risked lyrical diffuseness and the noisy nationalist rhetoric of *Song of the Exposition* (1871). Concentration of meaning in wit was not his strength, and his later poems reek of induced ecstasies. His finest work indeed generates his international myth: 'Solitary, singing in the West, / I strike up for a New World'.

E.N.W.M.

see also American Poetry

Whittemore, Reed (1919–), is an American poet and editor of *Furioso* and *The Carleton Miscellany*. His poems are anecdotal and satirical. Among contemporary Americans he is nearly unique in his combination of the comic, the intelligent and the moving.   D.H.

Wilbur, Richard (1921–), graduated from Amherst College in 1942. In the war he served in the American infantry in Italy and France, where he began to write poems. Afterwards he entered Harvard University Graduate School, and took his M.A. in 1947. He was a Junior Fellow in Harvard's Society of Fellows (1947–50), and was Assistant Professor of English there (1950–54). He was a Guggenheim Fellow (1952–3), a Prix de Rome Fellow (1954–5), and an Associate Professor of English at Wellesley College (1955–7). At present he is Professor of English at Wesleyan University. His books of poems are: *The Beautiful Changes* (1947), *Ceremony* (1950), *Things of this World* (1956), *Poems 1943–1956* (England, 1957), and *Advice to a Prophet* (1961). In 1957 he received the Pulitzer Prize and the National Book Award for *Things of this World*. He has edited *A Bestiary* (1955), a complete edition of **Poe**'s poems (1959), and has translated Molière. He collaborated with Lillian Hellman and others in writing *Candide*, a comic opera, in 1957.

Richard Wilbur's poems are characterised by elegance, grace and care. His early work showed attentive reading of Marianne **Moore** and Wallace **Stevens**, but these influences largely disappeared in his second book. His language is distinguished by discreet classical references, etymological puns, and remarkably accurate epithets. He is not averse to an occasional inversion, believing that artificiality is a quality of art. In subject matter he is commonly concerned with an asceticism of the imagination—his 'tall camels of the spirit' which are proud that they can endure without water. 'Caught Summer is always an imagined time.' In autumn,

> the envious mind
> Which could not hold the summer in
>   my head

While bounded by that blazing
                    circumstance
Parades these barrens in a golden trance,
Remembering the wealthy season dead,
And by an autumn inspiration makes
A summer all its own. Green boughs
                                arise
Through all the boundless backward of
                             the eyes.
And the soul bathes in warm conceptual
                               lakes.

In an elegant couplet Wilbur satirises his own practice: 'We milk the cow of the world, and as we do / We whisper in her ear, "You are not true".' In his most recent work he has concentrated more on things of this world, and less on the subjective creation of a substitute world. D.H.
see also American Poetry

Wilde, Oscar [Fingal O'Flahertie Wills] (1856–1900), is remembered chiefly as a writer of sparkling, highly civilised comedies. Most of his verse is languid, ornate and trivial, but *The Ballad of Reading Gaol* has a poignancy and a vividness born of the degradation he suffered in a place where

The hangman with his little bag
     Went shuffling through the gloom.
                                   J.P.

Williams, William Carlos (1883–1963), was born in Rutherford, New Jersey, and lived there most of his life. Medical studies took him early to Europe, where he renewed a college acquaintance with **Pound** and, in London, met **Yeats**. Marriage (1912) and a thriving general practice settled him in Rutherford, although he revisited Europe after the First World War. *In the American Grain* (1925), his eighth book, probes and establishes an Americanism he needed in a prose style which is magnificently native. A number of awards culminated in his appointment as fellow of the

Library of Congress; alleged leftist principles prevented him from serving. Central to his remarkably fine and large output are: *Paterson*, Books I–V (1946–58), *Make Light of It* (collected stories, 1950), *Collected Later Poems* (1950), *Collected Earlier Poems* (1951), *Autobiography* (1951), a novel trilogy—*White Mule, In the Money, The Build-Up* (1937–52), *The Desert Music and other poems* (1957), *Selected Essays* (1954), *Selected Letters* (1957), *Many Loves and other plays* (1961) and *Pictures from Brueghel* (1962).

Williams's poems contain a generosity of spirit, a humane warmth, ability to translate daily life and ordinary objects into an unsentimental order of personal and universal significance, which are unique in modern poetry and rare at any time. His ironical but tenderly empirical attitudes refused the abstract philosophical; the serene vision of *Paterson V* is not betrayed by the crackerbarrel wisdom of old age. Williams nearly despaired only over the wasted potentiality and deadening sources of constructive life in America. His ear for rhythm was practically perfect, his handling of the poetic line was in advance of his time and extremely influential in American poetry since 1945.

The **Imagism** of his early short poems is entirely modified by a striving for values rather than visual description: the well-known *The Red Wheelbarrow* is therefore typical, but less subtle than *This Is Just To Say*. *To Elsie* demonstrates Williams's controlled anger for the ordinary American existence under 'imaginations which have no / peasant traditions to give them character'. Hypo-critical disguises are exploded in the funeral of *Tract*: 'Go with some show of inconvenience; sit openly —/ to weather as to grief'. *Yachts* brilliantly allegorises the competitive spirit by which the beautifully powerful sustain their conquest:

. . . the horror of the race dawns
          staggering the mind,
the whole sea become an entanglement
          of watery bodies
lost to the world bearing what they
          cannot hold.
  Broken,
beaten, desolate, reaching from the
          dead to be taken up
they cry out, failing, failing! their cries
          rising
in waves still as the skillful yachts pass
          over.

Most of Williams's simplest, shortest poems manage an image of his sharp awareness of the human condition, and *Paterson*, throughout its variable styles and organisational devices, sounds 'this note of reality, this sense of the poem being in touch with something dense, not something that the writer has densified by mixing quick-drying ideas with it' (Kenner). This 'directed meditation' on the loss and possible recovery of community—a version of the great American theme of lost utopia—is firmly constructed out of experienced language—the heard vernacular, the official report, the news item, the private letter. The order of the poem reconciles social incoherence and fragmentary life is redeemed as it is in the tradition of American poems to which *Paterson* belongs, the syntheses of *The Bridge*, *Notes Towards a Supreme Fiction*, the *Cantos*, *The Waste Land*, and *The People, Yes*: and is far less literary than these. In his effort to affirm, Williams was too content to present raw material as art, out of a cussed desire to appear not the literary but the average man. He possessed some of the blindness of the primitivist. But mostly one is willing to respond to his plea:

    Hear me out
        for I too am concerned

and every man
    who wants to die in peace in his
      bed besides.

                E.N.W.M.

see also American Poetry *and* Imagery

Winchilsea, Anne Finch, Countess of (1661–1720), is a good representative of the kind of English poet we must call occasional. She was celebrated by **Pope** as Ardelia, and praised by **Wordsworth**. Both Pope and **Shelley**, curiously enough, imitated a couplet from her poem, *The Spleen*.   D.H.

Winters, [Arthur] Yvor (1900–1968), spent his childhood in California and Chicago. He studied at the universities of Chicago, Colorado, and Stanford. He taught at schools in New Mexico coal camps, at the University of Idaho, and at Stanford, where he became professor of English. His first book of poems, *The Immobile Wind*, was published in 1921. He has written several important books of criticism, three of them now collected in one volume, *In Defense of Reason*, two others called *The Function of Criticism* and *Forms of Discovery*, and a study of E. A. **Robinson**. He was awarded the Bollingen Prize for his *Collected Poems* (1960).

Winters' poetry has been neglected for years, partly because of the unpopularity of his better-known critical works, and partly because most of it runs counter to the 'modernist' revolution. He was, however, publishing experimental poetry in his early twenties, free verse embodying a view of life as a series of ecstatically perceived fragments:

    Adventurer in
living fact, the poet
mounts into the spring,
upon his tongue the taste of
air becoming body: is

embedded in this crystalline precipitate of time.

Since that time he came to view the writing of poetry as 'a technique of comprehension', involving full use of the rational powers and moral judgement that he had deliberately avoided in his earliest work. The poet may still be 'embedded' in his subject matter, but he now tries to view it in a context which can enable him to understand it. The discipline of his style does not reject experience—rather it is a means of simultaneously conveying it, in all its richness and variety, and evaluating it, since the conveying has little meaning without the evaluation. As Allen **Tate** has said, Winters 'brings his experience to order and form, and then order and form are themselves part of the experience'. The process of writing a poem is for him similar to the process described in his *Sir Gawaine and the Green Knight.* Donald Stanford has said, 'the theme of [this] poem is recurrent in Winters' poetry —the immersion into sensation, the plunge into particulars to the point of disintegration, and the recovery'. The Green Knight's Lady clings with the strength of the actual and particular, which one must both invite and resist before one can understand them:

By practice and conviction formed,
With ancient stubbornness ingrained,
Although her body clung and swarmed,
My own identity remained.

The 'recovery', the placing of experience, the understanding, is equivalent to the making of a poem:

I left the green bark and the shade
Where growth was rapid, thick, and still;
I found a road that men had made
And rested on a drying hill.

In a review of Winters' *Collected Poems*, Tate wrote: 'He has achieved an impressive clarity because he respects the limits of language more than the inner light; a true elegance, because he declines to invite the reader into the irrelevance of his private sensibility; and controlled power, because his insights are not asserted but earned. At least six poems, *A Vision, Sir Gawaine, The California Oaks, The Journey, The Marriage,* and *To the Holy Spirit,* I would place with the best American poetry of their century.'

T.G.

Wordsworth, William (1770–1850), was born at Cockermouth, Cumberland, in the Lake District, on 7 April, 1770, the second oldest of five children of John and Anne Cookson Wordsworth. His father was law agent and rent-collector for Lord Lonsdale, and the family was at this period reasonably well off. William attended the Hawkshead Grammar School, near Windermere, until his matriculation at St John's College, Cambridge. By this time he was an orphan, under the charge of guardians. He was an indifferent scholar at Cambridge, and when he graduated had little sense of his future vocation. In the year after his graduation he went to France (having been there once before, during a summer vacation from Cambridge), where he contracted not only radical republican sympathies but also an affair with one Annette Vallon, to whom his illegitimate daughter, Caroline, was born in 1792. Wordsworth returned to England, where his political sympathies gradually changed as the fortunes of liberty in France declined. Supported by a bequest from a friend, he settled, with his sister Dorothy, near Bristol. It was here that he met **Coleridge**, and that their famous friendship began. In 1798 the two poets published the *Lyrical Ballads* together, and in the same year they visited Germany. In 1799 Wordsworth and his sister settled in the Lake District. In 1802, having come into a patrimony long delayed by litigation, he married Mary Hutchinson. In 1813 he was granted the sinecure of Distributor of Stamps for Westmorland. His life meanwhile was a quiet one; the production of editions of his poems was steady and his reputation, especially after 1815, steadily increased. In 1839 he was honoured by Oxford University with a degree of Doctor of Civil Law, and in 1843 he became Poet Laureate.

When Wordsworth says:

Sweet is the lore which Nature brings;
Our meddling intellect
Mis-shapes the beauteous forms of
                     things:
We murder to dissect,

what he is protesting against and what he recommends are fairly well agreed about by his critics. His poetry is a protest against eighteenth-century intellectualistic and analytical habits of mind, and a recommendation in favour of what the imagination can do to combat or to transcend these habits, since their tendency is not only brutally to divide the objects of nature from one another but also brutally to divorce the mind of man from the world which he contemplates. A. N. Whitehead, for example, finds Wordsworth the hero of a 'protest on behalf of value'. He says that Wordsworth 'alleges against science its absorption in abstractions' and grasps 'the whole of nature in the tonality of the particular instance'. Wordsworth hears in nature 'a thousand blended notes' and says that 'To her fair works did Nature link / The human soul that through me ran,' and he laments the fact that man persists in

schematising nature and in divorcing himself from it by his exclusive reliance on his analytical or abstractive powers. Man has thwarted his own capabilities for 'feeling', for 'wise passiveness', for the exercise of that imagination which is 'Reason in her most exalted mood', which perceives not the distinctions between things but their unity, and which discovers in the processes of things, the moments as they change, the seasons as they pass and the days in their diurnal round, a single principle which binds all things together, which 'rolls through all things', and which is capable of revealing itself to the mind as the religious creative principle itself.

Since Wordsworth's great subject is the relation of the mind to nature, it follows that his scenes are most frequently natural scenes described by a solitary observer to himself, or to another, a dear friend, perhaps a sister, so intimate with himself as to be almost one with himself. This is not to say that he is uninterested in the problems of social intercourse; it is to say that for him the great teacher of love is not to be found in the society of men. It is to be found rather in the natural, the unconscious, the unintellectual and spontaneous harmony and order of nature. Indeed, his greatest long poem, *The Prelude*, may be described as the story of an ardent attempt and a deeply felt failure to discover in society, in politics or in abstract philosophy the possibilities of love, and the story of a return at last to nature as the only paradigm for what it was he sought. The return, that is to say, to poetry, since poetry for Wordsworth is defined primarily as the right contemplation of that nature in which can be discerned symbols of the eternal, the unchanging and the immutable, and therefore of a tranquillity which he identifies with love.

Those who exemplify the unifying powers of the imagination, whether consciously or not, include not only the poet but a number of rustic and simple figures who are close to 'the beautiful and permanent forms of nature' and who are uninstructed in, and therefore uncorrupted by, the ways of the world. The child, the idiot, the shepherd, some beautiful and innocent young girl; or an old man, a beggar, a wandering veteran, an ancient leech-gatherer, one who has survived his passions and his attachments to the world in which the intellect operates divisively and analytically. These figures are specially open to 'the whole of nature as involved in the tonality of the particular instance'; through 'outward shows of sky and earth' (to use Wordsworth's phrase) come 'impulses of deeper birth', evidences of unity. These figures are a lesson and a reproach to the ordinary man, the (so to speak) dweller in cities, with all his propensities for destructive intellectualism and analysis.

For Whitehead and for other critics— for example, Basil Willey, R. D. Havens, Bennett Weaver, Edmund Wilson, Newton Stallknecht, and many others, however much they differ in various respects— Wordsworth is the great hero of unification, the unification of object and object in nature, and of the mind of man with that which it perceives. As Wilson says (*Axel's Castle*, 1931): '. . . a Romantic poet like Wordsworth has come to feel the falsity of this assumption [that man is apart from nature]: he has perceived that the world is an organism, that nature includes planets, mountains, vegetation and people alike . . . , that all are involved in the same great entity'. But other writers have argued that while in one way Wordsworth was certainly just such a hero, in another a powerful counter-current can be felt, pulling towards

its own kind of abstractness, pulling away from the concrete and towards the metaphysical. G. Wilson Knight gives an account of the poetry by which it is a great deal less concrete than Whitehead's account might lead us to expect. D. G. James and John Jones both argue that the joining of mind to nature was ultimately a failure for Wordsworth and that his final goal had to be, in Jones' phrase, 'outside the world'. David Perkins speaks of the 'Wordsworthian withdrawal' and he shares with David Ferry the sense that the endings of both *Tintern Abbey* and the ode, *Intimations of Immortality*, which assert themselves to be celebrations of the mind's capacity to make its peace with nature, are really pessimistic in tone and suggest the failure of that peace-making. The latter critic suggests an absolute conflict in Wordsworth. While on the one hand he may be understood as desiring the healthy sense of man's living oneness with nature, on the other he desired the obliteration of personality in a kind of death, a very different sort of oneness. Consider the following poem:

A slumber did my spirit seal;
   I had no human fears:
She seem'd a thing that could not feel
   The touch of earthly years.
No motion has she now, no force;
   She neither hears nor sees;
Roll'd round in earth's diurnal course,
   With rocks, and stones, and trees.

The poet's original failure was in not having related this girl organically to the universe of which she has now tragically become part. He had thought of her in abstraction from nature; nature has now taught him how 'the whole of nature is involved in the tonality of the particular instance'. But the poem may be read another way as well, emphasising the grandeur of the concluding two lines, to suggest that her fate is superior to his, left alive as he is. She has been merged into that final unconsciousness which perhaps he desires.

Twentieth-century views of Wordsworth have been extremely diverse and are consequently hard to summarise. There have been studies based importantly upon the biography, for example on Wordsworth's affair with Annette Vallon or his relationship with his sister Dorothy; arguments over the degree to which Wordsworth was or was not a Christian; examinations of his Hartleianism and of his rejection of Hartley; investigations of the connection between his poetry and his politics; attacks on the later poetry and passionate defences of it. He cannot be said to have been ignored. In this article the writer has attempted to give a brief review of the attitudes towards Wordsworth's poetry which seem to be most significant. He would only call attention more especially to three other important works, Herbert Lindenberger's *On Wordsworth's Prelude*, Geoffrey Hartman's brilliant and challenging *Wordsworth's Poetry, 1787–1814*, and Mary Moorman's great biography, *William Wordsworth*.

It has not been possible, within the limits of this article, to do justice to the dazzling virtuosity and variety with which Wordsworth's great themes are expressed, in ballad-imitations, in sonnets, in stanzaic forms of great originality and beauty, and in a blank verse (especially that of *Tintern Abbey*, *The Prelude*, and Books I, II, and IV of *The Excursion*) unrivalled since **Milton**. Nor has it been possible to discuss the great political sonnets of 1802–4, which have their own somewhat different theme; nor the subject of the later poetry which has occasioned so much controversy; nor that

of the critical theories set forth in the 'Preface' to the second edition of the *Lyrical Ballads* (1800) and in the 'Preface' to the edition of 1815.   D.F.
see also Criticism and Poetry *and* Imagery

Wright, James (1927–), is an American poet who has written in two styles. His first is narrative or expository of character, sometimes like E. A. **Robinson**. More recently his poetry has become visionary, almost surrealistic. While the first poems were, successful, the second seem to include more possibilities of growth. D.H.

Wyatt, Sir Thomas (1503–42), was born in Allington Castle in Kent, and was educated at St John's College, Cambridge. He married in 1520, but separated from his wife six years later. He was not only a poet but a soldier and courtier and, above all, a diplomat, taking part in important missions abroad. In 1536 he was imprisoned, allegedly for having been Anne Boleyn's lover. He was released after six weeks, apparently restored to favour. But when his friend, Thomas Cromwell, was executed in 1540, he was once more imprisoned, this time for 'papist tendencies'. He was in the Tower of London for three months, and was then freed, to perform further duties for the King until his death of a fever in 1542.

The most accurate texts of Wyatt's poetry are found in manuscript collections, though for many years he was known only from the work included in Richard Tottel's anthology, *Songes and Sonettes* (1557), where his original metre had been considerably 'reformed'.

The poetry is of four kinds: balets (songs), translations, satires, and the series of *Penitential Psalms*. Most critics prefer the balets: Kenneth Muir calls 'some fifty of them . . . the best lyrics written in English before the great Elizabethans'. Their subject matter accords with the medieval conventions of courtly love, most of them following the formula of the lament about the cruelty of the poet's mistress. They vary a good deal in quality, from the lifelessness of

> Vengeaunce shall fall on thy disdain,
> That makest but game on ernest pain;
>   Thinck not alone vnder the sonne
> Vnquyt to cause thy lovers plain,
> All tho my lute and I have done,

to the powerful stanza starting his best-known poem:

> They fle from me that sometyme did
>   me seke
>   With naked fote stalking in my
>   chambre.
> I have sene theim gentill tame and meke
>   That nowe are wyld and do not
>   remembre
> That sometyme they put theimself in
>   daunger
> To take bred at my hand; and nowe
>   they raunge
> Besely seking with a continuell chaunge.

Perhaps the clearest contrast between these two passages is in the movement. In the first it is heavy and wooden, contributing nothing to the statement made; in the second it is halting and tentative, abetting the wistful feeling with which he evokes the creatures of past love.

Much has been made of the resemblance between Wyatt's and **Donne**'s love poetry; Sir Edmund Chambers speaks of the poise with which each watches 'his own emotions in detachment, with a finger on the burning pulse'. Though this is true, it is unlikely that Wyatt's tone can be called 'dramatic' in the same way as Donne's. Most of Wyatt's lyrics are written as songs in which he circles round a given point, or as narrative-meditations in which he proceeds from one point to another foreseen from the start. They lack the element of dramatic surprise found in Donne at his best and worst. Even in 'They fle from me' the feeling develops as a natural result of the situation described rather than as an unpredicted reaction to it, and the 'surprise ending' of the last two lines is strictly traditional.

H. A. Mason dissents from the general opinion of the balets, considering that Wyatt was in most of them 'merely supplying material for social occasions'. And though he finds most of the translations 'of little interest', he considers a few of them more distinguished than any of the balets. In the best of them, for example 'Whoso list to hunt', based on Petrarch, he proves that Wyatt is implicitly criticising the original while he translates it. It should be added that one cause for the lower opinion most critics have of the translations is that in many of them the metre is extremely irregular. Various reasons have been suggested for this irregularity, the most convincing being Muir's, that Wyatt was experimenting in such poems with a syllabic line.

Thomas **Warton** remarked that 'Wyatt may justly be deemed the first polished English satirist'. In 'Mine owne John Poynz' Wyatt writes an 'imitation of Horace', rendering the given theme in contemporary and personal terms. In the satire starting 'My mothers maydes' he retells the fable of the Country Mouse and the Town Mouse with a Chaucerian vigour and particularity:

> She fested her, that joy it was to tell
>   The faere they had: they drancke the
>   wyne so clere.
> And as to pourpose now and then it fell

She chered her with 'How, syster, what
chiere?'
Amyddes this joye befell a sorry
chaunce
That well awaye! the straunger
bought full dere
The fare she had; for as she loked
ascaunce,
Vnder a stole she spied two stemying
Ise
In a rownde hed with sherp erys . . .

The *Penitential Psalms* are also written in *terza rima* (though linked by poems in stanzas). Mason speaks of the 'supple strength' of the writing in 'Psalm 130',

but in general they have been neglected by the critics.   T.G.
see also Foreign Influences on English Poetry

Wylie, Elinor [Hoyt] (1885–1928), was an American poet and novelist, much admired in the nineteen-twenties but now largely unread. She wrote poems which derived from Scots ballads, as well as from the more fashionable **Donne**. She was often precise and sometimes intense, and deserves better than her present obscurity.   D.H.

Y

Yeats, W[illiam] B[utler] (1865–1939), was born in Dublin, of parents who were both members of distinguished Anglo-Irish families. His father, John Butler Yeats, had left the legal profession to become a painter. Yeats has said that his father's studio was the most important influence on his own development. He grew up in Dublin, London, and Sligo, where he usually spent his summers. The landscape of Sligo and to a lesser extent that of Galway and Clare formed the basis of Yeats' sensibility. He was badly educated at schools in London and Dublin and felt quite unprepared to enter Trinity College, Dublin, the family university.

Instead he entered the literary world and the field of Irish nationalist politics. His first poem appeared in 1885 and from then on he published continuously. His services to the Irish nationalist cause

were many. In the eighteen-nineties he attempted to revive the Young Ireland Movement by founding literary societies in London and Dublin; later he took the leading part in various attempts to establish an Irish theatre which culminated in the founding of the Abbey Theatre in 1904; he served in the Irish Senate from 1922 to 1928. These engagements and others provided the subject matter of much of his poetry.

From the eighteen-nineties to the nineteen-twenties Yeats was one of the landmarks on the London literary scene, though he usually spent part of each year in Ireland, in Dublin and at Coole Park, County Galway. He settled in Ireland with his family in 1922. During his later years he lived abroad for long periods.

From 1889 to 1916 his most important personal association was with Maud Gonne, to whom most of his early love poems were addressed. After her ultimate refusal to marry him in 1916, he turned to other plans for settling his personal life;

these led to his marriage with Georgie Hyde-Lees in 1917. They had two children: Anne and Michael. Yeats' last years were a long struggle against ill-health, though he wrote as actively as ever. He died in southern France on 28 January, 1939. In 1948 his body was brought back to Ireland and entombed under Ben Bulben in Drumcliffe Churchyard. On his tombstone is inscribed the epitaph he wrote in 1938:

> Cast a cold eye
> On life, on death.
> Horseman, pass by!

Yeats' early poetry up through *The Wind Among the Reeds* (1899) took two main directions. One led to many artificial ballads based on Irish folklore and legend, to poems such as *The Fiddler of Dooney*. The other led to many densely symbolic personal lyrics, often love poems, written in a hushed, opalescent tone, to poems like *The Secret Rose*:

> Far-off, most secret, and inviolate Rose,
> Enfold me in my hour of hours . . .
> I, too, await
> The hour of thy great wind of love and
> hate.
> When shall the stars be blown about the
> sky,
> Like the sparks blown out of a smithy,
> and die?
> Surely thine hour has come, thy great
> wind blows,
> Far-off, most secret, and inviolate Rose?

Such poems seem to be staged in a closed arcanum where the symbolic rose is worshipped. The air in this arcanum is heavy at times, the decoration sometimes over-elaborate and rich; still, it is a pleasant, even intoxicating place, if a little uncanny. By writing these early poems Yeats learned his trade. By 1899

his artistic means were adequate; he was able to express what he had to say in a finished style.

During the decade 1899–1909 Yeats wrote very few lyric poems, but devoted his attention to exploring subjects derived from Irish heroic legend in a series of plays and narrative poems. By 1909, when he began again to write lyrics regularly, he had developed the belief that a poem should be a 'personal utterance', that the voice of a poet is the voice of a man, that this is so because poetry is memorable speech and speech comes from a man; this belief enabled him to break through to a greater art. From now on his poems are nearly always personal utterances, that could have been written by no one else yet they are, perhaps surprisingly, more and more poems of public speech. Perhaps the greatest paradox in Yeats' development as a poet is that he became truly a public poet only after he became a private one, addicted to personal utterances; eventually he came to express whatever was nearest to hand, say a statuette of lapis lazuli in his study, in the mode of public speech.

Yeats' breakthrough is clearly seen in *Responsibilities* (1914), in poems such as *September 1913* and *To a Shade* which comment on men and events. His style, partly because of the criticism of Ezra **Pound**, is drier; the sun seems to have dispelled the Celtic Twilight.

> What need you, being come to sense,
> But fumble in a greasy till
> And add the halfpence to the pence
> And prayer to shivering prayer, until
> You have dried the marrow from the
> bone?
> For men were born to pray and save:
> Romantic Ireland's dead and gone,
> It's with O'Leary in the grave.

His next collection, *The Wild Swans at Coole* (1919), is one of his finest books.

His mood seems reminiscent and nostalgic, partly because he saved the poems of public speech, inspired by the Easter Rebellion of 1916, for *Michael Robartes and the Dancer* (1921). In *The Wild Swans at Coole* he uses what is nearest to him and most familiar, a walk along Coole Water, to express a state of mind and emotion which everyone who has lived fifty years has experienced. As he does this he achieves a diction and rhetoric that can truly be called noble:

> The trees are in their autumn beauty,
> The woodland paths are dry,
> Under the October twilight the water
> Mirrors a still sky;
> Upon the brimming water among the
> stones
> Are nine-and-fifty swans.

By the time of this volume, what Yeats called 'the System' was beginning to affect his poetry. The System, derived partly from the automatic writing of Mrs Yeats, partly from Yeats' meditations on this, partly from reading, occupied him for the rest of his life. It was finally set forth in the second version of *A Vision* (1937). The System includes an analysis of human personalities according to the phases of the moon, a cyclic theory of history, and much else. After about 1922 it seldom obtrudes directly into Yeats' poetry, though emblems derived from it such as the gyre and the winding stair haunt all his later verse.

Public speech prevails in the great poems Yeats wrote during the nineteen-twenties, though this diction frequently contrasts with poems in a metaphysical mode, the mode which came to prevail in the nineteen-thirties. These contrasting modes can be found in *The Tower* (1928). *Nineteen Hundred and Nineteen* is in the mode of public speech:

> Many ingenious lovely things are gone
> That seemed sheer miracle to the
> multitude,
> Protected from the circle of the moon
> That pitches common things about.

Two songs from a Play uses the metaphysical mode:

> I saw a staring virgin stand
> Where holy Dionysus died,
> And tear the heart out of his side,
> And lay the heart upon her hand
> And bear that beating heart away;
> And then did all the Muses sing
> Of Magnus Annus at the spring,
> As though God's death were but a play.

Poems in both modes are more and more concerned with Unity of Being, the central theme of Yeats' later poetry. He spent the early part of his life perfecting the doctrine of Unity of Being, the later part of his life inculcating it, beginning with his important essay of 1919 'If I were Four-and-Twenty'. Yeats magnificently expresses Unity of Being in the final stanza of *Among School Children*:

> Labour is blossoming or dancing where
> The body is not bruised to pleasure soul,
> Nor beauty born out of its own despair,
> Nor blear-eyed wisdom out of
> midnight oil.
> O chestnut-tree, great-rooted blossomer,
> Are you the leaf, the blossom or the
> bole?
> O body swayed to music, O brightening
> glance,
> How can we know the dancer from the
> dance?

He continued to write poems of public speech in the nineteen-thirties, as in *Lapis Lazuli*:

> I have heard that hysterical women say
> They are sick of the palette and
> fiddle-bow,

Of poets that are always gay,
For everybody knows or else should
                                know
That if nothing drastic is done
Aeroplane and Zeppelin will come out,
Pitch like King Billy bomb-balls in
Until the town lie beaten flat.

But poems at once gnomic and metaphysical establish the tone of *The Winding Stair* (1933) and *A Full Moon in March* (1935). This aspect of Yeats' art culminates in such a cryptic poem as *There* from *Supernatural Songs*:

There all the barrel-hoops are knit,
There all the serpent-tails are bit,
There all the gyres converge in one,
There all the planets drop in the Sun.

The final mode in Yeats' poetry, while all the other modes continue, is a rollicking lyricism. The circle closes in a series of poems in ballad metre reminiscent of the poems Yeats wrote in the eighteen-eighties and nineties, though the late poems are infinitely superior technically to the early ones. Their refrains, for example, are marvellously controlled and marvellously controlling. Typical of *New Poems* (1938) and *Last Poems* (1939) are *A Model for the Laureate* and *High Talk*. *A Model for the Laureate*—the title itself is a major irony—goes in part like this:

The Muse is mute when public men
Applaud a modern throne:
Those cheers that can be bought or sold,
That office fools have run,
That waxen seal, that signature.

For things like these what decent man
Would keep his lover waiting,
  Keep his lover waiting?

                                C.B.B.

see also Foreign Influences on English Poetry *and* Symbolism.

Young, Andrew (1885–   ), is a Scottish nature poet. He was awarded the Queen's Medal for Poetry in 1952. David Daiches has called his poems 'traditional in form, highly original in sensibility and precision of observation'. His collected poems were published in 1960.   D.H.

Young, Edward (1683–1765), after a career as tragedian (*Busiris*, 1719; *Revenge*, 1721) and fashionable prose satirist (*The Universal Passion*, 1725–8), became rector of Welwyn, Hertfordshire, in 1730. His most famous and distinguished poem, *The Complaint, or Night Thoughts on Life, Death, and Immortality* (1724–5), with its evocation of gloom and melancholia, is pre-romantic, despite many Augustan characteristics: the balanced statement of man's limited achievement ('To waft a feather or to drown a fly'); the maxim ('Procrastination is the thief of time'); the appeal to 'being's endless chain'; the didactic derivation of general truths. Yet the poem contains no easy Augustan assurances, for Young complains of the wars, the famines, 'how groaning hospitals eject their dead'. William **Blake**, who similarly depicted London, later provided thirty illustrative watercolours for *Night Thoughts*.   J.G.

For further reading

Some poets whose works are listed in the text are not included in this bibliography.

ADAMS, LÉONIE
Poems, by LÉONIE ADAMS, Mayflower Publishing Co., 1954
Poems, a Selection, by LÉONIE ADAMS, Funk & Wagnalls, New York, 1954

AIKEN, CONRAD
Selected Poems of Conrad Aiken, Oxford University Press, New York and London, 1961

AKENSIDE, MARK
The Poetical Works of Mark Akenside, edited by the REV. A. DYCE, Little, Brown & Co., Boston, 1864
The Poetical Works of Mark Akenside, edited by C. C. CLARKE. Nimmo, Edinburgh, 1868

ALABASTER, WILLIAM
Sonnets, by WILLIAM ALABASTER, Oxford University Press, London, 1959

AMERICAN POETRY
Modern American Poets, selected by CONRAD AIKEN, Martin Secker, London, 1922
A Comprehensive Anthology of American Poetry, edited by CONRAD AIKEN, Random House, New York, 1945
Essay on Rime, by KARL SHAPIRO, Reynal & Hitchcock, New York, 1945
A History of American Poetry, 1900–1940, by H. GREGORY and MARYA ZATURENSKA, Harcourt Brace, New York, 1946
On the Limits of Poetry, by ALLEN TATE, Swallow and W. MORROW, Denver, Colorado, 1948
The Oxford Book of American Verse, edited by F. O. MATTHIESSEN, Oxford University Press, London and New York, 1950

Modern American Poetry, edited by B. RAJAN, Dobson, London, 1950.
Achievement in American Poetry 1900–1950, by LOUISE BOGAN, Regnery, Chicago, 1951
Oxford Anthology of American Literature, Oxford University Press, New York, 1952
The Faber Book of Modern American Verse, edited by W. H. AUDEN, Faber, London, 1956
The Continuity of American Poetry, by R. H. PEARCE, Princeton University Press, Princeton, N.J., 1961

ANGLO-SAXON POETRY
Epic and Romance, by W. P. KER, 2nd edition, Macmillan, London and New York, 1908
An Anglo-Saxon Verse Book, by W. J. SEDGEFIELD, Manchester University Press and Longmans, Manchester, London, and New York, 1922
The Anglo-Saxon Poetic Records, edited by G. P. KRAPP and E. V. K. DOBBIE, 6 vols, Columbia University Press, New York, 1931–53, and Routledge, London, 1932–54
Anglo-Saxon Poetry: an Essay with Specimen Translations in Verse, by G. BONE, Clarendon Press, Oxford, and Oxford University Press, New York, 1943
The Earliest English Poetry, by C. W. KENNEDY, Oxford University Press, London and New York, 1943
Anglo-Saxon England, by SIR F. M. STENTON, 2nd edition, Clarendon Press, Oxford, and Oxford University Press, New York, 1947
The Literature of the Anglo-Saxons, by G. K. ANDERSON, Oxford University Press, London, and Princeton University

Press, Princeton, N.J., 1949, revised edition 1966

The Beginnings of English Society, by D. WHITELOCK, (Pelican History of England), Penguin Books, Harmondsworth, Middx., and Baltimore, 1952

The Beginnings of English Literature (to Skelton, 1509), by W. L. RENWICK and H. ORTON (Introductions to English Literature), 2nd edition, Cresset Press, London, and Dover Publications, New York, 1952

Anglo-Saxon Poetry, selected and translated by R. K. GORDON, (Everyman Library, revised edition), Dent, London, and Dutton, New York, 1954

Beowulf: a Verse Translation into Modern English, by E. MORGAN, Hand & Flower Press, Aldington, Kent, 1952, University of California Press, 1962.

Early English Christian Poetry: Translated into Alliterative Verse, with Critical Commentary, by C. W. KENNEDY, Hollis & Carter, London, and Oxford University Press, New York, 1952

Beowulf, with the Finnesburg Fragment, edited by C. L. WRENN, revised edition, Harrap, London, 1958

Beowulf: an Introduction to the Study of the Peom, by R. W. CHAMBERS, 3rd edition, Cambridge University Press, Cambridge and New York, 1959

An Anthology of Old English Poetry, by C. W. KENNEDY, Oxford University Press, New York, 1960

A Critical History of Old English Literature, by STANLEY B. GREENFIELD, New York University Press, New York, 1965, and University of London Press, London, 1966.

Poems from the Old English, translated by BURTON RAFFEL, University of Nebraska Press, n.p., 1960

The Earliest English Poems, translated by MICHAEL ALEXANDER, Penguin Books, Harmondsworth, Middx., 1966

ARNOLD, MATTHEW
The Poetical Works of Matthew Arnold, edited by C. B. TINKER and H. F. LOWRY,

Oxford University Press, London, 1950

Matthew Arnold, by LIONEL TRILLING, 2nd edition, Allen & Unwin, London, 1949

Matthew Arnold, by J. D. JUMP, Longmans, London, 1955

AUDEN, W. H.
Poems, (1930), by W. H. AUDEN, 2nd edition, Faber, London, 1933

The Orators, (1932), by W. H. AUDEN, 2nd edition, Faber, London, 1934

Look, Stranger, by W. H. AUDEN, Faber, London, 1936

Another Time, by W. H. AUDEN, Faber, London, 1940

New Year Letter, by W. H. AUDEN, 2nd edition, Faber, London, 1942

For the Time Being, by W. H. AUDEN, Faber, London, 1945

Collected Shorter Poems, 1930–1944, by W. H. AUDEN, Faber, London, 1950

The Collected Poems of W. H. Auden, Random House, New York, 1945

W. H. Auden, (Penguin Poets), Penguin Books (in association with Faber), Harmondsworth, Middx., 1958

The Age of Anxiety, by W. H. AUDEN, Faber and Random House, London and New York, 1948

Nones, by W. H. AUDEN, Faber and Random House, London and New York, 1952

The Shield of Achilles, by W. H. AUDEN, Faber and Random House, London and New York, 1955

Homage to Clio, by W. H. AUDEN, Faber and Random House, London and New York, 1960

The Dyer's Hand, by W. H. AUDEN, Faber and Random House, London and New York, 1963

The Enchaféd Flood, (criticism), by W. H. AUDEN, Faber and Random House, London and New York, 1951

About the House, by W. H. AUDEN, Faber and Random House, London and New York, 1968

Auden: an Introductory Essay, by RICHARD HOGGART, Chatto & Windus, London, 1951

The Making of the Auden Canon, by J. W. BEACH, University of Minnesota Press, Minneapolis, 1957

AUSTRALIAN POETRY

The Bush, by B. O'DOWD, Lothian Press, Melbourne, 1912

Poems, by C. BRENNAN, Lothian Press, Melbourne, 1913

Satyrs and Sunlight, by H. McCRAE, Fanfrolico Press, London, 1928

Collected Poems, by J. S. NEILSON, Lothian Press, Melbourne and Sydney, 1934

Moonlight Acre, by R. D. FITZGERALD, Melbourne University Press, Melbourne, 1938

One Hundred Poems, by K. L. SLESSOR, Angus & Robertson, London, 1944

The Moving Image, by JUDITH WRIGHT, Meanjin, Melbourne, 1946

Under Aldebaran, by JAMES McAULEY, Melbourne University Press, Melbourne, 1946

A Drum for Ben Boyd, by F. WEBB, Angus & Robertson, London, 1948

Selected Verse, by J. MANIFOLD, Dobson, London, 1948

Woman to Man, by JUDITH WRIGHT, Angus & Robertson, London, 1949

Between Two Tides, by R. D. FITZGERALD, Angus & Robertson, London, 1952

Leichhardt in Theatre, by F. WEBB, Angus & Robertson, Sydney, 1952

This Night's Orbit, by R. D. FITZGERALD, Melbourne University Press, Melbourne, 1953

Birthday, by F. WEBB, Advertiser Press, Adelaide, 1954

The Wandering Islands, by A. D. HOPE, Edwards & Shaw, Sydney, 1955

The Two Fires, by JUDITH WRIGHT, Angus and Robertson, London, 1955

A Vision of Ceremony, by JAMES McAULEY, Angus & Robertson, Sydney, 1956

The Penguin Book of Australian Verse, edited by J. THOMPSON, K. SLESSOR and R. G. HOWARTH, Penguin Books, Harmondsworth, Middx., 1958

Inside the Whale, by E. JONES, Cheshire, Melbourne, 1959

Socrates, by F. WEBB, Angus & Robertson, London, 1961

Poems, by A. D. HOPE, Hamish Hamilton, London, 1960, and Viking Press, New York, 1961

BARKER, GEORGE

Collected Poems 1930–1955, by GEORGE BARKER, Faber, London, 1957

The True Confession of George Barker, by GEORGE BARKER, Parton Press, London, 1957

BARNES, WILLIAM

Selected Poems, by WILLIAM BARNES, (Muses Library), Routledge, London, 1950

BEAUMONT AND FLETCHER

Works of Beaumont and Fletcher, edited by A. GLOVER and A. R. WALLER, Cambridge University Press, Cambridge, 1905–13

BEDDOES, THOMAS LOVELL

Selected Plays and Poems, by T. L. BEDDOES, Routledge, London, 1950

The Making of a Poet, by H. W. DONNER, Blackwell, Oxford, 1935

The Browning Box, by H. W. DONNER, Oxford University Press, London, 1935

BELLOC, HILAIRE

Verse, by HILAIRE BELLOC, Nonesuch Press, London, 1954

Verse, by HILAIRE BELLOC, (Penguin Poets), Penguin Books, Harmondsworth, Middx., 1960

BENÉT, STEPHEN VINCENT

John Brown's Body, by STEPHEN VINCENT BENÉT, Farrar & Rinehart, New York, 1941

Selected Works, by STEPHEN VINCENT BENÉT, Farrar & Rinehart, New York, 1942

Selected Poetry and Prose, by STEPHEN VINCENT BENÉT, Holt, New York, 1960

BETJEMAN, SIR JOHN

Selected Poems of John Betjeman, Murray, London, 1956

Collected Poems of John Betjeman, Murray, London, 1958

Summoned by Bells, by JOHN BETJEMAN, (verse autobiography), Murray, London, 1960

High and Low, Murray, London, 1966

BINYON, LAWRENCE

Collected Poems, by LAWRENCE BINYON. Macmillan, London, 1931

North Star, by LAWRENCE BINYON, Macmillan, London, 1941

Burning Leaves, by LAWRENCE BINYON, Macmillan, London, 1944

Madness of Merlin, by LAWRENCE BINYON, Macmillan, London, 1947

BISHOP, ELIZABETH

North and South, by ELIZABETH BISHOP, Houghton, Mifflin & Co., Boston, Mass., 1946

Poems, by ELIZABETH BISHOP, Chatto & Windus, London, 1956

Questions of Travel, by ELIZABETH BISHOP, Farrar, Strauss & Giroux, New York, 1965

BLAKE, WILLIAM

Blake's Vala, by H. M. MARGOLIOUTH, Oxford University Press, London, 1956

The Works of William Blake, edited by G. KEYNES, Nonesuch Press, London, 1957

William Blake, edited by J. BRONOWSKI, (Penguin Poets), Penguin Books, Harmondsworth, Middx., 1958

Life of William Blake, by A. GILCHRIST, (Everyman Library), Dent, London, 1945

Life of William Blake, by MONA WILSON, Hart-Davis, London, 1948

'A Bibliography of William Blake', by G. KEYNES, in *Anatomy of Criticism* (essays), Grolier Club, New York, 1957

BLUNDEN, EDMUND

Edmund Blunden: a selection of his poetry and prose, by K. HOPKINS, Hart-Davis, London, 1950

BOTTRALL, RONALD

Selected Poems of Ronald Bottrall, Editions Poetry, London, 1946

The Collected Poems of Ronald Bottrall, Sidgwick & Jackson, London, 1961

BRADSTREET, ANNE

Works, by ANNE BRADSTREET, Peter Smith, New York, 1932 (reprint)

BRIDGES, ROBERT

Poetical Works of Robert Bridges, (Oxford Standard Authors), Oxford University Press, London, 1953

Notes on the Testament of Beauty, by N. C. SMITH, Oxford University Press, London, 1931

BRONTË, EMILY

Complete Poems of Emily Brontë, Oxford University Press, London, 1941

BROOKE, RUPERT

Poetical Works of Rupert Brooke, Faber, London, 1946

John Webster and Elizabethan Drama, by RUPERT BROOKE, Sidgwick & Jackson, London, 1916

Letters from America, by RUPERT BROOKE, Sidgwick & Jackson, London, 1916

BROWNING, ELIZABETH BARRETT

Poetical Works of Elizabeth Barrett Browning, (Oxford Standard Authors), Oxford University Press, London, 1932

The Life of Elizabeth Barrett Browning, by G. B. TAPLIN, Yale University Press, New Haven, Conn., 1957

BROWNING, ROBERT

Works of Robert Browning, edited by A. BIRRELL, Macmillan, New York, 1912

A Browning Handbook, by W. C. DEVANE, revised edition, Croft's, New York, 1955

The Infinite Moment, and Other Essays on Robert Browning, by WILLIAM RAYMOND, University of Toronto Press, Toronto, 1950

The Life of Robert Browning (with notices of his writing, his family, and his friends), by W. H. GRIFFIN and H. C. MINCHIN, revised edition, Methuen, London, 1938

A Commentary upon Browning's 'The Ring

and the Book', by A. K. COOK, Oxford University Press, London and New York, 1920

The Poetry of Experience: The Dramatic Monologue in Modern Literary Tradition, by ROBERT LANGBAUM, Random House, New York, and Chatto & Windus, London, 1957

Browning's Characters: A Study in Poetic Technique, by PARK HONAN, Yale University Press, New Haven, Conn., 1961

BRYANT, WILLIAM CULLEN

The Life and Writings of William Cullen Bryant, Appleton, New York, 1883–4

The Poetical Works of William Cullen Bryant, (Oxford Standard Authors), Oxford University Press, London, 1914

Gotham Yankee: a Biography of William Cullen Bryant, by H. H. PECKHAM, Vantage Press, New York, 1951

BURNS, ROBERT

Poetical Works of Robert Burns, edited by J. L. ROBERTSON, (Oxford Standard Authors), O.U.P. London, 1910

Robert Burns, by DAVID DAICHES, Bell, London, 1952

The Burns Encyclopedia, by Maurice Lindsay, Hutchinson, London, 2nd edition 1970

BUTLER, SAMUEL

Characters and Passages from Notebooks, edited by A. R. WALLER, (Cambridge English Classics), Cambridge University Press, Cambridge 1908

Satires and Miscellaneous Poetry of Samuel Butler, edited by R. LAMAR, (Cambridge English Classics), Cambridge University Press, Cambridge, 1928

BYRON, LORD

Poems, by LORD BYRON, (Everyman Library), Dent, London, 1948

His Very Self and Voice, by E. LOVELL, Macmillan, New York, 1954

Byron: a Biography, by L. A. MARCHAND, Murray, London, 1957

Byron's Don Juan: a Critical Study, by ELIZABETH F. BOYD, Rutgers University Press, New Brunswick, N. J., 1958

CAMERON, NORMAN

Collected Poems, 1905–1953, by NORMAN CAMERON, Hogarth Press, London, 1957

CAMPBELL, ROY

Collected Poems, by ROY CAMPBELL, 3 vols, Bodley Head, London, 1949–60

Roy Campbell, by D. WRIGHT, (Writers and their Work), Longmans, for the British Council, London, 1961

CAMPION, THOMAS

Works of Thomas Campion, edited by P. VIVIAN, (Oxford English Texts), Clarendon Press, Oxford, 1909

Songs of Rosseter's Book of Airs, and First, Second, Third and Fourth Books of Airs, by THOMAS CAMPION, (English School of Lutenist Song Writers), Stainer & Bell, London, 1921–6

England's Musical Poet: Thomas Campion, by M. M. KASTENDIECK, Oxford University Press, New York, 1938

Elizabethan Lyrics, by CATHERINE ING, Chatto & Windus, London, 1951

The Works of Thomas Campion, edited by WALTER R. DAVIS, Doubleday & Co., 1967

CANADIAN POETRY

The Book of Canadian Poetry, edited by A. J. M. SMITH, Gage, Toronto, 1948

Creative Writing in Canada, by D. PACEY, Ryerson Press, Toronto, 1952

The Penguin Book of Canadian Verse, edited by R. GUSTAFSON, Penguin Books, Harmondsworth, Middx., 1958

CAREW, THOMAS

The Poems of Thomas Carew, edited by RHODES DUNLAP, (Oxford English Texts), Oxford University Press, London, 1949

CARROLL, LEWIS

Complete Works of Lewis Carroll, Nonesuch Press, Faber, London, 1939

Some Versions of Pastoral, by WILLIAM EMPSON, new edition, Chatto & Windus, London, 1950

The Field of Nonsense, by ELIZABETH SEWELL, Chatto & Windus, London, 1952

CAUSLEY, CHARLES
Union Street, by CHARLES CAUSLEY, Hart-Davis, London, 1957
Poets of the 1939–1945 War, by R. N. CURREY, (Writers and their Work), Longmans, for the British Council, London, 1960

CHAPMAN, GEORGE
Poems and Plays of George Chapman, edited by T. M. PARROTT, Routledge, London, 1910
George Chapman: Sa vie, sa poésie, son théâtre, sa pensée, by J. JACQUOT, (Annales de l'Université de Lyon), Les Belles Lettres, Paris, 1951
English Literature in the Sixteenth Century, excluding Drama, by C. S. LEWIS, (Oxford History of English Literature, Vol. 3), Clarendon Press, Oxford, and Oxford University Press, New York, 1954

CHATTERTON, THOMAS
Poetical Works of Thomas Chatterton, Bell, London, 1961
'Thomas Chatterton', essay in *The Age of Johnson,* edited by F. W. HILLES, Yale University Press, New Haven, Conn., 1949
A Life of Thomas Chatterton, by E. H. W. MEYERSTEIN, Ingpen & Grant, London, 1930

CHAUCER, GEOFFREY
The Complete Works of Geoffrey Chaucer, edited by W. SKEAT, 7 vols, Oxford University Press, London, 1894
The Complete Works of Geoffrey Chaucer, edited with notes and glossary by F. N. ROBINSON, Oxford University Press, London, 1933
The Canterbury Tales: a New Translation, by NEVILL COGHILL, Penguin Books, Harmondsworth, Middx., 1951
Chaucer: a Bibliographical Manual, by E. P. HAMMOND, Macmillan, New York, 1908
Sources and Analogues of Chaucer's Canterbury Tales, edited by W. F. BRYAN and G. DEMPSTER, University of Chicago Press, Chicago, 1941

A Chaucer Handbook, by R. D. FRENCH, Bell, London, 1947
Bibliography of Chaucer 1908–53, by DUDLEY D. GRIFFITH, Washington, 1955
Chaucer and the French Tradition, by C. MUSCATINE, California, 1957
Chaucer and the Medieval Sciences, by W. C. Curry, Barnes & Noble, New York, 1960
Chaucer's Early Poetry, by WOLFGANG CLEMEN, Methuen, London, 1960
A Preface to Chaucer, by D. W. ROBERTSON, Princeton, 1963
The Flowering of the Middle Ages, edited by JOAN EVANS, Thames & Hudson, 1966
The Court of Richard II, by GERVASE MATTHEW, John Murray, London, 1968

CHESTERTON, G. K.
New and Collected Poems of G. K. Chesterton, Palmer, London, 1929

CHURCHILL, CHARLES
The Poetical Works of Charles Churchill, edited by D. GRANT, Clarendon Press, Oxford, 1956
Charles Churchill, Poet, Rake and Rebel, by W. C. BROWN, University of Kansas Press, Lawrence, Kansas, 1953

CLARE, JOHN
Poems of John Clare, edited by J. W. TIBBLE, Dent, London, 1938
Poems of John Clare's Madness, edited by GEOFFREY GRIGSON, Routledge, London, 1949
Selected Poems of John Clare, edited by GEOFFREY GRIGSON, Routledge, London, 1960
John Clare: His Life and Poetry, by J. W. and A. TIBBLE, Heinemann, London, 1956

CLASSIC and ROMANTIC
Two Pioneers of Romanticism: Joseph and Thomas Warton, by SIR EDMUND GOSSE, British Academy Lecture, London, 1915
Romance, by WALTER RALEIGH, Milford, London, 1917
Classical and Romantic, by H. J. C. GRIERSON, (Leslie Stephen Lecture), Cambridge University Press, Cambridge, 1923

Romanticism, by L. ABERCROMBIE, Secker & Warburg, 1927

From Classic to Romantic, by W. J. BATE, Harvard University Press, Cambridge, Mass., 1946

The Mirror and the Lamp, by M. H. ABRAMS, Oxford University Press, London, 1953

CLEVELAND, JOHN

Works of John Cleveland in *Minor Poets of the Caroline Period,* Vol. 3, edited by G. SAINTSBURY, Clarendon Press, Oxford, 1921

CLOUGH, ARTHUR HUGH

The Poems of A. H. Clough, edited by H. F. LOWRY and others, Clarendon Press, Oxford, 1951

Arthur Hugh Clough, by J. I. OSBORNE, Constable, London, 1919

Ten Victorian Poets, by F. L. LUCAS, Cambridge University Press, Cambridge, 1948

The Uncommitted Mind, by KATHERINE CHORLEY, Oxford University Press, London, 1962

Arthur Hugh Clough, by ISOBEL ARMSTRONG, (Writers and their Work), Longmans, for the British Council, London, 1962

COLERIDGE, SAMUEL TAYLOR

The Poetical Works of S. T. Coleridge, edited by E. H. COLERIDGE, Oxford University Press, London, 1912

Coleridge on the Imagination, by I. A. RICHARDS, Routledge, London, 1934

Inquiring Spirit: a new presentation of Coleridge from his published and unpublished prose and unpublished prose writings, by KATHLEEN COBURN, Routledge, London, and Pantheon, New York, 1951

Coleridge, by HUMPHREY HOUSE, Hart-Davis, London, 1953

Coleridge, by KATHLEEN RAINE, Longmans, London, 1953

COLLINS, WILLIAM

Works of William Collins in *Minor Poets of the Eighteenth Century,* edited by H. L'A. FAUSSET, Dent, London, 1930

William Collins, by D. F. ROTA, (Everyman Library), Dent, London, 1953

COTTON, CHARLES

The Poems of Charles Cotton, edited by J. BUXTON, Harvard University Press, Cambridge, Mass., 1958

COWLEY, ABRAHAM

Poetry and Prose, by ABRAHAM COWLEY, (with Thomas Sprat's Life, and Observations by Dryden, Addison and others), (Clarendon Series of English Literature), Oxford University Press, London, 1949

COWPER, WILLIAM

The Poetical Works of William Cowper, edited by H. S. MILFORD, 4th edition, Oxford University Press, London, 1950

The Correspondence of William Cowper, edited by T. WRIGHT, 4 vols, Hodder & Stoughton, London, 1904

The Stricken Deer, or The Life of Cowper, by LORD DAVID CECIL, Constable, London, 1929, and Oxford University Press, New York, 1930

William Cowper, by NORMAN NICHOLSON, John Lehmann, London, 1951

William Cowper, by NORMAN NICHOLSON, (Writers and their Work), Longmans, for the British Council, London, 1960

William Cowper, an essay and a bibliography of Cowperian Studies, by LODWICK HARTLEY, University of North Carolina Press, Chapel Hill, N.C., 1960

CRABBE, GEORGE

The Poetical Works of George Crabbe, edited by A. J. and R. M. CARLYLE, Oxford University Press, London, 1908

The Life and Works of the Rev. George Crabbe, by GEORGE CRABBE, JR., Murray, London, 1847

CRANE, HART

Collected Poems, by HART CRANE, Liveright, New York, 1933

The Letters of Hart Crane, edited by BROM WEBER, Hermitage, New York, 1952

Hart Crane: the Life of an American Poet, by P. HORTON, Norton, New York, 1937

Hart Crane, by BROM WEBER, Bradley, New York, 1948

CRANE, STEPHEN
The Works of Stephen Crane, edited by
W. FOLLETT, Knopf, New York, 1925–6
The Collected Poems of Stephen Crane, edited
by W. FOLLETT, Knopf, New York and
London, 1930

CRASHAW, RICHARD
Poetical Works of Richard Crashaw, (Oxford
English Texts), Oxford University Press,
London, 1927
*Richard Crashaw: a Study in Baroque
Sensibility*, by A. WARREN, Faber, London,
1957

CRITICISM AND POETRY
On Translating Homer, by MATTHEW
ARNOLD, Longmans, London, 1862
Shakespearean Tragedy, by A. C. BRADLEY,
Macmillan, London, 1904
Elizabethan Critical Essays, edited by
GREGORY SMITH, Oxford University
Press, London, 1904
Essay on Dramatic Poesie, by JOHN DRYDEN,
Oxford University Press, London, 1904
On Shakespeare, by SAMUEL JOHNSON,
Oxford University Press, London, 1908
'Apologie for Poetrie', by Sir Philip Sidney,
in *English Critical Essays, 16th–18th
centuries*, edited by E. D. JONES, (World's
Classics), Oxford University Press,
London, 1922
Principles of Literary Criticism, by I. A.
RICHARDS, Routledge, London, 1926
Practical Criticism, by I. A. RICHARDS,
Routledge, London, 1929
Revaluation, by F. R. LEAVIS, Chatto &
Windus, London, 1936
Miscellaneous Criticism of S. T. Coleridge,
edited by T. M. RAYSOR, Constable,
London, 1936
Essays in Criticism, by MATTHEW ARNOLD,
Macmillan, London, 1938
Poetics, by ARISTOTLE, translated by I. BY-
WATER, Oxford University Press, London,
1940
Preface to 'Lyrical Ballads' by WILLIAM
WORDSWORTH in *Lyrical Ballads*, by
WILLIAM WORDSWORTH and S. T.
COLERIDGE, (English Classics), Methuen,
London, 1940

In Defence of Reason, by YVOR WINTERS,
Swallow, Denver, 1947
Seven Types of Ambiguity, by WILLIAM
EMPSON, new edition, Chatto & Windus,
London, 1949
New Bearings in English Poetry, by F. R.
LEAVIS, new edition, Chatto & Windus,
London, and G. W. Stewart, New York,
1950
Timber, or Discoveries, by BEN JONSON,
(Temple Classics, new edition), Dent,
London, 1951
Selected Essays, by T. S. ELIOT, 2nd edition,
Faber, London, 1951
'Conversations with Drummond', by Ben
Jonson, in *Complete Works of Ben Jonson*,
edited by HERFORD & SIMPSON, Oxford
University Press, London, 1925–52
The Common Pursuit, by F. R. LEAVIS,
Chatto & Windus, London, 1952
The Sacred Wood, by T. S. ELIOT, 7th
edition, Methuen, London, 1953
Letters of John Keats, edited by H. E. ROLLINS,
Oxford University Press, London, 1954
Letters to Robert Bridges, by GERARD MANLEY
HOPKINS, Oxford University Press, Lon-
don, 1955
Biographia Literaria, by S. T. COLERIDGE,
(Everyman Library), Dent, London, 1956
Lives of the Poets, by SAMUEL JOHNSON,
(Everyman Library, new edition), Dent,
London, 1961
Shakespearean Criticism, by S. T. COLERIDGE,
(Everyman Library, new edition), Dent,
London, 1961
The Literary Critics, by GEORGE WATSON,
Pelican Books, Harmondsworth, Middx.,
1962

CUMMINGS, E. E.
Collected Poems, by E. E. CUMMINGS,
Harcourt Brace, New York, 1938
Verse, by E. E. CUMMINGS, Horizon, London,
1947
A History of American Poetry, 1900–1940, by
H. GREGORY and M. ZATURENSKA,
Harcourt Brace, New York, 1946
E. E. Cummings: the Art of his Poetry, by
N. FRIEDMAN, Oxford University Press,
London, 1960

The Modern Poets, by M. L. ROSENTHAL, Oxford University Press, New York, 1961

DANIEL, SAMUEL
The Verse and Prose of Samuel Daniel, edited by A. B. GROSART, printed for private circulation in Aylesbury by Hazell, Watson & Viney, 1885–96
English Literature in the Sixteenth Century, excluding Drama, by C. S. LEWIS, (Oxford History of English Literature, Vol. 3), Clarendon Press, Oxford, and Oxford University Press, New York, 1954

DARLEY, GEORGE
The Complete Works of George Darley, edited by R. COLLES, (Muses Library), Routledge, London, and Dutton, New York, 1908

D'AVENANT, SIR WILLIAM
Works of Sir William D'Avenant in *Works of the English Poets,* Vol. 6, edited by A. CHALMERS, London, 1810
Sir William D'Avenant, by A. HARBAGE, University of Pennsylvania Press, Philadelphia, Pa., and Oxford University Press, London, 1935
Sir William D'Avenant, by A. H. NETHERCOT, University of Chicago Press, Chicago, 1938

DAVIDSON, JOHN
Ballads and Songs, by JOHN DAVIDSON, Lane, London, 1894
New Ballads, by JOHN DAVIDSON, Lane, London, 1897

DAVIES, SIR JOHN
The Complete Poems of Sir John Davies, edited by A. B. GROSART, Chatto & Windus, London, 1876
The Poet as Philosopher, by MABEL D. HOLMES, University of Pennsylvania Press, Philadelphia, Pa., 1921
Five Poems, by E. M. TILLYARD, Chatto & Windus, London, 1948

DAVIES, W. H.
The Collected Poems of W. H. Davies, edited by SIR OSBERT SITWELL, Cape, London, 1948

DAY LEWIS, CECIL
Collected Poems, 1954, by C. DAY LEWIS, Cape, London, 1954
Virgil's Georgics, translated by C. DAY LEWIS, Cape, London, 1940
Word over All, by C. DAY LEWIS, Cape, London, 1943
The Poetic Image, by C. DAY LEWIS, (Clark Lectures), Cape, London, 1947
Virgil's Aeneid, translated by C. DAY LEWIS, Hogarth Press, London, 1952
An Italian Visit, by C. DAY LEWIS, Cape, London, 1953
Pegasus, and Other Poems, by C. DAY LEWIS, Cape, London, 1958
The Gate, and Other Poems, by C. DAY LEWIS, Cape, London, 1962

DE LA MARE, WALTER
Collected Poems, by WALTER DE LA MARE, Faber, London, 1942
Walter de la Mare: a study of his Poetry, by H. C. DUFFIN, Sidgwick & Jackson, London, 1949

DENHAM, SIR JOHN
The Poetical Works of John Denham, edited by T. H. BANKS, Yale University Press, New Haven, Conn., 1928

DIAPER, WILLIAM
The Complete Works of William Diaper, edited by DOROTHY BROUGHTON, Routledge, London, and Harvard University Press, Cambridge, Mass., 1952

DICKINSON, EMILY
The Poems of Emily Dickinson, edited by THOMAS JOHNSON, Little, Brown & Co., Boston, 1960
Emily Dickinson's Poetry: Stairway of Surprise, by C. ANDERSON, Rinehart & Winston, New York, 1960
Collected Essays, by A. TATE, Swallow, Denver, Colorado, 1959

DONNE, JOHN
The Poems of John Donne, edited by H. J. C. GRIERSON, 2 vols, Oxford University Press, London, 1912

John Donne: Divine Poems, edited by HELEN GARDNER, Clarendon Press, Oxford, 1952

Complete Poetry and Selected Prose of John Donne, edited by J. HAYWARD, 4th edition, Nonesuch Press, London, 1955

John Donne: Elegies and Songs and Sonnets, edited by HELEN GARDNER, Clarendon Press, Oxford, 1965

John Donne: Satires and Verse-Letters, edited by W. MILGATE, Clarendon Press, Oxford, 1967

Donne the Craftsman, by P. LEGOUIS, HENRI DIDIER, Paris, 1928

Selected Essays, by T. S. ELIOT, 2nd edition, Faber, London, 1951

The Sermons of John Donne, edited by G. R. POTTER and E. M. SIMPSON, 10 vols, Cambridge University Press, Cambridge, and University of California Press, Berkeley, Cal., 1953

The Monarch of Wit, by J. B. LEISHMAN, Hutchinson, London, 1954

John Donne, by K. W. GRANSDEN, Longmans, London, 1954

DOUGHTY, C. M.
The Darkling Plain, by JOHN HEATH-STUBBS, Eyre & Spottiswoode, London, 1950

DOUGLAS, GAVIN
Poetical Works of Gavin Douglas, edited by JOHN SMALL, 4 vols, Edinburgh, 1874

Virgil's 'Aeneid' translated into Scottish Verse by Gavin Douglas, edited by D. F. C. COLDWELL, 4 vols in preparation, (Scottish Text Society), Blackwood, Edinburgh, Vols. 2 (1957) and 3 (1959)

Gavin Douglas: a Selection from his Poetry, edited by SYDNEY GOODSIR SMITH, Oliver & Boyd, Edinburgh, 1959

DOWSON, ERNEST
Poetical Works of Ernest Dowson, edited by D. FLOWER, Cassell, London, 1950

Ernest Dowson, by M. LONGAKER, 2nd edition, University of Pennsylvania Press, Philadelphia, Pa., 1945

The Stories of Ernest Dowson, edited by M. LONGAKER, W. H. Allen, London, 1949

The Last Romantics, by G. HOUGH, Duckworth, London, 1949

The Letters of Ernest Dowson, edited by D. FLOWER and A. MAAS, London, 1967

DRAYTON, MICHAEL
Works of Michael Drayton, edited by J. W. HEBEL, K. TILLOTSON and B. H. NEWDIGATE, Blackwell, Oxford, 1931–41

Michael Drayton and his Circle, by B. H. NEWDIGATE, Blackwell, Oxford, 1941

DRUMMOND, WILLIAM
The Poetical Works of William Drummond, edited by L. E. KASTNER, Manchester University Press, Manchester, 1913

DRYDEN, JOHN
The Poetical Works of Dryden, edited by G. R. NOYES, Houghton Mifflin, Boston, 1950

The Poems of John Dryden, by J. KINSLEY, Clarendon Press, Oxford, 1958

Essays of John Dryden, edited by W. P. KER, Clarendon Press, Oxford, 1926

John Dryden, by GEORGE SAINTSBURY, (English Men of Letters), Macmillan, London, 1881

The Poetry of John Dryden, by MARK VAN DOREN, Harcourt Brace, New York, 1920, and Minority Press, Cambridge, 1931

John Dryden: the Poet, the Dramatist, the Critic, by T. S. ELIOT, Holliday, New York, 1932

John Dryden, by D. NICHOL SMITH, (Clark Lectures), Cambridge University Press, Cambridge, 1950

The Life of John Dryden, by CHARLES E. WARD, University of North Carolina Press, Chapel Hill, N.C., and Oxford University Press, London, 1961

DUNBAR, WILLIAM
The Poems of William Dunbar, edited by W. M. MACKENZIE, 3rd edition, Faber, London, 1960

William Dunbar: a Biographical Study, by J. W. BAXTER, Oliver & Boyd, Edinburgh 1952

For further reading

English Literature in the Sixteenth Century, excluding Drama (Book I, chapter 1), by C. S. LEWIS, (Oxford History of English Literature), Clarendon Press, Oxford, and Oxford University Press, New York, 1954

DYER, JOHN

Works of John Dyer in *Minor Poets of the Eighteenth Century*, edited by H. L'A. FAUSSET, (Everyman Library), Dent, London, 1930

EBERHART, RICHARD

Collected Poems 1930–1960, by RICHARD EBERHART, Chatto & Windus, London, 1960, and Oxford University Press, New York, 1961

Selected Poems 1939–1965, by RICHARD EBERHART, New Directions Press, New York, 1966

Thirty-One Sonnets, by RICHARD EBERHART, Eakins Press, New York, 1967

Shifts of Beings, by RICHARD EBERHART, Oxford University Press, New York, 1968

The Modern Poets, by M. L. ROSENTHAL Oxford University Press, New York, 1960

ELIOT, T. S.

Poems 1909–1935, by T. S. ELIOT, Faber, London, 1936

Four Quartets, by T. S. ELIOT, Faber, London, 1944

Selected Essays, by T. S. ELIOT, 2nd edition, Faber, London, 1951

On Poetry and Poets, by T. S. ELIOT, Faber, London, 1959

The Cocktail Party, by T. S. ELIOT, Faber, London, 1950

The Confidential Clerk, by T. S. ELIOT, Faber, London, 1954

Murder in the Cathedral, by T. S. ELIOT, 4th edition, Faber, London, 1938

The Family Reunion, by T. S. ELIOT, Faber, London, 1954

The Elder Statesman, by T. S. ELIOT, Faber, London, 1959

To Criticize the Critic, by T. S. ELIOT, Faber, London, 1965

The Art of T. S. Eliot, by HELEN GARDNER, Oxford University Press, London, 1949

The Invisible Poet: T. S. Eliot, by HUGH KENNER, W. H. Allen, London, 1960

T. S. Eliot: a Collection of Critical Essays, edited by HUGH KENNER, Prentice-Hall, New York, 1962

New Bearings in English Poetry, by F. R. LEAVIS, Chatto & Windus, London, and G. W. Stewart, New York, 1950

Axel's Castle, by EDMUND WILSON, Scribner's, New York, 1931

EMERSON, RALPH WALDO

Complete Works of R. W. Emerson, Macmillan, London, 1886

The Life of Waldo Emerson, by R. L. RUSK, Scribner's, New York, 1949

Eight American Authors, (a review of research and criticism), edited by F. STOVALL, Modern Language Association of America, New York, 1956

EMPSON, WILLIAM

Collected Poems, by WILLIAM EMPSON, Chatto & Windus, London, 1955

Preliminary Essays, by JOHN WAIN, Macmillan, London, 1957

ENGLISH POETRY IN AFRICA

Poems from Black Africa, edited by LANGSTON HUGHES, Indiana University Press, 1963

An Anthology of West African Verse, edited by OLUMBE BASSIR, Ibadan University Press, 1954

Modern Poetry from Africa, edited by MOORE and BEIER, Penguin, London, 1963 and 1968

A Book of African Verse, edited by REED and WAKE, Heinemann, London, 1964

Darkness and Light, edited by PEGGY RUTHERFORD, Faith Press, London, 1958

Poems, by J. P. CLARK, Mbari, Ibadan, 1962

A Reed in the Tide, by J. P. CLARK, Longmans, London, 1965

Idanre, by WOLE SOYINKA, Methuen, London, 1967

Satellites, by LENRIE PETERS, Heinemann, London, 1967

Song of Lawino, by OKOT P'BITEK, East

African Publishing House, Nairobi, 1968

The Orphan, by OKELLO OCULI, East African Publishing House, Nairobi, 1968

Mortality, by M. J. C. ECHERUO, Longmans, London, 1968

Icheke, by OKOGBULE WANODI, Mbari, Ibadan, 1964

The Shadows of Laughter, by KWESI BREW, Longmans, London, 1968

Black Orpheus, published in Ibadan since 1957

Transition, published in Kampala since 1961

Okeame, published in Accra since 1961

The Classic, published in Johannesburg since 1964

The African Image, by EZEKIAH MPHAHLELE, Faber, London, 1962

Introduction to African Literature, edited by ULLI BEIE, Longmans, London, 1967

Literature and Thought of Modern Africa, by CLAUDE WAUTHIER, Pall Mall, London, 1966

A History of Neo-African Literature, by JANHEINZ JAHN, Faber, London, 1968

African Literature and The Universities, edited by GERALD MOORE, Ibadan University Press, 1965

The Chosen Tongue, by GERALD MOORE, Longmans, London, 1969

'EVERYMAN' AND THE MIRACLE PLAYS

The York Mystery Plays, by LUCY Y. SMITH, Oxford University Press, London, 1885

The Medieval Stage, by E. K. CHAMBERS, Oxford University Press, London, 1903

Everyman and the Medieval Miracle Plays, edited by A. C. CAWLEY, (Everyman Library, new edition), Dent, London, 1956

FEARING, KENNETH

Collected Poems of Kenneth Fearing, Random House, New York, 1940

Afternoon of a Pawnbroker, by KENNETH FEARING, Harcourt Brace, New York, 1943

Stranger at Coney Island, by KENNETH FEARING, Harcourt Brace, New York, 1948

FITZGERALD, EDWARD

The Rubáiyát of Omar Khayyám, rendered into English by EDWARD FITZGERALD, Collins, London, 1953

The Letters of Edward FitzGerald, edited by J. M. COHEN, Centaur Press, London, 1960

FLECKER, JAMES ELROY

The Collected Poems of James Elroy Flecker, edited by J. C. SQUIRE, Knopf, New York, 1921

FLETCHER, GILES AND PHINEAS

The Poetical Works of Giles and Phineas Fletcher, edited by F. S. BOAS, (Cambridge English Classics), Cambridge University Press, Cambridge, 1909

FORD, JOHN

The Works of John Ford, edited by W. GIFFORD with additions by A. DYCE, Toovey, London, 1869

The Plays of John Ford, edited by HAVELOCK ELLIS, Hill & Wang, New York, 1957

FROST, ROBERT

Complete Poems of Robert Frost, Holt, Rinehart & Winston, New York, 1949

In the Clearing, by ROBERT FROST, Holt, Rinehart & Winston, New York, 1962

The Poetry of Robert Frost, by REUBEN A. BROWER, Oxford University Press, New York, 1963

The Major Themes of Robert Frost, by RADCLIFFE SQUIRES, University of Michigan Press, 1963; Cresset, London, 1963

Robert Frost, the Early Years, by LAWRENCE THOMPSON, Holt, Rinehart & Winston, New York, 1966

FUGITIVE GROUP

The Fugitive Group: a Literary Study, by LOUISE COWAN, Louisiana State University Press, Baton Rouge, La., 1959

The Fugitives: a Critical Account, by J. M. BRADBURY, University of North Carolina Press, Chapel Hill, N.C., 1958

The Burden of Time, by JOHN L. STEWART, Princeton University Press, Princeton, N.J., 1965

FULLER, ROY
Collected Poems of Roy Fuller, Deutsch, London, 1962
New Poems, Deutsch, London, 1968
Poets of the 1939–1945 War, edited by R. N. CURREY, (Writers and their Work), Longmans, for the British Council, London, 1960

GASCOIGNE, GEORGE
The Works of George Gascoigne, edited by J. W. CUNLIFFE, 2 vols, (Cambridge English Classics), Cambridge University Press, Cambridge, 1904
George Gascoigne: Elizabethan, Courtier, Soldier and Poet, by C. T. PROUTY, Columbia University Press, New York, 1942

GASCOYNE, DAVID
Poems, 1937–1941, by DAVID GASCOYNE, Editions Poetry, London, 1943
A Vagrant, and other poems, by DAVID GASCOYNE, John Lehmann, London, 1950
Night Thoughts: poems, by DAVID GASCOYNE, Deutsch, London, 1956

GAY, JOHN
The Poetical Works of John Gay, edited by G. C. FABER, Oxford University Press, London, 1926

GOLDING, ARTHUR
The XV Books of P. Ovidius Naso entytuled Metamorphosis translated oute of Latin into English meeter, by ARTHUR GOLDING, W. Seres, London, 1567
ABC of Reading, by EZRA POUND, New Directions, Norfolk, Conn., 1951

GOLDSMITH, OLIVER
The Poetical Works of Oliver Goldsmith, edited by AUSTIN DOBSON, (Oxford Standard Authors), Oxford University Press, London, 1906
The Life of Oliver Goldsmith, by AUSTIN DOBSON, Walter Scott, London, 1888, and Dodd, Mead & Co., New York, 1899
Oliver Goldsmith, by RALPH M. WARDLE, University of Kansas Press, Lawrence, Kan., 1957, and Constable, London, 1958

The Search for Good Sense, by F. L. LUCAS, Cassell, London, 1958

GOWER, JOHN
The Complete Works of John Gower, edited by G. C. MACAULAY, 4 vols, Oxford University Press, London, 1899–1902
John Gower: Moral Philosopher and Friend of Chaucer, by JOHN H. FISHER, Methuen, 1965

GRAVES, ROBERT
Robert Graves: Poems Selected by Himself, (Penguin Poets), Penguin Books, Harmondsworth, Middx., 1957, and Garden City Books, New York, 1958
Collected Poems, by ROBERT GRAVES, Cassell, London, 1959
Robert Graves, by MARTIN SEYMOUR-SMITH, (Writers and their Work), Longmans, for the British Council, London, 1956
A Gathering of Fugitives, by LIONEL TRILLING, Beacon Press, Boston, 1956, and Secker & Warburg, London, 1957
Robert Graves, by J. M. COHEN, (Writers and Critics), Oliver & Boyd, Edinburgh, 1960

GRAY, THOMAS
The Poetical Works of Thomas Gray, edited by WHIBLEY and PAGE, (Oxford Standard Authors), Oxford University Press, London, 1937
Thomas Gray, by R. W. K. CREMER, Cambridge University Press, Cambridge, 1955

GREVILLE, SIR FULKE
Poems and Dramas of Fulke Greville, First Lord Brooke, edited by G. BULLOUGH, Oliver & Boyd, Edinburgh, 1939
English Literature in the Sixteenth Century, excluding Drama, by C. S. LEWIS, (Oxford History of English Literature, Vol. 3), Clarendon Press, Oxford, and Oxford University Press, New York, 1954
Remains, edited by G. A. WILKES, Oxford, 1965

GUNN, THOM
Fighting Terms, by THOM GUNN, Fantasy

Press, Oxford, 1954, and Hawk's Well
Press, New York, 1959
The Sense of Movement, by THOM GUNN,
Faber, London, 1957, and University of
Chicago Press, Chicago, 1959
My Sad Captains, by THOM GUNN, Faber,
London, 1961
Selected Poems (with TED HUGHES), Faber,
London, 1962
Positives, Faber, London, 1966
Touch, Faber, London, 1967

HAMILTON, SIR GEORGE ROSTREVOR
Selected Poems and Epigrams, by G. R.
HAMILTON, Heinemann, London, 1945

HARDY, THOMAS
Selected Poems of Thomas Hardy, edited by
JOHN CROWE RANSOM, Macmillan, London, 1961
Thomas Hardy, by EDMUND BLUNDEN,
Macmillan, London, 1942

HAWKER, ROBERT STEPHEN
Poetical Works of Robert Stephen Hawker,
edited by E. A. WALLIS, Lane, London,
1899
The Vicar of Morwenstow, by S. BARING
GOULD, 12th edition, Methuen, London,
1949

HENRYSON, ROBERT
*The Poems and Fables of Robert Henryson,
Schoolmaster of Dunfermline*, by H. HARVEY
WOOD, Oliver & Boyd, Edinburgh, 1933
Scottish Poetry: a Critical Survey, by
J. KINSLEY, Cassell, London, 1955
The Scottish Tradition in Literature, by
K. WITTIG, Oliver & Boyd, Edinburgh,
1958

HERBERT, EDWARD, LORD CHERBURY
*The Poems, English and Latin, of Edward,
Lord Herbert*, edited by G. C. MOORE,
Clarendon Press, Oxford, 1923
The Autiobiography of Edward, Lord Herbert,
edited by S. LEE, Routledge, London, and
Dutton, New York, 1906

HERBERT, GEORGE
The Works of George Herbert, edited by

F. E. HUTCHINSON, (Oxford English
Texts), Clarendon Press, Oxford, 1941
A Reading of Herbert, by R. TUVE, Faber,
London, 1952

HERRICK, ROBERT
The Poetical Works of Robert Herrick,
edited by F. W. MOORMAN, Clarendon
Press, Oxford, 1921
*Robert Herricke: a Biographical and Critical
Study*, by F. W. MOORMAN, Lane,
London, 1910
Robert Herrick, by F. DELATTRE, Paris, 1912

HODGSON, RALPH
Poems, by RALPH HODGSON, Macmillan,
London, 1917
The Skylark and Other Poems, by RALPH
HODGSON, Macmillan, London, 1959

HOOD, THOMAS
The Complete Works of Thomas Hood, edited
by T. HOOD and FRANCES F. BRODERIP,
Ward, Lock & Co., London and New
York, 1882–4

HOPKINS, GERARD MANLEY
The Poems of Gerard Manley Hopkins, edited
by W. H. GARDNER and N. H. MACKENZIE,
4th edition, Oxford University Press,
London and New York, 1967
*Poems and Prose of Gerard Manley Hopkins, a
selection*, edited by W. H. GARDNER,
Penguin Books, Harmondsworth, Middx,
1953, 10th impression, 1967
*The Letters of Gerard Manley Hopkins to
Robert Bridges*, edited by C. C. ABBOTT,
Oxford University Press, London and
New York, 1955
*The Correspondence of Gerard Manley
Hopkins and R. W. Dixon*, edited by
C. C. ABBOTT, Oxford University Press,
London and New York, 1956
*The Sermons and Devotional Writings of
Gerard Manley Hopkins*, edited by C.
DEVLIN, Oxford University Press, London and New York, 1959
Further Letters of Gerard Manley Hopkins,
edited by C. C. ABBOTT, 2nd edition,
Oxford University Press, London and
New York, 1956

The Journals and Papers of Gerard Manley Hopkins, edited by H. HOUSE and G. STOREY, 2nd edition, Oxford University Press, London and New York, 1959

Gerard Manley Hopkins: an Essay towards the Understanding of his Poetry, by W. A. M. PETERS, Oxford University Press, London and New York, 1948

Gerard Manley Hopkins: a Study of Poetic Idiosyncrasy in Relation to Poetic Tradition, by W. H. GARDNER, 2 vols, Oxford University Press, London and New York, 1966 (reissue of edition by Secker & Warburg, 1944–9)

Immortal Diamond: Studies in Gerard Manley Hopkins, edited by NORMAN WEYAND and RAYMOND V. SCHODER, Sheed & Ward, London, 1949

New Bearings in English Poetry, by F. R. LEAVIS, Chatto & Windus, London, and G. W. Stewart, New York, 1950

The Common Pursuit, by F. R. LEAVIS, Chatto & Windus, London, 1952

HOUSEMAN, A. E.

The Collected Poems of A. E. Housman, edited by J. W. CARTER, Cape, London, 1939

The Triple Thinkers, by E. WILSON, John Lehmann, London, 1952

A Buried Life, by P. WITHERS, Cape, London, 1940

A. E. Housman, by I. SCOTT-KILVERT, Longmans, for the British Council, London, 1955

A. E. Housman: Scholar and Poet, by N. MARLOW, Routledge, London, 1958

HUNT, LEIGH

Poetical Works of Leigh Hunt, Moxon, London, 1832

HYMNS, SONGS AND CAROLS

The Hymns of Wesley and Watts, by BERNARD LORD MANNING, Epworth Press, London, 1942

Songs and Lyrics from the Elizabethan Playbooks, by F. S. BOAS, Cresset Press, London, 1947

Hymns as Poetry, edited by T. INGRAM and D. NEWTON, Constable, London, 1956

Songs of the Restoration Theatre, edited by P. J. STEAD, Methuen, London, 1948

Representative Verse of Charles Wesley, selected and edited by FRANK BAKER, Epworth Press, London, 1962

IMAGISM

Imagism and the Imagists: a Study in Modern Poetry, by G. HUGHES, Stanford University Press, Palo Alto, California, 1931

Imagism: a Chapter for the History of Modern Poetry, by STANLEY K. COFFMAN JR., University of Oklahoma, Norman, Oklahoma, 1951

The Poetry of Ezra Pound, by HUGH KENNER, Faber, London, 1951

INDIAN POETRY IN ENGLISH

Ancient Ballads and Legends of Hindustan, by TORU DUTT, Routledge, London, 1882

Love Songs and Elegies, by MANMOHAN GHOSE, Elkin Matthews, London, 1898

The Golden Threshold, by SAROJINI NAIDU, Heinemann, London, 1905

Eastern Themes in English Verse by British and Indian Poets, Oxford University Press, Bombay and Madras, 1918

An Anthology of Modern Indian Poetry, edited by GWENDOLINE GOODWIN, (Wisdom of the East), Murray, London, 1927

Collected Poems and Prayers, by AUROBINDO GHOSE, 2 vols, Sri Aurobindo Ashram, Pondicherry, India, 1942

JAMES I OF SCOTLAND

The Kings Quair, by JAMES I OF SCOTLAND, edited by W. M. MACKENZIE, Faber, London, 1939

JARRELL, RANDALL

Selected Poems, by RANDALL JARRELL, Knopf, New York, 1955, and Faber, London, 1956

The Lost World, by RANDALL JARRELL, Eyre & Spottiswoode, London, 1966, and Collier-Macmillan, New York, 1965

Selected Poems, by RANDALL JARRELL, Atheneum, New York, 1966

The Modern Poets, by M. L. ROSENTHAL, Macmillan, New York, 1960

'Notes on American Poetry after 1945', by R. FITZGERALD, in *The American Review,* No. 4, Spring 1961, United States Information Service, London

Randall Jarrell 1914–1965, edited by ROBERT LOWELL, PETER TAYLOR and ROBERT PENN WARREN, Farrar, Strauss & Giroux, New York, 1967

JEFFERS, ROBINSON
Collected Poems of Robinson Jeffers, Random House, New York, 1948

A Bibliography of the Works of Robinson Jeffers, by S. S. ALBERTS, Random House, New York, 1933

Robinson Jeffers, by RADCLIFFE SQUIRES, University of Michigan Press, Ann Arbor, Michigan, 1956

JOHNSON, LIONEL
The Complete Poems of Lionel Johnson, edited by I. FLETCHER, Unicorn Press, London, 1953

JOHNSON, SAMUEL
Poems of Samuel Johnson, edited by D. NICHOL SMITH and E. L. MCADAM, Oxford University Press, London, 1941

The Common Pursuit, by F. R. LEAVIS, Chatto & Windus, London, 1952

JONES, DAVID
In Parenthesis, by DAVID JONES, Faber, London, 1937

The Anathemata, by DAVID JONES, Faber, London, 1952

JONSON, BEN
The Complete Works of Ben Jonson, edited by C. H. HERFORD and PERCY and EVELYN SIMPSON, 11 vols, Clarendon Press, Oxford, 1925–1952

Poems of Ben Jonson, edited by GEORGE BURKE JOHNSTON, (Muses Library), Routledge, London, 1954

Poets and Playwrights, by E. E. STOLL, University of Minnesota Press, Minneapolis, 1930

Revaluation, by F. R. LEAVIS, Chatto & Windus, London, 1936

Ben Jonson: Poet, by G. B. JOHNSTON, Harvard University Press, Cambridge, Mass., 1945

Selected Essays, by T. S. ELIOT, 2nd edition, Faber, London, 1951

Elizabethan Lyrics, by CATHERINE ING, Chatto & Windus, London, 1952

Ben Jonson, J. B. BAMBOROUGH, Longmans, London, 1959

Ben Jonson: a Study of the Plain Style, by W. TRIMPI, Stamford, 1962

KAVANAGH, PATRICK
Ploughman and other Poems, by PATRICK KAVANAGH, Macmillan, London, 1936

The Green Fool, by PATRICK KAVANAGH, Michael Joseph, London, 1938

The Great Hunger, by PATRICK KAVANAGH, Cuala Press, Dublin, 1942

A Soul for Sale, by PATRICK KAVANAGH, Macmillan, London, 1947

Tarry Flynn, by PATRICK KAVANAGH, Pilot Press, London, 1948

Come Dance with Kitty Stobling and other Poems, by PATRICK KAVANAGH, Longmans, London, 1960

Collected Poems, by PATRICK KAVANAGH, MacGibbon & Kee, London, 1964

Self Portrait, by PATRICK KAVANAGH, Dolmen Press, Dublin, 1964

Pulled Weeds on the Ridge, by JAMES PLUNKETT, *The Bell,* Vol. XVII, Number 12, March 1952

The Cobbler's Song, by JOHN HEWITT, *Threshold,* Vol. 5, Number 1, Spring-Summer 1961

A Few Thoughts about P. K., by JOHN JORDAN, *Poetry Ireland,* Number 4, Summer 1964

The Writings of Patrick Kavanagh, by DOUGLAS SEALY, *Dublin Magazine,* Vol. 4, Numbers 3 & 4, Winter 1965

Patrick Kavanagh as Critic, by ALAN WARNER, *Dublin Magazine,* Vol. 7, Number 1, Spring 1968 (an edition containing a special tribute to Patrick Kavanagh).

KEATS, JOHN

The Poems of John Keats, edited by G. THORN DRURY, Routledge, London, 1905

John Keats: His Life and Poetry, His Friends, Critics and After-Fame, by SIR SIDNEY COLVIN, Macmillan, London, 1917

Keats and Shakespeare, by J. MIDDLETON MURRY, Oxford University Press, London, 1925

'John Keats: a Critical Essay', in *Collected Essays,* by ROBERT BRIDGES, Oxford University Press, London, 1927–36

The Evolution of Keats' Poetry, by C. L. DINNEY, 2 vols, Harvard University Press, Cambridge, Mass., 1936

Revaluation, by F. R. LEAVIS, Chatto & Windus, London, 1936

'John Keats', in *Essays in Criticism* (2nd Series), by M. ARNOLD, Macmillan, London, 1938

The Mystery of Keats, by J. MIDDLETON MURRY, Oxford University Press, London, 1949

John Keats: The Living Year, by ROBERT GITTINGS, Heinemann, London, 1954

On the Poetry of Keats, by E. C. PETTET, Cambridge University Press, Cambridge, 1956

KING, HENRY

The English Poems of Henry King, edited by L. MASON, Yale University Press, New Haven, Conn., 1914

The Poems of Henry King, edited by J. SPARROW, Nonesuch Press, London, 1925

The Poems of Bishop Henry King, edited by J. R. BAKER, Swallow, Denver, Colorado, 1960

KIPLING, RUDYARD

Verse, by RUDYARD KIPLING, Hodder & Stoughton, London, 1940, and Doubleday, New York, 1945

A Choice of Kipling's Verse, edited with an introduction by T. S. ELIOT, Faber, London, 1941

Rudyard Kipling: His Life and Work, by C. CARRINGTON, Macmillan, London, 1955

LANDOR, WALTER SAVAGE

The Complete Works of Walter Savage Landor, edited by T. E. WELBEY and S. WHEELER, 16 vols, Chapman & Hall, London, 1927–36

Walter Savage Landor: a Biography, by R. H. SUPER, New York University Press, New York, and Allen & Unwin, London, 1954

LANGLAND, WILLIAM

The Vision of William concerning Piers the Plowman, in three parallel texts together with *Richard the Redeless,* by WILLIAM LANGLAND, edited with preface, notes and a glossary, by W. W. SKEAT, Oxford University Press, London, 1886

The Vision of Piers Plowman newly rendered into Modern English, by H. W. WELLS, Sheed & Ward, London, 1935

Piers Plowman: the 'C' Text and its Poet, by E. TALBOT DONALDSON, Yale University Press, New Haven, Conn., 1949

Piers Plowman: the 'A' Version, edited by G. KANE, University of London Press, London, 1960

Articles by S. MOORE in *Modern Philology,* Vol. II, pp. 177–93, and by M. W. BLOOMFIELD in Speculum, Vol. 14 (1939), pp. 215–32

Man's Unconquerable Mind, by R. W. CHAMBERS, (pp. 88–171), Cape, London, 1939

The Pardon of Piers Ploughman, by NEVILLE COGHILL, British Academy, Gollancz Memorial Lecture, London, 1945

Piers Plowman and the Scheme of Salvation, by R. W. FRANK, Yale, 1957

Piers Plowman, an Introduction by ELIZABETH SALTER, Blackwell, Oxford, 1962

Piers Plowman, an essay in criticism, by JOHN LAWLOR, Arnold, London, 1962

Piers Plowman, the Evidence for Authorship, by GEORGE KANE, Athlone Press, London, 1965

The Flowering of the Middle Ages, edited by JOAN EVANS, Thames & Hudson, London, 1966

The Court of Richard II, by GERVASE MATTHEW, John Murray, London, 1966

LANIER, SIDNEY
The Centennial Edition of the Works of Sidney Lanier, edited by C. R. ANDERSON, 10 vols, Johns Hopkins Press, Baltimore, Md., 1945

LARKIN, PHILIP
The Less Deceived: Poems, by PHILIP LARKIN, Marvell Press, Hessle, Yorkshire,

LAWRENCE, D. H.
Selected Poems of D. H. Lawrence, edited by KENNETH REXROTH, New Directions, Norfolk, Conn., 1948
Selected Poems of D. H. Lawrence, Penguin Books, Harmondsworth, Middx., 1950
The Complete Poems of D. H. Lawrence, edited by J. REEVES, 3 vols, Heinemann, London, 1957
The Shaping Spirit, by A. ALVAREZ, Chatto & Windus, London, 1958, and re-titled *Stewards of Excellence,* Scribner's, New York, 1958

LEAR, EDWARD
The Complete Nonsense of Edward Lear, edited by H. JACKSON, Faber, London, 1947
The Works of Edward Lear, Penguin Books, Harmondsworth, Middx., 1956
Edward Lear: Landscape Painter and Nonsense Poet, by A. DAVIDSON, Murray, 1968

LINDSAY, VACHEL
Collected Poems, by VACHEL LINDSAY, Macmillan, New York, 1952 (revised edition with illustrations by the author)
Vachel Lindsay: a Poet in America, by E. L. MASTERS, Scribner's, New York, 1935
The West-going Heart: a Life of Vachel Lindsay, by ELEANOR RUGGLES, Norton, New York, 1959

LODGE, THOMAS
The Complete Works of Thomas Lodge 1580–1683, edited by E. W. GOSSE, Hunterian Club, Glasgow, 1883

LONGFELLOW, HENRY WADSWORTH
Poetical Works of Henry Wadsworth Long-fellow, Oxford University Press, London and New York, 1957
Longfellow: a Full-Length Portrait, by E. C. WAGENKNECHT, Longmans, New York, 1955

LOVELACE, RICHARD
The Poems of Richard Lovelace, edited by C. H. WILKINSON, Clarendon Press, Oxford, 1925

LOWELL, AMY
The Complete Poetical Works of Amy Lowell, Houghton Mifflin, Boston, 1955
A Shard of Silence: selected poems of Amy Lowell, edited by G. R. RUIHLEY, Twayne, New York, 1957

Amy Lowell, by H. GREGORY, T. Nelson, New York, 1958

LOWELL, ROBERT
Lord Weary's Castle, by ROBERT LOWELL, Harcourt Brace, New York, 1946
The Mills of the Kavanaughs, by ROBERT LOWELL, Harcourt Brace, New York, 1951
Life Studies, by ROBERT LOWELL, Farrar, Straus & Cudahy, New York, 1959
Robert Lowell: the first twenty years, by H. STAPLES, Faber, London, 1962

LYDGATE, JOHN
The Minor Poems of John Lydgate, by H. N. MacCRACKEN, (Early English Text Society), Oxford University Press, London, 1911–34
A Critical Edition of John Lydgate's Life of Our Lady, edited by J. A. LAURITIS, V. F. GALLAHER, and R. A. KLINEFELTER. Duquesne University Press, Pittsburgh, Pa., 1961

MACDIARMID, HUGH
Collected Poems of Hugh MacDiarmid, Macmillan, New York, and Oliver & Boyd, Edinburgh, 1962
Introduction by DAVID DAICHES to *A Drunk Man Looks at a Thistle,* by HUGH MAC-DIARMID, Caledonian Press, Glasgow, 1953

The Scottish Tradition in Literature, by K. WITTIG, Oliver & Boyd, Edinburgh, 1958

Hugh MacDiarmid: A Festschrift, edited by K. D. DUVAL and SIDNEY GOODSIR SMITH, Duval, Edinburgh, 1962

MACLEISH, ARCHIBALD

Collected Poems 1917–1952, by ARCHIBALD MACLEISH, Houghton Mifflin, Boston, 1952

Modern Poetry and the Tradition, by CLEANTH BROOKS, University of North Carolina Press, Chapel Hill, North Carolina, 1939

MACNEICE, LOUIS

Collected Poems 1925–1948, by LOUIS MACNEICE, Faber, London, 1949

Ten Burnt Offerings, by LOUIS MACNEICE, Faber, London, 1952

Autumn Sequel, by LOUIS MACNEICE, Faber, London, 1954

Visitations, by LOUIS MACNEICE, Faber, London, 1958

Solstices, by LOUIS MACNEICE, Faber, London, 1961

MARLOWE, CHRISTOPHER

The Works of Christopher Marlowe, edited by R. H. CASE, Methuen, London, 1931

The Death of Christopher Marlowe, by J. L. HOTSON, Nonesuch Press, London, 1925

Christopher Marlowe, by UNA ELLIS-FERMOR, Methuen, London, 1927

The School of Night, by M. C. BRADBROOK, Cambridge University Press, Cambridge, 1936

Christopher Marlowe, by F. S. BOAS, Oxford University Press, London, 1940

The Tragicall History of Christopher Marlowe, by J. BAKELESS, Harvard University Press, Cambridge, Mass., 1942

Christopher Marlowe, by P. H. KOCHER, University of North Carolina Press, Chapel Hill, N.C., 1946

Shakespeare and Elizabethan Poetry, by M. C. BRADBROOK, Chatto & Windus, 1951

The Overreacher, by H. LEVIN, Harvard University Press, Cambridge, Mass., 1952

Marlowe and the Early Shakespeare, by F. P. WILSON, Oxford University Press, London, 1953

English Literature in the Sixteenth Century, excluding Drama, by C. S. LEWIS, (Oxford History of English Literature, Vol. 3), Clarendon Press, Oxford, and Oxford University Press, New York, 1954

Christopher Marlowe, by P. HENDERSON, (Writers and their Work), Longmans, for the British Council, London, 1956

Mythology and the Renaissance Tradition in English Poetry, by DOUGLAS BUSH, Pageant Book Co., New York, 1957

MARQUIS, DON

The Best of Don Marquis, with an introduction by C. MORLEY, Garden City Books, New York, 1959

MARVELL, ANDREW

Poems and Letters of Andrew Marvell, edited by H. M. MARGOLIOUTH, (Oxford English Texts), 2nd edition, Oxford University Press, London, 1952

Poems of Andrew Marvell, edited by H. MACDONALD, (Muses Library), Routledge, London, 1952

Selected Essays, by T. S. ELIOT, 2nd Edition, Faber, London, 1951

The Poetry of Andrew Marvell, by F. W. BRADBROOK, Penguin Books, Harmondsworth, Middx., 1956

The School of Donne, by A. ALVAREZ, Chatto & Windus, London, 1961

MASEFIELD, JOHN

Poems, by JOHN MASEFIELD, Heinemann, London, 1923

Salt Water Poems and Ballads, Macmillan, New York, 1953

Old Rigger and Other Verses, Macmillan, New York, 1965

MELVILLE, HERMAN

The Collected Works of Herman Melville, Constable, London, 1922–6

Collected Poems, by HERMAN MELVILLE, Hendricks House, New York, 1947

'Herman Melville', by R. P. WARREN, in the *Kenyon Review*, Vol. 8, 1946

Clarel, by HERMAN MELVILLE, Hendricks House, New York, 1960

MEREDITH, GEORGE

Selected Poetical Works of George Meredith, with notes by G. M. TREVELYAN, Longmans, London, 1955

The Poetry and Philosophy of George Meredith, by G. M. TREVELYAN, Constable, London, 1912

George Meredith: His Life and Work, by J. LINDSAY, Lane, London, 1956

A Troubled Eden: Nature and Society in the works of George Meredith, by NORMAN KELVIN, Edinburgh, 1961

MERWIN, W. S.

A Mask for Janus, by W. S. MERWIN, Yale University Press, New Haven, Conn., and Oxford University Press, London, 1952

The Dancing Bears, Yale University Press, New Haven, Conn., 1954

The Moving Target, Atheneum, New York, 1963

The Lice, Atheneum, New York, 1967

Green with Beasts, by W. S. MERWIN, Hart-Davis, London, 1956

A Drunk in the Furnace, by W. S. MERWIN, Hart-Davis, London, 1960

MEYNELL, ALICE

Poems of Alice Meynell, Burns Oates, London, 1923

MIDDLE ENGLISH LYRIC

English Lyrics of the Thirteenth Century, edited by CARLETON BROWN, Oxford University Press, London, 1932

The Index of Middle English Verse, edited by C. BROWN and R. H. ROBBINS, (Index Society), Columbia University Press, New York, 1943

Medieval Latin Lyrics, by HELEN WADDELL, 5th edition, Constable, London, 1948

English Lyrics of the Fourteenth Century, edited by CARLETON BROWN, 2nd edition, Oxford University Press, London, 1952

Medieval English Lyrics, edited by R. T. DAVIES, London, 1963

MIDDLETON, THOMAS

Works of Thomas Middleton, edited by A. H. BULLEN, Houghton Mifflin, Boston, 1885–6

MILTON, JOHN

Works, edited by F. A. PATTERSON and others, 20 vols, Columbia University Press, New York, and Oxford University Press, London, 1931–40

John Milton: Complete Poems and Major Prose, edited by MERRITT Y. HUGHES, Odyssey Press, New York, 1957

English Literature in the Earlier Seventeenth Century, by DOUGLAS BUSH (Oxford History of English Literature, Vol. 5), revised edition, Clarendon Press, Oxford, 1962 (with revised bibliography of Milton, 1966). See also Miltonic items under 'D.B.' in list of contributors to this Encyclopedia.

Milton: Modern Essays in Criticism, edited by ARTHUR E. BARKER (with copious references), paperback, Oxford University Press, New York and London, 1965

MOORE, MARIANNE

The Complete Poems of Marianne Moore, Faber, London, and Viking Press, New York, 1968

MOORE, THOMAS STURGE

Selected Poems of T. Sturge Moore, edited by MARIE STURGE MOORE, 4 vols, Macmillan, London, 1931–32

W. B. Yeats and T. Sturge Moore: their Correspondence 1901–1937, edited by URSULA BRIDGE, Routledge, London, 1953

MORRIS, WILLIAM

The Collected Works of William Morris, edited by MAY MORRIS, Longmans, London and New York, 1910–15

Selected Writings of William Morris, edited by G. D. H. COLE, Nonesuch Press, London, 1948

MUIR, EDWIN

The Collected Poems of Edwin Muir, Faber, London, 1960, revised edition, 1963

Edwin Muir, by J. C. HALL, (Writers and their Work), Longmans, for the British Council, London, 1956

'Edwin Muir', by MICHAEL HAMBURGER, in *Encounter,* Vol. 15, No. 6, London, December 1960

Edwin Muir: Man and Poet, by PETER BUTTER, Oliver & Boyd, Edinburgh, 1966

MUSIC AND POETRY

Source Readings in Music History, by O. STRUNK, Norton, New York, 1950, and Faber, London, 1952

The Works of Henry Purcell, various editors, 28 vols, Novello, London, 1876–

The English School of Lutenist Song Writers, by E. H. FELLOWES, Stainer & Bell, London, 1922–5

English Folk Song, by C. J. SHARP, 3rd edition, Methuen, London, 1934

A History of Song, by D. STEVENS, Hutchinson, London, 1960, second edihou 1970.

MYTH AND POETRY

BIBLIOGRAPHICAL NOTE. In modern criticism, the connections between myth and poetry have been developed out of the studies of ritual in anthropology and of dreams of psychology. Both studies trace the workings of unconscious or subconscious processes to the points at which they show analogies to literary form, the analogies of ritual and drama being particularly close. Frazer's *Golden Bough,* 1894, a work which eventually expanded into twelve volumes (1911–15), is a study of a single Classical rite (the King of the Wood at Nemi), which leads into an encyclopedic survey of magic and ritual. Though ostensibly a work of anthropology, it is really a work of Classical scholarship, and its greatest influence has been literary. E. K. Chamber's *Medieval Stage,* 1903, Gilbert Murray's *Rise of the Greek Epic,* 1907, Francis Cornford's *The Origin of Attic Comedy,* 1914, Jane Harrison's *Themis,* 1912 (where the

chapter contributed by Murray is of particular importance), Bertha Phillpotts' *The Elder Edda and Ancient Scandinavian Drama,* 1920, Enid Welsford's *The Court Masque,* 1927, Theodore Gaster's *Thespis,* 1950, are a few of Frazer's descendants in criticism. Another, Jessie Weston's *From Ritual to Romance,* 1920, is an acknowledged influence on Eliot's *Waste Land,* which also specifically mentions Frazer.

Freud's *Interpretation of Dreams,* 1899, and the book which shows the influence of Frazer on him, *Totem and Taboo,* 1913, began a series of studies relating the study of myth to dreams. Jung's work, especially *Psychology and Alchemy,* 1944, is even more closely related than Freud's to literary studies. Maud Bodkin's *Archetypal Patterns in Poetry,* 1934, is a pioneering effort at uniting psychological and critical approaches to myth. Rank's *Myth of the Birth of the Hero,* 1914, and, more recently, Joseph Campbell's *Hero with a Thousand Faces,* 1949, Lord Raglan's *The Hero,* 1936, Robert Graves' *The White Goddess,* 1948, and several books by Mircea Eliade, the best known being *The Myth of the Eternal Return,* 1954 (reissued as *Cosmos and History,* 1959), are attempts to combine the psychological and anthropological approaches with literary criticism. D. H. Lawrence's *Fantasia of the Unconscious,* 1922, is one of many literary responses to the influence of Freud.

N.F.

NASH, OGDEN

Verse from 1929 on, by OGDEN NASH, Little, Brown & Co., Boston, 1959

NASHE, THOMAS

The Works of Thomas Nashe, 5 vols, edited by R. B. MCKERROW, (including a critical article), A. H. Bullen, London, 1904–10

The Complete Works of Thomas Nashe, edited by F. B. WILSON, Blackwell, Oxford, 1958

NEMEROV, HOWARD

The Image and the Law, by HOWARD

NEMEROV, Holt, New York, 1947

Guide to the Ruins, by HOWARD NEMEROV, Random House, New York, 1950

The Salt Garden, by HOWARD NEMEROV, Little, Brown & Co., Boston, Mass., 1956

Mirrors and Windows, by Howard Nemerov, Univ. of Chicago Press, Chicago, 1958

New and Selected Poems, by Howard Nemerov, Univ. of Chicago Press, Chicago, 1960

The Next Room of the Dream, by Howard Nemerov, Univ. of Chicago Press, Chicago, 1962

The Blue Swallows, by Howard Nemerov, Univ. of Chicago Press, Chicago, 1962

NEW CRITICISM

Seven Types of Ambiguity, by WILLIAM EMPSON, Chatto & Windus, London, 1930, and New Directions, New York, 1947

Modern Poetry and the Tradition, by CLEANTH BROOKS, University of North Carolina Press, Chapel Hill, N.C., 1939

The New Criticism, by J. C. RANSOM, New Directions, Norfolk, Conn., 1941

Das Sprachliche Kunstwerk, by W. KAYSER, Francke Verlag, Bern, Switzerland, 1948

A Glossary of the New Criticism, by W. ELTON, Modern Poetry Association, Chicago, 1949

New Bearings in English Poetry, by F. R. LEAVIS, new edition, Chatto & Windus, London, and G. W. Stewart, New York, 1950

A History of Modern Criticism, Vols, 1 and 2, by R. WELLEK, Yale University Press, New Haven, Conn., 1955

Theory of Literature, by R. WELLEK and A. WARREN, Cape, London, 1956

The Apologists for Poetry, by MURRAY KRIEGER, University of Minnesota Press, Minneapolis, Minn., 1956

The Fugitives: a Critical Account, by JOHN MASON BRADBURY, University of North Carolina Press, Chapel Hill, N.C., 1958

Collected Essays, by ALLEN TATE, Swallow, Denver, Colorado, 1959

The New Romantics, by RICHARD FOSTER, Indiana University Press, Bloomington, Indiana, 1962

NEW ZEALAND POETRY

An Anthology of New Zealand Verse, edited by R. CHAPMAN and J. BENNETT, Oxford University Press, London and New York, 1956

In Fires of No Return, selected poems by J. K. BAXTER, Oxford University Press, London and New York, 1958

New Zealand Literature, a Survey, by E. H. McCORMICK, Oxford University Press, London and New York, 1959

The Penguin Book of New Zealand Verse, edited by A. CURNOW, Penguin Books, Harmondsworth, Middx., and Baltimore, 1960

A Small Room with Large Windows, selected poems by A. CURNOW, Oxford University Press, London, 1961

Howrah Bridge, poems by J. K. BAXTER, Oxford University Press, London, 1962

Recent Poetry in New Zealand, by C. D. DOYLE, Collins, London, 1965

Pig Island Letters, by JAMES K. BAXTER, Oxford University Press, London, 1967

OSSIAN

The Poems of Ossian, translated by James Macpherson, edited by W. SHARP, John Gaunt, Edinburgh, 1926

OWEN, WILFRED

Poems of Wilfred Owen, edited by EDMUND BLUNDEN, Chatto & Windus, London, 1933

Poems of Wilfred Owen, New Directions, Norfolk, Conn., 1949

Siegfried's Journey 1916–20, by SIEGFRIED SASSOON, Faber, London, 1945

War Poets, 1914–18, edited by EDMUND BLUNDEN, (Writers and their Work), Longmans, for the British Council, London, 1958

PARKER, DOROTHY

Collected Poems: Not So Deep as a Well, by DOROTHY PARKER, Viking Press, New York, 1936

PARNELL, THOMAS

Works of Thomas Parnell in *Minor Poets of the Eighteenth Century,* edited by H. L'A.

FAUSSET, (Everyman Library), Dent, London, 1930

PATMORE, COVENTRY
Selected Poems of Coventry Patmore, edited by D. PATMORE, Chatto & Windus, London, 1931
English Metrists, by T. S. OMOND, Oxford University Press, London, 1921
The Life and Times of Coventry Patmore, by D. PATMORE, Constable, London 1949
Further Letters of Gerard Manley Hopkins, including his Correspondence with Coventry Patmore, edited by C. C. ABBOTT, 2nd edition, Oxford University Press, London, 1956
The Mind and Art of Coventry Patmore, by J. C. REID, Routledge, London, 1957

PEELE, GEORGE
The Works of George Peele, edited by A. H. BULLEN, Nimmo, London, 1888
The Life and Minor Works of George Peele, edited by D. H. HORNE, Yale University Press, New Haven, Conn., 1952–

PLOMER, WILLIAM
Collected Poems, by WILLIAM PLOMER, Cape, London, 1960

POE, EDGAR ALLAN
The Complete Works of Edgar Allan Poe, edited by JAMES A. HARRISON, 17 Vols, (Virginia Edition), New York, 1902
The Poems of Edgar Allan Poe, edited by KILLIS CAMPBELL, Boston, 1917
The Complete Poems and Stories of Edgar Allan Poe, edited by A. H. QUINN, and E. H. O'NEIL, Knopf, New York, 1946
The Complete Poems of Edgar Allan Poe, edited by RICHARD WILBUR, Dell, New York, 1959

POPE, ALEXANDER
The Twickenham edition of the poems of Alexander Pope, edited by J. BUTT, Methuen, London, 1950
The Iliad, translated by A. POPE, (The World's Classics), Oxford University Press, London, 1906

The Poetical Career of Alexander Pope, by R. K. ROOT, Princeton University Press, Princeton, N.J., 1938
On the Poetry of Pope, by G. TILLOTSON, Clarendon Press, Oxford, 1950

POUND, EZRA
The Cantos of Ezra Pound, Faber, London, 1964
Ezra Pound, The Collected Shorter Poems, Faber, London, 1968
Ezra Pound: A Collection of Essays to be Presented to Ezra Pound on His Sixty-Fifth Birthday, edited by PETER RUSSELL, Peter Nevill, London and New York, 1950
The Poetry of Ezra Pound, by HUGH KENNER, Faber and New Directions, London and New York, 1951
Ezra Pound and the Cantos, by H. H. WATTS, Routledge, London, 1951
Some essays in Motive and Method in the Cantos of Ezra Pound, edited by L. LEARY, Columbia University Press, New York, 1954
Ezra Pound's Mauberley: A Study in Composition, by J. J. ESPEY, University of California Press, Berkeley and Los Angeles, 1955
Annotated Index to the Cantos of Ezra Pound, (Cantos I–LXXXIV), edited by J. H. EDWARDS and W. W. VASSE, University of California Press, Berkeley and Los Angeles, 1957
Ideas into Action: a Study of Pound's Cantos, (the first 30), by CLARK EMERY, University of Miami Press, Coral Gables, Florida, 1958
A Primer of Ezra Pound, by M. L. ROSENTHAL, Macmillan, New York, 1960
Ezra Pound and Sextus Propertius—A Study in Creative Translation by J. P. SULLIVAN, Faber, London, 1964
Ezra Pound—Perspectives, (Essays by various hands), edited by NOEL STOCK, Henry Regnery Co., Chicago, 1965
Ezra Pound—Poet as Sculptor, by DONALD DAVIE, Routledge, London, 1965
Reading the Cantos, by NOEL STOCK, Random House, New York, 1966
Ezra Pound—22 Versuche über einen Dichter,

edited by Eva Hesse, Athenäum Verlag, Frankfurt-am-Main, 1967

PRAED, WINTHROP

The Poems of Winthrop Mackworth Praed, edited by Derwent Coleridge, Moran, London, 1864, and Middleton, New York, 1865

Selected Poems of Winthrop Mackworth Praed, edited by K. Allott, (Muses Library), Routledge, London, 1953

PRIOR, MATTHEW

The Works of Matthew Prior, edited by H. B. Wright and M. K. Spears, Oxford University Press, London, 1959

The Life of Matthew Prior, by F. Bickley, Pitman, London and New York, 1914

PROSODY, FORMS OF VERSE, AND SOME USAGES

The Rationale of Verse, by E. A. Poe, in the *Southern Literary Messenger,* 1848

A Study of Metre, by T. S. Omond, Grant Richards, New York, 1903

Elizabethan Critical Essays, edited by G. G. Smith, 2 vols, Clarendon Press, Oxford, 1904

Historical Manual of English Prosody, by George Saintsbury, Macmillan, London, 1910

The History of English Prosody, by George Saintsbury, 3 vols, 2nd edition, Macmillan, London, 1923

Cambridge Bibliography of English Literature, Cambridge University Press, Cambridge, 1940

QUARLES, FRANCIS

The Works of Francis Quarles, edited by A. B. Grosart, 3 vols, (Chertsey Worthies Library), Constable, London, 1880–81

Francis Quarles, by E. James, (University of Texas Studies in English), University of Texas Press, Austin, Texas, 1943

RAINE, KATHLEEN

Collected Poems, by Kathleen Raine, Hamish Hamilton, London, 1956

RALEGH, SIR WALTER

The Poems of Sir Walter Ralegh, edited by Agnes Latham, Routledge, London, 1951

Sir Walter Ralegh: a Study in Elizabethan Scepticism, by E. A. Strathmann, Columbia University Press, New York, 1951

The Queen and the Poet, by Walter Oakeshott, Faber, London, 1960

RAMSAY, ALLAN

Allan Ramsay: Works, edited by B. Martin and J. W. Oliver, (Scottish Text Society), Blackwood, Edinburgh, 1951–3

Allan Ramsay, by B. Martin, Harvard University Press, Cambridge, Mass., 1931

RANSOM, JOHN CROWE

Selected Poems, by John Crowe Ransom, Knopf, New York, 1945, and Eyre & Spottiswoode, London, 1948

'The Poetry of John Crowe Ransom', by Vivienne Koch, in *Modern American Poetry,* edited by B. Rajan, Dobson, London, 1950

'John Ransom's Poetry', in *Poetry and the Age,* by Randall Jarrell, Knopf, New York, 1953, and Faber, London, 1955

READ, SIR HERBERT

Collected Poems, by Sir Herbert Read, 2nd edition, Faber, London, 1953

Moon's Farm, by Sir Herbert Read, Faber, London, 1955

REED, HENRY

A Map of Verona, by Henry Reed, Cape, London, 1956

RELIGION AND POETRY

'Sources of the Liturgical Drama' in *Chief Pre-Shakespearean Drama,* edited by John Quincy Adams, Houghton Mifflin, New York, and Harrap, London, 1924

'Arnold and Pater' in *Selected Essays,* by T. S. Eliot, Faber, London, 1932

Principles of Art, by R. G. Collingwood. Clarendon Press, Oxford, 1938

The Glass of Vision, by A. Farrer, (chapter on Prophecy and Poetry), Dacre Press, Black, London, 1948

Ancient Art and Ritual, by JANE HARRISON, Oxford University Press, London, 1948

'Johnson as Critic and Poet' in *On Poetry and Poets,* by T. S. ELIOT, Faber, London, 1957

Centuries, Poems and Thanksgivings, by T. TRAHERNE, Clarendon Press, Oxford, and Oxford University Press, New York, 1958

The Image of the City, by CHARLES WILLIAMS, Clarendon Press, Oxford, 1958

RIDING, LAURA

Collected Poems, by LAURA RIDING, Cassell, London, 1938

ROBINSON, EDWIN ARLINGTON

Collected Poems, by E. A. ROBINSON, Macmillan, London, 1932, and New York, 1937

Edwin Arlington Robinson, by YVOR WINTERS, New Directions, Norfolk, Conn., 1946

On the Limits of Poetry, by ALLEN TATE, Swallow and W. Morrow, New York, 1948

The Shores of Light, by E. WILSON, W. H. Allen, London, and Farrar, Straus & Cudahy, New York, 1952

ROCHESTER, JOHN WILMOT, EARL OF

The Poems of John Wilmot, Earl of Rochester, edited by V. DE S. PINTO, (Muses Library), Routledge, London, 1953

The Rochester–Savile Letters, 1671–1680, edited by J. H. WILSON, Ohio State University Press, Columbus, Ohio, 1941

The Famous Pathologist, or The Noble Mountebank, by Thomas Alcock and John Wilmot, Earl of Rochester, edited with an introduction and commentary by V. DE S. PINTO, Sisson & Parker Ltd. for the University of Nottingham, Nottingham, 1961

John Wilmot, Earl of Rochester: his Life and Writings, by J. PRINZ, Mayer & Muller, Leipzig, 1927

'Life and Death of John, Earl of Rochester', by G. BURNET, in *English Biography in the Seventeenth Century,* edited by V. DE S. PINTO, Harrap, London, 1951

Restoration Carnival, by V. DE S. PINTO, Folio Society, London, 1954

Enthusiast in Wit: Portrait of John Wilmot, Earl of Rochester, by V. DE S. PINTO, Routledge, London, and University of Nebraska Press, Lincoln, Neb., 1962

The Restoration Court Poets, British Council and Longmans, Green, London, 1965

ROETHKE, THEODORE

Collected Poems, by THEODORE ROETHKE, Doubleday, New York, 1966

ROSENBERG, ISAAC

The Collected Works of Isaac Rosenberg, edited by GORDON BOTTOMLEY and D. W. HARDING, London, Chatto & Windus, 1937: new enlarged edition, 1968

'Aspects of the Poetry of Isaac Rosenberg', by D. W. HARDING in *Scrutiny,* Vol. 3 (1934–35), pp. 358–369, Cambridge University Press, 1963

English Poetry of the First World War, by JOHN H. JOHNSTON, Princeton, University Press: Princeton N.J., Oxford University Press, London, 1964, ch. 6

Heroes' Twilight, by BERNARD BERGONZI, Constable, London, 1965 (esp. pp. 109–121).

'Isaac Rosenberg: The war, class, and the Jews' by JON SILKIN in *Stand,* Vol. 4, no. 3, pp. 35–38

ROSSETTI, CHRISTINA

The Poetical Works of Christina Georgina Rossetti, edited by W. M. ROSSETTI, Macmillan, London, 1904

Christina Rossetti: a Portrait with Background, by MARYA ZATURENSKA, Macmillan, New York, 1949

ROSSETTI, DANTE GABRIEL

The Works of Dante Gabriel Rossetti, edited by W. ROSSETTI, Ellis, London, 1911

Dante and Ourselves, by NICOLETTE M. GRAY, Faber, London, 1947

The Last Romantics, by G. HOUGH, Duckworth, London, 1949

Dante Gabriel Rosetti: a Victorian Romantic, by O. DOUGHTY, Muller, London, 1949

The Letters of Dante Gabriel Rossetti, edited by O. DOUGHTY and J. R. WAHL, 4 vols., Oxford, 1965–67

Rossetti–Macmillan Letters, edited by L. M. PACKER, London, 1963

SACKVILLE, SIR THOMAS

The Works of Thomas Sackville, Lord Buckhurst and Earl of Dorset, edited by the Rev. the Hon. REGINALD SACKVILLE-WEST, with a biographical note, J. R. Smith, London, 1859

The MS. of Sackville's Contribution to the Mirror for Magistrates, by MARGUERITE HEARSAY, Sidgwick & Jackson, London, 1932

The Complaint of Henry Duke of Buckingham, including the Induction, or Thomas Sackville's Contribution to the Mirror for Magistrates, edited by MARGUERITE HEARSAY, Yale University Press, New Haven, Conn., 1936

Knole and the Sackvilles, by VICTORIA SACKVILLE-WEST (chapter on Thomas Sackville, with quotations from various critics of his work), Benn, London, 1949

SANDBURG, CARL

Collected Poems, by CARL SANDBURG, Harcourt Brace, New York, 1950

On Native Grounds, by A. KAZIN, Cape, London, 1942

SASSOON, SIEGFRIED

Collected Poems, by SIEGFRIED SASSOON, Faber, London, 1947

War Poets 1914–1918, edited by EDMUND BLUNDEN, (Writers and their Work), Longmans, for the British Council, London, 1958

SATIRE

The Rise of Formal Satire in English, by R. M. ALLEN, London, 1899

Verse Satire in English Before the Renaissance, by S. M. TUCKER, Columbia University Press, New York, 1908

English Satire and Satirists, by H. WALKER, Dent, London, 1925

Satirical Verse, edited by EDWARD LUCIE SMITH, Penguin, London, 1968

SCIENCE AND POETRY

Aesthetic as a Science of Expression and General Linguistic, by BENEDETTO CROCE, (translated by D. Ainslie), Owen & Vision, London, 1953

The New Science, by G. VICO, (translated by T. G. Bergin and M. H. Fisch), Cornell University Press, Ithaca, N.Y., 1948

Principles of Literary Criticism, by I. A RICHARDS, 2nd edition, Routledge, London, 1926

Science and Poetry, by I. A. RICHARDS, Kegan Paul, London, 1926

Practical Criticism, by I. A. RICHARDS, Routledge, London, 1929

The Four Ages of Poetry, by T. C. PEACOCK, the *Defence of Poetry,* by P. B. SHELLEY, and the *Essay on Shelley,* by ROBERT BROWNING, edited in one volume by P. BRETT-SMITH, Blackwell, Oxford, 1937

The Origins of Modern Science, 1300–1800, by H. BUTTERFIELD, new edition, Bell, London, 1957

Tracks in the Snow, by R. TODD, Grey Walls Press, London, 1946

Inquiring Spirit: a new presentation of Coleridge from his published and unpublished prose writings, by KATHLEEN COBURN, Routledge, London, and Pantheon, New York, 1951

SCOTT, SIR WALTER

Scott's Poetical Works, edited with an introduction by L. M. WATT, Collins, London, 1942

Sir Walter Scott, by J. BUCHAN, Cassell, London, 1952

Sir Walter Scott, Bt., by H. J. C. GRIERSON, Constable, London, 1938

SHAKESPEARE, WILLIAM

Complete Works of William Shakespeare, edited by P. ALEXANDER, new edition, Collins, London, 1951

A New Variorum Edition of Shakespeare, edited by H. H. FURNESS and others, Lippincott, London and Philadelphia, 1871–

Shakespeare: His Mind and Art, by E. DOWDEN, Routledge, London, 1875

For further reading

Shakespearean Tragedy, by A. C. BRADLEY, Macmillan, London, 1904

Johnson on Shakespeare, by WALTER RALEIGH, Oxford University Press, London, 1908

The Works of Shakespeare, edited by A. QUILLER-COUCH and J. D. WILSON, Cambridge University Press, Cambridge, 1921–

William Shakespeare: a Study of Facts and Problems, by SIR E. K. CHAMBERS, Clarendon Press, Oxford, 1930

Shakespeare's Life and Art, by P. ALEXANDER, Nisbet, London, 1939

Shakespeare and Spenser, by W. B. C. WATKINS, Princeton University Press, Princeton, N.J., and Oxford University Press, London, 1950

The Common Pursuit, by F. R. LEAVIS, Chatto & Windus, London, 1952

The Works of William Shakespeare, edited by W. J. CRAIG and others, (Arden Edition), Methuen, London, 1951–, and Harvard University Press, Cambridge, Mass., 1953–

The Development of Shakespeare's Imagery, by W. H. CLEMEN, Methuen, London, 1953

The Wheel of Fire, by G. W. KNIGHT, 4th edition, Metheun, London, 1954

English Literature in the Sixteenth Century, excluding Drama, by C. S. LEWIS, (Oxford History of English Literature, Vol. 3), Clarendon Press, Oxford, and Oxford University Press, New York, 1954

Essays and Lectures on Shakespeare, by S. T. COLERIDGE, edited by T. M. RAYSOR, (Everyman Library, new edition), Dent, London, and Dutton, New York, 1960

SHAPIRO, KARL

Essay on Rime, by KARL SHAPIRO, Reynal & Hitchcock, New York, 1945

Poems 1940–53, by KARL SHAPIRO, Random House, New York, 1953

Poems of a Jew, by KARL SHAPIRO, Random House, New York, 1958

The Bourgeois Poet, Random House, New York, 1964

Selected Poems, Random House, New York, 1968

SHELLEY, PERCY BYSSHE

Works of P. B. Shelley, edited by T. HUTCHINSON, Oxford University Press, London, 1934

Literary Studies, by W. BAGEHOT, Vol. 1, (Everyman Library), Dent, London, 1911

Revaluation, by F. R. LEAVIS, Chatto & Windus, London, 1936

Shelley, by N. I. WHITE, 2 vols, Secker & Warburg, London, 1947

The Nascent Mind of Shelley, by A. M. D. HUGHES, Oxford University Press, London, 1947

English Poetry, by L. VIVANTI, Faber, London, 1950

Shelley, Godwin, and their Circle, by H. N. BRAILSFORD, 2nd edition, Oxford University Press, London, 1951

Shelley, by STEPHEN SPENDER, (Writers and their Work), Longmans, for the British Council, London, 1952

The True Voice of Feeling, by SIR HERBERT READ, Faber, London, 1953

Shelley at Work, by N. ROGERS, Oxford University Press, London, 1956

The Starlit Dome, by G. WILSON KNIGHT, Methuen, London, 1959

SHIRLEY, JAMES

The Dramatic Works and Poems of James Shirley, edited by A. DYCE, Murray, London, 1833

The Poems of James Shirley, edited by R. L. ARMSTRONG, (thesis), King's Crown Press, New York, 1941

SIDNEY, SIR PHILIP

The Complete Works of Sir Philip Sidney, edited by A. FEUILLERAT, (Cambridge English Classics), Cambridge University Press, Cambridge, 1912–23

Sir Philip Sidney, by MONA WILSON, Duckworth, London, 1931

Silver Poets of the Sixteenth Century, edited by G. BULLETT, (Everyman Library), Dent, London, and Dutton, New York, 1947

English Literature in the Sixteenth Century, excluding Drama, by C. S. LEWIS, (Oxford History of English Literature, Vol. 3),

Clarendon Press, Oxford, and Oxford University Press, New York, 1954

Sir Philip Sidney, by F. S. BOAS, Staples Press, London, 1955

Sir Philip Sidney, by K. MUIR, (Writers and their Work), Longmans, for the British Council, London, 1960

Sidney's Poetry, by D. KALSTONE, Harvard, 1965

SITWELL, DAME EDITH
Collected Poems of Edith Sitwell, Macmillan, London, 1962

SITWELL, SACHEVERELL
Collected Poems, by SACHEVERELL SITWELL, Duckworth, London, 1948

Selected Works, by SACHEVERELL SITWELL, Hale, London, 1955

SKELTON, JOHN
The Complete Poems of John Skelton, Laureate, edited by P. HENDERSON, revised edition, Dent, London, 1949

Skelton: the Life and Times of an Early Tudor Poet, by H. L. R. EDWARDS, Cape, London, 1949

John Skelton, Laureate, by W. NELSON, Columbia University Press, New York, 1939

SMART, CHRISTOPHER
The Collected Poems of Christopher Smart, edited by N. CALLAN, 2 vols, (Muses Library), Routledge, London, 1949, and Harvard University Press, Cambridge, Mass., 1950

Poems by Christopher Smart, edited by R. BRITTAIN, Oxford University Press, London, and Princeton University Press, Princeton, N.J., 1950

Rejoice in the Lamb: a Song from Bedlam, edited by W. F. STEAD, Cape, London, 1939

Jubilate Agno, by CHRISTOPHER SMART, Hart-Davis, London, 1954

SOUTH AFRICAN POETRY IN ENGLISH
Poetical Works, by T. PRINGLE, E. Moxon, London, 1837

Africa: Verses, by A. S. CRIPPS, Oxford University Press, London, 1939

Fifty Years of Rhodesian Verse, edited by J. SNELLING, Blackwell, Oxford, 1939

A New Centenary Book of South African Verse, edited by F. C. SLATER, Longmans, London, 1945

Selected Poems, by F. C. SLATER, Oxford University Press, London, 1947

Collected Poems, by ROY CAMPBELL, 3 vols, Bodley Head, London, 1949

An Unknown Border, by A. DELIUS, Balkema, Cape Town, 1954

A Critical Survey of South African Poetry in English, by G. M. MILLER and H. SERGEANT, Balkema, Cape Town, 1957

The Last Division, by A. DELIUS, Human & Rousseau, Cape Town, 1959

Stranger to Europe, by GUY BUTLER, Balkema, Cape Town, 1959

Monologue of a Deaf Man, by DAVID WRIGHT, Deutsch, London, 1959

A Book of South African Verse, edited by GUY BUTLER, Oxford University Press, London, 1959

Testament of a South African, by R. MAC-NABB, Fortune Press, London, 1960

Collected Poems, by WILLIAM PLOMER, Cape, London, 1960

A Corner of the World, by ANTHONY DELIUS, Human and Rousseau, Cape Town, 1962

Sjambok, by DOUGLAS LIVINGSTONE, Oxford University Press, London, 1964

Floating Island, by RUTH MILLER, Human and Rousseau, Cape Town, 1965

Only a Setting Forth, by ADÈLE NAUDÉ, Human and Rousseau, Cape Town, 1965

The Land at my Door, by PERSEUS ADAMS, Human and Rousseau, Cape Town, 1965

South of the Zambesi, by GUY BUTLER, Abelard-Schuman, London, 1966

One Life, by SYDNEY CLOUTS, Purnell, Cape Town, 1967.

Set in Brightness, by ANNE WELSH, Purnell, Cape Town, 1968

SOUTHEY, ROBERT
Poems of Robert Southey, edited by J. FITZ-GERALD, Oxford University Press, London, 1909

For further reading

Southey, by J. SIMMONS, Collins, London, 1945, and Yale University Press, New Haven, Conn., 1948

Robert Southey and His Age: the Development of a Conservative Mind, by GEOFFREY CARNALL, Clarendon Press, Oxford, 1960

Southey, by E. DOWDEN, (English Men of Letters), Harper, New York, 1880

SOUTHWELL, ROBERT

The Complete Poems of Robert Southwell, edited by A. GROSART, (Fuller Worthies Library), Constable, London, 1872

SPENDER, STEPHEN

Collected Poems 1928–53, by STEPHEN SPENDER, Faber, London, 1954

SPENSER, EDMUND

Works, Variorum Edition, edited by E. GREENLAW and others, with a Life, by A. C. JUDSON, 11 vols, Johns Hopkins Press, Baltimore, and Oxford University Press, London, 1932–57

English Literature in the Sixteenth Century, excluding Drama, by C. S. LEWIS (Oxford History of English Literature, Vol. 3), Clarendon Press, Oxford, and Oxford University Press, New York, 1954

The Poetry of Edmund Spenser, by WILLIAM NELSON, Columbia University Press, New York, 1963

The Poetry of The Faerie Queene, by PAUL J. ALPERS, Princeton University Press, Princeton, N.J., 1967

STEIN, GERTRUDE

The Third Rose: Gertrude Stein and her World, by J. M. BRINNIN, Weidenfeld & Nicolson, London, 1960

The Yale Edition of the Unpublished Writings of Gertrude Stein, 6 vols, Yale University Press, New Haven, Conn., 1951

STEPHENS, JAMES

Collected Poems, by JAMES STEPHENS, (revised and enlarged edition), Macmillan, London, 1954

STEVENS, WALLACE

The Collected Works of Wallace Stevens,

Knopf, New York, 1954, and Faber, London, 1955

Selected Poems of Wallace Stevens, selected by the author, Faber, London, 1953

Opus Posthumous, by WALLACE STEVENS, edited by SAMUEL FRENCH NORTH, Faber, London, and Knopf, New York, 1957

The Shaping Spirit, by WILLIAM VAN O'CONNER, Regnery, Chicago, 1950

Wallace Stevens, by R. PACK, Rutgers University Press, New Brunswick, N.J., 1958

Wallace Stevens, by FRANK KERMODE, (Writers and Critics), Oliver & Boyd, Edinburgh, 1960

The Achievement of Wallace Stevens: a Critical Anthology, edited by ASHLEY BROWN and ROBERT S. HALLER, Lippincott, Philadelphia, 1962

The Act of the Mind: Essays on the Poetry of Wallace Stevens, edited by ROY HARVEY PEARCE and J. HILLIS MILLER, Johns Hopkins Press, Maryland, 1965

Stevens' Poetry of Thought by FRANK DUGGET, Johns Hopkins Press, Maryland, 1966

SUCKLING, SIR JOHN

The Works of Sir John Suckling in Prose and Verse, edited by A. H. THOMPSON, Routledge, London, and Dutton, New York, 1910

SURREY, HENRY HOWARD, EARL OF

Poems of Henry Howard, Earl of Surrey, edited by F. M. PADELFORD, University of Washington Publications, Seattle, 1928

Henry Howard, Earl of Surrey, by E. CASADY, Modern Language Association of America, New York, 1938

SWIFT, JONATHAM

The Poems of Jonathan Swift, edited by H. WILLIAMS, Clarendon Press, Oxford, 1937

Swift, by L. STEPHEN, (English Men of Letters), Macmillan, London, 1882

Jonathan Swift, by J. MIDDLETON MURRY, (Writers and their Work), Longmans, for the British Council, London, 1955

SWINBURNE, ALGERNON CHARLES

Works of Algernon Charles Swinburne,

edited by E. GOSSE, and T. J. WISE, Heinemann, London, 1925–7

Swinburne, by H. NICOLSON, (English Men of Letters), Macmillan, London, 1926

Swinburne, by H. C. J. GRIERSON, (Writers and their Work), Longmans, for the British Council, London, 1953

Five Poems, by E. M. W. TILLYARD, Chatto & Windus, London, 1948

Swinburne: a Literary Biography, translation of *La Jeunesse de Swinburne*, by G. LAFOURCADE, Bell, London, 1932

SYMBOLISM

Message Poétique du Symbolisme, by G. MICHAUD, Nizet, Paris, 1947

The Symbolist Movement, by K. CORNELL, Yale University Press, New Haven, Conn., 1951

Symbolism from Poe to Mallarmé, by J. CHIARI, Rockliff, London, 1956

The Symbolist Poem, edited by EDWARD ENGELBERG, E. P. Dutton, New York, 1967

SYMONS, ARTHUR

Poems, by ARTHUR SYMONS, 2 vols, Heinemann, London, 1901

TATE, ALLEN

Poems, by ALLEN TATE, Charles Scribner's Sons, New York, 1960: Swallow Paperbook, Denver, Colorado, 1961. *Poems 1920–1945: A Selection* by ALLEN TATE, Eyre & Spottiswoode, London, 1947

Collected Essays, by ALLEN TATE, Swallow Press, Denver, Colorado, 1959 (esp. pp. 248–262).

The Fugitives: A Critical Account, by JOHN M. BRADBURY, The University of North Carolina Press, Chapel Hill, 1958

Southern Renascence: The Literature of the Modern South, edited by LOUIS D. RUBIN JR, and ROBERT D. JACOBS, The Johns Hopkins Press, Baltimore, 3rd impression 1961 (esp. pp. 352–67)

The Last Alternatives: A Study of the Works of Allen Tate, by ROGER K. MEINERS, Swallow Press, Denver, Colorado, 1963

Allen Tate, by GEORGE HEMPHILL, University of Minnesota Pamphlets on American Writers, no. 39, 1964

TAYLOR, EDWARD

The Poems of Edward Taylor, edited by D. STANFORD, Yale University Press, New Haven, Conn., 1960

Abridged paperback edition with a new Introduction by the Editor, Yale University Press, 1963

TENNYSON, ALFRED, LORD

Poems 1830–1870, by ALFRED, LORD TENNYSON, (Oxford Standard Authors), Oxford University Press, London, 1953

Tennyson: Aspects of his Life, Character and Poetry, by SIR HAROLD NICOLSON, 2nd edition, Constable, London, 1925

Six Tennyson Essays, by SIR CHARLES TENNYSON, Cassell, London, 1954

THOMAS, DYLAN

Collected Poems 1934–52, by DYLAN THOMAS, Dent, London, 1952

Innovation and Tradition, anonymous, (New World Writing Mentor Selection), The Times Publishing Co., London, 1953, and New American Library of World Literature, New York, 1954

'Dylan Thomas', by KARL SHAPIRO, in *Poetry Magazine*, Modern Poetry Association, Chicago, November 1955

Dylan Thomas: a Bibliography, by J. A. ROLPH, Dent, London, 1956

Letters to Vernon Watkins, by DYLAN THOMAS, edited by VERNON WATKINS, Dent and Faber, London, and New Directions, New York, 1957

Dylan Thomas, by R. SANESI, Lerici editori, Milan, 1960

THOMAS, EDWARD

Collected Poems, by EDWARD THOMAS, Faber, London, 1949

Edward Thomas: a Biography and a Bibliography, by R. P. ECKERT, Dent, London, 1937

As It Was . . . World Without End, by HELEN THOMAS, Heinemann, London, 1935

New Bearings in English Poetry, by F. R. LEAVIS, Chatto & Windus, London, and G. W. Stewart, New York, 1950

Edward Thomas, by HENRY COOMBES, Chatto & Windus, London, 1956

THOMAS, R. S.
Song at the Year's Turning: Collected Poems, by R. S. THOMAS, Hart-Davis, London, 1955
Poetry for Supper, by R. S. THOMAS, Hart-Davis, London, 1958
Tares, (including *Judgement Day*), by R. S. THOMAS, Hart-Davis, London, 1961
Not that he brought the Flowers, Hart-Davis, London, 1968

THOMPSON, FRANCIS
The Works of Francis Thompson, edited by W. MEYNELL, (Oxford Standard Authors), Oxford University Press, London, 1913

THOMSON, JAMES (1700–1748)
The Complete Poetical Works of James Thomson, edited by J. L. ROBERTSON, Froude, Oxford, 1908
Thomson, Poet of the Seasons, by DOUGLAS GRANT, Cresset Press, London, 1951

THOMSON, JAMES (1834–82)
Poetical Works of James Thomson, edited by BERTRAM DOBELL, 2 vols, London, 1895
The City of Dreadful Night, and Other Poems, by JAMES THOMSON, Methuen, London, 1932

THOREAU, HENRY DAVID
Collected Poems of H. D. Thoreau, edited by CARL BODE, Packard, Chicago, 1943

TOURNEUR, CYRIL
The Works of Cyril Tourneur, edited by A. NICOLL, Fanfrolico Press, London, 1930

TOWNSHEND, AURELIAN
Aurelian Townshend's Poems and Masks, edited by E. K. CHAMBERS, Clarendon Press, Oxford, 1912

TRAHERNE, THOMAS
Centuries, Poems and Thanksgivings, by THOMAS TRAHERNE, (Oxford English Texts), Oxford University Press, London, 1958

Thomas Traherne, by G. I. WADE, Oxford University Press, London, and Princeton University Press, Princeton, N.J., 1944

TRANSLATION
Essay on the Principles of Translation, by A. F. TYTLER, (Everyman Library), Dent, London, 1907
Some Remarks on Translation and Translators, by J. S. PHILLIMORE, Oxford University Press, London, 1919
Translators and Translations, by J. P. POSTGATE, Bell, London, 1922
Essays in Poetry and Prose, by JOHN DRYDEN, (Clarendon Series of English Literture), Clarendon Press, Oxford, 1925
Preface to *Translation of 'The Iliad',* by ALEXANDER POPE, (World's Classics), Oxford University Press, London, 1934
Modern Translation, by E .S. BATES, Oxford University Press, London, 1936
On Translation, a symposium, edited by REUBEN BROWER, Harvard University Press, Cambridge, Mass., 1959
Dryden's Aeneid and its Seventeenth Century Practitioners, by L. PROUDFOOT, Manchester University Press, Manchester, 1960
The Craft and Context of Translation, edited by W. ARROWSMITH and R. SHATTUCK, University of Texas Press, Austin, Texas, 1961

VAN DOREN, MARK
Collected Poems, by MARK VAN DOREN, Holt, New York, 1939
Selected Poems, by MARK VAN DOREN, Holt, New York, 1954
Autobiography, by MARK VAN DOREN, Harcourt Brace, New York, 1958
Collected and New Poems, by Mark Van Dorea, Hill & Wang, NewYork, 1968
100 Poems selected by the author, Hill & Wang, New York, 1967

VAUGHAN, HENRY
The Works of Henry Vaughan, edited by L. C. MARTIN, (Oxford English Texts), 2nd edition, Oxford University Press, London, 1958

Henry Vaughan: a Life and Interpretation, by
F. E. HUTCHINSON, Clarendon Press,
Oxford, 1947

WALLER, EDMUND
The Poems of Edmund Waller, edited by
G. THORN DRURY, (Muses Library),
Routledge, London, 1891

WARREN, ROBERT PENN
Brother to the Dragons, by ROBERT PENN
WARREN, Random House, New York,
1953
Selected Poems, 1923–66, Random House,
New York, 1966

WARTON, JOSEPH AND THOMAS
The Three Wartons: a Choice of their Verse,
edited by E. PARTRIDGE, Scholartis Press,
London, 1927

WEBSTER, JOHN
The Works of John Webster, edited by F. L.
LUCAS, 4 vols, Chatto & Windus,
London, 1927
John Webster and the Elizabethan Drama, by
R. BROOKE, 2nd impression, Sidgwick &
Jackson, London, 1917
John Webster, a Concise Bibliography, by S. A.
TANNENBAUM, New York, 1941
Sources of 'The White Devil', by G. BOKLUND,
Uppsala, 1957
The White Devil and *The Duchess of Malfi*,
by JOHN WEBSTER, revised editions,
Chatto & Windus, London, 1958
The Jacobean Drama, by UNA ELLIS-FERMOR,
4th edition, Methuen, London, 1958
The White Devil, by JOHN WEBSTER, edited
by J. R. BROWN, Methuen, London, 1960
John Webster's Borrowing, by R. W. DENT,
University of California Press, Berkeley
and Los Angeles, 1960

WHEELWRIGHT, JOHN
Selected Poems of John Wheelwright, New
Directions, New York, 1941

WHITMAN, WALT
Complete Poetry and Prose of Walt Whitman,
edited with an introduction by M.

COWLEY, Garden City Books, New York,
1954
*Complete Poetry and Selected Prose of Walt
Whitman*, edited by E. HOLLOWAY, None-
such Press, Faber, London, 1938
Poetry and the Age, by RANDALL JARRELL,
Knopf, New York, 1953, and Faber,
London, 1955
*The Solitary Singer: a Critical Biography of
Walt Whitman*, by G. W. ALLEN,
Macmillan, New York, 1955
Walt Whitman, by G. DUTTON, (Writers
and Critics), Oliver and Boyd, Edinburgh,
1961

WILBUR, RICHARD
The Beautiful Changes, and other poems, by
RICHARD WILBUR, Reynal & Hitchcock,
New York, 1947
Ceremony, and other poems, by RICHARD
WILBUR, Harcourt Brace, New York,
1950
Things of This World, by RICHARD WILBUR,
Harcourt Brace, New York, 1956
Poems 1943–56, by RICHARD WILBUR, Faber,
London, 1957
Molière's 'Misanthrope', translated by
RICHARD WILBUR, Harcourt Brace, New
York, 1955, and Faber, London, 1958
Advice to a Prophet, by RICHARD WILBUR,
Harcourt Brace, New York, 1961, and
Faber, London, 1962
Tartuffe, by MOLIÈRE, translated by RICHARD
WILBUR, Harcourt Brace, New York,
and Faber, London, 1963

WILDE, OSCAR
Works of Oscar Wilde, edited by G. F.
MAINE, Collins, London, 1909
Letters of Oscar Wilde, edited by R. HART-
DAVIS, Hart-Davis, London, 1952

WILLIAMS, WILLIAM CARLOS
Selected Poems, by WILLIAM CARLOS
WILLIAMS, New Directions, Norfolk,
Conn., 1949
*The Collected Later Poems of William Carlos
Williams*, New Directions, Norfolk,
Conn., 1950
The Collected Earlier Poems of William

For further reading

Carlos Williams, New Directions, Norfolk, Conn., 1951

Pictures from Brueghel and other poems, by WILLIAM CARLOS WILLIAMS, MacGibbon & Kee, London, 1964 and New Directions, 1967

Paterson, by WILLIAM CARLOS WILLIAMS, 5 vols, New Directions, Norfolk, Conn., 1946–58

The Desert Music and other poems, by WILLIAM CARLOS WILLIAMS, Random House, New York, 1954

Journey to Love, by WILLIAM CARLOS WILLIAMS, Random House, New York, 1955

Gnomon, by HUGH KENNER, McDowell, Obolensky, New York, 1958

WINCHILSEA, ANNE FINCH, COUNTESS OF

The Poems of Anne, Countess of Winchilsea, Reynolds, Chicago, 1903

WINTERS, YVOR

Collected Poems, by YVOR WINTERS, Swallow, Denver, Colorado, 1960

Sequoia (special issue on Yvor Winters), contributions by MARIANNE MOORE and others, Associated Students of Stanford University, Stanford, California, Winter, 1961

The Early Poems of Yvor Winters, 1920–1928, Swallow, Denver, 1966

WORDSWORTH, WILLIAM

The Prelude, by WILLIAM WORDSWORTH, edited by E. DE SELINCOURT, Oxford University Press, London, 1928

Poetical Works of William Wordsworth, edited by E. DE SELINCOURT and HELEN DARBISHIRE, Oxford University Press, London, 1940–54

The Mind of a Poet, by R. D. HAVENS, Johns Hopkins Press, Baltimore, Md., 1941

The Poet Wordsworth, by HELEN DARBISHIRE, Oxford University Press, London, 1950

The Egotistical Sublime, by J. JONES, Chatto & Windus, London, 1954

William Wordsworth, by MARY MOORMAN, Oxford University Press, London, 1957-65

Wordsworth's Poetry, by GEOFFREY HARTMAN, 1787–1814, Yale University Press, New Haven and London, 1964

WRIGHT, JAMES

St Judas, Wesleyan University Press, Middletown, 1958

The Branch Will not Break, Wesleyan University Press, Middletown, 1963

Shall We Gather at the River, Wesleyan University Press, Middletown, 1968

The Green Wall, by JAMES WRIGHT, Yale University Press, New Haven, Conn., and Oxford University Press, London, 1957

WYATT, SIR THOMAS

Collected Poems of Sir Thomas Wyatt, edited by K. MUIR, (Muses Library), Routledge, London, 1949

Unpublished Poems by Sir Thomas Wyatt and his Circle, edited by K. MUIR, Liverpool University Press, Liverpool, 1961

WYLIE, ELINOR

Collected Poems of Elinor Wylie, Knopf, New York, 1932

YEATS, W. B.

The Collected Poems of W. B. Yeats, 2nd edition, Macmillan, London, 1952

Collected Plays, by W. B. YEATS, Macmillan, London, 1952

Autobiographies, by W. B. YEATS, Macmillan, London, 1955

Mythologies, by W. B. YEATS, Macmillan, London, 1959

Essays and Introductions, by W. B. YEATS, London, 1961

Explorations, by W. B. YEATS, Macmillan, London, 1962

The Poetry of W. B. Yeats, by LOUIS MAC-NEICE, Faber & Faber, London and New York, 1947

The Identity of Yeats, by R. ELLMANN, Macmillan, London, 1954

The Lonely Tower, by T. R. HENN, 2nd edition, Methuen, London, 1965

The Letters of W. B. Yeats, by A. WADE, Hart-Davis, London, 1954

Prolegomena to the Study of Yeats' Poems, by

366

G. B. SAUL, University of Pennsylvania Press, Philadelphia, Pa., 1958

Bibliography of the Writings of W. B. Yeats, by A. WADE, revised edition, Hart-Davis, London, 1958

Yeats Scholarship and Criticism, by H. ADAMS, (Texas Studies in Literature and Language, III, 439–51), Texas University Press, Austin, Texas, 1962

YOUNG, ANDREW

Out of the World and Back, by ANDREW YOUNG, Rupert Hart-Davis, London, 1958

Collected Poems of Andrew Young, Rupert Hart-Davis, London, 1960

YOUNG, EDWARD

The Complete Works of Edward Young, edited by JOHN DORAN and JAMES NICHOLS, 2 vols, W. Tegg, London, 1854, (with a Life of Young by John Doran)

Edward Young and His Fear of Death: a Study in Romantic Melancholy, by C. WICKER, University of New Mexico Press, Albuquerque, New Mexico, 1952

A Bibliography of Edward Young's Night Thoughts, by H. J. PETTIT, (University of Colorado Studies in Language and Literature), University of Colorado Press, Boulder, Colorado, 1954

Notes on the contributors

A.H. Arnold P. Hinchliffe

Lecturer in English Literature, University of Manchester. Publications include articles on American poetry in *Studii Americani*, *Texas Studies in Language and Literature* and *Twentieth Century*, and *Modern Drama*, *Harold Pinter*, New York, 1967, *A Casebook on the 'Wasteland'*, London, 1968, and a pamphlet of poems, *Private File*.

A.R. Anne Ridler

Writer and editor. Publications include several books of verse and verse plays, and a biography of *Olive Willis and Downe House*, London, 1967.

A.S. Anne Stevenson

Instructor in English, the Cambridge School, Massachusetts. Publications include poems in the *Paris Review*, *Poetry* (Chicago), and the *Saturday Review*.

A.W. Andrews Wanning

Professor of English, Bard College, New York. Publications include contributions to *Focus*, the *Partisan Review*, and the *Southern Review*. Editor, the Laurel *Donne*.

B.B. Bernard Bergonzi

Senior Lecturer in English, Warwick University. Publications include *Descartes and the Animals*, (poems), 1954, *The Early H. G. Wells*, Manchester, 1961, *Heroes' Twilight: A Study of the Literature of the Great War*, London, 1965, and (as editor) *Innovations: Essays on Art and Ideas*, London, 1968

B.BO. Buddhadeva Bose

Bengali poet and author, founder-editor

of *Kavita*, a Bengali poetry magazine, formerly professor of Comparative Literature at Jadavpur University, Calcutta. Publications include numerous titles in Bengali, and two in English, *An Acre of Green Grass*, Calcutta, 1948, and *Tagore: Portrait of a Poet*, Bombay, 1962. English versions of his poems and short stories, made by himself, have appeared in magazines in India and the United States.

B.D. Bonamy Dobrée

Emeritus Professor of English Literature, University of Leeds. Hon. LL.D., Canterbury, 1968. Publications include *Restoration Comedy*, Oxford, 1924, *Histriophone*, London, 1925, *Restoration Tragedy*, Oxford, 1929, *Modern Prose Style*, Oxford, 1934, *The Broken Cistern*, London, 1954, and Indiana, 1955, and *English Literature in the Early Eighteenth Century*, Oxford, 1959. Editor of *The Letters of Lord Chesterfield*, London, 1932, and of the Everyman editions of the works of Dryden (1948) and of Pope (1956).

C.B. Carl Bode

Professor of English, University of Maryland. Publications include books of verse, *The Half-World of American Culture*, 1965, and contributions to the *Encyclopedia Americana*, the *Encyclopaedia Britannica*, and the *Dictionary of American Biography*. Editor of *Collected Poems of Henry Thoreau*, 1948.

C.B.B. Curtis B. Bradford

Oakes Ames Profesor of English, Grinnell College. Publications include *Yeats at Work*, 1956, and various articles.

C.B-R. Christine Brooke-Rose

Writer. Publications include *A Grammar of Metaphor*, (criticism), London, 1958, several novels, including *Out, Such* and *Between*, London, 1964, 1966 and 1968

C.K.S. C. K. Stead

Associate Professor of English, University of Auckland, New Zealand. Publications include *Whether the Will is Free*, (Poems 1954–62), Auckland, 1964, *The New Poetic: Yeats to Eliot*, London, 1964, World's Classics *New Zealand Short Stories*, London, 1966

C.M. Charles Madge

Professor of Sociology, University of Birmingham. Publications include books of verse, *Britain by Mass-Observation*, (with Tom Harrisson), Harmondsworth, Middlesex, 1939, *War-time pattern of Saving and Spending*, Cambridge, 1943, and *Society in the Mind*, 1964

D.B. Douglas Bush

Gurney Professor of English Emeritus, Harvard University. Publications include two volumes on mythology in English poetry, *The Renaissance and English Humanism*, Toronto, 1939, *English Literature in the Earlier Seventeenth Century*, Oxford, rev. 1962, *Science and English Poetry*, New York and London, 1950, *John Milton*, ibid., 1964, *John Keats*, ibid., 1966. Editor of *Keats: Selected Poems and Letters*, Boston, 1959, *Complete Poetical Works of John Milton*, Boston and London, 1965–66.

D.E.S. Donald E. Stanford

Professor of English, Louisiana State University, and Co-editor of the *Southern Review*. Publications include books of verse, *Edward Taylor* (University of Minnesota Pamphlets of American Literature), and contributions to the *Southern Review, Kenyon Review, Poetry,* and *American Literature*. Editor of *The Poems of Edward Taylor*, New Haven, Conn., 1960.

D.F. David Ferry

Professor of English, Wellesley College, Massachusetts. Publications include *The Limits of Mortality, an Essay on Wordsworth's Major Poems*, 1959, *On the Way to the Island*, (poems), 1960, and various poems and articles.

D.H. Donald Hall

Associate Professor of English, University of Michigan. Publications include several books of verse and a prose memoir. Editor of several anthologies of English and American poetry. Co-editor of this *Encyclopedia*.

D.L.H. Donald L. Hill

Assistant Professor of English, University of Michigan. Publications include reviews and articles on Victorian and modern writers, and a book on the poet, Richard Wilbur, New York, 1967.

D.W. David Wright

Writer and editor. Has published four books of verse and several anthologies including *The Mid-Century: English Poetry 1940–50* and *Longer Contemporary Poems*.

E.L. Edward Lowbury

Author of *Time for Sale*, 1961, *Daylight Astronomy*, 1968, and other books of poems: represented in *Palgrave's Golden Treasury* and other anthologies. Member of Scientific Staff, Medical Research Council.

E.M. Edwin Morgan

Senior Lecturer in English, University of Glasgow. Publications include books of verse, *Beowulf: A verse Translation into Modern English*, Aldington, Kent, 1952, and contributions to the *Chicago Review*, the *Critical Quarterly*, the *Listener*, the *Partisan Review*, and *Twentieth Century*.

E.N.W.M. E. N. W. Mottram

Lecturer in American Literature, King's

College and the Institute of United States Studies, University of London.

F.L.L. F. L. Lucas (d.1967)
Reader in English, University of Cambridge. Publications include *Ten Victorian Poets*, Cambridge, 1930, *Decline and Fall of the Romantic Ideal*, Cambridge, 1936, *Literature and Psychology*, London, 1951, and Michigan, 1957, *Style*, London and New York, 1955, *The Search for Good Sense*, London and New York, 1958, *The Art of Living*, London and New York, 1959, and *The Greatest Problem*, London, 1960, and New York, 1961. Editor of *The Works of John Webster*, London, 1927, *The White Devil* and *The Duchess of Malfi*, London, 1958.

G.A.O. G. A. Over (d.1965)
Lecturer in English Literature, University of Leeds.

G.B. Guy Butler
Professor of English, Rhodes University, South Africa. Publications include *The Dam*, (Play), Cape Town, 1952, *The Dove Returns*, (play), London, 1956, *Cape Charade*, (play), Cape Town, 1968, *Stranger to Europe*, (verse), Cape Town, 1959, *South of the Zambesi*, (verse), London, 1966. Editor of *A Book of South African Verse*, London, 1959, *When Boys were Men*. London, 1968. Editor of *New Coin*, a poetry quarterly.

G.C. Glauco Cambon
Professor of Comparative and Italian Literature, Rutgers University, New Jersey. Publications include *The Inclusive Flame*, (criticism), Indiana, 1962, *Recent American Poetry*, 1962, *The Inclusive Flame*, 1963, *La Lotta con Proteo*, 1963, and contributions to the *Italian Quarterly*, the *Modern Language Quarterly*, *Poetry* (Chicago), and the *Sewanee Review*.

G.F. George Fraser
Lecturer in English, University of Leicester. Publications include *The Traveller has Regrets*, (poems), 1947,

The Modern Writer and His World, London, 1953, and *Vision and Rhetoric*, London, 1959.

G.G. Geoffrey Grigson
Poet. Editor of *New Verse 1933–1939*. Publications include *Collected Poems*, 1963, *A Skull in Salop*, 1967, *Poems and Poets*, 1968.

G.H. Geoffrey Hill
Lecturer in English Literature, University of Leeds. Publications include two books of poems: *For the Unfallen*, London, 1959 and *King Log*, London: Chester Springs, Pa, 1968.

G.Mac. George MacBeth
B.B.C. talks producer. Publications include *A Form of Words*, (poems), 1954, and poems in *Encounter*, the *Listener*, the *London Magazine*, the *New Statesman*, the *Paris Review*, and the *Spectator*, *The Penguin Book of Animal Verse*, (editor), London, 1965, *The Colour of Blood*, (poems), 1967, and *The Night of Stones*, (poems), 1968.

G.M. Gerald Moore
Lecturer in African Studies, University of Sussex. Publications include *African Literature and the Universities*, 1965, *The Chosen Tongue*, 1969, and *Seven African Writers*, 1962.

H.G. Helen Gardner, Dame
Merton Professor of English Literature, University of Oxford. Publications include *The Art of T. S. Eliot*, London and New York, 1949, *The Business of Criticism*, Oxford, 1959, *A Reading of 'Paradise Lost'*, Oxford, 1965. Editor of *John Donne: The Divine Poems*, Oxford, 1952, and *John Donne: Elegies and Songs and Sonnets*, Oxford, 1965, and of *The Metaphysical Poets*, Penguin Poets, 1957, and Oxford, 1961.

H.K. Hugh Kenner
Professor of English, University of California (Santa Barbara). Publications

include *The Poetry of Ezra Pound,* London and New York, 1951, *Wyndham Lewis,* London and New York, 1954, *Dublin's Joyce,* London and Indiana, 1956, *Gnomon, essays on contemporary literature,* New York, 1958, *The Art of Poetry,* New York, 1959, *The Invisible Poet: T. S. Eliot,* New York, 1959, and London, 1960, *Samuel Beckett,* London and New York, 1961, *The Stoic Comedians,* London and Boston, 1963, *The Counterfeiters,* Indiana, 1968, and various articles and reviews.

H.M.M. H. M. McLuhan

Professor of English and Director, Centre for Culture and Technology, University of Toronto. Publications include: *The Mechanical Bride,* Toronto, 1951, *The Gutenberg Galaxy,* Toronto, 1962, *Understanding Media,* New York, 1964, *Explorations in Communications,* Boston 1966, *The Medium is the Message,* New York, 1967, *War and Peace in the Global Village,* New York and Toronto, 1968, *Through the Vanishing Point: Space in Poetry and Painting,* (with Harley Parker), New York, 1968, and *Counterblast,* New York, 1968.

I.F. Ian Fletcher

Lecturer in English Literature, University of Reading, Publications include *Orisons,* (poems), 1947, and contributions to *Essays in Criticism,* the *London Magaazine,* the *New Statesman,* the *Times Literary Supplement,* and *Victorian Studies.* Editor of *The Complete Poems of Lionel Johnson,* London, 1953.

J.C.H. J. C. Hall

Writer and editor. Publications include *Edwin Muir,* London, 1956, and books of verse.

J.C.M. J. C. Maxwell

Reader in English Literature, University of Oxford. Editor of *Titus Andronicus,* London, 1953, revised 1968, *Pericles, Prince of Tyre, Timon of Athens,* and *Cymbeline,* Cambridge, 1956, 1957, and 1960, and of *Poems,* London, 1966.

J.C.R. John Crowe Ransom

Professor Emeritus, Kenyon College, Gambier, Ohio. Publications include several books of verse and of criticism. Formerly editor of the *Kenyon Review* (1939–59).

J.G. James Gindin

Professor, Department of English, University of Michigan. Publications include *Postwar British Fiction: New Accents and Attitudes,* Los Angeles, Calif., 1962, and London, 1963, and contributions to *Modern Fiction Studies, Wisconsin Studies in Contemporary Literature,* and *The Michigan Quarterly Review.*

J.H-S. John Heath-Stubbs

Lecturer in English Literature, College of St Mark & St John. Publications include several books of verse and criticism. Editor (with David Wright) of *The Faber Book of Twentieth Century Verse,* London, 1953.

J.L. John Lehmann

Writer and editor. Publications include books of verse, *A Nest of Tigers* (the Sitwells in their times), London, 1963, and three volumes of autobiography. Editor of several books of verse and prose; formerly editor of the *London Magazine* and of *New Writing.*

J.M.C. J. M. Cohen

Writer and editor. Publications include *History of Western Literature,* Harmondsworth, Middlesex, 1956. Translator of (Penguin Classics): *Don Quixote,* 1950, *Rousseau's Confessions,* 1953, and *Gargantua and Pantagruel,* 1955. Editor of *The Penguin Book of Comic and Curious Verse,* 1952, *The Penguin Book of Spanish Verse,* 1956, *The Baroque Lyric,* London, 1963, and *Poetry of This Age* (2nd ed.), London, 1966.

J.P. John Press

Deputy Representative, British Council, Paris. Publications include books of verse and the following works of criticism: *The Fire and the Fountain,* London, 1955, *The Chequer'd Shade,* London, 1958, and *Rule and Energy,* London, 1963.

J.P.B. J. Philip Brockbank
Professor of English, University of York. Publications include a number of contributions to *Shakespeare Survey* and to *Stratford Studies,* and *Marlowe: Dr Faustus,* London, 1962. He is general editor with Brian Morris of the *New Mermaid* series of plays, and has edited *Volpone* in that series (1968).

J.W. John Waller, Bt., Kt.T.
Writer. Publications include several books of verse. Editor of *The Collected Poems of Keith Douglas,* London, 1951 and 1967, Greenwood Award for Poetry, 1947. Founder-editor, *Kingdom Come,* republished, London, 1968.

K.R. Kathleen Raine
Writer. Publications include *Collected Poems,* London, 1956, *William Blake and Traditional Mythology,* London, 1963.

L.M. Louis MacNeice (d. 1963)
Writer and B.B.C. producer. Publications include several books of verse, *The Poetry of W. B. Yeats,* London and New York, 1941, and a verse translation of Goethe's *Faust.*

L.S. Louis Simpson
Professor, State University of New York at Stony Brook. Publications include four books of verse, a novel, a critical study of James Hogg, and *An Introduction to Poetry.*

M.B. Marius Bewley
Professor of English, Rutgers University, New Brunswick, N.J. Publications include *The Complex Fate,* London and New York, 1952, and *The Eccentric Design,* London, 1959.

M.D. Maureen Duffy
Writer. Publications include *That's How*

It Was, London, 1962, *The Microcosm,* and other novels, a book of verse, *Lyrics for the dog lover,* 1968, and poems in *The Arts,* the *Guinness Book of Verse,* the *Listener,* and *Outposts.*

M.K.S. Monroe K. Spears
Moody Professor of English, Rice University, Texas. Publications include *The Poetry of W. H. Auden,* Oxford, 1963, and *Hart Crane,* Minnesota, 1965.

N.C. Nevill Coghill
Merton Professor of English Literature, University of Oxford, 1957–66. Publications include *Visions from Piers Plowman,* London, 1949, *The Canterbury Tales, a new translation,* Harmondsworth, Middlesex, 1951, and *The Poet Chaucer,* London, 1959.

N.C.C. Nirad C. Chaudhuri
Writer and broadcaster. Publications include *The Autobiography of an Unknown Indian,* London, 1959, and New York, 1960, *A Passage to England,* London, 1959, and New York, 1960, and contributions to the *Atlantic Monthly, Encounter,* the *New English Review,* and various Indian periodicals.

N.F. Northrop Frye
Principal, Victoria College, University of Toronto. Publications include *Fearful Symmetry, a study of William Blake,* Princeton, 1947, and *Anatomy of Criticism,* Princeton, 1957.

N.N. Norman Nicholson
Writer. Publications include several books of verse and verse drama, *H. G. Wells,* London, 1947, *William Cowper,* London, 1950, and books on travel and topography.

P.D. Patric Dickinson
Gresham Professor in Rhetoric at the City University, London. Writer and broadcaster. Publications include *The World I See,* London, 1960, *This Cold Universe,* London, 1964, and other books of poetry.

P.P. Peter Pears
Concert singer. Has broadcast talks on 'Translation' and 'Words and Music'.

R.C. Rivers Carew
Joint editor of the *Dublin Magazine*. Publications include a book of verse and contributions to *A Review of English Literature*, the *Hibbert Journal*, *The Encyclopaedia Britannica Year Book*, and various Irish periodicals.

R.S. Radcliffe Squires
Professor of English, University of Michigan. Publications include books of verse and critical studies of Robinson Jeffers, Robert Frost and Frederic Prokosch.

R.S.T. R. S. Thomas
Vicar of Aberdaron, North Wales. Publications include several books of verse. Editor of *The Batsford Book of Country Verse*.

R.W. Richard Wilbur
Professor of English, Wesleyan University, Connecticut. Publications include several books of verse. Editor of *The Complete Poems of Edgar Allan Poe*, New York, 1959.

S.C. Seymour Chatman
Professor, Department of Speech, University of California, Berkeley. Publications include *A Theory of Meter*, Hague, 1966, and *Essays on the Language of Literature*, Boston, 1967.

S.G.S. Sydney Goodsir Smith
Writer. Publications include several books of verse, and *A Short Introduction to Scottish Literature*, Edinburgh, 1951. Editor of *Gavin Douglas, a Selection from his Poetry*, Edinburgh, 1959

S.K.C. Stanley K. Coffman, Jr.
Professor of English, Bowling Green State University. Publications include *Imagism: A Chapter for the History of Modern Poetry*, Oklahoma, 1951, and contributions to *Books Abroad*, *Modern Philology*, and *Publications of the Modern Language Association of America*.

S.S. Stephen Spender
Writer and editor. Publications include several books of verse and of criticism. Co-editor of *Horizon* (1939–41), and of *Encounter* from 1953 till 1965. Co-editor of this *Encyclopedia*.

T.G. Thom Gunn
Writer. Publications include several books of verse, and contributions to the *London Magazine*, *Poetry* (Chicago), the *Spectator*, and the *Yale Review*.

T.J.G. Thomas Jay Garbáty
Associate Professor of English, University of Michigan. Publications include articles on medieval literature in the *Journal of American Folklore*, the *Journal of English and Germanic Philology*, and *Publications of the Modern Language Association of America*.

V.B. Vincent Buckley
Senior Lecturer in English, University of Melbourne. Publications include *The World's Flesh*, (poems), Melbourne, 1954, *Essays in Poetry, mainly Australian*, Melbourne, 1957, and *Poetry and Morality*, London, 1959. Editor of *Australian Poetry, 1958*, Sydney, 1958.

V.deS.P. V. de S. Pinto
Emeritus Professor of English, University of Nottingham. Publications include *The English Renaissance*, London, 1938, *Crisis in English Poetry*, London, 1951, *English Biography in the Seventeenth Century*, London, 1951, *Restoration Carnival*, London, 1954, *The Common Muse* (with A. E. Rodway), London, 1957, *Enthusiast in Wit, Portrait of John Wilmot, Earl of Rochester*, London and Lincoln, Neb., 1962, *William Blake*, London, 1965, *The Restoration Court Poets*, London, 1965; Editor of *The Poems of John Wilmot, Earl of Rochester*, London, 1953, 2nd rev. ed., 1964.

V.S-W. Victoria Sackville-West
(d.1962)
Publications include *Knole and the Sackvilles*, London, 1949, and several novels, biographies, and books of verse.

V.W. Vernon Watkins (d.1967)
Bank clerk. Publications include several books of verse. Editor of *Letters to Vernon Watkins, by Dylan Thomas*, London, 1957.

W.A.A. William A. Armstrong
Professor of English Literature, Westfield College, University of London. Publications include *The Elizabethan Private Theatres: Facts and Problems*, London, 1958, and contributions to *English*, *English Studies*, the *Review of English Studies*, and the *Shakespeare Survey*.

W.H.G. W. H. Gardner
Emeritus Professor of English, University of Natal, South Africa. Publications include *Salamander in Spring, and other poems*, London, 1933, and *Gerard Manley Hopkins: a study of poetic idiosyncrasy in relation to poetic tradition*, 2 vols, Oxford, 1966. Co-editor of *Poems of Gerard Manley Hopkins*, 4th edition, Oxford, 1967.

W.J.O. Walter J. Ong, S.J.
Professor of English, St Louis University, has served also as visiting professor at New York University, the University of California, Indiana University, and the University of Chicago. Publications include *Ramus, Method, and the Decay of Dialogue*, Harvard, 1958, the two collections *The Barbarian Within*, New York, 1962, and *In the Human Grain*, New York,

1967, and his Yale University Terry Lectures, *The Presence of the Word*, Yale, 1967, as well as contributions to the *Kenyon Review*, the *Sewanee Review*, the *Saturday Review*, *Speculum*, *Studies in Philology*, *Studies in Theology*, and the *Yale Review*.

W.L.S. W. Leonard Stevens
Instructor in English, Phillips Exeter Academy, New Hampshire.

W.M.M. W. Moelwyn Merchant
Professor of English, University of Exeter. Publications include *Shakespeare and the Artist*, London, 1959, and various articles. Editor of *Wordsworth*, London and Harvard, 1955.

W.W.R. W. W. Robson
Fellow of Lincoln College, Oxford. Publications include *Critical Essays*, London, 1966, and *The Signs among Us*, London, 1968.

X.J.K. X. J. Kennedy
Associate Professor of English, Tufts University, Massachusetts. Publications include *Nude Descending a Staircase*, (poems), New York, 1961, and poems in the *Cornhill Magazine*, the *New Yorker*, the *Paris Review* and *Poetry*.

Y.B. Yves Bonnefoy
Writer. Publications include *Du Mouvement et de l'Immobilité de Douve*, Paris, 1953, *Hier régnant désert*, Paris, 1958, *L'Improbable*, (essays), Paris, 1959, *Pierre é'crite*, 1964, and various articles and translations of Shakespeare.

Acknowledgments

Great care has been taken to trace all the owners of copyright material used in this book. If any have been inadvertently overlooked or omitted, acknowledgment will gladly be made in any future edition.

We are indebted to the owners of copyright for permission to include the following quotations:

An extract from *Selected Poems of Conrad Aiken,* published by the Oxford University Press, New York and London, in 1961, reprinted by permission of the Oxford University Press, New York.

An extract from 'New Love' by Richard Aldington in *Some Imagist Poets,* published by the Houghton Mifflin Company, Boston, in 1915, reprinted by permission of the Houghton Mifflin Company.

An extract from 'Birthday Poem' in *Collected Shorter Poems by W. H. Auden,* reprinted by permission of Faber & Faber Ltd, London.

An extract from 'The Memorial' in *Poems of Many Years* by Edmund Blunden, published by Collins, Publishers, London, and reprinted by permission of A. D. Peters, London.

An extract from 'The Islands' by Charles Brasch in *The Penguin Book of New Zealand Verse,* reprinted by permission of Charles Brasch.

An extract from 'The Wanderer' in *Poems 1913* by Christopher Brennan, reprinted by permission of the Lothian Publishing Co. Pty Ltd, Melbourne.

An extract from 'Low Barometer' in *Collected Poems of Robert Bridges,* reprinted by permission of the Clarendon Press, Oxford.

An extract from 'Wagner' by Rupert Brooke, reproduced by permission of Sidgwick & Jackson Limited, London, from *The Collected Poems of Rupert Brooke,* and reprinted by permission of McClelland & Stewart Ltd, Canada.

An extract from 'Home Thoughts' in *Stranger to Europe* by Guy Butler, published by A. A. Balkema Ltd, Cape Town, in 1959, reprinted by permission of A. A. Balkema Ltd.

An extract from 'The Sling' in *Collected Poems of Roy Campbell,* Vol. I, reprinted by permission of The Bodley Head Ltd, London.

An extract from *The Flaming Terrapin* by Roy Campbell, reprinted by permission of Jonathan Cape Ltd, London.

'On Some South African Novelists' from *Adamastor* by Roy Campbell, published by Faber & Faber Ltd, London, and reprinted by permission of Curtis Brown Ltd, London.

Extracts from 'Voyages II' and 'The Bridge' in *The Collected Poems of Hart Crane,* copyright © R, 1961 by Liveright Publishing Corp., reprinted by permission of Liveright, Publishers, New York.

Extracts from *The Collected Poems of E. E. Cummings,* published by Harcourt, Brace & World Inc., New York, in 1938, reprinted by permission of Harcourt, Brace & World Inc.

Acknowledgments

An extract from 'Tomb of an Ancestor' in *At Dead Low Water* by Allen Curnow, published by the Caxton Press, Christchurch, New Zealand, in 1949, reprinted by permission of Allen Curnow.

An extract from *The Collected Poems of C. Day Lewis,* published by Jonathan Cape Ltd, London, in 1954, reprinted by permission of Jonathan Cape Ltd.

An extract from *The Last Division* by Anthony Delius, published by Human & Rousseau (Pty) Ltd, Cape Town, in 1959, reprinted by permission of Human & Rousseau.

An extract from 'Seal, Terns, Time' in *Collected Poems 1930–1960* by Richard Eberhart, published by Chatto & Windus Ltd, London, in 1960, reprinted by permission of the Oxford University Press, New York.

Extracts from 'Ash Wednesday', 'Gerontion', 'The Love Song of J. Alfred Prufrock' and 'The Wasteland' in *Collected Poems 1909–1935* by T. S. Eliot, published by Faber & Faber Ltd and reprinted by permission of Faber & Faber Ltd.

An extract from *Selected Essays of T. S. Eliot,* published by Faber & Faber Ltd, London, required by permission of Faber & Faber Ltd.

Extracts from 'The Pasture', 'Birches' and 'After Apple-picking' in *The Complete Poems of Robert Frost*, published by Jonathan Cape Limited, copyright Holt, Rinehart & Winston Inc, and reprinted by permission of Laurence Pollinger Limited.

Extracts from 'A Lost Season', 'Ambiguities' and 'The Ides of Marche' by Roy Fuller, reprinted by permission of André Deutsch Ltd, London.

An extract from 'Sings Harry' in *Sings Harry, and other poems* by Dennis Glover, published by the Caxton Press, Christchurch, New Zealand, in 1951, 2nd edition 1957, re-printed by permission of Dennis Glover.

An extract from 'Vanity' in *Collected Poems 1955* by Robert Graves, published by Doubleday & Co. Inc., New York, reprinted by permission of International Authors N.V.

Extracts from *A Procession of Dead Days* and *The Subalterns* by Thomas Hardy, reprinted by permission of Macmillan Company Ltd, London.

An extract from *The Wandering Islands* by A. D. Hope, published by Edwards & Shaw, Sydney, in 1956, reprinted by permission of Edwards & Shaw.

Extracts from 'Bredon Hill', 'Could Man be Drunk for Ever', 'Eight O'Clock' and 'When First my Way to Fair I took' in *Collected Poems of A. E. Housman,* published by Jonathan Cape Ltd, London, in 1939, reprinted by permission of The Society of Authors, London.

An extract from 'Autumn' by T. E. Hulme in *Speculations,* edited by Herbert Read, reprinted by permission of Routledge & Kegan Paul Ltd, London.

An extract from *Double Axe* by Robinson Jeffers, published by Random House Inc., New York, in 1948, reprinted by permission of Random House Inc.

Extracts from 'Mandalay' in *Barrack Room Ballads,* 'Recessional' in *The Five Nations,* 'Divided Destinies' in *Departmental Ditties,* and 'McAndrews Hymn' in *The Seven Seas,* published by Methuen & Co Ltd, and reprinted by permission of Mrs George Bambridge.

An extract from 'The Open Door' in *Brazilian Sketches,* published by Macmillan & Co Ltd, London, and reprinted by permission of Mrs George Bambridge.

An extract from 'Hymn of the Triumphant Airman' in *Rudyard Kipling's Verse* (Definitive edition), reprinted by permission of

Mrs George Bambridge.

An extract from 'Love on the Farm' in *The Complete Poems of D. H. Lawrence*, published by William Heinemann Ltd, and reprinted by permission of Laurence oPllinger Limited and the Estate of the Late Mrs Frieda Lawrence.

An extract from 'The Eagle that is Forgotten', reprinted by permission of the publisher from *Collected Poems of Vachel Lindsay*, copyright © 1913 by the Macmillan Company, New York.

An extract from 'The Traveling Bear' by Amy Lowell in *Some Imagist Poets*, published by the Houghton Mifflin Company, Boston, in 1915, reprinted by permission of the Houghton Mifflin Company.

An extract from 'Dunbarton' in *Life Studies* by Robert Lowell, reprinted by permission of Farrar, Straus & Cudahy Inc., New York.

An extract from 'Falling Asleep over the Aeneid' in *Poems 1938–1949* by Robert Lowell, published by Faber & Faber Limited and reprinted by permission of Faber & Faber Limited.

An extract from 'O Wha's the Bride', reprinted by permission of Oliver & Boyd Limited, Scotland, from *Collected Poems of Hugh MacDiarmid*, copyright 1962 by Christopher Murray Grieve.

An extract from 'Epistle to be left in the Earth' by Archibald MacLeish, reprinted by permission of the Houghton Mifflin Company, Boston.

Extracts from 'Smooth Gnarles Crape Myrtle' and 'Poetry' in *Collected Poems* by Marianne Moore, reprinted by permission of Faber & Faber Limited, London.

An extract from 'Ecce Homunculus' by R. A. K. Mason in *No New Thing*, published by Unicorn Press, Auckland, New Zealand, 1934, and reprinted by permission of R. A. K. Mason.

Extracts from 'The Myth' and 'One Foot in Eden' by Edwin Muir, reprinted by permission of Faber & Faber Ltd, London.

An extract from 'The Orange Tree' in *The Collected Poems of John Shaw Neilson*, published by the Lothian Publishing Co. Pty Ltd, Melbourne, in 1934, reprinted by permission of the Lothian Publishing Company.

An extract from 'Strange Meeting' in *Poems* by Wilfred Owen, reprinted by permission of Chatto & Windus Ltd, London.

Extracts from 'The Devil Dancers' and 'The Scorpion' in *Collected Poems of William Plomer*, published by Jonathan Cape Ltd, London, in 1960, reprinted by permission of Jonathan Cape Ltd.

Extracts from 'Canto 20', 'Canto 93', 'Canto 98', 'Hugh Selwyn Mauberley' and 'Lustra' by Ezra Pound, reprinted by permission of Arthur V. Moore.

An extract from 'The Cachalot' in *The Collected Poems of E. J. Pratt*, 2nd edition, published by Macmillan & Co. Ltd, London, in 1926, reprinted by permission of Macmillan & Co. Ltd.

Extracts from 'Blue Girls', 'Captain Carpenter', 'Dead Boy' and 'Painted Head' by John Crowe Ransom, reprinted by permission of Alfred A. Knopf Inc., New York.

An extract from *Collected Poems of Edwin Arlington Robinson*, reprinted by permission of the Macmillan Company, New York.

Extracts from 'Miniver Cheevy' by Edwin Arlington Robinson, reprinted by permission of Charles Scribner's Sons, New York.

An extract from a poem by Theodore

Acknowledgments

Extracts from 'The Return' and 'Praise to the End' by Theodore Roethke reprinted by permission of A. M. Heath and Co. Ltd.

Extracts from 'Louse Hunting' and 'The Dead Man's Dump' in *Collected Poems* by Isaac Rosenberg, published by Chatto & Windus Ltd, and reprinted by permission of Chatto & Windus Ltd.

An extract from 'Saturday Sundae' in *Overtures* by F. R. Scott, published by Ryerson Press, Toronto, reprinted by permission of F. R. Scott.

Extracts from 'Madam Mouse Trots' and 'Still Falls the Rain' by Edith Sitwell, reprinted by permission of David Higham Associates Ltd, London.

An extract from 'Pastoral' by Sacheverell Sitwell, reprinted by permission of David Higham Associates Ltd, London.

Extracts from 'Final Soliloquy of the Interior Paramour', 'Notes toward a Supreme Fiction', 'The Glass of Water', 'The Idea of Order at Key West' and 'The Man on the Dump' by Wallace Stevens, reprinted by permission of Alfred A. Knopf Inc., New York.

An extract from *The Wolves, poems* (1960) by Allen Tate, reprinted by permission of Eyre & Spottiswoode Ltd, London.

'Do not go gentle into that good night' and extracts from *Collected Poems* by Dylan Thomas, and 'Twenty-four years' in *The Map of Love* by Dylan Thomas, reprinted by permission of J. M. Dent & Sons Ltd.

Extract from 'Asphodel, That Greeny Flower', William Carlos Williams *Pictures from Brueghel and other poems* copyright © 1959 by William Carlos Williams, reprinted by permission of New Directions Publishing Corporation, New York, and MacGibbon & Kee, London.

Extracts from 'Adlestrop', 'But These Things Also', 'March the Third', 'Old Man', 'Tall Nettles' and 'The Unknown Bird' in *Collected Poems of Edward Thomas,* published by Faber & Faber Ltd, London, in 1936, reprinted by permission of Mrs Helen Thomas.

An extract from 'Seeing is believing' in *A farewell to Van Gogh* by Charles Tomlinson, published by the Oxford University Press, reprinted by permission of Oxford University Press, London.

An extract from 'Friday's Child' by Wilfred Watson, reprinted by permission of Faber & Faber Ltd, London.

Extracts from 'I' and 'In the Elegy Season' by Richard Wilbur, reprinted by permission of Faber & Faber, Ltd, London.

An extract from 'Yachts' in *The Collected Earlier Poems of William Carlos Williams,* copyright © 1938, 1951, by William Carlos Williams, reprinted by permission of New Directions, Publishers, New York.

An extract from *The Collected Later Poems of William Carlos Williams,* copyright © 1944, 1948, 1950, by William Carlos Williams, reprinted by permission of New Directions, Publishers, New York.

An extract from 'Asphodel, that Greeny Flower' by William Carlos Williams, published in 1955 by Random House Inc. in *Journey to Love* by William Carlos Williams and in 1962 by New Directions in *Pictures from Brueghel* by William Carlos Williams, reprinted by permission of Random House Inc., New York.

Extracts from *Collected Poems of Yvor Winters* published by Routledge & Kegan Paul Limited and reprinted by permission of Routledge & Kegan Paul Limited.

An extract from 'Woman to Man' in *Woman to Man* by Judith Wright, published by Angus & Robertson Ltd, Sydney, in 1949, reprinted by permission of Angus & Robertson Ltd.

Extracts from 'Under Ben Bulben', 'The Secret Rose', 'September 1913', 'The Wild Swans at Coole', 'Nineteen Hundred and Nineteen', 'Two Songs from a Play', 'Among School Children', 'Lapis Lazuli', 'Supernatural Songs,' 'There' and 'A Model for the Laureate' in *Collected Poems of W. B. Yeats*, published by Macmillan & Co Ltd, and reprinted by permission of Mrs W. B. Yeats (Bertha Georgie Yeats).

INDEX OF POETS QUOTED

Aiken, Conrad, 1
Aldington, Richard, 140
Arnold, Matthew, 12, 110-11, 232
Auden, W. H., 14

Beddoes, Thomas Lovell, 20
Blake, William, 24, 220, 228, 233
Blunden, Edmund, 25
Brasch, Charles, 198
Brennan, Christopher, 16
Bridges, Robert, 26, 241
Brontë, Emily, 27
Brooke, Rupert, 27
Browning, Elizabeth Barrett, 28, 235
Browning, Robert, 29-30, 221, 231
Bryant, William Cullen, 31
Burns, Robert, 31-2
Butler, Guy, 288
Butler, Samuel, 33, 244
Byron, Lord, 34, 222, 244, 247, 264

Campbell, Roy, 36, 244, 286-7
Campion, Thomas, 37, 246
Carew, Thomas, 41-2
Carroll, Lewis, 42
Chapman, George, 43, 231, 313
Chatterton, Thomas, 44
Chaucer, Geoffrey, 47, 48, 49, 137, 227
Churchill, Charles, 44
Clare, John, 50, 51
Cleveland, John, 54
Clough, Arthur Hugh, 223
Coleridge, Samuel Taylor, 56, 228
Collins, William, 57
Cotton, Charles, 236
Cowley, Abraham, 58
Cowper, William, 59
Crabbe, George, 60
Crane, Hart, 61
Crashaw, Richard, 62, 107
Cummings, E. E., 75, 76
Curnow, Allen, 199

Daniel, Samuel, 76, 216, 234, 244
D'Avenant, Sir William, 77
Davies, Sir John, 77, 78, 236
Day Lewis, Cecil, 78-9
Diaper, William, 80
Dickinson, Emily, 5, 80-1, 234, 255
Donne, John, 84-5, 219, 263-4
Douglas, Gavin, 86
Dowson, Ernest, 86, 224
Drayton, Michael, 87, 216
Dryden, John, 66, 88, 89, 90, 215, 221, 231, 264, 311
Dunbar, William, 91
Durrell, Lawrence, 91

Eberhart, Richard, 92
Eliot, T. S., 93, 94, 95, 96, 226
Emerson, Ralph Waldo, 5, 97
Etherege, Sir George, 225

Fairburn, A. R. D., 198
FitzGerald, Edward, 100, 110, 236
Freneau, Philip, 2
Frost, Robert, 114, 115
Fuller, Roy, 117
Fanshawe, Sir Richard, 237

Gascoigne, George, 118, 216
Gilbert, W. S., 225
Glover, Dennis, 198, 229
Goldsmith, Oliver, 119
Goldsmith, Oliver (Canadian), 39
Gower, John, 120
Graves, Robert, 121
Gray, Thomas, 108, 121-2
Greene, Robert, 236
Greville, Sir Fulke, Lord Brooke, 123

Hales, Friar Thomas, 104
Hardy, Thomas, 124, 241
'H.D.', 140

Henryson, Robert, 125, 126
Herbert, George, 127, 254
Herrick, Robert, 127, 128, 226
Hood, Thomas, 221, 226
Hope, A. D., 18
Hopkins, Gerard Manley, 130, 131, 132, 232
Housman, A. E., 132, 133
Hulme, T. E., 141

Jeffers, Robinson, 145
Johnson, Samuel, 146, 228
Jonson, Ben, 148, 220, 227, 243, 246

Keats, John, 136, 151-2, 216, 240
King, Henry, 153-4, 227
Kipling, Rudyard, 154, 155, 247, 286

Landor, Walter Savage, 155-6, 219, 244
Langland, William, 157-8, 224, 263
Lawrence, D. H., 159
Lear, Edward, 160
Lindsay, Vachel, 161
Lodge, Thomas, 227
Longfellow, Henry Wadsworth, 162, 222
Lovelace, Richard, 220
Lowell, Amy, 140
Lowell, Robert, 163-4
Lydgate, John, 164

MacDiarmid, Hugh, 165
MacLeish, Archibald, 166
Marlowe, Christopher, 168, 230
Marvell, Andrew, 107, 169-70, 171, 219
Mason, R. A. K., 198
Meredith, George, 172, 223
Milton, John, 138, 179, 180, 181, 182, 183, 217, 223, 228, 229, 232, 240
Moore, Marianne, 138-9, 183
Muir, Edwin, 184

Index of Poets Quoted

Nashe, Thomas, 191, 222
Neilson, John Shaw, 16

Owen, Wilfred, 200, 226

Patmore, Coventry, 201–2
Peele, George, 202
Pickthall, Marjorie, 40
Plomer, William, 287
Poe, Edgar Allan, 204
Pope, Alexander, 206, 207, 208, 217, 228–9, 244, 264, 312, 313
Pound, Ezra, 138, 140, 141, 211, 212, 213
Pratt, E. J., 40
Pringle, Thomas, 286
Prior, Matthew, 215, 221

Quarles, Francis, 248

Raine, Kathleen, 248
Ralegh, Sir Walter, 249, 250–2
Ramsay, Allan, 220
Ransom, John Crowe, 251
Read, Sir Herbert, 252
Reeves, William Pember, 197
Ridler, Anne, 253
Robinson, Edwin Arlington, 4–5, 257
Rochester, John Wilmot, Earl of, 258–9
Roethke, Theodore, 259

Rosenberg, Isaac, 260
Rossetti, Christina, 225, 260
Rosetti, Dante Gabriel, 238, 261

Sackville, Sir Thomas, Lord Buckhurst and Earl of Dorset, 230, 262
Sangster, Charles, 40
Sassoon, Siegfried, 263
Scott, F. R., 40
Scott, Sir Walter, 221
Shakespeare, William, 69–70, 136, 224, 230, 237, 270–1, 272, 273
Shelley, Percy Bysshe, 220, 235, 247, 274, 275–6
Sidney, Sir Philip, 277, 278
Sitwell, Dame Edith, 279
Sitwell, Sacheverell, 279–80
Skelton, John, 238, 263, 280–1
Slater, F. C., 286
Smart, Christopher, 220, 225, 282
Smithyman, Kendrick, 199
Southey, Robert, 223, 288
Spenser, Edmund, 174, 175, 237, 239, 290, 291
Stevens, Wallace, 235, 293–4, 295
Suckling, Sir John, 41, 237, 295
Surrey, Henry Howard, Earl of, 240, 296
Swift, Jonathan, 223, 297
Swinburne, Algernon Charles, 219, 223, 231, 298

Tate, Allen, 303
Taylor, Edward, 303–4
Tennyson, Alfred, Lord, 71, 72, 135, 137–8, 225, 231, 232, 236, 244, 247, 304–5
Thomas, Dylan, 241, 306
Thomas, Edward, 308
Thompson, Francis, 220
Thomson, James (1700–48), 220, 230, 309
Tomlinson, Charles, 139
Traherne, Thomas, 310–11

Vaughan, Henry, 316

Waller, Edmund, 317–18
Watson, Wilfred, 41
Watts, Isaac, 234, 238, 254
Webster, John, 319–20
Wesley, Charles, 253
Whitman, Walt, 5, 233, 320
Whittier, John Greenleaf, 4
Wilbur, Richard, 322–3
Wilde, Oscar, 323
Williams, William Carlos, 139, 324
Winters, Yvor, 324–5
Wordsworth, William, 71, 72, 136, 220, 230, 326, 327
Wotton, Sir Henry, 244
Wright, Judith, 17
Wyatt, Sir Thomas, 105, 226, 227, 239, 329–30

Yeats, W. B., 227, 331, 332–3

GENERAL INDEX

Articles in the *Encyclopedia* are indicated by page numbers in **bold type**. Page numbers are also given for other references in the text and for the lists of books for further reading. Verse quotations are indexed separately on pages 381-2.

Adali-Mortty, G., 98
Adams, Léonie, **1**, *books* 334
Adams, Perseus, 288, *books* 361
African Poetry, *see* English Poetry in Africa *and* South African Poetry in English
Aiken, Conrad, **1**, *books* 334
Akenside, Mark, **1**, *books* 334
Alabaster, William, **1**, *books* 334
alcaics, 223
Aldington, Richard, 139
alexandrine, 231
alliteration, 224-5
Allonby, Margaret, 288
American Poetry, **1-7**, *books* 334, *see also* names of poets
amphibrach, 217
amphimacer, 217
anapaest, 217
anapaestic measure, 221-2
Anglo-Saxon Poetry, **8-12**, *books* 334-5
anti-bacchius, 217
Aristotle, 63, 192
Armattoe, Raphael, 98
Arnold, Matthew, **12-13**, 55, 63, 70-72, 88, 102, 110-11, 152, 233, 243, 252, 313, *books* 335
Ashbery, John, 7
assonance, 226
Auden, W. H., 7, 8, **13-15**, 97, 112, 133, 166, 167, 187, 242, 281, *books* 335-6
Augustan Age, 54, 108-9, 208
Aurobindo, Sri, 142
Australian Poetry, **15-18**, *books* 336
Awoonor-Williams, George, 98

Babalola, Adebayo, 98
bacchic, 217
bacchic measure, 222

bacchius, *see* bacchic
ballad, 242-3, *see also* Popular Peotry
ballade, 238-9
Barker, George, **18-19**, 113, *books* 336
Barnes, William, **19**, 110, *books* 336
Barnfield, Richard, **19**
Baxter, James K., 199
Baylebridge, William, 16
Beaumont, Francis, and Fletcher, John, **19-20**, 74, *books* 336
Beddoes, Thomas Lovell, **20**, *books* 336
Bell, Currer, Ellis and Acton, *see* Brontë, Emily
Belloc, Hilaire, **20-1**, 111, *books* 336
Benét, Stephen Vincent, **21**, *books* 336
Beowulf, *see* Anglo-Saxon Poetry
Berrigan, Ted, 7
Berryman, John, **21**, 259
Betjeman, Sir John, **21**, 209, 211, *books* 336-7
Binyon, Lawrence, **21**, *books* 337
Bishop, Elizabeth, **21**, *books* 337
Bishop, John Peale, **21**
Blackburn, Paul, 7
Blake, William, **21-4**, 109, 188, 213, 220, 228, 233, 254, 284, 299, 311, *books* 337
blank verse, 229-30
Blunden, Edmund, **24-5**, 201, *books* 337
Bogan, Louise, **25**
'bohemian' behaviour, 284
Bottrall, Ronald, **25**, *books* 337
Bradstreet, Anne, 2, 3, 4, **25**, *books* 337
Brasch, Charles, 198
Brennan, Christopher, 16

Breton, Nicholas, **25**
Brettell, N. H., 288
Brew, Kwesi, 98, *books* 345
Bridges, Robert, **25-6**, 129, 215, 232, 242, *books* 337
Brontë, Emily, **26-7**, *books* 337
Brooke, Rupert, **27**, 113, *books* 337
Brooks, Cleanth, 116, 166, 192
Brooks, Van Wyck, 3
Browne, William, **27**
Browning, Elizabeth Barrett, **27-8**, *books* 337
Browning, Robert, **28-30**, 102, 110, 114, 172, 213, 221, 231, 235, 236, 312, *books* 337-8
Bryant, William Cullen, 2, 4, **30-1**, *books* 338
burden, *see* refrain
Burke, Kenneth, 192
Burns, Robert, **31-2**, 109, *books* 338
Burns metre, 241
Butler, Guy, 287, *books* 361
Butler, Samuel, **32-3**, 244, *books* 338
Bynner, Witter, **33**
Byron, Lord, 12, **33-5**, 50, 54, 60, 109-10, 133, 183, 189, 222, 225, 243, 258, 259, 264, *books* 338

Cædmon, 8
caesura, 217
Cameron, Norman, **35**, *books* 338
Campbell, Roy, **35-6**, 38, 234, 244, 286-7, *books* 338
Campion, Thomas, **36-8**, 76, 102, 185, 246, *books* 338
Canadian Poetry, **38-41**, *books* 338
Cannell, Skipwith, 140

Canute, King, 177
Carew, Thomas, **41-2**, 310, books 338
carols, *see* Hymns, Songs and Carols
Carroll, Lewis, **42**, books 338
catalectic line, *see* catalexis
catalexis, 218, 220
Causley, Charles, **42**, 242, books 339
Cavalier Poets, *see* Carew, Herrick, Lovelace *and* Suckling
Channing, W. E., 2
Chapman, George, **42-3**, 106-7, 167, 231, 313, books 339
Chatterton, Thomas, **43-4**, books 339
Chattopadhyaya, Harindranath, 142
Chaucer, Geoffrey, **44-9**, 65, 104-5, 119, 125, 137, 164, 227, 229, 237, 245, 265, books 339
Cherbury, Lord, *see* Herbert, Edward
Chesterton, G. K., **50**, 111, books 339
choriambics, 223
chorus, *see* refrain
Churchill, Charles, **50**, 224, books 339
Cilliers, Charl J. F., 288
Clare, John, 25, **50-1**, books 339
Clark, J. P., 98
Classic and Romantic, **51-4**, 108-10, 252, books 339-40
Cleveland, John, **54**, books 340
Clough, Arthur Hugh, **54-5**, 223, 314, books 340
Clouts, Sydney, 288, books 361
Coleridge, Samuel Taylor, 8, 53, **55-7**, 67-70, 88, 109, 192, 215, 227-8, 299, 301, 325, books 340
Collins, William, **57-8**, 109, 243, books 340
Comte, Auguste, 267
Corbet, Richard, **58**
Cotton, Charles, **58**, 227, books 340
counterpoint, 232
Cournos, John, 140
Cowley, Abraham, **58**, 107-8, books 340
Cowper, William, **58-60**, 109, 134, 189, 313, books 340
Crabbe, George, **60-1**, books 340

Crane, Hart, 3, 4, 5, 6, **61**, 116, 142, books 340
Crane, Stephen, **61-2**, books 341
Crashaw, Richard, 42, **62-3**, 101, 107, 227, books 341
Creeley, Robert, 7
Cripps, A. S., 286
Criticism and Poetry, **63-75**, books 341
Croce, Benedetto, 191, 266
Cummings, E. E., **75-6**, books 341-2
Curnow, Allen, 199
Currey, R. N., 287
Cynewulf, 8, 10

dactyl, 217
dactylic measure, 220-21
Daniel, Samuel, **76-7**, 106, 216, 240, 244, books 342
Darley, George, **77**, books 342
Datta, Madhusudan, 142, 143
D'Avenant, Sir William, **77**, books 342
Davidson, Donald, 116-17
Davidson, John, **77**, 243, books 342
Davies, Sir John, **77-8**, 236, books 342
Davies, W. H., **78**, books 342
Day Lewis, Cecil, **78-9**, books 342
decasyllable, 228-9
Dekker, Thomas, **79**, 318
De la Mare, Walter, **79**, 187, books 342
Denham, Sir John, 58, **79**, books 342
Diaper, William, **79-80**, 243, books 342
Dickinson, Emily, 35, **80-1**, 171, 234, 255, books 342
dimeter, *see* duple metres
dissonance, 226
Donne, John, 10, 41, **81-6**, 87, 127, 130, 133, 135, 153, 219, 240, 243, 263-4, 316, 329, books 342-3
Doolittle, Hilda, *see* 'H.D.'
Doughty, C. M., **86**, books 343
Douglas, Gavin, 86, 90, 313, books 343
Dowson, Ernest, **86-7**, 111, books 343

Drayton, Michael, **87**, 216, 231, 240, 245, books 343
Drummond, William, Earl of Hawthornden, 64, **87**, books 343
Dryden, John, 49, 50, 58, 65-6, 67, **87-90**, 102, 152, 186, 218, 231, 236, 243, 264, 313, 317, books 343
Dunbar, William, **90-1**, 104, books 343-4
duple metres, 217, 219-20
Durrell, Lawrence, **91**
Dutt, Toru, 142, 143
Dyer, Sir Edward, **92**, 228, 276
Dyer, John, **92**, books 344

Eberhart, Richard, 8, **92-3**, books 344
Echeruo, Michael, 98
eclogue, 243
elegy, 243
Eliot, T. S., 3, 4, 8, 13, 39, 63, 72-4, **93-6**, 114, 116, 120, 130, 137, 138, 141, 168, 171, 184, 190, 191-2, 205, 214, 225, 236, 240, 250, 255, 291, 292, 302, 313, books 344
elision, 216
Emerson, Ralph Waldo, 2, 3, 4, 5, **96-7**, 293, 299, 309, 320, books 344
Empson, William, 73, 95, **97**, 192, 236, 241, books 344
end-stopped line, 230
English Poetry in Africa, **97-9**, books 344-5, *see also* South African Poetry in English
enjambement, 230
epic, 245
epigram, 243-4
epistle, 244-5
epitaph, 243
'Everyman' and the Miracle Plays, **99**, books 345
eye-rhyme, 225-6

Fair, C. A., 288
Fairbridge, Kingsley, 288
Fairburn, A. R. D., 286
Fairfax, Edward, **100**, 312
falling metre, *see* trochaic metre
Fearing, Kenneth, **100**, books 345
feminine ending, 231
Fergusson, Robert, 31

Field, Barron, 15
Finch, Anne, *see* Winchilsea, Anne Finch, Countess of
fingering, 232
FitzGerald, Edward, 60, **100**, 236, 312, *books* 345
Fitzgerald, R. D., 17
Flecker, James Elroy, **101**, *books* 345
Fletcher, Giles, **101**, *books* 345
Fletcher, John, *see* Beaumont Francis, and Fletcher, John
Fletcher, John Gould, 140
Fletcher, Phineas, **101**, *books* 345
Flint, F. S., 139
Ford, Ford Madox, 140
Ford, John, **101**, 318, *books* 345
Foreign Influences on English Poetry, **101-13**
fourteener, 231
free verse, 233
Freneau, Philip, 2, 4
Frost, Robert, 5, 7, 38, **113-16**, 307, *books* 345
Fugitive Group, **116-17**, 302, *books* 345
Fuller, Roy, **117**, *books* 346

galliambics, 223
Gardner, Isabella, **118**
Gascoigne, George, **118**, 216, 232, *books* 346
Gascoyne, David, 113, **118**, *books* 346
Gay, John, **118**, 186, 243, *books* 346
Ghose, Aurobindo, *see* Aurobindo, Sri
Ghose, Manmohan, 142, 143
Gilbert, W. S., **118**, 186, 190, 225
Ginsberg, Allen, 3, 4, 7
Glover, Dennis, 198, 229-30
Golding, Arthur, **118-19**, 313, *books* 346
Goldsmith, Oliver, **119**, *books* 346
Goldsmith, Oliver (Canadian), 39
Gordon, Adam Lindsay, 15-16
Gouldsbury, Cullen, 286
Gower, John, **119-20**, *books* 346
Graves, Robert, 25, 35, 65, 116, 119, **120-1**, 242, 281, *books* 346
Gray, Thomas, 13, 67, 90, 108, **121-2**, 200, 236, *books* 346

Greene, Robert, **122**, 202, 236
Greville, Sir Fulke, Lord Brooke, 106, **122-3**, *books* 346
Grieve, Christopher Murray, *see* MacDiarmid
Guest, Edgar, **123**, 209, 210
Gunn, Thom, 113, **123**, *books* 346-7

Hales, Friar Thomas, 104
Hall, Donald, **123**
Hall, Joseph, 263
Hamilton, Sir George Rostrevor, **123**, 244, *books* 347
Hardy, Thomas, **123-4**, 241, *books* 347
Harpur, Charles, 15, 16
Harvey, Gabriel, 276
Hawker, Robert Stephen, **124-5**, *books* 347
Hawthornden, Earl of, *see* Drummond, William
Hayford, Gladys Casely, 98
Hazlitt, William, 70
'H.D.', 5, 139, 141, 313
Hecht, Antony, **125**
Hemans, Mrs Felicia, 210, 211
hendecasyllable, 231
Henley, W. E., **125**
Henryson, Robert, 90, **125-6**, *books* 347
Herbert, Edward, Lord Cherbury, **126**, 236, *books* 347
Herbert, George, **126-7**, 130, 133, 242, 316, *books* 347
heroic couplet, 234
Herrick, Robert, 102, **127-9**, 186, 226, *books* 347
hexameter, 222
Higo, Aig, 198
Hill, Geoffrey, **129**
Hillyer, Robert, **129**
Hodgson, Ralph, **129**, 227, *books* 347
Hood, Thomas, 8, 119, **129**, 221, *books* 347
Hope, A. D., 18
Hopkins, Gerard Manley, 7, 8, 26, 56, **129-32**, 201, 215, 232, 255, *books* 347-8
Horace, 64
Housman, A. E., 63, **132-3**, 186, 234, *books* 348
Howard, Henry, *see* Surrey, Henry Howard, Earl of
Hughes, Ted, 113, **133**
Hulme, T. E., 141-2, 192

Hunt, Leigh, **133**, *books* 348
Hymns, Songs and Carols, **133-4**, *books* 348

iamb, 217
iambic metre, 219-20
iambic pentameter, *see* blank verse
Imagery, **134-9**
Imagism, 5, 138, **139-42**, 323, *books* 348
Indian Poetry in English, **142-3**, *books* 348
internal rhyme, 225
Isherwood, Christopher, 13

James I of Scotland, **144**, *books* 348
Jarrell, Randall, **144**, 183, 322, *books* 348-9
Jeffers, Robinson, **144-5**, *books* 349
Johnson, Lionel, 111, **145**, *books* 349
Johnson, Louis, 199
Johnson, Samuel, 50, 57, 58, 60, 65-7, 88, **145-6**, 200, 228, 254, 272, 317, 318, *books* 349
Jones, David, **146-7**, *books* 349
Jones, Evan, 18
Jones, Leroi, 7
Jonson, Ben, 27, 41, 64, 73-4, 79, 82, 87, 100, 128, **147-8**, 153, 220, 243, 312, *books* 349
Joyce, James, 140
jubilatio, *see* Music and Poetry

Kavanagh, Patrick, **149**, *books* 349
Keats, John, 102, 109, 133, 136, **150-3**, 188, 200, 216, 237, 240, 253, *books* 350
Kendall, Henry, 15, 16
King, Henry, **153-4**, 227, 243, *books* 350
Kipling, Rudyard, **154-5**, 239-40, 286, *books* 350
Koch, Kenneth, 7
Kunitz, Stanley, 166, **155**
Kyd, Thomas, **155**, 270

Lal, P., 143
Landor, Walter Savage, 88, **155-6**, 219, 244, 274, 297, *books* 350

Langland, William, 104,
156-8, 213–14, 224, 263,
books 350
Lanier, Sidney, **158**, 218,
books 351
Larkin, Philip, 113, **158-9**,
books 351
Lawrence, D. H., 73, 140,
159-60, 233, 259, *books*
351
Lear, Edward, **160-61**, *books*
351
Leavis, F. R., 73, 192
leonine rhyme, *see* internal
rhyme
Lerner, Laurence, 287
Lewis, Wyndham, **161**, 214
limerick, *see* Lear
Lindsay, Norman, 17
Lindsay, Vachel, **161**, 238,
books 351
line measurement, 226
Livingstone, Douglas, 288,
books 361
Lodge, Thomas, **161-2**, 227,
books 351
Lomax, Alan and John, 4,
209
Longfellow, Henry
Wadsworth, **162**, 210,
222–3, *books* 351
Lovelace, Richard, **162**,
220, *books* 351
Lowell, Amy, 5, 139–40,
162, *books* 351
Lowell, James Russell, 3, 4,
162
Lowell, Robert, 3, 113, 155,
162-4, *books* 351
Lydgate, John, 48, **164**,
books 351
Lyly, John, 161, **164**, 271
lyrical poetry, 242
Lytle, Andrew, 116

McAuley, James, 17
McClelland, D. C., 268
McClure, Michael, 7
McCrae, Hugh, 16
MacDiarmid, Hugh, **165-6**,
books 351–2
McGinley, Phyllis, **166**
MacLeish, Archibald, 4, 6,
166, 236, *books* 352
Macnab, Roy, 288
MacNeice, Louis, 13, **166-7**,
236, *books* 352
Macpherson, James, *see*
Ossian
Madge, Charles, 287
Makars, *see* Henryson
Manifold, John, 17–18

Marlowe, Christopher, 87,
167-8, 230, 259, 313,
books 352
Marquis, Don, **168**, *books* 352
Marsh, Edward, 27
Marston, John, **168**, 263
Marvell, Andrew, 13, 94,
107, **169-71**, 219, 243,
books 352
Masefield, John, **171**, 245.
books 352
Mason, Madeline, 240
Mason, R. A. K., 197
Masters, Edgar Lee, 5, **171**
Matthiessen, F. O., 3–4, 6
Melville, Herman, 2, **171**,
books 352–3
Meredith, George, 223, 240,
171-2, *books* 353
Merwin, W. S., **172**, *books*
353
Metaphor, 172–6
Metaphysical Poets, 97, 254,
see also Carew, Cowley,
Crashaw, Donne, Herbert
(George), Marvell, Religion
and Poetry *and* Vauchan
metre, 218
metrics, *see* Prosody, Forms
of Verse, and Some
Usages *and* New
Directions in Metrics
Meynell, Alice, **176**, *books*
353
Middle English Lyric, 103,
177-8, *books* 353
Middleton, Thomas, **178**,
books 353
Millay, Edna St Vincent, **178**
Miller, Ruth, 288, *books* 361
Milton, John, 65, 101, 108,
109, 122, 138, 143,
178-83, 184, 186, 189,
223, 229, 232, 240, 243,
254, *books* 353
Miracle plays, *see* 'Everyman'
and the Miracle Plays
molossus, 217
Moore, Marianne, 5, 6,
138–9, 142, **183**, *books* 353
Moore, Merrill, 116
Moore, Thomas, 40, **183**
Moore, Thomas Sturge,
183, *books* 353
Moraes, Dom, 143
Moralities, *see* 'Everyman'
and the Miracle Plays
Morris, William, 111, **184**,
226, 236, *books* 353
Muir, Edwin, 166, **184**,
books 354
Music and Poetry, **184-7**,
books 354

Mystery plays, *see*
'Everyman' and the
Miracle Plays
Myth and Poetry, 187–90,
books 354

Naidu, Sarojini, 142
narrative poetry, 245
Nash, Ogden, **190**, *books*
354
Nashe, Thomas, 147, **190-1**,
202, *books* 354
Naudé, Adèle, *books* 361
Ndu, Pol N., 98
Neilson, John Shaw, 16
Nemerov, Howard, **191**,
books 354–5
New Criticism, **191-2**,
books 355
New Directions in Metrics,
192-6
New Zealand Poetry,
197-9, *books* 355

octave, 236
octosyllable, 227–8
ode, 246
O'Dowd, Bernard, 16
Okara, Gabriel, 98
Okigbo, Christopher, 98, 99
Oldham, John, 264
Olson, Charles, 7
Osadebay, Dennis, 98
Ossian, 109, **200**, *books* 355
ottava rima, 237
Owen, Wilfred, 25, 198,
200-1, 226, *books* 355

paeon, 232
Parker, Dorothy, **201**, *books*
355
Parnell, Thomas, **201**, *books*
355–6
Pater, Elias, 288
Patmore, Coventry, **201-2**,
309, *books* 356
p'Bitek, Okot, 98, *books*
344–5
Peele, George, 37, **202**,
books 356
Peters, Lenrie, 98, *books*
344
Pickthall, Marjorie, 40
Piers Plowman, see
Langland
pindaric ode, 246
Pitter, Ruth, **202**
Plomer, William, **202-3**,
286–7, *books* 356

Poe, Edgar Allan, 2, 3, 79, **203-4**, 217, 299–300, *books* 356

Poetry and Publishing:
—Britain, **204-5**
—United States, **205**

Pope, Alexander, 32, 54, 58, 67, 108, 145, 186, **205-9**, 217, 228–9, 231, 243, 244, 245, 264, 311–12, 313, 317, 318, 324, *books* 356

Popular Poetry, **209-11**

poulter's measure, 234

Pound, Ezra, 3, 4, 5, 6, 7, 112, 119, 120, 139–41, 161, 162, 192, 205, **211-14**, 233, 240, 308, 312, 314, 317, 323, 331, *books* 356-7

Praed, Winthrop, **214**, *books* 357

Pratt, E. J., 38, 40

Pre-Raphaelites, 111, *see also* Patmore, Rossetti (Christina) *and* Rossetti (D. G.)

Prince, F. T., 287

Pringle, Thomas, 285–6

Prior, Matthew, **215**, 221, *books* 357

Prosody, Forms of Verse, and Some Usages, **215-47**, *books* 357

publishing, of poetry, *see* Poetry and Publishing

Purcell, Edward, *see* FitzGerald, Edward

Putnam, Phelps, **247**

pyrrhic, 217

Quarles, Francis, **248**, *books* 357

quatrain, 236

quintet, 236

Quintilian, 53, 64

Raine, Kathleen, **248**, *books* 357

Ralegh, Sir Walter, 106, 167, **248-50**, 289, *books* 357

Ramsay, Allan, 242, **250**, *books* 357

Ransom, John Crowe, 5–6, 114, 116–17, 171, 191–2, **250-2**

Read, Sir Herbert, **252**, *books* 357

Redgrove, Peter, 113, **252**

Reed, Henry, **252**, *books* 357

Reeves, William Pember, 197

refrain, 226

Religion and Poetry, **252-5**, *books* 357-8

Rexroth, Kenneth, **255**

rhyme, 225

rhyme royal, 237

Richards, I. A., 73, 192, 255

Riding, Laura, 116, 120, **255-6**, *books* 358

rising metre, *see* iambic metre

Robinson, Edwin Arlington, 2, 4–5, 96, **256-7**, 324, *books* 358

Robinson, Michael Massey, 15

Rochester, John Wilmot, Earl of, **257-9**, 264, *books* 358

Roethke, Theodore, **259**, *books* 358

Romantic Movement, 34, 51–4, 55, 77, 109–10, 111

rondeau, 239

rondel, 239

Rosenberg, Isaac, **259-60**, *books* 358

Rossetti, Christina, 240, **260-1**, *books* 358

Rossetti, Dante Gabriel, 100, 111, 225, 238–9, **261**, 314, *books* 358-9

Rowley, Thomas, *see* Chatterton, Thomas

Roy, Dilip Kumar, 142

Sackville, Sir Thomas, Lord Buckhurst and Earl of Dorset, 230, 237, **262**, *books* 359

Sandburg, Carl, 4, **262-3**, *books* 359

Sangster, Charles, 40

Santayana, George, 3

sapphics, 238

Sassoon, Siegfried, 200, **263**, *books* 359

Satire, **263-4**, *books* 359

Schwartz, Delmore, 255, **264**

Science and Poetry, **264-8**, *books* 359

Scott, F. R., 40

Scott, Sir Walter, 221, **268**, *books* 359

Scottish Chaucerians, *see* Dunbar *and* Henryson

septet, 237

Service, Robert, **268**

sestina, 239–40

Shakespeare, William, 36, 66, 68–70, 109, 118, 134, 136, 148, 151, 155, 162, 168, 186, 189, 195, 208, 224, 230, 237, 240, 254, **269-73**, *books* 359-60

Shapiro, Karl, **273**, *books* 360

Shelley, Percy Bysshe, 68, 109, 133, 135–6, 188, 220, 235, 236, 237, 243, 247, 254, **273-6**, 299, 324, *books* 360

Shirley, James, **276**, *books* 360

Sidney, Sir Philip, 64, 92, 106, 240, 248, **276-8**, *books* 360-1

Silkin, Jon, **278**

Simpson, Louis, **278**

Sinclair, Keith, 199

Sir Gawayne and the Grene Knight, 104, 158, 245

Sitwell, Dame Edith, 68, 217, **278-9**, *books* 361

Sitwell, Sir Osbert, 278

Sitwell, Sacheverell, 278, **279-80**, *books* 361

sixaine, 236–7

Skelton, John, 105, 226, 237–8, 242, 263, **280-1**, *books* 361

Skelton, Robin, **282**

Skeltonic, 280

Slater, F. C., 286

Slessor, Kenneth, 17

Smart, Christopher, 220, 227, **282**, *books* 361

Smithyman, Kendrick, 199

Snodgrass, William Dewitt, **282-3**

Society and the Poet, **283-5**

song, 245–6, *see also* Hymns, Songs and Carols

sonnet, 240

sonetto caudato, *see* tailed sonnet

South African Poetry in English, **285-8**, *books* 361

Southey, Robert, 88, 223, 274, **288**, *books* 361-2

Southwell, Robert, 106, **288**, *books* 362

Soyinka, Wole, 98, *books* 344

Spender, Stephen, **288-9**, *books* 362

Spenser, Edmund, 106, 109, 150, 174–5, 239, 240, 276, **289-92**, 309, *books* 362

Spenserian stanza, 237

spondee, 217

sprung rhythm, 232-3, *see also* Hopkins, Gerard Manley
staff, *see* stanza
stanza, 235
Stein, Gertrude, 5, 214, **292**, *books* 362
Stephens, James, **292**, *books* 362
Stevens, Wallace, 3, 4, 113, 142, 235, **292-5**, *books* 362
Stewart, Douglas, 18
Suckling, Sir John, 237, **295**, *books* 362
Sumer is i-cumen in, see Middle English Lyric
Surrealism, 57, 113, 268
Surrey, Henry Howard, Earl of, 105-6, 240, **295-6**, *books* 362
Swift, Jonathan, 206, 223-4, **296-7**, *books* 362
Swinburne, Algernon Charles, 100, 151, 215, 231, 239, **297-8**, 314, 319, *books* 362-3
Symbolism, 57, **298-302**, *books* 363
Symons, Arthur, 52, **302**, 314, *books* 363

Tagore, Rabindranath, 142
tailed sonnet, 240
Tate, Allen, 4, 6, 61, 80, 116-17, 192, **302-3**, 325, *books* 363
Taylor, Edward, 2, 3, **303-4**, *books* 363
Tennyson, Alfred, Lord, 9, 60, 71, 100, 110, 137, 201, 203, 210-11, 218, 223, 231, 232, 243, 244, **304-6**, 314, *books* 363
tercet, 235-6
terza rima, see tercet
Thomas, Dylan, 113, 241, 242, **306-7**, *books* 363
Thomas, Edward, 27, 113, **307-8**, *books* 363-4
Thomas, R. S., 113, **308-9**, *books* 364
Thompson, Francis, 176, 220, **309**, *books* 364
Thomson, James (1700-48), 109, **309**, *books* 364

Thomson, James (1834-82), 230, **309**, *books* 364
Thoreau, Henry David, **309**, *books* 364
Tomlinson, Charles, 139
Tourneur, Cyril, **309-10**, *books* 364
Townshend, Aurelian, **310**, *books* 364
Traherne, Thomas, 253, **310-11**, 316, *books* 364
Translation, **311-15**, *books* 364
tribrach, 217
trimeter, *see* triple metres
triolet, 241
triple metres, 217, 220-4
triplet, 235
trochaic metre, 220
trochee, 217
Troubadours, 102-3, 177
Tupper, Martin, 210, 211

Upward, Allen, 140

Van der Post, Laurens, 287
Van Doren, Mark, **315**, *books* 364
Vaughan, Henry, 109, 130, 237, 311, **315-16**, *books* 364-5
verse forms, *see* Prosody, Forms of Verse, and Some Usages
Viereck, Peter, **316**
vilanelle, 241

Waley, Arthur, 112, 174, **317**
Waller, Edmund, 108, 186, **317-18**, *books* 365
Wanode, Okogbule, 98, *books* 345
Warren, Robert Penn, 6, 116-17, **318**, *books* 365
Warton, Joseph, **318**, *books* 365
Warton, Thomas, **318**, 329, *books* 365
Watkins, Vernon, 242, **318**
Watson, Wilfred, 41
Watts, Isaac, 134, 234, 238, **318**

Webb, Francis, 17
Webster, John, **318-20**, *books* 365
Welsh, Anne, 361
Wesley, Charles, 134
Wheelwright, John, **320**, *books* 365
Whitman, Walt, 2, 3, 4, 5, 7, 96, 233, 294, **320-2**, *books* 365
Whittemore, Reed, **322**
Whittier, John Greenleaf, 4
Wigglesworth, Michael, 2
Wilbur, Richard, 3, **322-3**, *books* 365
Wilde, Oscar, 190, **323**, *books* 365
Williams, William Carlos, 2, 3, 4, 5, 6, 7, 139, 140, 142, **323-4**, *books* 365-6
Winchilsea, Anne Finch, Countess, of **324**, *books* 365
Winters, Yvor, 61, 115, 257, 303, **324-5**, *books* 366
Wordsworth, William, 42, 53, 55-6, 70, 71-2, 77, 90, 109, 136-7, 180, 193, 220, 230, 245, 254, 324, **325-8**, *books* 366
Wotton, Sir Henry, 244
Wright, David, 287, *books* 361
Wright, James, **328**, *books* 366
Wright, Judith, 17
Wyatt, Sir Thomas, 105, 226, 234, 239, 240, **328-30**, *books* 366
Wylie, Elinor, **330**, *books* 366

Yeats, W. B., 23, 111-12, 120, 143, 183, 214, 226, 232, 259, 292, 302, 323, **330-3**, *books* 366-7
Young, Andrew, **333**, *books* 367
Young, Edward, **333**, *books* 367

Zukofsky, Louis, **7**